The Multicultural Dictionary of Proverbs

The Multicultural Dictionary of Proverbs

Over 20,000 Adages from More Than 120 Languages, Nationalities and Ethnic Groups

HAROLD V. CORDRY

McFarland & Company, Inc., Publishers
Jefferson, North Carolina, and London

For Janice

British Library Cataloguing-in-Publication data are available

Library of Congress Cataloguing-in-Publication Data

Cordry, Harold V., 1943–
The multicultural dictionary of proverbs : over 20,000 adages from more than 120 languages, nationalities and ethnic groups / Harold V. Cordry.
p. cm.
Includes bibliographical references and indexes. 
ISBN 0-7864-0251-2 (library binding : 50# alkaline paper)
1. Proverbs. I. Title
PN6405.C67 1997
082—dc20 96-33264
CIP

Manufactured in the United States of America

McFarland & Company, Inc., Publishers
Box 611, Jefferson, North Carolina 28640

Contents

Acknowledgments

A collection such as this is the product of many years' gathering. Though I have drawn most heavily from such centuries-old collections as those of Heywood, Herbert and Fuller, I decided only recently to pursue the idea of publication, and I fear that I may unknowingly have included specimens from contemporary collectors. Whether that be the case or not, I feel obliged to acknowledge my indebtedness to Burton Stevenson, compiler of the formidable *Macmillan Home Book of Proverbs, Maxims, and Famous Phrases*; to William George Smith, compiler of *The Oxford Dictionary of English Proverbs*; and especially to Wolfgang Mieder, compiler of *The Prentice Hall Encyclopedia of World Proverbs*, whose scholarship in the field sets the standard by which the rest of us are to be judged.

I wish also to express my gratitude to Kay Bradt, Jan Boyd, Anne Liebst and Claudia Hey, of the Baker University library staff; to supportive colleagues and to foreign students at three universities who helped with translation and provided proverbs from their homelands; and to my mother-in-law, Donna DeuPree, who helped to make it all come together.

My deepest thanks go to my wife, Janice, without whom there would be nothing at all.

Preface

This book was conceived initially as a compendium of proverbial wisdom, embodying the horse sense, street-smarts and native sagacity of peoples from around the world and dating to the dim beginnings of our recorded past. As a definitive record of the observations and judgments of those who learned about life by living it, but who rarely recorded their findings, it was to contain everything from instructions for teaching old dogs new tricks to cautionary advice concerning the laundering of dirty linen. And so it does. But the present work is not the book I intended it to be.

For as my collection grew, I found myself increasingly fascinated by the striking similarity of proverbs from dissimilar cultures in different times and different places, and by the fundamental universality of human experience which the proverbs so clearly reflect. To be sure, a proverb found among the Lugbara people of Central Africa may not have originated among the Lugbara; indeed, virtually all proverbs originated at some earlier time—"*old* proverb" is a redundancy—and a great many of them, no doubt, in some other place. Their currency, however, at any identifiable time or place attests to their validity in accurately depicting life as it was experienced by those people who used them—or who continued to use them—and in prescribing appropriate responses to its various challenges and quandaries.

Space considerations precluded repetition of more or less identical proverbs from two or more sources. Had they been included, the book might have been many inches thicker, though still without any basis for being thought comprehensive; nor, I think, would it have been more useful. Despite the omissions, however, the universality of response to the human experience remains clear. One proverb speaks of a jungle, another of a desert, another of ice, yet all convey the message that we must be wary of unseen danger.

Thus, I have arranged the proverbs not by source but by topic, to facilitate comparison, and not by their figurative meaning but, to the extent that I was able, by whatever topic they seemed to be addressing. Some proverbs being more diffuse than others with regard to their applicability, I sought to assist readers further by means of cross-references and topical indexing.

Most proverbs are attributed by language, some by nationality or ethnic group, depending on where they were found and on how earlier collectors had catalogued them. Wherever priority could be determined, I cited the earlier source. The book therefore contains comparatively few American proverbs, not because they are less common here, but because so many of them may be easily traced to other cultures and nationalities.

A number of proverbs were found in works of literature, but in general such proverbs were not recorded if earlier appearances were discovered. Proverbs appearing in the works of Shakespeare, Cervantes and several other major authors, however, were routinely recorded and cited, even when similar proverbs were found in Latin or Greek. In such instances, the earlier appearances were listed as well so that readers might compare them.

All but a few of the Scottish proverbs were found in the original dialect, and because they are more or less translatable by speakers of English, they have been retained in their original form, with interpolated translations of difficult words and phrases.

A few of the proverbs in this collection might well be considered maxims. If, for example, one defines a maxim as a rule of conduct and a proverb as a comment or observation with regard to the universal experience of life, the distinction is not always clear. Many proverbs, after all, in their essence, are at least implicit rules of conduct. And translation alone may very well turn one into the other. So rather than eliminate proverbs which some might consider maxims, I have chosen to include maxims which some might consider proverbs.

H.C., *1996*

The Dictionary

Abasement *see* **Shame**

Ability *see also* **Blindness; Dexterity; Excellence; Limitations; Proficiency; Quality; Self-Confidence; Self-Reliance; Skill; Talent**

1. A man can do no more than he can. *English*
2. A man who can't sing is always striving to sing. *Latin*
3. A wee mouse can creep under a great cornstack. *Scottish*
4. Ability is a poor man's wealth. *English*
5. As we advance in life, we learn the limits of our abilities. *English (Froude)*
6. Attempt only what you are able to perform. *Latin (Cato)*
7. Dogs gnaw bones because they cannot swallow them. *English*
8. Everyone must row with the oars he has. *English*
9. From each according to his abilities, to each according to his needs. *German (Marx)*
10. Gentility without ability is waur [worse] than plain begging. *Scottish*
11. He is good that failed never. *Scottish*
12. He is not poor who has a competency. *Latin (Horace)*
13. He rides sicker [sure] that fell never. *Scottish*
14. It is a great ability to be able to conceal one's ability. *French (La Rochefoucauld)*
15. Let him who knows the instrument play upon it. *Spanish (Cervantes)*
16. Man is capable of all things. *French (Montaigne)*
17. Many can drive an ox; few can plough. *Latin*
18. Many can pack the cards that cannot play. *English*
19. Most men don't lack the will but the ability. *American*
20. My heart bids me do it, if do it I can, and it is a thing possible to do. *Greek (Homer)*
21. One man can speak and seven can sing. *German*
22. One man excels in one thing, another in another. *Latin*
23. Put the man to the mare that can manage the mare. *Scottish*
24. The winds and waves are always on the side of the ablest navigators. *English (Gibbon)*
25. There is no school for ability. *Turkish*
26. Those who have the fewest teeth chew the most. *Dutch*
27. Who ties well, unties well. *Spanish*

Absence *see also* **Leaving; Parting**

28. A good thing is esteemed more in its absence than in its enjoyment. *Latin*
29. A little absence does much good. *French*
30. A man who speaks ill of an absent friend, or fails to take his part if attacked by another, is a scoundrel. *Latin (Horace)*
31. Absence diminishes little passions and increases great ones. *French (La Rochefoucauld)*
32. Absence doth sharpen love, presence strengthens it. *English (Overbury)*
33. Absence is a shrew. *English*
34. Absence is love's foe: far from the eyes, far from the heart. *Spanish*
35. Absence is the death of love. *Spanish (Calderon)*
36. Absence is the enemy of love. *Spanish*
37. Absence makes the heart grow fonder. *English (Bayly)*
38. Absent, none without fault; present, none without excuse. *French*
39. Achilles absent was Achilles still. *Greek (Homer)*
40. Always toward absent lovers love's tide flows stronger. *Latin (Propertius)*
41. Distance sometimes endears friendship, and absence sweeteneth it. *English*
42. Distance weakens love. *Latin (Claudian)*
43. Even enemies, when absent, should not be harmed. *Latin (Cato)*
44. Far from the eyes, far from the heart. *French*
45. Friends dwelling afar off are not friends. *Greek*
46. Friends, though absent, are still present. *Latin (Cicero)*
47. Friendship, like love, is destroyed by long absence, though it may be increased by short intermissions. *English (Johnson)*
48. Greater things are believed of those who are absent. *Latin (Tacitus)*
49. He is guilty who is not at home. *Ukrainian*
50. He that is absent is soon forgotten. *English*
51. He that is absent will not be the heir. *Latin*
52. He that quits his place loses it. *French*

53. He who has departed is forgotten as time goes on. *Japanese*

54. He's a silly body that's never missed. *Scottish*

55. His absence is gude [good] company. *Scottish*

56. If a person is away, his right is away. *Moorish*

57. If the dog is not at home, he barks not. *African*

58. It is commonly known that the absent know by a ringing in their ears that they are being talked about. *Latin (Pliny)*

59. Let no one be willing to speak ill of the absent. *Latin (Propertius)*

60. Long absence changes a friend. *French*

61. Long absent, soon forgotten. *English*

62. Nearest is dearest. *German*

63. Never through long absence is true love forgotten. *French*

64. Never were the absent in the right. *Spanish*

65. Our hours in love have wings; in absence, crutches. *English (Cibber)*

66. Out of mind, when out of view. *English (Gay)*

67. Out of sight, out of mind. *Greek (Homer)*

68. Out of the eye, out of the heart. *Yiddish*

69. Present to the eye, present to the mind. *Chinese*

70. Salt water and absence always wash away love. *English (H. Nelson)*

71. Separation secures manifest friendship. *Indian*

72. So near and yet so far. *Latin (Martial)*

73. The absent are always at fault. *Dutch*

74. The absent are never without blame, nor the present without excuse. *Spanish*

75. The absent are never without fault, nor the present without excuse. *American (Franklin)*

76. The absent feel and fear every ill. *Spanish (Cervantes)*

77. The absent get farther off every day. *Japanese*

78. The coaches won't run over him. [He is in jail.] *English*

79. The dead and absent have no friends. *Spanish*

80. The rarer seen, the less in mind. *English (Googe)*

81. The remedy for love is land between. *English*

82. The silence resulting from absence has destroyed many a friendship. *Latin*

83. They are aye [always] good that are away. *Scottish*

84. They may see me being absent to be present. *English (Lyly)*

85. Tho' lost to sight, to mem'ry dear. *English (G. Linley)*

86. True love is never forgotten through long absence. *French*

87. Unminded, unmoaned. *English (Heywood)*

88. What the eye does not see the heart does not care about [or grieve over]. *Arabic*

89. What the eye rarely sees, the heart soon despises. *Latin*

90. What the eye sees not, the heart craves not. *Dutch*

91. What the eye sees not, the heart rues not. *English*

92. What the eyes see not, does not break the heart. *Spanish (Cervantes)*

93. Whoso absents himself, his share absents itself. *Arabic*

Absolution *see also* **Confession; Forgiveness; Pardon**

94. The blackest sin is cleared with absolution. *English (Shakespeare)*

Abstinence *see also* **Diet; Longevity; Moderation; Self-Denial; Temperance**

95. Abstinence from doing is often as generous as doing, but it is not so apparent. *French (Montaigne)*

96. Abstinence is the best medicine. *American*

97. It is easier to abstain than to restrain. *French*

98. Many diseases may be cured by abstinence. *Latin (Celsus)*

99. The abstinent run away from what they desire / But carry their desires with them. *Bhagavad-Gita*

100. To abstain that we may enjoy. *French (Rousseau)*

Abundance *see also* **Excess; Quantity; Sufficiency**

101. Abundance is no fault. *French*

102. Abundance, like want, ruins many. *Chinese (Confucius)*

103. Abundance of a thing does no harm. *French*

104. An abundance of a good thing is not cause for unhappiness. *Tunisian*

105. Better be rough with plenty than genteel with poverty. *American*

106. Flowers in both hands. [Having two good things at the same time.] *Japanese*

107. He kensna [knows not] the pleasures o' plenty wha [who] ne'er felt the pains o' poverty. *Scottish*

108. He that has routh [plenty] o' butter may butter his bread on baith [both] sides. *Scottish*

109. If one swain scorns you, you will soon find another. *Latin (Virgil)*

110. In a house where there is plenty, supper is soon cooked. *Spanish*

111. In plenty, think of want; in want, do not presume on plenty. *Chinese*

112. One can never have too much of a good thing. *American*

113. Plenty breeds pride. *American*

114. Plenty destroys passion. *Latin*

115. Plenty is na [no] dainty. *Scottish*

116. Plenty is nae plague. *Scottish*

117. Plenty maks dainty. *Scottish*

118. Plough well and deep and you will have plenty of corn. *Spanish*

119. Store is no sore. Who hath many pease may put the mo in the pot. *English*

120. There are as good fish in the sea as ever came out of it. *English*

121. There is much meat in God's storehouse. *Danish*

122. There's seldom a cake but there's more of the make. *English*

123. 'Tis pleasant to have a large heap to take from. *Latin*

Abuse *see also* **Child-Rearing; Discipline; Discipline and Women; Excess**

124. If you abuse others, you can't squawk if you are given a taste of your own medicine. *American*

125. The abuse of a thing does not forbid its use. *Latin*

126. The best things may be abused. *English (Lyly)*

127. To throw pumpkin water in someone's eyes. *Zulu*

Abuse of Women *see* Discipline and Women; Husbands and Wives; Marriage

Acceptance *see also* Forbearance; Submission

128. A man must plow with such oxen as he has. *American*

129. As you have made your bed, so you must lie in it. *French*

130. Do not kick against the pricks. *Greek*

131. Happy is he who forgets what cannot be altered. *German*

132. If you don't like it, you must lump it. *American*

133. If you rightly bear your cross it will bear you. *Latin*

134. If you should find your house on fire, go up and warm yourself by it. *Spanish*

135. Let's not cry over spilled milk. *American*

136. Never grieve for what you cannot help. *American*

137. One must needs like what he cannot hinder. *English*

138. Past cure, past care. *American*

139. Take no sorrow of the thing lost which may not be recovered. *Greek*

140. Take people as they are. *American*

141. Take the bad with the good. *American*

142. Take the bit and the buffet with it. *American*

143. Take the rough with the smooth. *American*

144. Take things as they come. *American*

145. The superior man is content in a state of poverty; the intelligent man submits himself to his destiny. *Chinese*

146. To kiss the rod. *French*

147. We accepted the misfortune but the misfortune did not accept us. *Tunisian*

148. What can't be brushed must be stroked. *German*

149. What can't be cured must be endured. *Italian*

150. What cannot be altered must be borne, not blamed. *English*

151. What's done is done. *American*

152. When a thing is done, make the best of it. *German*

153. When everyone tells you that you are an ass, thank God and bray. *Moorish*

154. When what you wish does not happen, wish for what does happen. *Arabic*

155. You have to take the bitter with the better. *American*

156. You must plow with such oxen as you have. *American*

Accidents *see also* Error(s)

157. A horse may stumble on four feet. *Dutch*

158. A ridiculous accident has often been the making of many. *Latin*

159. Accidents will happen. *American*

160. Accidents will occur in the best regulated families. *English (Dickens)*

161. Even genii sometimes drop their swords. *Chinese*

162. Nothing is or can be accident with God. *American (Longfellow)*

163. Nothing under the sun is accidental. *German (Lessing)*

164. Spilt salt is never all gathered. *Spanish*

165. Spilt wine is worse than water. *English*

166. The greatest events often arise from accidents. *American*

167. There is no ladle which never strikes the edge of the pot. *Chinese*

168. There's many a slip 'twixt the cup and the lip. *English*

169. What men call accident is the doing of God's providence. *American*

170. Whatever can happen to one man can happen to every man. *Latin (Publilius Syrus)*

Accomplices *see* Complicity; Guilt

Accomplishment *see also* Achievement; Deeds; Words and Deeds

171. Labors accomplished are pleasant. *Latin*

172. No day should pass without something being done. *Latin*

173. No sooner said than done, so acts your man of worth. *Latin (Ennius)*

174. Who begins too much accomplishes too much. *German*

Accumulation *see also* Gradualness; Quantity; Size; Trifles

175. Drop by drop fills the tub. *English*

176. Eat many meals, and you will grow fat. *Arabic*

177. Every great thing only consists of many small particles united. *Latin*

178. Every little bit helps, as the sow said when she snapped at a gnat. *Danish*

179. From small things a great heap is made. *Latin*

180. Gathering gear [money, property] is weel liket wark [work]. *Scottish*

181. Gear [money, property] is easier gotten than guided. *Scottish*

182. Grain by grain the hen fills her crop. *English*

183. Greatness is nothing but many littles. *Latin*

184. Light gains make a heavy purse. *English*

185. Little and often fattens the bank-roll. *American*

186. Little and often fills the purse. *Italian*

187. Little and often make much at last. *German*

188. Little by little the bird builds its nest. *English*

189. Little drops produce the shower. *Latin*

190. Many drops of water will sink a ship. *English*

191. Many little leaks sink a ship. *American*

192. Many littles mak a mickle [make a lot]. *Scottish*

193. Many smalle maken a great. *English (Chaucer)*

194. Many ventures make a full-freight. *English*

195. Moderate gains fill the purse. *Italian*

196. Mony pickles [small quantities] make a mickle [a lot]. *Scottish*

197. Mony sma's [many smalls] mak a great. *Scottish*

198. One hair added to another makes a beard. *Lebanese*

199. Plate by plate the armor is made. *French (Rabelais)*

200. Rubbish accumulates, mountains arise. *American*

201. Sma' winnings mak a heavy purse. *Scottish*

202. The whole ocean is made up of single drops. *English*

203. There will grow from straws a mighty heap. *Latin*

Accuracy *see also* Precision

204. Accuracy is the twin brother of honesty; inaccuracy, of dishonesty. *American (C. Simmons)*

Accusation *see also* Blame; Calumny; Reputation; Scandal; Slander

205. A blow of a frying-pan smuts [leaves a mark], if it does not hurt. *Spanish*

206. A man is his own near friend, and no man is expected to incriminate himself. *Babylonian Talmud*

207. A serious accusation, even lightly made, does harm. *Latin (Publilius Syrus)*

208. Accusation is proof when Malice and Force sit on the bench. *American*

209. Accuse not a servant unto his master. *Bible*

210. Even doubtful accusations leave a stain behind them. *English*

211. Every accusation against a fallen man gains credence. *Latin*

212. Evil report travels farther than any applause. *English*

213. He who accuses himself cannot be accused by another. *Latin (Publilius Syrus)*

214. If the cap fits, wear it. *English*

215. It is safer not to accuse a bad man than to acquit him. *Latin*

216. It is well not to lend too easy an ear to accusations. *Latin (Publilius Syrus)*

217. Lay it on thick and some of it will stick. *English*

218. No man is bound to accuse himself. *English*

219. No one is obliged to accuse himself. *Latin*

220. Report hangs the man. *French*

221. When foxes pack the jury box, the chicken is always found guilty as accused. *American*

Achievement *see also* Accomplishment; Deeds; Words and Deeds

222. A thing well done is its own reward. *American*

223. By their fruits ye shall know them. *Bible*

224. He was born on an eating mat [i.e., in comfortable circumstances]. *Zulu*

225. He was born on manure [i.e., born into poverty]. *Zulu*

226. It is not enough to aim, you must hit. *Italian*

227. That which is well done is first done. *American*

228. The greatest things are done by the aid of small ones. *English*

229. The higher the ape goes, the more he shows his tail. *English*

Acquaintance *see also* Friends and Friendship

230. Him you know is better than him you do not know. *Tunisian*

231. Short acquaintance brings repentance. *English*

232. Sudden acquaintance brings long repentance. *English*

233. The more acquaintance the more danger. *English*

234. The worst of those you know is better than the best of those you do not know. *Tunisian*

235. They that know one another, salute afar off. *English*

Acquisition *see also* Accumulation; Greed

236. It's easy to get, but hard to keep what you get. *American*

237. The more you heap / The worse you cheap. *English*

238. Things hardly attained [i.e., obtained with difficulty] are long [or longer] retained. *English*

239. What we acquire without sweat we give away without regret. *American*

Acrimony *see* Anger

Action *see also* Activity; Good Deeds; Idleness; Laziness; Thought and Action; Words and Deeds

240. Action is eloquence. *English (Shakespeare)*

241. Action is the proper fruit of knowledge. *English*

242. Action may not always bring happiness, but there is no happiness without action. *English (Disraeli)*

243. Action overcomes cold; inaction overcomes heat. *Chinese (Laotse)*

244. Action should culminate in wisdom. *Bhagavad-Gita*

245. Actions are ours; their consequences belong to heaven. *English (Sidney)*

246. Always act as if your acts were seen. *Spanish (Gracián)*

247. Heaven never helps the man who will not act. *Greek (Sophocles)*

248. In base times active men are of more use than virtuous. *English (Bacon)*

249. Let us be judged by our actions. *Latin*

250. Merit consists in action. *Latin*

251. One can only do by doing. *French*

252. Our grand business is not to see what lies dimly at a distance, but to do what lies clearly at hand. *English (Carlyle)*

253. Renunciation and activity both liberate, / but to work is better than to renounce. *Bhagavad-Gita*

254. That action is best which procures the greatest happiness for the greatest numbers. *English (Hutchinson)*

255. The best of the sport is to do the deed and say nothing. *English*

256. The deed proves the man. *French*

257. The flighty purpose never is o'ertook unless the deed go with it. *English (Shakespeare)*

258. The more we do, the more we can do; the more busy we are the more leisure we have. *English (Hazlitt)*

259. The shortest answer is doing. *English*

260. The test of a man lies in action. *Latin (Pindar)*

261. Virtues are perceived in actions. *Latin (Cicero)*

262. Who acts not when he should, acts not when he would. *French*

263. You may gape long enough ere a bird fall into your mouth. *English*

Activity *see also* **Action; Inactivity**

264. Better wear out than rust out. *English*

265. Better wear shoon [shoes] than sheets. *Scottish*

266. Constant occupation prevents temptation. *English*

267. Every noble activity makes room for itself. *American (Emerson)*

268. Fools are aye fond o' flittin'. *Scottish*

269. Grass grows not on the highway. *English*

270. Occupy yourself, and you will be out of harm's way. *Latin (Ovid)*

271. The mill gains by going, not by standing still. *Spanish*

272. The millstone does not become moss-grown. *German*

273. The rust of the mind is the destruction of genius. *Latin (Seneca)*

274. The used key is always bright. *English*

275. The used plow shines, standing water stinks. *English*

276. Who more busy than they that have least to do? *English*

277. Who moves, picks up; who stands still, dries up. *English*

Adaptability *see also* **Acceptance; Circumstance(s); Conformity; Custom; Fashion; Flexibility; Habit; Necessity**

278. A wise man will make tools of what comes to hand. *English*

279. Adapt thyself to the estate which is thy portion. *Latin (Marcus Aurelius)*

280. Adapt yourself to the times. *American*

281. Be good with the good and bad with the bad. *Latin (Plautus)*

282. He is a wise man who accommodates himself to the occasion. *Latin*

283. He is wise, who suits himself to the occasion. *Latin*

284. He who changes his ways loses his happiness. *Syrian*

285. I dance to the tune that is played. *Spanish*

286. I strive to mold circumstances to myself, not myself to circumstances. *Latin (Horace)*

287. One should be compliant with the times. *Latin (Theodosius II)*

288. Since the house is on fire let us warm ourselves. *Italian*

289. Suit self to circumstances. *Chinese*

290. Treat a thousand dispositions in a thousand ways. *Latin (Ovid)*

291. We can accustom ourselves to anything. *Latin*

292. Were I a nightingale, I would act the part of a nightingale; were I a swan, the part of a swan. *Greek (Epictetus)*

293. Whosoever adapteth himself shall be preserved to the end. *Chinese (Laotse)*

Addition *see also* **Accumulation; Gradualness; Quantity**

294. Addition is the miser's sum of happiness. *American*

295. An addition to the family is often a subtraction. *American*

Adequacy *see* **Excess; Quantity; Sufficiency**

Adjustment *see* **Adaptability; Conformity; Flexibility**

Admiration

296. Admiration is the daughter of ignorance. *American (Franklin)*

297. Fools admire, but men of sense approve. *English (Pope)*

298. Things not understood are admired. *English*

299. We always like those who admire us, but we do not always like those whom we admire. *French (La Rochefoucauld)*

Adolescence *see* **Aging; Children and Childhood; Youth; Youth and Old Age**

Advancement *see also* **Progress**

300. Flight towards preferment will be but slow without some golden feathers. *English*

301. Hard is the path from poverty to renown. *Latin*

302. Having mastered the lesser difficulties, you will more safely venture on greater achievements. *Latin*

303. He can carry the ox, who has carried the calf. *English*

304. Who does not advance fails. *Latin*

Advantage *see also* **Winning and Losing**

305. Every advantage has its disadvantage. *Latin*

306. Every advantage has its tax. *American (Emerson)*

307. Fortune turns everything to the advantage of those she favors. *French (La Rochefoucauld)*

308. He has the best end o' the string. *Scottish*

309. He that has one eye is a prince among those that have none. *English*

310. It's them as take advantage that get advantage i' this world. *English (G. Eliot)*

311. Kick him again; he's down. *American*

312. Let nothing slip that will advantage you. *Latin (Cato)*

313. To be born with a silver spoon in the mouth. *English*

314. When fortune is on our side, popular favor bears her company. *Latin (Publilius Syrus)*

Adventure

315. Those who seek adventures do not always find happy ones. *Spanish (Cervantes)*

316. Who seeks adventure finds blows. *French*

Adversity *see also* **Affliction; Good and Bad; Misfortune; Suffering**

317. A gem is not polished without friction, nor a man perfected without trials. *Chinese*

318. A noble heart, like the sun, showeth its greatest countenance in its lowest estate. *English (Sidney)*

319. Adversity flatters no man. *French*

320. Adversity has no friends. *Latin (Tacitus)*

321. Adversity is the diamond dust Heaven polishes its jewels with. *English (Leighton)*

322. Adversity is the first path to truth. *English (Byron)*

323. Adversity is the touchstone of friendship. *French*

324. Adversity is the trial of courage. *French*

325. Adversity is the trial of principle. Without it man hardly knows whether he is honest or not. *English (Fielding)*

326. Adversity makes a great man. *Japanese*

327. Adversity makes a man, luck makes monsters. *French*

328. Adversity makes a man wise, not rich. *Japanese*

329. Adversity makes men, prosperity makes monsters. *American*

330. Adversity makes us wise — until the next misfortune comes. *American*

331. Adversity reminds men of religion. *Latin (Livy)*

332. Adversity tries virtue — and finds it guilty. *American*

333. Adversity tries virtue. *Arabic*

334. After crosses and losses, men grow humbler and wiser. *American (Franklin)*

335. Be not elated by fortune, be not depressed by adversity. *Greek (Cleobulus)*

336. Be patient in adversity and cautious in prosperity. *American*

337. Better be wise by the misfortunes of others than by your own. *Greek (Aesop)*

338. Fire is the test of gold; adversity is the test of strong men. *Latin (Seneca)*

339. For one man who can stand prosperity, there are a hundred that will stand adversity. *English (Carlyle)*

340. Forgetting trouble is the way to cure it. *Latin*

341. Greater dooms win greater destinies. *Greek (Heraclitus)*

342. He knows not his own strength that hath not met adversity. *English (Bacon)*

343. He that has no cross will have no crown. *English (Quarles)*

344. He that never was acquainted with adversity has seen the world but on one side. *English (Johnson)*

345. If thou faint in the day of adversity, thy strength is small. *Bible*

346. In adversity a man is saved by hope. *Greek (Menander)*

347. In the adversity of our friends we often find something that does not displease us. *French (La Rochefoucauld)*

348. In this wild world, the fondest and the best are the most tried, most troubled, and distrest [distressed]. *English (Crabbe)*

349. Let each man turn his mind to his own troubles. *Latin*

350. Light troubles speak; the weighty are struck dumb. *Latin (Seneca)*

351. Never trouble trouble till trouble troubles you. *American*

352. No land without stones, no meat without bones. *American*

353. No man can smile in the face of adversity and mean it. *American (Howe)*

354. One must never make a stand against adversity. *Latin*

355. Prosperity is no just scale; adversity is the only balance to weigh friends. *Greek (Plutarch)*

356. Shut your doors and sit in your house, yet trouble will fall from the skies. *Chinese*

357. Sweet are the uses of adversity. *English (Shakespeare)*

358. Sweet is the remembrance of troubles when you are in safety. *Greek*

359. Take warning by the mischance of others, that others may not take warning by thine. *Persian (Sa'di)*

360. The drowning man is not troubled by rain. *Persian*

361. The philosopher coins adversity into spiritual riches. *American*

362. The wicked grow worse, and good men better for trouble. *American*

363. The wind in a man's face makes him wise. *French*

364. The worse the passage the more welcome the port. *English*

365. The worst is not / So long as we can say "This is the worst." *English (Shakespeare)*

366. There is no education like adversity. *English (Disraeli)*

367. Tribulation brings understanding. *Latin*

368. Trouble is to man what rust is to iron. *Yiddish*

369. We can bear adversity but not self-contempt. *American*

370. We must seek some other cause than the gods for our troubles. *Greek*

371. What anyone bears willingly he bears easily. *Latin*

372. When an elephant is in trouble, even a frog will kick him. *Hindi*

373. When troubles are few, dreams are few. *Chinese*

374. Who troubles others has not rest himself. *Italian*

375. Wisdom is a good purchase, though we pay dear for it. *English*

Advertising *see also* **Quality**

376. Gude ale needs nae wisp. *Scottish*

377. It sells itself. *Spanish*

378. No man cries stinking fish. *English*

379. Puffed goods are putrid. *Latin*

380. The sign brings customers. *French*

Advice *see also* **Heedlessness**

381. A fool is a fine counselor for a wise man. *French*

382. A fool may put somewhat in a wise body's head. *English*

383. A hundred sage counsels are lost upon one who cannot take advice; a hundred bits of wisdom are lost upon the unintelligent. *Panchatantra*

384. Advice after mischief is like medicine after death. *Danish*

385. Advice comes after the rabbit has escaped. *Spanish*

386. Advice given in the midst of a crowd is disgusting. *Arabic*

387. Advice is a stranger; if welcome he stays for the night; if not welcome he returns home the same day. *Malagasy*

388. Advice is judged by results, not by intentions. *Latin (Cicero)*

389. Advice is like snow; the softer it falls the longer it dwells upon, and the deeper it sinks into the mind. *English (Coleridge)*

390. Advice is seldom welcome; and those who want it the most always like it the least. *English (Lord Chesterfield)*

391. Advice is something the wise don't need and fools won't take. *American*

392. Advice should be viewed from behind. *Swedish*

393. Advice when most needed is least heeded. *English*

394. Advice whispered is not worth a pea. *Spanish*

395. Advice: the smallest current coin. *American (Bierce)*

396. Advise a fool and you'll be his enemy. *Egyptian*

397. Advise none to marry or go to war. *American*

398. Advise with wit. *Latin*

399. Advisement is good before the need. *English (Chaucer)*

400. Advisers are not payers. *French*

401. Advisers get away with it: they never pay the penalty of their advice. *American*

402. An adviser may give you a helping hand to the poorhouse. *American*

403. An enemy may chance to give good counsel. *English*

404. As a bamboo conduit makes a round jet of water / So taking counsel together rounds men to one mind. *Malay*

405. Ask advice, but use your own common sense. *Yiddish*

406. Avysement is good before the nede [need]. *English (Chaucer)*

407. Bad counsel confounds the adviser. *Latin*

408. Be niggards of advice on no pretence; / For the worst avarice is that of sense. *American (Franklin)*

409. Be slow of giving advice, ready to do a service. *Italian*

410. Beware of him who is benefited by the advice he offers thee. *Babylonian Talmud*

411. Come not to the counsel uncalled. *Latin*

412. Counsel after action is like rain after harvest. *American*

413. Counsel breaks not the head. *English*

414. Counsel is no command. *English*

415. Counsel is nothing against love. *Italian*

416. Counsel will make a man stick to his own mare. *English*

417. Distrust the advice of the interested. *Greek (Aesop)*

418. Don't give me advice, give me money. *Spanish*

419. Every man, however wise, needs the advice of some sagacious friend in the affairs of life. *Latin (Plautus)*

420. Everybody knows good counsel except him that has need of it. *German*

421. Everyone has judgment to sell. *Italian*

422. Evil counsel marches with seven-league boots. *American*

423. Fools need advice most, but wise men only are the better for it. *American (Franklin)*

424. Friendly counsel cuts off many foes. *English (Shakespeare)*

425. Give advice to all; but be security for none. *English*

426. Give every man thine ear, but few thy voice; take each man's censure, but reserve thy judgment. *English (Shakespeare)*

427. Give neither counsel nor salt till you are asked for it. *Italian*

428. Giving advice is sometimes only showing our wisdom at the expense of another. *English (Shaftesbury)*

429. Good advice is as good as an eye in the hand. *French*

430. Good advice is often annoying, bad advice never is. *French*

431. Good advice is worth a camel. *Lebanese*

432. Good counsel brings good fruit. *American*

433. Good counsel comes overnight. *German*

434. Good counsel is a pearl beyond price. *American*

435. Good counsel never comes too late. *German*

436. Good medicine is bitter to the mouth, but will cure illness; sincere advice is harsh to the ear, but will remedy misconduct. *Korean*

437. Good medicine [i.e., advice] is bitter to the taste. *Chinese*

438. Gude counsel is abune [above] a' price. *Scottish*

439. Happy counsel flows from sober feasts. *Greek (Homer)*

440. Harsh counsels have no effect: they are like hammers which are always repulsed by the anvil. *French (Helvétius)*

441. Haste and anger hinder gude counsel. *Scottish*

442. Hazard not your wealth on a poor man's advice. *Spanish*

443. He asks advice in vain who will not follow it. *French*

444. He is best of all men who follows good advice. *Greek (Zeno)*

445. He is more obstinate for being advised. *English*

446. He tells me my way, and knows not his own. *English*

447. He that builds by the wayside has many advisers. *Dutch*

448. He that kisseth his wife in the market place shall have people enough to teach him. *English*

449. He that speers a' opinions comes ill speed. *Scottish*

450. He that will not hear must feel. *German*

451. He that winna be counselled canna be helped. *Scottish*

452. He who builds according to every man's advice will have a crooked house. *Danish*

453. He who counsels aids. *Latin (Plautus)*

454. He who is wise and consults others is a whole man, he who has a wise opinion of his own and seeks no counsel from others is half a man, and he who has no

opinion of his own and seeks no advice is no man at all. *Arabic*

455. He who will not accept an old man's advice will someday be a beggar. *Chinese*

456. He who will not go to heaven needs preaching. *German*

457. How is it possible to expect that mankind will take advice, when they will not so much as take warning? *Irish (Swift)*

458. If a man love to give advice, it is a sure sign that he himself wanteth it. *English (Lord Halifax)*

459. If the counsel is good, take it even from a fool. *American*

460. If you want good advice, consult an old man. *Portuguese*

461. If you want to get into the bog, ask five fools the way to the forest. *Livonian*

462. If you want to succeed, consult three old people. *Chinese*

463. If you won't take advice, you can't be helped. *American*

464. If your strength is small, don't carry heavy burdens; if your words are worthless, don't give advice. *Chinese*

465. In giving advice, seek to help, not to please, your friend. *Greek (Solon)*

466. In the multitude of counselors there is safety. *Bible*

467. In vain he craves advice that will not follow it. *English*

468. It is bad advice that cannot be altered. *Latin*

469. It is easier to know how to do a thing than to do it. *Chinese*

470. It is easy for a man in health to preach patience to the sick. *American*

471. It is easy when we are in prosperity to give advice to the afflicted. *Greek (Aeschylus)*

472. It is not often that any man can have so much knowledge of another as is necessary to make instruction useful. *English (Johnson)*

473. Less advice [or counsel] and more hands. *German*

474. Love to be advised, not praised. *French*

475. Many receive advice, few profit by it. *Latin (Publilius Syrus)*

476. More know the pope and a peasant than the pope alone. *Venetian*

477. Neither salt nor advice should be given unless asked for. *Italian*

478. Never advise a man to go to the halter or to the altar. *American*

479. Never give advice unasked. *German*

480. Never trust the advice of a man in difficulties. *Greek (Aesop)*

481. No enemy is worse than bad advice. *Greek (Sophocles)*

482. Nobody can give you wiser advice than yourself. *Latin (Cicero)*

483. Nothing is given so freely as advice. *French*

484. One can advise comfortably from a safe port. *German (Schiller)*

485. One who is not wise for himself cannot be well advised. *Italian (Machiavelli)*

486. People give nothing so willingly as advice. *American*

487. Seek advice of the old, and then do the opposite. *Tunisian*

488. Seek counsel of him who makes you weep, and not of him who makes you laugh. *Arabic*

489. Take help of many, counsel of few. *Danish*

490. Teeth placed before the tongue give good advice. *Italian*

491. The advice of fools is worthless. *American*

492. The counsels of old age give light without heat, like the sun in winter. *French (Vauvenargues)*

493. The worst men are often the best advisers. *American*

494. There is no helping him who will not be advised. *Italian*

495. There is nothing which we receive with so much reluctance as advice. *English (Addison)*

496. There never came ill of good advisement. *Scottish*

497. There's no advice like a father's — even if you don't take it. *American*

498. They that will not be counseled, cannot be helped. *American (Franklin)*

499. Those who school others, oft should school themselves. *English (Shakespeare)*

500. Though auld and wise still tak advice. *Scottish*

501. Though you are a prudent old man, do not despise counsel. *Spanish*

502. 'Tis easier to advise the suffering than to bear suffering. *Greek (Euripides)*

503. To accept good advice is but to increase one's own ability. *German (Goethe)*

504. To give counsel to a fool is like throwing water on a goose. *Danish*

505. Wait for the season when to cast good counsels upon subsiding passion. *English (Shakespeare)*

506. We are all wise for other people, none for himself. *American (Emerson)*

507. We ask advice, but we mean approbation. *English* (Colton)

508. We give advice by the bucket, but take it by the grain. *American (W.R. Alger)*

509. We give nothing so freely as advice. *French (La Rochefoucauld)*

510. We may give advice, but we cannot inspire conduct. *French (La Rochefoucauld)*

511. We treat advisers as we treat doctors: we do as we damned please as soon as their backs are turned. *American*

512. Whatever advice you give, be short. *Latin (Horace)*

513. When a man seeks your advice he generally wants your praise. *English (Chesterfield)*

514. When a thing is done, advice comes too late. *English*

515. When error is committed, good advice comes too late. *Chinese*

516. When we are well, it is easy to give good advice to the sick. *Latin (Terence)*

517. Where's the man who counsel can bestow, / Still pleased to teach, and yet not proud to know? *English (Pope)*

518. Who cannot give good counsel? 'Tis cheap, it costs them nothing. *English (Burton)*

519. Who works in the public square will have many advisers. *Spanish*

520. Worthless is the advice of fools. *Latin*

521. Write down the advice of him who loves you, though you like it not at present. *Italian*

Affectation *see also* **Ostentatiousness; Pretense**

522. Affectation is a greater enemy [or injury] to the face than small-pox. *English*

Affection

523. Cold hand, warm heart. *German*

524. Most affections are habits or duties we lack the courage to end. *French (Montherlant)*

525. Most people would rather get than give affection. *Greek (Aristotle)*

526. Our affections are our life. We live by them; they supply our want. *American (Channing)*

527. The affections are like lightning: you cannot tell where they will strike till they have fallen. *French (Lacordaire)*

528. The affections cannot keep their youth any more than men. *American (Emerson)*

Affinity *see also* **Association; Likeness; Recognition; Resemblance; Similarity**

529. A fly to a fly. *Telugu*

530. A jackdaw always sits near a jackdaw. *Greek*

531. A raven will not peck out the eye of another raven. *Polish*

532. An ass is beautiful in the eyes of an ass, a sow in those of a sow. *Latin*

533. An ox goes with an ox; a horse with a horse. *Japanese*

534. Birds of a feather flock together, and so with men, like to like. *Hebrew*

535. Birds of a feather flock together. *German*

536. But like to like, the collier and the devil. *English*

537. Cat after kind. *Scottish*

538. Every sheep with its fellow [or its like]. *Spanish*

539. Everybody likes those like himself. *Wolof*

540. Everyone to his equal. *American*

541. How God ever brings like to like. *Greek (Homer)*

542. Jackdaw always perches by jackdaw. *Latin*

543. Like calls to like. *Japanese*

544. Like draws to like, a scabbed [scared] horse to an auld dyke [old wall]. *Scottish*

545. Like draws to like, the whole world over. *English*

546. Like is dear to like. *Greek*

547. Like likes like. *Latin*

548. Like pleases like. *Greek*

549. Like readily gathers together with like. *Latin (Cicero)*

550. Like to like, and Nan for Nicholas. *English*

551. Like to like, Jack to Lizzie. *Dutch*

552. Like will to like, as the devil said to the collier. *English*

553. Like will to like, as the devil said to the charcoal-burner. *German*

554. Like will to like. *Greek*

555. The bird flies to its own. *Latin*

556. The grasshopper is dear to the grasshopper, the ant loves the ant. *Latin*

Affliction *see also* **Adversity; Good and Bad; Misfortune, Suffering**

557. Affliction and adversity make men better. *Japanese*

558. Affliction is a school of virtue; it corrects levity, and interrupts the confidence of sinning. *English (Atterbury)*

559. Affliction is not sent in vain from the good God who chastens those that he loves. *English (Southey)*

560. Affliction smarts most in the most unhappy state. *English (Browne)*

561. Afflictions are sometimes blessings in disguise. *American*

562. Afflictions are the good man's treasure — but he'd rather bury it than bear it. *American*

563. As sure as God puts his children into the furnace of affliction, he will be with them in it. *English (Spurgeon)*

564. As threshing separates the wheat from the chaff, so does affliction purify virtue. *English (Burton)*

565. God afflicts those whom He loves. *American*

566. Heaven but tries our virtue by affliction, and oft the cloud that wraps the present hour serves but to brighten all our future days. *American (J. Brown)*

567. If afflictions refine some, they consume others. *English*

568. If you would not have affliction visit you twice, listen at once to what it teaches. *Scottish (Burgh)*

569. The afflicted person was once thought sacred, but now he's considered a fool. *American*

570. The good man piles up woe, the bad man piles up dough. *American*

Affront *see also* **Injury; Insult; Offense**

571. A murder may be forgiven, an affront never. *Chinese*

Age *see also* **Aging; Maturity; Old Age; Women and Age; Youth; Youth and Old Age**

572. A man need not look in your mouth to know how old you are. *English*

573. Age makes many a man white but not better. *Danish*

574. Age steals away all things, even the mind. *Latin (Virgil)*

575. Every man at forty is a fool or a physician. *English*

576. Every man desires to live long, but no man would be old. *Irish (Swift)*

577. He who has no sense at thirty will never have any. *French*

578. If a man reach forty and yet be disliked by his fellows, he will be so to the end. *Chinese (Confucius)*

579. Men have as many years as they feel, women as many as they show. *Italian*

580. No wise man ever wished to be younger. *Irish (Swift)*
581. Oil, wine and friends improve with age. *Spanish*
582. Old enough to lie without doors. *English*
583. One is as old as one's heart. *American*
584. To be happy, we must be true to nature, and carry our age along with us. *English (Hazlitt)*
585. When he dies for age, you may quake for fear. *Scottish*
586. You're only as old as you feel. *American*

Aggravation
587. A nail in the wound. *Latin (Cicero)*
588. You rub the sore / When you should bring the plaster. *English (Shakespeare)*

Aging *see also* **Age; Maturity; Wrinkles**
589. Age will not be defied. *English (Bacon)*
590. As we grow old we become both more foolish and more wise. *French (La Rochefoucauld)*
591. At 20 years of age the will reigns; at 30 the wit; at 40 the judgment. *American*
592. Being young is a fault which improves daily. *Swedish*
593. Oh, sweet youth, how soon it fades! *English*
594. Sweet joys of youth, how fleeting! *English (Moore)*
595. The older the worse. *English*
596. The vigor of our days passes like a flower of the spring. *Latin*
597. We shall never be younger. *English*

Agreement *see also* **Alternatives; Compromise; Disagreement**
598. A bad agreement is better than a good lawsuit. *English*
599. A lean agreement is better than a fat sentence. *Italian*
600. Agree, for the law is costly. *English*
601. Agreement is made more precious by disagreement. *Latin (Publilius Syrus)*
602. Agreement with two people, lamentation with three. *Kashmiri*
603. Can two walk together, except they be agreed? *Bible*
604. If all pulled in one direction, the world would keel over. *Yiddish*
605. If there were no fools or scoundrels in the world, all people would agree on everything. *American*
606. "Let us agree not to step on each other's feet," said the cock to the horse. *English*
607. Make your flutes agree. (Settle your differences.) *French*
608. My idea of an agreeable person is a person who agrees with me. *English (Disraeli)*
609. No two on earth in all things can agree. *American*
610. There is no accord where every man would be lord. *English*
611. They agree like bells; they want nothing but hanging. *English*
612. When all men say you are an ass, it is time to bray. *Spanish*
613. When two men are of one mind, clay may be turned into gold. *Chinese*

Agriculture *see* **Farmers and Farming**

Aid *see* **Assistance; Collaboration; Cooperation; Divine Assistance; Man and God; Prayer; Unity**

Ailment *see* **Disease; Illness**

Aiming Too High *see also* **Ambition; Aspiration**
614. A child may crush a snail, but it will not crush a tortoise. *Oji*
615. A thing which cannot be lifted should never be undertaken. *Yoruba*
616. Asses sing badly because they pitch their voices too high. *German*
617. Attempt nothing beyond your strength. *Latin*
618. By jumping at the moon you may fall in the mud. *American*
619. Don't put your hat higher than you can reach. *Jamaican*
620. He that hewes over hie, the spaill [chips] will fall into his eye. *Scottish*
621. He who stands on tiptoe does not stand firm. *Chinese (Laotse)*
622. Hew not too high, / Lest the chips fall in thine eye. *English*
623. If you take big paces, you leave big spaces. *Burmese*
624. Men would be Angels, Angels would be gods. *English (Pope)*
625. Not if you burst yourself will you equal him. *Latin (Horace)*
626. One may miss the mark by aiming too high as too low. *English*
627. People are always neglecting something they can do in trying to do something they can't do. *American (Howe)*
628. Slight not what's near through aiming at what's far. *Greek (Euripides)*
629. The ambitious bullfrog puffed and puffed until he burst. *American*
630. The bear wants a tail and cannot be a lion. *Latin*
631. The camel that was seeking horns lost his ears. *Hebrew*
632. The crab would catch a hare! *Latin*
633. The leech wants to become a snake. *Mauritius Creole*
634. The poor, wishing to imitate the powerful, perish. *Latin*
635. There is no eel so small but it hopes to become a whale. *American*
636. Vaulting ambition...o'erleaps itself. *English (Shakespeare)*
637. What is too high, that let fly. *English*
638. Who aims at things beyond his reach, the greater will be his fall. *Latin*

Alcohol *see* Drinking and Drunkenness; Wine

Alertness *see* Caution; Listening; Watchfulness

Alternatives *see also* Choice; Parts and Wholes; Preference; Taste

639. A bad bush is better than the open field. *American*

640. A bad camel is better than a good field. *Arabic*

641. A bad field is better than a good camel. *Arabic*

642. A barley-corn is better than a diamond to a cock. *English*

643. A bit in the morning is better than a thump in the back with a stone. *English*

644. A bit in the morning is better than nothing all day. *English*

645. A broken pot is better than none. *American*

646. A little bite is as good as a feast. Gĩkũyũ

647. A little is better than nothing. *Wolof*

648. A lively devil is better than a frigid angel. *Lebanese*

649. A thin bush is better than no shelter. *American*

650. A trout in the pot is better than a salmon in the sea. *Irish*

651. As good eat the devil as the broth he's boiled in. *English*

652. Bannocks [oat-cakes] is better than na kind o' bread. *Scottish*

653. Barefoot-tea [i.e., an unsubstantial meal] is better than an empty belly. *Belizean Creole*

654. Better a bird in the hand than a thousand on the house. *Romanian*

655. Better a bird in the hand than three in the wood. *English*

656. Better a blind horse than an empty halter. *Danish*

657. Better a false "Good morning" than a sincere "Go to hell." *Yiddish*

658. Better a finger aff as aye wagging. *Scottish (Scott)*

659. Better a handful of bees than a basketful of flies. *Moroccan*

660. Better a hawk in the hand than two in flight. *Icelandic*

661. Better a lean horse than a toom [empty] halter. *Scottish*

662. Better a leveret in the kitchen than a wild boar in the forest. *Livonian*

663. Better a red face than a black heart. *Portuguese*

664. Better a sparrow in the hand than a vulture on the wing. *Spanish (Cervantes)*

665. Better a sparrow in the hand than two flying. *Portuguese*

666. Better a wee fire that warms nor a meikle [than a great one] that burns. *Scottish*

667. Better a wren in the hand than a crane in the air. *French*

668. Better an egg in peace, than an ox in war. *English*

669. Better an egg today than a hen tomorrow. *Italian*

670. Better be mad with all the world than wise alone. *French*

671. Better be the head of a cat than the tail of a lion. *Italian*

672. Better be the head of a pike [or a sprat] than the tail of a sturgeon. *English*

673. Better be the head of the yeomanry than the tail of the gentry. *English*

674. Better bend than break. *American*

675. Better bowlegs than no legs at all. *American*

676. Better break your leg than your neck. *American*

677. Better coarse cloth than the naked thighs. *Danish*

678. Better finger off nor ay warkin. *Scottish*

679. Better give the wool than the sheep. *English*

680. Better go without medicine than call in an unskillful physician. *Japanese*

681. Better half an egg nor [i.e., than] an empty shell. *Scottish*

682. Better haud wi' the hound than rin wi' the hare. *Scottish*

683. Better have a mouse in the pot as no flesh. *Scottish*

684. Better nae ring nor [i.e., than] the ring of a rush [or rash]. *Scottish*

685. Better old debts nor [i.e., than] old sores. *Scottish*

686. Better play at small game than stand out. *English*

687. Better sit still than rise an' fa'. *Scottish*

688. Better small fish than an empty dish. *Scottish*

689. Better spare at the breird [brim] than at the bottom. *Scottish*

690. Better the head of a dog than the tail of a lion. *English*

691. Better the head of an ass, than the tail of a horse. *English*

692. Better the ill ken'd [bad known] than the gude unken'd [good unknown]. *Scottish*

693. Better to be the head of a cat than the tail of a lion. *Italian*

694. Better to be the head of a lizard than the tail of a dragon. *Italian*

695. Better to rule than be ruled by the rout. *English*

696. Better to trust in God than in his saints. *French*

697. Better walk before than behind a police horse. *American*

698. Better weak beer than lemonade. *American*

699. Choose rather to be the tail of lions than the head of foxes. *Hebrew*

700. Half a loaf is better than no bread. *English*

701. Half a loaf is better than none. *American*

702. He fled from the sword and hid in the scabbard. *Yoruba*

703. Horseradish is not sweeter than garden radish. *Russian*

704. It is better to lose the saddle than the horse. *Italian*

705. It's better to have a little than nothing. *American*

706. It's better to have a sparrow today than a wild turkey tomorrow. *Hungarian*

707. One bird in the net is better than a hundred flying. *Hebrew*

708. Sma' fish are better than nae [no] fish [or better than nane (none)]. *Scottish*

709. Smoke that blinds rather than cold that makes me ill. *Syrian*

710. Somewhat is better than nothing. *Irish*

711. Take it or leave it. *American*

712. The voter must often choose between Tweedledum and Tweedledee. *American*

713. Throw no gift at the giver's head; / Better is half a loaf than no bread. *English*

714. Vinegar in hand is better than halvah to come. *Persian*

715. Who cannot catch fish must catch shrimps. *Chinese*

716. Who will not feed the cats, must feed the mice and rats. *German*

Ambiguity *see* Approximation; Vagueness

Ambition *see also* Aiming Too High; Aspiration

717. A great mark is soonest hit. *American*

718. A man's worth is no greater than the worth of his ambitions. *Latin (Marcus Aurelius)*

719. Ambition can creep as well as soar. *English (Burke)*

720. Ambition destroys its possessor. *Babylonian Talmud*

721. Ambition is but avarice on stilts and masked. *English (Landor)*

722. Ambition is no cure for love. *Scottish*

723. Ambition is not a vice of little people. *French (Montaigne)*

724. Ambition is the growth of every clime. *English (Blake)*

725. Ambition is the last infirmity of noble minds. *American*

726. Ambition is the only power that combats love. *English (Cibber)*

727. Ambition makes more trusty slaves than need. *English (Jonson)*

728. Ambition makes people diligent. *German*

729. Ambition obeys no law but its own appetite. *English*

730. An upstart is a sparrow eager to be betrothed to a hornbill. *Malay*

731. Be wise; / Soar not too high to fall; but stoop to rise. *English (Massinger)*

732. Black ambition stains a public cause. *English (Pope)*

733. Every ambitious man is a captive and every covetous one a pauper. *Arabic*

734. Every little fish would become a whale. *American*

735. Every man believes that he has a greater possibility. *American (Emerson)*

736. First, say to yourself what you would be; and then do what you have to do. *Greek* (Epictetus)

737. Fling away ambition: by that sin fell the angels. *American*

738. Golden dreams make men awake hungry. *English*

739. He begins to die that quits his desires. *English*

740. He who cannot do always wants to do. *Italian*

741. He who opens his heart to ambition closes it to repose. *Italian*

742. He who would leap high must take a long run. *Danish*

743. He who would rise in the world should veil his ambition with the forms of humanity. *Chinese*

744. He will shoot higher who shoots at the sun than he who aims at a tree. *English (Sidney)*

745. If the string is long, the kite will fly high. *Chinese*

746. If you love, love a moon; if you steal, steal a camel. *Egyptian*

747. Keep your eye upon the goal. *Latin*

748. Learn to creep before you run. *English*

749. Man is naturally ambitious, but water flows downward. *Chinese*

750. No bird soars too high, if he soars with his own wings. *English (Blake)*

751. No tree has ever reached the sky. *Syrian*

752. Nothing arouses ambition so much in the heart as the trumpet-clang of another's fame. *Spanish (Gracián)*

753. Nothing humbler than ambition, when it is about to climb. *American (Franklin)*

754. Poor by condition, rich by ambition. *Chinese*

755. Seize what is highest, and you will possess what is in between. *Greek*

756. Stretch your feet only as your blanket allows. *Turkish*

757. The greatest evil which fortune can inflict on men is to endow them with small talents and great ambition. *French (Vauvenargues)*

758. The higher they rise, the steeper they fall. *American*

759. The highest branch is not the safest roost. *English*

760. The noblest spirit is most strongly attracted by the love of glory. *Latin (Cicero)*

761. The slave has but one master; the man of ambition has as many as there are people useful to his fortune. *French (La Bruyere)*

762. The tallest trees are most in the power of the winds, and ambitious men of the blasts of fortune. *American (Penn)*

763. The trap to the high-born is ambition. *English*

764. The true way is the middle one, halfway between deserving a place and pushing oneself into it. *Latin* (Gracian)

765. The wise man is cured of ambition by ambition. *French (La Bruyere)*

766. Things beyond our reach are not worth our consideration. *Latin*

767. Though ambition may be a fault in itself, it is often the mother of virtues. *Latin (Quintilian)*

768. 'Tis a laudable ambition, that aims at being better than his neighbors. *American (Franklin)*

769. To get what you want you must be prepared to kiss a dog on its mouth. *Tunisian*

770. To jump farther than the width of the ditch. *German*

771. To lick the sky with the tongue. *Arabic*

772. To take ambition from a soldier, is to rob him of his spurs. *English*

773. Too low they build, who build beneath the stars. *English (Edward Young)*

774. Too often those who entertain ambition, expel remorse and nature. *English (Shakespeare)*

775. Virtue is choked with foul ambition. *English (Shakespeare)*

776. What shall it profit a man, if he shall gain the whole world, and lose his own soul? *Bible*

777. Whatever you undertake let it be proportioned to your powers. *Latin*

778. Who never climbed high never fell low. *English*

Amendment *see also* Conscience; Irrevocableness; Penitence; Reform; Repentance

779. Amendment is not sin. *French*

780. Amendment is repentance. *English*

781. Be not afraid to amend your fault. *Chinese*

782. He'll mend when he grows better, like sour ale in summer. *Scottish*

783. In the end things will mend. *English*

784. It is easier to descend than ascend. *English*

785. It is easier to run from virtue to vice, than from vice to virtue. *English*

786. It's never too late to mend. *Spanish*

787. Least said, soonest mended. *English*

788. Ower sune [over soon] is easy mendit [easily mended]. *Scottish*

789. The course of a river is not to be altered. *Latin*

790. The descent to the infernal regions is easy, but to rise again to the air above is not. *Latin (Virgil)*

791. There's naething [nothing] but mends for misdeeds. *Scottish*

792. When a fault is known, it should be amended. *Chinese*

793. Who sins and mends, commends himself to God. *Spanish*

794. Who stumbles and does not fall mends his pace. *Spanish*

Amiability

795. Amiability begets riches. *Chinese*

Amount *see* Quantity

Amusement *see also* Humor; Jests and Jesting

796. Amusement is the happiness of those who cannot think. *English (Pope)*

797. Amusement to an observing mind is study. *English (Disraeli)*

Ancestry *see also* Heredity

798. He that boasts of his ancestors confesses that he has no value to himself. *Welsh*

799. There's nobbut [lit., not but] three generations atween clog and clog. *English*

Anger *see also* Temper

800. A headstrong man and a fool may wear the same cap. *English*

801. A man that does not know how to be angry does not know how to be good. *American (Beecher)*

802. An angry man is a madman's brother. *Lebanese*

803. An angry man stirreth up strife. *Bible*

804. Anger and folly walk cheek by jole; repentance treads on both their heels. *American (Franklin)*

805. Anger begins with folly and ends with prayer. *American*

806. Anger can't stand, without a strong hand. *English*

807. Anger dieth quickly with a good man. *English*

808. Anger ends in cruelty. *Indian*

809. Anger has no eyes. *Hindi*

810. Anger has nothing to do with counsel. *German*

811. Anger, if not restrained, is often more hurtful to us than the injury that provokes it. *Latin (Seneca)*

812. Anger is a bad adviser. *Hungarian*

813. Anger is a brief madness but it can do damage that lasts forever. *American*

814. Anger is a brief madness. *Latin (Horace)*

815. Anger is a fool. *Yiddish*

816. Anger is a stone cast into a wasp's nest. *Malabar*

817. Anger is a transient madness. *Latin*

818. Anger is as useless as the waves of the ocean without wind. *Chinese*

819. Anger is more hurtful than the injury that caused it. *English*

820. Anger is never without a reason, but seldom with a good one. *American (Franklin)*

821. Anger is one of the sinews of the soul; he that wants it hath a maimed mind. *English*

822. Anger is short-lived in a good man. *English*

823. Anger is the fever and frenzy of the soul. *American*

824. Anger makes dull men witty, but it keeps them poor. *English (Bacon)*

825. Anger manages everything badly. *Latin (Statius)*

826. Anger renders the man insane and the prophet dumb. *Hebrew*

827. Anger resteth in the bosom of fools. *Bible*

828. Anger warms the Invention, but overheats the Oven. *American (Franklin)*

829. Anger without power is folly. *German*

830. Anger's final resting-place is the bosom of fools. *American*

831. Anger's mair [more] hurtfu' than the wrang [wrong] that caused it. *Scottish*

832. Anger's short-lived in a gude man. *Scottish*

833. Angry men make themselves beds of nettles. *English (Richardson)*

834. Angry men seldom want woe. *English*

835. Beware of him that is slow to anger: he is angry for something, and will not be pleased for nothing. *American (Franklin)*

836. Beware the fury of a patient man. *English (Dryden)*

837. Choleric men are blind and mad. *English*

838. Come not between the dragon and his wrath. *English (Shakespeare)*

839. Concealed anger is to be feared; but hatred openly manifested destroys its chance of revenge. *Latin (Seneca)*

840. Dread the anger of the cornered sheep. *American*

841. Even a fly can show temper. *Latin*

842. Even a fly has wrath. *Latin*

843. Even the ant and the worm have their wrath. *Greek*

844. Even the ant has its gall. *Latin*

845. Fire that's closest kept burns most of all. *English (Shakespeare)*

846. Fire will not put out fire. Anger is not appeased by anger. *Latin*

847. Fury and anger carry the mind away. *Latin (Virgil)*

848. He best keeps anger who remembers that God is always looking upon him. *Greek (Plato)*

849. He got angry with the fleas and threw his fur coat into the oven. *Russian*

850. He got angry with the rat and set fire to the house. *Pakistani*

851. He has na gotten the first seat o' the midden the day. *Scottish*

852. He hath wit at will that with an angry heart can hold him still. *Scottish*

853. He that is angry is seldom at ease. *English*

854. He that is angry without a cause, shall be pleased without amends. *English*

855. He that is slow to anger is better than the mighty; and he that ruleth his spirit than he that taketh a city. *Bible*

856. He that will be angry for anything will be angry for naething. *Scottish*

857. He that's angry opens his mouth and steeks [shuts] his een [eyes]. *Scottish*

858. He's ne'er at ease that's angry. *Scottish*

859. However weak the hand, anger gives it strength. *Latin (Ovid)*

860. If you kick a stone because you are angry at it, you will only hurt your foot. *Korean*

861. If you look at your brother's faults you get angry; if you overlook them you get the grace of Heaven. *American*

862. Ill-will ne'er spak weel. *Scottish*

863. Ill words are bellows to a slackening fire. *English*

864. It is hidden wrath that harms. *Latin (Seneca)*

865. Let him come to himself, like MacKibbon's crowdy [porridge]. *Scottish*

866. Let not the sun go down upon your wrath. *Bible*

867. Like a mad dog, he snaps at himself. *Afghan*

868. Like a man who would not wash his feet in the tank because he was angry with it. *Tamil*

869. Like ice, anger passes away. *Latin (Ovid)*

870. Master anger. *Greek (Periander)*

871. No man is angry that feels not himself hurt. *English (Bacon)*

872. Rancor will out. *English (Shakespeare)*

873. She stamps like a ewe upon yeaning [lambing]. *Scottish*

874. Sturt [anger] pays nae debt. *Scottish*

875. Sweeter than honey is anger. *Turkish*

876. The anger of those in authority is always weighty. *Latin (Seneca)*

877. The angry beggar gets a stone instead of a handout. *American*

878. The angry man opens his mouth and shuts his eyes. *American*

879. The fire you kindle for your enemy often burns yourself more than him. *Chinese*

880. The greatest remedy for anger is delay. *Latin (Seneca)*

881. The pain of anger punishes the fault. *Greek (Homer)*

882. The tigers of wrath are wiser than the horses of instruction. *English (Blake)*

883. There is no old age for a man's anger, / Only death. *Greek (Sophocles)*

884. To be angry is to punish yourself for another's sins. *American*

885. To be angry is to revenge the faults of others on ourselves. *English (Pope)*

886. When a man is angry, he cannot be in the right. *Chinese*

887. When anger rises, think of the consequences. *Chinese (Confucius)*

888. When angry, count four; when very angry, swear. *American (Twain)*

889. When angry count ten; when very angry, a hundred. *American*

890. When passion is on the throne, reason is out of doors. *English (M. Henry)*

891. When the pot boils over it cools itself. *English*

892. Who spits against heaven, it falls in his face. *American*

893. Wrath killeth the foolish man. *Bible*

894. Wrath often consumes what goodness husbands. *Icelandic*

Animals

895. A man's best friend is his dog. *American*

896. Cats, like men, are flatterers. *English (Landor)*

897. Human beings have two feet less than other animals — that's the best that can be said about them. *American*

Annoyance *see* Interference; Meddling

Answers *see also* Questions; Questions and Answers; Response; Soft Words

898. A soft answer turneth away wrath. *Bible*

899. An answer is a word. *Scottish*

900. Every man shall kiss his lips that giveth a right answer. *Bible*

901. No answer is also an answer. *Danish*

902. Not all words require an answer. *Italian*

903. Silence is the best answer to a fool. *American*

904. The best answer is to roll up your sleeves and do the job yourself. *American*

905. To answer like a Scot. [To answer ambiguously.] *Scottish*

Antagonism

906. Though the mastiff be gentle, yet bite him not by the lip. *English*

Anxiety *see* Worry

Apathy *see* **Indifference**

Apology *see also* **Atonement; Confession; Forgiveness; Regret; Repentance**

907. A wound is not cured by the unbending of the bow. [Apology for an injury is not sufficient.] *Italian*

Appearance *see also* **Beauty; Clothes; Countenance; Deception; Face; Hypocrisy; Identity; Inference; Judging; Seeming; Vanity; Women and Their Bodies; Women and Vanity**

908. A black hen lays a white egg. *English*
909. A black plum is as sweet as a white. *English*
910. A blithe heart makes a blomand visage. *Scottish*
911. A bright-eyed blind man. [One who looks brighter than he is.] *Chinese*
912. A deformed body may have a beautiful soul. *American*
913. A dink [neat, trim] maiden aft maks a dirty wife. *Scottish*
914. A good horse cannot be of a bad color. *English*
915. A good presence is letters of recommendation. *English*
916. A grave and majestic outside is the palace of the soul. *Chinese*
917. A little body doth often harbor a great soul. *English*
918. A man cannot be known by his looks, nor can the sea be measured with a bushel basket. *Chinese*
919. A man, in order to establish himself in the world, does everything he can to appear established there. *French (La Rochefoucauld)*
920. A man may be old and yet have a youthful heart; a man may be poor and yet his will be undaunted. *Chinese*
921. A poor cask often holds good wine. *Latin*
922. A straight stick is crooked in the water. *English*
923. A white glove often conceals a dirty hand. *English*
924. A' are no thieves that dogs bark at. *Scottish*
925. A' cats are gray in the dark. *Scottish*
926. A's no gowd [gold] that glitters, nor maidens that wear their hair. *Scottish*
927. All cows are black in the dark. *Estonian*
928. All saint without, all devil within. *English*
929. Always scorn appearances and you always may. *American (Emerson)*
930. An ape is an ape, though decked with gold. *Latin*
931. An ape's an ape though he wears a gold ring. *Dutch*
932. An ass in a lion's hide. *English*
933. An ox with long horns, even if he does not butt, will be accused of butting. *Malay*
934. Appearance cheats. *Hungarian*
935. Appearances are deceitful. *French*
936. As they see you, so they describe you. *Polish*
937. Be what you appear to be. *Latin*
938. Beads about the neck and the devil in the heart. *Spanish*
939. Believe not that the stream is shallow because its surface is smooth. *Latin*
940. Bonnie feathers dinna aye mak [do not always make] bonnie birds. *Scottish*
941. By appearance an eagle, by intelligence a black cock. *Russian*
942. By the husk you may guess at the nut. *English*
943. Cats of all colors are black at night. *Hungarian*
944. Compliment an old hag on her lovely appearance and she'll take you at your word. *American*
945. Curly hair, curly thoughts. *Russian*
946. Cutting off a mule's ears won't make him a horse. *American*
947. Dirt glitters as long as the sun shines. *German (Goethe)*
948. Dirty troughs will serve dirty sows. *American*
949. Do not mistake a goat's beard for a fine stallion's tail. *Irish*
950. Don't rely on the label of the bag. *English*
951. Don't trust the weak appearance of the wolf or the disappearance of the cat: they'll both make a comeback. *American*
952. Even virtue is fairer in a fair body. *Latin (Virgil)*
953. Every glowworm is not a fire. *Italian*
954. Fair hair may hae [have] foul roots. *Scottish*
955. Fair without, foul within. *English*
956. Fine cage does not feed the bird. *French*
957. Fine words and an insinuating appearance are seldom associated with true virtue. *Chinese (Confucius)*
958. First impressions are most lasting. *Italian*
959. Foolish men mistake transitory semblances for eternal fact, and go astray more and more. *English (Carlyle)*
960. Froth is not beer. *Dutch*
961. Gude wares hae often come frae an ill market. *Scottish*
962. Habit maketh no monk, ne wearing of gilt spurs maketh no knight. *English (Chaucer)*
963. Handsome features are a silent recommendation. *Latin (Publilius Syrus)*
964. He has an ill look among lambs. *Scottish*
965. He is like a silvered pin, fair without but foul within. *English*
966. He looks as if he could swallow a cow. *Scottish*
967. He looks as if he would not muddy the water. *Spanish*
968. He looks as if the wood were fu' o' thieves. *Scottish*
969. He looks like the far end o' a French fiddle. *Scottish*
970. He smiles, but does the heart smile? *Congolese*
971. He that would no evil do, / Must do nought that's like thereto. *English*
972. He who observes the speaker more than the sound of his words, will seldom meet with disappointment. *American*
973. His heart is not upright whose eye looks askance. *Chinese*
974. Hit is not al gold that glareth. *English (Chaucer)*
975. I am black, but I am not the devil. *English*
976. If the beard were all, the goat might preach. *Danish*

977. If thou do na ill, do na ill like. *Scottish*

978. If you want a fine wife, don't pick her on a Sunday. *Spanish*

979. In painting a tiger, one can paint the skin, but it is impossible to paint the bones. *Chinese*

980. In the coldest flint there is hot fire. *English*

981. It is for its contents that one kisses a book. *Arabic*

982. It's no the cowl that maks the friar. *Scottish*

983. Judge not according to the appearance. *Bible*

984. Long whiskers cannot take the place of brains. *Russian*

985. Look to the mind, not to the outward appearance. *Greek (Aesop)*

986. Mair [more] than the deil [devil] wear a black manteel. *Scottish*

987. Men take more pains to mask than mend. *American (Franklin)*

988. Merit in appearance is more often rewarded than merit itself. *American*

989. Narrowness of waist shows narrowness of mind. *American*

990. Neither jewel, nor woman, nor linen by candlelight. *Italian*

991. Never let the prejudice of the eye determine the heart. *American*

992. Not all who go to church say their prayers. *Italian*

993. Not every man a huntsman who can blow a horn. *Latin*

994. Not everyone is a saint who goes to church. *Italian*

995. Not everyone with a blackened face can say, "I am a blacksmith." *Arabic*

996. Not everything round is a nut; not everything long is a banana. *Lebanese*

997. Often under a rough leaf a lovely fruit is hidden. *Italian*

998. Outside, fair; inside, foul. *American*

999. Outside show is a poor substitute for inner worth. *Greek (Aesop)*

1000. Outward appearances assuming the form of virtues. *Latin*

1001. Philosophers as far as the beard. *Latin*

1002. Small like a pea, but with the voice of an ogre. *Tunisian*

1003. So honour peereth in the meanest habit. *English (Shakespeare)*

1004. Telling the tree by its fruit. *Greek*

1005. The beard does not make the philosopher. *English*

1006. The devil is not so ugly as he is painted. *Italian*

1007. The fairest looking shoe may pinch the foot. *American*

1008. The fox changes his skin but remains the rogue. *German*

1009. The fox may grow gray, but never good. *English*

1010. The fox may lose his hair but not his tricks. *Dutch*

1011. The house may be imposing, but God knows what is inside it. *Omani*

1012. The Lord seeth not as man seeth; for man looketh on the outward appearance, but the Lord looketh on the heart. *Bible*

1013. The magician mutters, and knows not what he mutters. *Hebrew*

1014. The oleander is beautiful but bitter. *Moroccan*

1015. The prudent person will distrust most when appearances are fairest. *American*

1016. The title is one thing, the contents another. *Latin*

1017. The tonsure does not make the monk, nor the rough clothing. *Latin*

1018. The world is governed more by appearances than by realities. *American (Webster)*

1019. There is many a fair thing full false. *Scottish*

1020. There is no reliance to be placed on appearance. *Latin (Juvenal)*

1021. There never has been a red-haired saint. *Russian*

1022. They are not all cooks who carry a long knife. *Italian*

1023. They are not all friends who laugh with you. *German*

1024. They're no a' saints that get holy water. *Scottish*

1025. Things are not as they are, but as they are regarded. *Italian*

1026. Think not all things gold which you see glittering. *Latin*

1027. 'Tis not the habit that makes the monk. *English*

1028. Vice would be frightful if it did not wear a mask. *English*

1029. We are deceived by the appearance of right. *Latin (Horace)*

1030. We love good looks rather than what is practical, / Though good looks may prove destructive. *French (La Fontaine)*

1031. Where you think there are flitches of bacon there are not even hooks to hang them on. *Spanish*

1032. Wise as far as the beard. *Latin*

1033. Ye look like Let-me-be. *Scottish*

1034. Ye look liker [more like] a deil [devil] than a bishop. *Scottish*

1035. Yet gold all is not that doth golden seem. *English (Shakespeare)*

1036. You can't know a girl by her looks or a man by his books. *American*

Appetite *see also* Diet; Eating; Excess; Gluttony; Hunger; Moderation; Obesity

1037. A growing boy can never eat his fill; there's always room for more. *American*

1038. A stomach that is seldom empty despises common food. *Latin (Horace)*

1039. A well-governed appetite is a great part of liberty. *Latin (Seneca)*

1040. All the labor of man is for his mouth, and yet the appetite is not filled. *Bible*

1041. Appetite and reason are like two buckets — when one is up, the other is down. *English (Collier)*

1042. Appetite comes with eating. *French*

1043. Appetite does not need sauce. *Italian*

1044. Choose rather to punish your appetites than to be punished by them. *Latin (Tyrius)*

1045. He who checks his appetite avoids debt. *Chinese*

1046. It is the sign of an over-nice appetite to toy with many dishes. *Latin (Seneca)*

1047. Let the appetites be subject to reason. *Latin (Cicero)*

1048. No purse so fat as to buy back a lost appetite. *Japanese*

1049. One always has a good appetite at another's feast. *Yiddish*

1050. One quarter makes the other sell. *French*

1051. Put a knife to thy throat, if thou be a man given to appetite. *Bible*

1052. Reason should direct, and appetite obey. *Latin (Cicero)*

1053. Seek an appetite by hard toil. *Latin (Horace)*

1054. Taste, and you will feed. *Arabic*

1055. The eye is bigger than the belly. *English*

1056. There is no sauce but that of appetite. *French*

1057. There's no stomach a hand's breadth bigger than another. *Spanish (Cervantes)*

1058. What is earned with hard labor is eaten with pleasure. *Chinese*

1059. What one relishes, nourishes. *American (Franklin)*

1060. Where reason rules, appetite obeys. *American*

1061. Ye have a ready mouth for a ripe cherry. *Scottish*

Applause *see also* Appreciation; Approval; Honor; Praise

1062. Applause is the beginning of abuse. *Japanese*

1063. He seeks renown by public applause. *Latin*

1064. He who is greedy of applause never gives a cheer for a rival. *American*

1065. No man will disown the wish to earn the applause of men. *Latin (Persius)*

Appreciation *see also* Judging; Judgment; Taste; Understanding

1066. Neither cast ye pearls before swine, lest they trample them under their feet, and turn again and rend you. *Bible*

Appropriateness *see also* Inappropriateness; Proportion; Timeliness

1067. Set the saddle on the right horse. *Hebrew*

Approval *see also* Fame; Popularity; Praise

1068. Fools and bairns should not see half-done work. *Scottish*

1069. It is the wedding of the sickle and all the song is for the hoe. *Behar*

1070. It is well to buy oil as well as salt. *Latin*

1071. On a good day good things are to be spoken. *Latin*

1072. The better the day the better the deed. *English*

1073. The song should be for her whose wedding it is. *Behar*

1074. Virtue is increased by the smile of approval; and the love of renown is the greatest incentive to honorable acts. *Latin (Ovid)*

Approximation *see also* Vagueness

1075. An inch breaks no squares. [An inch more or less does not matter.] *English*

1076. An inch of a miss is as good as a mile. *English*

1077. As good twenty as nineteen. *English*

Argument *see also* Contention; Discord; Dispute; Fighting; Quarreling; Stress and Strain; Strife

1078. A knock-down argument; 'tis but a word and a blow. *English (Dryden)*

1079. A man convinced against his will is of the same opinion still. *American*

1080. Argument seldom convinces anyone contrary to his inclinations. *English*

1081. Avoid contesting with the powerful. *Latin*

1082. Debate destroys despatch. *English (Denham)*

1083. Do not argue against the sun. *Latin*

1084. Do not investigate facts by the light of arguments, but arguments by the light of facts. *Greek*

1085. In a heated argument we are apt to lose sight of the truth. *Latin*

1086. It takes two to start an argument. *American*

1087. It's easy as pie to get into an argument and hard as hell to get out. *American*

1088. Men's arguments often prove nothing but their wishes. *English (Colton)*

1089. The arguments of the strongest have the most weight. *French*

1090. The man who loves to argue is left without friends. *American*

1091. There are two sides to every question. *Greek*

1092. There is no such thing as a convincing argument, although every man thinks he has one. *American (Howe)*

1093. To strike with a leaden sword [i.e., a pointless argument]. *Latin*

1094. Truth becomes lost in the turmoil of arguments. *Latin*

1095. Understand your opponent before you answer him. *American*

1096. We may convince others by our arguments; but we can only persuade them by their own. *French (Joubert)*

1097. When the argument flares up the wise man quenches it by silence. *American*

1098. When you argue with a fool, be sure he isn't similarly engaged. *American*

1099. Wise men argue causes; fools decide them. *Scythian (Anacharsis)*

1100. With much argument and disputation, one often loses the truth. *German*

Arrogance

1101. Arrogance is a roadblock on the highway of wisdom. *American*

1102. Arrogance is a weed that grows maistly in the midden [mostly on the dunghill]. *Scottish*

1103. Arrogance is intolerable. *Latin*

1104. He's too big for his britches. *American*

1105. The weed of arrogance grows on a dunghill. *American*

Art and Artists *see also* **Art and Nature**

1106. A man may be an artist though he lacks the necessary tools. *American*

1107. An art requires a whole man. *American*

1108. An artist gains fame and fortune—after he is dead. *American*

1109. An artist lives everywhere. *Greek*

1110. An artist lives on fame, but he prefers bread and cheese. *American*

1111. Art hath no enemy but ignorance. *Latin*

1112. Art holds fast when all else is gone. *German*

1113. Art is by far weaker than necessity. *Greek (Aeschylus)*

1114. Art is long and life is short. *Greek (Hippocrates)*

1115. Art is long and time is fleeting. *American (Longfellow)*

1116. Art makes favor. *German*

1117. Every artist was first an amateur. *American*

1118. Good material often stands idle for want of an artist. *Latin (Seneca)*

1119. He who has learned any art may live in any place. *Spanish*

1120. In art, as in love, instinct is enough. *French (France)*

1121. It is a poor art that does not maintain the artisan. *Italian*

1122. It is the perfection of art when no trace of the artist appears. *Latin*

1123. Let each man exercise the art he knows. *Greek (Aristophanes)*

1124. Life is short, art is long. *Latin*

1125. Never judge a work of art by its defects. *American (Washington Allston)*

1126. The artist needs no religion beyond his work. *American*

1127. The best art conceals art. *American*

1128. The devil is master of all the arts. *American*

1129. The good artist is a successful failure. *American*

1130. The greatest art is the art of life. *American*

1131. The perfection of art is to conceal art. *Latin (Quintilian)*

1132. Without favor art is like a windmill without wind. *Danish*

Art and Nature

1133. All art is but imitation of nature. *Latin (Seneca)*

1134. Art helps nature, and experience art. *English*

1135. Art imitates nature. *American*

1136. Don't whiten ivory and spoil nature by art. *American*

1137. He who paints the flower cannot paint its fragrance. *Latin*

1138. Nature is the art of God. *Latin*

1139. Nature without an effort surpasses art. *Latin*

1140. Nature's gold is genuine; art makes it false. *American*

1141. Where art is displayed truth does not appear. *Latin*

Artfulness *see also* **Deception; Pretense**

1142. An artful fellow is the devil in a doublet. *English*

Asking *see also* **Answers; Denial; Questions; Questions and Answers; Refusal**

1143. A good asker should have a good nay-sayer. *Scottish*

1144. A man may speir [ask about] the gate [road] he kens [knows] fu' weel. *Scottish*

1145. Ask no favors and everywhere men are affable; if you don't drink it doesn't matter what price wine is. *Chinese*

1146. Ask the host if he has good wine. *Italian*

1147. Ask the patient, not the physician, where the pain is. *Polish*

1148. Ask the young people; they know everything. *French*

1149. Better ask twice than go wrong once. *German*

1150. Better to ask than go astray. *Italian*

1151. Do not give an opinion until it is asked for. *Latin*

1152. Every question requires not an answer. *American*

1153. He that asks faintly begs a denial. *Latin*

1154. He that has a tongue in his mouth can find his way anywhere. *English*

1155. He that speirs [asks] a' gets wit but o' pairt. *Scottish*

1156. He who asks timidly invites a refusal. *Latin (Seneca)*

1157. He who wants a great deal must not ask for a little. *Italian*

1158. He's a fool that asks ower muckle [too much], but he's a greater fool that gies it. *Scottish*

1159. I know well what I say when I ask for bread. *Spanish*

1160. If you are reluctant to ask the way, you will be lost. *Malay*

1161. If you do not ask their help, all men are good-natured. *Chinese*

1162. Lose nothing for asking. *English*

1163. Mair in a mair dish. [More in a larger dish.] *Scottish*

1164. Many a man asks the way he knows full well. *Scottish*

1165. Many things are lost for want of asking. *American*

1166. Misterful [needy] folk must not be menseful [i.e., hesitant about asking]. *Scottish*

1167. Never ask of him who has, but of him who wishes you well. *Spanish*

1168. Nothing ask, nothing have. *American*

1169. They are as wise that speir [ask] not. *Scottish*

1170. They give, to find a pretext for asking. *Latin*

1171. Who has a tongue can go to Rome. *Spanish*

Aspiration *see also* **Aiming Too High; Ambition**

1172. Heaven is not really high; the heart of man aspires higher and higher. *Chinese*

1173. Hitch your wagon to a star. *American (Emerson)*

1174. Not failure, but low aim, is crime. *American (James R. Lowell)*

1175. Power to do good is the true and lawful end of aspiring. *English (Bacon)*

1176. 'Tis not what man does which exalts him, but what man would do! *English (Browning)*

1177. Who digs hills because they do aspire, throws down one mountain to cast up a higher. *English (Shakespeare)*

Assertiveness

1178. A man may lose his goods for want of demanding them. *English*

1179. He never gets good business who does not dare to ask for it. *French*

Asses *see also* Folly; Fools and Folly; Learned Fools; Wisdom and Folly

1180. Many asses have only two legs. *Latin*

Assessment *see also* Judgment; Value; Worth

1181. No wise combatant underrates his antagonist. *American*

Assimilation *see* Adaptability; Conformity; Flexibility

Assistance *see also* Collaboration; Cooperation; Divine Assistance; Prayer; Unity

1182. A grain does not fill a sack but it helps its fellow. *Spanish*

1183. All rivers do what they can for the sea. *American*

1184. Assist him who is carrying his burden, but by no means him who is laying it aside. *Latin*

1185. Clapping with the right hand only will not produce a noise. *Malay*

1186. Don't lift me till I fall. *Irish*

1187. Even the just have need of help. *Italian*

1188. Every little bit helps. *American*

1189. Every ten years one man has need of another. *Italian*

1190. Everything helps, quoth the wren, when she pissed into the sea. *French*

1191. Four eyes see more than two. *Latin*

1192. Give a helping hand to a man in trouble. *Latin*

1193. God's help is nearer than the door. *American*

1194. He who greases his wheels helps his oxen. *Italian*

1195. He who helps everybody helps nobody. *Spanish*

1196. Help is good everywhere except at one's dinner. *Yiddish*

1197. Help the lame dog over the stile. *English*

1198. If you help everybody you help nobody. *American*

1199. In misfortune we need help, not lamentation. *Latin*

1200. It is a kindly act to help the fallen. *Latin*

1201. It is by helping one another that the lion is subdued. *Moroccan*

1202. It is easier to seize the tiger in the hills than to appeal to man for support. *Chinese*

1203. It is not necessary to light a candle to the sun. *English*

1204. Kick away the ladder and one's feet are left dangling. *Malay*

1205. Mutual assistance in despair will make this ugly world more fair. *American*

1206. Often we can help each other most by leaving each other alone; at other times we need the hand-grasp and the word of cheer. *American*

1207. One thing asks the help of another. *Latin*

1208. Slow help is no help. *English*

1209. Soon or late the strong needs the help of the weak. *French*

1210. The assistance of fools only brings injury. *Latin*

1211. The dog that starts the hare is as good as the one that catches it. *German*

1212. Three brothers, three castles. *Italian*

1213. Three helping each other are as good as six. *Spanish*

1214. Two heads are better than one. *English (Heywood)*

1215. Two men of one mind will make enough money to buy gold; each man for himself won't secure enough money to buy a needle. *Chinese*

1216. Vain is the help of man. *Bible*

1217. When a dog is drowning everybody brings him drink. *French*

1218. You lift it, I'll do the groaning. *Lettish*

1219. You must help an idle man thoroughly. [That is, if you help him at all.] *Yoruba*

Association *see also* Affinity; Bad Company; Company; Corruption; Example

1220. A man is known by the company he keeps. *American*

1221. All the gems in one place, all the snails in another. *Telugu*

1222. Birds of prey do not flock together. *Portuguese*

1223. Common oysters are in one spot and pearl oysters in another. *Telugu*

1224. Connected with a great man, you will advance. *Efik*

1225. Every man is like the company he is wont to keep. *Greek*

1226. Hatched in the same nest. *English*

1227. He is known by his companions. *Latin*

1228. He that lieth down with dogs, shall rise up with fleas. *Latin*

1229. He that sleeps wi' dogs maun rise wi' fleas. *Scottish*

1230. He who associates with wolves learns to howl. *Spanish*

1231. He who hunts with cats will catch mice. *Danish*

1232. He who mixes with vermilion becomes red. *Japanese*

1233. If you live with a lame person you will learn to limp. *Greek*

1234. It's better to rob with good men than pray with bad. *American*

1235. Keep company with good men and a good man you'll learn to be. *Chinese*

1236. Like a black-faced villain joining an oily-legged sinner. *Telugu*

1237. Mountain will not mingle with mountain. *Greek (Xenophon)*

1238. Near putrid fish you'll stink, near the epidendrum you'll be fragrant. *Chinese*

1239. Near vermillion one gets stained pink, near ink one gets stained black. *Chinese*

1240. Never entreat a servant to dwell with thee. *American (Franklin)*

1241. One often has need of someone less than oneself. *French (La Fontaine)*

1242. Sic [such] a man as thou wad [would] be, draw thee to sic companie. *Scottish*

1243. Tarred with the same stick. *Scottish (Scott)*

1244. Taught in the same school. *Latin*

1245. Tell me with whom thou goest and I'll tell thee what thou doest. *English*

1246. The fish that sooms [swims] in a dub [puddle, pool of water] will aye taste o' mud. *Scottish*

1247. The nearer you can associate yourself with the good, the better. *Latin (Plautus)*

1248. When the crane attempts to dance with the horse she gets broken bones. *American*

1249. Who consorts with the wise will become wise. *Greek*

1250. Who keeps company with the wolf will learn to howl. *English*

1251. You may know him by the company he keeps. *English*

1252. You sail in the same boat. [You are in the same danger.] *Latin*

Atonement *see* Amendment; Confession; Forgiveness; Repentance

Attempt *see* Action; Effort

Attentiveness *see* Listening; Watchfulness

Authority *see also* Leaders and Leadership; Kings and Rulers; Master and Man; Shared Authority

1253. After he had mounted, he put his legs in motion. *Arabic*

1254. All authority belongs to the people. *American* (Jefferson)

1255. Authority buries those who assume it. *Babylonian Talmud*

1256. Authority forgets a dying king. *English (Tennyson)*

1257. Authority is never without hate. *Greek (Euripides)*

1258. If you want to know a man, give him authority. *Montenegrin*

1259. Kiss the rod. *American*

1260. New faces / Have more authority than accustomed ones. *Greek (Euripides)*

1261. No beard, no authority. *Turkish*

1262. Nothing is more gratifying to the mind of man than power or dominion. *English (Addison)*

1263. People who are masters in their own house are never tyrants. *French (Napoleon I)*

1264. Though authority be a stubborn bear, yet he is oft led by the nose with gold. *English (Shakespeare)*

Avarice *see also* Greed

1265. A large morsel chokes a child. *Yoruba*

1266. An avaricious man is a horse which is laden with wine, and drinks water. *German*

1267. Avarice blinds wisdom. *Japanese*

1268. Avarice hoards itself poor; charity gives itself rich. *German*

1269. Avarice increases with the increasing pile of gold. *Latin (Juvenal)*

1270. Avarice increases with wealth. *English*

1271. Avarice is its own stepmother. *German*

1272. Avarice is never satisfied. *English*

1273. Avarice loses all in seeking to gain all. *American*

1274. Avarice overreaches itself. *American*

1275. Even the fountains thirst. [Avarice is never satisfied.] *Latin*

1276. Expel avarice from thy heart, and the fetters will be loosened from thy feet. *Arabic*

1277. Frugality is one thing, avarice another. *Latin (Horace)*

1278. He that has muckle [much] wad aye hae mair [would always have more]. *Scottish*

1279. It is not want but abundance that makes avarice. *English*

1280. Money lies nearest them that are nearest their graves. *American (Penn)*

1281. Poverty craves many things, but avarice more. *English*

1282. Poverty needs much, avarice everything. *Latin*

1283. Poverty wants many things, avarice all things. *Latin*

1284. Poverty wants some things, luxury many, avarice all things. *English (Cowley)*

1285. Riches with their wicked inducements increase; nevertheless, avarice is never satisfied. *Latin (Horace)*

1286. The avaricious man is ready to sell his share of the sun. *American*

1287. The love of money grows as money grows. *Latin (Juvenal)*

1288. The more a man has, the more he desires. *Italian*

1289. The more we have, the more we want. *English*

1290. The want of pelf increases with the pelf. *Latin (Juvenal)*

1291. The wretch whom avarice bids to pinch and spare, starves, steals and pilfers to enrich an heir. *American*

1292. There's no vice like avarice. *American*

1293. When all other sins are old, avarice is still young. *French*

1294. When spherical bodies can unite and embrace, then there will be friendship among the avaricious. *Latin*

Awkwardness

1295. A man with butter-fingers should not climb ropes. *American*

1296. Like a sow playing on a trump. *Scottish*

1297. Pigs may whistle, but they hae [have] an ill mouth for 't. *Scottish*

Babies

1298. A baby is an angel whose wings decrease as his legs increase. *French*

Bachelors *see also* **Courtship; Marriage**

1299. A bachelor's bed is the most pleasant. *Latin (Cicero)*

1300. A house without woman and firelight, is like a body without soul or sprite. *American (Franklin)*

1301. A lewd bachelor makes a jealous husband. *American*

1302. He that has not got a wife, is not yet a compleat man. *American (Franklin)*

1303. If you hate storm and strife lead a bachelor's life. *American*

1304. Nothing is better than a single life. *Latin (Horace)*

1305. Praise a wife, but remain a bachelor. *Italian*

1306. Praise married bliss but keep to your bachelor quarters. *American*

1307. Single long, shame at last. *Welsh*

1308. The fear of women is the basis of good health. *Spanish*

1309. There's a funny smell in a bachelor's house. *American*

1310. Who would avoid all strife, should be a bachelor. *Latin*

Backwardness

1311. To row one way and look another. *English*

1312. You bridle the horse by its tail. *French*

Bad Company *see also* **Association**

1313. Associating with the bad, you yourself will become bad. *Greek (Menander)*

1314. Bad companions quickly corrupt the godly. *American*

1315. "Bad company," said the thief, as he went to the gallows between the hangman and the monk. *Dutch*

1316. Be guided by the crow and you will come to the body of a dead dog. *Arabic*

1317. Better a saft [soft] road as bad company. *Scottish*

1318. Better be alone than in bad company. *English*

1319. Crime equalizes those whom it contaminates. *Latin*

1320. Evil communications corrupt good manners. *Bible*

1321. He keeps his road weel enough wha gets rid o' ill company. *Scottish*

1322. He that toucheth pitch shall be defiled therewith. *Bible*

1323. Rather go rob with good men than pray with bad. *Portuguese*

1324. Shun evil company. *Greek (Solon)*

1325. Solitude is better than bad company. *Arabic*

1326. The rotten apple spoils his companion. *American (Franklin)*

1327. To stay with a mother dog, not with a mother cow. [To stay with someone of bad character, rather than with someone of good character.] *Lugbara*

Badness *see also* **Evil; Good; Good and Bad; Good and Evil; Wickedness**

1328. A bad action leaves a worse hangover. *American*

1329. A good sheriff gets his man no matter how bad. *American*

1330. Bad is the wool that cannot be dyed. *Italian*

1331. Bad men leave their mark wherever they go. *Chinese*

1332. Bad mind, bad heart. *Latin (Terence)*

1333. He who hold the ladder is as bad as the thief. *English*

1334. In every pomegranate a decayed pip is to be found. *Latin*

1335. Nothing so bad but it might be worse. *American*

1336. Putrid flesh is all of a flavor. *Chinese*

1337. The bad refrain from sin from fear of punishment. *Latin*

1338. There is nothing so bad but may be of some use. *German*

Bad News *see* **News**

Bait

1339. A little bait catches a large fish. *American*

1340. Better shun the bait than struggle on the hook. *American*

1341. Fish, or cut bait. *American*

1342. The fish that nibbles at every bait will soon be caught. *American*

1343. Without bait you can't catch fish. *American*

Balance *see also* **Fairness**

1344. A just balance preserves justice. *Latin*

Baldness

1345. Balder than a pestle. *Latin*

Bargains *see also* **Business and Commerce; Buying and Selling; Value; Worth**

1346. A bargain is a bargain. *English*

1347. A bargain is always dear. *Yiddish*

1348. A good bargain is a pickpocket. *American*

1349. Cheap purchase is money lost. *Japanese*

1350. Dry bargains are seldom successful. *Scottish*

1351. He loses his time that comes early to a bad bargain. *Scottish*

1352. He that buys a house ready wrought / Hath many a pin and nail for nought. *Scottish*

1353. It is an ill bargain where no man wins. *Latin*

1354. On a good [or great] bargain, think twice. *Italian*

1355. One never has a good bargain with bad ware. *French*

1356. One word will not settle a bargain. *Chinese*

1357. Without drink bargains can't be hastened. *Latin*

1358. Ye'll ne'er mak a mark in your testament by that bargain. *Scottish*

Bashfulness

1359. A close mouth catcheth no flies. *English*

1360. Bashfulness is an enemy to poverty. *Latin*

1361. Bashfulness is an ornament to youth, but a reproach to old age. *Greek*
1362. Bashfulness is of no use to the needy. *Dutch*
1363. Bashfulness will not avail a beggar. *Latin*
1364. He wa'd fain be forward, if he wist [knew] how. *Scottish*
1365. If you are bashful, you'll have no children. *Yiddish*
1366. It is only the bashful that lose. *French*
1367. There is that destroyeth his own soul through bashfulness. *Bible*
1368. You are bashful like the armadillo. *Yoruba*

Beauty *see also* **Appearance; Deception; Face; Inference; Judging**

1369. A beautiful face is a silent commendation. *English (Bacon)*
1370. A beauty's smile covers a multitude of sins. *American*
1371. A comely face is a silent recommendation. *Latin (Publilius Syrus)*
1372. A dunghill will produce beautiful flowers. *American*
1373. A fair face is half a portion. *English*
1374. A fair hostess is a bad thing for the purse. *French*
1375. A good face needs no band, and a pretty wench no land. *English*
1376. A handsome landlady is bad for the purse. *French*
1377. A thing of beauty is a joy forever. *English (Keats)*
1378. A thousand dogs do not make a gazelle. *Iraqi*
1379. All orators are dumb, when beauty pleadeth. *English (Shakespeare)*
1380. Beaute sans bonte [beauties without fortunes], blessed were never. *English (Langland)*
1381. Beauties without fortunes have sweethearts plenty, but husbands none at all. *English*
1382. Beautiful enough if good enough. *Latin*
1383. Beautiful flowers are soon picked. *German*
1384. Beauty and folly are often companions. *Italian*
1385. Beauty and folly are old companions. *American (Franklin)*
1386. Beauty and wisdom are seldom conjoined. *Latin (Petronius)*
1387. Beauty blemished once forever's lost. *English (Shakespeare)*
1388. Beauty draws more than oxen. *English*
1389. Beauty draws us with a single hair. *English (Pope)*
1390. Beauty in distress is much the most affecting beauty. *English (Burke)*
1391. Beauty is a blossom. *English*
1392. Beauty is a fading flower. *Bible*
1393. Beauty is a good letter of introduction. *German*
1394. Beauty is a natural superiority. *Greek (Plato)*
1395. Beauty is a short-lived reign. *Greek (Socrates)*
1396. Beauty is an evil in an ivory setting. *Greek (Theocritus)*
1397. Beauty is another's good. *Greek (Bion)*
1398. Beauty is as good as ready money. *German*
1399. Beauty is but a flower, / Which wrinkles will devour. *English (T. Nash)*
1400. Beauty is heaven's gift. *Latin*
1401. Beauty is its own excuse for being. *American (Emerson)*
1402. Beauty is Nature's coin, must not be hoarded. *English (Milton)*
1403. Beauty is no inheritance. *English*
1404. Beauty is not caused, / It is. *American (E. Dickinson)*
1405. Beauty is only one layer. *Japanese*
1406. Beauty is only skin-deep. *English*
1407. Beauty is the flower of virtue. *Greek (Zeno)*
1408. Beauty is the gift of God. *Greek (Aristotle)*
1409. Beauty is truth, truth beauty. *English (Keats)*
1410. Beauty is worse than wine: it intoxicates both the holder and the beholder. *American*
1411. Beauty may have fair leaves, yet bitter fruit. *English*
1412. Beauty opens locked doors. *German*
1413. Beauty provoketh thieves sooner than gold. *English (Shakespeare)*
1414. Beauty will buy no beef. *English*
1415. Beauty without bounty avails nought. *English*
1416. Beauty without discipline, a rose without scent. *Danish*
1417. Beauty without virtue is a curse. *English*
1418. Beauty without virtue is a flower without perfume. *French*
1419. Beauty without virtue is a rose without fragrance. *American*
1420. Beauty won't buy your groceries. *American*
1421. Dear to the heart of girls is their own beauty. *Latin (Ovid)*
1422. Even the autumn of beauty is beautiful. *Macedonian (Archelaus)*
1423. Everything beautiful is lovable. *Latin*
1424. Everything has its beauty but not everyone sees it. *Chinese (Confucius)*
1425. Fair enough is good enough. *Latin*
1426. Fair flowers do not remain long by the wayside. *English*
1427. Fair maidens wear no purses. *Scottish*
1428. Favor is deceitful, and beauty is vain. *Bible*
1429. Goodness and bounty are better than fairness and beauty. *French*
1430. He hath made every thing beautiful in his time. *Bible*
1431. Here below, the beautiful is the useful. *French*
1432. Not that which is great is beautiful, but that which is beautiful is great. *Latin*
1433. One hair of a woman draws more than a bell-rope. *German*
1434. Over the greatest beauty hangs the greatest woe. *American*
1435. Prettiness dies quickly. *English*
1436. Rare is the union of beauty and modesty. *Latin (Juvenal)*
1437. She that is born a beauty is born married. *Italian*
1438. She that is born a beauty is half married. *French*

1439. The fairer the hostess the fouler the reckoning. *English*

1440. The heart's letter is read in the eyes. *English*

1441. The lady of beauteous face needs neither gauds nor turquoise ring. *Persian (Sa'di)*

1442. The most beautiful fig may contain a worm. *African*

1443. The time will come when you will hate the sight of a mirror. *Latin (Ovid)*

1444. The voice is the beauty of cuckoos; chastity is the beauty of women; learning is the beauty of the deformed; patience is the beauty of ascetics. *Sanskrit*

1445. There is no excellent beauty that hath not some strangeness in the proportion. *English (Bacon)*

1446. Three things soon pass away: Woman's beauty, the rainbow and the echo of the woods. *Kashmiri*

1447. Trust not too much in an enchanting face. *American*

1448. We cannot divide beauty into dollars. *Polish*

1449. We seize the beautiful and reject the useful. *French (La Fontaine)*

1450. What is beautiful is good, and who is good will soon also be beautiful. *Greek (Sappho)*

1451. When the candles are out all women are fair. *Greek (Plutarch)*

Bed *see also* Night; Sleep

1452. Age and wedlock bring a man to his nightcap. *English*

1453. Laith to bed, laith out o't. *Scottish*

1454. Too much bed makes a dull head. *American*

1455. When I go to bed I leave my troubles in my clothes. *Dutch*

1456. When you begin to turn in bed, it is time to turn out. *American*

Beggars and Begging

1457. A beggar can never be bankrupt. *English*

1458. A beggar's estate lies in all lands. *Dutch*

1459. Beggars are never bankrupts, but bankrupts can become beggars. *American*

1460. Beggars breed and rich men feed. *English*

1461. Beggars can't be choosers. *American*

1462. Beggars mounted run their horse to death. *English (Shakespeare)*

1463. Beggars must be no choosers. *English*

1464. Beggars' bags are bottomless. *German*

1465. Better a living beggar than a dead emperor. *French*

1466. Better it is to die than to beg. *Bible*

1467. Better to beg than steal, but better to work than beg. *Russian*

1468. God rejoices when one beggar scratches another. *Yiddish*

1469. He is a sorry beggar that may not gae by ane man's door. *Scottish*

1470. Not even his own parents are friends to a beggar. *Latin*

1471. Rather not to live at all than to live by alms. *French*

1472. That costs dear which is bought with begging. *Italian*

1473. The beggar may sing before the thief. *Latin (Juvenal)*

1474. The beggar who becomes rich has the pride of Lucifer. *American*

1475. The beggar's wallet has no bottom. *Italian*

1476. The mouth [of a traveler asking for food] does not despise. *Zulu*

1477. The petition of an empty hand is hazardous. *Latin*

1478. When it rains porridge the beggar has no spoon. *Danish*

1479. Who is not ashamed to beg, soon is not ashamed to steal. *German*

Beginning *see also* Beginning and Ending; Earliness; End

1480. A beard well lathered is half shaved. *Italian*

1481. A good beginning is half a battle. *English*

1482. A good salad is the prologue to a bad supper. *Italian*

1483. A happy beginning is half the work. *French*

1484. A house pulled down is half rebuilt. *French*

1485. A journey of a thousand miles begins with one step. *Japanese*

1486. A poor wedding is a prologue to misery. *American*

1487. A weak foundation destroys the work. *Latin*

1488. All things hath a beginning (God excepted). *Scottish*

1489. As soon as man is born he begins to die. *American*

1490. Beginning hot, middle lukewarm, ending cold. *German*

1491. Beware beginnings. *Greek*

1492. Clawing [scratching] and eating need but a beginning. *Scottish*

1493. Each goodly thing is hardest to begin. *English (Spenser)*

1494. Eating, drinking and cleaning need but a beginning. *Scottish*

1495. Every beginning is feeble. *Latin*

1496. "Every beginning is hard," as the thief said when he began by stealing an anvil. *German*

1497. Everything has a beginning. *Scottish*

1498. Everything is difficult at first. *Chinese*

1499. Everything must have a beginning. *Italian*

1500. Everything stands till it is begun. *Venetian*

1501. From small beginnings come great things. *American*

1502. He who would climb a ladder must begin at the bottom. *English*

1503. It is only the first step that counts. *French*

1504. It is the first step which is troublesome. *French*

1505. No threshold without God. *Russian*

1506. The beginning is not everything. *American*

1507. The beginning of the dollar is the bank shilling. *German*

1508. The beginnings of all things are small. *Latin (Cicero)*

1509. The difficult thing is to get foot in the stirrup. *Italian*

1510. The first step is all the difficulty. *French*

1511. The getting out of doors is the greatest part of the journey. *American*

1512. The golden rule of life is: make a beginning. *American*

1513. The half [i.e., the beginning] is better than the whole. *Greek (Hesiod)*

1514. The hardest step is over the threshold. *Italian*

1515. The most difficult mountain to cross is the threshold. *English*

1516. The sprout at length becomes a tree. *Latin*

1517. The threshold is the tallest mountain. *Slovenian*

1518. Things are always at best in their beginning. *French (Pascal)*

1519. Things bad begun make strong themselves by ill. *English (Shakespeare)*

1520. Thread and needle are half clothing. *Spanish*

1521. To be lucky at the beginning is everything. *Spanish (Cervantes)*

1522. To begin a matter is to have it half finished. *Spanish (Cervantes)*

1523. To break the ice. *Latin*

1524. To climb steep hills / Requires slow pace at first. *English (Shakespeare)*

1525. To make a commencement requires a mental effort. *Latin*

1526. Well begun is half done. *Latin (Horace)*

1527. What raging rashly is begun / Challengeth shame before half done. *English*

1528. Who begins amiss ends amiss. *English*

1529. Who begins and does not complete loses his pains. *French*

1530. Who will mount the ladder must needs begin at the lowest step. *German*

Beginning and Ending *see also* Beginning; End

1531. A bad beginning makes a bad ending. *Greek*

1532. A bad beginning often makes a good ending. *English*

1533. A begun turn is hauf [half] ended. *English*

1534. A begun work is half ended. *Scottish*

1535. "A begun turn is half ended," quo' the wife when she stuck the graip [a dung fork] in the midden [dunghill]. *Scottish*

1536. A good beginning makes a good ending. *English*

1537. A good life has a good ending. *French*

1538. A hard beginning maketh a good ending. *English*

1539. As a thing begins, so ends it still. *English*

1540. Bad beginnings, bad endings. *Latin (Livy)*

1541. Begin wi' needles and preens [pins], and end wi' horn'd nowte [black cattle]. *Scottish*

1542. Beginning and end shake hands together. *German*

1543. Better is the end of a thing than the beginning thereof. *Bible*

1544. Better ne'er begun than ne'er ended. *Scottish*

1545. Evil beginning hours may end in good. *English*

1546. From a bad beginning comes a bad ending. *Greek (Euripides)*

1547. Good beginnings make good endings. *French*

1548. Good to begin well, better to end well. *English*

1549. He that would eat a good dinner, let him eat a good breakfast. *English*

1550. If you know the beginning well, the end will not trouble you. *Wolof*

1551. If you start with a bang you often end with a bust. *American*

1552. It is better coming to the beginning of a feast than to the end of a fray. *English*

1553. It's gude to begin weel, but better to end weel. *Scottish*

1554. The end of a thing is better than the beginning. *Bible*

1555. Thing never begun hath never end. *French*

1556. Things hatched in discord are not speedily terminated. *Latin*

1557. Whate'er's begun in anger, ends in shame. *American (Franklin)*

1558. Whatever begins also ends. *Latin*

1559. You began better than you have finished; the last act is not equal to the first. *Latin (Ovid)*

1560. Zealous in the commencement, careless in the end. *Latin (Tacitus)*

Being

1561. I am, therefore all things are. *Latin*

1562. I eat, therefore I exist. *Latin*

Belief *see also* Credibility; Divine Assistance; God; Man and God; Prayer; Religion; Wishful Thinking

1563. A belief is not true because it is useful. *Swiss (Amiel)*

1564. He does not believe that does not live according to his belief. *English*

1565. Man prefers to believe what he prefers to be true. *English (Bacon)*

1566. Men's beliefs often change with the changing fashions. *American*

1567. No storm harms a man who believes. *Latin (Ovid)*

1568. The saint who cures no diseases has few pilgrims. *French*

1569. There is no belief in the saint unless he works miracles. *Italian*

1570. To believe with certainty we must begin with doubting. *Polish*

1571. We are prone to believe what we don't understand. *American*

1572. We believe what we wish and wish what we believe is good for us. *American*

1573. We soon believe what we desire. *American*

1574. Who quick believes late repents. *German*

Benefit *see also* Advantage; Gifts and Giving; Obligation

1575. A free man never asks for benefits or receives them. *American*

1576. Benefits are only agreeable as long as one can repay them. *Latin*

1577. Benefits are traced on the sand and injuries are graven on brass. *Latin*

1578. Benefits, like flowers, please most when they are fresh. *English*
1579. Benefits turn poison in bad minds. *American*
1580. Dogs never go into mourning when a horse dies. *English*
1581. He who confers a benefit on anyone loves him better than he is beloved. *Greek (Aristotle)*
1582. The last benefit is the most remembered. *American*
1583. To accept a benefit is to sell one's liberty. *Latin (Publilius Syrus)*
1584. When befriended, remember it; when you befriend, forget it. *American (Franklin)*
1585. When you confer a benefit on a worthy man you oblige all men. *Latin*
1586. You reap the crop of another. *Latin*

Benevolence
1587. He who does good to me and evil to others is the best of benefactors. *Lebanese*

Bereavement *see* **Death; Mourning**

Best *see also* **Quality; Superiority**
1588. In the deepest water is the best fishing. *English*
1589. The best always goes first. *Italian*
1590. The best cloth has uneven edges. *Spanish*
1591. The best fish swim near the bottom. *American*
1592. The best manure is under the farmer's foot. *Danish*
1593. The fairest apple hangs on the highest bough. *Scottish*
1594. The first pig, but the last whelp of a litter, is the best. *English*

Betrayal *see also* **Treachery**
1595. Betrayers are hated even by those whom they benefit. *Latin*
1596. He who will betray pipes sweet. *German*
1597. He won't betray in whom none will confide. *English (Congreve)*
1598. Turning the cat in the pan. [Becoming a traitor.] *English*
1599. When knaves betray each other, one can scarce be blamed or the other pitied. *American (Franklin)*

Better One Thing Than Another *see* **Alternatives**

Bible
1600. Even the devil will swear on a stack of Bibles. *American*

Birds *see also* **Affinity; Identity**
1601. A bird is known by its feathers. *Yiddish*
1602. A bird is known by its note and a man by his talk. *American*
1603. A bird may be caught by a snare that will not be shot. *Danish*
1604. Birds of prey do not sing. *German*
1605. Even when the bird walks, one feels that it has wings. *French*
1606. However high a bird may soar, it seeks its food on earth. *Danish*
1607. Such bird, such song. *Latin*

Birth *see also* **Good Breeding**
1608. A man is not completely born until he be dead. *American (Franklin)*
1609. Blest are those who were never born to see the sun. *Greek*
1610. He who is born, yells; he who dies is silent. *Russian*
1611. No man can help his birth. *Danish*
1612. No one is born with an axe in his hand. *German*
1613. We start dying the day we are born. *American*

Bitterness
1614. If you are bitter at heart, sugar in the mouth will not help you. *Yiddish*

Blame *see also* **Accusation; Conscience; Guilt; Fault-Finding; Shame**
1615. He must be pure who would blame another. *Danish*
1616. However stupid a man may be, he is clever when blaming others; however wise, he is a dolt when blaming himself. *Chinese*
1617. It will be a feather out o' your wing. *Scottish*
1618. It's easier to blame others than to pin the blame on ourselves. *American*
1619. Mony wyte [many blame] their wife for their ain [own] thriftless life. *Scottish*
1620. Put your finger in the fire and say it was your fortune. *English*
1621. When a dog is lost, they say the alligator has eaten it. [A person with a bad reputation naturally attracts blame.] *Belizean Creole*
1622. When the crow flew away, the pear fell. *Korean*

Blessings *see also* **Mixed Blessings**
1623. A double blessing is a double grace. *English (Shakespeare)*
1624. An injury may prove a blessing. *Latin (Ovid)*
1625. No human blessing lasts forever. *Latin (Plautus)*
1626. Nothing is blessed in every respect. *Latin (Horace)*

Blindness *see also* **Ability; Advantage; Handicaps; Limitations**
1627. A blind archer may kill a hare. *English*
1628. A blind horse makes straight for the pit. *Yiddish*
1629. A blind leader of the blind. *English*
1630. A blind man can sometimes find corn. *French*
1631. A blind man is no judge of colors. *Latin*
1632. A blind man may catch a crow. *English*
1633. A blind man may kill a hare. *English*
1634. A blind man may sometimes hit a cow. *English*
1635. A blind man who sees is better than a seeing man who is blind. *Persian*
1636. A blind man will not thank you for a looking-glass. *English*
1637. A man were better be half blind than have both his eyes out. *English*
1638. A nod is as good as a wink to a blind horse. *Irish*
1639. A pebble and a diamond are alike to a blind man. *American*

1640. Among the blind close your eyes. *Turkish*

1641. Associate with beggars but not with the blind. *Chinese*

1642. Blind man's holiday [i.e., twilight]. *English*

1643. Blinder than a beetle. *Latin*

1644. Every man's blind to his ain [own] cause. *Scottish*

1645. Every soil bears not everything. *French (Rabelais)*

1646. He has the greatest blind side who thinks he has none. *Dutch*

1647. He is blind enough, who sees not through the holes of a sieve. *Spanish (Cervantes)*

1648. He is blind with both eyes open. *American*

1649. He is very blind that cannot see the sun. *Italian*

1650. His eyes are like two burnt holes in a blanket. *Irish*

1651. In the country of the blind the one-eyed man is king. *American*

1652. Mettle is dangerous in a blind horse. *English*

1653. More blind than the cast-off skin of a serpent. [Alluding to the holes where the eyes had been.] *Latin*

1654. Naething sae bauld [nothing so bold] as a blind mear [mare]. *Scottish*

1655. One may have good eyes and see nothing. *Italian*

1656. The blind eat many a fly. *English*

1657. The blind horse goes straight on. *German*

1658. The blind horse is hardiest. *Scottish*

1659. The blind man wishes to show the way. *Latin*

1660. The blind man's wife needs no painting. *Spanish*

1661. The blind would lead the blind. *English*

1662. The eye is blind if the mind is troubled [or absent]. *Italian*

1663. The sky is not less blue because the blind man does not see it. *Danish*

1664. There are none so blind as those who won't see. *English*

1665. Though the cat winks a little, she is not blind. *English*

1666. To act with closed eyes. *Latin*

1667. We all have our blind spots. *American*

1668. We shall see, said the blind man. *French*

1669. When blind to blind / His guidance lends, / In some deep pool / Their journey ends. *Welsh*

1670. When the blind lead the blind they all fall into the ditch. *American*

1671. When the blind man carries the banner, woe to those who follow. *French*

1672. Woe to the mule that sees not her master. *English*

Blunders *see also* Error(s)

1673. A stumble may prevent a fall. *English*

1674. He that has much to do will do something wrong. *English (Johnson)*

1675. It is worse than a crime: it is a blunder. *French*

1676. The body pays for a slip of the foot and gold pays for a slip of the tongue. *Malay*

Blushing

1677. Better a blush on the cheek than a spot in the heart. *Spanish*

1678. Blushing is virtue's color. *Greek*

1679. He blushes: all is well. *Latin*

1680. Men blush less for their crimes than for their weaknesses. *French*

1681. The blush is beautiful, but it is sometimes inconvenient. *Italian (Goldoni)*

1682. Whoso blushes is guilty already. *French*

Boasting *see also* Exaggeration; Lies and Lying; Words and Deeds

1683. A vaunter and a liar are near akin. *Scottish*

1684. A vaunter and a liar is the same thing. *English (Chaucer)*

1685. Believe a boaster as you would a liar. *Italian*

1686. Big talk won't boil the pot. *American*

1687. Brag's a good dog, but that he hath lost his tail. *English*

1688. Brag's a good dog, if he be well set on; but he dare not bite. *English*

1689. Bragging abroad is like singing in the bath. *Turkish*

1690. Do not make yourself so big, you are not so small. *Hebrew*

1691. Empty barrels mak maist din [make the most noise]. *Scottish*

1692. Empty pitchers ring loudest. *English*

1693. Every gypsy praises his own horse. *Hungarian*

1694. Every man thinks his own geese are swans. *English*

1695. Great boast, small roast. *English*

1696. Great braggers are little doers. *American*

1697. Great smoke, little roast. *Italian*

1698. Great vaunters, little doers. *French*

1699. He makes idle boasting. *Latin*

1700. He that boasteth of himself affronteth his company. *English*

1701. He that boasts of his own knowledge proclaims his own ignorance. *English*

1702. He who killeth a lion when absent feareth a mouse when present. *English*

1703. His calves are bulls at the butchers and his bulls are calves at the tanners. *French*

1704. It's good to whip a boaster. *Yiddish*

1705. Men brag to hide their fears. *American*

1706. Nobody calls his own buttermilk sour. *Iranian*

1707. Nobody takes a beating like a braggart. *Yiddish*

1708. Only a jackass boasts of his own wisdom. *American*

1709. Only children brag before company. *American*

1710. The ass boasted that there was no voice equal to his, and no gait equal to that of his elder sister. *Tamil*

1711. The big drum beats fast but does not realize its hollowness. *Malay*

1712. The loudest bummer's no the best bee. *Scottish*

1713. The man who boasts boosts himself into the company of liars. *American*

1714. The noisiest drum has nothing in it but air. *English*

1715. They brag most that can do least. *American*

1716. To brag is not to plant bananas. *Accra*

1717. We hounds killed the hare, quoth the lapdog. *English*

1718. When a toad gapes, what a mouth, and what breath! *Chinese*

1719. Who is the greatest liar? He that talks most of himself. *Chinese*

Boisterousness

1720. Indulge not in boisterous mirth. *Latin*

Boldness *see also* Risk; Venture and Investment

1721. A bold attempt is half success. *American*

1722. A bold man has luck in his train. *Danish*

1723. A dog on his own dunghill is bold. *French*

1724. Audacity augments courage; hesitation, fear. *Latin (Publilius Syrus)*

1725. Better hazard once than always be in fear. *English*

1726. Bold resolution is the favorite of providence. *English*

1727. Boldly attempted [or ventured] is half won. *German*

1728. Boldness ever meets with friends. *Greek (Homer)*

1729. Boldness in business is the first, second and third thing. *English*

1730. Boldness is a bulwark. *Latin*

1731. Boldness leads a man to heaven and to hell. *Greek*

1732. By boldness great fears are concealed. *Latin*

1733. Choose an author as you would a friend. *Irish*

1734. Faint heart ne'er won fair lady. *English (Spenser)*

1735. Fortune favors the bold. *Latin (Virgil)*

1736. Fortune gives her hand to a bold man. *English*

1737. God himself favors the bold. *Latin*

1738. Good luck trails a bold man; misfortune trails the timid. *American*

1739. He that handles a nettle tenderly is soonest stung. *English*

1740. In doubtful matters boldness is everything. *Latin (Publilius Syrus)*

1741. It had need to be / A wily mouse that should breed in the cat's ear. *English*

1742. It is a bold mouse that makes her nest in the cat's ear. *American*

1743. Nip a nettle hard and it will not sting you. *East Anglian*

1744. No one reaches a high position without boldness. *Latin*

1745. Nothing so bold as a blind man. *English*

1746. The blind are bold but they stumble and fall. *American*

1747. Who bravely dares must sometimes risk a fall. *English (Smollet)*

1748. Who so bold as blind Bayard? *English*

Bondage

1749. If you resent your chains you are half-free. *American*

1750. You're not free if you drag your chains after you. *American*

Books and Reading

1751. A big book is a great evil. *Greek*

1752. A book may be as great a thing as a battle. *English (Disraeli)*

1753. A book that remains shut, is but a block. *English*

1754. A good book is your best friend. *American*

1755. A great book is a great evil. *Greek (Callimachus)*

1756. A room without books is a body without a soul. *Latin*

1757. A wicked book is the wickeder because it cannot repent. *American*

1758. As you read it out, it begins to grow your own. *Latin*

1759. Ask counsel of the dead [i.e., books]. *English*

1760. Beware of the man of one book. *Latin*

1761. Books and friends should be few and good. *Spanish*

1762. Books are a triviality. Life alone is great. *English (Carlyle)*

1763. Books are ships which pass through the vast seas of time. *English (Bacon)*

1764. Books give not wisdom where was none before. *American*

1765. Books have always had a good flavor; the fields of literature have no poor harvests. *Chinese*

1766. Books will speak plain when counselors blanch. *English (Bacon)*

1767. Every age hath its book. *Koran*

1768. Extensive reading is a priceless treasure. *Chinese*

1769. In reading of many books is distraction. *Latin*

1770. It is not wide reading but useful reading that tends to excellence. *Greek*

1771. Letters enter with the blood. *Spanish*

1772. Much, but not many. *Latin*

1773. No book is so bad but some profit may be gleaned from it. *Latin*

1774. Of making many books there is no end. *Bible*

1775. Read the whole if you wish to understand the whole. *Latin*

1776. Reading maketh a full man. *English (Bacon)*

1777. Something is learned every time a book is opened. *Chinese*

1778. The dead [i.e., books or old books] are the best counselors. *Latin*

1779. The fountain of wisdom flows through books. *Greek*

1780. There is no worse robber than a bad book. *Italian*

1781. 'Tis the good reader that makes the good book. *American (Emerson)*

1782. Too many books make us ignorant. *American*

1783. We cannot learn men from books. *American*

1784. Would you know the affairs of the empire, read the works of the ancients. *Chinese*

Boredom

1785. One must know how to be bored. *French*

1786. When time grows long it becomes a snake. *Maltese*

Bores

1787. The man who disagrees with you is a bore. *American*

1788. The secret of being a bore is to tell everything. *French (Voltaire)*

1789. The well-bred man should never consent to become a bore. *Latin (Ovid)*

1790. We often pardon those who bore us, but never those whom we bore. *French (La Rochefoucauld)*

Borrowing and Lending *see also* Credit and Creditors; Debt

1791. A borrowed cloak does not keep one warm. *Arabic*

1792. A borrowed len' [loan] should gae laughing hame. *Scottish*

1793. A good man sheweth favor, and lendeth. *Bible*

1794. A loan though old is no gift. *Hungarian*

1795. A long-continued loan usually confers ownership. *Irish*

1796. Be not made a beggar by banqueting upon borrowing. *Bible*

1797. Better a bad buy than a good loan. *American*

1798. Better buy than borrow. *Scottish*

1799. Better give a penny than lend twenty. *Italian*

1800. Big spenders are bad lenders. *American*

1801. Borrow from yourself. *Latin*

1802. Borrowed cat catches no mice. *Japanese*

1803. Borrowed clothes don't fit the body; borrowed thoughts don't fit the mind. *American*

1804. Borrowed garments never fit well. *English*

1805. Borrowed pots are apt to leak. *American*

1806. Borrowed wives, like borrowed books, are rarely returned. *American*

1807. Borrowers must be no choosers. *English*

1808. Borrowing brings sorrowing. *American*

1809. Borrowing is not much better than begging. *German*

1810. Borrowing is the mother of trouble. *Hebrew*

1811. Borrowing thrives but once. *German*

1812. Building and borrowing, / A sackful of sorrowing. *German*

1813. Does your neighbor's presence annoy you? Lend him money. *Italian*

1814. Don't lend or borrow salt or pepper; it will break friendship. If you must borrow it, don't pay it back. *American*

1815. Folks lend money only to the rich. *American*

1816. Have a horse of thine own, and thou may'st borrow another's. *Welsh*

1817. He begs frae them that hae borrowed frae him. *Scottish*

1818. He borrows like an angel and pays back like the devil himself. *American*

1819. He that borrows must pay again with shame or loss. *English*

1820. He that goes a borrowing goes a sorrowing. *English*

1821. He that lends his pot may see the his kail [broth] in his loof [the palm of the hand]. *Scottish*

1822. He that lends money to his friend has a double loss. *Scottish*

1823. He that lends you hinders you to buy. *Scottish*

1824. He that lippens [depends on, trusts to] to lent ploughs, his land will lang lie lea [unploughed]. *Scottish*

1825. He that stretches his hand must stretch his foot. *Gaelic*

1826. He that would have a short Lent, let him borrow money to be repaid at Easter. *American*

1827. He who borrows does not choose. *French*

1828. He who does not have to borrow lives without cares. *Yiddish*

1829. He who has but one coat cannot lend it. *Spanish*

1830. He who lends to the poor gets his interest from God. *German*

1831. I prefer buying to asking. *Latin*

1832. If you give the loan of your breeches don't cut off the buttons. *Irish*

1833. If you lend to the poor you get your interest from God. *American*

1834. If you want to know how much a dollar is still worth, try to borrow it from a friend. *American*

1835. If you'd lose a troublesome visitor, lend him money. *American (Franklin)*

1836. If you're looking for enemies lend money to your friends. *American*

1837. In borrowing an angel, in repaying a devil. *German*

1838. Lend and lose is the game of fools. *American*

1839. Lend money to an enemy, and thou'lt gain him; to a friend, and thou'lt lose him. *American (Franklin)*

1840. Lend not your money to a great man. *French*

1841. Lend to a friend what you can afford to lose. *Slovenian*

1842. Lend to one who will not repay, and you will provoke his dislike. *Chinese*

1843. Lend to your friend and ask payment of your enemy. *Spanish*

1844. Lend your money and lose your friend. *American*

1845. Lend your money to a city, but never to a man. *Japanese*

1846. Let the lender beware. *American*

1847. Money lent, an enemy made. *Portuguese*

1848. Neither a borrower nor a lender be. *English (Shakespeare)*

1849. Neither borrow nor lend, a custom to commend. *Polish*

1850. Pay on the spot and borrow a lot; pay slow and you'll get no dough. *American*

1851. People lend only to the rich. *French*

1852. Seldom loan comes laughing home. *American*

1853. That is but an empty purse that is full of other men's money. *English*

1854. The ant is not given to lending. *French*

1855. The borrower is a slave to the lender, the debtor to the creditor. *American*

1856. The borrower is a slave to the lender; the security to both. *American (Franklin)*

1857. The borrower is the servant of the lender. *Bible*

1858. They bow to you when borrowing, and you bow to them when collecting. *Russian*

1859. Though you borrow only a zloty, you'll be sorry. *Polish*

1860. To lend is to buy a quarrel. *Indian*

1861. To refuse a loan means temporary estrangement, to grant it means falling out forever. *Russian*

1862. We may just as well quarrel the noo [now], an' I'll keep the siller in my pouch. *Scottish*

1863. What you lend is lost. *Latin*

1864. Whether you lend or borrow, you will sink without trace. *Lebanese*

1865. Who lends loses double. *Italian*

1866. Who readily borrows, readily lies. *German*

1867. Would you know the value of money, go and borrow some. *Spanish*

1868. You buy yourself an enemy when you lend a man money. *Yiddish*

Boys *see also* Children and Childhood; Fathers and Sons; Heredity; Sons

1869. As the boy is, so is the man. *American*

1870. Boys will be boys. *American*

Bragging *see* Boasting; Exaggeration; Lies and Lying

Brains and Brawn *see also* Strength; Strength and Skill

1871. Brute strength without reason falls of its own weight. *Latin*

Bravery *see also* Courage; Heart; Heroes and Heroism; Valor

1872. A short sword for a brave man. *French*

1873. All are brave when the enemy flies. *Italian*

1874. All bravery stands upon comparisons. *English (Bacon)*

1875. Be brave, not ferocious. *Latin*

1876. Brave actions never want a trumpet. *English*

1877. Brave men are brave from the first. *French*

1878. Either a man or a mouse. *American*

1879. Fortune favors the brave. *Latin (Terence)*

1880. God Himself helps the brave. *Latin (Ovid)*

1881. Handle your tools without mittens. *Scottish*

1882. He has more guts than brains. *English*

1883. He has no guts in his brains. *English*

1884. He has spur metal in him. *Scottish*

1885. He who doesn't turn runs far. *American*

1886. It is easy to be brave from a safe distance. *Greek (Aesop)*

1887. Many are brave when the enemy flies. *Italian*

1888. No exile or danger can frighten a brave spirit. *American*

1889. None but the brave deserve the fair. *English (Dryden)*

1890. The brave are born from the brave and good. *Latin (Horace)*

1891. The brave man has no country but mankind. *American*

1892. The brave man is daring enough to forgive an injury. *American*

1893. The brave man may die, but he will never say "die." *Latin*

1894. The brave man's word is a coat of mail. *Turkish*

1895. The brave yield only to the brave. *Irish*

1896. There were brave men before Agamemnon. *Latin (Horace)*

1897. We're all brave when the enemy takes to its heels. *American*

1898. Wha daur [who dare] bell the cat? *Scottish*

1899. Who dares wins. *American*

Bread

1900. Another's bread costs dear. *Spanish*

1901. If you have bread, don't look for cake. *Yiddish*

1902. Man doth not live by bread alone. *Bible*

1903. Others' bread has seven crusts. *Italian*

1904. When God gives us bread, men will supply the butter. *Yiddish*

1905. Whose bread I eat, his song I sing. *German*

Breeding *see also* Good Breeding; Heredity

1906. Breed is stronger than pasture. *English*

1907. Boasting of one's merits is better than boasting of one's pedigree. *Arabic*

Brevity *see also* Loquaciousness; Quiet; Silence; Speaking

1908. A man may haud [hold] his tongue in an ill time. *Scottish*

1909. Brevity is pleasing. *Latin*

1910. Brevity is the soul of wit. *English (Shakespeare)*

1911. Brevity makes the master. *American*

1912. Contraction of words conceals the sense. *Yoruba*

1913. Few words are best. *English*

1914. Few words, but those from the heart. *Latin*

1915. Few words sufficeth to a wise man. *Scottish*

1916. Gie your tongue mair holidays than your head. *Scottish*

1917. He acts wisely who says little. *Latin*

1918. He that would live in peace and at ease, must not speak all he knows, nor judge all he sees. *American (Franklin)*

1919. Keep your tongue as deep as possible. *Zyryan*

1920. Let thy words be few. *Bible*

1921. Little said is soon amended. *Spanish (Cervantes)*

1922. Men of few words are the best men. *American*

1923. Never say what you think in another man's house, never open a door, and never ask questions. *Maltese*

1924. Reticence is a great gift. *Latin (Ovid)*

1925. Short and sweet. *English*

1926. The man is wise who speaks few things. *Latin*

1927. There is a time when nothing should be said, there is a time when some things may be said, but there is indeed no time in which everything can be said. *Latin*

1928. Who knows most speaks light. *Italian*

1929. Who says little has little to answer for. *German*

Bribery

1930. A bribe entereth everywhere. *English*

1931. A bribe will enter without knocking. *English*

1932. A greased mouth cannot say no. *Italian*

1933. Being blinded by bribes, he is in the dark. *English*

1934. Bribes buy both gods and men. *Latin*

1935. Every man has his price. *American*

1936. Money and friendship bribe justice. *American*

1937. Money will soothe the itching palm. *American*

1938. No lock will hold against the power of gold. *Spanish*

1939. To win the lady, first bribe her maid. *American*

Brides *see also* Weddings

1940. A bonny bride is soon buskit [kissed]. *Scottish*

1941. A sad bride makes a glad wife. *American*

1942. At the wedding feast the least eater is the bride. *Spanish*

1943. Happy the bride the sun shines on. *American*

1944. He who has the luck brings home the bride. *German*

1945. If everyone seek a handsome bride, what will become of the ugly ones? *Yiddish*

1946. The weeping bride makes a laughing wife. *German*

Brothers

1947. A brother is a friend given by nature. *French*

1948. A brother turned enemy is an enemy for life. *Yiddish*

1949. A man has no friend like a brother. *Osmanli*

1950. Am I my brother's keeper? *Bible*

1951. Between two brothers, two witnesses and a notary. *Spanish*

1952. Brothers keep careful accounts. *Chinese*

1953. Brothers quarrel like thieves inside a house, but outside their swords leap out in each other's defense. *Japanese*

1954. Do not trust a younger brother. *Arabic*

1955. Every man is his brother's keeper. *American*

1956. He has made a younger brother of him. *English*

1957. The wrath of brothers is the wrath of devils. *American*

1958. There is no strength in the legs of a brotherless man. *Persian*

1959. Though they are brothers their pockets are not sisters. *Turkish*

Building

1960. It is easier to pull down than to build. *Latin*

1961. Those who love building will soon ruin themselves, and need no other enemies. *Latin (Marcus Crassus)*

1962. Who builds cleans out his purse. *Italian*

Bullies

1963. A bully is always a coward. *American*

1964. A drubbed bully never says anything about the matter. *French*

1965. The bully bags a lion at a distance but runs when a mule starts kicking. *American*

Burdens *see also* Excess

1966. Bear ye one another's burdens. *Bible*

1967. Even a straw becomes heavy, if you carry it far enough. *Latin*

1968. It is base to flinch under a burden. *Latin*

1969. It is other people's burdens that kill the ass. *Spanish*

1970. It's not the burden but the overburden that kills the beast. *American*

1971. Light burdens borne far are heavy. *American*

1972. Light burdens, long borne, grow heavy. *English*

1973. Light grows the burden which is well borne. *Latin (Ovid)*

1974. Place the burden on the slow-paced ass. *Latin*

1975. The burden is equal to the horse's strength. *Hebrew*

1976. The burden is light on the shoulder of another. *Russian*

Business and Commerce *see also* Buying and Selling; Customers; Fair Dealing; Trade

1977. A handfu' o' trade is worth a gowpen [two hands cupped together] o' gold. *Scottish*

1978. A hundred tailors, a hundred weavers and a hundred millers make three hundred thieves. *American*

1979. A man o' mony trades may beg his bread on Sunday. *Scottish*

1980. A man without a smiling face must not open a shop. *Chinese*

1981. A toom [empty] purse makes a blate [bashful] merchant. *Scottish*

1982. A tradesman who cannot lie may shut up his shop. *French*

1983. As gude [good] merchants tine [lose] as win. *Scottish*

1984. Bargaining is as necessary to trade as poling to a vessel. *Chinese*

1985. Business is business. *American*

1986. Business is other people's money. *French*

1987. Business kills friendship. *German*

1988. Business makes men. *French*

1989. Business neglected is business lost. *American*

1990. Business tomorrow. *Greek*

1991. Drive thy business; let not that drive thee. *American (Franklin)*

1992. Everyone knows his own business. *French*

1993. Good ware makes good markets. *Latin*

1994. He is not a merchant bare, / That hath money, worth or ware. *English*

1995. He is not a merchant who always gains. *Dutch*

1996. He that kens [knows] what will be cheap or dear needs be a merchant but for half a year. *Scottish*

1997. He who can turn his hand to anything is not a fool; stock which never lies dead, naturally yields a profit. *Chinese*

1998. He who reckons without the host [i.e., without the person most concerned] must reckon twice. *Italian*

1999. He's fond o' trade that niffers wi' Auld Nick. *Scottish*

2000. How happy the life unembarrassed by the cares of business. *Latin*

2001. If you play with a fool at home, he'll play with you in the market. *English*

2002. If you would be a merchant fine, beware o' auld horses, herring and wine. *Scottish*

2003. In business one must be perfectly affable. *Chinese*

2004. In trade, competition prevents imposition. *American*

2005. Keep your shop, and your shop will keep you. *Japanese*

2006. Live together like brothers and do business like strangers. *Arabic*
2007. Love me as if I were your brother and do your accounts with me as if I were your enemy. *Tunisian*
2008. One who is in the trade can't be cheated. *Chinese*
2009. Penny wise and pound foolish. *Scottish*
2010. Sair [sore] cravers are aye ill payers. *Scottish*
2011. See [sell] for love and buy for siller [silver]. *Scottish*
2012. Small trades make great profits. *Chinese*
2013. Souters [cobblers] and tailors count hours. *Scottish*
2014. The art of the merchant lies more in getting paid than in making sales. *Spanish*
2015. The market is the place set apart where men may deceive each other. *Greek*
2016. There are customers for all sorts of goods. *Chinese*
2017. There are no foolish trades; there are only foolish people. *French*
2018. There may be trade to be done but no way found to do it. *Chinese*
2019. To make accounts without the host [i.e., without the person most concerned]. *Polish*
2020. To open a shop is easy, to keep it open an art. *Chinese*
2021. Trade has a golden foundation. *German*
2022. Trade is the mother of money. *English*
2023. Wares are good and bad; prices high and low. *Chinese*
2024. Well worth aw that gars the plough draw. [Good luck to all that keeps business going.] *Scottish*

Business and Pleasure

2025. Business before pleasure. *French*
2026. Don't mix business with pleasure. *American*

Buying and Selling *see also* Cost; Fair Dealing; Profit and Loss; Value; Worth; Worthlessness

2027. A miser and a liar bargain quickly. *Greek*
2028. A' the winning's in the first buying. *Scottish*
2029. As the market gaes [goes] the wares maun [must] sell. *Scottish*
2030. Ask but enough, and you may lower the price as you list. *Italian*
2031. Ask your purse what you should buy. *Scottish*
2032. Bad silver will only buy old sow's flesh. *Chinese*
2033. Be not too hasty to outbid another. *English*
2034. Before you calculate on buying, calculate on selling. *Chinese*
2035. Better to sell with regret than to keep with regret. *Swiss*
2036. Buy and sell, and your name will not perish. *Iraqi*
2037. Buy at a market, but sell at home. *English*
2038. Buy what ye dinna want, and ye'll sell what ye canna spare. *Scottish*
2039. Buy when it is market time. *German*
2040. Buyers and sellers dispute over a fraction of the cash. *Chinese*
2041. Buying and selling is but winning and losing. *English*
2042. Cheat me in price, but not in the goods I purchase. *Spanish*
2043. Dispute the price but don't dispute the weight. *Chinese*
2044. Don't buy a cat for a hare. *Italian*
2045. Don't buy a cat in a bag. *Hungarian*
2046. Don't buy a cat in a poke [game bag]. [That is, if you are buying a hare, look in the bag to make certain it isn't a cat.] *French*
2047. Don't buy a pig in a poke [a pouch or bag]. *English*
2048. Don't buy everything that is cheap, and you won't be greatly cheated. *Chinese*
2049. Don't loose the falcon till you see the hare. [Don't hand over the goods until you see the money.] *Chinese*
2050. Even an earthen jar should be tested before purchasing. *Sindhi*
2051. Even gold may be bought too dear. *German*
2052. Everything has its price. *American*
2053. Everything is worth what its purchaser will pay for it. *Latin (Publilius Syrus)*
2054. Fuel is not sold in a forest, nor fish on a lake. *Chinese*
2055. Good merchandise finds a ready buyer. *Latin*
2056. Good things soon find a purchaser. *Latin (Plautus)*
2057. Gude wares mak a quick market. *Scottish*
2058. Hale sale is gude sale. *Scottish*
2059. He has brought his pack to a braw [fine] market. *Scottish*
2060. He that blames would buy. *American*
2061. He that buyeth magistracy must sell justice. *English*
2062. He that buys a house ready wrought / Hath many a pin and nail for nought. *English*
2063. He that has gold may buy land. *Scottish*
2064. He that has nothing to sell loses his market. *Spanish*
2065. He that lacks [i.e., belittles] my mare may buy my mare. *Scottish*
2066. He that sells his wares for words maun [must] live by the loss. *Scottish*
2067. He who buys has need of eyes; / But one's enough to sell the stuff. *Welsh*
2068. He who buys the broom can also buy the handle. *Italian*
2069. He who buys what he cannot pay for sells what he would rather not. *German*
2070. He who buys what he doesn't need steals from himself. *Swedish*
2071. He who does not intend to pay is not troubled in making his bargain. *Spanish*
2072. He who has goods can sell them. *Wolof*
2073. He who pays cash will be treated like a partner. *Persian*
2074. He will never get a good thing cheap, that is afraid to ask the price. *American*
2075. He would sell even his share of the sun. *Italian*

2076. He'll no sell his hen on a rainy day. *Scottish*

2077. He's in great want of a bird that will give a groat for an owl. *English*

2078. High prices attract sellers from afar. *Chinese*

2079. Highways and streets have not all the thieves; shops have ten to one. *American*

2080. Hold back your goods for a thousand days and you will be able to sell at a profit. *Chinese*

2081. I prefer buying to asking. *Latin*

2082. I'll ne'er buy a blind bargain, or a pig in a pock [bag]. *Scottish*

2083. If fools went not to market, bad wares would not be sold. *Spanish*

2084. If you buy what you don't need you'll sell what do you need. *American*

2085. If you go out to buy anything, don't show your silver. *Chinese*

2086. If you would not be cheated, ask the price at three shops. *Chinese*

2087. It is better to buy than to sell. *Egyptian*

2088. It is folly to buy a cat in a sack. *French*

2089. It is well to buy when someone else wants to sell. *Italian*

2090. It isn't the buying that teaches, it is the selling. *Russian*

2091. Let the buyer beware. *Latin*

2092. Long standing and little offering makes a good price. *Scottish*

2093. Mony ane [many a one] opens his pack and sells nae [no] wares. *Scottish*

2094. More than one ass goes to market. *Italian*

2095. Never buy anything from or sell anything to your friend. *Italian*

2096. No one buys yams in the ground. *Accra*

2097. No one will get a bargain he does not ask for. *French*

2098. Nothing is to be had for nothing. *Greek (Epictetus)*

2099. One doesn't buy oats from geese. *Polish*

2100. One may buy by mistake, but one never sells by mistake. *Chinese*

2101. One should buy land and houses ready-made. *French*

2102. Pluck a goose without making it scream. *French*

2103. Rather sell than be poor. *Hebrew*

2104. Tak the head for the washing. *Scottish*

2105. Taste and try / Before you buy. *English*

2106. The buyer does not consider the seasons; he insists that his yam be as big as a log. *Yoruba*

2107. The buyer needs a hundred eyes, the seller not one. *Italian*

2108. The buying of bread undoes us. *English*

2109. There are more foolish buyers than sellers. *French*

2110. There are two fools in every market: one asks too little, one asks too much. *Russian*

2111. There is nothing to be gained by buying inferior goods. *Latin*

2112. There's a difference between "Will ye sell?" and "Will ye buy?" *Scottish*

2113. They buy gudes cheap that bring naething hame. *Scottish*

2114. To vaunt one's goods is good, but it is better to go where they are bought. *Wolof*

2115. Vinegar at a good price is sweeter than honey. *Arabic*

2116. We'll bark oursels ere we buy dogs sae dear. *Scottish*

2117. Well bought is half sold. *English*

2118. When asking a price, don't be afraid to ask a high one; when offering a price, don't be afraid to offer a low one. *Chinese*

2119. When buying fresh fish and vegetables, examine them first, then fix the price. *Chinese*

2120. When folk's ready to buy, ye can want to sell. *Scottish*

2121. When one cheats to high heaven in the price he asks, come down to earth in the price you offer. *Chinese*

2122. When the market is brisk the seller does not stop to wash the mud from his turnips. *Chinese*

2123. When you're able to buy, don't buy in such a way as to frighten the seller; when you're able to sell, don't sell in such a way as to frighten the buyer. *Chinese*

2124. While the dust is on your feet, sell what you have bought. *Hebrew*

2125. Who buys hath need of a hundred eyes; who sells hath enough of one. *English*

2126. Who does not open his eyes must open his purse. *German*

2127. Who will sell the cow must say the word. *English*

2128. Woo [wool] sellers ken aye [always know] woo buyers. *Scottish*

2129. You can sell with one eye but you need two eyes — or four — to buy without being gypped. *American*

2130. You can't buy peace of mind. *American*

2131. You must ask what is unjust that you may obtain what is just. *Latin*

Bystanders *see also* Idleness; Innocence

2132. The innocent bystander often gets beaten up. *American*

2133. To the bystander no work is too hard. *American*

Calamity

2134. Calamity is often a friend in disguise. *American*

2135. Calamity is the test of a brave mind. *American*

2136. Calamity is virtue's opportunity. *Latin*

Calumny *see also* Accusation; Reputation; Slander

2137. An honest man is not the worse because a dog barks at him. *Danish*

2138. Be thou as chaste as ice, as pure as snow, thou shalt not escape calumny. *English (Shakespeare)*

2139. Calumniate strongly and some of it will stick. *Latin*

2140. Calumny will soil virtue itself. *American*

2141. If you throw dirt at a man, some of it will stick. *American*

2142. "I'll not beat thee nor abuse thee," said the Quaker to his dog: "but I'll give thee an ill name." *Irish*

2143. Lying calumny alarms no one except the liar. *Latin*

2144. There are calumnies against which even innocence loses courage. *French*

Candor *see also* **Forthrightness; Frankness; Plain Speaking; Sincerity**

2145. Be not ashamed to say what you are not ashamed to think. *French (Montaigne)*

2146. Candor breeds hatred. *Latin*

2147. He calls a spade a spade. *Dutch (Erasmus)*

2148. Speak boldly and speak truly; shame the devil. *American*

2149. Speak out, hide not thy thoughts. *Greek (Homer)*

2150. Truths and roses have thorns about them. *English*

2151. We call a fig a fig, and a skiff a skiff. *Dutch (Erasmus)*

2152. We call figs figs, and a hoe a hoe. *Latin*

2153. Women confess their small faults that their candor may cover great ones. *American*

Capability *see* **Ability**

Capital *see also* **Business and Commerce; Money; Venture and Investment**

2154. A merchant without capital is like a farmer without an ox. *Chinese*

2155. Great capital, great profits. *Chinese*

2156. The field should be poorer than the farmer. [Don't start an enterprise without sufficient capital.] *Latin*

Care *see also* **Carefulness**

2157. A horn-spoon holds no poison. *Scottish*

2158. A man does not die of care: he dries up. *Russian*

2159. Another's cares will not rob you of sleep. *Yiddish*

2160. Behind the horseman sits black care. *Latin (Horace)*

2161. Better greet [cry] ower your gudes [over your goods] than after your gudes. *Scottish*

2162. Care is beauty's thief. *American*

2163. Care killed the cat. *French*

2164. Care will kill a cat, but ye canna live without it. *Scottish*

2165. Care's an enemy to life. *English (Shakespeare)*

2166. Care's no cure. *English*

2167. Cares deny all rest to weary limbs. *Latin (Virgil)*

2168. Cry you mercy killed my cat. *English*

2169. Hang sorrow, care 'll kill a cat. *English (Jonson)*

2170. Light cares speak, great ones are silent. *Latin (Seneca)*

2171. Many cares make the head white. *American*

2172. No hemlock is drunk out of earthenware. *Latin*

2173. Other folks' care kissed the ass. *Spanish*

2174. Other times, other cares. *Italian*

2175. Petty cares wear the soul out, drop by drop. *American*

2176. The rich are burdened with cares, but the poor are always eager to relieve them of the burden. *American*

2177. The world is like a vapor bath; the higher up one is, the more one sweats. *Polish*

2178. Too much care does more harm than good. *Latin*

2179. Too much care may be as bad as downright negligence. *English*

Carefulness *see also* **Care; Caution; Common Sense; Prudence; Watchfulness; Sense**

2180. Care and not fine stables makes a good horse. *Danish*

2181. Deviate a fraction and you lose a thousand miles. *Chinese*

2182. If you can't be good, be careful. *American*

2183. Measure a thousand times and cut once. *Turkish*

2184. Measure thrice [what thou buyest,] and cut [it but] once. *Italian*

2185. Measure twice, cut but once. *Russian*

2186. Measure your cloth ten times; you can only cut it once. *Russian*

2187. Measure your coat twice since you can only cut once. *American*

Carelessness

2188. A careless watch invites the thief. *Scottish*

2189. A careless watch invites the vigilant foe. *American*

2190. A reckless houssie [housewife] maks mony thieves. *Scottish*

2191. Careless folk are aye [always] cumbersome [troublesome]. *Scottish*

2192. Careless men come to a sudden and sorry end. *American*

2193. Careless shepherds make many a feast for the wolf. *American*

2194. He brings a staff to break his ain head. *Scottish*

2195. He that stumbles twice at ae stane [one stone] deserves to break his shin bane. *Scottish*

2196. He that's far frae [from] his gear [wealth, property, goods] is near his skaith [harm]. *Scottish*

2197. He would tine [lose] his lugs [ears] if they werena tacked to him. *Scottish*

2198. Ill herds mak fat foxes. *Scottish*

2199. Ill laying up maks mony [makes many] thieves. *Scottish*

2200. It's ower weel hoardit [stowed away] that canna be found. *Scottish*

2201. She that fa's ower a strae [straw] 's a tentless [careless] taupie [a foolish woman]. *Scottish*

2202. Slip shod's no for a frozen road. *Scottish*

2203. Throw not the child out with the bath. *Danish*

2204. Tine thimble, tine thrift. *Scottish*

2205. Tine [lose] needle, tine darg [a day's work]. *Scottish*

2206. Want of care does more harm than want of knowledge. *American*

Cause and Effect *see also* **Association; Bad Company; Causes; Coincidence; Consequence; Ends and Means; Heredity; Size; Trifles**

2207. A bad day never hath a good night. *English*

2208. A bad father has never a good son. *Latin*
2209. A bad mother wishes for good children. *English*
2210. A bad tree does not yield good apples. *Danish*
2211. A crooked stick will have a crooked shadow. *English*
2212. A good winter brings a good summer. *English*
2213. A hair's breadth at the bow is a mile beside the butt. *Chinese*
2214. A little leak will sink a great ship. *English*
2215. A little spark makes muckle [much] wark. *Scottish*
2216. A little stream drives a light mill. *English*
2217. A match will set fire to a large building. *American*
2218. A muffled cat was ne'er a gude hunter. *Scottish*
2219. A pestilence follows a famine. *Latin*
2220. A primsie damsel maks a daidlin' [dilly-dallying] dame. *Scottish*
2221. A ridiculous accident has often been the making of many. *Latin*
2222. A small leak will sink a great ship. *English*
2223. A small spark makes a great fire. *English*
2224. A spark may consume a city. *Hungarian*
2225. A spark may raise / An awful blaze. *English*
2226. Alas, by what trivial causes is greatness overthrown! *Latin*
2227. An ill life maks an ill death. *Scottish*
2228. An old crow does not croak for nothing. *Russian*
2229. An olite [active] mither maks a sweird [indolent] dochter. *Scottish*
2230. As you sow, so shall you also reap. *Latin (Cicero)*
2231. Bad chicken, bad egg; bad egg, bad chick. *American*
2232. Bad hen, bad egg. *Latin*
2233. By a mere spark a town is set on fire. *French*
2234. Corbies [ravens] dinna gather without [i.e., unless] they smell carrion. *Scottish*
2235. Despise not a small wound or a poor kinsman. *English*
2236. Ding down the nest and the rooks will flee awa. *Scottish*
2237. Do not make me kiss, and you will not make me sin. *English*
2238. Even a single hair casts its shadow. *Latin (Publilius Syrus)*
2239. Every fault has its fore. *Scottish*
2240. Every why has a wherefore. *American*
2241. Everything must have a cause. *Chinese*
2242. Farther east the shorter west. *Scottish*
2243. Fat flesh freezes soon. *Scottish*
2244. Fire is next akin to smoke. *Latin (Plautus)*
2245. From a little spark may burst a mighty flame. *Italian*
2246. From a small spark there will often be produced a great conflagration. *Latin*
2247. From a spark, a fire. *Latin*
2248. From the disease of one the whole flock perishes. *Latin (Juvenal)*
2249. Fry stanes [stones] wi' butter and the broo [juice] will be gude. *Scottish*
2250. Give him an inch and he'll take an ell. *English*
2251. Hail brings frost in the tail. *English*
2252. Happy is he who can trace effects to their causes. *Latin (Virgil)*
2253. He can run ill that canna gang [walk]. *Scottish*
2254. He must needs go that the devil drives. *English*
2255. He that corrects not youth, controls not age. *English*
2256. He who goes to the mill gets befloured. *English*
2257. Hunger and delay raise up anger. *Latin*
2258. Hunger sharpens anger. *Latin*
2259. If better were within, better would come out. *English*
2260. If nothing touches the bamboo tree, it does not make a sound. *African*
2261. If the knitter is weary the baby will have no new bonnet. *Irish*
2262. If you sow dragon's teeth, you will reap a crop of violence. *American*
2263. If you're living like a pig you'll die like a swine. *American*
2264. It is easier to suppress the first desire than to satisfy all that follow it. *English*
2265. It never thunders but it rains. *Italian*
2266. Liberty begets license. *Latin (Claudius)*
2267. Like saint, like offering. *English*
2268. More than one war has been kindled by a single word. *American*
2269. Nae [no] mills, nae meal. *Scottish*
2270. Nobody cries who has not been pinched. *Kenyan*
2271. Oft mouseth the cat after her mother. *English*
2272. One nail drives out another. *English*
2273. Out of cheap fish there will be sour soup. *Cheremis*
2274. Pleasure is often the introduction to pain. *Latin (Ovid)*
2275. Rich mixture maks gude mortar. *Scottish*
2276. Sharp stomachs make short devotion. *English*
2277. Sic reek [such smoke] as is therein comes out o' the lum [chimney]. *Scottish*
2278. Sic [such] as ye gie [give] sic will ye get. *Scottish*
2279. Slight means, great effect. *French*
2280. Small rain lays a great wind. *French*
2281. Sow thin, and mow thin. *Scottish*
2282. Strong is vinegar made from sweet wine. *Italian*
2283. Study invites study, idleness produces idleness. *Latin*
2284. Such a father, such a son. *English*
2285. Such a king, such a people. *Latin*
2286. Such a saint, such an offering. *English*
2287. Take away the cause, and the effect ceases; what the eye ne'er sees, the heart never rues. *Spanish (Cervantes)*
2288. The cause ceasing, the effect ceases also. *Latin*
2289. The cause lies hidden; the effect is most notorious. *Latin (Ovid)*
2290. The causes of events are more interesting than the events themselves. *Latin (Cicero)*

2291. The child saith nothing but what he heard at the fireside. *English*
2292. The higher the tree the sweeter the plooms, the richer the souter [cobbler] the blacker his thooms [thumbs]. *Scottish*
2293. The monk responds as the abbot sings. *French*
2294. The rat enters the trap, the trap catches it; if it did not go into the trap, the trap would not catch it. *Efik*
2295. The smallest insect may cause death by its bite. *Chinese*
2296. There ne'er was a fire without some reek [smoke]. *Scottish*
2297. There's aye some water where the stirkie [calf] drowns. *Scottish*
2298. There's nae reek [smoke] but there's some heat. *Scottish*
2299. There's no smoke without fire. *Czech*
2300. They that bourd wi' cats may count upon scarts [scratches]. *Scottish*
2301. Thirst comes from drinking. *Italian*
2302. To know truly is to know by causes. *English (Bacon)*
2303. Unless the vessel be pure, everything which is poured into it will turn sour. *Latin (Horace)*
2304. We may not expect a good whelp from a bad dog. *Hebrew*
2305. What can you expect from a pig but a grunt? *English*
2306. What follows conforms to what went before. *Greek*
2307. What will ye get frae [from] an oily pat but stink? *Scottish*
2308. When a dead tree falls, the woodpeckers share in its death. *Malay*
2309. When the mare hath a bald face, the filly will have a blaze. *English*
2310. When the root is worthless so is the tree. *English*
2311. When the stomach is full the heart is glad. *English*
2312. Where the deer's slain the blude will lie. *Scottish*
2313. Will there be smoke where there is no fire? *Hindi*
2314. With a spark of fire a heap of coals is kindled. *American*

Causes *see also* Cause and Effect

2315. A good cause and a good tongue: and yet money must carry it. *English*
2316. A good cause finds weapons to defend it. *American*
2317. A good cause makes a stout heart and a strong arm. *English*
2318. A good cause needs help. *French*
2319. Courage becomes knavery if the cause is bad. *American*
2320. Everything is the cause of itself. *American (Emerson)*
2321. He that hath the worst cause makes the most noise. *English*
2322. The best cause requires a good pleader. *Dutch*
2323. There is no wall without poles to support it. *Lugbara*
2324. They never fail who die in a great cause. *English (Byron)*
2325. Those whose cause is just will never lack / good arguments. *Greek (Euripides)*

Caution *see also* Care; Carefulness; Common Sense; Precaution; Prudence; Watchfulness

2326. A cautious man will observe the indications of character which nature reveals in others. *Latin*
2327. A word is sufficient for the wise. *Latin*
2328. An animal that fails to respect the hunter will sleep in the oven. *Yoruba*
2329. An excess of caution does no harm. *Latin*
2330. Be inwardly clever, but outwardly clownish; if you brag too much about your wisdom you are sure to come to grief. *Chinese*
2331. Better safe than sorry. *American*
2332. Better sit still than rise and fa'. *Scottish*
2333. Caution comes too late when we are in the midst of evils. *Latin (Seneca)*
2334. Caution is the mother of security. *Italian*
2335. Caution is the mother of tender beer glasses. *Dutch*
2336. Caution is the parent of safety. *Italian*
2337. Don't monkey with the buzz-saw. *American*
2338. Don't play with fire. *American*
2339. Don't take any wooden nickels. *American*
2340. Don't wade if your feet can't feel the river's bottom. *American*
2341. Don't wake a sleeping dog. *English*
2342. Fear to let fall a drop and you spill a lot. *Malay*
2343. Fields have eyes, and woods have ears. *English*
2344. He is the furthest from danger, who is on his guard even when in safety. *Latin (Publilius Syrus)*
2345. He that fears danger in time seldom feels it. *English*
2346. He that has but ae ee [one eye] maun tent [must take care of it] weel. *Scottish*
2347. He that observeth the wind shall not sow; and he that regardeth the clouds shall not reap. *Bible*
2348. He that will not sail till all dangers are over must never put to sea. *English*
2349. He who sees not the bottom let him not pass the water. *Italian*
2350. If not chastely, at all events cautiously. *Latin*
2351. If poor, act with caution. *Latin*
2352. If water be too clear it will contain no fish; if men are too cautious they will not be clever. *Chinese*
2353. If you dinna see the bottom don't wade. *Scottish*
2354. In eating, avoid choking; in walking, avoid stumbling. *Chinese*
2355. Let me skim the water with one oar, and with the other touch the sand. *Latin (Propertius)*
2356. Let sleeping dogs lie. *English*
2357. Partition walls have ears; and are there not listeners under the window? *Chinese*
2358. Praise the sea but keep on the land. *American*
2359. Safe bind, safe find. *English (Shakespeare)*

2360. The cautious wolf fears the pit, the hawk regards with suspicion the snare laid for her, and the fish the hook in its concealment. *Latin*

2361. To act the part of one deaf and dumb. [To avoid danger or involvement in a crime.] *Chinese*

2362. When free from trouble be on your guard; when trouble comes keep calm. *Chinese*

2363. When misfortune sleeps let no one wake her. *Spanish*

2364. When you ride a lion beware of his claws. *Arabic*

2365. With caution, one may go anywhere in the empire; if careless, everything will go wrong. *Chinese*

Censure *see also* **Criticism; Fault-Finding**

2366. Take each man's censure, but reserve thy judgment. *English (Shakespeare)*

Ceremony

2367. Ceremony is the smoke of friendship. *Chinese*

Certainty *see also* **Odds; Probability**

2368. As sure as a gun. *English*

2369. Be certain and on the level; to trust to chance is to dance with the devil. *American*

2370. Be sure you're right, then go ahead. *American (Crockett)*

2371. Don't change the cottage you live in for a castle in Spain. *American*

2372. He is a fool who leaves certainties for uncertainties. *Greek*

2373. He that leaves certainty and sticks to chance, / When fools pipe he may dance. *English*

2374. Never take things for granted. *American*

2375. Nothing is certain but death and taxes. *French*

2376. Nothing is certain but uncertainty. *Latin*

2377. Nothing is positively certain but uncertainty. *American*

2378. There is nothing sure under the sun. *American*

2379. Try before you trust. *American*

Challenge

2380. Any man can steer in a calm. *Latin*

2381. Easy to keep the castle that was never besieged. *English*

Chance *see also* **Odds; Opportunity; Possibility; Probability**

2382. A chance shot will kill the devil. *Irish*

2383. All passes, all breaks, all wearies. *French*

2384. Blind chance sweeps the world along. *Greek*

2385. Chance and valor are blended in one. *Latin*

2386. Chance contrives better than we ourselves. *Greek*

2387. Chance dispenses life with unequal justice. *American*

2388. Chance is a nickname of Providence. *French*

2389. Chance is another master. *Latin*

2390. Chance is blind. *French*

2391. Chance makes a football of man's life. *Latin (Seneca)*

2392. Chances rule men and not men chances. *Greek*

2393. Fortune and humor govern the world. *French (La Rochefoucauld)*

2394. He that waits for chance is never sure of his dinner. *French*

2395. Nothing must be left to chance. *French*

2396. Something must be left to chance. *American*

2397. There is many a slip 'twixt the cup and the lip. *Greek (Palladas)*

2398. What chance has made yours is not really yours. *Latin*

2399. Whom chance often passes by, it finds at last. *Latin*

Change *see also* **Diversity; Innovation; Novelty; Progress; Time; Transience; Variety; Women and Variability**

2400. A rowin' stane [rolling stone] gathers nae fog [no moss]. *Scottish*

2401. A winter night, a woman's mind, and a laird's purpose aften change. *Scottish*

2402. After high floods low ebbs. *Dutch*

2403. All things change them to the contrary. *English (Shakespeare)*

2404. All things change; nothing perishes. *Latin*

2405. Change doth unknit the tranquil strength of men. *English (Arnold)*

2406. Change in all things is sweet. *Greek*

2407. Change of pasture makes fat calves. *English*

2408. Change of scenery makes for health. *American*

2409. Changes are lightsome, and fools like them. *Scottish*

2410. Changes o' wark is a lightening o' hearts. *Scottish*

2411. Every change of place becomes a delight. *Latin (Seneca)*

2412. He who goes to Rome a beast, returns a beast. *Italian*

2413. I am not what I once was. *Latin (Horace)*

2414. Man is what he is, not what he was. *Spanish*

2415. Never swap horses crossing a stream. *American*

2416. O God, spare us from change. *Tunisian*

2417. O God, spare us from change. *Tunisian*

2418. She's a bad sitter that's aye in a flutter. *Scottish*

2419. Sit tight; you may do worse by changing your position. *American*

2420. The cook that's with you in the morning is against you in the afternoon. *American*

2421. The more it changes, the more it is the same thing. *French*

2422. The times are changing; we, too, are changing with them. *Latin*

2423. There is nothing permanent except change. *Greek*

2424. Things do not change; we change. *American (Thoreau)*

2425. Times change and we change with them. *Latin*

2426. To an optimist every change is a change for the better. *American*

2427. To turn the pigs into the grass. [To change the subject.] *French*

2428. "Unsicker [insecure, unsafe], unstable," quo' the wave to the cable. *Scottish*

2429. We do not always gain by changing. *American*

2430. Who changes his condition changes fortune. *Italian*

2431. Who would be constant in happiness must often change. *Chinese*

2432. Wood may remain ten years in the water, but it will never become a crocodile. *Congolese*

2433. Ye're fae [so] keen o' clockin' ye'll dee on the eggs. *Scottish*

2434. Ye're out and in, like a dog at a fair. *Scottish*

2435. You cannot step twice in the same river, for other waters are continually flowing in. *Greek (Heraclitus)*

Changeableness *see also* Change; Transience; Women and Variability

2436. More changeable than the chameleon. *Latin*

Character *see also* Reputation

2437. A character, like a kettle, once mended, always needs mending. *American*

2438. A lost wife can be replaced, but the loss of character spells ruin. *Malay*

2439. A man shows his character by what he laughs at. *German*

2440. A man will take a lifetime to build a good character and then destroy it by a single misstep. *American*

2441. A man's character depends on whether his friends are good or bad. *Japanese*

2442. A man's character is his guardian divinity. *Greek (Heraclitus)*

2443. A man's own character is the arbiter of his fortune. *Latin*

2444. Character is destiny. *Greek*

2445. Character is habit long continued. *Greek*

2446. Character is much easier kept than recovered. *American (Paine)*

2447. Character is what you are in the dark. *American (Moody)*

2448. Character, not happiness, is the end of life. *American*

2449. Every cask smells of the wine it contains. *Spanish*

2450. Every man's character is good in his own eyes. *Yoruba*

2451. His own character is the arbiter of everyone's fortune. *Latin (Publilius Syrus)*

2452. It matters not what you are thought to be, but what you are. *Latin*

2453. It's not only the feathers that make the bird. *American*

2454. Our characters are the result of our conduct. *Greek*

2455. Put more trust in character than in an oath. *Greek*

2456. There are four points in a good character from which all good traits take their origin — prudence, courage, continence, and justice. *Arabic*

2457. There are six faults which a man ought to avoid: The desire of riches, drowsiness, sloth, idleness, tediousness, fear, and anger. *Sanskrit*

2458. To a bad character good doctrine avails nothing. *Italian*

2459. Ye hae a streak o' carl-hemp in ye. [You have strength of mind.] *Scottish*

Charity *see also* Generosity; Gifts and Giving; Philanthropy

2460. A closed fist is the lock of heaven and the open hand is the key of mercy. *Arabic*

2461. Alms are the father [i.e., the best of] sacrifice. *Moslem*

2462. Alms do not exhaust the purse, nor a mass the day's duty. *Danish*

2463. Almsgiving never lightens the purse. *Spanish*

2464. As cold as charity. *English*

2465. As the rivers pour their waters back again into the sea, so what a man has lent is returned to him again. *Chinese*

2466. Avarice hoards itself poor; charity gives itself rich. *German*

2467. Better the heat of hell than the cold of charity. *American*

2468. Blessed is he that considereth the poor. *Bible*

2469. Cast thy bread upon the waters, for thou shalt find it after many days. *Bible*

2470. Charity begins at home, but should not end there. *French*

2471. Charity begins at home. *Latin*

2472. Charity begins with ourselves. *Dutch*

2473. Charity bread has hard crusts. *American*

2474. Charity gives herself rich; covetousness hoards itself poor. *German*

2475. Charity is not wasted, even if you are not thanked for it. *Hungarian*

2476. Charity shall cover the multitude of sins. *Bible*

2477. Charity well ordered begins at home. *Spanish*

2478. Did anyone ever become poor by giving alms? *Hindi*

2479. Do good and throw it in the sea. *Moorish*

2480. Do good even to the wicked; it is as well to shut a dog's mouth with a crumb. *Persian (Sa'di)*

2481. Do good to yourself and yours, and then to others if you can. *Italian*

2482. Don't make gratitude the price of charity. *Iranian*

2483. Gie [give] your heart to God and your alms to the poor. *Scottish*

2484. Give to the poor, and thou shalt have treasure in heaven. *Bible*

2485. He gives a benefit twice who gives quickly to a poor man. *Latin*

2486. He is truly great who hath a great charity. *German*

2487. He that gives his heart will not deny his money. *English*

2488. He that has no charity deserves no mercy. *English*

2489. He who depends on charity soon learns to fast. *American*

2490. Help thi kynne, Crist bit [biddeth], for ther bygynneth charitie. *English*

2491. If charity cost no money and benevolence caused no heartache, the world would be full of philanthropists. *Yiddish*

2492. It is not enough to help the feeble up, but to support him after. *American*

2493. One "Take this" is better than ten "God-help-you's." *German*

2494. Send your charity abroad wrapt in blankets. *American*

2495. She plays whore for apples and then bestows them upon the sick. *Hebrew*

2496. The best charity is justice to all. *American*

2497. The bread of charity is bitter. *American*

2498. The candle before lights better than the candle behind. [Said of posthumous charity.] *French*

2499. The charitable give out at the door, and God puts in at the window. *English*

2500. The highest charity is charity toward the uncharitable. *American*

2501. The longest road is that to the pocket. *Yiddish*

2502. The man who weeps for everyone soon loses his eyes. *Turkish*

2503. To give quickly is the best charity. *Hindi*

2504. When thou doest alms, let not thy left hand know what thy right doeth. *Bible*

2505. Who gives alms sows one and reaps one thousand. *Turkish*

2506. Who gives me small gifts will have me live. *French*

2507. With malice toward none, with charity for all. *American (Lincoln)*

Charm

2508. Charm costs no more than disgust. *Yiddish*

2509. Whatever charm thou hast, be charming. *Latin (Ovid)*

Chastity *see also* Virtue; Women and Virtue

2510. A chaste matron rules her husband in obeying him. *Latin (Publilius Syrus)*

2511. A simple maiden in her flower is worth a hundred coats-of-arms. *American*

2512. A woman who has sacrificed her chastity will hesitate at no other iniquity. *Latin (Tacitus)*

2513. An untempted woman cannot boast of her chastity. *French (Montaigne)*

2514. By no art can chastity, once injured, be made whole. *Latin (Ovid)*

2515. Chaste is she whom no one has asked. *Latin*

2516. Dear to heaven is saintly chastity. *English (Milton)*

2517. Give me chastity and continence, but not just now. *Latin (St. Augustine)*

2518. If you cannot be chaste, be cautious. *Spanish*

2519. More chaste than vestal's couch. *Latin*

2520. The most cautious pass for the most chaste. *Spanish*

2521. The only chaste woman is the one who has not been asked. *Spanish*

2522. The unchaste woman can never be chaste again. *American*

2523. The unchaste woman will hesitate at no wickedness. *American*

2524. There are few good women who are not weary of their trade. *French (La Rochefoucauld)*

2525. Who can find a virtuous woman? for her price is far above rubies. *Bible*

Cheapness *see also* Bargains; Buying and Selling; Value; Worth

2526. Cheap goods always prove expensive. *American*

2527. Cheap purchase is money lost. *Japanese*

2528. Cheap things are not good; good things are not cheap. *Chinese*

2529. Cheapest is dearest. *American*

2530. Dear is cheap, cheap is dear. *American*

2531. If you want to buy cheap, buy from a needy fool. *Spanish*

2532. Light cheap, lither yield. [Little yield from what costs little.] *English*

2533. Nothing is cheap if you don't want it. *Latin (Cato)*

2534. The best is the cheapest. *French*

2535. When cheap meat boils you will smell what you have saved. *Arabic*

Cheating *see also* Buying and Selling; Crime and Criminals; Deception; Fraud; Lies and Lying

2536. A skillful cheat needs no assistance. *German*

2537. He that cheats in daffin [sport] winna be honest in earnest. *Scottish*

2538. Heads, I win; tails, you lose. *American*

2539. If you've cheated him of his birthright, at least give him the mess of lentils. *Yiddish*

2540. It is fair and just to cheat the cheater. *Spanish*

2541. The cheater winds up by cheating himself. *American*

2542. The man who cheats you once will cheat you a hundred times. *Arabic*

2543. Three things are men most likely to be cheated in: a horse, a wig, and a wife. *American (Franklin)*

Cheerfulness

2544. A cheerful look makes a dish a feast. *English*

2545. A man of gladness seldom falls into madness. *English*

2546. All succeeds with those who are cheerful. *French*

2547. Be cheerful, if you are wise. *Latin (Martius)*

2548. Cheerful company shortens the miles. *German*

2549. Fortune comes to a smiling house. *Japanese*

2550. He that sings drives away his troubles. *Spanish*

2551. If you cultivate a cheerful disposition in misfortune you will reap the advantage of it. *Latin (Plautus)*

2552. The sign of wisdom is a continual cheerfulness. *French*

2553. When the Spaniard sings, he is either mad or he has nothing. *Spanish*

Child-Rearing *see also* Discipline and Children; Parents and Children

2554. A child may have too much of his mother's blessing. *English*

2555. Bachelors' wives and auld maids' bairns [children] are aye weel bred. *Scottish*

2556. Beat your child once a day. If you don't know why, he does. *Chinese*

2557. Bring up your beloved child with a stick. *American*

2558. Children are what you make them. *French*
2559. Children have more need of models than of critics. *French*
2560. For betere is childe unbore [unborn] / Than unbuhsum [unbuxom, i.e., disobedient]. *English*
2561. For [i.e., far] betere is child unborn / Thenne unbeten. *English*
2562. Gie a bairn [child] his will and a whelp its fill and nane o' them will e'er do weel. *Scottish*
2563. Gold must be beaten, and a child scourged. *Hebrew*
2564. He has been rowed [rolled up] in his mother's sark [shirt] tail. *Scottish*
2565. He is better fed nor [than] nurtured. *Scottish*
2566. He that does not beat his child will later beat his own breast. *Turkish*
2567. He that spareth his rod hateth his son. *Bible*
2568. He who spares the rod hates his son. *Latin*
2569. It is better to bind children by respect than by fear. *Latin*
2570. Let thy child's first lesson be obedience, and the second will be what thou wilt. *American (Franklin)*
2571. Obedience is the first duty of a child. *American*
2572. Pampering a child is like a bear's hug; it may crush it to death. *American*
2573. Spare the rod, spoil the child. *English*
2574. Teach your child to hold his tongue; he'll learn fast enough to speak. *American*
2575. The best horse needs breaking, and the aptest child needs teaching. *American*
2576. Where the teacher strikes roses will grow. *Turkish*
2577. Who will not obey father, will have to obey stepfather. *Danish*

Childhood *see* Child-Rearing; Children and Childhood

Children and Childhood *see also* Child-Rearing; Parents and Children

2578. A child is fed with milk and praise. *English*
2579. A child's hand and a pig's trough must always be full. *American*
2580. A daft [foolish, merry] nurse maks a wise wean [child]. *Scottish*
2581. A pet child has many names. *Danish*
2582. A quiet child is plotting mischief— or has done it. *American*
2583. A ragged colt may make a good horse. *English*
2584. As long as a child does not cry, it does not matter what pleases it. *Russian*
2585. Better the child should cry than the father. *German*
2586. Childhood and youth are vanity. *Bible*
2587. Childhood is the sleep of reason. *French (Rousseau)*
2588. Children and chicken, must ever be picking. *English*
2589. Children, drunkards and fools cannot lie. *Latin*
2590. Children pick up words as pigeons peas, and utter them again as God shall please. *English*
2591. Children should be seen, not heard. *American*
2592. Even a child is known by his doing. *Bible*
2593. Gude bairns [children] are eith [easy] to lear [easy to learn [i.e., to teach]. *Scottish*
2594. Gude bairns [children] get broken brows. *English*
2595. Happy is that child whose father goeth to the devil [i.e., whose father acquires wealth]. *English*
2596. It is soon known which trees will bear fruit. *Latin*
2597. Just as the twig is bent the tree's inclined. *English (Pope)*
2598. The devil could not be everywhere so he made children. *American*
2599. When a child stumbles, a good angel puts his hands under. *Yiddish*
2600. When children stand quiet they have done something wrong. *American*
2601. When the child cuts its teeth, death is on the watch. *Spanish*
2602. When the child is christened come godfathers enough. *French*
2603. Woman and bairns [children] layne [conceal] what they ken na [what they know not]. *Scottish*
2604. You can do anything with children if you only play with them. *German*

Choice *see also* Better; Dilemma; Indecision; Possession; Preference; Taste; Vacillation

2605. Between the shrine and the stone. *Latin*
2606. He that chooses takes the worst. *French*
2607. He that has a choice has trouble. *Dutch*
2608. It's difficult to choose between two blind goats. *Irish*
2609. Man is a choosing animal but he often chooses the worst. *American*
2610. One can't make the bed and save the sheet. *French*
2611. One does not eat acorns when he has pearls. *German*
2612. One should choose one's bedfellow whilst it is daylight. *Swedish*
2613. Picking out melons in a melon patch, the more one does it the more one gets confused. *Chinese*
2614. The burden of one's own choice is not felt. *American*
2615. The lass that has mony wooers aft wales [chooses] the warst. *Scottish*
2616. There is a small choice in rotten apples. *Spanish*
2617. There is no banquet but some dislike something in it. *English*
2618. There's no choice among stinking fish. *American*
2619. There's small choice in rotten apples. *English (Shakespeare)*
2620. Where bad's the best, naught must be the choice. *English*

Church *see also* God; Man and God; Religion

2621. A church debt is the devil's salary. *American*
2622. A church is four walls and God within. *French*

2623. Bring yourself to church, not your Sunday clothes. *American*
2624. Except the Lord build the house, they labor in vain that build it. *Bible*
2625. He who is near the church is often far from God. *French*
2626. If you go to church for an evil purpose, you go to God's house on the devil's errand. *American*
2627. In the visible church the true Christians are invisible. *German*
2628. Let the devil get into the church and he'll mount the altar. *American*
2629. The nearer to the church, the further from God. *English*

Circumspection *see also* **Carefulness; Caution; Prudence; Watchfulness**

2630. Let not your tongue cut your throat. *Arabic*
2631. That which you know, know not; and that which you see, see not. *Latin (Plautus)*

Circumstance(s) *see also* **Change**

2632. A coal-heaver is a lord in his own house. *French*
2633. A thoroughbred horse is not dishonored by its saddle. *Syrian*
2634. As time changes, counsel changes. *Portuguese*
2635. Different times, different folk. *Danish*
2636. Fruit ripens not well in the shade. *English*
2637. Suit yourself to circumstances. *Chinese*
2638. The chameleon says, "Speed is good, and slowness is good." *Oji*
2639. The partridge loves peas, but not those that go into the pot with it. *Wolof*
2640. Turn your coat according to the wind. *German*
2641. Yield to circumstances. *Chinese*

Cities *see also* **Town and Country**

2642. A city that is set on a hill cannot be hid. *Bible*
2643. A great city, a great solitude. *Greek*
2644. Cities should be walled with the courage of their dwellers. *Greek*
2645. Do not dwell in a city where a horse does not neigh nor a dog bark. *Hebrew*
2646. Do not dwell in a city whose governor is a physician. *Hebrew*
2647. God the first garden made, and the first city Cain. *English (Cowley)*
2648. In cities vice is hidden with most ease. *American*
2649. It is the men who make the city, not walls or ships. *Greek*
2650. 'Tis the men, not the houses, that make the city. *English*
2651. Unless the Lord keepeth the city, the watchman waketh in vain. *Latin*

Citizens and Citizenship *see also* **Country**

2652. Every subject's duty is the king's, but every subject's soul is his own. *English (Shakespeare)*

Civility *see also* **Courtesy; Politeness**

2653. Civility costs nothing. *American*
2654. "It's aye gude to be ceevil," quo' the auld wife when she beckit to the deevil. *Scottish*
2655. There is nothing that costs less than civility. *Spanish*

Clarity

2656. It would be clear enough even to a blind man. *Latin*
2657. Not to create confusion in what is clear, but to throw light on what is obscure. *Latin (Horace)*

Cleanliness

2658. A clean-fingered housewife and an idle, folk say. *English*
2659. A clean hand is happy. *English*
2660. "A clean thing's kindly," quo' the wife when she turn'd her sark [shirt] after a month's wear. *Scottish*
2661. Be thou clean. *Bible*
2662. Cleanliness is next to godliness. *Latin*
2663. Cleanliness is the key of prayer. *Arabic*
2664. Empty, swept, and garnished. *Bible*
2665. One keep-clean is better than ten make-cleans. *American*
2666. Poverty comes from God, but not dirt. *Hebrew*
2667. There is nothing so crouse [cheerful] as a new-washen house. *Scottish*
2668. Wash your hands often, your feet seldom, and your head never. *English*

Clemency *see also* **Leniency; Pardon; Punishment**

2669. Clemency alone makes us equal to the gods. *Greek*
2670. Clemency is the remedy for cruelty. *Latin*
2671. Sometimes clemency is cruelty, and cruelty clemency. *Italian*

Cleverness

2672. All clever men are birds of prey. *English*
2673. Clever and strong people never make mistakes. *Chinese*
2674. Clever for a lifetime; foolish for a moment. *Chinese*
2675. Clever men are sometimes dupes of their own cleverness. *Chinese*
2676. Cleverness does not take the place of knowledge. *American*
2677. Cleverness is serviceable for everything, sufficient for nothing. *French*
2678. Don't be so clever; cleverer ones than you are in jail. *Russian*
2679. Good is wisdom to possess, and better still is cleverness. *Bulgarian*
2680. He who would be too clever makes a fool of himself. *Yiddish*
2681. Let them be handsome so long as I'm clever. *Yiddish*
2682. The desire of appearing clever often prevents our becoming so. *French (La Rochefoucauld)*
2683. There is nothing so difficult that cleverness cannot overcome it. *Latin*
2684. Three fools are equal to one clever man; three clever men equal to one district magistrate. *Chinese*

2685. What's the use of cleverness, if foolishness serves? *Yiddish*
2686. When luck joins in the game, cleverness scores double. *Yiddish*
2687. Wiles help weak folk. *Scottish*
2688. Wisdom comes by cleverness, not by time. *Latin*

Closeness *see* **Nearness**

Clothes *see also* **Appearance; Deception; Fashion; Inference; Prejudice**

2689. A man is estimated by his clothes — and a horse by its saddle. *Chinese*
2690. A monkey remains a monkey though dressed in silk. *American*
2691. A negligent dress is becoming to men. *Latin*
2692. A smart coat is a good letter of introduction. *Dutch*
2693. A stick dressed up does not look like a stick. *Spanish*
2694. Abroad, a man's clothes are looked at; at home, the man himself. *Chinese*
2695. An ape is an ape, a varlet's a varlet, / Though they be clad in silk or scarlet. *English*
2696. Apes are apes though clothed in scarlet. *English (Jonson)*
2697. Apes are apes though you clothe them in velvet. *German*
2698. Bonny feathers dinna aye mak' bonny birds. *Scottish*
2699. Clothes do much to make a man. *French*
2700. Clothes don't make the man. *American*
2701. Clothes make people. *German*
2702. Clothes make the man. *American*
2703. Dress a little toad, and it will look pretty. *Spanish*
2704. Dress does not give knowledge. *Spanish*
2705. Dress slowly when you are in a hurry. *French*
2706. Eat to please thyself, but dress to please others. *American (Franklin)*
2707. Fair feathers make fair fowls. *English*
2708. Fair fowles hes fair feathers. *Scottish*
2709. Fine clothes do not make the gentleman — except when he travels abroad. *American*
2710. Gude claes [clothes] open a' doors. *Scottish*
2711. He who wears a ten-bob suit must needs have a ten-bob mind. *Irish*
2712. If it ser' me to wear, it may ser' you to look at. *Scottish*
2713. If she is beautiful, she is overdressed. *Latin*
2714. If you want a wife, choose her on Saturday, not on Sunday. *Spanish*
2715. In your own country, your name; in other countries, your dress. *Hebrew*
2716. It's hard to make clothes fit a miserable man. *American*
2717. It's not the gay coat that makes the gentleman. *English*
2718. It's not the habit that makes the monk. *American*
2719. Man is judged by his clothes; a horse by its saddle. *Chinese*
2720. Man is like a tree trunk; entirely dependent on clothing. *Chinese*
2721. Many come to bring their clothes to church rather than themselves. *American*
2722. Meat and cloth make the man. *Scottish*
2723. Mendings are honorable; rags are abominable. *American*
2724. No fine clothes can hide the clown. *English*
2725. No one in a shabby coat is treated with respect. *Latin*
2726. No one respects an old ewe who is decked out lamb fashion. *American*
2727. Reynard is still Reynard, though he put on a cowl. *English*
2728. Showy clothes attract most. *Latin*
2729. Silk goes with everything. *Iraqi*
2730. Swank clothes open all doors. *American*
2731. That which covers thee discovers [i.e., reveals] thee. *Spanish*
2732. The clothes make the man. *Dutch*
2733. The coat is quite new; only the holes are old. *Russian*
2734. The coat makes the man. *Latin*
2735. The dress does not make the friar. *Spanish*
2736. The habit does not make the monk. *French (Rabelais)*
2737. The jackdaw, stripped of her stolen colors, provokes our laughter. *Latin*
2738. The judicial gown does not make the judge nor the surplice the priest. *American*
2739. The outer dress covers the petticoat. *Yiddish*
2740. The peasant saw himself in fine breeches, and he was as insolent as could be. *Spanish*
2741. The tailor makes the man. *English (Jonson)*
2742. The white coat does not make the miller. *Italian*
2743. There is often a royal heart under a torn cloak. *Danish*
2744. Those who have fine clothes in their chests can wear rags. *Italian*
2745. Though manners make, yet apparel shapes. *Italian*
2746. Three-tenths according to a man's abilities; seven-tenths according to his costume. *Chinese*
2747. Through tattered clothes small vices do appear; / Robes and furred gowns hide all. *English (Shakespeare)*
2748. Trappings do not make the horse; clothes do not make the man. *American*
2749. Who arrays himself in other men's garments is stripped on the highway. *Spanish*
2750. Wisdom does not consist in dress. *Latin*
2751. You can't get warm on another's fur coat. *Yiddish*

Coarseness *see* **Vulgarity**

Coercion *see also* **Force; Motivation**

2752. A wise man does nothing by constraint. *Latin (Cicero)*
2753. Bliss itself is not worth having, / If we're by compulsion blest. *English (Moore)*
2754. Forced prayers are no gude for the soul. *Scottish*

2755. It is a part of the nature of man to resist compulsion. *Latin (Tacitus)*
2756. Oppression causeth rebellion. *English*
2757. The bird that can sing and won't sing must be made to sing. *English*
2758. You may force a man to shut his eyes but you can't make him sleep. *Danish*
2759. You may take a horse to the water, but you can't make him drink. *English*

Coffee
2760. Coffee should be black as Hell, strong as death, and sweet as love. *Turkish*

Cohabitation *see also* Association
2761. A separate hole is to be preferred though it be but a rathole. Tamil
2762. If there are more women in the house than hearths, there is no peace in it. *Swiss*
2763. Two bears cannot live in one cave. *Cheremis*

Coincidence
2764. The sparrow flying behind the hawk thinks the hawk is fleeing. *Japanese*

Coldness
2765. A dog's nose and a maid's knees are always cold. *American*
2766. Everyone feels the cold according as he is clad. *Spanish*
2767. What keeps out the cold keeps out the heat. *Italian*

Collaboration *see also* Assistance; Cooperation; Unity
2768. By the hands of many a great work is made light. *Latin*
2769. If everyone would mend one, all would be mended. *English*
2770. One finger cannot lift a pebble. *Iranian*
2771. Twa [two] heads are better than ane [one], though they're but sheep's anes. *Scottish*
2772. "Twa [two] heads are better than ane [one]," as the wife said when she and her dog gaed [went] to the market. *Scottish*
2773. Two are an army against one. *Latin*
2774. Two eyes see more than one. *English*

Comfort *see also* Ease
2775. Is there no balm in Gilead? *Bible*
2776. It is good sheltering under an old hedge. *English*
2777. It is good sleeping in a heal [whole] skin. *Scottish*
2778. Muckle [much] sorrow comes to the scrae [shoe], e'er the heat come to the tae [toe]. *Scottish*
2779. When I break my leg it is no comfort to me that another has broken his neck. *Danish*

Command *see also* Kings and Rulers; Leaders and Leadership
2780. He who demands does not command. *Italian*
2781. It is a fine thing to command though it be but a herd of cattle. *Spanish*

Commerce *see* Business and Commerce

Commitment *see also* Decision
2782. As good be hanged for a sheep as a lamb. *English*
2783. Don't take hold of a leopard's tail, but if you do, don't let go. *Ethiopian*
2784. Either a man or a mouse. *English*
2785. Either make a spoon or spoil a horn. *English*
2786. Either win the horse or lose the saddle. *English*
2787. He that is at sea must either sail or sink. *Danish*
2788. He that is embarked with the devil must make the passage along with him. *English*
2789. He that takes the devil into his boat must carry him over the sound. *English*
2790. If you dip your arm into the pickle-pot, let it be up to the elbow. *Malay*
2791. If you ferry at all, ferry right over. *Chinese*
2792. If you have to kill a snake, kill it once and for all. *Japanese*
2793. In for a penny in for a pound. *English*
2794. It is all the same whether a man has both legs in the stocks or one. *German*
2795. It is the first shower that wets. *Italian*
2796. Ne'er go to the deil wi' a dishclout in your hand. *Scottish*
2797. Neck or nothing, for the king loves no cripples. *English*
2798. Once you have said, "Here I am," don't try to say that you are not there. *Haitian Creole*
2799. Over shoes, over boots. *English*
2800. Perhaps hinders folk from lying. *French*
2801. Such things must be if we sell ale. *English*
2802. The cat loves fish, but she is loath to wet her feet. *English*
2803. The whole hog or none. *English*
2804. There is nothing like being bespattered for making one defy the slough. *French*
2805. Whatsoever thy hand findeth to do, do it with all thy might. *English*
2806. You may as well be hung for a sheep as a lamb. *English*
2807. You should eat plentifully of the flesh of the turtle or not at all. *Latin*

Common Sense *see also* Carefulness; Caution; Folly; Fools and Folly; Prudence; Sense; Watchfulness
2808. A kennel is not the place to keep sausages. *Danish*
2809. A man may love his house well and yet not ride on the ridge. *English*
2810. A windy day is not the day for thatching. *Irish*
2811. An ounce o' wit is worth a pound o' lear [learning]. *Scottish*
2812. An ounce of mother-wit is worth a pound of clergy. *Scottish*
2813. Ask the patient, not the physician, where the pain is. *Polish*
2814. Barefooted folk shouldna tread on thorns. *Scottish*

2815. Common sense is not so common. *French*

2816. Common sense is the wick of the candle. *American (Emerson)*

2817. Do not remove a fly from your friend's forehead with a hatchet. *Chinese*

2818. Don't throw out the baby with the bath water. *American*

2819. I had rather ride on an ass that carries me than a horse that throws me. *English (Herbert)*

2820. Learning is worthless without mother-wit. *Spanish (Cervantes)*

2821. Let us not throw the rope after the bucket. *Spanish*

Community *see also* **Neighbors; Shared Misfortune**

2822. Rain does not fall on one roof alone. *Cameroonian*

2823. What is not good for the swarm is not good for the bee. *Latin (Marcus Aurelius)*

2824. Your own safety is at stake when your neighbor's wall is ablaze. *Latin (Horace)*

Companions and Companionship *see also* **Association; Bad Company**

2825. Among thorns grow the roses. *Italian*

2826. An agreeable companion on a journey is as good as a carriage. *Latin (Publilius Syrus)*

2827. Man should take as companion one older than himself. *Wolof*

2828. No road is long with good company. *Turkish*

2829. One ripe fruit between two green. *French*

2830. Society is no comfort / To one not sociable. *English (Shakespeare)*

2831. The best company must part. *French*

2832. The shortest road's where the company's gude. *Scottish*

2833. The smaller the company, the greater the feast. *Yiddish*

2834. They're keen o' company that tak the dog on their back. *Scottish*

2835. To have the universe bear one company would be a great consolation in death. *Latin (Publilius Syrus)*

2836. Two are better than one. *American*

2837. Two is company, three's a crowd. *American*

2838. With merry company the dreary way is endured. *Spanish*

Company *see* **Association; Bad Company; Companions and Companionship; Shared Misfortune**

Comparison *see also* **Difference; Perspective; Relativity**

2839. Acorns were good till bread was found. *Latin*

2840. An itch is worse than a smart. *English*

2841. Comfort is not known if poverty does not come before it. *Irish*

2842. Comparison, more than reality, makes men happy or wretched. *English*

2843. Comparisons are odious. *American*

2844. Comparisons make enemies of our friends. *Greek*

2845. Fleas are not lobsters. *English*

2846. I can tell by my pot how the others boil. *French*

2847. I murmured because I had no shoes, until I met a man who had no feet. *Persian*

2848. Illness gives us the taste for health. *Hungarian*

2849. Kings' cauff's [chaff's] worth ither [other] folk's corn. *Scottish*

2850. Nothing is good or bad but by comparison. *English*

2851. Were there no fools there would be no wise men. *German*

2852. Where there are no fish even a crawfish calls herself a fish. *American*

2853. Who has never tasted what is bitter does not know what is sweet. *German*

2854. You are comparing a rose to an anemone. *Latin*

2855. You compare the bee to the grasshopper. *Latin*

2856. You compare the moorhen to the swan. *Latin*

Compensation *see also* **Consolation**

2857. If you are ugly, learn how to dance. *Nyanja*

Competence *see also* **Ability**

2858. A small competence is best. *Latin*

Competition *see also* **Winning and Losing**

2859. A good bone never falls to a good dog. *French*

2860. Ane [one] beggar is wae that another by the gate gae. *Scottish*

2861. Compete not with a friend. *Latin*

2862. Competition is the life of trade. *American*

2863. Competition makes a horse-race. *Latin*

2864. In the grave dust and bones jostle not for the wall. *American*

2865. One barber shaves not so close but another finds work. *English*

2866. One dog growls when the other goes into the kitchen. *German*

2867. Rivalry is good for mortals. *Greek*

2868. The only competition worthy of a wise man is with himself. *American*

2869. The race is not to the swift, nor the battle to the strong. *English*

Complacency

2870. Fat hens are aye [always] ill layers. *Scottish*

2871. Fat hens lay few eggs. *German*

2872. Fat paunches make lean pates. *Scottish*

2873. He that is too secure is not safe. *English*

2874. The path is smooth that leadeth on to danger. *English (Shakespeare)*

Complaint *see also* **Discontent; Dissatisfaction**

2875. A good dog never barketh about a bone. *Scottish*

2876. A tarrowing bairn [complaining child] was never fat. *Scottish*

2877. A wheel not greased will creak. *Latin*

2878. He behoves to have meal enow that sal stop ilka man's mou' [that will stop every man's mouth]. *Scottish*

2879. He needs much butter who would stop every man's mouth. *Dutch*

2880. He that falls by himself never cries. *Turkish*

2881. It is better to try to forget your troubles than to speak of them. *French*

2882. It's no use crying over spilled milk. *American*

2883. Never yowl till you're hit. *Irish*

2884. The horse that pulls at the collar is always getting the whip. *French*

2885. The horseshoe which clatters wants a nail. *Spanish*

2886. The worst wheel of the cart makes the most noise. *Latin*

2887. We should all endure our own grievances rather than detract from the comforts of others. *Latin (Cicero)*

2888. Wise men ne'er wail their present woes. *English (Shakespeare)*

Completeness *see also* Completion; End

2889. All or nothing at all. *American*

2890. All or nothing. *American*

2891. Complete as a whole, and complete in every part. *Latin*

Completion *see also* Completeness; End

2892. A deed done has an end. *Italian*

2893. A thing done is no to do. *Scottish*

Complicity *see also* Guilt

2894. A common blot is held no stain. *English*

2895. A crime in which many are implicated goes unpunished. *Latin (Lucan)*

2896. He sins as much who holds the sack as he who puts into it. *French*

2897. He that hinders not a mischief is guilty of it. *Latin*

2898. He who hold the ladder is as bad as the thief. *English*

2899. It is a fraud to connive at a fraud. *Latin*

2900. The receiver is as bad as the thief. *English*

2901. Wrongdoers and assenting parties are equally punishable. *Latin*

Compliment *see also* Applause; Approval; Fair Words; Good Words; Praise

2902. Compliments cost nothing, yet many pay dear for them. *German*

2903. It hurteth not the toung [tongue] to geue fayre woordes [to speak fair words]. *English (Heywood)*

2904. What compliments fly when beggars meet! *English*

Compromise *see also* Alternatives; Choice; Possession

2905. A bird in the cage is worth a hundred at large. *Italian*

2906. A bird in the cage is worth a dozen in your neighbor's garden. *American*

2907. A bird in the hand is worth twa [two] fleeing by. *Scottish*

2908. A bird in the hand is worth two in the bush. *Greek*

2909. A penny in the pocket is worth ten outside of it. *Lebanese*

2910. A pullet in the pen is worth a hundred in the fen [mire]. *English*

2911. A sparrow in the hand is worth a vulture flying. *Spanish*

2912. A sparrow in the hand is worth more than a goose flying in the air. *French*

2913. Ae bird i' the hand is worth ten fleeing. *Scottish*

2914. Better a lean agreement than a fat judgment. *Italian*

2915. Give and take. *Greek*

2916. Hard against hard was never good. *German*

2917. He that canna do as he would maun [must] do as he may. *Scottish*

2918. He that hath a good harvest must be content with some thistles. *English*

2919. He who cannot do what he wishes, must needs do as he can. *Latin*

2920. If flesh is not to be had, fish must content us. *Latin*

2921. If the mountain will not go to Mahomet, let Mahomet go to the mountain. *English*

2922. If thou hast not a capon, feed on an onion. *English*

2923. If you are deaf and blind, smell the paint. *Arabic*

2924. If you can't lick 'em, join 'em. *American*

2925. If you cannot drive an ox, drive a donkey. *Latin*

2926. Lose a leg rather than your life. *American*

2927. One bird in the hand is worth four in the air. *Latin*

2928. Too soft, and you will be squeezed; too hard, and you will be broken. *Arabic*

2929. You cannot drive straight on a twisting lane. *Russian*

Compulsion *see also* Coercion; Force

2930. Half a will is worth a dozen compulsions. *Russian*

Concealment

2931. A candle under a bushel. *Latin*

2932. A cup concealed in the dress is rarely honestly carried. *Latin*

2933. An open countenance often conceals close thoughts. English

2934. Have an open face, but conceal your thoughts. *Italian*

2935. He who conceals his disease cannot expect to be cured. *Ethiopian*

2936. Hide nothing from thy minister, physician and lawyer. *American*

2937. One cannot hide an awl in a sack. *Russian*

2938. Surely in vain the net is spread in the sight of any bird. *English*

2939. Wolves can't catch what dogs do not expose. *French (La Fontaine)*

Conceit *see also* Self-Importance; Vanity

2940. Buy him at his own price and sell him at yours and you'll make no bargain. *English*

2941. Can't we prepare a meal without your carrot? [In reference to one who takes too much upon himself.] *Chinese*

2942. He looks on others as nonentities. *Chinese*

2943. His eye beholds an empty world; within its range no man appears. *Chinese*
2944. The bigger a man's head, the worse his headache. *Persian*
2945. The smaller the mind, the greater the conceit. *Greek (Aesop)*
2946. There is more hope of a fool, than of him that is wise in his own conceit. *Bible*
2947. Ye're like me, and I'm nae sma drink. *Scottish*

Conciseness *see also* **Brevity**
2948. In trying to be concise I become obscure. *Latin (Horace)*

Conclusion *see* **Completion; Completeness; End**

Conditions *see also* **Adaptability; Circumstance(s); Flexibility**
2949. Condition makes, condition breaks. *American*

Conduct *see also* **Golden Rule; Morality**
2950. A man may talk like a wise man, but act like a fool. *American*
2951. Act so in the valley that you need not fear those who stand on the hill. *Danish*
2952. An insolent lord is not a gentleman. *English*
2953. Ane [one] never tires by doing gude. *Scottish*
2954. As the occasion, so the behavior. *Spanish (Cervantes)*
2955. Bad conduct soils the finest ornament more than filth. *Latin (Plautus)*
2956. Be aye [always] the same thing you wad be ca'd [you would be called]. *Scottish*
2957. Be what ye seem, and seem what ye are. *Scottish*
2958. Be with a man deaf and hearing, silent and speaking. *Hebrew*
2959. Behavior is the mirror in which everyone shows his image. *German (Goethe)*
2960. Consider not what you may do, but what it will become you to do. *Latin (Claudius)*
2961. Do on the hill as ye wad do in the ha' [hall]. *Scottish*
2962. Do the likeliest and hope the best. *Scottish*
2963. Do weel, an' doubt nae [no] man; do ill, an' doubt a' [all] men. *Scottish*
2964. Do weel, and dread nae [no] shame. *Scottish*
2965. Do weel and hae [have] weel. *Scottish*
2966. Do what thou oughtest, and come what come can. *English (Herbert)*
2967. Do what ye ought and let come what will. *Scottish*
2968. Don't strike a man when he is down. *Russian*
2969. Don't tell all you know, don't believe all you hear, don't do everything you're capable of. *American*
2970. Don't throw dirt into the fountain from which you must drink. *American*
2971. Even God is terrified at the actions of His creatures. *American*
2972. He that sings on Friday shall weep on Sunday. *American*
2973. He that will not live a saint can never die a martyr. *English*
2974. He that would live at peace and rest, / Must hear, and see, and say the best. *English*
2975. Hear, see, and hold your peace, if you would live in peace. *Italian*
2976. If not seemly, do it not; if not true, say it not. *Greek*
2977. It is not gain that is gain; it is upright conduct. *Chinese*
2978. Keep hame [home] and hame will keep you. *Scottish*
2979. Let every man be swift to hear, slow to speak. *Bible*
2980. Mind your till, and till your mind. *American*
2981. Never order a man to do what you're afraid to do yourself. *American*
2982. Never repent of a good action. *American*
2983. Never take anything for granted. *American*
2984. Never tread on a sore toe. *American*
2985. Nothing is more adroit than irreproachable conduct. *French*
2986. The wise man doesn't tell what he does, but never does what can't be told. *American*
2987. To a crazy ship all winds are contrary. *American*
2988. Weel is that weel does. *Scottish*

Confession *see also* **Absolution; Forgiveness; Guilt**
2989. A fault once denied is twice committed. *French*
2990. A fault [or sin] confessed is half redressed [forgiven]. *French*
2991. A fool that confesses is a fool that progresses. *American*
2992. A generous confession disarms slander. *English*
2993. A sin confessed is half forgiven. *Italian*
2994. Confess and be hanged. *English*
2995. Confess'd faut [fault] is half amends. *Scottish*
2996. Confession is good for the soul. *American*
2997. Confession of a fault makes half amends for it. *English*
2998. Confession of our faults is the next thing to innocence. *Latin (Publilius Syrus)*
2999. Sin confessed is forgiveness asked. *Arabic*

Confidence *see also* **Arrogance**
3000. Assurance is two-thirds of success. *Gaelic*
3001. Confidence begets confidence. *Latin*
3002. Confidence cannot find a place wherein to rest in safety. *Latin (Virgil)*
3003. Confidence does more to make conversation than wit. *French (La Rochefoucauld)*
3004. Confidence in an unfaithful man in time of trouble is like a broken tooth, and a foot out of joint. *Bible*
3005. Confidence is a plant of slow growth. *English*
3006. Confidence is wont to come slowly in matters of great moment. *Latin (Ovid)*
3007. Confidence placed in another often compels confidence in return. *Latin (Livy)*
3008. Confidence should arise from beneath, and power descend from above. *French*
3009. Confident because of our caution. *Greek*

3010. Let every man's hope be in himself. *Latin*
3011. Self-confidence is the first requisite of great undertakings. *American*
3012. They are able because they seem [to themselves] to be able. *Greek (Virgil)*
3013. They can conquer who believe they can. *Latin (Virgil)*
3014. They succeed, because they think they can. *Latin (Virgil)*
3015. To conquer you must believe you can. *American*

Confidences *see* Secrets and Secrecy; Trust; Women and Secrets; Women and Trustworthiness

Confinement
3016. A bird in a cage is less than half a bird. *American*
3017. A bird in a cage puts all heaven in a rage. *American*
3018. A cat that is locked up may change into a lion. *Dutch*
3019. Nightingales won't sing in a cage. *American*
3020. The captive eagle in the zoo envies the free sparrow who steps in to look around. *American*

Conflict *see also* Contention; Discord; Strife
3021. Two Sir Positives can scarce meet without a skirmish. *English*
3022. When at close quarters aim low. *English*

Conformity *see also* Custom; Fashion
3023. After the land's manner is mannerly. *German*
3024. Among the one-eyed, close one eye. *Arabic*
3025. At Rome do as Rome does. *English*
3026. Do as your neighbor does or shut the door. *Tunisian*
3027. If you go to a country where they worship the calf, pick grass and feed it. *Lebanese*
3028. It is hard to live in Rome and strive against the pope. *English*
3029. Trumpet in a herd of elephants; / Crow in the company of cocks; / Bleat in a flock of goats. *Malay*
3030. When in Rome, do as the Romans do. *American*
3031. When you are at Rome, do as you see. *Spanish (Cervantes)*
3032. When you are at Rome, live as Romans live. *Latin (St. Ambrose)*
3033. When you enter a town, swear by its gods. *Arabic*
3034. Wherever you be, do as you see. *Spanish*
3035. You must howl with wolves if you wish to be one of their herd. *Latin*

Confusion *see* Order

Connections *see also* Relatives
3036. It's gude to be sib [related] to siller [silver]. *Scottish*

Conquest *see also* Winning and Losing
3037. Conquer thyself. *Chinese*
3038. Conquered, we conquer. *Latin*
3039. Divide and rule. *Latin*
3040. He went forth conquering and to conquer. *Bible*
3041. I came, I saw, I conquered. *Latin (Caesar)*
3042. Prudent men enjoy more conquests than passionate ones. *American*
3043. The conquered are always wrong. *American*
3044. The conquerer is always right. *American*
3045. The conquerer may please the conquered according to his pleasure. *Latin*
3046. The conquering cause was pleasing to the gods. *Latin*
3047. The honor of the conquest is rated by the difficulty. *French*
3048. The man who conquers sticks to his guns. *American*
3049. There is no pain in the wound received in the moment of victory. *Latin (Publilius Syrus)*
3050. They conquer who believe they can. *Latin*
3051. To conquer others you must first conquer yourself. *American*
3052. To rejoice in conquest is to take joy in the loss of human life. *Chinese*
3053. We triumph without glory when we conquer without danger. *French*

Conscience *see also* Guilt
3054. A bad conscience is a snake in one's heart. *Yiddish*
3055. A clear conscience is a wall of brass. *Latin*
3056. A clear conscience is absolutely essential to happiness. *American*
3057. A good conscience is a continual feast. *English (Bacon)*
3058. A good conscience is a soft pillow. *American*
3059. A good conscience is God's eye. *Russian*
3060. A good conscience is the best divinity. *English*
3061. A good conscience knows no fear. *American*
3062. A guilty conscience needs no accuser. *French*
3063. A mind conscious of guilt is its own accuser. *Latin*
3064. A peace above all earthly dignities, / A still and quiet conscience. *English (Shakespeare)*
3065. A quiet conscience sleeps in thunder, but rest and guilt live far asunder. *American (Franklin)*
3066. A quiet conscience sleeps in thunder. *English*
3067. A safe conscience makes a sound sleep. *American*
3068. A scar on the conscience is the same as a wound. *Latin*
3069. A sinful heart makes feeble hand. *Scottish (Scott)*
3070. An evil act has a witness in the heart. *Danish*
3071. An evil conscience breaks many a man's neck. *English*
3072. An evil conscience is often quiet, but never secure. *Latin (Publilius Syrus)*
3073. An ill conscience can never hope well. *English*
3074. Conscience is a god to all mortals. *Greek*
3075. Conscience is as a thousand witnesses. *Latin*
3076. Conscience is as good as a thousand witnesses. *Italian*

3077. Conscience is the avenging angel in the mind. *American*
3078. Conscience is the chamber of justice. *English*
3079. Conscience makes cowards of us all. *American*
3080. Deaf to the voice of conscience. *Latin*
3081. Even when there is no law, there is conscience. *Latin (Publilius Syrus)*
3082. Every sound alarms. *Latin (Virgil)*
3083. Fear nothing but your own conscience. *American*
3084. Happy is he that chastens himself. *English*
3085. He that commits a fault thinks everyone speaks of it. *English*
3086. He that excuses himself accuses himself. *French*
3087. He that has a muckle [big] nose thinks ilka ane [everyone] is speaking o't. *Scottish*
3088. He that has no conscience has nothing. *French (Rabelais)*
3089. He that hath had one of his family hanged may not say to his neighbor, "Hang up this fish." *Hebrew*
3090. He who has no conscience has nothing. *French*
3091. If you have no observers, be afraid of yourself. *American*
3092. In the court of his own conscience no guilty man is acquitted. *American*
3093. It is always term time in the court of conscience. *American*
3094. It is neither safe nor prudent to do aught against conscience. *German (Luther)*
3095. Keep conscience clear, then never fear. *American (Franklin)*
3096. Let your conscience be your guide. *American*
3097. No whip cuts so sharply as the lash of conscience. *American*
3098. O coward conscience, how dost thou afflict me. *English (Shakespeare)*
3099. One who has a straw tail is always afraid of its catching fire. *Italian*
3100. The best friend is a clean conscience. *Welsh*
3101. The conscience of the dying belies their life. *French*
3102. The worm of conscience consorts with the owl. *German (Schiller)*
3103. Thus conscience does make cowards of as all. *English (Shakespeare)*
3104. What you take lightly on your conscience you'll feel heavily on your back. *American*
3105. Ye're busy to clear yourself when naebody files you. *Scottish*

Consent *see also* Acceptance

3106. Consenting against his inclination. *Latin*
3107. No injury can be complained of by a consenting party. *Latin*

Consequence *see also* Cause and Effect; End; Ends and Means; Outcome

3108. The thread follows the needle. *Yoruba*
3109. Where they chop wood, chips fly. *Polish*
3110. Who plays with cats will have scratches. *Algerian*

Consistency

3111. A foolish consistency is the hobgoblin of little minds. *American (Emerson)*
3112. A wise man wavers, a fool is fixed. *Scottish*
3113. It is natural for a wise man to change his opinion; a fool keeps on changing like the moon. *Latin*
3114. It is often consistency to change the mind. *Italian*
3115. Most of us are consistently inconsistent. *American*
3116. The color of the odoo [a kind of fruit] does not change. *Lugbara*
3117. Wise men change their minds, fools never. *Spanish*

Consolation *see also* Encouragement; Hope

3118. If I have lost the ring I still have the fingers. *Italian*
3119. The last shall be first. *Bible*

Conspicuousness

3120. Some people are conspicuous by their presence and others by their absence. *American*

Constancy *see also* Faithfulness

3121. Constancy is the foundation of virtues. *English (Bacon)*
3122. Constant in nothing but inconstancy. *English (Pope)*
3123. One man; two loves. No good ever comes of that. *Greek (Euripides)*

Contamination *see also* Corruption; Disease

3124. One sickly sheep infects the flock. *English*

Contempt

3125. Contempt is the sharpest reproof. *American*
3126. Contempt will sooner kill an injury than revenge. *American*
3127. Fare-ye-weel, Meg Dorts, and e'en 's ye like. *Scottish*
3128. I'll get a better fore-speaker than you for nought. *Scottish*
3129. If this be a feast I hae been at mony. *Scottish*
3130. Many can bear adversity, but few contempt. *English*

Contentment

3131. A blythe heart maks a blomand [bloomin'] look. *Scottish*
3132. A contented man is always rich. *Latin*
3133. A contented mind is a continual feast. *English*
3134. A contented mind is a specific for making gold. *Tamil*
3135. A harvest of peace is produced from a seed of contentment. *Kashmiri*
3136. A little house well filled, a little land well tilled, and a little wife well willed are great riches. *American*
3137. A man must plough with such oxen as he hath. *English*
3138. Be content the sea hath fish enough. *English*
3139. Be content with your lot; one cannot be first in everything. *Greek (Aesop)*
3140. Being on sea, sail; being on land, settle. *English*

3141. Better a sparrow in the hand than a heath-hen on a knot. *Polish*

3142. Content is more than a kingdom. *English*

3143. Content is the philosopher's stone, that turns all it touches into gold. *English*

3144. Content lodges oftener in cottages than palaces. *English*

3145. Content makes poor men rich; discontent makes rich men poor. *American (Franklin)*

3146. Content surpasses wealth. *French*

3147. Contented poverty is an honorable estate. *Greek*

3148. Contented with your lot, you will live wisely. *Latin*

3149. Contentment is an impregnable fortress. *Greek*

3150. Don't rouse evil [or the devil] when it is sleeping. *Polish*

3151. Enjoy your little, while the fool seeks for more. *English*

3152. Gnaw the bone which is fallen to thy lot. *English*

3153. Happiness belongs to those who are contented. *Greek (Aristotle)*

3154. He has enough who is content. *Italian*

3155. He is poor who does not feel content. *Japanese*

3156. He that cannot get bacon must be content with cabbage. *Danish*

3157. He that desires but little has no need of much. *English*

3158. He that is contented with his poverty is wonderfully rich. *English*

3159. He who is content can never be ruined. *Chinese*

3160. He who wants content can't find an easy chair. *English*

3161. If you are contented with your lot, you will live wisely. *Latin*

3162. If you haven't a capon, feed on an onion. *Spanish*

3163. If you would know contentment, let your deeds be few. *Greek (Democritus)*

3164. It is better to enjoy what we possess than to hanker after other things. *Latin*

3165. Let everyone be content with what God has given him. *Portuguese*

3166. Let your mind, happily contented with the present, care not what the morrow will bring with it. *Latin (Horace)*

3167. Little gear [property, wealth], less care. *American*

3168. My bread is baked, my jar is full. *Arabic*

3169. Nae [no] cows, nae care. *Scottish*

3170. No man is content with his own lot. *Latin*

3171. Nothing will content him who is not content with a little. *Greek*

3172. One ought to speak well of what is well. *French*

3173. Our content is our best having. *English (Shakespeare)*

3174. Poor and content is rich, and rich enough. *English (Shakespeare)*

3175. Remain within your own sphere. *Latin*

3176. Ruse [praise] the foord as ye find it. *Scottish*

3177. Since we have loaves, let us not look for cakes. *Spanish*

3178. The best of blessings — a contented mind. *Latin*

3179. The goat must browse where she is tied. *English*

3180. The greatest wealth is contentment with a little. *English*

3181. The superior man is content with poverty; the intelligent man submits to destiny. *Chinese (Confucius)*

3182. Think not on what you lack as much as on what you have. *Greek*

3183. To be content with little is true happiness. *American*

3184. To have no wants is wealth. *Latin*

3185. True happiness is in a contented mind. *American*

3186. We lessen our wants by lessening our desires. *English*

3187. When once at sea, do not long to be on shore. [Be satisfied with your calling in life.] *Latin*

3188. When we have not what we like, we must like what we have. *French*

3189. Where there is content there is abundance. *Latin*

3190. Who is rich? He that is content. Who is that? Nobody. *American*

3191. Who is rich? He that rejoices in his portion. *Talmud*

3192. Who is well seated should not budge. *German*

Contention *see also* Argument; Discord; Dispute; Fighting; Quarreling; Stress and Strain; Strife

3193. Religious contention is the Devil's harvest. *French*

3194. The contentions of a wife are a continual dropping. *Bible*

3195. The issue of all contention is uncertain. *Latin*

Contradiction

3196. Never will a judgment be / Without its contradictory. *Welsh*

Contrast *see also* Difference

3197. Contrasts mutually set off each other. *Latin*

3198. Even a tin knocker will shine on a dirty door. *Irish*

3199. Lilies are whitest in a blackamoor's hand. *English*

Contrivance

3200. Contrivance is better than force. *French*

Control

3201. He that is at sea has not the wind in his hands. *Dutch*

3202. I strive to mold circumstances to myself, not myself to circumstances. *Latin (Horace)*

Convenience

3203. Convenience makes thieves. *French*

3204. It is easy to fetch water when a river is near. *American*

Conversation *see also* Speaking

3205. A man is not better than his conversation. *German*

3206. A man's conversation is the mirror of his thoughts. *Chinese*
3207. Confidence contributes more to conversation than wit. *French (La Rochefoucauld)*
3208. Conversation makes one what he is. *English*
3209. Conversation ministers to a mind diseased. *Latin*
3210. Education begins a gentleman; conversation completes him. *English*
3211. He that converses not knows nothing. *English*
3212. One evening's conversation with a superior man, is better than ten years of study. *Chinese*
3213. Reading makes a full man — meditation a profound man — discourse a clear man. *American (Franklin)*
3214. Speak not but what may benefit others or yourself; avoid trifling conversation. *American*
3215. When I saw you I knew half of you; when we spoke I knew everything. *Maltese*
3216. When you speak to a man, look on his eyes; when he speaks to thee, look on his mouth. *American*
3217. You learn more by talking to others than by talking to yourself. *American*
3218. Your conversation is the mirror of your thoughts. *American*

Conviction
3219. Not he who has many ideas, but he who has one conviction may become a great man. *American*

Cooks and Cooking
3220. If you cook with straw, the food stays raw. *Yiddish*
3221. Where there are six cooks, there is nothing to eat. *Polish*

Cooperation *see also* **Assistance**
3222. Hands wash each other. *Zulu*
3223. One finger cannot extract a thorn. *Lugbara*
3224. One hand washes the other. *Jamaican*

Correction
3225. Correction brings fruit. *Dutch*
3226. Correction is good when administered in time. *American*
3227. For whom the Lord loveth he correcteth. *Bible*
3228. He that chastens one chastens twenty. *English*
3229. He that chastiseth one amendeth many. *English*

Corruption
3230. After one vice a greater follows. *Spanish*
3231. An egg-thief becomes a camel-thief. *Persian*
3232. Bad thoughts sprout worse deeds, bad deeds sprout worse thoughts. *American*
3233. Corruption of the best becomes the worst. *English*
3234. Corruption will find a dozen alibis for its evil deeds. *American*
3235. Corruption wins not more than honesty. *English (Shakespeare)*
3236. He who does not eat garlic does not smell of it. *Lebanese*
3237. If the camel once get his nose in the tent, his body will soon follow. *Arabic*
3238. One rotten apple spoils the barrel. *American*
3239. Still water breeds worms. *Italian*
3240. The best things corrupted become the worst. *Latin*
3241. The hog that is filthy tries to make others so. *American*
3242. The road to vice is not only downhill, but steep. *Latin*
3243. The unrighteous penny corrupts the righteous pound. *English*

Cost *see also* **Buying and Selling; Value; Worth**
3244. Fools pursue pleasure regardless of the cost. *American*
3245. Free sitters grumble most at the play. *Chinese*
3246. Merry is the feast-making till we come to the reckoning. *English*
3247. Much never cost little. *Spanish*
3248. Never pleasure without repentance. *English*
3249. That which costs little is lightly esteemed. *Spanish (Cervantes)*
3250. The best things in life are free. *American*
3251. The cost takes away the relish [or taste]. *French*
3252. The more cost, the more honour. *Scottish*
3253. What costs little is little respected. *American*
3254. What costs nothing is worth nothing. *American*

Counsel *see* **Advice**

Countenance *see* **Appearance; Face**

Counting
3255. He that counts all costs will never put plough in the earth. *American*
3256. He that reckons without his host, must reckon over again. *French*
3257. Ower narrow counting culyes [gains] nae kindness. *Scottish*
3258. To swallow gudgeons ere they're catched / And count their chickens ere they're hatched. *English (Butler)*
3259. When angry count ten; when very angry, a hundred. *American*

Country *see also* **Citizens and Citizenship; Town and Country**
3260. Country is dear, but liberty dearer still. *Latin*
3261. My country, right or wrong. *American (Decatur)*
3262. The man without a country is an exile from life and hope. *American*
3263. To a brave man every soil is his country. *Latin (Ovid)*

Courage *see also* **Bravery; Heart; Heroes and Heroism; Valor**
3264. A man of courage is never in need of weapons. *American*
3265. A stout heart breaks bad luck. *Spanish*
3266. A wight [strong, bold] man ne'er wanted a weapon. *Scottish*
3267. Courage in danger is half the battle. *Latin*

3268. Courage is that virtue which champions the cause of right. *Latin*
3269. Courage mounteth with occasion. *English (Shakespeare)*
3270. Courage scorns the death it cannot shun. *English (Dryden)*
3271. Even savage animals, if kept shut up, forget their courage. *Latin*
3272. Fearless courage is the foundation of victory. *American*
3273. Good courage breaks bad luck. *American*
3274. It is courage that wins, and not good weapons. *Spanish*
3275. Rage avails less than courage. *French*
3276. True courage grapples with misfortune. *Latin*
3277. Wealth lost, something lost; honor lost, much lost; courage lost, all lost. *German (Goethe)*
3278. Who has not courage should have legs. *Italian*
3279. Without justice, courage is weak. *American (Franklin)*
3280. You can't answer for your courage if you have never been in danger. *French*

Court *see also* Judges; Judging; Judgment; Justice; Law; Lawyers; Lawsuits

3281. A friend in court is worth a penny in a man's purse. *English*
3282. At court there are many hands but few hearts. *German*
3283. "Hame's hamely," quo' the deil when he found himsel in the Court o' Session. *Scottish*
3284. Hell and the court-room are always open. *American*
3285. Who has seen the court has seen the world. *French*
3286. Whoso lives in court shall die in the jail. *American*

Courtesy *see also* Manners; Politeness

3287. All doors open to courtesy. *English*
3288. As courteous as a dog in a kitchen. *English*
3289. Be not niggardly of what costs thee nothing, as courtesy, counsel, and countenance. *American (Franklin)*
3290. Cap in hand never did anyone harm. *Italian*
3291. Courtesy is cumbersome to him that kens it na [knows it not]. *Scottish*
3292. Courtesy on one side never lasts long. *French*
3293. Fou [full] o' courtesy, fou o' craft. *Scottish*
3294. Leave off first for manners' sake. *Bible*
3295. Less of your courtesy and more of your purse. *English*
3296. Lip courtesy pleases much and costs little. *Spanish*
3297. One dram of courtesy is worth a whole pound of discourtesy. *English*
3298. The courteous learns his courtesy from the discourteous. *Turkish*
3299. The fox is all courtesy and all craft. *American*
3300. To enrich a favor by a courteous manner in conferring it. *Latin*
3301. Too much courtesy is discourtesy. *Japanese*
3302. Virtue and courtesy go hand in hand. *American*

Courtship *see also* Men and Women; Wives: Choosing a Wife

3303. A lass that has mony wooers aft wails the warst. *Scottish*
3304. A man chases a woman until she catches him. *American*
3305. A man may woo where he will, but he will wed where his hap is. *Scottish*
3306. A wooer should open his ears more than his eyes. *Norwegian*
3307. Better woo ower the midden [dunghill] than ower the muir [moor]. [Woo close to home.] *Scottish*
3308. Bitin' and scratchin' is Scots folk's wooing. *Scottish*
3309. Blessed is the wooing / That is not long a-doing. *English (Burton)*
3310. Boys win girls best with flattery. *American*
3311. Courting and wooing bring dallying and doing. *English*
3312. Every Jack will find a Jill. *Scottish*
3313. Flee, and she follows; follow, and she'll flee. *Latin (Martial)*
3314. He that woos a maid, must seldom come in her sight; / But he that woos a widow, must woo her day and night. *English*
3315. He that would the daughter win, / Must with the mother first begin. *German*
3316. He's a cake and pudding courtier. *Scottish*
3317. It is time to marry when the woman woos the man. *English*
3318. Many court in poetry and after marriage live in prose. *American*
3319. Men are April when they woo, December when they wed. *English (Shakespeare)*
3320. Nature framed all women to be won. *American*
3321. Nipping and scarting's [pinching and scratching's] Scotch folk's wooing. *Scottish*
3322. Sunday wooin' draws to ruin. *Scottish*
3323. 'Tis best to woo where you can see the smoke. *Dutch*
3324. Wha may woo without cost? *Scottish*

Covetousness

3325. A covetous man does nothing that he should till he dies. *Latin*
3326. A covetous man is gude to nane, but warst to himsel. *Scottish*
3327. All covet, all lose. *English*
3328. Covet not the property of others. *Latin*
3329. Covet nothing over much. *American*
3330. Covetous men's chests are rich, not they. *English*
3331. Covetousness brings nothing home. *English*
3332. Covetousness bursts the bag. *Spanish*
3333. Covetousness is the father of unsatisfied desires. *Yoruba*
3334. Covetousness starves other vices. *English*
3335. He who covets is always poor. *Latin*
3336. If you covet wealth you won't get it; if you don't covet, it will come of itself. *Chinese*

3337. Mony ane [many a one] lacks what they fain wad hae [would have] in their pack. *Scottish*
3338. Muckle would aye hae mair. [Much would always have more.] *Scottish*
3339. Naething comes out o' a close hand. *Scottish*
3340. The covetous are always in want. *Latin (Horace)*
3341. The sharper soon cheats the covetous man. *Spanish*
3342. The world is too small for the covetous. *Latin*
3343. Those who covet much want much. *Latin*
3344. Warn men against covetousness, for wealth thus coveted provokes the wrath of heaven. *Chinese*
3345. We covet not that of which we know not. *Latin*
3346. When all sins grow old covetousness is young. *English*
3347. Ye come o' the M'Taks, but no o' the M'Gies. *Scottish*

Cowardice

3348. A coward calls himself cautious and a miser thrifty. *Latin*
3349. A coward's fear maks a brave man braver. *Scottish*
3350. A coward's fear may make a coward valiant. *English*
3351. A frog never bites, a Brahman never fights. *Telugu*
3352. A man without guts lives on his knees. *American*
3353. A wee thing fleys [frightens] cowards. *Scottish*
3354. Better be a coward than foolhardy. *French*
3355. Between two cowards, he has the advantage who first detects the other. *Italian*
3356. Coward against coward, the assailant conquers. *Spanish*
3357. Cowardice is the mother of cruelty. *French*
3358. Cowards are cruel. *English*
3359. Cowards call themselves cautious and misers thrifty. *American*
3360. Cowards die daily, the brave but once. *American*
3361. Cowards die many times before their deaths. *English (Shakespeare)*
3362. Cowards do not count in battle; they are there, but not in it. *Greek*
3363. Cowards' weapons neither cut nor pierce. *Italian*
3364. Drive a rat into a corner, and he'll jump at you. *English*
3365. He that has no heart let him have heels. *Italian*
3366. He that strikes my dog wad strike mysel if he daur'd. *Scottish*
3367. He that's rede [afraid] for windlestraes [stalks of ryegrass] should never sleep on leas. *Scottish*
3368. He wasna the inventor o' gunpowder. *Scottish*
3369. Like the cat, fain fish wad ye eat, but ye are laith to weet your feet. *Scottish*
3370. Many would be cowards if they had courage enough. *English*
3371. One coward makes ten. *German*
3372. Strength avails not a coward. *Italian*
3373. The coward threatens only when he is safe. *German*
3374. To see what is right and not to do it is the part of a coward. *Chinese*
3375. Who cannot strike the ass may strike the saddle. *Italian*

Craftiness

3376. Craft against vice I must apply. *English (Shakespeare)*
3377. He can best avoid a snare who knows how to set one. *Latin (Publilius Syrus)*
3378. Never fight an enemy whilst it is possible to cheat him. *English*
3379. The fox knows many tricks, but the hedgehog's one trick is the best of all. *Latin (Zenobius)*

Credibility *see also* Belief; Credulity; Gullibility; Trust; Truth

3380. A lie becomes true when one believes it. *German*
3381. We are slow to believe that which, if true, would grieve us. *Latin (Ovid)*
3382. When fish come from the river-bottom and tell you the alligator has a belly-ache, believe it. [Believe someone who is in a position to know.] *Belizean Creole*

Credit and Creditors *see also* Borrowing and Lending; Debt

3383. A poor man has no credit. *Latin*
3384. Better take eight hundred than sell for a thousand on credit. *Chinese*
3385. Buying on credit is robbing next year's crop. *American*
3386. Credit cuts off customers. *Chinese*
3387. Credit is better than ill won gear [wealth, property, goods]. *Scottish*
3388. Credit is dead; bad pay killed it. *Italian*
3389. Credit keeps the croun o' the causey [causeway]. *Scottish*
3390. Creditors are a superstitious sect, great observers of set days and times. *American (Franklin)*
3391. Creditors have better memories than debtors. *Spanish*
3392. He that is hasty to give credit is light-minded. *Bible*
3393. He who loses credit can lose nothing else. *Latin*
3394. Lost credit is like a broken mirror. *American*
3395. Nothing seems expensive on credit. *Czech*
3396. Take the cash and let the credit go. *Persian (Omar Khayyám)*
3397. The creditors are a superstitious sect, great observers of set days and times. *American*
3398. Who gets drunk on credit gets doubly drunk. *Bulgarian*
3399. Who sells on credit has much custom but little money. *German*
3400. You can make an enemy out of your best friend by lending him money. *American*

Credulity *see also* Belief; Gullibility; Naivete

3401. Better be too credulous than too skeptical. *Chinese*

3402. If ye believe a' ye hear, ye may eat a' ye see. *Scottish*

Crime and Criminals *see also* Killing; Leniency; Murder; Pardon; Punishment and Retribution

3403. A crook who robs a crook is a thief in need—and a thief indeed. *American*
3404. A man may thrive on crime, but not for long. *Greek*
3405. Crime leaves a trail like a water-beetle; / Like a snail it leaves its shine; / Like a horse-mango it leaves its reek. *Malay*
3406. Crime requires further crime to conceal it. *Latin (Seneca)*
3407. Crime which is prosperous and lucky is called virtue. *Latin (Seneca)*
3408. Crimes may be secret, yet not secure. *English*
3409. Every man enjoys his own crimes. *Latin*
3410. He acts the third crime that defends the first. *American*
3411. Heaven takes care that no man secures happiness by crime. *Italian*
3412. If you commit a crime in the mind you may transmit it into action. *American*
3413. If you share your friend's crime, you make it your own. *Latin*
3414. Interest is half the crime. *American*
3415. It is unlawful to overcome crime by crime. *American*
3416. It takes one [i.e., a crook] to know one. *American*
3417. No crime is founded upon reason. *Latin*
3418. No crook finds a jail nice enough to suit him. *American*
3419. No one lives who is without a crime. *Latin*
3420. Petty crimes are punished; great ones are rewarded. *American*
3421. Successful crime is called virtue. *Latin*
3422. The act itself does not constitute a crime, unless the intent be criminal. *Latin*
3423. The contagion of crime is like that of the plague. *French*
3424. The greater the man, the greater the crime. *American*
3425. The number of malefactors authorizes not the crime. *English*
3426. We easily forget crimes known only to ourselves. *French*
3427. Who is content with one crime only? *Latin*
3428. Who profits by a crime commits the crime. *Latin*

Criticism *see also* Blame; Censure; Fault-Finding; Name-Calling

3429. Clean your finger, before you point at any spots. *American (Franklin)*
3430. Criticism is easy; art, difficult. *French*
3431. "Crooked carlin [old woman]," quo' the cripple to his wife. *Scottish*
3432. Does the lofty Diana care about the dog barking at her? *Latin*
3433. Don't throw stones at your neighbors', if your own windows are glass. *American (Franklin)*
3434. Every reproach against an accused man is contemptible. *Latin*
3435. He can see a louse as far away as China but not the elephant on his nose. *Malay*
3436. He should have a hale pow [head] / That calls his neighbour nitty-know [lousy-head]. *Scottish*
3437. He should have clean fingers who would blow another's nose. *Danish*
3438. He that has a roof of glass should not throw stones at his neighbor's. *Spanish*
3439. He that mocks a cripple ought to be whole. *Italian*
3440. He that seeks motes gets motes. *Scottish*
3441. Hear no ill of a friend, nor speak any of an enemy. *American (Franklin)*
3442. If you're out to beat a dog, you're sure to find a stick. *Yiddish*
3443. It is folly to censure him whom all the world adores. *Latin (Publilius Syrus)*
3444. It's easier to pull down than to build. *American*
3445. It's easy to be critical; it's hard to be correct. *American*
3446. Ne'er say "ill-fallow" to him ye deal wi'. *Scottish*
3447. Ne'er speak ill o' the deil [devil]. *Scottish*
3448. Ne'er speak ill o' them whase bread ye eat. *Scottish*
3449. People who live in glass houses shouldn't throw stones. *American*
3450. The blow of a whip raises a welt, but a blow of the tongue crushes bones. *Bible*
3451. The man that sits on the bank always hurls well. *Irish*
3452. They damn what they do not understand. *Latin*
3453. To say harsh things soothingly. *Greek*
3454. When a man's coat is threadbare, it is easy to pick a hole in it. *English*
3455. When I did weel, I heard it never; when I did ill, I heard it ever. *English*
3456. Wherein thou judgest another, thou condemnest thyself. *Bible*
3457. Who hath glass windows of his own must take heed how he throws stones. *English*
3458. Who laughs at crooked men should walk very straight. *English*

Cross Purposes

3459. Both ends against the middle. *American*
3460. The horse thinks one thing, and he that saddles it another. *Spanish*

Crowds *see* Mobs

Cruelty

3461. A cruel heart ill suits a manly mind. *Greek*
3462. All the world will beat the man whom fortune buffets. *English*
3463. Cruelty is a tyrant that is always attended by fear. *English*
3464. I must be cruel, only to be kind. *English (Shakespeare)*

3465. The claws of a leopard spare no one. *Lugbara*
3466. To kindness from thy heart be kinder still: / To cruelty be hard against thy will. *Welsh*

Crying *see also* **Women and Tears**
3467. An orphan's tear falls not in vain. *Russian*
3468. Even when the gates of prayer are shut, the gates of tears are open. *Hebrew*
3469. He loves thee well that makes thee weep. *Spanish*
3470. He wastes his tears who weeps before the judge. *Italian*
3471. In tears was I born, and after tears I die. *Greek*
3472. In youth, one has tears without grief; in age, grief without tears. *French*
3473. Nothing dries sooner than tears. *Latin*
3474. Of what good is a silver cup, if it is filled with tears? *Yiddish*
3475. Onion tears do not touch the heart. *Yiddish*
3476. Tears are often the telescope by which men see far into heaven. *American (H.W. Beecher)*
3477. Tears are sometimes as weighty as words. *Latin*
3478. Tears are the silent language of grief. *French*
3479. Tears benefit not the wounded. *Greek*
3480. Tears in mortal miseries are vain. *Greek (Homer)*
3481. Tears soothe suffering eyes. *German*
3482. The tears of other people are only water. *Russian*
3483. The tears of the night equal the smiles of the day. *French*
3484. When the heart is full, the eyes overflow. *Yiddish*

Culpability *see* **Blame; Guilt**

Cunning
3485. A cunning man is overmatched by a cunning man and a half. *American*
3486. Cunning is no burden. *German*
3487. Cunning proceeds from want of capacity. *American (Franklin)*
3488. Cunning surpasses strength. *German*
3489. Monkey's wisdom. [Shallow cunning.] *Japanese*
3490. Put her in the mortar and she will seven times avoid being hit by the pestle. *Marathi*
3491. The bait hides the hook. *American*
3492. The greatest cunning is to have none at all. *French*
3493. The lion puts on the fox's skin when cunning is more fruitful than force. *American*
3494. The most cunning are the first caught. *French*
3495. What the lion cannot, the fox can. *German*
3496. When the fox preaches, beware of your geese. *American*

Cures *see* **Remedies**

Curiosity
3497. A man should live if only to satisfy his curiosity. *Yiddish*
3498. Be not curious in unnecessary matters. *Bible*
3499. Curiosity is born of jealousy. *French*
3500. Curiosity killed the cat. *American*
3501. Curious Varvara's nose was torn off. *Russian*
3502. Enquire not what boils in another's pot. *English*
3503. He that peeps in at his neighbor's window may chance to lose his eyes. *Arabic*
3504. Let curiosities alone. *Latin*
3505. Look through a keyhole, and your life will be sore. *American*

Cursing
3506. A curse will not strike out an eye unless a fist goes with it. *Danish*
3507. A thousand curses never tore a shirt. *Arabic*
3508. Cussing the weather is mighty poor farming. *American*
3509. Don't curse the crocodile's mother before you cross the river. *African*
3510. The fouler his language, the fouler the man. *American*
3511. The lips that curse shall want bread. *Polish*

Custom *see also* **Conformity; Habit; Heredity**
3512. A bad custom is like a good cake — better broken than kept. *English*
3513. A cake and a bad custom ought to be broken. *French*
3514. A custom breaks a law. *Yiddish*
3515. A custom more honored in the breach than in the observance. *English (Shakespeare)*
3516. A good custom is surer than law. *Greek (Euripides)*
3517. An ancient custom obtains the force of nature. *Latin (Cicero)*
3518. As times are, so are the customs. *American*
3519. Bad customs, like good cakes, should be broken. *American*
3520. Break the legs o' an ill custom. *Scottish*
3521. Choose what is best; custom will make it agreeable and easy. *Greek*
3522. Custom becomes, as it were, another nature. *Latin (Cicero)*
3523. Custom is a deceiving schoolmistress. *French*
3524. Custom is a master that makes a slave of reason. *American*
3525. Custom is a tyrant. *Latin*
3526. Custom is another law. *Latin*
3527. Custom is mummified by habit and glorified by law. *American*
3528. Custom is second nature. *Latin (St. Augustine)*
3529. Custom is the guide of the ignorant. *English*
3530. Custom is the master of all things. *Latin*
3531. Custom is the reason of fools. *American*
3532. Custom makes all things easy. *English*
3533. Different times, different customs. *Latin*
3534. For use almost can change the stamp of nature. *English (Shakespeare)*
3535. In every country its own custom. *Spanish*
3536. In sondry londes sondry ben usages. [Different customs in different lands.] *English (Chaucer)*
3537. Let old customs be no prescription and set a good one against a bad. *English*

3538. Never can custom conquer nature. *Latin*
3539. Nice customs curtsey to great kings. *English (Shakespeare)*
3540. Old custom without truth is but an old error. *English*
3541. Old customs are good customs. *French*
3542. Old customs, if they be evil customs, are better broken than kept. *English*
3543. Other times, other customs. *Italian*
3544. Outside in accordance with custom; within our doors as it pleases us. *Latin*
3545. So many countries, so many customs. *French*
3546. Something must be allowed to custom. *Latin*
3547. To change a custom is as bad as death. *Spanish*
3548. Use will make a man live in a lion's den. *English*
3549. We are more sensible of what is done against custom than against nature. *Greek*
3550. What is in accordance with custom needs no excuse. *Italian*

Customers *see also* Business and Commerce; Buying and Selling

3551. Customers are to be valued; goods are mere grass. *Chinese*
3552. It's better to handle a tough customer with kid gloves. *American*
3553. No matter how shoddy the goods, you can always find a customer. *American*
3554. One is full, the other is hungry; to whom do people sell? *Accra*
3555. The customer is always right. *American*
3556. What the customer fears is being taken in. *Chinese*

Cynicism

3557. A cynic is a man who knows the price of everything and the value of nothing. *English (Wilde)*

Damnation *see* Devil; Hell

Danger

3558. A common danger causes common action. *American*
3559. A danger is never overcome without danger. *Latin*
3560. A snake lies concealed in the grass. *Latin*
3561. Barking dogs don't bite. *Indian*
3562. Better face a danger than be always in fear. *Italian*
3563. Common danger produces agreement. *Latin*
3564. Danger and delight grow on one stalk. *English*
3565. Danger comes on us more speedily when we treat it with contempt. *Latin*
3566. Danger deviseth shifts; wit waits on fear. *English (Shakespeare)*
3567. Danger is next neighbor to security. *English*
3568. Danger is sauce for prayers. *American (Franklin)*
3569. Danger is sweet. *Latin*
3570. Dangers are conquered by dangers. *American*
3571. Fear the goat from the front, the horse from the rear, and man from all sides. *Russian*
3572. Great men live dangerously; small men don't take chances. *American*
3573. He is happy whom other men's perils make wary. *Latin*
3574. He that loveth danger shall perish therein. *Bible*
3575. He who dares dangers overcomes them before he incurs them. *Latin*
3576. He who sees danger perishes in it. *Spanish*
3577. If you take a leap in the dark you usually land in a pit. *American*
3578. It's dangerous to dig pits for other folks: you'll fall in yourself. *American*
3579. Look before you leap, / For snakes among sweet flowers do creep. *English*
3580. There is delight in danger and danger in delight. *American*
3581. There is no person who is not dangerous to someone. *French*
3582. We least dread the danger that is nearest. *Latin*
3583. Where there is no danger there is no glory. *French*
3584. Wise men say nothing in dangerous times. *English*
3585. Without danger the game grows cold. *Latin*
3586. Without danger we cannot be beyond danger. *American*

Daughters *see also* Heredity; Fathers and Daughters; Mothers and Daughters; Parents and Children; Wives: Choosing a Wife

3587. A daughter married is a daughter lost. *Spanish*
3588. A house full of daughters is a cellar full of sour beer. *Dutch*
3589. A married daughter is but a neighbor. *Serbian*
3590. An undutiful daughter will prove an unmanageable wife. *American (Franklin)*
3591. Daughters an' dead fish are nae keeping ware. *Scottish*
3592. Daughters pay nae debts. *Scottish*
3593. Every daughter is a handful of trouble. *Arabic*
3594. He who has daughters is always a shepherd. *Spanish*
3595. Marry your son when you will, and your daughter when you can. *Spanish*
3596. My son is my son till he's got him a wife; my daughter's my daughter all the days of her life. *English*
3597. The worst store is a maid unbestowed. *Welsh*
3598. Twa daughters and a back door are three stark thieves. *Scottish*

Daughters-In-Law *see also* Mothers-in-Law

3599. A bad daughter-in-law is worse than a thousand devils. *Japanese*

Deafness

3600. Deaf people always hear better than they say they do. *American*
3601. He hearsna at that ear. *Scottish*
3602. He's horn deaf on the side o' his head. *Scottish*
3603. None so deaf as those that will not hear. *English*
3604. You talk to a deaf man. *Latin*

Death *see also* Mortality; Life; Transience

3605. A dead man does not make war. *Yiddish*
3606. A dead man feels no cold. *American*

3607. A dead mouse feels no cold. *English*

3608. A good death does honor to a whole life. *Italian*

3609. A good death is better than a bad life. *Yiddish*

3610. A man can only die once. *American*

3611. A thousand pounds and a bottle of hay are all one at domesday. *English*

3612. Account ye no man happy till he die. *Greek*

3613. All men are born richer than they die. *German*

3614. As dead as a doornail. *English*

3615. Better to die once for all than to live in continual terror. *Greek*

3616. Dead men are free men. *Scottish*

3617. Dead men do nae harm. *Scottish*

3618. Dead men do not bite. *Greek*

3619. Dead men tell no tales. *American*

3620. Death always comes too early or too late. *English*

3621. Death brings to a level spades and scepters. *Latin*

3622. Death comes in and speirs [asks] nae questions. *Scottish*

3623. Death defies the doctor. *Latin*

3624. Death does not blow a trumpet. *Danish*

3625. Death does not take the old but the ripe. *Russian*

3626. Death foreseen never comes. *Italian*

3627. Death is a black camel which kneels at every man's gate. *Turkish*

3628. Death is a camel that lies down at every door. *Persian*

3629. Death is a great leveler. *American*

3630. Death is in strange places [i.e., one never knows when (or where) death may strike]. *Zulu*

3631. Death is no chooser. *Yiddish*

3632. Death is rest from labor and misery. *Latin*

3633. Death is shameful in flight, glorious in victory. *Latin*

3634. Death is sometimes a gift. *Latin*

3635. Death is the receipt for all evils. *French*

3636. Death lays his impious touch on all things rare. *Latin*

3637. Death levels all things. *Latin*

3638. Death never would own, / That he took upon loan. *Welsh*

3639. Death o'ertakes the man who flees. *Latin*

3640. Death pays all debts. *French*

3641. Death rather than a toilsome life. *Greek*

3642. Death reveals the truth. *Yiddish*

3643. Death rides on every passing breeze. *English*

3644. Death takes no bribes. *American (Franklin)*

3645. Death takes no denial. *Greek*

3646. Death takes us piecemeal, not at a gulp. *Latin (Seneca)*

3647. Death veils all faults. *Iraqi*

3648. Death — the gate of life. *Latin*

3649. Death's gude proof. *Scottish*

3650. Do not expect good from another's death. *Latin (Cato)*

3651. Do not speak evil of the dead. *Greek (Chilo)*

3652. Dying is as natural as living. *English*

3653. Even hares insult a dead lion. *Latin*

3654. Everyone is wont to praise him who is no more. *Greek (Thucydides)*

3655. Flowers and buds fall, and the old and ripe fall. *Malay*

3656. Food for Acheron. *Latin (Plautus)*

3657. Forgetfulness and silence are the privileges of the dead. *Latin*

3658. He but sleeps the holy sleep. *Greek*

3659. He doth sin that doth belie the dead. *English (Shakespeare)*

3660. He hath lived ill that knows not how to die well. *English*

3661. He lives in fame who dies in virtue's cause. *English (Shakespeare)*

3662. He slippet awa like a knotless thread. *Scottish*

3663. He that lives most, dies most. *American*

3664. He went over to the majority. *Latin*

3665. He who you say has passed away has simply posted on ahead. *Latin*

3666. He whom the gods love dies young. *Greek (Menander)*

3667. He'll neither dee nor do weel. *Scottish*

3668. Hope is fawin' while death is mawin'. *Scottish*

3669. It is folly to die of the fear of death. *Latin (Seneca)*

3670. It is only the dead who do not return. *French*

3671. It is the part of a fearful mind to wish for death. *Latin*

3672. It is uncertain where death may await thee, therefore expect it everywhere. *Latin*

3673. It takes four living men to carry one dead man out of the house. *Italian*

3674. It's better to die with honor than to live in infamy. *American*

3675. Let the dead bury the dead. *Bible*

3676. Live mindful of death. *Latin*

3677. Me dead, the world is dead. *Italian*

3678. Neither dread your last day nor desire it. *Latin*

3679. Neither the sun nor death can be looked at steadily. *French (La Rochefoucauld)*

3680. Never the grave gives back what it has won. *German*

3681. No one dies before his time. *Yiddish*

3682. No one laments the death of a suicide. *Sudanese*

3683. No one needs a calendar to die. *Yiddish*

3684. Nobly to die were better than to save one's life. *Greek*

3685. Not death is dreadful but a shameful death. *Greek*

3686. Now he lives in Abraham's bosom. *Latin (St. Augustine)*

3687. O death, where is thy sting? O grave, where is thy victory? *Bible*

3688. O Death! the poor man's dearest friend. *Scottish (Burns)*

3689. One cannot die twice. *Russian*

3690. Serve the living, bury the dead. *American*

3691. Shrouds have no pockets. *American*

3692. Speak well of the dead. *Latin*

3693. The Angel of Death has many eyes. *Yiddish*

3694. The best go first, the bad remain to mend. *English*

3695. The dead are always in the wrong. *French*

3696. The dead are soon forgotten. *American*

3697. The dead ride fast. *German*

3698. The fear of death is worse than death itself. *Latin*

3699. The last garment is made without pockets. *Italian*

3700. The less of this cold world the more of heaven. *English (Milton)*

3701. The life of the dead is in the memory of the living. *Latin*

3702. The Lord gave, and the Lord hath taken away; blessed be the name of the Lord. *Bible*

3703. The sense of death is most in apprehension. *English (Shakespeare)*

3704. There is no man who does not die his own death. *Latin*

3705. To die quickly is a privilege. *French*

3706. To die well is the chief part of virtue. *Greek*

3707. To die without fear of death is a desirable death. *Latin*

3708. To whom life was heavy, the earth is light. *Polish*

3709. We count it death to falter, not to die. *Greek*

3710. We die as we live. *Turkish*

3711. We live in jest, but we die in earnest. *Russian*

3712. When death lifts the curtain it's time to be startin'. *Scottish*

3713. When one is dead, it is for a long time. *French*

3714. When the snake is dead, his venom is dead. *French*

3715. When you die, even your tomb shall be comfortable. *Russian*

3716. With one foot in the grave. *English*

Debt *see also* Borrowing and Lending; Credit and Creditors

3717. A debt and gratitude are different things. *Latin*

3718. A debtor does not get angry. *Accra*

3719. A hundred cartloads of anxiety will not pay an ounce of debt. *Italian*

3720. A little debt makes a debtor, a great one an enemy. *English*

3721. A poor man's debt maks muckle din [much noise]. *Scottish*

3722. A pound of care won't pay an ounce of debt. *French*

3723. A sick man sleeps, but not a debtor. *Spanish*

3724. A small loan makes a debtor; a great one, an enemy. *Latin (Publilius Syrus)*

3725. Better go to bed supperless than rise in debt. *Spanish*

3726. Debt is a grievous bondage to an honorable man. *Latin*

3727. Debt is the worst poverty. *English*

3728. Debts are like children; the smaller they are, the more they scream. *Spanish*

3729. Debts turn freemen into slaves. *Greek*

3730. Early to rise and late to bed lifts again the debtor's head. *English*

3731. From a bad payer, get what you can. *American*

3732. Good debts become bad unless called in. *Latin*

3733. Happy is the man who is out of debt. *Latin*

3734. He is rich enough who owes nothing. *French*

3735. He robs Peter to pay Paul. *American*

3736. He that pays his debt begins to make a stock. *Scottish*

3737. He that pays his debts increases his wealth. *French*

3738. He who oweth is always in the wrong [i.e., he must accept blame to avoid incurring his creditors' displeasure]. *English*

3739. He's rich that has nae debt. *Scottish*

3740. Ill payers are aye gude cravers. *Scottish*

3741. It is hard to pay for bread that has been eaten. *Danish*

3742. No man is impatient with his creditors. *Talmud*

3743. O' ill debtors men get aiths [i.e., promises]. *Scottish*

3744. Only a dog has no debts. *Yiddish*

3745. Out of debt, out of danger. *English*

3746. Owe no man anything, but to love one another. *Bible*

3747. Pay what you owe, and be cured of your complaint. *Spanish*

3748. Say nothing of my debts unless you mean to pay them. *English*

3749. Sins and debts are aye mair [always more] than we think them. *Scottish*

3750. Sweet at the on-taking but soor in the aff-putting. *Scottish*

3751. The debts go to the next heir. *German*

3752. The man in debt is a jump ahead of the sheriff. *American*

3753. The second vice is lying; the first is running in debt. *American (Franklin)*

3754. The sick man sleeps when the debtor cannot. *American*

3755. We all have more than each man knows / Of sins, of debts, of years, of foes. Persian

3756. Without debt, without care. *Italian*

3757. You can't pay your debts with tears. *Yiddish*

Decay

3758. All that rises sets, and everything which grows decays. *American*

3759. All things deteriorate in time. *Latin (Virgil)*

Deception *see also* Appearance; Beauty; Fraud; Hypocrisy; Identity; Inference; Judging; Seeming

3760. A clean glove often hides a dirty hand. *English*

3761. A fair face may hide a foul heart. *English*

3762. A fair face may make a foul bargain. *English*

3763. A wolf often lies concealed in the skin of a lamb. *Latin*

3764. A' are no friends that speak us fair. *Scottish*

3765. Aggression, perfidy, and deceit — all will rise against their perpetrator. *Arabic*

3766. Be not caught by the cunning of those who appear in a disguise. *Latin (Horace)*

3767. Behind the cross stands the devil. *English*

3768. Deceit is a spider's web that traps the deceiver. *American*

3769. Deceive the deceivers. *Latin*

3770. Deceiving a deceiver is no knavery. *English*

3771. Deception follows on the heels of deception. *Latin (Terence)*

3772. Dissimulation is a coward's virtue. *French*

3773. Distrust justifies deceit. *French*

3774. False with one can be false with two. *English*

3775. Feigned love is worse than hatred. *Latin*

3776. Full of courtesy, full of craft. *English*

3777. He can say, "My jo," an' think it na. *Scottish*

3778. He cries wine and sells vinegar. *English*

3779. He is not deceived who is knowingly deceived. *American*

3780. He looks one way and rows another. *American*

3781. He sleeps as dogs do when wives sift meal. *Scottish*

3782. He sleeps as dogs do when wives talk. [He pretends to sleep.] *Scottish*

3783. He wears twa faces aneath ae cowl. *Scottish*

3784. He who digs a hole for another may fall in himself. *Russian*

3785. He who has once used deception will deceive again. *Latin*

3786. Honey is sweet, but the bee stings. *English*

3787. I like not fair terms and a villain's mind. *English (Shakespeare)*

3788. If the same man deceives us twice, we deserve ruin. *American*

3789. If the world will be gulled, let it be gulled. *English (Burton)*

3790. If you must be fooled, though wise, be the fool of virtue, not of vice. *Persian*

3791. Let no man deceive you with vain words. *Bible*

3792. Mouth of ivy, heart of holly. *Irish*

3793. My tongue may swear, but I act as I please. *Latin*

3794. No deceit is so veiled as that which lies concealed behind the semblance of courtesy. *Latin (Cicero)*

3795. No one can keep a mask on long. *Latin (Seneca)*

3796. Nothing is more like an honest man than a rogue. *French*

3797. O what a tangled web we weave, / When first we practice to deceive! *Scottish (Scott)*

3798. Of ten bald men nine are deceitful, and the tenth is dumb. *Chinese*

3799. One may outwit another, but not all the others. *French*

3800. One may smile, and smile, and be a villain. *English (Shakespeare)*

3801. Slight are the outward signs of evil thought. *English (Byron)*

3802. The bald are deceitful, the blind are perverse, and the one-eyed are even more wicked. *Chinese*

3803. The cross on his breast and the devil in his acts. *Spanish*

3804. The cross on his breast, and the devil in his heart. *English*

3805. The deceitful have no friends. *Hindi*

3806. The fox preaches to the hens. *French*

3807. The honeyed tongue hath its poison. *Latin (Publilius Syrus)*

3808. The soft speeches of the wicked are full of deceit. *Latin*

3809. The surest way to be deceived is to think oneself more clever than others. *French*

3810. The words of a saint, and the claws of a cat. *Spanish*

3811. 'Tis time to fear when tyrants seem to kiss. *American*

3812. To be true to the perfidious is perfidy and to deceive the deceitful is lawful. *Arabic*

3813. Tongue double, brings trouble. *American (Franklin)*

3814. Vice deceives us when dressed in the garb of virtue. *Latin (Juvenal)*

3815. Vice is most dangerous when it puts on the garb of virtue. *English*

3816. We are usually deceived by that which we love. *French (Molière)*

3817. When the devil prays he is out to deceive you. *Spanish*

3818. When the devil says his paternosters he wants to cheat you. *French*

3819. When you seek to deceive your neighbor, be more wary than he is when trying to deceive you. *Arabic*

3820. Who makes the fairest show means most deceit. *English (Shakespeare)*

3821. Who would not be deceived must have as many eyes as hairs on his head. *German*

Decision *see also* Choice; Commitment; Dilemma; Indecision

3822. Pills are to be swallowed, not chewed. *German*

3823. Settled once, settled forever. *Latin*

3824. Speedy execution is the mother of good fortune. *English*

3825. Swift decisions are not sure. *Greek*

3826. The die is cast. *Latin*

3827. When you decide, let it be once for all. *Latin*

3828. Who shall decide, when doctors disagree? *American*

Decorum *see also* Conduct; Politeness

3829. Let them cant about decorum / Who have characters to lose. *Scottish (Burns)*

3830. Observe decorum even in your sport. *Latin*

Deduction *see* Inference

Deeds *see also* Accomplishment; Action; Activity; Good Deeds

3831. A man is not good or bad for one action. *English*

3832. A widow is known by her weeds, a man by his deeds. *American*

3833. Deeds are love, and not fine speeches. *Spanish*

3834. Deeds are males, words are females. *Italian*

3835. Deeds make the old man. *Latin (Ovid)*

3836. Do deeds worth praise and tell you them at night. *English (Shakespeare)*

3837. Great soul, great deed. *German*

3838. He fills his lifetime with deeds, not with inactive years. *Latin (Ovid)*

3839. He that returns a good for evil obtains the victory. *English*

3840. If you love me, John, your acts will tell me so. *Spanish*

3841. It is no profit to have learned well, if you neglect to do well. *Latin (Publilius Syrus)*

3842. Living requires less life than doing. *French*

3843. Many things, base when doing, please when done. *Latin*

3844. No deed that sets an example of evil brings joy to the doer. *Latin*

3845. Only deeds give strength to life. *German*

3846. The braggart talks most, the doer least, for deeds are silent. *American*

3847. The deed is forgotten but its results remain. *Latin*

3848. The gods know the deeds of the righteous. *Latin*

Defeat *see also* Surrender; Yielding

3849. Defeat is a school in which truth always grows strong. *American (Beecher)*

3850. Man learns little from victory, but much from defeat. *Japanese*

3851. They went forth to battle but they always fell. *Ossian*

3852. Woe to the vanquished! *Latin*

Defense *see also* Preparedness

3853. A combined defense is the safest. *Latin*

3854. Arms carry peace. *English*

3855. Attack is the best defense. *American*

3856. If the fence is secure the dogs will not enter. *Chinese*

3857. If the sky falls, hold up your hands. *Spanish*

3858. One knife makes the other stay in the sheath. *Italian*

3859. The best defense is a good offense. *American*

3860. The fox knew much, but the cat one great thing [i.e., how to climb]. *Latin*

3861. The loaded gun terrifies one man; the unloaded gun terrifies two. *Persian*

3862. The robber and the cautious traveler each carry a sword; one uses it as a means of attack, the other as a means of defense. *Latin (Ovid)*

Deference

3863. Give place to your superiors. *Latin (Terence)*

Delay *see also* Deliberation; Future; Lateness; Postponement; Procrastination; Timeliness; Today and Tomorrow

3864. A delay is not necessarily a denial. *American*

3865. A whet is not let [i.e., stopping to sharpen the scythe is no hindrance]. *English*

3866. All delay is irksome, but it teaches us wisdom. *Latin (Publilius Syrus)*

3867. An auld horse may die waiting for the grass. *Scottish*

3868. Be wise today;'tis madness to defer. *English (Young)*

3869. By-and-by is easily said. *English (Shakespeare)*

3870. By hesitation the opportunity is lost. *Latin (Publilius Syrus)*

3871. By the street of By-and-by, one arrives at the house of Never. *Spanish*

3872. Defer no time; delays have dangerous ends. *English (Shakespeare)*

3873. Defer not till tomorrow to be wise, / Tomorrow's sun to thee may never rise. *English (Congreve)*

3874. Delay is preferable to error. *American* (Jefferson)

3875. Delays are dangerous but they make things sure. *American*

3876. Delays are dangerous. *Scottish*

3877. Delays increase desires and sometimes extinguish them. *American*

3878. Every delay that postpones our joys is long. *Latin*

3879. He that gives time to resolve, gives time to deny, and warning to prevent. *English*

3880. He that will not sail till he has a full fair wind, will lose many a voyage. *American*

3881. He who delays, gathers. *Spanish*

3882. He who stays till tomorrow stays at the back. *Osmanli*

3883. However the fool delays, the day does not delay. *French*

3884. Lang tarrying taks a' the thanks awa. *Scottish*

3885. Look before you leap. *English*

3886. Opportunity is often lost by pausing. *Latin*

3887. Prudent pauses forward business. *English*

3888. Stay but a while, you lose a mile. *Dutch*

3889. That which had no force in the beginning can gain no strength from the lapse of time. *American*

3890. The cow may dee [die] ere the grass grows. *Scottish*

3891. The Roman [i.e., Fabius Cunctator] conquered by delay. *Latin*

3892. The tide tarieth no man. *English (Heywood)*

3893. There is danger in delay. *Latin*

3894. Tide and wind stay no man's pleasure. *English (Southwell)*

3895. Two anons and a by-and-by is an hour-and-a-half. *English*

3896. When a man's life is at stake, no delay is too long. *Latin*

3897. When God says today, the devil says tomorrow. *German*

3898. Who has time let him not wait for time. *Italian*

3899. Ye're as lang tuning your pipes as anither wad play a spring [a cheerful tune]. *Scottish*

3900. You may delay, but time will not. *American (Franklin)*

Deliberation *see also* Delay; Night; Procrastination

3901. A good dinner helps deliberation. *Latin*

3902. Add a sprinkling of folly to your long deliberations. *Latin (Horace)*

3903. Consideration gets as many victories as rashness loses. *English*

3904. Consideration gets as many victories as rashness. *American*
3905. Consideration is the parent of wisdom. *English*
3906. Deliberate about serious matters: it's the safest form of delay. *American*
3907. Deliberate before you act. *English*
3908. First consider, then begin. *German*
3909. Night is the mother of councils. *English*
3910. Our pillow should be our counselor. *Latin*
3911. Ponder long before you act. *Latin*
3912. Rome deliberates, Saguntum perishes. *Latin*
3913. Sleep on it. *American*
3914. Sleep over it and you will come to a decision. *Spanish*
3915. Take counsel of one's pillow. *Russian*
3916. That delay is our surest protection which enables us to deliberate on the merits of our intentions. *Latin (Publilius Syrus)*
3917. The night brings counsel. *Latin*
3918. Think today and speak tomorrow. *English*
3919. 'Tis best to pause, and think, ere you rush on. *English (Byron)*
3920. What is to be once resolved on should be first often well considered. *Latin (Publilius Syrus)*
3921. While we are making up our minds as to when we shall begin, the opportunity is lost. *Latin (Quintilian)*
3922. While we discuss matters, the opportunity passes by. *Latin*

Demagoguery

3923. Demagogues are the mob's lackies. *Greek*
3924. Demagogues try to ride two horses at the same time. *American*

Denial *see also* Questions and Answers; Refusal; Response; Soft Words

3925. A civil denial is better than a rude grant. *English*
3926. A good denial — the best point in law. *Irish*
3927. Better a friendly denial than unwilling compliance. *German*
3928. He who denies all confesses all. *Italian*
3929. He who says overmuch "I love not," is in love. *Latin*
3930. If the wild boar say it is not his footprint, still it is his. *Accra*
3931. To deny all is to confess all. *Spanish*
3932. To offer much is one way of denying. *Italian*

Dependence

3933. Every man bows to the bush he gets bield [shelter] frae. *Scottish*
3934. He seeks to live like a parasite. *Latin*
3935. He sits wi' little ease that sits on his neighbour's coattail. *Scottish*
3936. He that rides ahint [behind] another doesna faddle when he pleases. *Scottish*
3937. It is a wretched position to be dependent on others for support. *Latin*
3938. Sometimes a good crutch is better than a bad foot. *Chinese*
3939. The bitter bread of dependence is hard to chew. *American*
3940. The dependent man must dine late and eat the leftovers. *American*
3941. The man who is being carried does not realize how far away the town is. *Nigerian*
3942. To depend on one's own child is blindness in one eye; to depend on a stranger, blindness in both eyes. *Malay*
3943. To eat off another man's plate. *Latin*
3944. Wae [woe] to him that lippens to [depends on] ithers for tippence. *Scottish*

Desert *see also* Merit; Punishment and Retribution

3945. A bad cat deserves a bad rat. *French*
3946. A good bone never comes to a good dog. *French*
3947. A good cat deserves a good rat. *French*
3948. A good dog deserves a good bone. *English*
3949. A mended lid for a cracked pot. *Japanese*
3950. As the work is, so is the pay. *Polish*
3951. By rearing a tiger one makes trouble for oneself. *Japanese*
3952. Great deservers grow intolerable presumers. *American*
3953. He who has shipped the devil must carry him over the sound. *English*
3954. He who stumbles twice over one stone deserves to break his shins. *English*
3955. If strokes are good to give, they are good to receive. *English*
3956. Let him drink as he has brewen. *Scottish*
3957. Let him fry in his own grease. *English*
3958. Let the blacksmith wear the chains he has made. *Latin*
3959. Riches fall not always to the lot of the most deserving. *Latin*
3960. Somebody may come to kame [comb] your hair wi' a cutty stool [a small stool]. *Scottish*
3961. Though the power be wanting, the will deserves praise. *Latin (Ovid)*
3962. What is deservedly suffered must be endured. *Latin*
3963. What's sauce for the goose is sauce for the gander. *English*
3964. You made this mess yourself, and now you must eat it all up. *Latin (Terence)*

Desirability *see also* Desire

3965. A good thing is soon snatched up. *English*
3966. Sweet is the apple when the keeper is away. *Latin*
3967. The figs on the far side of the hedge are sweeter. *Serbian*
3968. The sweetest grapes hang highest. *German*

Desire *see also* Desirability; Worth; Value

3969. Desire beautifies what is ugly. *Spanish*
3970. Desires are nourished by delays. *American*
3971. Every man is led by his own desire. *Latin*
3972. He who can't do, always wants to do. *Italian*
3973. If you desire many things, many things will seem but a few. *American (Franklin)*
3974. Learn to level down your desires rather than level up your means. *Greek*
3975. No one desires what is unknown. *Latin*

3976. There is no pleasure that does not pall, and all the more if it costs nothing. *Spanish*

3977. To wish to be cured is half way to the cure. *Latin (Seneca)*

3978. We desire nothing so much as what we ought not have. *Latin*

3979. When desire dies, fear is born. *Spanish (Gracián)*

3980. When desire has the most, it longs for more. *Latin (Ovid)*

Despair

3981. A man may be damned for despairing to be saved. *American*

3982. Despair aggravates our weakness. *French*

3983. Despair doubles our strength. *French*

3984. Despair gives courage to a coward. *English*

3985. Despair has often gained battles. *French*

3986. Every sheet has parted. [Every hope is gone.] *Latin*

3987. He is desperate that thinks himself so. *English*

3988. Never despair. *Latin (Horace)*

3989. When water covers the head, a hundred fathoms are as one. *Persian*

Desperation *see also* Necessity

3990. A bad bush is better than the open field. *American*

3991. A cornered cat becomes as fierce as a lion. *American*

3992. A drowning man would catch at razors. *Italian*

3993. A hungry man will eat gravel. *Egyptian*

3994. A man has many enemies when his back is to the wall. *American*

3995. A rat at bay dares to bite a cat. *Korean*

3996. Any port in a storm. *English*

3997. Do not seek to escape from the flood by clinging to a tiger's tail. *Chinese*

3998. He is at his wit's end. *Scottish*

3999. He is desperate that thinks himself so. *English*

4000. He that is carried down the torrent catches at everything. *American*

4001. He that is drowning shouts though he be not heard. *American*

4002. Necessity urges desperate measures. *Spanish*

Destiny *see also* Fate

4003. Air [early] day or late day, the tod's [fox's] hide finds aye [always] the flaying knife. *Scottish*

4004. Destiny leads the willing but drags the unwilling. *American*

4005. Each man suffers his own destiny. *Latin*

4006. It is the fate of the coconut husk to float, for the stone to sink. *Malay*

4007. It is wise to submit to destiny. *Chinese*

4008. No man of woman born can shun his destiny. *Greek*

4009. One meets his destiny often in the road he takes to avoid it. *French*

4010. The destiny assigned to every man is suited to him. *Greek*

4011. The dice of Zeus have always lucky throws. *Greek*

4012. The intelligent man submits himself to his destiny. *Chinese*

4013. When a thing is shapen, it shall be. *English (Chaucer)*

4014. Where shall the ox go, but he must labor? *English*

4015. Where shall the ox go, where he shall not labor, since he knows how? *Portuguese*

4016. You can't fight destiny; submit to it. *American*

Determination *see also* Will

4017. He'll either win the horse or tine [lose] the saddle. *Scottish*

4018. He'll make a spune or spoil a horn. *Scottish*

4019. Let us do or die. *Scottish (Burns)*

4020. Set hard heart against hard hap. *English*

4021. The determined man won't change his position until hell freezes over. *American*

4022. The vermin finally determine the fate of ancient houses and whores. *American*

4023. There is nothing that cannot be achieved with a firm resolve. *Japanese*

4024. To him who is determined it remains only to act. *Italian*

4025. Yield not to calamity, but face her boldly. *Latin (Virgil)*

Detraction *see also* Accusation; Criticism; Fault-Finding; Name-Calling; Slander

4026. A detractor is his own foe and a triple threat to all. *American*

4027. Detraction is a weed that only grows on dunghills. *American*

4028. If the fool has a hump, no one notices it; if the wise man has a pimple, everybody talks about it. *Livonian*

4029. It is only at the trees laden with fruit that people throw stones. *French*

4030. Take a bit of mud and dab it on the wall: if it does not stick it will leave its mark. *Arabic*

4031. The best-bearing trees are the most beaten. *Italian*

4032. The man of little mind and less heart is always belittling. *American*

4033. The man that makes a character, makes foes. *American*

4034. The man who detracts from the worth of other men brings his own worth into question. *American*

4035. Throw much dirt, and some will stick. *Latin*

4036. Weak men are crushed by detraction; but the brave hold on and succeed. *American*

Devil

4037. As gude eat the deil [devil] as sup the kail he's boil'd in. *Scottish*

4038. Call not the devil; he'll come fast enough without. *Danish*

4039. Devils must be driven out with devils. *German*

4040. Don't paint the devil blacker than he is. *French*

4041. Each man for himself and the devil for all. *Italian*

4042. Give the devil his due. *American*

4043. He that is afraid of the devil does not grow rich. *Italian*
4044. It is not easy to walk on the devil's ice. *Danish*
4045. Raise no more devils than you can lay. *German*
4046. Resist the devil, and he will flee from you. *Bible*
4047. Talk of the devil and he'll appear. *Latin*
4048. The deil bides his time. *Scottish*
4049. The deil gaes awa when he finds the door steekit [barred] against him. *Scottish*
4050. The deil made souters [cobblers] sailors that can neither steer nor row. *Scottish*
4051. The deil was sick, the deil a monk wad be; the deil grew hale, syne deil a monk was he. *Scottish*
4052. The deil will tak little or he want a'. *Scottish*
4053. The deil [devil] aye drives his hogs to an ill market. *Scottish*
4054. The deil's a busy bishop in his ain diocese. *Scottish*
4055. The deil's cow calves twice in ae year. *Scottish*
4056. The deil's gude when he's pleased. *Scottish*
4057. The deil's nae waur [worse] than he's ca'd [called]. *Scottish*
4058. The deil's ower grit [intimate] wi' you. *Scottish*
4059. The devil can cite scripture for his purpose. *English (Shakespeare)*
4060. The devil catches most souls in a golden net. *German*
4061. The devil corrects sin. *Italian*
4062. The devil hawks his wares within the house of God. *American*
4063. The devil is ae gude [always good] to beginners. *Scottish*
4064. The devil is good to his own. *American*
4065. The devil is good to some. *English*
4066. The devil is not always at a poor man's door. *French*
4067. The devil is not always at one door. *English*
4068. The devil is not so black as he is painted. *German*
4069. The devil is not so black [or ugly] as he is painted. *Italian*
4070. The devil is not so frightful as he is painted. *Polish*
4071. The devil is not so ugly as he is painted. *Italian*
4072. The devil lurks behind the cross. *French*
4073. The devil never sleeps. *American*
4074. The devil take the hindmost. *Latin*
4075. The devil, when he is old, becomes a hermit. *French*
4076. The devil's flour goes all to chaff. *Italian*
4077. The virtue of the devil is in the loins. *Latin*
4078. Where the devil cannot put his head he puts his tail. *Italian*

Devotion

4079. Devotion has mastered the hard way. *Latin*

Dexterity *see also* Skill

4080. Dexterity comes by experience. *American*

Diet *see also* Eating; Gluttony; Health; Obesity

4081. Better lose a supper than have a hundred doctors. *Spanish*
4082. By suppers more have been killed than Galen ever cured. *English*
4083. Cheese and bread make the cheeks red. *American*
4084. Cheese and salt meat should be sparingly eat. *American*
4085. Cheese is wholesome when it is given with a sparing hand. *American*
4086. Cheese, it is a peevish elf; it digests all things but itself. *American*
4087. Diet cures more than the lancet. *English*
4088. Eat few suppers, and you'll need few medicines. *American (Franklin)*
4089. Eat in measure and defy the doctor. *Scottish*

Difference *see also* Contrast; Novelty; Variety

4090. A scepter is one thing, a ladle another. *Latin*
4091. All covet, all lose. *English*
4092. All feet tread not in one shoe. *English*
4093. As like as an apple to an oyster. *American*
4094. As like in taste as chalk and cheese. *American*
4095. As mony heads, as mony wits. *Scottish*
4096. Different men like different things. *Latin*
4097. Different pursuits suit different ages. *Latin*
4098. Differing in words, not in reality. *Latin*
4099. Every shoe fits not every foot. *English*
4100. Forthy [therefore] men seyn ech contree hath his laws. *English (Chaucer)*
4101. His e'ening sang and his morning sang are no baith alike. *Scottish*
4102. It does not fall to the lot of all to smell of musk. *Latin*
4103. No dish pleases all palates alike. *English*
4104. One egg is not so much like to another. *Latin*
4105. So many heads, so many counsels. *French*
4106. The owl has one note, the crow another. *Latin*
4107. The parrot utters one cry, the quail another. *Latin*
4108. The same shoe does not fit every foot. *Latin*
4109. There are fagots and fagots. *French (Molière)*
4110. There's a difference between the piper and his bitch. *Scottish*
4111. There's some difference between Peter and Peter. *Spanish*
4112. Two goods seldom meet, / What's good for the plant is ill for the peat. *Scottish*
4113. You should not hate everyone whose nose is different from yours. *German*

Difficulty *see also* Adversity

4114. A smooth sea never made a skillful mariner. *English*
4115. All things are difficult before they are easy. *English*
4116. Difficulties are things that show what men are. *Greek (Epictetus)*
4117. Difficulty is the daughter of idleness. *English*
4118. Difficulty makes desire. *English*
4119. Every path has its puddle. *English*
4120. Having a mouth and eating rice by the nose. *Bengalese*
4121. He is a foolish swimmer who swims against the

stream, when he might take the current sideways. *Latin (Ovid)*

4122. He who accounts all things easy will have many difficulties. *Chinese (Laotse)*

4123. It is difficulties which show what men are. *Greek*

4124. It's ill taking corn frae [from] geese. *Scottish*

4125. Nothing is so difficult but that man will accomplish it. *Latin (Horace)*

4126. The best things are most difficult. *Greek*

4127. The greater the difficulty, the greater the glory. *Latin*

4128. There's a word in my wame [womb], but it's ower far doun. *Scottish*

4129. Through difficulties to the stars. *Latin*

4131. 'Tis very ill driving black hogs in the dark. *American*

4130. To look for a needle in a haystack. *English*

4132. What is worth while must needs be difficult. *Latin*

4133. What's too hard for a man must be worth looking into. *Kenyan*

Diffidence

4134. Diffidence is the right eye of prudence. *English*

4135. He that spares to speak spares to speed. *Scottish*

4136. Say aye "No," and ye'll ne'er be married. *Scottish*

4137. Ye canna preach out o' your ain pu'pit. *Scottish*

4138. Ye maun hae't baith simmered [summered] and wintered. *Scottish*

4139. Ye're as mim [prim] as a May puddock [toad]. *Scottish*

Dignity

4140. It is easier to grow in dignity than to make a start. *Latin*

4141. It is thou must honor the place, not the place thee. *English*

4142. The house should derive dignity from the master, not the master from the house. *Latin (Cicero)*

Dilemma *see also* Choice; Decision

4143. A precipice ahead, wolves behind. *Latin*

4144. Among enemies choose the least. *Spanish*

4145. Between dog and wolf. *French*

4146. Between hammer and anvil. *Latin*

4147. Between hawk and buzzard. *English*

4148. Between Scylla and Charybdis. *Greek*

4149. Go forward and fall—go backward and mar all. *English*

4150. I am in a dilemma. I have caught a Tartar. *English*

4151. I hold a wolf by the ears. *Latin (Terence)*

4152. In all things man's choice is not between the good and the bad, but between the bad and the worse. *French*

4153. O' twa ills choose the least. *Scottish*

4154. Of evils one should select the least. *Greek*

4155. Of harmes two the lesse is for to cheese. *English (Chaucer)*

4156. Of two evils choose neither. *English*

4157. Of two evils I have chose the least. *English (Prior)*

4158. Of two evils the least is always to be chosen. *Latin*

Diligence

4159. A diligent man ever finds that something remains to be done. *Latin*

4160. By diligence and patience, the mouse bites in two the cable. *American (Franklin)*

4161. Care and diligence bring luck. *English*

4162. Diligence is a great teacher. *Arabic*

4163. Diligence is an inestimable treasure, and prudence a defensive charm. *Chinese*

4164. Diligence is everything. *Greek*

4165. Diligence is the mother of good luck. *French*

4166. Honor springs from diligence; and riches from economy. *Chinese*

4167. The diligent spinner has a large shift. *American (Franklin)*

4168. There is no poverty that can overtake diligence. *Korean*

4169. To perfect diligence nothing is difficult. *Chinese*

Dirtiness

4170. Dirt bodes luck. *Scottish*

4171. Dirt defies the king. *Scottish*

4172. Dirt pairts gude company. *Scottish*

4173. He is in mourning for his washerwoman. [His clothes are dirty.] *French*

4174. Never cast dirt into the fountain of which you sometimes drink. *Hebrew*

4175. The clartier [dirtier] the cosier. *Scottish*

4176. The mair [more] dirt the less hurt. *Scottish*

4177. Ye may be godly, but ye'll ne'er be cleanly. *Scottish*

Disadvantage *see* Advantage

Disagreement *see also* Agreement; Disputes

4178. Gree like tykes and swine. *Scottish*

4179. No and yes often cause long disputes. *Danish*

4180. The children of the same mother do not always agree. *Wolof*

4181. The potter is at odds with the potter. *Greek (Hesiod)*

4182. They agree like cats and dogs. *American*

4183. They agree like harp and harrow. *English*

4184. They agree like London clocks. *English*

4185. They agree like pickpockets at a fair. *English*

4186. They'll gree better when they gang [go] in by different kirk [church] doors. *Scottish*

4187. Three Spaniards, four opinions. *Spanish*

4188. Two cats and a mouse, / Two wives in a house, / Two dogs and a bone, / Never agree in one. *English*

4189. Two dogs never agree over one bone. *French*

4190. Two of a trade seldom [or never] agree. *English*

4191. We may talk this and talk that [i.e., disagree with each other], [but] it is because we do not understand each other. *Yoruba*

4192. With a dear friend, a thousand cups of wine are too few; when opinions disagree, even half a sentence is too much. *Chinese*

Discipline *see also* Child-Rearing; Discipline and Women; Motivation; Punishment and Retribution

4193. A dog belonging to a harsh master does not become wise. *Bemba*
4194. A resty horse must have a sharp spur. *English*
4195. A sharp goad for a stubborn ass. *French*
4196. A whip for the horse, a bridle for the ass, and a rod for the fool's back. *Bible*
4197. If you beat spice it will smell the sweeter. *English*
4198. Love well, whip well. *English*
4199. No inclinations are so fierce that they may not be subdued by discipline. *Latin*
4200. One whip is good enough for a good horse; for a bad one, not a thousand. *American*
4201. Oughts are nothing unless they've strokes to them. *English*
4202. The mind is best taught with a sharp whip. *Latin*
4203. To educate without severity shows a teacher's indolence. *Chinese*
4204. Woe to the house where there is no chiding. *English*

Discipline and Children *see also* Child-Rearing; Discipline

4205. If you do not understand with your ears, you will understand with your buttocks. *Lugbara*

Discipline and Women

4206. A good horse and a bad horse need the spur; a good woman and a bad woman need the stick. *Italian*
4207. A nut-tree, an ass, and a woman are useless if blows are spared. *Latin*
4208. A spaniel, a wife, and a walnut tree, / The more you beat 'em the better they be. *English*
4209. Beat a woman with a hammer and you'll make gold. *Russian*
4210. Govern a horse with a bit and a shrew with a stick. *Danish*
4211. There are three things which are no good without beating — a walnut tree, an ass and a woman. *Danish*

Discontent *see also* Contentment

4212. A man's discontent is his worst evil. *American*
4213. Admiring others' lots, we hate our own. *Latin*
4214. He that hath nothing is not contented. *English*
4215. He that wants content canna sit easy in his chair. *Scottish*
4216. No fortune is so good but that you may find something to grumble about. *Latin (Publilius Syrus)*
4217. The discontented man finds no easy chair. *American (Franklin)*
4218. The grass is always greener on the other side of the fence. *American*
4219. The neighbor's cooking always smells better. *Maltese*
4220. They need muckle [much] that naething [nothing] will content. *Scottish*
4221. Who is not satisfied with his condition is a great fool. *German*

Discord *see also* Argument; Contention; Dispute; Fighting; Quarreling; Stress and Strain; Strife

4222. A house divided against itself cannot stand. *Bible*
4223. Discord gives a relish for concord. *Latin (Publilius Syrus)*
4224. He who incites to strife is worse than he who takes part in it. *Greek (Aesop)*
4225. One house cannot keep two dogs. *Latin*
4226. One tree won't hold two robins. *Latin*
4227. The mother of dissension is less than a gnat. *Gaelic*
4228. Two sparrows upon one ear of corn make ill agreement. *English*
4229. Where no wood is, there the fire goeth out: so where there is no tale-bearer, the strife ceaseth. *Bible*

Discouragement *see* Despair

Discretion *see also* Prudence; Tact

4230. A close mouth catches nae flees. *Scottish*
4231. A dram of discretion is worth a pound of wisdom. *German*
4232. A' that's said in the kitchen shouldna be told in the ha'. *Scottish*
4233. A' the truth shouldna aye be tauld. *Scottish*
4234. All that is said in the kitchen should not be heard in the hall. *English*
4235. All things are gude unsay'd. *Scottish*
4236. All truth is not good to tell. *French*
4237. All truth must not be told at all times. *Italian*
4238. An ounce of discretion is worth a pound of wit [or knowledge]. *English*
4239. An ounce of discretion is worth more than a pound of knowledge. *Italian*
4240. As a jewel of gold in a swine's snout, so is a fair woman which is without discretion. *Bible*
4241. Discreet women have neither eyes nor ears. *French*
4242. Discretion in speech is more than eloquence. *American*
4243. Don't tell tales out of school. *American*
4244. He wha tells his wife a' is but newly married. *Scottish*
4245. I'll keep my mind to mysel, and tell my tale to the wind. *Scottish*
4246. I'll say naething, but I'll yerk [writhe] at the thinking. *Scottish*
4247. If you are not a sailor don't handle a boat-hook. *Chinese*
4248. In a discreet man's mouth a public thing is private. *American (Franklin)*
4249. Keep well thy tongue and keep thy friendship. *English (Chaucer)*
4250. Keep your gab [mouth] steekit [shut] when ye kenna [know not] your company. *Scottish*

4251. Keep your mouth and keep your friend. *Danish*

4252. Know not what you know, and see not what you see. *Latin*

4253. Let the kirk [church] stand in the kirkyard. *Scottish*

4254. Shoot not beyond the mark. *Latin*

4255. Tell everybody your business and they will do it for you. *Italian*

4256. The better part of valor is discretion. *English (Shakespeare)*

4257. The doctor who would heal another's hurt should not show his own. *Swedish*

4258. The eye has a veil. *Arabic*

4259. Think what you like, say what you ought. *French*

4260. To put his finger on his lips. [To refuse to reveal what he knows.] *Latin*

4261. Valor can do little without discretion. *English*

4262. Wash your dirty linen at home. *English*

Discussion *see also* **Argument; Conversation; Dispute; Quarreling**

4263. Discussion is the anvil upon which the spark of truth is struck. *American*

4264. Free and fair discussion will ever be found the firmest friend to truth. *American*

4265. He who is not open to conviction, is not qualified for discussion. *American*

4266. People do not [i.e., should not] talk while moving. *Lugbara*

Disease *see also* **Illness; Physicians; Remedies**

4267. Disease is not of the body but of the place. *Latin*

4268. Diseases are the interest on pleasures. *English*

4269. Diseases are the tax on pleasures. *English*

4270. Meet the disease on its way. *Latin*

4271. The beginning of health is to know the disease. *Spanish*

4272. There is no curing a sick man who believes himself in health. *French*

4273. To hide disease is fatal. *Latin*

Dishonesty *see also* **Buying and Selling; Cheating; Crime and Criminals; Deception; Fraud; Honesty; Lies and Lying**

4274. Avoid dishonest gain: no price can recompence the pangs of vice. *American (Franklin)*

4275. He that oppresses honesty ne'er had ony. *Scottish*

4276. He's fail'd wi' a fu' hand. *Scottish*

4277. Nothing is profitable which is dishonest. *Latin*

4278. Speir [ask] at Jock Thief if I be a leal [honest] man. *Scottish*

4279. There are mair [more] knaves in my kin than honest men in yours. *Scottish*

4280. Ye fand it where the Hielandman fand the tangs [tongs]. *Scottish*

4281. Ye're an honest man, and I'm your uncle—that's twa big lees. *Scottish*

Disposition

4282. Man's disposition, like water, distinguishes between high and low; the world is ever changing, like a cloud. *Chinese*

4283. Rather fear the man whose disposition is a two-edged sword, than the savage tiger of the mountains. *Chinese*

4284. Though a snake get into a bamboo tube it is hard to change its wriggling disposition. *Chinese*

4285. When you see into man's disposition, you perceive that all is false. *Chinese*

Dispute *see also* **Argument; Conflict; Contention; Disagreement; Discord; Fighting; Quarreling; Stress and Strain; Strife**

4286. As ass's arguments and a donkey's shadow are not matters for dispute. *American*

4287. Between wrangling and disputing truth is lost. *American*

4288. By too much disputing, truth is lost. *French*

4289. Great disputing repels truth. *English*

4290. He who disputes with the stupid must have sharp answers. *German*

4291. The pain of dispute exceeds by much its utility. *American*

4292. There is more disputing about the shell than the kernel. *American*

4293. To dispute about a donkey's shadow. *Latin*

4294. To dispute about smoke. *Latin*

4295. True disputants are like true sportsmen; their whole delight is in the pursuit. *English (Pope)*

Dissatisfaction *see* **Discontent**

Distance *see also* **Nearness**

4296. A good way round is not roundabout. *German*

4297. Far from court, far from care. *French*

4298. Far from Jupiter, far from thunder. *Latin*

4299. From a distance it is something; nearby it is nothing. *French*

4300. Go farther and fare worse. *English*

4301. The further we go, the further behind. *English*

4302. The furthest way about's the nearest way home. *English*

4303. Water comes to the mill from afar. *Portuguese*

4304. Water far off will not put out a fire near at hand. *Italian*

Distraction

4305. The eyes are blind when the mind is preoccupied. *Latin (Publilius Syrus)*

4306. When dogs fight among themselves, the wolf devours the sheep. *Hungarian*

4307. When the snipe and the mussel fight with each other, the fisherman catches them both. *Chinese*

Distrust *see also* **Suspicion; Trust; Watchfulness**

4308. A rogue always suspects deceit. *Spanish*

4309. A Tyrone woman will never buy a rabbit without a head for fear it's a cat. *Irish*

4310. At the gate which suspicion enters, love goes out. *English*

4311. Distrust is the mother of safety. *French*

4312. I fear the Greeks even when they bring gifts. *Latin (Virgil)*

4313. Our distrust justifies the deceit of others. *French (La Rochefoucauld)*

4314. Trust in God, but tie your camel. *Persian*

4315. Words will not do for my aunt, for she does not trust even deeds. *Spanish*

Diversity *see also* Man; Opinion; Variety

4316. As many men as there are existing, so many are their different pursuits. *Latin (Horace)*

Divided Interest *see also* Simultaneity

4317. A lass that has many wooers often fares the worst. *English*

4318. Drive not too many ploughs at once, some will make foul work. *English*

4319. He that hath many irons in the fire, some of them will cool. *English*

4320. He who carries two melons in one hand is sure to drop at least one of them. *Arabic*

4321. If you chase two hares, you will not catch either. *Russian*

4322. If you run after two hares, you will catch neither. *Latin*

4323. It's good to be off wi' the old love / Before ye be on wi' the new. *Scottish*

4324. Jack of all trades and master of none. *English*

4325. Nothing is more foolish than to dabble in too many things. *Latin*

4326. To do two things at once is to do neither. *Latin (Publilius Syrus)*

4327. You cannot hold onto two cows' tails at once. *Upper Volta*

Divided Loyalty *see also* Subordinates

4328. A good horse cannot wear two saddles, nor a loyal minister serve two masters. *Chinese*

4329. Divided in heart, divided in practice. *Chinese*

4330. He falls short of his duty to both who tries to serve two masters. *Latin*

4331. He who serves two masters has to lie to one. *Portuguese*

4332. He who serves two masters serves neither. *Italian*

4333. Hobbling, put your trust in God. *Arabic (Mahomet)*

4334. No man can serve two masters. *English*

4335. No man can serve two masters: for either he will hate the one, and love the other; or else he will hold to the one, and despise the other. *Bible*

4336. Render unto the Caesar the things that are Caesar's and unto God the things that are God's. *Bible*

4337. Two calls confuse a dog. *Acholi*

Divine Assistance *see also* God; Man and God; Prayer

4338. Call Minerva to aid, but bestir yourself. *Greek*

4339. For a web begun God sends a thread. *Italian*

4340. Get thy spindle and thy distaff ready, and God will send the flax. *English*

4341. Get your rock and spindle ready, God will send the tow. *Scottish*

4342. God builds the nest of the blind bird. *Turkish*

4343. God comes at last when we think he is farthest off. *Italian*

4344. God cometh with leaden feet, but striketh with iron hands. *English*

4345. God feeds even the worm in the earth. *Yiddish*

4346. God gives birds their food, but they must fly for it. *Dutch*

4347. God gives, but man must open his hand. *German*

4348. God gives food but does not cook it. *American*

4349. God gives the milk but not the pail. *German*

4350. God help you to a hutch [a poor cottage], for ye'll never get a mailing [farm]. *Scottish*

4351. God helps everyone with what is his own. *Spanish*

4352. God helps him who amends himself. *Spanish*

4353. God helps the sailor, but he must row. *American*

4354. God helps the strongest. *German*

4355. God helps them that help themselves. *Latin*

4356. God helps three sorts of people — fools, children and drunkards. *French*

4357. God is a good worker, but he loves to be helped. *Basque*

4358. God lends a helping hand to him who works hard. *Greek (Aeschylus)*

4359. God measures the cold to the shorn lamb. *French*

4360. God moderates all at His pleasure. *French (Rabelais)*

4361. God never send'th mouth but he sendeth meat. *English (Heywood)*

4362. God never shuts one door but he opens another. *Irish*

4363. God orders cold according to the cloth. *Italian*

4364. God puts a good root in the little pig's way. *French*

4365. God send'th cold after clothes. *English*

4366. God sends meat an' the de'il sends cooks. *Scottish*

4367. God sends men claith [cloth] as they hae cauld [have cold]. *Scottish*

4368. God sends men cold as they have clothes to. *Scottish*

4369. God sends the cure before the plague. *Yiddish*

4370. God sends the thread to cloth which is begun. *French*

4371. God tempers the cold to our clothes. *Yiddish*

4372. God who sends the wound sends the medicine. *Spanish (Cervantes)*

4373. God will provide, but a bundle of straw will not be amiss. *Spanish*

4374. God will provide — if only God would provide until he provides. *Yiddish*

4375. God will provide. *Bible*

4376. God's help is nearer nor [i.e., than] the fair e'en. *Scottish*

4377. He who gives us teeth will give us bread. *Yiddish*

4378. Help thyself, and God will help thee. *Scottish*

4379. Hope in the Lord, but exert yourself. *Russian*
4380. In praying to God you must use your hammer. *Spanish*
4381. It's God that feeds the craws [crows], that neither till, harrow, nor saws. *Scottish*
4382. It's little o' God's might that maks a poor man a knight. *Scottish*
4383. Pray to God and ply the hammer. *Spanish*
4384. Pray to God but continue to row to the shore. *Russian*
4385. Prayer and practice is good rhyme. *Scottish*
4386. Praying to God, and hammering away. *Spanish*
4387. Put your trust in God, but tie up the leg of your camel. *Arabic*
4388. Spend, and God will send. *English*
4389. Spend, and God will send; spare, and be bare. *Scottish*
4390. The man whom heaven helps / has friends enough. *Greek (Euripides)*
4391. Trust in God, but mind your business. *Russian*
4392. Trust in the Lord, but pass the ammunition. *American*
4393. Try first thyself, and after call in God; / For to the worker God himself lends aid. *Greek (Euripides)*
4394. Use the means and God will give the blessing. *English*
4395. When God will not, the saints cannot. *Italian*
4396. Without divine assistance we can achieve nothing. *Latin*

Divorce
4397. Better a tooth out than always aching. *English*
4398. Divorce is the sacrament of adultery. *French*
4399. The betrothed of good is evil, / The betrothed of life is death, / The betrothed of love is divorce. *Malay*

Doctors *see* Physicians

Double-Dealing *see* Duplicity

Doubt
4400. By doubting we come at the truth. *Latin (Cicero)*
4401. Doubt the worst and hope for the best. *American*
4402. He that doubteth is damned. *Bible*
4403. He who doubts nothing knows nothing. *American*
4404. He who holds out but a doubtful hope of succor to the afflicted, denies it. *Latin (Seneca)*
4405. Honest doubt is better than faith in a pious fraud. *American*
4406. Some say she do, and some say she don't. *American*
4407. The wise are prone to doubt. *Greek*
4408. To believe a business impossible is the way to make it so. *English*
4409. When doubt is doubted death is clouted. *American*
4410. When in doubt do nowt. *English*
4411. When in doubt, leave it out. *American*
4412. Where doubt ends, peace of mind begins. *American*
4413. Where doubt is, truth is. *American*
4414. With a grain of salt. *Latin*

Dowries *see also* Marriage
4415. A great dowry is a bed full of brambles. *Scottish*
4416. A tocherless [dowerless] dame sits long at hame [home]. *Scottish*
4417. Better a tocher [dower] in her than wi' her. *Scottish*
4418. Having accepted a dowry, I have lost an empire. *Latin*
4419. There is nothing false about a girl who has no dowry. *Russian*
4420. Well-dowered wives bring evil and loss to their husbands. *Latin (Plautus)*
4421. Where there is a dowry there is danger. *Irish*
4422. Who takes a wife for her dower turns his back on freedom. *French*

Dreams
4423. After a dream of a wedding, comes a corpse. *English*
4424. All men of action are dreamers. *American*
4425. Don't build castles in the air. *American*
4426. Dream of a funeral and hear of a marriage. *American*
4427. Dreams are from Zeus. *Greek*
4428. Dreams go by contraries. *American*
4429. Love's dreams prove seldom true. *American*
4430. Only in dreams does the happiness of the earth dwell. *American*
4431. To believe in one's dreams is to spend all of one's life asleep. *Chinese*
4432. Who lives in a silver bed has golden dreams. *German*

Dress *see also* Clothes; Fashion; Women and Clothes
4433. It's not the gown that adorns the man but the man the gown. *Polish*

Drinking and Drunkenness
4434. A cup in the hand is worth all else. *Chinese*
4435. A dreigh [dry] drink is better than a dry sermon. *Scottish*
4436. A drink is shorter than a tale. *Scottish*
4437. A drunkard can soon be made to dance. *Danish*
4438. A drunken man cannot lie. *English*
4439. A drunken night makes a cloudy morning. *English*
4440. A drunken woman is only herself. *Russian*
4441. A fou [drunk] man and a hungry horse aye make haste hame. *Scottish*
4442. A fou [drunk] man's a true man. *Scottish*
4443. A hot drink is as good as an overcoat. *Latin*
4444. A man who can't hold his liquor shouldn't drink. *American*
4445. A red nose maks a ragget back. *Scottish*
4446. A red-nosed man may be a teetotaller but no one will believe it. *American*
4447. A thousand will drink themselves to death before one dies of thirst. *German*

4448. A young drunkard, an old pauper. *Yiddish*
4449. After all mourning one drinks. *French*
4450. Ale-sellers shouldna be tale-tellers. *Scottish*
4451. Ale that would make a cat speak. *English*
4452. An aching for wine — a wine-ache. *Latin*
4453. And dronkennesse is eek [also] a foul record / Of any man, and namely [especially] in a lord. *English (Chaucer)*
4454. As drunk as a beggar. *English*
4455. As drunk as a lord. *English*
4456. As drunk as a wheelbarrow. *English*
4457. As drunk as David's sow. *English*
4458. As he brews so shall he drink. *English (Jonson)*
4459. At the first cup man drinks wine; at the second cup wine drinks wine; at the third cup wine drinks man. *Japanese*
4460. Bacchus opens the gate of the heart. *Latin*
4461. Bacchus scatters carking cares. *Latin*
4462. Better to trip with the feet than with the tongue. *Greek*
4463. Bread as long as there is any, wine by measure. *French*
4464. Candy is dandy, but liquor is quicker. *American*
4465. Cobblers and tinkers are the best ale-drinkers. *English*
4466. Death and drink-draining are near neighbours. *Scottish*
4467. Do not drink more wine than you are able to carry. *Chinese*
4468. Double drinks are gude for drouth. *Scottish*
4469. Drink and drouth come na aye thegither [not always together]. *Scottish*
4470. Drink does not drown care, but waters it, and makes it grow faster. *American (Franklin)*
4471. Drink little that ye may drink lang. *Scottish*
4472. Drink nothing without seeing it; sign nothing without reading it. *Portuguese*
4473. Drink wine and have the gout; drink none and have it too. *English*
4474. Drink wine and let the water go to the mill. *Italian*
4475. Drunk at e'en and dry in the morning. *Scottish*
4476. Drunk folk seldom take harm. *Scottish*
4477. Drunkards beget drunkards. *Greek*
4478. Drunken talk doesn't remain in the mind. *Chinese*
4479. Drunkenness does not creat vice; it merely reveals it. *Latin*
4480. Drunkenness is voluntary madness. *Latin*
4481. Drunkenness, that worst of evils, makes some men fools, some beasts, some devils. *American (Franklin)*
4482. Drunks don't think their own thoughts. *Russian*
4483. Dry bargains bode ill. *Scottish*
4484. Eat a bit before you drink. *English*
4485. Eating and drinking / Shouldn't keep us from thinking. *English*
4486. Ever drunk, ever dry. *English*
4487. Every inordinate cup is unblessed, and the ingredient is a devil. *English (Shakespeare)*
4488. Every month one should get drunk at least once. *French*
4489. Excessive joy breeds sorrow; excess of wine, disorder. *Chinese*
4490. Fair chieve [comes] good ale, it makes many folks speak as they think. *English*
4491. Fair fa' the wife, and weel may she spin, that counts aye the lawin' wi' a pint to come in. *Scottish*
4492. For a bad night, a mattress of wine. *Spanish*
4493. Full bottles and glasses make swearers and asses. *American*
4494. Give him something to drink, and you will see whose son he is. *Hungarian*
4495. Give wine to them that are in sorrow. *English*
4496. God's aye kind to fou [drunk] folk and bairns [children]. *Scottish*
4497. Good ale is meat, drink and cloth. *English*
4498. Good drink drives out bad thoughts. *Danish*
4499. Grief is put to flight and assuaged by generous draughts. *Latin*
4500. He speaks in his drink what he thinks in his drouth. *Scottish*
4501. He that drinks fast, pays slow. *American (Franklin)*
4502. He that is drunk is gone from home. *English*
4503. He that spills the rum loses that only; he that drinks it, often loses both that and himself. *American (Franklin)*
4504. He who drinks much beer must drink water. *Sumerian*
4505. He, who is always drinking and stuffing, / Will in time become a ragamuffin. *English*
4506. He who quarrels with a drunken man injures one who is absent. *Latin*
4507. He who sins when drunk will have to atone for it when sober. *Latin*
4508. He's as fou's a fiddler [as drunk as a fiddler]. *Scottish*
4509. He's gane aff at the nail. *Scottish*
4510. He's waur to water than to corn. *Scottish*
4511. His head is fu' o' bees. *Scottish*
4512. I wish ye may hae as muckle [have as much] Scotch as tak ye to your bed. *Scottish*
4513. I would appeal to Philip, but to Philip sober. *Latin*
4514. I'm no that fou [drunk], but I'm gayly yet. *Scottish*
4515. If you cannot carry your liquor when you are young, you will be a water-carrier when you are old. *Greek*
4516. If you get the best of whiskey, it will get the best of you. *American*
4517. In wine there is truth. *Latin*
4518. Intoxication is not the wine's fault but the man's. *Chinese*
4519. It's a dry tale that doesna end in a drink. *Scottish*
4520. It's drink will ye and no drink shall ye. *Scottish*
4521. Keep in the stoup [jug] was ne'er a gude fellow. *Scottish*
4522. Laith [loath] to the drink and laith fra it. [Slow to begin, difficult to stop.] *Scottish*

4523. Late hours and love and wine lead not to moderation in anything. *Latin*

4524. Let but the drunkard alone, and he will fall of himself. *Hebrew*

4525. Lips gae, laps gae, drink and pay. *Scottish*

4526. Mad drunkenness discloses every secret. *Latin*

4527. Many a child is hungry because the saloonkeeper is rich. *American*

4528. Medicine may heal imagined sickness, but wine cannot dispel real sorrow. *Chinese*

4529. Mony ane [many a one] kens [knows] the gudefellow that doesna ken the gudefellow's wife. *Scottish*

4530. Mony words wad hae muckle drink. [Many words would have much drink.] *Scottish*

4531. More are drowned in the goblet than in the sea. *German*

4532. More men are drowned on land than in the sea. *American*

4533. Ne'er count the lawin' [a tavern reckoning] wi' a toom [empty] quaich [small, shallow drinking cup]. *Scottish*

4534. Never go out to drink on a winter night. *Greek*

4535. No fool is silent over his cups. *Greek*

4536. No wine, no company; no wine, no conversation. *Chinese*

4537. Nothing is more hurtful to health than much wine. *Latin*

4538. O' a' meat i' the warld the drink gaes best doun. *Scottish*

4539. One can never drink all the wine there is for sale. *Chinese*

4540. One fit of intoxication dispels three anxieties. *Chinese*

4541. One that will drink till the ground looks blew. *English (Heywood)*

4542. Only what I drink is mine. *Polish*

4543. Our fathers, who were wondrous wise, / Did wash their throats before they washed their eyes. *English*

4544. Over the bottle many a friend is found. *Yiddish*

4545. Over the wine cup conversation is light. *Chinese*

4546. Pint stoups [jugs] hae lang lugs [ears]. *Scottish*

4547. Pleasure in drinking, fatigue on the road. *Sumerian*

4548. "Saft's [soft is] your horn, my friend," quo' the man when he took haud o' the cuddy's lug [ear]. *Scottish*

4549. Saki is the best of all medicines. *Japanese*

4550. Sir John Barleycorn's the strongest knight. *English*

4551. Tak a hair o' the dog that bit you. *Scottish*

4552. That's a tale o' twa [two] drinks. *Scottish*

4553. The ass that carries wine drinks water. *American*

4554. The best cure for drunkenness is, while sober, to see a drunken man. *Chinese*

4555. The devil places a pillow for a drunken man to fall upon. *Canadian*

4556. The drunkard is always talking of wine. *Italian*

4557. The drunkard is convicted by his praises of wine. *Latin (Horace)*

4558. The fool sucks wisdom, as the porter sups, / And cobblers grow fine speakers in their cups. *English*

4559. The glass antagonizes, the glass advises. *Polish*

4560. The malt is above the water. [The man is drunk.] *English*

4561. The mawt's aboon the meal wi' him. [The malt's above the meal—i.e., the man is drunk.] *Scottish*

4562. The smith hath always a spark in his throat. [The smith is always thirsty.] *Scottish*

4563. The sober man's secret is the drunken man's speech. *Russian*

4564. The tavern will not spoil a good man, nor the church mend a bad one. *Polish*

4565. The wise drunkard is a sober fool. *German*

4566. There are more old drunkards than old doctors. *French*

4567. There is a devil in every berry of the grape. *Koran*

4568. There is no deceit in a brimmer. *English*

4569. There is nothing more like a madman than a drunken person. *Latin*

4570. There's a special Providence watches ower drunk men and bairns [children]. *Scottish*

4571. There's no bad brandy for a drunkard. *Yiddish*

4572. There's plenty o' raible [nonsense] when drink's on the table. *Scottish*

4573. They speak o' my drinking, but ne'er think o' my drouth. *Scottish*

4574. They that drink langest live langest. *Scottish*

4575. Thirst comes with drinking, when the wine is good. *French*

4576. Thirst departs with drinking. *French*

4577. Thought when sober, said when drunk. *English*

4578. Thousands drink themselves to death before one dies of thirst. *German*

4579. Three glasses of wine can set everything to rights. *Chinese*

4580. Three glasses of wine fulfill the principles of true politeness; to get drunk banishes a thousand worries. *Chinese*

4581. To a drunken man, everything is on a big scale; to a man of leisure, days and months are long. *Chinese*

4582. To dispute with a drunkard is to debate with an empty house. *Latin (Publilius Syrus)*

4583. To drink like frogs. *Latin*

4584. To take a hair of the same dog. *English*

4585. Too much wine will make a sane man mad. *Latin*

4586. Under a bad cloak there is often a good drinker. *Spanish*

4587. We can drink till all look blue. *English (Ford)*

4588. Wet your wizen [throat] or else it'll gizen [become leaky from drought]. *Scottish*

4589. "Wha can help sickness?" quo' the wife when she lay in the gutter. *Scottish*

4590. What is in the heart of the sober man is on the tongue of the drunken man. *Latin*

4591. What is one keg of beer among one man? *American*

4592. What soberness conceals, drunkenness reveals. *Latin*

4593. What the sober man has in his heart, the drunken man has on his lips [or tongue]. *Latin*

4594. What ye do when you're drunk ye may pay for when ye're dry. *Scottish*

4595. When drink enters, wisdom departs. *American*

4596. When drink's in, wit's out. *Scottish*

4597. When drinking wine, remember the poverty of your family. *Chinese*

4598. When inspired by wine that is the time for business. *Chinese*

4599. When the bag's fu' the drone gets up. *Scottish*

4600. When the beer goes in the wit goes out. *Danish*

4601. When the cock is drunk, he forgets about the hawk. *Ashanti*

4602. When the gudeman drinks to the gudewife, a' wad be weel; when the gudewife drinks to the gudeman, a's weel. *Scottish*

4603. When the wine enters, out goes the truth. *American (Franklin)*

4604. When the wine goes in the wisdom goes out. *Dutch*

4605. When the wine is in, murder will out. *Hebrew*

4606. When wine sinks, words swim. *English*

4607. Where wine enters, modesty goes out. *Italian*

4608. Who has drunk will drink. *French*

4609. Whom has not the inspiring bowl made eloquent? *Latin (Horace)*

4610. Wine brings forth the truth. *Latin*

4611. Wine can both help and hinder business. *Chinese*

4612. Wine carries no rudder. *Latin*

4613. Wine disorders man's nature. *Chinese*

4614. Wine gladdeneth the heart of man. *English*

4615. Wine hath drowned more men than the sea. *English*

4616. Wine is a discoverer [i.e., revealer] of secrets. *Chinese*

4617. Wine is given to bring mirth, not drunkenness. *Latin*

4618. Wine is the best broom for troubles. *Japanese*

4619. Wine is the mirror of the mind. *Latin*

4620. Wine mars beauty and destroys the freshness of youth. *Latin*

4621. Wine unlocks the breast. *Latin*

4622. Wine wears no breeches. [That is, causes a man to reveal himself, so to speak, for what he is.] *French*

4623. Wine wears no mask. *English*

4624. Wisdom is clouded by wine. *Latin*

4625. Ye had been smelling the bung. *Scottish*

4626. You cannot distinguish between a drunken man and a mad until they have slept. *Danish*

4627. You drink flood and ebb. *Efik*

Duplicity

4628. He has bread in one hand and a stone in the other. *American*

4629. He howls with the wolves when he is in the wood, and bleats with the sheep in the field. *Dutch*

4630. He runs with the hound and holds with the hare. *Scottish*

4631. He says to the thief, "Steal"; and to the house-owner, "Take care of thy goods." *Arabic*

4632. To carry two faces under one hood. *English*

4633. To run with the hare and hold with the hounds. *English*

4634. To sit on two seats. *Latin*

Duty *see also* Obligation

4635. Do well the duty that lies before you. *Greek*

4636. Duties are ours, events are God's. *American*

4637. Duty before pleasure. *American*

4638. Duty determines destiny. *English*

4639. God obligeth no man to more than he hath given him ability to perform. *Koran*

4640. He seen his duty and he done it. *American*

4641. In doing what we ought we deserve no praise. *Latin*

4642. It is an honor to have remembered one's duty. *Latin*

4643. The path of duty is near at hand; men seek it in what is remote. *Japanese*

4644. The path of duty lies in the thing that is nearby, but men seek it in things far off. *Chinese*

Earliness *see also* Early Rising; Morning

4645. An hour in the morning is worth two at night. *English*

4646. Early sow, early mow. *English*

4647. Early start makes easy stages. *American*

4648. Early to bed, and early to get married. *Yiddish*

4649. Go early to the fish market, and late to the shambles. *English*

4650. He rises over early that is hangit or noon [hanged before noon]. *Scottish*

4651. Soon fire, soon ash. *Dutch*

4652. Soon grass, soon hay. *Dutch*

4653. Soon ripe, soon rotten. *Scottish*

4654. Soon ripe, soon rotten; soon wise, soon foolish. *Dutch*

4655. Soon tod [toothed], soon with God. *English*

4656. The foremost hound grips the hare. *Scottish*

4657. What is soon done, soon perishes. *Latin*

Early Rising *see also* Earliness; Morning

4658. By always rising early in the morning you won't make the dawn come any sooner. *Spanish*

4659. Early rising is most conducive to health. *Latin*

4660. Early rising is the first thing that puts a man to the door. *Scottish*

4661. Early to bed and early to rise makes a man healthy, wealthy and wise. *German*

4662. Early to rise has virtues three: / 'Tis healthy, wealthy, and godlie. *English*

4663. Early up, and never the nearer. *English*

4664. Getting up early and getting married early are not regretted. *Zyryan*

4665. Go to bed with the lamb, and rise with the lark. *English*

4666. God helps the early riser. *English*

4667. He that will deceive the fox, must rise betimes. *Spanish*

4668. He that will thrive must rise at five; / He that hath thriven may lie till seven. *English*

4669. He who does not rise with the sun does not enjoy the day. *Spanish*

4670. He who rises early finds the way short. *Wolof*
4671. I wad rather hear the lark sing nor the [than] mouse cheep. *Scottish*
4672. If you rise too early, the dew will wet you. *Wolof*
4673. Out early and watch, labor and catch. *Spanish*
4674. Rise early and you will see: take pains and you will grow rich. *Portuguese*
4675. Rise when the day daws [dawns], bed when the night fa's [falls]. *Scottish*
4676. Rise with the sun and enjoy the day. *American*
4677. The cow that's first up gets the first o' the dew. *Scottish*
4678. The early bird catches the worm. *English*
4679. The first bird gets the first grain. *Danish*
4680. They that rise wi' the sun hae their wark weel begun. *Scottish*
4681. They wha are early up, and hae nae business, hae either an ill wife, an ill bed, or an ill conscience. *Scottish*
4682. To him who rises early in the morning God gives help and lends his hand. *French*
4683. To rise betimes makes one healthy, virtuous, and rich. *Latin*
4684. Too much bed makes a dull head. *English*

Ease *see also* Ability; Comfort; Dexterity; Facility; Leisure; Rest; Skill

4685. A dog's life, hunger and ease. *English*
4686. A life of ease is the most unpleasant thing in the world. *Irish*

Eating *see also* Gluttony; Obesity

4687. A fu' wame [belly] maks a strong back. *Scottish*
4688. A full belly makes a dull brain. *American (Franklin)*
4689. A full belly supports moral precepts. *Burmese*
4690. A good eater is a happy man. *American*
4691. A good meal ought to begin with hunger. *French*
4692. A kiss and a drink o' water mak but a wersh [insipid, tasteless] breakfast. *Scottish*
4693. A man must eat though every tree were a gallows. *Dutch*
4694. A more generous supper may follow a light dinner. *Latin*
4695. A rich man, when he will; a poor man, when he can. *Greek*
4696. A rich mouthful, a heavy groan. *English*
4697. A rough bane [bone] maks a fu' wame [belly]. *Scottish*
4698. A wamefu's a wamefu' [a belly full's a belly full] were but o' bear cauf [barley chaff]. *Scottish*
4699. A warmed-up dinner was never worth much. *French*
4700. After a pear, wine or the priest. *French*
4701. All goes down gutter lane. *English*
4702. An apple at night puts the dentist to flight. *American*
4703. An eating horse never foundered. *Scottish*
4704. As a man eats, so he works. *German*
4705. At table it becomes no one to be bashful. *Latin*
4706. Bad meals kill more than the best doctors ever cured. *American*
4707. Beefstakes and porter are gude belly mortar. *Scottish*
4708. Better a good dinner than a fine coat. *French*
4709. Better pay the baker than the doctor. *French*
4710. Better plays the fu' wame [belly] than the new coat. *Scottish*
4711. Broken bread and brown ale winna bide lang. *Scottish*
4712. Broken bread maks hale bairns [children]. *Scottish*
4713. Butter is gold in the morning, silver at noon, lead at night. *English*
4714. Cabbage twice cooked is death. *American*
4715. Corn him weel, he'll work the better. *Scottish*
4716. Diet cures mair [more] than the doctors. *Scottish*
4717. Diet cures more than pills. *American*
4718. Dine lightly and sup more lightly still. *Spanish*
4719. Dine lightly, and sup more plentifully; sleep high up and live long. *Spanish*
4720. Drink and frankfurters for a dime kill a man before his time. *American*
4721. Eat and drink measurely, and defy the mediciners. *English*
4722. Eat, and welcome; fast, and heartily welcome. *English*
4723. Eat at pleasure, drink by measure. *English*
4724. Eat measurelie and defy the mediciners. *Scottish*
4725. Eat the fruit and don't ask about the tree. *Turkish*
4726. Eat to live, but do not live to eat. *Greek*
4727. Eat well, drink well — and do your duty well. *American*
4728. Eat your fill, but pouch nane [pocket none], is gardener's law. *Scottish*
4729. Eaten meat is ill to pay. *Scottish*
4730. Eating and drinking takes away one's stomach. *French*
4731. Eating teaches drinking. *Italian*
4732. Eatweel's drinkweel's brother. *Scottish*
4733. Every beast but man keeps to a single dish. *American*
4734. Feed sparingly and defy the physician. *English*
4735. Feeding out o' course maks mettle out o' kind. *Scottish*
4736. Fill fu' and haud [keep] fu' maks a stark [strong] man. *Scottish*
4737. Fresh pork and new wine kill a man before his time. *American*
4738. From a great supper comes a great pain; that you may sleep lightly sup lightly. *Latin*
4739. Graceless meat maks folk fat. *Scottish*
4740. Gude kail is half meat. *Scottish*
4741. He puts his meat in an ill skin. *Scottish*
4742. He puts in a bad purse that puts in his pechan [stomach]. *Scottish*
4743. He sups ill who eats all at dinner. *French*
4744. He that eats a boll o' meal in bannocks [scones] eats a peck o' dirt. *Scottish*
4745. He that never eats much, will never be lazy. *American (Franklin)*

4746. He who eats the meat, let him pick the bone. *Spanish*

4747. He who is ashamed to eat is ashamed to live. *French*

4748. He's like a bagpipe, ne'er heard till his wame's [belly's] fu'. *Scottish*

4749. If 'twerena for the belly the back wad wear gowd [gold]. *Scottish*

4750. If I were to fast for my life, I would eat a good breakfast in the morning. *English*

4751. If you eat it for supper, you can't have it for breakfast. *Spanish*

4752. It is by the head that the cow gives the milk. *Scottish*

4753. Leave off with an appetite. *American*

4754. Let your meat close your mouth. *Scottish*

4755. Light suppers make long lives. *Scottish*

4756. Little odds between a feast and a fu' wame [belly]. *Scottish*

4757. Manners in eating count for something. *Latin*

4758. Meat and mass ne'er hindered wark. *Scottish*

4759. More die of food than famine. *English*

4760. More people are killed by supper than by the sword. *Danish*

4761. Naething sooner maks a man auld-like than sitting ill to his meat. *Scottish*

4762. Not with whom you are bred, but with whom you are fed. *Spanish*

4763. Often and little eating makes a man fat. *English*

4764. One is what he eats. *German*

4765. Quick at meat, quick at work. *English*

4766. Seven make a banquet; nine make a clamor. *Latin*

4767. Sound sleep cometh of moderate eating. *Bible*

4768. Spread the table and contention will cease. *Hebrew*

4769. Stop short of your appetite. *Latin*

4770. Stuffing hauds [keeps] out storms. *Scottish*

4771. Suppers kill mair [more] than doctor's cure. *Scottish*

4772. Teeth serve as a fence to the mouth. *Wolof*

4773. Tell me what you eat, and I will tell you what you are. *French*

4774. The back and the belly hauds [keeps] ilka ane [everyone] busy. *Scottish*

4775. The belly carries the legs. *American*

4776. The broth makes the soldier. *French*

4777. The muses starve in a cook's shop. *American (Franklin)*

4778. The pleasures of the palate treat us like Egyptian thieves who strangle those they embrace. *American*

4779. The soup makes the soldier. *French*

4780. The stomach carries the heart, and not the heart the stomach. *Spanish (Cervantes)*

4781. The way to a man's heart is through his stomach. *American*

4782. Their sole reason for living lies in their palate. *Latin*

4783. There is a good deal in a man's mode of eating. *Latin (Ovid)*

4784. There's aye a glum look where there's cauld crowdy [cold gruel]. *Scottish*

4785. There's death in the pot. *Latin*

4786. They may ken [know] by your beard what has been on your board. *Scottish*

4787. Three good meals a day is bad living. *American (Franklin)*

4788. To lengthen thy life, lessen thy meals. *American (Franklin)*

4789. We are what we eat. *American*

4790. Wersh [insipid, tasteless] parritch [oatmeal porridge], neither gude to boil, fry, nor sup cauld [cold]. *Scottish*

4791. What in your wame's [belly's] no in your testament. *Scottish*

4792. What is food to one may be poison to another. *Latin*

4793. Who eats his dinner alone must saddle his horse alone. *Spanish*

4794. Who goes to bed thirsty rises healthy. *French*

4795. Who sups well sleeps well. *Italian*

4796. You require flesh if you want to be fat. *Latin*

Eavesdropping *see also* Children and Childhood; Secrets and Secrecy

4797. He that keeks [peeps] through a keyhole may see what will vex him. *Scottish*

4798. He who listens at doors hears much more than he desires. *French*

4799. Listen at the keyhole and you'll hear news of yourself. *Scottish*

4800. Listen at the keyhole; you will hear ill of yourself as well as of your neighbor. *Spanish*

4801. Listeners seldom hear good of themselves. *American*

4802. Listeners [or eavesdroppers] hear no good of themselves. *French*

4803. Take care what you say before a wall. *Persian*

4804. Walls have ears. *English*

Economy *see also* Frugality; Profit and Loss; Saving and Spending; Thrift; Waste

4805. Cold water has to be carried; hot water has to be heated. [Don't be wasteful.] *Chinese*

4806. Don't start economizing when you are down to your last dollar. *American*

4807. Economy is the easy chair of old age. *American*

4808. Economy is the wealth of the poor and the wisdom of the rich. *French*

4809. Economy is too late at the bottom of the purse. *Latin*

4810. From small profits, and many expenses, comes a whole life of sad consequences. *American*

4811. Kail [broth] spares bread. *Scottish*

4812. Live within your means and save for a rainy day. *American*

4813. Two can live cheaper than one. *American*

Education

4814. A silly bairn [a good child] is eith to lear [easy to teach]. *Scottish*

4815. All pursuits are mean in comparison with learning. *Chinese*

4816. Bend the willow while it is young. *English*
4817. Better unborn than untaught. *Greek (Plato)*
4818. Better unfedde than un-taughte. *English*
4819. Better untaught than badly taught [or ill-taught]. *English*
4820. Between three and thirteen, thraw [bend] the woodie while it's green. *Scottish*
4821. By nature all men are alike, but by education widely different. *Chinese*
4822. Despise school and remain a fool. *English*
4823. Educated men are as much superior to the uneducated as the living are to the dead. *Greek*
4824. Education is an ornament in prosperity and a refuge in adversity. *Greek*
4825. Education is the poor man's haven. *Latin*
4826. Education leads to an immortal treasure. *Latin*
4827. Education makes the man. *American*
4828. High-born children are taught to be polite and virtuous; low-born sons are taught violence and evil. *Chinese*
4829. Highly fed and lowly taught. *English (Shakespeare)*
4830. Husbandry and letters are the two chief professions. *Chinese*
4831. If fields are left untilled the granaries will be empty; if your books are left unread your descendants will be ignorant. *Chinese*
4832. If men do not learn, they are not equal to the brutes. *Chinese*
4833. In spite of colleges and schools, the world remains a ship of fools. *American*
4834. In the instruction of sons and grandsons be sure to teach them a trade; plant the mulberry and the wild mulberry, but don't plant many flowers. *Chinese*
4835. It is only the ignorant who despise education. *Latin (Publilius Syrus)*
4836. Nothing in all the world can be done without instruction. *Chinese*
4837. Nothing is worth more than a mind well instructed. *American*
4838. Of such importance is early training. *Latin (Virgil)*
4839. Only the educated are free. *Greek*
4840. Superior men are good without instruction; medium men are good with it; but low fellows are bad even with it. *Chinese*
4841. Teach your descendants the two proper roads — literature and farming. *Chinese*
4842. Teach your son in the hall; your wife, on the pillow. *Chinese*
4843. The foundation of every society is education of its youth. *Greek*
4844. The mulberry twig is bent, when it is young. *Chinese*
4845. The roots of education are bitter, but the fruit is sweet. *Greek*
4846. Though an affair be small, it must be attended to, or it will not be completed; though a son be good, he must be instructed or he will remain ignorant. *Chinese*
4847. 'Tis education forms the common mind; / Just as the twig is bent the tree's inclined. *English (Pope)*
4848. To educate children requires a proper method. *Chinese*
4849. To instruct children and wives you must begin from the very first. *Chinese*
4850. To rear a boy without educating him is to rear an ass; to rear a girl without educating her is to rear a pig. *Chinese*
4851. Too much and too little education hinders the mind. *French*
4852. Train up a child in the way he should go, and when he is old will not depart from it. *English*
4853. Well fed, ill taught. *French*
4854. What is learned in the cradle lasts till the grave. *Hungarian*
4855. What Johnny learned, John will do. *German*
4856. What smarts teaches. *English*
4857. What we first learn we best ken [know]. *Scottish*
4858. You pay more for your schooling than your learning is worth. *English*
4859. You shall have the whetstone. [To make you sharper.] *English*

Efficacy *see* Ends and Means

Efficiency

4860. For one reward to follow up two matters. *Latin*
4861. It is a goodly thing to take two pigeons with one bean. *Latin*
4862. Keep no more cats than will catch mice. *American*
4863. Make good use of your time; it flies fast. *Latin (Ovid)*
4864. No sooner said than done. *American*
4865. To bring down two apples with one stick. *Dutch*
4866. To catch two pigeons with one bean. *English*
4867. To hit two marks with one arrow. *Persian*
4868. To kill two birds with one stone. *English*
4869. To kill two flies with one clapper. *German*
4870. To kill two flies with one slap [or flap]. *English*
4871. To kill two rabbits with one crook. *Portuguese*
4872. To make two friends with one gift. *Italian*
4873. To make two hits with one stone. *French*
4874. To stop two gaps with one bush. *English*
4875. To stop two mouths with one morsel. *English*
4876. To take two boars in one thicket. *Latin*
4877. To take two pigeons with one bean. *Italian*
4878. To whiten two walls from the same lime-pot. *Latin*
4879. Two doves with one arrow. *Persian*
4880. Weel done, soon done. *Scottish*

Effort

4881. A still bee gathers no honey. *English*
4882. As good sit still as rise up and fall. *English*
4883. Birds fly not into our mouths ready roasted. *Latin*
4884. By going gains the mill, and not by standing still. *Portuguese*
4885. By labor fire is got out of a stone. *Dutch*
4886. By trying, the Greeks got into Troy. *Greek (Theocritus)*

4887. Elbow-grease is the best polish. *English*

4888. God gives food to the birds, but they must look for it. *German*

4889. God helps them that help themselves. *American (Franklin)*

4890. Good luck enters by dint of cuffs. *Spanish*

4891. Hand and foot. [With all one's strength and resolution.] *Latin*

4892. He beat the bushes without taking the birds. *French (Rabelais)*

4893. He that gapes till he be fed will gape till he be dead. *English*

4894. He that stays in the valley shall never get over the hill. *English*

4895. He that will conquer must fight. *English*

4896. He that will to Cupar, maun [must (go)] to Cupar. *Scottish (Scott)*

4897. He that would have the fruit must climb the tree. *English*

4898. He that would have the kernel must crack the shell. *American*

4899. He who would eat the kernel must crack the shell. *Latin (Plautus)*

4900. Hope and strive is the way to thrive. *English*

4901. If the wind will not serve, take to the oars. *Latin*

4902. If you don't enter a tiger's den, you can't get his cubs. *Chinese*

4903. If you don't scale the mountain you can't view the plain. *American*

4904. Lambs don't run into the mouth of the sleeping wolf. *Danish*

4905. Naethin [nothing] is got without pains but dirt and lang [long] nails. *Scottish*

4906. No endeavor is in vain; / Its reward is in the doing. *American (Longfellow)*

4907. No one knows what he can do till he tries. *Latin (Publilius Syrus)*

4908. No pear falls into a shut mouth. *Italian*

4909. No sweet without some sweat. *English*

4910. Nothing can come of nothing. *English (Shakespeare)*

4911. Nothing comes for nothing. *Latin (Lucretius)*

4912. Nothing falls into the mouth of a sleeping fox. *French*

4913. Nothing is got without pain but dirt and long nails. *English*

4914. Put a stout heart to a stey [steep] brae. *Scottish*

4915. Roasted pigeons will not fly into one's mouth. Pennsylvania *Dutch*

4916. Seldom lies the deil [devil] dead by the dyke side. *Scottish*

4917. Short shooting loses the game. *English*

4918. Sink or swim. *English*

4919. The dog that trots about finds a bone. *Gipsy*

4920. The gods sell all good things for labor. *Greek*

4921. The mill gets by going. *English*

4922. The ripest fruit will not fall into your mouth. *Chinese*

4923. The scraping hen will get something; the crouching hen nothing. *English*

4924. They that sow in tears shall reap in joy. *Bible*

4925. Tooth and nail. *English*

4926. Try and Trust will move mountains. *English*

4927. What's worth doing is worth doing well. *American*

4928. Whatever you do, do with all your might. *Latin*

4929. When the winds fail, take to the oars. *Latin*

4930. Without pains, no gains. *English*

4931. You never know what you can do till you try. *American*

Effortlessness

4932. Going downhill no one is old. *Japanese*

4933. He that's carried down the stream need not row. *American*

Egoism

4934. He is a fool and ever shall, that writes his name upon a wall. *English*

Eloquence

4935. Eloquence avails nothing against the voice of gold. *Latin*

4936. Eloquence enough, but little wisdom. *Latin (Sallust)*

4937. Eloquence is the child of knowledge. *English*

4938. He has the gift o' gab. *Scottish*

4939. He is eloquent enough for whom truth speaks. *Latin*

4940. I can scarce believe ye, ye speak sae fair. *Scottish*

4941. It is the heart which makes men eloquent. *Latin*

4942. Many are the friends of the golden tongue. *Welsh*

4943. Often there is eloquence in a silent look. *Latin*

4944. Their own eloquence is fatal to many. *Latin*

4945. There is nothing so eloquent as a rattlesnake's tail. *American Indian*

4946. When money talks no eloquence can prevail against it. *American*

4947. Who can speak well can lie well. *Japanese*

Emotion(s) *see* Feeling

Empathy

4948. There is a road from heart to heart. *American*

Emptiness *see also* Fullness

4949. Empty hands allure no hawks. *Latin*

4950. Empty heads are always erect. *Estonian*

4951. Empty rooms make ladies foolish. *French*

4952. Empty vessels make the most sound. *Latin*

4953. It is hard for an empty bag to stand upright. *English*

4954. Nature abhors a vacuum. *Latin*

4955. The empty vessel makes the most sound. *Latin*

4956. There is plenty of sound in an empty barrel. *Russian*

4957. Toom pokes [empty bags] will strive. *Scottish*

4958. Toom [empty] bags rattle. *Scottish*

Emulation *see also* Example; Imitation

4959. Emulation begets emulation. *Latin*

4960. Emulation is the whetstone of wit [or talent]. *Latin*

4961. For emulation hath a thousand sons / That one by one pursue. *English (Shakespeare)*
4962. To emulate is to envy. *American*

Encouragement *see also* Hope

4963. A dead mouse feels no cold. *English*
4964. A flow will have an ebb. *English*
4965. A joyful evening may follow a sorrowful morning. *English*
4966. A rainy morn oft brings a pleasant day. *English*
4967. A' is na tint [all is not lost] that's in peril [or hazard]. *Scottish*
4968. A's no tint that fa's bye. *Scottish*
4969. After a storm comes a calm. *English*
4970. After black clouds, clear weather. *American*
4971. After clouds comes clear [or fair] weather. *English*
4972. After clouds sunshine. *Latin*
4973. After darkness comes light. *Latin*
4974. After high floods, low ebbs. *Dutch*
4975. After rain comes fair weather. *French*
4976. After rain comes sunshine. *American*
4977. After the evil will not a good time come? *Italian*
4978. All clouds are not rain clouds. *Latin*
4979. All is not lost that is in danger. *English*
4980. All is not yet lost that lyeth in peril. *French*
4981. Although you sit in a corner, they'll notice you. *Polish*
4982. As gude fish in the sea as ever came out o't. *Scottish*
4983. As the devil said to Noah, "It's bound to clear up." *English*
4984. Bad fortune is good for something. *French*
4985. Be the day never so long, at length cometh evensong. *English*
4986. Behind the clouds is the sun still shining. *American (Longfellow)*
4987. Better times perhaps await us who are now wretched. *Latin (Virgil)*
4988. Better [time] will be. *French*
4989. Beware of desperate steps; the darkest day, / Live till tomorrow, will have passed away. *English (Cowper)*
4990. Blaw the wind ne'er sae fast, it will lown [lower] at the last. *Scottish*
4991. By dint of going wrong, all will come right. *French*
4992. Come what come may, / Time and the hour runs through the roughest day. *English (Shakespeare)*
4993. Earth has no sorrows that Heaven cannot heal. *Irish*
4994. Every cloud has a silver lining. *American*
4995. Every flow has its ebb. *Scottish*
4996. He that is down need fear no fall. *English (Bunyan)*
4997. He who bravely endures evils, in time reaps the reward. *Latin (Plautus)*
4998. He who lies on the ground cannot fall. *Latin*
4999. Heaviness may endure for a night, but joy cometh in the morning. *English*
5000. Hold on, and wait for the grasshoppers [i.e., better times]. *Latin (Juvenal)*
5001. I'd charm her with the magic of a switch. *Scottish (Burns)*
5002. If one swain scorns you, you will soon find another. *Latin (Virgil)*
5003. If things look bad today they may look better tomorrow. *Latin*
5004. If today will not, tomorrow may. *English*
5005. Ill blows the wind that profits nobody. *English (Shakespeare)*
5006. Ill is the eve of well. *Italian*
5007. In man's most dark extremity / Oft succor dawns from heaven. *Scottish (Scott)*
5008. It is a long lane that has no turning. *English*
5009. It is at the narrowest part of the defile that the valley begins to open. *Persian*
5010. It is day still while the sun shines. *English*
5011. It is possible for a ram to kill a butcher. *English*
5012. It's always darkest before the dawn. *American*
5013. It's an ill air where nothing's to be gained. *English*
5014. It's an ill wind that blaws naebody gude. *Scottish*
5015. Let folk bode weel and do their best. *Scottish*
5016. Neither storm nor war lasts forever. *French*
5017. Never say, "die!" *Latin*
5018. Now it rains, and again the sun shines forth brightly in the heavens. *Latin*
5019. Providence has not entirely deserted us. *Latin*
5020. The darkest hour is that before dawn. *English*
5021. The day will be long, but there will be an end to it. *French (Damiens)*
5022. The first hundred years are the hardest. *American*
5023. The good time will come. *French*
5024. The longest day must have an end. *English*
5025. The longest night must end. *American*
5026. The man who has nothing has nothing to lose. *Russian*
5027. The tide never goes out so far, but it always comes back again. *English*
5028. The waur [worse] luck now, the better anither time. *Scottish*
5029. The wind keeps not always in one quarter. *English*
5030. There are other fish in the sea. *American*
5031. There is a good time coming. *Latin*
5032. There is life in a mussel. *English*
5033. There is no ill but comes for good. *Spanish*
5034. There is no month which does not return. *French*
5035. There is nothing so bad in which there is not something of good. *Hebrew*
5036. There's aye [always] life in a living man. *Scottish*
5037. There's life in a mussel although it be little. *Scottish*
5038. There's life in a mussel as long as it cheeps [squeaks]. *Scottish*
5039. There's mony a tod [fox] hunted that's no killed. *Scottish*
5040. There's remede for a' but stark dead. *Scottish*

5041. There's seldom a cake but there's more of the make. *English*
5042. They that get neist [next] best are no ill aff. *Scottish*
5043. Things at the worst will cease, or e'en climb upward / To what they were before. *English (Shakespeare)*
5044. Time and thinking tame the strongest grief. *English*
5045. Tine [lose] heart, tine a'[lose all]. *Scottish*
5046. 'Tis a long run that never turns. *English*
5047. 'Tis day still, while the sun shines. *English*
5048. What may be mayna be. *Scottish*
5049. When bale is hext, boot is next. *English*
5050. When misery is highest help is nighest. *English*
5051. When the night's darkest the dawn is nearest. *English*
5052. When the tale of bricks is doubled Moses comes. *Hebrew*
5053. When things are at the worst they will sometimes mend. *English (Byron)*
5054. Where one door shuts, another opens. *English*
5055. While life remains it is well. *Latin*
5056. With life many things are remedied. *Spanish (Cervantes)*
5057. Weeping may endure for a night, but joy cometh in the morning. *Bible*

End

5058. All things move on to their end. *French (Rabelais)*
5059. At the end of the work you may judge of the workmen. *English*
5060. End good, all good. *German*
5061. Everything has an end, and a pudding has twa [two]. *Scottish*
5062. Everything has an end, except a sausage, which has two. *Danish*
5063. Everything hath an end. *English*
5064. Great trees are long in growing, but they are rooted up in a single hour. *Latin (Quintus Curtius)*
5065. In everything consider the end. *French*
5066. Nothing is ill that ends well. *English*
5067. The end crowns all. *English (Shakespeare)*
5068. The end crowns the work. *Latin*
5069. The end of a corsair is to drown. *Italian*
5070. The end praises the life, and the evening the day. *Italian*
5071. The end praises the work. *French*
5072. The end to the work, a crown. *Russian*
5073. The evening brings a' hame. *Scottish*
5074. There is not such a long day which would not have an evening. *Hungarian*
5075. There's the end o' an auld sang. *Scottish*

Ends and Means *see also* Cause and Effect; Great and Small; Method; Remedies; Size; Trifles; Will

5076. A crafty person is consumed by other crafty people. *Zulu*
5077. A fire is not extinguished by fire. *Italian*
5078. A fog cannot be dispelled with a fan. *Japanese*
5079. A gude day's darg [a good day's work] may be done wi' a dirty spade. *Scottish*
5080. A hand may first, and then a lip be kiss'd. *English (Byron)*
5081. A hard knot requires a hard wedge. *Latin*
5082. A horse deprived of his food won't work. *Latin*
5083. A knife is soon found for bread. *Yiddish*
5084. A light breath fans the flame, a violent gust extinguishes it. *Latin*
5085. A man may lead a horse to the water, but four-and-twenty cannot gar him drink. *Scottish*
5086. A man may live upon little but he cannot live upon nothing. *American*
5087. A mole can undermine the strongest rampart. *American*
5088. A necessary evil. *Latin*
5089. A stick is soon found to beat a dog. *Dutch*
5090. A want of pence stops all your marketing. *Latin*
5091. A wedge is driven out by a wedge. *Cheremis*
5092. A whetstone, though it can't itself cut, makes tools cut. *English*
5093. All's fair in love and war. *English*
5094. All's well that ends well. *English (Shakespeare)*
5095. An onion will not produce a rose. *Latin*
5096. Bad grass does not make good hay. *English*
5097. By a single effort two ends are accomplished. *Chinese*
5098. By fair means or foul. *English*
5099. By good means or bad. *Latin*
5100. By hook or by crook. *English*
5101. Dirty water does not wash clean. *Italian*
5102. Do not spur the horse with whip but with oats. *Cheremis*
5103. Doing evil to avoid an evil cannot be good. *German*
5104. Don't appoint a crooked politician to investigate graft. *American*
5105. Don't excavate a mountain to catch a rat. *American*
5106. Don't fan the sun with a peacock's feather. *American*
5107. Drumming is not the way to catch a hare. *English*
5108. Either by might or by sleight. *English*
5109. Even by small things are great ends helped. *Latin*
5110. Every man's nose will not make a shoeing horn. *English*
5111. Every reed will not make a pipe. *English*
5112. Every soil does not bear the same fruit. *Latin*
5113. Fight fire with fire. *American*
5114. Follow the river and you will find the sea. *French*
5115. Foul water will quench fire. *English*
5116. Give the devil rope enough, and he will hang himself. *English*
5117. Go home and make a net if you desire to get fishes. *Chinese*
5118. Good pastures make fat sheep. *American*
5119. Green wood will burn if there is enough dry wood with it. *Turkish*
5120. Hard things alone will not make a wall. *Latin*
5121. He argues in vain who argues without means. *Latin*

5122. He fishes in troubled waters. [To catch gudgeons you must stir up the mud.] *Latin*

5123. He gives a pea to get a bean. *French*

5124. He is not a good mason who refuses any stone. *Italian*

5125. He must have fingers of iron that will flay the devil. *Danish*

5126. He must have iron nails that scratches a bear. *Russian*

5127. He rives [dismantles] the kirk [church] to thatch the choir. *Scottish*

5128. He that has a good head does not want for hats. *French*

5129. He that has teeth has not bread, he that has bread has not teeth. *Italian*

5130. He that has twa [two] herds is able to get the third. *Scottish*

5131. He that wad eat the kernel maun [must] crack the nut. *Scottish*

5132. He that wants to strike a dog ne'er wants a stick. *Scottish*

5133. He that will have the kernel, must crack the shell. *English*

5134. He that will take the bird must not scare it. *English*

5135. He that would have eggs must endure the cackling of hens. *English*

5136. He who has no mother sucks his grandmother. *Wolof*

5137. He who wants to shoot the general must first shoot his horse. *Japanese*

5138. He who would catch fish must not mind getting wet. *American*

5139. He who would have a hare for breakfast must hunt overnight. *American*

5140. However high the tree, the shortest axe can reach its trunk. *Chinese*

5141. I don't care how, as long as I get it. *Latin*

5142. If I cannot move the powers above, Acheron itself shall be appealed to. *Latin (Virgil)*

5143. If I had no plough, you would have had no corn. *Greek*

5144. If the cat had wings she'd choke all the birds in the air. *American*

5145. If the lion's skin cannot, the fox's shall. *English*

5146. If the plough cannot reach it, the harrow can. *Chinese*

5147. If there are no horses, saddle the dogs. *Arabic*

5148. If we see a dog there is no stone and if we see a stone there is no dog. *Tamil*

5149. If you cut down the woods, you'll catch the wolf. *American*

5150. If you don't crack the shell, you can't eat the nut. *Russian*

5151. If you want to clear the stream get the hog out of the spring. *American*

5152. Ill beef ne'er made gude broo. *Scottish*

5153. Ill-gotten gain brings loss. *Greek (Euripides)*

5154. Ill-gotten goods do no good. *German*

5155. Ill-gotten goods seldom prosper. *English*

5156. In strife who inquires whether stratagem or courage was used? *Latin (Virgil)*

5157. It is difficult to fly without wings. *Latin (Plautus)*

5158. It is ill baking without meal or water. *English*

5159. It is ill to make a blown horn of a tod's [fox's] tail. *English*

5160. It takes a good many mice to kill a cat. *American*

5161. It's the bait that lures, not the fisherman or the reel. *American*

5162. Ivory does not come from a rat's mouth. *Chinese*

5163. Jack will never make a gentleman. *English*

5164. Kill two birds with one stone. *American*

5165. Lay on more wood; ashes give money. *English*

5166. Learning has sour roots, but pleasant fruits. *Latin*

5167. Let him alone with the Saint's Bell, and give him rope enough. *English*

5168. Let not a god interfere unless where a god's assistance is necessary. *Latin (Horace)*

5169. Little chips kindle the fire, and great logs sustain it. *Portuguese*

5170. Little dogs start the hare, the great get her. *English*

5171. Mony [many] ways to kill a dog though ye dinna hang him. *Scottish*

5172. Ne'er do ill that gude [good] may come o 't. *Scottish*

5173. No gains without pains. *English*

5174. No means, no market. *English*

5175. Often it is better to take the indirect way rather than the direct. *Latin*

5176. One arrow does not bring down two birds. *Turkish*

5177. One beats the bush and another catcheth the bird. *English*

5178. One gets nothing for nothing. *French*

5179. One heat another heat expels. *English (Shakespeare)*

5180. One wedge drives out another. *Russian*

5181. Out of nothing nothing is made. *Latin*

5182. Peace is obtained by war. *Latin (Cornelius Nepos)*

5183. Pick up the hen and you can gather all the chickens. *Ashanti*

5184. Pour not water on a drowning mouse. *English*

5185. Pray don't burn my house to roast your eggs. *American (Franklin)*

5186. Quietly, if you can; if not, by any means. *Latin*

5187. Restive horses must be roughly dealt with. *English*

5188. Set a sprat to catch a mackerel. *English*

5189. Set a thief to catch a thief. *English*

5190. Set hard heart against hard hap. *English*

5191. Shaving is better than plucking the hair. *Wolof*

5192. Show the fatted calf but not the thing that fattened him. *Irish*

5193. Some Cupid kills with arrows, some with traps. *English (Shakespeare)*

5194. That which is good for the back is good for the head. *English*

5195. The bust of Mercury cannot be cut from every wood. *Latin*

5196. The cat would eat fish, but is loth to wet her feet. *English (Chaucer)*

5197. The end doesn't justify the means. *American*

5198. The end justifies the means. *American*

5199. The end of fishing is not angling, but catching. *English*

5200. The finest edge is made with the blunt whetstone. *English (Lyly)*

5201. The fox barks not when he would steal the lamb. *English (Shakespeare)*

5202. The grape is not ripened by the rays of the moon. *Latin*

5203. The honest man lives according to his means. *American*

5204. The little dogs find, but the big ones get the hare. *Italian*

5205. The noisy fowler catches no birds. *English*

5206. The oak is felled by many strokes. *Latin*

5207. The result justifies the deed. *Latin*

5208. The right way leads to the right place. *American*

5209. The rough net is not the best catcher of burdes. *English (Heywood)*

5210. The sacrifice of an ox will not bring us all we want. *Latin*

5211. The well is deep, the rope is short. *Arabic*

5212. The workmanship surpassed the material. *Latin*

5213. There are many ways of skinning a cat. *American*

5214. There are more ways to kill a dog than hanging. *English*

5215. There are more ways to the wood than one. *English*

5216. There is more than one way out of the woods. *American*

5217. There's mair [more] ways than ane o' keepin' craws frae [from] the stack. *Scottish*

5218. There's no making a good arrow of a pig's tail. *Spanish*

5219. There's no making a sieve of an ass's tail. *Greek*

5220. Though little fire grows great with little wind, / Yet extreme gusts will blow out fire and all. *English (Shakespeare)*

5221. Throw a brick to produce a gem. *Chinese*

5222. Throwing your cap at a bird is not the way to catch it. *English*

5223. To a boiling pot flies come not. *English*

5224. To a rogue a rogue and a half. *French*

5225. To cast oil into the fire is not the way to quench it. *English*

5226. To cure evil by evil. *Latin*

5227. To dig with golden spades. [To waste means.] *Latin*

5228. To fright a bird is not the way to catch her. *English*

5229. To hand over the bow is to hand over the arrow. *Chinese*

5230. To make any gain some outlay is necessary. *Latin (Plautus)*

5231. To obtain that which is just we must ask that which is unjust. *Latin*

5232. To put a racehorse to the plough. *English*

5233. To remove the hairs from a horse's tail, one by one must be plucked out. *Latin*

5234. To repel force by force. *Latin*

5235. To stop the hand is the way to stop the mouth. *Chinese*

5236. To throw the sausage to catch a flitch of bacon. *German*

5237. Two dry sticks will kindle a green one. *English*

5238. Use the little to get the big. *Chinese*

5239. What hands have built, hands can pull down. *German (Schiller)*

5240. When a dog comes a stone cannot be found; when a stone is found the dog does not come. *Telugu*

5241. When a man will throw at a dog he soon finds a stone. *German*

5242. When the end is lawful, the means are also lawful. *Latin*

5243. Where you cannot climb over, you must crawl under. *Irish*

5244. Whether you boil snow or pound it you can have but water of it. *English*

5245. Who asks whether the enemy was defeated by strategy or valor? *Latin (Virgil)*

5246. Who desires the end, desires the means. *French*

5247. Who wants to hit a dog will find a stick. *Polish*

5248. Whoso is desirous of beating a dog will readily find a stick. *French*

5249. With a rogue you must catch a rogue. *German*

5250. With a thief one catches a thief. *Dutch*

5251. Without oars you cannot cross in a boat. *Japanese*

5252. Without pains, no prize. *German*

5253. Would you shear a donkey for wool! *Latin*

5254. Yelping curs will rouse mastiffs. *Scottish*

5255. You can't beat something with nothing. *American*

5256. You can't catch trout with dry trousers. *American*

5257. You can't get something for nothing. *American*

5258. You can't go far in a row-boat without oars. *American*

5259. You can't make a drum from a ratskin. *Omani*

5260. You can't make a good cloak out of a bad cloth. *American*

5261. You can't make a horn of a pig's tail. *English*

5262. You can't make a rope of sand. *American*

5263. You can't make bricks without straw. *American*

5264. You can't make horn of a pig's tail. *English*

5265. You can't put out a fire with oil. *American*

5266. You can't tame a bear with a whistle. *American*

5267. You cannot catch a fox with a bait. *Latin*

5268. You cannot draw oil from a wall. *French*

5269. You cannot get blood from a turnip. *Italian*

5270. You cannot make a good hunting horn of a pig's tail. *Danish*

5271. You cannot make a sieve out of an ass's tail. *German*

5272. You cannot make a silk purse out of a sow's ear. *English*

5273. You cannot make a sparrow-hawk out of a buzzard. *French*

5274. You cannot make omelettes [or little cakes] without breaking eggs. *Spanish*

5275. You cannot make velvet of a sow's ear. *English*

5276. You cannot trade without capital. *Chinese*

5277. You cannot write in the chimney with charcoal. *Russian*

5278. You catch no hares with drums. *French*

5279. You may lose a fly to catch a trout. *American*

5280. You must crack the nuts before you can eat the kernel. *Irish*

5281. You must endure what is painful to secure that which is profitable. *Latin (Publilius Syrus)*

5282. You must have good luck to catch hares with a drum. *Danish*

5283. You must lose a fly, to catch a trout. *English*

5284. You must risk a small fish to catch a big one. *French*

5285. You must wet your fingers to take up salt. *Chinese*

5286. You seek wool from an ass. *Greek*

Endurance *see also* Perseverance

5287. A man may bear till his back breaks. *English*

5288. As long runs the fox as he feet hath. *Scottish*

5289. Every trial is to be overcome by endurance. *Latin (Virgil)*

5290. He that can't endure the bad, will not live to see the good. *Yiddish*

5291. He that endures is not overcome. *English (Chaucer)*

5292. He that shall endure unto the end, the same shall be saved. *Bible*

5293. He that tholes [endures] overcomes. *Scottish*

5294. Nothing befalls any man which he is not fitted to endure. *Greek*

5295. There is no greater misfortune than not to be able to endure misfortune. *American*

5296. To endure what is unendurable is true endurance. *Japanese*

Enemies *see also* Friends and Enemies

5297. A man's foes shall be they of his own household. *Bible*

5298. An enemy is a perpetual spy. *American*

5299. An enemy never sleeps. *French*

5300. Be my enemy, but go to my mill. *Spanish*

5301. Be thine enemy an ant, see in him an elephant. *Turkish*

5302. Better a thousand enemies outside the house than one inside. *Arabic*

5303. Do not speak ill of an enemy, but think it. *Latin*

5304. Don't believe your enemy even when he's telling the truth. *American*

5305. Enemies' promises were made to be broken. *Greek (Aesop)*

5306. Enmity is anger watching the opportunity for revenge. *Latin*

5307. Even from a foe a man may learn wisdom. *Greek*

5308. Every wise man dreadeth his enemy. *English (Chaucer)*

5309. Fortune can give no greater advantage than discord among the enemy. *Latin*

5310. Four things everyone has more of than he knows — sins, debts, years and foes. *Persian*

5311. He that gives honor to his enemy is like to an ass. *Hebrew*

5312. He who feeds a wolf strengthens his enemy. *Danish*

5313. He who surpasses or subdues mankind, / Must look down on the hate of those below. *English (Byron)*

5314. His must be a very wretched fortune who has no enemy. *Latin*

5315. If thine enemy hunger, feed him; if he thirst, give him drink: for in so doing thou shalt heap coals of fire on his head. *Bible*

5316. If you have no enemies it is a sign fortune has forgot you. *English*

5317. It is a most miserable lot to be without an enemy. *Latin (Publilius Syrus)*

5318. Learn even from an enemy. *Latin*

5319. Little enemies and little wounds must not be despised. *German*

5320. Love your enemies, for they tell you your faults. *American (Franklin)*

5321. Love your enemy — but don't put a gun in his hand. *American*

5322. No man is without enemies. *Arabic*

5323. No tears are shed when an enemy dies. *Latin*

5324. Of enemies the fewer the better. *Spanish*

5325. Once an enemy, always an enemy. *English*

5326. Rejoice not over the greatest enemy being dead. *Bible*

5327. The body of a dead enemy always smells sweet. *Latin*

5328. The enemy who is avaricious, subject to passion, unruly, treacherous, violent, fearful, unsteady or foolish, is easily defeated. *Sanskrit*

5329. The fox thrives best when he is most cursed. *English*

5330. There is no little enemy. *French*

5331. Water sleeps, the enemy wakes. *Turkish*

5332. When the angry dogs bark, you know you're getting places. *American*

5333. Your enemy makes you wise. *Italian*

Enjoyment *see also* Pleasure

5334. Enjoyment is the grace of God. *Hindi*

5335. Even the heart has its boundaries. *Japanese*

5336. Every blade of grass has its share of the dews of heaven. *Chinese*

Enough *see* Sufficiency

Enterprise *see* Effort

Enthusiasm *see also* Zeal

5337. He freezes who does not burn. *Latin*

5338. Nothing great was ever achieved without enthusiasm. *American*

Envy *see also* Ambition; Jealousy

5339. A brave man is able to bear envy. *Latin*
5340. A wise man cares not for what he cannot have. *English*
5341. After honor and state, follow envy and hate. *Dutch*
5342. An envious man grows lean at another's fatness. *Latin (Horace)*
5343. As a moth gnaws at a garment, so does envy consume a man. *American*
5344. As rust corrupts iron, so envy corrupts man. *Greek*
5345. Be jealous of your neighbor, but don't envy him. *Egyptian*
5346. Envy and wrath shorten the life. *Bible*
5347. Envy does not enter an empty house. *Danish*
5348. Envy feeds on the living; it ceases when they are dead. *American*
5349. Envy goes beyond avarice. *French*
5350. Envy has no holidays. *Latin*
5351. Envy is an early riser. *Danish*
5352. Envy is blind, and is only clever in depreciating the virtues of others. *Latin (Livy)*
5353. Envy is left-handed praise. *American*
5354. Envy is the enemy to honor. *Latin*
5355. Envy is the sincerest form of flattery. *American*
5356. Envy is the sorrow of fools. *German*
5357. Envy ne'er does a good turn but when it means an ill ane [one]. *Scottish*
5358. Envy never enriched any man. *English*
5359. Envy never has a holiday. *Latin*
5360. Envy never rests. *Arabic*
5361. Envy no man. *Latin*
5362. Envy shoots at others and wounds herself. *Swedish*
5363. Envy slays itself by its own arrows. *Greek*
5364. Envy waits on boasting. *Latin*
5365. Even a beggar envies another beggar. *Greek (Hesiod)*
5366. He who goes unenvied shall not be admired. *Greek (Aeschylus)*
5367. I would rather my enemies envy me than I envy them. *Latin*
5368. If envy were a fever, all the world would be ill. *Danish*
5369. It is the nature of the unfortunate to be spiteful, and to envy those who are well to do. *Latin (Plautus)*
5370. Money is the most envied, but the least enjoyed; health is the most enjoyed, but the least envied. *American*
5371. Nothing can allay the rage of biting envy. *Latin*
5372. Nothing sharpens sight like envy. *American*
5373. Our neighbor's crop seems better than our own. *Latin*
5374. The ass went seeking for horns and lost his ears. *Arabic*
5375. The brave or the fortunate can afford to laugh at envy. *Latin (Publilius Syrus)*
5376. The crow went to learn the ways of the goose, but lost its own. *Behar*
5377. The dog of envy barks at a celebrity. *American*
5378. The dog with the bone is always in danger. *American*
5379. The envious die, but envy never. *French*
5380. The envious grow thin at others' prosperity. *Latin*
5381. The envious heart procures mickle smart. *Scottish*
5382. The ox longs for the gaudy trappings of the horse; the lazy packhorse would fain plough. *Latin (Horace)*
5383. The toothless man envies those who can eat well. *Latin*
5384. To all apparent beauties blind, each blemish strikes an envious mind. *American (Franklin)*
5385. You may envy everyone, but no one envies you. *Latin (Martius)*
5386. Your pot broken seems better than my whole one. *Spanish*

Equality

5387. A mare is not fit to go into battle. *Chinese*
5388. All fingers are equal in the clenched fist. *Russian*
5389. All men are created equal. *American*
5390. Ask me what is my virtue, not what is the color of my skin. *Arabic*
5391. Equality begins in the grave. *French*
5392. Equality breeds no war. *Greek*
5393. Every man is as good as his neighbor. *American*
5394. Freedom without equal opportunity is a myth. *American*
5395. In the bath-house all are equal. *Yiddish*
5396. It is good that equals consort together. *Efik*
5397. Six feet of earth make all men of one size. *American*
5398. The wise man marries his equal; the fool marries above or beneath him. *American*
5399. The world belongs to the whole world. *Japanese*
5400. We are all born equal and distinguished only by virtue. *Latin*
5401. Wire tie wire. [Equally matched.] *Belizean Creole*

Equanimity

5402. A full cup must be carried steadily. *English*
5403. In hard times, no less than in prosperity, preserve equanimity. *Latin*

Era

5404. Accusing the times is but excusing ourselves. *English*

Error(s) *see also* Accidents

5405. A clock that stands still is better than one that goes wrong. *Yiddish*
5406. A known mistake is better than an unknown truth. *Arabic*

5407. Any man may make a mistake; none but a fool will persist in it. *Latin*

5408. Erring is not cheating. *German*

5409. Error cannot be defended but by error. *English*

5410. Error is always in haste. *English*

5411. Error is no payment. *Italian*

5412. Error is prolific. *Latin*

5413. Error is the force that welds men together. *Russian (Tolstoy)*

5414. Error, though blind herself, sometimes brings forth children that can see. *American*

5415. Every age confutes old errors and begets new. *English*

5416. Folly is the product of all countries and ages. *English*

5417. He who is wrong fights against himself. *Egyptian*

5418. Him who errs forgive once but never twice. *Spanish*

5419. I can pardon everybody's mistakes but my own. *Latin*

5420. It is a good man that never stumbles, and a good wife that never grumbles. *American*

5421. It is disgraceful to stumble against the same stone twice. *Greek*

5422. It is human to err. *Latin*

5423. It is not allowed a man to err twice in war. *Latin*

5424. Love truth, but pardon error. *French*

5425. Mak ae [one] wrang step, an' doun ye gae. *Scottish*

5426. Man is the child of error. *Arabic*

5427. Mistakes occur through haste, never through doing a thing leisurely. *Chinese*

5428. No horse is so good, but that he will at times stumble. *Latin*

5429. No one who lives in error is free. *Greek*

5430. Not every error is not to be called folly. *Latin*

5431. One error breeds more. *American*

5432. The best brewer sometimes makes bad beer. *German*

5433. The best man stumbles. *American*

5434. The last error shall be worse than the first. *Bible*

5435. The shortest errors are always the best. *French*

5436. The wisest of the wise may err. *Greek*

5437. To err is human, but to persevere in error is the act of a fool. *Latin (Cicero)*

5438. To err is human, to repent divine; to persist devilish. *American (Franklin)*

5439. Truth belongs to the man, error to his age. *German (Goethe)*

5440. We learn by trial and error. *American*

5441. What man is not guilty of slight errors? *Chinese*

5442. When the learned man errs, he errs with a learned error. *Arabic*

5443. Who errs and mends, commends himself to God. *Spanish*

5444. Who errs in the tens errs in the thousands. *Italian*

5445. Ye hae ca'd your pigs to an ill market. *Scottish*

Escape

5446. He escaped from the smoke and fell into the fire. *Zyryan*

5447. He has not escaped who drags his chain. *French*

5448. He who flees will fight again. *Latin (Tertullian)*

5449. The horse that draws his halter has not quite escaped. *English*

5450. The mouse that has but one hole is quickly taken. *Latin*

5451. There is no need of spurs when the horse is running away. *Latin (Publilius Syrus)*

Estrangement

5452. A broken friendship may be soldered, but will never be sound. *English*

5453. Better kind fremit, than fremit kindred. [Better kind strangers than estranged kindred.] *Scottish*

Evidence *see also* Proof

5454. I believe in death, because of the bones. *Wolof*

5455. The rat betrayed by his own track perishes. *Latin*

Evil *see also* Badness; Good and Evil; Wickedness

5456. A house is subject to three evils—rain, a bad woman and smoke. *Latin*

5457. A strong remedy for evils is ignorance of them. *Latin*

5458. All spirits are enslaved which serve things evil. *English (Shelley)*

5459. An evil lesson is soon learned. *American*

5460. An evil life is a kind of death. *Spanish*

5461. Better to have a red face than a black heart. *Portuguese*

5462. By a brave endurance of unavoidable evils, we conquer them. *Latin*

5463. By excess evil, evil dies. *English*

5464. Doing evil is fun, but it's cheaper to be good. *American*

5465. Evil boomerangs: it strikes your conscience. *American*

5466. Evil conduct is the root of misery. *Chinese*

5467. Evil enters like a needle and spreads like an oak tree. *Ethiopian*

5468. Evil is fittest to consort with evil. *Latin*

5469. Evil shall have that evil well deserves. *English (Chaucer)*

5470. He would sink a ship freighted with crucifixes. *Provencal*

5471. In every company there is some evil person, par Dieu. *English (Chaucer)*

5472. In the world it is only the heart of man that is evil. *Chinese*

5473. Never do evil that good may come of it. *Italian*

5474. No one becomes at once completely vile. *Latin*

5475. No time is too brief for the wicked to accomplish evil. *Latin*

5476. Of evils we must choose the least. *Greek*

5477. One evil breeds another. *Latin*

5478. Pleasant are the beginnings of evil, but the end is sad. *Polish*

5479. Recompense to no man evil for evil. *Bible*
5480. Submit to the present evil, lest a greater one befall you. *Latin*
5481. Sufficient unto the day is the evil thereof. *Bible*
5482. That which is evil is soon learned. *English*
5483. The authors of great evils know best how to remove them. *Latin*
5484. The best-known evils are the most tolerable. *Latin*
5485. The devil gets up to the belfry by the vicar's skirts. *English*
5486. The devil is a busy bishop in his own diocese. *English*
5487. The evil which issues from thy mouth falls into thy bosom. *Spanish*
5488. The worse the evil, the more calmly we face it. *Italian*
5489. There is no evil without its compensation. *Latin (Seneca)*
5490. There is no greater evil than not to be able to bear what is evil. *Latin*

Exactness *see* Accuracy; Precision

Exaggeration *see also* Boasting; Lies and Lying

5491. Don't gild the lily. *American*
5492. Every fish that escapes appears greater than it is. *Turkish*
5493. He makes a lion of a mouse. *Latin*
5494. Present fears / Are less than horrible imaginings. *English (Shakespeare)*
5495. The cow that was eaten by the wolf was the one that gave most milk. *Russian*
5496. The wolf is always said to be more terrible than he is. *English*
5497. Things rumored lessen in importance as they assume reality. *Latin*
5498. To express a matter the size of a needle as if it were the size of a cudgel. *Japanese*
5499. To make a pitchfork out of a needle. *Polish*
5500. We always weaken whatever we exaggerate. *French*
5501. You make a mountain of a mole-hill. *English*
5502. You make an elephant of a mouse. *Latin*

Example *see also* Preachers and Preaching

5503. A good example is the best sermon. *English*
5504. Ae [one] scabbit [frightened] sheep will smit [infect] a hail hirsel [a whole flock]. *Scottish*
5505. An ill lesson is easy learned. *Scottish*
5506. Ane [one] will gar [make] a hundred lee [lie]. *Scottish*
5507. As the auld [old] cock craws the young cock learns; aye tak care what ye do afore the bairns [children]. *Scottish*
5508. As the old birds sing, so the young ones twitter. *German*
5509. As the old cock crows, so crows the young. *English*
5510. As the old cock crows, the young one learns. *Irish*
5511. As the old hen crows, so crow her chicks. *American*
5512. Before an ill wife be gude, even if she was a' turn'd to tongue. *Scottish*
5513. By looking at squinting people you learn to squint. *Latin (Ovid)*
5514. Do as I say, not as I do. *American*
5515. Do as the friar saith, not as he doth. *Spanish*
5516. Easy learning the cat the road to the kirn [churn]. *Scottish*
5517. Example is the greatest of all seducers. *French*
5518. Follow example in drawing your calabash. *Chinese*
5519. Follow the good and learn to be better. *American*
5520. From the old ox the young one learns to plough. *English*
5521. Gambling sire, gambling son. *English*
5522. He does not sing his father's songs [i.e., does not follow his father's example]. *Latin*
5523. He preaches best who lives best. *English*
5524. He preaches well who lives well. *Spanish (Cervantes)*
5525. He teaches me to be good that does me good. *English*
5526. If ae [one] sheep loup [leap] the dyke a' the rest will follow. *Scottish*
5527. If the prior gambles, what can you expect of the friars? *Spanish*
5528. If ye gang [lit., go] a year wi' a cripple ye'll limp at the end o 't. *Scottish*
5529. Live near a lame man, and you will soon learn to limp. *Latin*
5530. Long is the road to learning by precepts, but short and successful by examples. *Latin (Seneca)*
5531. Mocking's catching. *Scottish*
5532. Nothing more contagious than a bad example. *French*
5533. Practice what you preach. *American*
5534. Precept begins, example accomplishes. *French*
5535. Precepts invite, but examples drag us to conclusions. *Latin*
5536. Precepts lead, examples draw. *Latin*
5537. Profit by good example. *Latin*
5538. Setting too good an example is a kind of slander seldom forgiven; 'tis scandalum magnatum. *American*
5539. The best mode of instruction is to practice what we preach. *English*
5540. The crab instructs its young, "Walk straight ahead — like me." *Hindi*
5541. The example of good men is visible philosophy. *English*
5542. The misfortune of the foolish is a warning to the wise. *Latin*
5543. The path of precept is long; that of example short. *Latin*
5544. The whole community is ordered by the king's example. *Latin*
5545. The young cock crows as he hears the old one. *English*
5546. The young pig grunts like the old sow. *English*
5547. They do more harm by their evil example than by their actual sin. *Latin*

5548. To follow a man like his shadow. *Latin*
5549. Vice grows to be a custom through the example of a prince. *Latin*
5550. We live more by example than by reason. *Latin*
5551. What is shown by example, men think they may justly do. *Latin*
5552. What the eye has seen, the hand may do. *Hindi*
5553. Ye're like Brackley's tup [ram]—ye follow the lave [rest]. *Scottish*
5554. You cannot show the wolf to a bad dog. *French*

Excellence *see also* Ability; Perfection; Quality; Skill

5555. Either dance well or quit the ballroom. *Greek*

Exception

5556. All but saves many a man. *Danish*
5557. All would be well if it were not for the "buts." *German*
5558. Almost and hardly save many a lie. *English*
5559. Almost kills no man. *Danish*
5560. Almost never killed a fly. *German*
5561. Almost was never hanged. *English*
5562. The exception proves [i.e., tests] the rule. *Latin*
5563. There's an exception to every rule. *American*

Excess *see also* Burdens; Extremes; Moderation

5564. A baited cat may grow as fierce as a lion. *English*
5565. A bow o'erbent will weaken. *English*
5566. A lengthy sermon is intolerable. *Latin*
5567. A little more breaks the horse's back. *American*
5568. A little wind kindles; much puts out the fire. *English*
5569. A man may love his house weel, and no ride on the riggin [roof] o 't. *Scottish*
5570. A' owers [overs] are ill, but ower the water and ower the hill. *Scottish*
5571. All excess turns into vice. *Latin*
5572. All work and no play makes Jack a dull boy. *English*
5573. Better no doctor at all than three. *Polish*
5574. Cherries are bitter to the glutted blackbird. *American*
5575. Cold cools the love that kindles over hot. *Scottish*
5576. Double-charging will break even a cannon. *English*
5577. Enough, even to loathing. *Latin*
5578. Even honey occasions satiety. *American*
5579. Even sugar itself may spoil a good dish. *English*
5580. Even too much praise is a burden. *English*
5581. Every excess becomes a vice. *Latin*
5582. Excess in anything becomes a vice. *Latin*
5583. Excess of delight palls the appetite. *English*
5584. For everything in excess is opposed to nature. *Greek (Hippocrates)*
5585. Great virtues driven to excess become great faults. *American*
5586. He goes beyond the bounds. *Latin*
5587. He has mair [more] floor than he has flail for. *Scottish*
5588. He that embraces too much holds nothing fast. *French*
5589. He that exceeds the commission must answer for it at his own cost. *German*
5590. He who blows his nose too hard makes it bleed. *English*
5591. He who does all he may, does not do well. *Italian*
5592. He who does too much often does little. *Italian*
5593. He who pitches too high won't get through his song. *English*
5594. He's crackt with larnin'. *Scottish*
5595. Honey cloys. *Latin*
5596. I cannot find you baith [both] tales and ears. *Scottish*
5597. If the sailors become too numerous the ship sinks. *Arabic*
5598. In excess nectar poisons. *Hindi*
5599. It bursts the bag. *Italian*
5600. It is not the burden but the over-burden that kills the beast. *English*
5601. It is the superfluous things for which men sweat. *Latin*
5602. It is vain to do that by a multitude which a few can accomplish. *Latin*
5603. It's no the burden, but the owerburden, that kills the beast. *Scottish*
5604. Keep no more cats than will catch mice. *English*
5605. Leave off the play [or jest] when it is merriest. *Spanish*
5606. Make a bridge of gold for the flying enemy. *English*
5607. Make not thy tail broader than thy wings. [Don't have more attendants or servants than you need.] *English*
5608. Many doctors, death accomplished. *Czech*
5609. Many irons in the fire; some will cool. *English*
5610. More than enough is too much. *English*
5611. No feast to a miser's. *English*
5612. Nothing in excess. *Greek (Solon)*
5613. Nothing too much; no excess. *Greek*
5614. O'er meikle o' ae thing [too much of one thing] is gude for naething. *Scottish*
5615. Often he who does too much, does little. *Italian*
5616. One can have too much of a good thing. *German*
5617. One may be surfeited with eating tarts. *French*
5618. One's too few, three's too many. *English*
5619. Overdoing is doing nothing to the purpose. *English*
5620. Overdone is as bad as underdone. *Japanese*
5621. Overdone is worse than underdone. *American*
5622. Ower [over] hot, ower cauld [cold]. *Scottish*
5623. Possession is the grave of pleasure. *English*
5624. Satiety causes disgust; abundance begets indifference. *American*
5625. Satiety has killed more men than hunger. *Latin*
5626. Stretch a bow to the very full, / And you will wish you had stopped in time. *Chinese (Laotse)*

5627. Superfluities do not hurt. *Latin*

5628. The ape claspeth her young so long that at last she killeth them. *English*

5629. The ass endures the load but not the overload. *Spanish*

5630. The child hates him who gives it all it wants. *Wolof*

5631. The cord breaketh at last by the weakest pull. *Spanish*

5632. The foot which is with walking sore / But worse becomes by walking more. *Welsh*

5633. The full stomach turns from the honey of Hybla. *Latin (Petronius)*

5634. The last drop makes the cup run over. *English*

5635. The mill that is always grinding grinds coarse and fine together. *Irish*

5636. The pot that boils too much loses flavor. *Portuguese*

5637. They prayed so hard for good weather that drought set in. *Russian*

5638. They were never fain that fidg'd [shrugged their shoulders], nor fu' that licket dishes. *Scottish*

5639. Through much enduring come things that cannot be endured. *Latin*

5640. 'Tis the last straw that breaks the camel's back. *English*

5641. To beat the dog already punished. *Latin*

5642. To go beyond is as wrong as to fall short. *Chinese (Confucius)*

5643. To go beyond the bounds. *Latin*

5644. To kick a man when he is down. *English*

5645. To kill with kindness. *English*

5646. To overshoot the mark. *Latin*

5647. To pour water on a drowned mouse. *English*

5648. Too clever by half. *English*

5649. Too good is stark naught. *English*

5650. Too good to be true. *English*

5651. Too hasty to be a parish clerk. *English*

5652. Too hot to handle. *American*

5653. Too hot to hold. *English*

5654. Too many boatmen will run the boat up to the top of a mountain. *Japanese*

5655. Too many cooks make the porridge too salty. *Dutch*

5656. Too many cooks spoil the broth. *English*

5657. Too many tirewomen make the bride ill-dressed. *Spanish*

5658. Too much breaks the bag. *Spanish*

5659. Too much consulting confounds. *English*

5660. Too much is stark nought. *Welsh*

5661. Too much is worse than too little. *Japanese*

5662. Too much of a good thing is not good. *English*

5663. Too much of a thing is good for nothing. *American*

5664. Too much of a thing nauseates. *Latin*

5665. Too much of anything is bad. *Latin (Terence)*

5666. Too much of one thing is good for nothing. *English*

5667. Too much of ought / Is good for nought. *English*

5668. Too much pudding will choke a dog. *English*

5669. Too much spoileth; too little is nothing. *English*

5670. Too much taking heed is loss. *English*

5671. Too much water drowns the miller. *English*

5672. Too too will in two. [If something is bent too far it will break.] *English*

5673. Too wise to live long. *English*

5674. Two fools in one house is over many. *Scottish*

5675. Two hungry [insufficient] meals make the third a glutton. *English*

5676. Very slight violence will break that which has once been cracked. *Latin (Ovid)*

5677. When the wame's [belly's] fu' the banes [bones] wad [would] be at rest. *Scottish*

5678. When the well is full it will run over. *Scottish*

5679. Where does the ant die except in sugar? *Malay*

5680. Who does too much, often does little. *English*

5681. With so many roosters crowing, the sun never comes up. *Italian*

Exchange

5682. Exchange is no robbery. *English*

5683. Fair exchange is no robbery. *American*

Excuses

5684. A bad excuse is better than none (at all). *English*

5685. A bad reaper never gets a good sickle. *Gaelic*

5686. A bad workman never gets a good tool. *English*

5687. A bad workman quarrels with his tools. *American*

5688. A fine shot never killed a bird. *Italian*

5689. A poor dancer will blame her gown. *Polish*

5690. A poor excuse is better than none. *American*

5691. A' things wytes [blames] that no weel fares. *Scottish*

5692. An ass may account for, but can't excuse his conduct. *American*

5693. An excuse which was uncalled for becomes an obvious accusation. *Latin*

5694. An ill laborer quarrels with his tools. *English*

5695. Any excuse is better than none. *American*

5696. Any excuse is good provided it avails. *Italian*

5697. Any excuse will serve when one has not a mind to do a thing. *Italian*

5698. Bad excuses are worse than none. *English*

5699. Every sluggard has his excuse. *American*

5700. Every vice has its excuse ready. *Latin (Publilius Syrus)*

5701. Find a sluggard without a scuse, and find a hare without a muse [an escape passage]. *English*

5702. He is a bad shot who cannot find an excuse. *German*

5703. He that does amiss never lacks excuses. *Italian*

5704. He who does not know how to dance says the floor is uneven. *Egyptian*

5705. He who does not want to pray says the door of the mosque is closed. *Arabic*

5706. He who excuses himself, accuses himself. *French*

5707. How pitiable is he who cannot excuse himself! *Latin*

5708. I readily find excuses for myself. *Latin*

5709. If you excuse yourself, you accuse yourself. *American*

5710. Make excuses for another, never for yourself. *Latin*

5711. No crime lacks justification. *Zulu*

5712. One unable to dance blames the unevenness of the floor. *Malay*

5713. Stumbling is the excuse of a lame horse. *Hindi*

5714. The archer that shoots ill has a lie ready. *Spanish*

5715. The cunning fox has a bag of excuses. *American*

5716. The girl who can't dance says the band can't play. *Yiddish*

5717. The losing horse blames the saddle. *English*

5718. The singer covers up the wrong note with a cough. *German*

5719. The wrongdoer is never without excuses. *American*

5720. Where no good reason can avail her, / Be sure excuses will not fail her. *Welsh*

5721. "Who can help sickness?" quoth the drunken wife, when she lay in the gutter. *English*

Exercise *see also* Fitness; Health

5722. After a meal you will stand or walk a mile. *Italian*

5723. After dinner rest; after supper walk. *Venetian*

5724. After dinner set awhile, after supper walk a mile. *Scottish*

5725. After dinner you must stand awhile, or walk a thousand paces. *German*

5726. After eating stand or walk a mile. *Latin*

5727. After eating walk a hundred paces. *Sanskrit*

5728. After good wine a good horse. *French*

5729. Before supper walk a little, after supper do the same. *Latin*

5730. Bodily exercise profiteth little; but godliness is profitable unto all things. *Bible*

5731. Use legs and have legs. *English*

Exile

5732. Exiles feed on hope. *Greek*

5733. He suffers exile who denies himself to his country. *Latin*

5734. No exile from his country ever escaped from himself. *Latin*

Expectation *see also* Hope; Prematureness

5735. Do not expect everything, everywhere, from everyone. *Latin*

5736. Expect to be treated as you have treated others. *American*

5737. If you sow the wind expect to reap the whirlwind. *American*

5738. Long looked for comes at last. *English*

5739. Nothing is so good as it seems beforehand. *English (G. Eliot)*

5740. Prospect is often better than possession. *English*

Expedience

5741. Cauld parritch [porridge] are sooner het again than new anes made. *Scottish*

5742. Soon enough if well enough. *English*

Expendability

5743. A man overboard, a mouth the less. *Dutch*

Expense *see also* Cost; Value; Worth

5744. Beware of little expenses: a small leak will sink a great ship. *American (Franklin)*

5745. Far-sought and dear-bought is gude for ladies. *Scottish*

5746. Those things please more, which are more expensive. *Latin (Juvenal)*

Experience *see also* Knowledge; Learning

5747. A burnt bairn [child] fire dreads. *Scottish*

5748. A burnt child fears the fire and a bitten child the dog. *Danish*

5749. A dog which has been beaten with a stick is afraid of its shadow. *Italian*

5750. A fisherman once stung will be wiser. *Latin*

5751. A fox is not caught twice in the same trap. *Greek*

5752. A good scare is worth more to a man than good advice. *American (Howe)*

5753. A new broom sweeps clean, but the old brush knows the corners. *Irish*

5754. A scalded cat fears [or dreads] cold water. *Scottish*

5755. A scalded dog dreads cold water. *French*

5756. A sensible man judges of present by past events. *Greek (Sophocles)*

5757. A shipwrecked man fears every sea. *Latin*

5758. A's but lip-wit that wants experience. *Scottish*

5759. An ass does not stumble twice over the same stone. *French*

5760. An auld dog bits sicker [certain]. *Scottish*

5761. An auld [old] knave is nae bairn [no child]. *Scottish*

5762. An auld [old] mason maks a gude [good] barrowman. *Scottish*

5763. An old bird is not caught with chaff. *English*

5764. An old broom knows the dirty corners best. *Irish*

5765. An old dog does not bark for nothing. *Italian*

5766. An old fox is not to be caught in a trap. *Latin*

5767. An old fox needs not to be taught tricks. *English*

5768. An old knave is no babe. *English*

5769. An old man's saying is rarely untrue. *Danish*

5770. Avoid the ford on which your friend was drowned. *Welsh*

5771. Believe him who speaks from experience. *Latin*

5772. Better ae [one] wit bought than twa [two] for nought. *Scottish*

5773. Better learn frae [from] your neebor's scathe [injury] than frae your ain [own]. *Scottish*

5774. Biggin' [a small house] and bairns [children] marrying are arrant masters. *Scottish*

5775. Bought wit is best. *English*

5776. Boys avoid the bees that stung 'em. *English*

5777. Burnt bairns [children] dread the fire. *Scottish*

5778. By falling we learn to go safely. *English*

5779. By working in the smithy one becomes a smith. *French*

5780. Each believes naught but his experience. *Greek*

5781. Empty the glass if you would judge of the drink. *Latin*

5782. Every day learns from the one that went before, but no day teaches the one that follows. *Russian*

5783. Experience bought by suffering teaches wisdom. *American*

5784. Experience bought with sorrow teaches. *Latin*

5785. Experience is a comb which nature gives us when we are bald. *Chinese*

5786. Experience is gude, but aften dear bought. *Scottish*

5787. Experience is the best teacher. *American*

5788. Experience is the blind man's dog. *American*

5789. Experience is the looking-glass of the intellect. *Arabic*

5790. Experience is the mother of all things. *Italian*

5791. Experience is the teacher of fools. *Latin*

5792. Experience keeps a dear school, yet fools will learn in no other. *American (Franklin)*

5793. Experience may teach a fool. *Scottish*

5794. Experience teaches fools, and fools will learn nae [no] other way. *Scottish*

5795. Experience teaches. *Latin*

5796. Experience tests the truth. *American*

5797. Experience without learning is better than learning without experience. *English*

5798. Fortunate is he whom the dangers of others have rendered cautious. *Latin*

5799. Had you sic [such] a shoe on ilka [each] foot it would gar you shackle [shackle you]. *Scottish*

5800. Hand in use is father o' lear [learning, skill]. *Scottish*

5801. Happy is the man made wary by others' perils. *Latin*

5802. He gets his wisdom cheaply who gets it at another's cost. *Latin*

5803. He has tasted both sweet and bitter. *Chinese*

5804. He knows the roads by which he has escaped before. *Latin*

5805. He knows the water best who has waded through it. *Danish*

5806. He may bear a bull that hath borne a calf. *Latin*

5807. He that cheats me ance [once], shame fa' him; if he cheats me twice, shame fa' me. *Scottish*

5808. He that has been bitten by a serpent fears a rope. *Hebrew*

5809. He that has been hurt, fears. *Latin*

5810. He that has been wrecked shudders even at still water. *Latin (Ovid)*

5811. He that stumbles, if he does not fall, quickens his pace. *Spanish*

5812. He who has been bitten by a snake fears a piece of string. *Persian*

5813. He who has been burned by hot broth will blow even on cold water. *Korean*

5814. He who has once burned his mouth always blows his soup. *German*

5815. He who has tried it, is afraid of it. *Latin*

5816. He who is once bitten by a snake, will not walk in the grass. *Chinese*

5817. He who is one day older than you is a year wiser. *Arabic*

5818. He who suffers, remembers. *Latin*

5819. He who suffers shipwreck a second time cannot blame Neptune. *Latin (Publilius Syrus)*

5820. He who was first an acolyte, and afterward an abbot [or curate], knows what the boys do behind the altar. *Spanish*

5821. I know by my own pot how others boil. *French*

5822. If a man deceive me once, shame on him; if he deceive me twice, shame on me. *English*

5823. If a' things were to be done twice ilka ane [everyone] wad be wise. *Scottish*

5824. If you drink the water you will know the spring. *Chinese*

5825. If you haven't been deceived by others you will never learn the trade. *Chinese*

5826. If you want to know the road down the mountain, ask those who have trodden it. *Chinese*

5827. If young folk had experience, and old folk strength! *American*

5828. In doing, we learn. *American*

5829. Injuries put us on our guard. *Latin*

5830. It has caused injury and will do so again. *Latin*

5831. It is best to learn wisdom by the experience [or follies] of others. *Latin*

5832. Learn to see in another's misfortune the ills which you should avoid. *Latin (Publilius Syrus)*

5833. Let another's shipwreck be your sea-mark. *English*

5834. Listen to the voice of experience, but also make use of your brains. *American*

5835. New nets don't catch old birds. *Italian*

5836. No man is a good physician who has never been sick. *Arabic*

5837. Old birds are not caught with cats. *Dutch*

5838. Old birds only laugh when you try to catch them with chaff. *American*

5839. Old crows are hard to catch. *German*

5840. Once bit, twice shy. *English*

5841. One learns by doing. *American*

5842. One man's fault is another man's lesson. *English*

5843. One sight is better than a thousand lessons. *Chinese*

5844. One thorn of experience is worth a whole wilderness of warning. *American*

5845. One who has been bitten by a serpent is alarmed by a lizard. *Italian*

5846. One year bitten by a snake; three years afraid of grass ropes. *Chinese*

5847. Only after you have crossed the river can you ridicule the crocodile. *Ashanti*

5848. Only he who has traveled the road knows where the holes are deep. *Chinese*

5849. Only the wearer knows where the shoe pinches. *English*

5850. Profit by your experience. *American*

5851. Put an old cat to an old rat. *American*

5852. Rats know the ways of rats. *Chinese*

5853. Sad experience leaves no room for doubt. *English (Pope)*

5854. Scalded cats fear even cold water. *English*
5855. Suffering brings experience. *Greek (Aeschylus)*
5856. The animal escapes the trap, and stands in dread of a bent stick. *Efik*
5857. The first time, even a duck dives in tail-first. *Turkish*
5858. The fish which has once felt the hook, suspects it in every food which offers. *Latin (Ovid)*
5859. The frog in the well knows nothing of the great ocean. *Japanese*
5860. The horses of hope gallop, but the asses of experience go slowly. *Russian*
5861. The langer we live the mair ferlies [more wonders] we see. *Scottish*
5862. The man who has been beaten with a firebrand runs away at the sight of a firefly. *Senegalese*
5863. The proof o' the puddin's the preein' [the tasting] o 't. *Scottish*
5864. The remembrance of the deeds of past ages is our best guide in the future. *Chinese*
5865. The snake knows its own hole. *Chinese*
5866. The tiger that has once tasted blood is never sated with the taste of it. *English*
5867. The world is a whet-stone and man a knife. *American*
5868. Their harms, our arms. *English*
5869. There is danger when a dog has once tasted flesh. *Latin*
5870. There is no hunting but with old hounds. *French*
5871. There's beild [protection] beneath an auld [old] man's beard. *Scottish*
5872. They say, best men are moulded out of faults. *English (Shakespeare)*
5873. To-day is yesterday's pupil. *English*
5874. To learn from other men's mistakes to prevent your own. *Latin (Terence)*
5875. We are aye to learn as lang as we live. *Scottish*
5876. What does not poison, fattens. *Italian*
5877. What I do not know does not make me hot. *German*
5878. What smarts teaches. *English*
5879. Who knows what hurts himself, knows what hurts others. *Malagasy*
5880. Wisdom rides upon the ruins of folly. *English*
5881. Wise men learn by other men's mistakes; fools, by their own. *Latin*
5882. Wit's never bought till it's paid for. *English*
5883. Wyse ben by foles harm chastysed. [Wise men learn by fools' mistakes.] *English (Chaucer)*
5884. Ye're ower auld-sarrant to be fleyed wi' bogles [too old to be frightened by bugbears]. *Scottish*
5885. Years know more than books. *American*
5886. You don't know how difficult a thing is until you try to do it. *Chinese*
5887. You must spoil before you spin. *English*
5888. You shall know by experience. *Latin*

Experimentation

5889. A barber learns to shave by shaving fools. *English*
5890. Make your experiment on a worthless subject. *Latin*

Explanation

5891. The unknown is explained by what is still more unknown. *Latin*

Exploitation

5892. If you let them lay the calf on your back it will not be long before they clap on the cow. *Italian*

Exposure

5893. Guard yourself from being found out, so that you may be at fault freely. *French*
5894. It is ill to be a villain, but it is worse to be found out. *Italian*
5895. Murder will out. [Mordre wol out.] *English (Chaucer)*

Extravagance

5896. A fat kitchen, a lean legacy. *German*
5897. He that has not bread to spare should not keep a dog. *English*
5898. He who buys what he doesn't need steals from himself. *Swedish*
5899. He who spends more than he should / Shall not have to spend when he would. *English*
5900. Kindle a candle at baith [both] ends and it'll soon be done. *Scottish*
5901. Narrow gathered, widely spent. *Scottish*
5902. Silk and satins put out the kitchen fire. *English*
5903. Unable to keep yourself, you are keeping dogs. *Latin*
5904. Wyte [blame] your teeth if your tail be sma. *Scottish*

Extremes *see also* Excess

5905. Ane [one] may like to be lo'ed [loved], but wha would mool in wi' a moudiewart [move in with a mole]? *Scottish*
5906. Ane may like the kirk [church] weel enough, and no ride on the riggin [the ridge of the roof] o 't. *Scottish*
5907. Don't go to extremes. *American*
5908. Extremes in nature equal ends produce. *English (Pope)*
5909. Extremes meet. *French*
5910. Extremity of right is wrong. *Latin*
5911. He gangs frae the jilt [a dash of water] to the gellock [an iron crowbar]. *Scottish*
5912. He lo'ed mutton weel that lick'd where the ewie [ewe] lay. *Scottish*
5913. He starts at straes, and lets windlins [bottles of straw or hay] gae. *Scottish*
5914. He stumbles at a strae, and loups [leaps] ower a linn [a waterfall between two rocks]. *Scottish*
5915. He's either a' honey or a' dirt. *Scottish*
5916. If the deil [devil] be laird, ye'll be tenant. *Scottish*
5917. If the lift [firmament] fa' the laverocks [larks] will be smoored [smothered]. *Scottish*
5918. It maun e'en be ower shoon, ower boots wi' me now. *Scottish*
5919. It's best to be cautious and to avoid extremes. *American*
5920. Man's extremity is God's opportunity. *English*

5921. There is a point at which even justice does injury. *Greek (Sophocles)*

5922. Too far east is west. *Dutch*

Eyes *see also* **Eyes and Ears; Face; Seeing and Hearing**

5923. A twitching of the left eye denotes wealth; that of the right eye signifies calamity. *Chinese*

5924. An evil eye can see no good. *Danish*

5925. If thine eye offend thee, pluck it out, and cast it from thee. *Bible*

5926. If you don't look with the eye, you will lose out of the pocket. *Yiddish*

5927. Love is allured by gentle eyes. *Latin (Ovid)*

5928. One eye has more faith than two ears. *Yiddish*

5929. The eye is a window that looks upon the heart. *Osmanli*

5930. The eye is not satisfied with seeing. *Bible*

5931. The eye is small, yet it sees the whole world. *Yiddish*

5932. The eye is the mirror of the soul. *English*

5933. The eyes are a balance of which the heart forms the weight. *Turkish*

5934. The eyes do not go wrong if the mind rules them. *Latin*

5935. The eyes of a fool are in the ends of the earth. *Bible*

5936. The face is the portrait of the mind; the eyes, its informers. *Latin*

5937. The present eye praises the present object. *English (Shakespeare)*

5938. What I can see with my eyes, I point out with my finger. *Spanish*

5939. Who has only one eye, guards it well. *French*

5940. Your eyes are bigger than your stomach. *American*

Eyes and Ears *see also* **Eyes; Seeing and Hearing**

5941. Believe half of what you see, nothing of what you hear. *Jamaican*

5942. The ear is less trustworthy than the eye. *Greek*

5943. The ears can endure an injury better than the eye. *Latin*

5944. The eyes are as ignorant as the ears are knowing. *Greek*

5945. The eyes believe themselves, the ears believe other people. *Greek*

5946. The eyes serve for ears to the deaf. *Italian*

Face *see also* **Appearance**

5947. A dimple in the chin, the devil within. *Irish*

5948. A face like a benediction. *Spanish*

5949. A face that only a mother could love. *American*

5950. A face that resembles nothing but itself. *Russian*

5951. A fine face, but eats vile things. *Arabic*

5952. A good face is worth more than gold. *Chinese*

5953. A man is known by the eye, and the face discovers [i.e., reveals] wisdom. *English*

5954. A man's face is the reflex of his state of mind. *Chinese*

5955. An open countenance often conceals close thoughts. *English*

5956. An ugly face should not curse the mirror. *Russian*

5957. Everyone is satisfied with his own face. *Yiddish*

5958. His face would hang him. *English*

5959. In the forehead and the eye / The lecture of the mind doth lie. *English*

5960. It's weel that our fauts [faults] are no written in our face. *Scottish*

5961. Men's characters are not always written on their foreheads. *English*

5962. Men's faces are not to be trusted. *Latin*

5963. Merit is often belied by the countenance. *Latin*

5964. Often a noble face hides filthy ways. *Greek (Euripides)*

5965. Often a silent face has voice and words. *Latin*

5966. The countenance free, the thoughts close. *Italian*

5967. The countenance is the index of the mind. *American*

5968. The face is the index of the heart. *Latin*

5969. The face of an eagle, the heart of a chicken. *American*

5970. There's no art to find the mind's construction in the face. *English (Shakespeare)*

5971. We know men's faces, not their minds. *Chinese*

5972. When the disposition is friendly, the face pleases. *Latin*

5973. When you paint a dragon, you paint his skin; but you cannot paint the bones. When you know a man, you know his face but not his heart. *Chinese*

5974. You may judge a man by his countenance. *Latin*

5975. Your face betrays your years. *Latin*

Facility *see also* **Ability; Dexterity; Ease; Skill**

5976. A bald head is soon shaven. *English*

5977. That which is easily done is soon believed. *English*

Fact and Fiction *see also* **Truth and Falsehood**

5978. Fiction intended to please, should resemble truth as much as possible. *Latin*

5979. I shall speak facts; but some will say I deal in fiction. *Latin (Ovid)*

5980. Truth is stranger than fiction. *English (Byron)*

Facts

5981. A single fact is worth a ship-load of argument. *American*

5982. Facts are stubborn things. *American*

5983. Facts do not cease to exist when they are ignored. *American*

5984. One fact is stronger than a dozen texts or pretexts. *American*

Failure

5985. A man may be down but he's never out. *American*

5986. A miss is as good as a mile. *American*

5987. He is gude [good] that failed ne'er. *Scottish*

5988. He that lies on the ground cannot fall. *Yiddish*
5989. In the dictionary of youth there is no such word as failure. *English*
5990. One learns by failing. *French*

Fair Dealing *see also* Business and Commerce; Buying and Selling

5991. A false balance is abomination to the Lord: but a just weight is his delight. *Bible*
5992. Good weight and measure is heaven's treasure. *English*
5993. It's nae sin to tak a gude price, but in [there is sin] gieing ill measure. *Scottish*
5994. Just scales and full measures injure no man. *Chinese*
5995. Weight and measure save a man trouble. *Spanish*

Fair Words *see also* Good Words; Smooth Words; Soft Words

5996. Fair and softly, as lawyers go to heaven. *English*
5997. Fair speech turns elephants away from the garden path. *Swahili*
5998. Fair words and foul deeds cheat wise men as well as fools. *English*
5999. Fair words make fools fain [i.e., pleased]. *Latin*
6000. Fair words winna mak the pat boil [will not make the pot boil]. *Scottish*
6001. Fair words won't feed a cat. *Italian*
6002. Fair words — but look to your purse. *Italian*
6003. Fair [or fine] words butter no parsnips. *English*

Fairness *see also* Balance; Justice

6004. A fox should not be of the jury at a goose's trial. *American*
6005. Listen to both sides. *American*
6006. Soft and fair goes far. *English (Dryden)*
6007. Turnabout is fair play. *American*

Faith *see also* Divine Assistance; Man and God; Religion; Prayer

6008. As thou to me, so I to thee. *German*
6009. Be thou faithful unto the end. *Bible*
6010. Faith is certitude without proofs. *French*
6011. Faith is the substance of things hoped for, the evidence of things not seen. *Bible*
6012. Faith without works is dead. *Bible*
6013. Fight the good fight of faith. *Bible*
6014. He who will not keep faith with God, will not keep faith with man. *Welsh*
6015. "I have kept the faith." *Bible*
6016. I know that my redeemer liveth. *Bible*
6017. If you don't keep faith with man you can't keep faith with God. *American*
6018. In the affairs of this world, men are saved, not by faith, but by the want of it. *American*
6019. It will profit me nothing if I have no faith in it. *French*
6020. It's easier to lose faith than to find it again. *American*
6021. Keep the faith. *American*
6022. Knowledge of things divine escapes us through want of faith. *Greek*
6023. Little men are men of little faith; big men have the faith to move mountains. *American*
6024. Love demands faith, and faith steadfastness. *Italian*
6025. Men's faiths are wafer-cakes. *English (Shakespeare)*
6026. The just shall live by faith. *Bible*
6027. The ship of him who confides in God founders not. *American*
6028. We walk by faith, not by sight. *American*
6029. What faith is there in the faithless? Greek

Faith and Reason *see also* Faith

6030. The way to see by faith is to shut the eye of reason. *American (Franklin)*

Faithfulness *see also* Fidelity; Husbands and Wives; Marriage; Marriage and Infidelity; Women and Trustworthiness

6031. He who has a bonny wife needs mair than twa een [two eyes]. *Scottish*
6032. The back door is the one that robs the house. *Italian*
6033. The right hand does not cut off the left one. *Swahili*
6034. There is no faith in women, horses or swords. *Persian*

Fallibility *see* Accidents

False Generosity

6035. Broad thongs are cut from other men's leather. *Latin*
6036. He is the best gentleman, who is the son of his own deserts. *English*
6037. Hens are free o' [i.e., with] horse corn. *Scottish*
6038. No one is so open-handed as he who has nothing to give. *French*
6039. Of my gossip's loaf a large slice for my godson. *Spanish*
6040. Steal the goose, and give the giblets in alms. *English*
6041. Steal the pig, and give away the pettitoes for God's sake. *Spanish*
6042. They are aye gudewilly [lit., good-willed] o' their horse that hae nane. *Scottish*
6043. They are free of fruit that want an orchard. *English*

False Piety

6044. Hypocritical piety is double iniquity. *English*

Falsehood *see* Lies and Lying

Fame *see also* Reputation

6045. A bull does not enjoy fame in two herds. *Rhodesian*
6046. After five generations the fame of both superior and mean men disappears. *Chinese*
6047. All fame is dangerous: good bringeth envy; bad, shame. *English*
6048. Fame grows like a tree with hidden life. *Latin*
6049. Fame hides her head among the clouds. *Latin (Virgil)*

6050. Fame is a magnifying glass. *English*
6051. Fame is as ephemeral as the famous. *Greek*
6052. Fame is the last infirmity of noble minds. *American*
6053. Fame is the perfume of heroic deeds. *Greek*
6054. Fame is the shadow of virtue. *Latin*
6055. Fame is the spur that the clear spirit doth raise, / To scorn delights, and live laborious days. *English (Milton)*
6056. Fame must be won; honor must not be lost. *German*
6057. From fame to infamy is a much traveled road. *American*
6058. Honest fame awaits the truly good. *Latin*
6059. It is a wretched thing to lean on the fame of others. *Latin*
6060. Let us now praise famous men. *Bible*
6061. Renown is the mother of virtues. *Greek*
6062. She acquires momentum as she advances. *Latin (Virgil)*
6063. She comes unlook'd for, if she comes at all. *English (Pope)*
6064. Some have fame and others live in shame. *American*
6065. Some have the fame and others card the wool. *Spanish*
6066. The top of a pinnacle now, firewood soon. *Burmese*
6067. There are many paths to the top of the mountain, but the view is always the same. *Chinese*
6068. True fame is never the gift of chance. *Greek*

Familiarity

6069. A cowherd does not fear a cow. *Accra*
6070. A maid aft seen and a gown aft worn are disesteemed and held in scorn. *Scottish*
6071. A rose too often smelled loses its fragrance. *Spanish*
6072. A thing too much seen is little prized. *French*
6073. Be thou familiar, but by no means vulgar. *English (Shakespeare)*
6074. By the familiarity of the master the servant is spoiled. *Latin*
6075. Familiarity breeds contempt — and children. *American (Twain)*
6076. Familiarity breeds contempt. *Latin*
6077. Few men are admired by their servants. *French (Montaigne)*
6078. Go to your brother's house, but not every day. *Spanish*
6079. I have lived too near the woods to be scared by owls. *American*
6080. It's ill living where everybody knows everybody. *English*
6081. No man is a hero to his valet. *French*
6082. Over-great familiarity genders despite. *Scottish*
6083. Ower muckle hameliness [too much familiarity] spoils gude courtesy. *Scottish*
6084. Play with an ass and he'll whisk his tail in your face. *Spanish*
6085. That which a man knows best he must use most. *French*
6086. The herb one knows one should bind to one's finger. *French*
6087. The sound of the bell does not drive away rooks. *American*
6088. To preserve friendship a wall must be put between. *French*

Family *see also* Brothers; Fathers and Sons; Mothers and Daughters; Parents and Children; Relatives

6089. All happy families resemble one another; every unhappy family is unhappy in its own way. *Russian (Tolstoy)*
6090. An ounce of blood is worth more than a pound of friendship. *Spanish*
6091. Blood is thicker than water. *American*
6092. Every large family has at least one black sheep. *American*
6093. Govern a family as you would cook a small fish — very gently. *Chinese*
6094. He that flies from his own family has far to travel. *Latin*
6095. He that hath wife and children hath given hostages to fortune. *English (Bacon)*
6096. In a united family, happiness springs up of itself. *Chinese*
6097. It is easier to rule a kingdom than to regulate a family. *Chinese*
6098. Men with the smallest incomes have the largest families. *American*
6099. Mistakes happen in the best regulated families. *American*
6100. Nobody's family can hang up the sign, "Nothing the matter here." *Chinese*
6101. Some families are like potatoes; all that is good of them are under ground. *American*
6102. There is no method of managing stupid wives and disobedient children. *Chinese*
6103. Wife and children are bills of charges. *English*

Fancy *see also* Fantasy; Imagination

6104. Children, the weak-minded, and the timid are full of fancy. *American*
6105. Ever let the fancy roam; pleasure never is at home. *American*
6106. Every fancy you consult, consult your purse. *American*
6107. False fancy brings real misery. *American*
6108. Fancy may kill or cure. *English*
6109. Fancy passes [i.e., or surpasses] beauty. *English*
6110. Fancy runs most furiously when a guilty conscience drives it. *American*
6111. Geniuses have great imaginations but little fancy. *American*
6112. It is the fancy, not the reason of things, that makes us so uneasy. *American*
6113. When we become fancy-sick there is no cure. *American*

Fantasy *see also* Dreams; Fancy; Imagination

6114. To build castles in the air. *English*

Farmers and Farming

6115. A bad farmer's hedge is full of gaps. *Gaelic*
6116. Each man reaps his own farm. *Latin*
6117. He that tilleth the land shall be satisfied with bread. *Bible*
6118. Let us seek bread with the plough. *Latin*
6119. Praise a great estate, but cultivate a small one. *Latin*
6120. The foot of the farmer manures the field. *Danish*
6121. The man who plants corn sows holiness. *Persian*
6122. The master's eye is the best fertilizer. *Latin*
6123. The way of cultivation is not easy. *Latin*

Fashion *see also* Conformity; Clothes; Custom

6124. As good be out of the world as out of the fashion. *English*
6125. Better be out o' the warld than out o' fashion. *Scottish*
6126. Fashion is more powerful than any tyrant. *Latin*
6127. Follow the fashion, or quit the world. *French*
6128. Fools invent fashions; wise men follow them. *French*
6129. For fashion's sake, as dogs go to church. *English*
6130. For fashion's sake — as dogs gae [go] to market. *Scottish*
6131. It is in vain to mislike the current fashion. *English*
6132. Men after the modern fashion and asses after the ancient. *Italian*
6133. The fashion of this world passeth away. *Bible*
6134. The fashion wear out more apparel than the man. *English (Shakespeare)*
6135. What has been the fashion once will be the fashion again. *Japanese*

Fate *see also* Fortune

6136. A light spirit can bear a heavy fate. *American*
6137. All things are produced by fate. *Greek*
6138. Between cup and lip hovers the hand of the dark powers. *American*
6139. Don't tempt fate. *American*
6140. Every bullet has its billet. *American*
6141. Everyone is the maker of his own fate. *English*
6142. Fate leads the willing, drags the unwilling. *Greek*
6143. For man is man, and master of his fate. *English (Tennyson)*
6144. From no place can you exclude the fates. *Latin*
6145. If you're fated to be drowned, you'll drown in a spoonful of water. *Yiddish*
6146. Man blindly works the will of fate. *German*
6147. Many have come upon their fate while shunning fate. *Latin*
6148. Men at some time are masters of their fates. *English (Shakespeare)*
6149. Nae [no] fleeing frae [from] fate. *Scottish*
6150. No man can escape his fate. *Egyptian*
6151. No man can fight his own doom. *American*
6152. No man can make his own hap. *Scottish*
6153. No one is made guilty by fate. *Latin*
6154. That which God writes on thy forehead thou wilt come to. *Koran*
6155. The fated will happen. *Gaelic*
6156. The fates lead the willing, and drag the unwilling. *Latin (Seneca)*
6157. The fates will find a way. *Latin*
6158. There's no flying from fate. *American*
6159. To one man feast, to another famine. *Polish*
6160. Two things a man should not be angry at: what he can help, and what he can't. *American*
6161. We make our fortunes and we call them fate. *American*
6162. What must be, must be. *American*
6163. What will be, will be. *Italian*
6164. Whither the fates lead, virtue will follow. *Latin*
6165. Will is over-ruled by fate. *English*
6166. You cannot avoid your fate, even by getting up early. *Russian*

Fathers and Daughters *see also* Daughters; Fathers; Parents and Children

6167. The lucky man has a daughter for his first-born. *Spanish*
6168. Who does not beat his daughters, will one day strike his knees in vain. *Turkish*

Fathers and Fatherhood *see also* Child-Rearing; Fathers and Daughters; Fathers and Sons; Parents and Children

6169. A father is a banker provided by nature. *French*
6170. A father loves his children in hating their faults. *French*
6171. A father's blessing cannot be drowned in water nor consumed by fire. *Russian*
6172. A father's love for all others is air. *Spanish*
6173. Happy is he that is happy in his children. *English*
6174. He knows not what love is that has not children. *Italian*
6175. If you live without being a father you will die without being a human being. *Russian*
6176. It is a wise father that knows his own child. *English (Shakespeare)*
6177. One father supports ten children better than ten children one father. *German*
6178. To rear and not educate is a father's fault. *Chinese*
6179. What sweeter gift from nature has fallen to the lot of man than his children? *Latin (Cicero)*

Fathers and Sons *see also* Heredity; Parents and Children; Sons

6180. A foolish son is the calamity of his father; and the contentions of a wife are a continual dropping. *Bible*
6181. A son pays his father's debts. *Chinese*
6182. An ungrateful son is a wart on his father's face. *Afghani*
6183. As the baker, so the buns; as the father, so the sons. *American*
6184. He that has his father for judge goes safe to the trial. *Spanish*

6185. He that has sons or sheep will not want vexation. *Spanish*

6186. He that honoreth his father shall have a long life. *Bible*

6187. He that spareth his rod hateth his son. *Bible*

6188. He who has riches and no sons is not really rich; he who has sons but not money cannot be considered poor. *Chinese*

6189. He who hath but one hog, makes him fat; and he who hath but one son, makes him a fool. *Italian*

6190. It is a wise child that knows its own father. *Greek (Homer)*

6191. It is not a father's anger but his silence that a son dreads. *Chinese*

6192. Niggard father, spendthrift son. *French*

6193. Raw dads mak fat lads. *Scottish*

6194. The child is father to the man. *English (Wordsworth)*

6195. The father, in praising his son, extols himself. *Chinese*

6196. The son disgraces himself when he blames his father. *Chinese*

6197. The ungrateful son is a wart on his father's face; to leave it is a blemish, to cut it off is pain. *Afghanistani*

6198. To a hoarding father succeeds an extravagant son. *Spanish*

6199. When cares overwhelm you, take your son on your lap. *Egyptian*

6200. When your son's shoe becomes as big as yours, stop associating with him. [Let him be independent.] *Tunisian*

6201. Whom should he bear with if not with his own father? *Latin*

Fatness *see* Eating; Obesity

Fault Finding *see also* Criticism

6202. A house built by the wayside is either too high or too low. *American*

6203. Baboons laugh at each other's foreheads. *Zulu*

6204. Clean your finger before you point at my spots. *English*

6205. Clodius impeaches the adulterers. *Latin*

6206. Death said to the man with his throat cut, "How ugly you look." *English*

6207. Every clown can find fault, though it would puzzle him to do better. *English*

6208. Every peasant can find fault; to do better would puzzle him. *German*

6209. Faults are thick when love is thin. *Welsh*

6210. Fools aye [always] see ither folks' fauts [faults] and forget their ain [own]. *Scottish*

6211. He may find faut that canna mend. *Scottish*

6212. If we had no faults, we should not take so much pleasure in remarking them in others. *French (La Rochefoucauld)*

6213. If you are a child do not deride a short man. [You may grow no taller yourself.] *Oji*

6214. It is peculiarly a fool's habit to discern the faults of others, and to forget his own. *Latin (Cicero)*

6215. Many speak of my drinking, but few of my thirst. *American*

6216. Men should not be told of the faults which they have mended. *American*

6217. None are prevented by their own faults from pointing out those of another. *Latin*

6218. One ass nicknames another "Long-ears." *English*

6219. Point not at others' spots with a foul finger. *English*

6220. Said the pot to the kettle, "Get away, black-face." *Spanish (Cervantes)*

6221. The coal is making fun of the cinder. *Kenyan*

6222. The colander said to the needle, "Get away, you have a hole in you." *Hindu*

6223. The frying-pan says to the kettle, "Avaunt, black brows!" *English*

6224. The hunchback sees not his own hump, but that of his neighbor [or brother]. *French*

6225. The kettle blackens the frying pan [or the stove]. *French*

6226. The kettle calls the pot black, / The kiln calls the oven burnt-house. *English*

6227. The most faulty always find fault. *American*

6228. The Most High God sees, and bears: my neighbor knows nothing, and yet is always finding fault. *Persian*

6229. The pan says to the kettle, "Get away, lest you stain me." *Italian*

6230. The pot reproaches the kettle because it is black. *Dutch*

6231. The raven chides blackness. *English*

6232. The raven said to the rook, "Stand away, black-coat." *English*

6233. The saucepan laughs at the pipkin. *Italian*

6234. The shovel scoffs at the poker. *French*

6235. The sieve says to the needle: You have a hole in your tail. *Pakistani*

6236. The sooty oven mocks the black chimney. *English*

6237. Those see nothing but faults that seek for nothing else. *English*

6238. "Thou art a bitter bird," said the raven to the starling. *English*

6239. To see the mote in another's eye and not the beam in your own. *Bible*

6240. We see only the faults of others. *Yiddish*

6241. We see the faults of others but not our own. *American*

6242. When you would arraign your neighbor's faults, think first of your own. *Greek*

6243. You can find faults in an angel if you look hard enough. *American*

Faults *see also* Blame; Error(s); Guilt; Perfection

6244. A fault once denied, is twice committed. *English*

6245. A good fisherman may let an eel slip from him. *French*

6246. A man must have his faults. *Latin*

6247. Are there not spots on the very sun? *French*

6248. Avoid great faults by keeping away from small ones. *American*

6249. Bad men excuse their faults; good men leave them. *American*

6250. Condemn the fault and not the actor of it? *English (Shakespeare)*

6251. Every bean has its black. *English*

6252. Every rose has its prickles. *English*

6253. Faultless to a fault. *English (Browning)*

6254. Faults are committed within the walls of Troy and also without. [There is fault on both sides.] *Latin (Horace)*

6255. God keep the cat out o' our gate, for the hens canna flee. *Scottish*

6256. Happy the man when he has not the defects of his qualities. *French*

6257. He has no fault except that he has no fault. *Latin*

6258. He is dead that is faultless. *American*

6259. He is lifeless that is faultless. *English*

6260. He may find faut [fault] that canna mend. *Scottish*

6261. He rode sicker [sure] that ne'er fell. *Scottish*

6262. He that shoots always right forfeits his arrow. *Welsh*

6263. He who wants a mule without fault must go afoot. *Spanish*

6264. If the best man's faults were written on his forehead, it would make him pull his hat over his eyes. *Welsh*

6265. Ilka bean has its black. *Scottish*

6266. It is a sound head that has not a soft piece in it. *English*

6267. It's weel that our fauts [faults] are no written in our face. *Scottish*

6268. Lifeless, faultless. *English*

6269. Love him who tells you your faults in private. *Hebrew*

6270. Love your friend with his faults. *Italian*

6271. Men's faults do seldom to themselves appear. *English (Shakespeare)*

6272. No one is born without faults. *Latin*

6273. Only great men have great faults. *French*

6274. Small faults indulged are little thieves that let in greater. *English*

6275. The best driver will sometimes upset. *French*

6276. The brightest of all things, the sun, hath its spots. *English*

6277. The fault is as great as he that commits it. *Spanish*

6278. The fault of another is a good teacher. *German*

6279. The fault of the ass must not be laid on the pack-saddle. *Spanish*

6280. The man who denies his faults, never atones for them. *Latin*

6281. The priest errs at the altar. *Italian*

6282. The real fault is to have faults and not to amend them. *Chinese (Confucius)*

6283. To each man at his birth nature has given some fault. *Latin (Propertius)*

6284. Use men as you would use wood; because one inch is worm-eaten, you would never throw away the whole trunk. *American*

6285. We never confess our faults except through vanity. *French (La Rochefoucauld)*

6286. Who but the sages are free from faults? *Chinese*

Favors *see also* Good Deeds; Gratitude; Ingratitude; Obligation; Service; Thanks

6287. A favor bestowed by a hard man is bread made of stone. *Latin*

6288. A favor ill placed is great waste. *English*

6289. A favor is half granted when graciously refused. *Latin (Publilius Syrus)*

6290. A favor to come is better than a hundred received. *Italian*

6291. Death plays no favorites. *American*

6292. Don't ask a man for a favor before he has had his lunch. *American*

6293. Don't ask as a favor what you can take by force. *Spanish*

6294. Favor deserves favor. *Russian*

6295. Favors should never be forced upon others against their will. *Latin*

6296. Favors unused are favors abused. *Scottish*

6297. Fools refuse favors. *English*

6298. He has received a favor who has granted one to a deserving person. *Latin*

6299. He receives more favors who knows how to return them. *Latin (Publilius Syrus)*

6300. He that canna gie [cannot give] a favour shouldna [should not] seek ane [one]. *Scottish*

6301. He that doth a good turn looketh for a good turn. *English*

6302. He who will not grant a favor has no right to ask one. *Latin (Publilius Syrus)*

6303. If a man confers a benefit upon another, that benefit is not lost [to himself]. *Kanuri*

6304. If you accept favors from crooked men, you sell yourself down the river. *American*

6305. It's a sort of favor to be denied at first. *Scottish*

6306. Love will last; favors will blast. *American*

6307. Never remember the benefits conferred nor forget the favors received. *Greek*

6308. Only a pig depends on the favors of swine. *American*

6309. The favor of ignoble men is won only by ignoble means. *Latin*

6310. The first time it is a favor, the second time a rule. *Chinese*

6311. The greater the favor, the greater the obligation. *Latin*

6312. The man who confers a favor would rather not be repaid in the same coin. *Greek (Aristotle)*

6313. To confer favors happily three things are necessary — promptness, discrimination and secrecy. *Arabic*

6314. To do a favor slowly is to begrudge it; to consent slowly shows unwillingness. *Latin*

6315. When you buy a vase cheap, look for the flaw; when a man offers favors, look for the motive. *Japanese*

Fear *see also* Courage

6316. A slave to fear creates a hell on earth. *American*

6317. All fearfulness is folly. *Italian*

6318. Be duly afraid, and there is no danger. *Irish*

6319. Better pass a danger once than be always in fear. *Italian*

6320. Courage is often caused by fear. *French*

6321. Early and provident fear is the mother of safety. *English (Burke)*

6322. Even the bravest are frightened by sudden terrors. *Latin*

6323. Extreme fear can neither fight nor fly. *English (Shakespeare)*

6324. Fear always springs from ignorance. *American (Emerson)*

6325. Fear drives out pain. *Syrian*

6326. Fear follows crime and is its punishment. *French (Voltaire)*

6327. Fear guards the vineyard. *Italian*

6328. Fear has large eyes. *Polish*

6329. Fear has lead in its feet. *Russian*

6330. Fear him who fears thee, though he be a fly and thou an elephant. *Persian (Sa'di)*

6331. Fear in love has no luck. *German*

6332. Fear is a great inventor. *French*

6333. Fear is a hindrance to all virtue. *Latin*

6334. Fear is not a lasting teacher of duty. *Latin*

6335. Fear is the beginning of wisdom. *Spanish*

6336. Fear is the father of cruelty. *American*

6337. Fear is the mother of foresight. *American (H. Taylor)*

6338. Fear kills more than illness. *American*

6339. Fear lends wings. *French*

6340. Fear makes lions tame. *German*

6341. Fear makes men ready to believe the worst. *Latin*

6342. Fear mothers safety but it often smothers it. *American*

6343. Fear, not clemency, restrains the wicked. *Latin*

6344. Fear not tomorrow's mischance. *Turkish*

6345. Fear reveals ignoble minds. *Latin*

6346. Fear springs from ignorance. *American*

6347. Fear the man who fears you. *Yiddish*

6348. Fearing his own shadow. *Latin*

6349. Frightened at bugbears. *English*

6350. He fears the very flies. *Latin*

6351. He has not learned the lesson of life who does not every day surmount a fear. *American (Emerson)*

6352. He must fear many whom many fear. *Latin*

6353. He that fears you present will hate you absent. *English*

6354. He who fears a sparrow will never sow millet. *Russian*

6355. He who fears his servants is less than a servant. *Latin (Publilius Syrus)*

6356. He who seeks to terrify others is more in fear himself. *Latin (Claudian)*

6357. His heart is in his mouth. *American*

6358. If you are feared by many, beware of many. *Greek*

6359. If you fear death you're already dead. *American*

6360. If you fear leaves, don't go into the woods. *French*

6361. If you fear to suffer, you suffer from fear. *American*

6362. If you wish to fear nothing, consider that everything is to be feared. *Latin*

6363. In extreme danger fear feels no pity. *Latin (Caesar)*

6364. It is foolish to fear what cannot be avoided [or overcome]. *Latin*

6365. It was fear that first made gods in the world. *Latin*

6366. Men who fear to live are in love with fear. *American*

6367. Never lose honor through fear. *Spanish*

6368. No one loves the man whom he fears. *Greek (Aristotle)*

6369. Nobody would be afraid if he could help it. *American*

6370. Nothing is terrible except fear itself. *English (Bacon)*

6371. Our fears are always more numerous than our dangers. *Latin (Seneca)*

6372. Our fears vanish as the danger approaches. *Latin (Seneca)*

6373. Ships fear fire more than water. *American*

6374. Terror closes the ears of the mind. *Latin*

6375. The fear of God makes the heart shine. *American*

6376. The fear of war is worse than war itself. *English*

6377. The greater the fear, the nearer the danger. *Danish*

6378. The less there is of fear, the less there is of danger. *Latin*

6379. There is nae [no] medicine for fear. *Scottish*

6380. There's nae remede [no remedy] for fear but cut aff [off] the head. *Scottish*

6381. To the timorous the air is filled with demons. *Hindi*

6382. We have nothing to fear but fear itself. *American*

6383. What we fear comes to pass more speedily than what we hope. *Latin (Publilius Syrus)*

6384. When our actions do not, / Our fears do make us traitors. *English (Shakespeare)*

6385. Who causes fear is himself most fearful. *Latin*

6386. Who knows how to fear, knows how to go safely. *Latin*

6387. Whom they fear they hate. *Latin*

Feasibility *see* **Common Sense; Ends and Means; Practicality; Prudence**

Feasts and Feasting *see also* **Gluttony**

6388. A great feast lasts a short while. *Yiddish*

6389. After a feast a man scratches his head. *French*

6390. Feast today, fast tomorrow. *Latin*

6391. Feasting is the physician's harvest. *English*

6392. Feasting makes no friendship. *English*

6393. It's good feasting in another's hall. *Dutch*

6394. The first in banquets but the last in fight. *Greek*

6395. Time enough to keep the feast when it comes. *French*

Feeling

6396. Feeling hath no fellow. *English*

6397. If you wish me to weep, you must first feel grief. *Latin (Horace)*

6398. It's with feelings as with waters: the shallow murmur but the deep are dumb. *American*

6399. Seeing's believing, but feeling's the truth. *English*

6400. There are subjects upon which we cannot reason, we can only feel. *American*

6401. Trust not to thy feeling. *Latin*

Feuds and Feuding

6402. An old feud soon becomes new. *Italian*

Fickleness *see also* Inconsistency; Women and Variability

6403. A fickle memory is bad; a fickle course of conduct is worse; but a fickle heart and purposes, worst of all. *American*

6404. Everything by starts, and nothing long. *American*

Fidelity *see also* Faithfulness; Marriage and Infidelity; Trust; Women and Trustworthiness

6405. Fidelity indeed is a noble virtue, yet justice is nobler still. *American*

6406. Fidelity, purchased with money, money can destroy. *Latin (Seneca)*

6407. He that is won with a nut, may be lost with an apple. *English*

6408. Prosperity asks for fidelity; adversity exacts it. *Latin*

6409. The fidelity of barbarians depends on fortune. *Latin*

Fighting *see also* Argument; Contention; Discord; Dispute; Fighting; Stress and Strain; Strife; Quarreling

6410. Do not fight against two adversaries. *Latin*

6411. In a fight the rich man tries to save his face, the poor man his coat. *Russian*

6412. Never contend with a man who has nothing to lose. *Spanish (Gracián)*

6413. The fight is over when the enemy is down. *Latin*

6414. Tulying [fighting] dogs come halting home. *Scottish*

6415. We are at great disadvantage when we fight with someone who has nothing to lose. *Italian*

6416. Whoever contends with the great sheds his own blood. *Persian (Sa'di)*

Firmness *see also* Purpose

6417. The firm purpose is equal to the deed. *American*

6418. When firmness is sufficient, rashness is unnecessary. *American*

First *see* Priority

Fishing

6419. He is a poor fisherman that will not wet his feet. *German*

6420. He who holds the hook is aware in what waters many fish are swimming. *Latin*

6421. The gods do not deduct from man's alloted span the hours spent in fishing. *Babylonian*

6422. There's no taking trout with dry breeches. *Spanish*

Fitness *see also* Appropriateness; Exercise; Health

6423. As fit as a fiddle. *English*

6424. As fit as a fritter for a friar's mouth. *English*

6425. Sickly body, sickly mind. *German*

6426. The kite that can outspeed his prey, / Owes to his leanness that he may. *Welsh*

Flattery

6427. A flatterer is a fool who despises me or a knave who wants to cheat me. *Chinese*

6428. A flatterer is a secret enemy. *Hungarian*

6429. A flatterer's mouth worketh ruin. *Bible*

6430. A flatterer's throat is an open sepulchre. *Italian*

6431. A flattering speech is a honeyed poison. *Latin*

6432. A man that flattereth his neighbor spreadeth a net for his feet. *Bible*

6433. A softspoken compliment is honied poison. *Latin*

6434. Approve not of him who commends all you say. *American (Franklin)*

6435. As a wolf is like a dog, so is a flatterer like a friend. *English*

6436. Beware of one who flatters unduly; he will also censure unjustly. *Arabic*

6437. Every flatterer lives at the expense of the person who listens to him. *French (La Fontaine)*

6438. Flatterers and dogs soil their own masters. *German*

6439. Flatterers are cats that lick before and scratch behind. *German*

6440. Flattery brings friends, but the truth begets enmity. *Latin (Terence)*

6441. Flattery is a vice — disguised as a virtue. *American*

6442. Flattery is sweet food to those who can swallow it. *American*

6443. Flattery is the close attendant of great fortune. *Latin*

6444. Flattery is the food of fools. *American*

6445. Flattery is the handmaid of the vices. *Latin*

6446. Flattery sits in the parlor when plain dealing is kicked out of doors. *English*

6447. For flattery is the bellows blows up sin. *English (Shakespeare)*

6448. For over-warmth, if false, is worse than truth. *English (Byron)*

6449. He can wile the flounders out o' the sea. *Scottish*

6450. He that loves to be flattered is worthy o' the flatterer. *English (Shakespeare)*

6451. How closely flattery resembles friendship! *Latin*

6452. If he's your flatterer he can't be your friend. *American*

6453. If you reward the chap who flatters you, you are begging for his flattery. *American*

6454. It is easier for men to flatter than to praise. *German*

6455. It is less shameful to steal than to flatter. *Yiddish*

6456. Just praise is only a debt but flattery is a poisoned gift. *American*

6457. Love in secret, but flatter him you hate. *Egyptian*

6458. Not kings alone—the people, too, have their flatterers. *American*

6459. One catches more flies with a spoonful of honey than with twenty casks of vinegar. *French*

6460. The bird maun flicher [must flatter] that has but ae [one] wing. *Scottish*

6461. The coin that is most current is flattery. *American*

6462. The flatterer scratches you where you itch. *American*

6463. The flatterer's bite is poisonous. *American*

6464. The flattery of a bad man conceals treachery. *Latin*

6465. The man who delights in flattery pays by a late repentance. *Latin*

6466. The man who flatters you is a liar: the greater the flattery the bigger the liar. *American*

6467. The most dangerous of wild beasts: a slanderer; of tame ones: a flatterer. *Greek*

6468. The most detestable race of enemies is flatterers. *Latin (Tacitus)*

6469. The only benefit of flattery is that by hearing what we are not, we may be instructed what we ought to be. *American*

6470. The same man cannot be both friend and flatterer. *American (Franklin)*

6471. There is no remedy for the bite of a flatterer. *Latin*

6472. To flatter one who separates us is good, but it is better to flatter one who strikes us. *Wolof*

6473. We wad [would] wheedle a laverock [lark] frae the lift [from the firmament]. *Scottish*

6474. When flatterers meet, the devil goes to dinner. *English*

6475. When fortune flatters, she does it to betray. *Latin (Publilius Syrus)*

6476. When the flatterer pipes, the devil dances. *English*

6477. When the hand ceases to scatter, the mouth ceases to praise. *Irish*

6478. Who paints me before, blackens me behind. *Italian*

6479. Your flattery is so much bird lime. *Latin*

Flexibility *see also* Acceptance; Adaptability; Circumstance(s); Conformity; Custom; Fashion; Habit; Necessity; Submission

6480. A man who will never change his mind is he who has no mind to change. *American*

6481. Be firm or mild as the occasion may require. *Latin (Cato)*

6482. Best to bend while it is a twig. *English*

6483. Better bend the neck than bruise the forehead. *Danish*

6484. Better to bend [or bow] than to break. *English*

6485. Muddy though it be, say not, "Of this water I will not drink." *Spanish*

6486. That which bends does not break. *Lebanese*

6487. That which would become a hook, must bend itself betimes. *German*

6488. There is no use in saying, "Such a way I will not go, or such water I will not drink." *Italian*

6489. When the wind is great, bow before it; when the rain is heavy, yield to it. *Chinese*

6490. Young twigs will bend but not old trees. *Dutch*

Folly *see also* Fools and Folly; Learned Fools; Wisdom and Folly

6491. As the fool thinks so the bell tinks. *English*

6492. Follies are miscalled the crimes of Fate. *Greek (Homer)*

6493. Folly and beauty walk hand in hand. *American*

6494. Folly has more followers than discretion. *Spanish*

6495. Folly has the wings of an eagle, but the eyes of an owl. *Dutch*

6496. Folly is a bonny dog, but a bad ane [one]. *Scottish*

6497. Folly is a self-chosen misfortune. *Greek*

6498. Folly is the most incurable of diseases. *Spanish*

6499. Folly is wont to have more followers and comrades than discretion. *Spanish (Cervantes)*

6500. For every fool there are two more. *Polish*

6501. It is folly to drown on dry land. *English*

6502. It is well to advise folly, not to punish it. *Latin*

6503. It is well to profit by the folly of others. *Latin*

6504. No country or age has a monopoly on human folly. *American*

6505. Profit by the folly of others. *American*

6506. The first degree of folly, is to conceit one's self wise; the second to profess it; the third to despise counsel. *American (Franklin)*

6507. The folly of one man is the fortune of another. *English (Bacon)*

6508. The malady that is incurable is folly. *Spanish*

6509. The most exquisite folly is made of wisdom spun too fine. *American (Franklin)*

6510. The shame is not in having once been foolish, but in not cutting the folly short. *Latin (Horace)*

6511. There is no folly like love. *Welsh*

6512. To pretend folly on occasion is the highest of wisdom. *Latin*

6513. To throw the rope after the bucket. *English*

6514. What use is wisdom when folly reigns? *Yiddish*

6515. When folly passes by, reason draws back. *Japanese*

6516. Where the old are foolish, the child learns folly. *German*

6517. Whoever falls sick of folly is long in getting cured. *Spanish*

6518. You can tell a fool by his laugh. *Polish*

6519. You cannot conceal folly except by silence. *Latin*

Food *see* **Cooks and Cooking; Eating; Hunger**

Fools and Folly *see also* **Learned Fools**

6520. A dry stick and a fool can be broken, not bent. *American*

6521. A fool always finds a greater fool to admire him. *French (Boileau)*

6522. A fool and his money are soon parted. *Scottish*

6523. A fool at forty will ne'er be wise. *Scottish*

6524. A fool demands much, but he's a greater fool that gives it. *English*

6525. A fool is fulsome. *English*

6526. A fool is he who comes to preach or prate, / When men with swords their right and wrong debate. *Italian*

6527. A fool is like other men as long as he is silent. *Danish*

6528. A fool may sometimes speak to the purpose. *Greek*

6529. A fool repays a salve by a stab, and a stab by a salve. [He mistakes friends for foes and vice versa.] *Latin*

6530. A fool shoots; God guides the bullet. *Russian*

6531. A fool talks of folly. *Latin*

6532. A fool when he hes [has] spoken hes all done. *Scottish*

6533. A fool winna gie [will not give] his toy for the Tower o' London. *Scottish*

6534. A fool's belle is sone [soon] runge. *French (Romaunt of the Rose)*

6535. A fool's bolt is soon shot. *Scottish*

6536. A fool's head never grows white. *French*

6537. A fool's lips are the snare of his soul. *Bible*

6538. A fool's loaf is eaten first. *French*

6539. A fool's soul is ever dancing on the tip of his tongue. *Arabic*

6540. A fool's speech is a bubble of air. *English*

6541. A fool's tongue is long enough to cut his own throat. *English (Shakespeare)*

6542. A foolish head makes for weary feet. *Arabic*

6543. A foolish judge passes quick sentence. *French*

6544. A gowk [one easily imposed upon] at Yule'll no be bright at Beltane. *Scottish*

6545. A knavish speech sleeps in a foolish ear. *English (Shakespeare)*

6546. A nod frae [from] a lord is a breakfast for a fool. *Scottish*

6547. A prating fool shall fall. *Bible*

6548. A prosperous fool is a grievous burden. *Greek (Aeschylus)*

6549. A self-made fool is worse than a natural one. Gĩkũyũ

6550. A snickering man is a fool; a giggling woman a castaway. *Chinese*

6551. A thoughtless body's aye thrang [always busy]. *Scottish*

6552. A white wall is a fool's paper. *Italian*

6553. A' [all] fails that fools think. *Scottish*

6554. All fools are slaves. *Latin*

6555. Almost all men are fools. *Latin*

6556. An ill weed grows of its own accord. *French*

6557. As a dog returneth to his vomit, so a fool returneth to his folly. *Bible*

6558. As fain [glad] as a fool is o' a fair day. *Scottish*

6559. Better be a fool than a knave. *English*

6560. Better fleech [flatter] a fool than fight him. *Scottish*

6561. Change of weather is the discourse of fools. *Spanish*

6562. Come a' to Jock Fool's house and ye'll get bread and cheese. *Scottish*

6563. Daffin [sport, folly] does naething. *Scottish*

6564. Daffin and want o' wit mak auld [old] wives donnart [dull]. *Scottish*

6565. Do not seek to escape from the flood by clinging to a tiger's tail. *Chinese*

6566. Dogs and bairns [children] are aye fain o' fools. *Scottish*

6567. Don't fool with a fool. *Yiddish*

6568. Don't give your eggs to a fool to carry. *American*

6569. Don't speak of a stone to a fool lest it be cast at your head. *American*

6570. Every man hath a fool in his sleeve. *English*

6571. Fashious [troublesome] fools are easiest flisket [annoyed, fretful]. *Scottish*

6572. Fine clothes may disguise, but foolish words will disclose a fool. *Greek (Aesop)*

6573. Fool's set far trysts. *Scottish*

6574. Foolish men have foolish dreams. *French*

6575. Foolish pity spoils a city. *English*

6576. Fools and bairns [children] shouldna see half-done wark. *Scottish*

6577. Fools and obstinate men make rich lawyers. *Spanish*

6578. Fools are aye fortunate. *Scottish*

6579. Fools are aye seeing ferlies [wonders]. *Scottish*

6580. Fools are fain o' naething. *Scottish*

6581. Fools are fain of flitting. *Scottish*

6582. Fools are fain of right nought. *Scottish*

6583. Fools are fond o' a' they foregather wi'. *Scottish*

6584. Fools are never uneasy. *German (Goethe)*

6585. Fools are not planted or sowed, they grow of themselves. *Russian*

6586. Fools are the worst thieves; they rob you of time and temper. *American*

6587. Fools cannot hold their tongues. *English (Chaucer)*

6588. Fools die for want of wisdom. *Bible*

6589. Fools go in crowds. *French*

6590. Fools grow without watering. *Italian*

6591. Fools laugh at their ain sport. *Scottish*

6592. Fools let for trust. *Scottish*

6593. Fools multiply folly. *American (Franklin)*

6594. Fools must not be set on eggs. *German*

6595. Fools rush in through the door; for folly is always bold. *Spanish (Gracián)*

6596. Fools should have no chappin' sticks [no means of mischief]. *Scottish (Scott)*

6597. For as the crackling of thorns under a pot, so is the laughter of the fool. *English*

6598. Fortune and women are fond of [or partial to] fools. *German*

6599. Fortune favors fools. *Latin*

6600. God alone understands fools. *French*

6601. God gave fools mouths not that they might talk, but eat. *Turkish*

6602. God help the fool, quoth Pedley. *English*

6603. He doesna ken [does not know] what end o' him's upmost. *Scottish*

6604. He is a fool indeed who expects sense from a fool. *French*

6605. He is a fool that thinks what others think not. *Spanish*

6606. He is a fool who buys an ox to have cream. *German*

6607. He is a fool who does not know which way the wind blows. *Italian*

6608. He is a fool who makes his doctor his heir. *French*

6609. He is a fool who spares the children after having killed the father. *Latin*

6610. He is not the fool that the fool is, but he that with the fool deals. *Scottish*

6611. He maun hae [must have] leave to speak that canna haud [hold] his tongue. *Scottish*

6612. He that plays wi' fools and bairns [children] maun e'en play at the chucks [marbles]. *Scottish*

6613. He that pleads his ain [own] cause has a fool for his client. *Scottish*

6614. He that speaks to himsel speaks to a fool. *Scottish*

6615. He who is born a fool is never cured. *English*

6616. He's a fool who buys an ox to have good cream. *American*

6617. He's gane aff at the nail. *Scottish*

6618. He's no the fool that the fool is, but he that wi' the fool deals. *Scottish*

6619. How ill white hair becomes a fool. *English (Shakespeare)*

6620. I hae gien [have given] a stick to break my ain [own] head. *Scottish*

6621. If all fools wore white caps, we should look like a flock of sheep. *Russian*

6622. If every fool wore a crown most of us would be kings. *Welsh*

6623. If fools ate no bread, corn would be cheap. *German*

6624. If God listened to the fool, the world would have another face. *Yiddish*

6625. If you want to make a fool of yourself, you'll find a lot of people ready to help you. *American*

6626. If you were born a fool, you also die a fool. *Zyryan*

6627. It is folly to make a mallet of one's fish. *French*

6628. It is ill-manners to silence a fool, and cruelty to let him go on. *American (Franklin)*

6629. Knaves and fools divide the world. *English*

6630. Let a bear robbed of her cubs meet a man, rather than a fool in his folly. *Bible*

6631. Live a fool, die a fool. *Yiddish*

6632. Many an injury comes from a fool's speech. *Latin*

6633. More fools, more fun. *French*

6634. Most fools think they are only ignorant. *American (Franklin)*

6635. Muckle [much] fails that fools think. *Scottish*

6636. Nane but fools and knaves lay wagers. *Scottish*

6637. Nane ferlie mair [none wonder more] than fools. *Scottish*

6638. Never show a fool a job half-done. *Yiddish*

6639. No creature smarts so little as a fool. *English (Pope)*

6640. No fool like an old fool. *English*

6641. No one is a fool always, everyone sometimes. *English*

6642. On a fool's beard the barber learns to shave. *French*

6643. One fool makes many. *English*

6644. One fool may make a disturbance which forty wise men may not be able to quiet. *French*

6645. Pheasants are fools if they invite the hawk to dinner. *English*

6646. Send a fool to the market and a fool he will return. *English*

6647. Sloth and silence are a fool's virtues. *American (Franklin)*

6648. Speak not of stones to a fool lest he cast them at thy head. *Turkish*

6649. Take from a fool, but give him nothing. *Saudi Arabian*

6650. Talk sense to a fool / and he calls you foolish. *Greek (Euripides)*

6651. That's like seekin' for a needle in a windlin o' strae. *Scottish*

6652. The dulness of the fool is the whetstone of the wits. *English (Shakespeare)*

6653. The family of fools is ancient. *American (Franklin)*

6654. The fool is always beginning to live. *Latin*

6655. The fool is generally able to get a good meal but the cunning rogue is rightly left hungry. *Chinese*

6656. The fool shall not enter into heaven, let him be ever so holy. *English (Blake)*

6657. The fool thinks nothing done right unless he has done it himself. *Latin*

6658. The fool who falls into the fire rarely falls out of it. *Arabic*

6659. The foolish and perverse fill the lawyer's purse. *American*

6660. The fools do more hurt in the world than the rascals. *American*

6661. The gravest fish is an oyster; the gravest bird's an ool; the gravest beast's an ass; an' the gravest man's a fool. *Scottish*

6662. The height o' nonsense is supping soor milk wi' a brogue. *Scottish*

6663. The learned fool writes his nonsense in better language than the unlearned; but still 'tis nonsense. *American (Franklin)*

6664. The more foolish the man is, the more insolent does he grow. *Latin*

6665. The more riches a fool hath, the greater fool he is. *English*

6666. The thinking of a bad thought, the uttering of a bad speech, and the doing of a bad deed—this is the character of a fool. *Burmese*

6667. The treasure of a fool is always in his tongue. *Latin*

6668. The way of a fool is right in his own eyes. *Bible*

6669. The wise man draws more advantage from his enemies, than the fool from his friends. *American (Franklin)*

6670. The wise man knows the fool, but the fool does not know the wise man. *English*

6671. The words of fools are like the cypress: they are tall and large, but they bear no fruit. *American*

6672. There are bearded fools. *English*

6673. There is no need to fasten a bell to a fool. *Danish*

6674. There's little wit in the pow [head] that lights the candle at the lowe [flame]. *Scottish*

6675. There's no fool like an old fool. *American*

6676. Those who realize their folly are not true fools. *Chinese (Chuang Tzu)*

6677. Thrust not your finger into a fool's mouth. *Dutch*

6678. 'Tis wisdom sometimes to seem a fool. *English*

6679. To a fool an elephant has a tail at both ends. *American*

6680. To be intimate with a foolish friend, is like going to bed to a razor. *American (Franklin)*

6681. To hit a policeman over the head and then to take refuge with the sheriff. *Spanish*

6682. To irritate the hornets. *French (Rabelais)*

6683. To jump into the water to escape the rain. *French*

6684. To make one hole to stop up another. *French*

6685. To put one's hand into a wasps' nest. *German*

6686. To put one's head in a bees' byke. *Scottish*

6687. Twa [two] fools in ae [one] house are a pair ower mony [too many]. *Scottish*

6688. We have all been fools in our time. *Latin*

6689. What fools these mortals be! *English (Shakespeare)*

6690. When a fool finds a horse shoe he thinks aye [always] the like will do. *Scottish*

6691. When a fool is sent to market, the storekeepers rejoice. *Yiddish*

6692. When beans are in flower [i.e., in the spring], fools are in full strength. *French*

6693. When the horse has been stolen, the fool shuts the stable. *French*

6694. Who is born a fool is never cured. *Italian*

6695. Who knows a fool must know his brother; for one will recommend another. *American*

6696. Wipe wi' the water and wash wi' the towel. *Scottish*

6697. Wise men learn by others' harms, fools scarcely by their own. *American (Franklin)*

6698. With fools it is always holiday. *Latin*

6699. "Ye're a fine sword," quo' the fool to the wheat braird [blade]. *Scottish*

6700. Ye're as daft as ye're days auld. *Scottish*

6701. You can't serve dog's flesh at a banquet. [Don't expect much of fools.] *Chinese*

6702. You have left the sheep with the wolf for safe custody. *Latin*

6703. You seek for fruit in the garden of Tantalus. *Latin*

Forbearance *see also* Acceptance; Tolerance

6704. Bear and forbear. *Latin (Ovid)*

6705. Bear and forbear is gude philosophy. *Scottish*

6706. Bear with others and you shall be borne with. *Latin*

6707. If you are capable of submitting to insult you ought to be insulted. *Latin (Juvenal)*

6708. If you would have a hen lay, you must bear with her cackling. *American*

6709. Impatience does not diminish but augments the evil. *English*

6710. It's all in a day's work. *American*

6711. There is a limit at which forbearance ceases to be a virtue. *English (Burke)*

6712. Thole [suffer, endure] weel's gude for burning. *Scottish*

6713. To bear our fate is to conquer it. *American*

6714. What we can't change we must bear without despair. *American*

Forbidden Fruit *see also* Stealing

6715. Forbid a fool a thing, an' that he'll do. *Scottish*

6716. Forbid us a thing, that thing desyren we. *English (Chaucer)*

6717. Forbidden fruit is sweet. *Bible*

6718. Forbidden ware sells twice as dear. *English*

6719. Nothing so good as forbidden fruit. *English*

6720. Stolen bread stirs the appetite. *French*

6721. Stolen fruit is sweet [or sweetest]. *English*

6722. Stolen kisses are always sweeter. *English (Hunt)*

6723. Stolen sweets are best. *English*

6724. Stolen waters are sweet, and bread eaten in secret is pleasant. *Bible*

6725. That which we are not permitted to have we delight in; that which we can have is disregarded. *Latin (Seneca)*

6726. The sweetness of stolen things shouts. *Acholi*

6727. Things forbidden have a secret charm. *Greek*

6728. To drink Falernian wine, the sweeter for being stolen. *Latin (Juvenal)*

6729. What is permitted us we least desire. *Latin*

Force *see also* Coercion; Motivation

6730. A rotting leaf is overcome by force: how else could it rot? *American*

6731. An old wise man's shadow is better than a young buzzard's sword. *English*

6732. Force finds a way. *Latin*

6733. Force without counsel falls of its own weight. *Latin*

6734. Force without foresight aften fails. *Scottish*

6735. If a man won't think as you do, make him do as you think. *American*

6736. If it cannot be done by washing, then it must be done by mangling. *Russian*

6737. Let the sword decide after stratagem has failed. *Arabic*

6738. No mouth speaks louder than the cannon's mouth. *American*

6739. Power backed by force alone must tremble. *American*

6740. The armed prophets conquer, the unarmed perish. *American*

6741. The last argument of kings [i.e., the sword]. *Latin*

6742. The stick is the surest peacemaker. *French*

6743. Who overcomes / By force, hath overcome but half his foe. *English (Milton)*

6744. Who will not be ruled by the rudder, must be ruled by the rock. *English*

Foreigners and Foreignness

6745. The more I see of foreigners, the more I love my own. *French*

Foresight *see also* Forethought; Precaution; Preparedness; Warning

6746. A danger foreseen is half avoided. *English*

6747. Foreseen, the blow comes more lightly. *Latin*

6748. Gude foresight furthers the wark. *Scottish*

6749. He is wise who looks ahead. *Latin*

6750. He who can see three days ahead may be rich for three thousand years. *Japanese*

6751. He who does not look before finds himself behind. *French*

6752. He who does not look before him must take misfortune for his earnings. *Danish*

6753. If one knew that he would fall, he would lie down. *Polish*

6754. If one knew where he would fall, he would spread straw there. *Russian*

6755. Look for squalls, but don't make them. *American*

6756. 'Tis easy to see, hard to foresee. *American (Franklin)*

6757. Who looks not before finds himself behind. *English*

Forethought *see also* Foresight; Lateness; Precaution; Preparedness; Tardiness

6758. A steek in time saves nine. *Scottish*

6759. A stitch in time saves nine. *English*

6760. A strong man who is without forethought is the father of laziness. *Yoruba*

6761. A wise man carries his cloak in fair weather, and a fool wants his in rain. *Scottish*

6762. Ane [one] word before is worth twa behint [two afterward]. *Scottish*

6763. After greet heet cometh cold; / No man cast his pilche [fur garmet] away. *English (Chaucer)*

6764. Afttimes the cautioner pays the debt. *Scottish*

6765. Although it rain, cast not away the watering pot. *Malay*

6766. Dig a well before you are thirsty. *Chinese*

6767. Don't throw away the old bucket until you know whether the new one holds water. *Swedish*

6768. Forecast is better than hard work. *English*

6769. Forethought is better than repentance. *Greek (Dionysius of Halicarnassus)*

6770. Forethought is easy, repentance difficult. *Chinese*

6771. Forewarned, forearmed. *Latin*

6772. Have a care not to commence an undertaking of which you may repent. *Latin*

6773. He who has no anxious thoughts for the future will find trouble close at hand. *Chinese*

6774. It is not at the altar that we should consider the course we would take. *Latin*

6775. It's gude to hae your cog [a wooden dish] out when it rains kail [broth]. *Scottish*

6776. Light your lamp before it becomes dark. *Arabic*

6777. Look whair thou licht before thou lowp / And slip na certainty for howp. *Scottish*

6778. The superior man speaks beforehand, not when all is finished. *Chinese*

6779. The wise man digs a well before he steals a minaret. *Arabic*

6780. Think of the going out before you enter. *Arabic*

6781. To be wise beyond the script. [Look toward tomorrow.] *Latin*

6782. When ye christen the bairn [child] ye should ken what to ca't. *Scottish*

6783. You can't hatch chickens from fried eggs. Pennsylvania *Dutch*

Forgetting and Forgetfulness *see also* Memory

6784. He is lucky who forgets what cannot be mended. *German*

6785. It is as sometimes good not to remember all we know. *Latin (Publilius Syrus)*

6786. Let us forget what the earth covers. *Yiddish*

6787. Men are men; the best sometimes forget. *English (Shakespeare)*

Forgiveness *see also* Absolution; Pardon; Punishment; Revenge

6788. A sin concealed is half forgiven. *Italian*

6789. An injury forgiven is better than an injury revenged. *Danish*

6790. Forgive and forget. *American*

6791. Forgive another often, yourself never. *Latin*

6792. Forgive any sooner than thyself. *French*

6793. Forgive yourself nothing; others much. *German*

6794. He who doth the injury never forgives the injured man. *English*

6795. He who forgives gains the victory. *Yoruba*

6796. He who forgives readily only invites offense. *French*

6797. He who is the offender is never the forgiver. *English*

6798. It is human nature to hate him whom you have injured. *Latin (Tacitus)*

6799. Let bygones be bygones. *English*

6800. Only when the fault is forgotten is forgiveness complete. *Arabic*

6801. The injured often forgive but those who injure neither forgive nor forget. *American*

6802. The worst of men are those who will not forgive. *English*

6803. 'Tis more noble to forgive, and more manly to despise, than to revenge an injury. *American (Franklin)*

6804. To err is human, to forgive divine. *English (Pope)*

6805. To forgive everyone is as much cruelty as to forgive no one. *Greek*

6806. To forgive is beautiful. *Greek*

6807. To understand is to forgive. *French*

6808. Where there is no money there is no forgiveness of sins. *German*

6809. Write injuries in dust, benefits in marble. *English*

Forthrightness *see also* **Candor; Frankness; Sincerity**

6810. Better speak bauldly [boldly] out than aye be grumplin'. *Scottish*

6811. Calling figs figs, and a skiff a skiff. *Greek (Aristophanes)*

Fortitude *see* **Bravery; Courage; Heart**

Fortune *see also* **Destiny; Fate; Luck; Misfortune**

6812. A blind hen can sometimes find her corn. *French*

6813. A blind man may by fortune catch a hare. *English*

6814. A blind man may sometimes shoot a crow. *Dutch*

6815. A blind pigeon may sometimes find a grain of wheat. *Danish*

6816. A change in fortune hurts a wise man no more than a change of the moon. *American (Franklin)*

6817. A drop of fortune [or luck] is better than a cask of wisdom. *Latin*

6818. A fool may meet with good fortune, but only the wise man profits by it. *English*

6819. A fortunate man may be anywhere. *English*

6820. A good man's fortune may grow out of heels. *English (Shakespeare)*

6821. A just fortune awaits the deserving. *Latin*

6822. A lucky bastard is still a bastard; fortune doesn't change his birth. *American*

6823. A partridge has dropped in the yard. *Zulu*

6824. Against fortune nothing avails. *French*

6825. Against fortune the carter cracks his whip in vain. *French*

6826. All your eggs have two yolks apiece. *German*

6827. All your geese are swans. *English*

6828. An ounce of fortune is worth a pound of forecast. *English*

6829. Be not arrogant when fortune smiles, or dejected when she frowns. *Latin (Ausonius)*

6830. Bear good fortune modestly. *Latin*

6831. Beauty will sit and weep, fortune will sit and eat. *Tamil*

6832. Blind fortune pursues blind rashness. *French*

6833. Born of a white hen. *Latin*

6834. Born with a silver spoon in his mouth. *English*

6835. Call me not fool till Heaven has sent me fortune. *English (Shakespeare)*

6836. Cast ye owre the house riggen, and ye'll fa' on your feet. *Scottish*

6837. Come with the wind, gone with the water. *Latin*

6838. Every man's fortune is molded by his character. *Latin*

6839. Every wind is against a leaky ship. *Danish*

6840. Everyone is the author of his own good fortune. *French*

6841. Everything may be borne except good fortune. *Italian*

6842. Fling him into the Nile, and he will come up with a fish in his mouth. *English*

6843. Fortune and futurity are no to be guessed at. *Scottish*

6844. Fortune and misfortune are neighbors. *German*

6845. Fortune and Venus help the bold. *Latin*

6846. Fortune brings in some boats that are not steer'd. *English (Shakespeare)*

6847. Fortune, by being too lavish of her favors on a man, only makes a fool of him. *Latin (Publilius Syrus)*

6848. Fortune can take away riches, but not courage. *Latin*

6849. Fortune can take from us only what she has given us. *French*

6850. Fortune comes to her who seeks her. *Italian*

6851. Fortune comes to the merry gate. *Japanese*

6852. Fortune does not stand waiting at anyone's door. *Dutch*

6853. Fortune effects great changes in brief moments. *Latin*

6854. Fortune favors fools. *Latin*

6855. Fortune favors the cheerful. *English*

6856. Fortune gains the bride. *Scottish*

6857. Fortune gives too much to many, to no one enough. *Latin (Martius)*

6858. Fortune, good or bad, does not last forever. *Arabic*

6859. Fortune has wings. *German*

6860. Fortune hath in her honey gall. *English (Chaucer)*

6861. Fortune helps the daring, but repulses the timid. *Latin*

6862. Fortune helps the hardy. *Scottish*

6863. Fortune is a woman; if you neglect her today, do not expect to regain her tomorrow. *French*

6864. Fortune is accumulated by drops and poured out by pails. *Slovenian*

6865. Fortune is blind. *Latin*

6866. Fortune is blind, but not invisible. *French*

6867. Fortune is easy to find but hard to keep. *American*

6868. Fortune is fickle. *American*

6869. Fortune is gentle to the lowly. *Latin*

6870. Fortune is like glass: it breaks when it is brightest. *Latin (Publilius Syrus)*

6871. Fortune is not far from the brave man's head. *Turkish*

6872. Fortune is not on the side of the faint-hearted. *Greek*

6873. Fortune is on the side of the bold. *American*

6874. Fortune is round; it makes one a king, another a beggar. *Dutch*

6875. Fortune is the companion of virtue. *Latin*

6876. Fortune is the good man's prize, but the bad man's bane. *Chinese*

6877. Fortune knocks, but fools do not answer. *Danish*

6878. Fortune knocks once at least at every man's door. *Italian*

6879. Fortune knows neither reason nor law. *Greek*

6880. Fortune makes a fool of him whom she favors too much. *Latin (Publilius Syrus)*

6881. Fortune makes kings and fools. *German*

6882. Fortune makes kings out of beggars and beggars out of kings. *German*

6883. Fortune molds human affairs as she pleases. *Latin*

6884. Fortune never seems so blind as to those upon whom she has bestowed no favors. *French (La Rochefoucauld)*

6885. Fortune, not riches, rules the life of men. *Greek*

6886. Fortune often knocks at the door, but the fool does not invite her in. *Danish*

6887. Fortune rarely brings good or evil singly. *English*

6888. Fortune sells what we think she gives. *French*

6889. Fortune sides with him who dares. *Greek (Virgil)*

6890. Fortune smiles on the brave, and frowns upon the coward. *Latin*

6891. Fortune sometimes favors those she afterwards destroys. *Italian*

6892. Fortune to one is mother, to another stepmother. *English*

6893. Fortune truly helps those who are of good judgment. *Greek (Euripides)*

6894. Fortune turns like a mill wheel; now you are at the top, and then at the bottom. *Spanish*

6895. Fortune turns on her wheel the fate of kings. *Latin*

6896. Fortune wearies with carrying one and the same man always. *English*

6897. Fortune will call at the smiling gate. *Japanese*

6898. From twelve eggs he gets thirteen chickens. *German*

6899. Good comes to some while they are sleeping. *American*

6900. Good fortune and bad are necessary to man to make him capable. *French*

6901. Good fortune is not known until it is lost. *Spanish*

6902. Good fortune wears a pretty dress, but its underclothes do not bear investigation. *Russian*

6903. Greater qualities are needed to bear good fortune than bad. *French*

6904. Hap and mishap govern the world. *English*

6905. Have fortune and go to sleep. *Italian*

6906. He dances well to whom fortune pipes. *English*

6907. He extracts milk even from a barren goat. *German*

6908. He fell today; I may fall tomorrow. *Latin*

6909. He has luck that brings home the bride. *German*

6910. He is a horse with four white feet. *French*

6911. He planted pebbles and took potatoes. *Greek*

6912. He that falls today may rise tomorrow. *English*

6913. He that hath no ill-fortune will be troubled with good. *American (Franklin)*

6914. He who can bear fortune must also beware of fortune. *Latin*

6915. He who hath no ill fortune is cloyed with good. *English*

6916. He who is born to misfortune stumbles as he goes, and though he fall on his back will fracture his nose. *German*

6917. His bread fell into the honey. *Spanish*

6918. His hens lay eggs with two yolks. *German*

6919. If fortune assist you, your teeth can break an anvil; but should it desert you, your teeth will be broken by eating flummery. *Persian*

6920. If fortune favors you, go and sleep at ease. *Persian*

6921. If he threw up a penny on the roof, down would come a dollar to him. *German*

6922. Industry is Fortune's right hand, and Frugality her left. *English*

6923. Into the mouth of a bad dog falls many a good bone. *English*

6924. It is an ill wind that blows no good to Cornwall [alluding to the salvage value of shipwrecks]. *English*

6925. It is easier to get a favor from fortune than to keep it. *Latin (Publilius Syrus)*

6926. It is the fortunate who should praise fortune. *German*

6927. Jack gets on by his stupidity. *German*

6928. No one is satisfied with his fortune, nor dissatisfied with his intellect. *French*

6929. None know the unfortunate and the fortunate do not know themselves. *American*

6930. Not only is Fortune blind herself, but she blinds those whom she favors. *Latin*

6931. Once in each man's life fortune smiles. *Latin*

6932. Seldom are men blessed with good fortune and good sense at the same time. *Latin*

6933. Some have the hap, some stick in the gap. *American*

6934. The bird of prosperity has lodged on his head. *Turkish*

6935. The blind catch a flea! *Osmanli*

6936. The blind man has picked up a coin. *Portuguese*

6937. The brave man carves out his fortune. *Spanish*

6938. The footsteps of fortune are slippery. *Latin*

6939. The goddess of fortune dwells in the feet of the industrious; the goddess of misfortune dwells in the feet of the sluggard. *Tamil*

6940. The good bone never falls to a good dog. *French*

6941. The good fortunes of life fall to the lot even of the base. *Latin*

6942. The meat has fallen on the hairy side. *Zulu*

6943. The most friendly fortune trips up your heels. *French*

6944. The most wretched fortune is safe, for it fears nothing worse. *Latin*

6945. The ox that tossed me threw me upon a good place. *Spanish*

6946. The sun once stood still, the wheel of fortune, never. *Spanish*

6947. The unfortunate are counted fools. *English*

6948. The vulgar follow Fortune's glances. *Latin (Ovid)*

6949. The wheel of fortune is forever in motion. *American*

6950. The wheel of fortune turns quicker than a mill wheel. *Spanish*

6951. The worst pig gets the best acorn. *Portuguese*

6952. There is no fence against fortune. *English*

6953. There is nothing so intolerable as a fortunate fool. *Latin*

6954. They make their fortune who are stout and wise. *Italian*

6955. 'Tis better to be fortunate than wise. *English (Webster)*

6956. To-morrow morning I found a horseshoe. *English*

6957. We are all bound up with fortune. *Latin (Seneca)*

6958. We are corrupted by good fortune. *Latin (Tacitus)*

6959. We must master our good fortune, or it will master us. *Latin (Publilius Syrus)*

6960. What fortune has given, she cannot take away. *Latin*

6961. When bad fortune comes, a man will be bitten by a dog although mounted on a camel. *Persian*

6962. When fortune closes one door, she opens another. *German*

6963. When fortune knocks, open the door. *German*

6964. When fortune opens one door, she opens another. *German*

6965. When fortune reaches out her hand one must seize it. *German*

6966. When fortune smiles on thee, take advantage. *English*

6967. When the fountain has gone up, it comes down. *Persian*

6968. When you're in ill luck, a snake can bite you even with its tail. *Martinique Creole*

6969. Where fortune is wanting, diligence is useless. *Spanish*

6970. Where God and cruel fortune call, let us follow. *Latin*

6971. Who can put trust in the strength of the body or in the stability of fortune? *Latin (Cicero)*

6972. Whom fortune favors the world favors. *German*

6973. With a fortunate man all things are fortunate. *Greek*

6974. You used to be a baker, though now you wear gloves. *Spanish*

Frankness *see also* Candor; Forthrightness; Sincerity

6975. There is no wisdom like frankness. *American*

Fraud *see also* Deception; Hypocrisy; Insincerity

6976. A few things gained by fraud destroy a fortune otherwise honestly won. *Latin*

6977. Dead flies cause the ointment of the apothecary to send forth a stinking savor. *English*

6978. Fraud and cunning are the weapons of the weak. *American*

6979. Fraud deals in generalities. *Latin*

6980. Fraud is always in a terrible hurry. *American*

6981. Frost and fraud both end in foul. *American*

6982. To hang up a sheep's head and sell dog's flesh. *Japanese*

Freedom and Liberty

6983. A bean in liberty is better than a comfit in prison. *English*

6984. All the arts of pleasure grow when suckled by freedom. *German*

6985. Better be a bird in the wood than one in the cage. *Italian*

6986. Better be a free bird than a captive king. *Danish*

6987. Better free in a foreign land than a serf at home. *American*

6988. Better starve free than be a fat slave. *Greek (Aesop)*

6989. Country is dear, but liberty dearer still. *Latin*

6990. Eternal vigilance is the price of liberty. *American*

6991. Fetters of gold are still fetters, and silken cords pinch. *English*

6992. Freedom is a fair thing. *Scottish*

6993. Freedom is only in the land of dreams. *German (Schiller)*

6994. He is not free who drags his chain. *French*

6995. If we lose our freedom we have nothing else to lose. *American*

6996. Injurious is the gift that takes away freedom. *Italian*

6997. It is not good to have too much liberty. *French (Pascal)*

6998. Lean liberty is better than fat slavery. *English*

6999. Liberty is given by nature even to mute animals. *Latin*

7000. Liberty is not license: you endanger liberty by abusing it. *American*

7001. Liberty is the choice of working or starving. *English (Johnson)*

7002. Liberty, like charity, must begin at home. *American*

7003. Liberty, when it begins to take root, is a plant of rapid growth. *American (Washington)*

7004. Loud coos the doo when the hawk's no whistling; loud cheeps the mouse when the cat's no rustling. *Scottish*

7005. No bad man is free. *Greek*

7006. No man is free who is not master of himself. *Greek*

7007. No man loveth his fetters, be they made of gold. *English (Heywood)*

7008. No outward tyranny can reach the mind. *American*

7009. Nothing brings more pain than too much pleasure; nothing more bondage than too much liberty. *American (Franklin)*

7010. O sweet name of liberty! *Latin*

7011. Only a free soul will never grow old. *German*

7012. Proclaim liberty throughout the land unto all the inhabitants thereof. *Bible*

7013. Sell not virtue to purchase wealth, nor liberty to purchase power. *American (Franklin)*

7014. The blood of tyrants waters the tree of liberty and makes it grow strong and tall. *American*

7015. The God who gave us life, gave us liberty at the same time. *American (Jefferson)*

7016. The grouch is the guardian of our freedom. *American*

7017. The truth makes us free. *American*

7018. The worst crimes have been committed in the name of liberty. *American*

7019. They are not all free who scoff at their chains. *German*

7020. 'Tis folly to love fetters, though they be of gold. *Latin*

7021. To speak his thought is every free man's right. *Greek (Homer)*

7022. Weel kens the mouse when the cat's oot o' the house. *Scottish*

7023. What in some is called liberty, in others is called license. *Latin*

7024. Where liberty dwells, there is my country. *American (Franklin)*

7025. Where the Spirit of the Lord is, there is liberty. *Bible*

7026. Who has lost his freedom has nothing else to lose. *German*

Freedom and Slavery *see also* Slavery

7027. Freedom — the name of virtue; slavery — of vice. *Greek*

7028. He is still a slave whose limbs alone are freed. *American*

7029. Retain a free mind, though a slave, and slave thou shalt not be. *Greek*

7030. The blow that liberates the slave sets the master free. *American*

Friends and Enemies *see also* Friends and Friendship

7031. A dead enemy is as good as a cold friend. *American*

7032. A friend cannot be known in prosperity nor an enemy in adversity. *English*

7033. A reconciled friend, a double foe. *Spanish*

7034. An enemy will agree, but a friend will argue [i.e., will admonish you]. *Russian*

7035. An open enemy is better than a false friend. *German*

7036. An open enemy is better than an indiscreet friend. *American*

7037. Be on guard against thy friends. *Greek*

7038. Better a good enemy than a bad friend. *Yiddish*

7039. Better be friends at a distance than neighbors and enemies. *Italian*

7040. Beware of your enemy twice, but beware of your friend a thousand times. *Syrian*

7041. Consider that a friend may be made out of an enemy. *Latin (Seneca)*

7042. Do good to thy friend to keep him, to thy enemy to gain him. *American (Franklin)*

7043. Faithful are the wounds of a friend; but the kisses of an enemy are deceitful. *Bible*

7044. False friends are waur [worse] than bitter enemies. *Scottish*

7045. Friends are as dangerous as enemies. *English (De Quincey)*

7046. Friends become foes, and foes are reconciled. *Latin*

7047. From my friends God defend me, from my enemies I can defend myself. *German*

7048. He is wise that can make a friend of a foe. *Scottish*

7049. He makes no friend, who never made a foe. *English (Tennyson)*

7050. He that is not with me is against me. *Bible*

7051. He who has a thousand friends has not a friend to spare, / And he who has one enemy shall meet him everywhere. *Arabic (Ali Ibn-abi-Talib)*

7052. He who has no enemy, has not any friend. *Latin*

7053. He's a man o' wise mind that o' a foe can mak a friend. *Scottish*

7054. If you never tell your secret to a friend, you will never fear him when he becomes your enemy. *Greek*

7055. Invite your friend to a feast, but leave your enemy alone. *Greek*

7056. My friends can do no wrong and my enemies can do no right. *American*

7057. One enemy can do more hurt than ten friends can do good. *Irish (Swift)*

7058. One enemy is too many, and a hundred friends are not sufficient. *German*

7059. Peel a fig for your friend, a peach for your enemy. *English*

7060. The best friend often becomes the worst enemy. *German*

7061. The friend looks at the head, the enemy at the foot. *Turkish*

7062. The friendship of the wicked changes to fear, and fear to hate. *French*

7063. The greatest enmity is better than uncertain friendship. Hindu

7064. The lucky man's enemy dies, and the unlucky man's friend. *Russian*

7065. There is no formality among friends. *Omani*

7066. Treat your friends as if they will become your enemies, and your enemies as if they will become your friends. *Latin*

7067. You've never made a friend if you've never made a foe. *American*

7068. Your best friend is your worst enemy. [Even your best friend can't be trusted fully]. *Belizean Creole*

Friends and Friendship *see also* Absence; Friends and Enemies; Love and Friendship

7069. A blazing friendship goes out in a flash. *American*

7070. A brother may not be a friend, but a friend will always be a brother. *American (Franklin)*

7071. A faithful friend is an image of God. *French*

7072. A faithful friend is the medicine of life. *Bible*

7073. A false friend and a shadow attend only while the sun shines. *American (Franklin)*

7074. A false friend has honey in his mouth, gall in his heart. *German*

7075. A false friend is worse than an open enemy. *American*

7076. A father's a treasure; a brother's a comfort; a friend is both. *American (Franklin)*

7077. A friend, a single soul dwelling in two bodies. *Greek*

7078. A friend in need is a friend indeed. *English*

7079. A friend is best found in adversity. *English*

7080. A friend is never known till one has need. *English*

7081. A friend is not so soon gotten as lost. *English*

7082. A friend is often best known by his loss. *German*

7083. A friend married is a friend lost. *Norwegian (Ibsen)*

7084. A friend must not be wounded, even in jest. *Latin*

7085. A friend should bear a friend's infirmities. *English (Shakespeare)*

7086. A friend that will go to the scaffold with you. *Latin*

7087. A friend that you buy with presents, will be bought from you. *English*

7088. A friend to all is a friend to none. *Greek*

7089. A friend to everybody and to nobody is the same thing. *Spanish*

7090. A friend's dinner is soon dight [dished]. *Scottish*

7091. A friend's eye is a good mirror. *Gaelic*

7092. A friend's frown is better than a fool's smile. *Hebrew*

7093. A friend's ne'er kin'd [known] till he's needed. *Scottish*

7094. A good friend is better than silver and gold. *Dutch*

7095. A good friend is my nearest relation. *English*

7096. A good friend is worth more than a near relation. *Spanish*

7097. A good friend never offends. *English*

7098. A handful of friends is better than a wagon of gold. *Slovak*

7099. A lost friendship is an enmity won. *German*

7100. A loving heart and a leal within is better than gowd [gold] and gentle kin. *Scottish*

7101. A man dies as often as he loses a friend. *English (Bacon)*

7102. A man may see his friend in need that wouldna see his pow [head] bleed. *Scottish*

7103. A new friend is like new wine; when it has aged you will drink it with pleasure. *Bible*

7104. A quarrel with a friend is like pepper in food — it makes the friendship stronger. *Hungarian*

7105. A stone from the hands of a friend is an apple. *Tunisian*

7106. A superior man breaks off a friendship without any unpleasantness. *Chinese*

7107. A sure friend is known in a doubtful matter. *Latin (Ennius)*

7108. A true friend does sometimes venture to be offensive. *English*

7109. A true friend is known in the day of adversity. *Turkish*

7110. A true friend is tested in adversity. *Latin (Ennius)*

7111. A true friend is the best possession. *American (Franklin)*

7112. A true friend is the wine of life. *American*

7113. A wa' between best preserves friendship. *Scottish*

7114. Above our life we love a steadfast friend. *English (Marlowe)*

7115. Admonish your friends in private; praise them in public. *Latin (Publilius Syrus)*

7116. Ae gude [one good] friend is worth mony [many] relations. *Scottish*

7117. Affront your friend in daffin' [sport], and tine him in earnest. *Scottish*

7118. Aft [oft] counting keeps friends lang thegither [long together]. *Scottish*

7119. An old friend is a mount for a black day. *Osmanli*

7120. An old friend is better than two new ones. *Russian*

7121. An old friend is like a ready-saddled horse. *Afghani*

7122. An untried friend is like an uncracked nut. *Russian*

7123. Ants will not go to an empty granary, and friends will not visit us when our wealth is gone. *Latin (Ovid)*

7124. As close as batty an bench. *Belizean Creole*

7125. Be a friend to yourself and others will befriend you. *French*

7126. Be more ready to visit a friend in adversity than in prosperity. *Greek*

7127. Be not too thick with anybody; your joys will be fewer, and so will your pains. *Latin (Martius)*

7128. Be slow in choosing a friend, but slower in changing him. *Scottish*

7129. Before you make a friend eat a bushel of salt with him. *Latin*

7130. Better a fremit freend than a freend fremit. [Better a stranger made a friend than a friend made a stranger.] *Scottish*

7131. Better be a nettle in the side of your friend than his echo. *American (Emerson)*

7132. Better one true friend than a hundred relations. *Italian*

7133. Between two friends, a notary and two witnesses. *Spanish*

7134. Between two friends two words. *French*

7135. Beware of a reconciled friend as of the devil. *Spanish*

7136. Beware of fair-weather friends. *American*

7137. Broken friendship may be soldered, but never made sound. *Spanish*

7138. Buy friendship wi' presents, and it will be bought frae [from] you. *Scottish*

7139. Change your friend ere ye hae need. *Scottish*

7140. Change your pleasures, but not your friends. *French (Voltaire)*

7141. Desert not old friends for new ones. *Hindi*

7142. Even the best of friends must part. *American*

7143. Every man's friend is no man's friend. *Latin (Cicero)*

7144. Everyone dances as he has friends in the ballroom. *Portuguese*

7145. Fall not out with a friend for a trifle. *English*

7146. Familiar paths and old friends are the best. *German*

7147. Fate makes relatives, but choice makes friends. *French*

7148. Few there are that will endure a true friend. *English*

7149. Fire is the test of gold, adversity of friendship. *American*

7150. "For better acquaintance-sake," as Sir John Ramsay drank to his father. *Scottish*

7151. Forsake not an old friend, for a new one does not compare with him. *Bible*

7152. Fresh fish and poor friends soon grow ill-fau-r'd [ill-favored]. *Scottish*

7153. Fresh fish and unwelcome friends stink before they are three days old. *Scottish*

7154. Friends agree best at a distance. *French*

7155. Friends and mules fail us at hard passes. *French*

7156. Friends are far from a man who is unfortunate. *Latin*

7157. Friends are like fiddle-strings; they must not be screwed too tight. *English*

7158. Friends are lost by calling often and calling seldom. *Gaelic*

7159. Friends are the true scepters of princes. *American (Franklin)*

7160. Friends are thieves of time. *Latin*

7161. Friends disappear with the dregs from the empty wine casks. *Latin*

7162. Friends have all things in common. *Greek*

7163. Friends living far away are not friends. *Greek*

7164. Friends should be judged by their acts, not their words. *Latin (Livy)*

7165. Friends show their love / in times of trouble, not in happiness. *Greek (Euripides)*

7166. Friends tie their purse with a thread of cobweb. *Italian*

7167. Friendship cannot stand always on one side. *English*

7168. Friendship either finds or makes equals. *Latin (Publilius Syrus)*

7169. Friendship excels relationship. *Latin*

7170. Friendship is a furrow in the sand. *Tongan*

7171. Friendship is a plant which must be watered. *German*

7172. Friendship is but a name. *Latin*

7173. Friendship is equality. *Greek*

7174. Friendship is love with understanding. *American*

7175. Friendship is not to be bought at a fair. *English*

7176. Friendship is the marriage of the soul. *French*

7177. Friendship is the most sacred of all moral bonds. *American*

7178. Friendship lasts as long as the pot boils. *Latin*

7179. Friendship should be unpicked, not rent. *Italian*

7180. Friendship that flames goes out in a flash. *English*

7181. Friendship's full of dregs. *English (Shakespeare)*

7182. Get to know new friends, but don't forget the old ones. *Bulgarian*

7183. Give out that you have many friends, and believe that you have few. *French*

7184. Go a mile to see a sick man, go two miles to make peace between two men, and go three miles to visit a friend. *Arabic*

7185. Happy is he whose friends were born before him. *English*

7186. Have few friends, though much acquaintance. *English*

7187. He does good to himself who does good to his friends. *Latin*

7188. He is a friend to none who is a friend to all. *Swedish*

7189. He is my friend that succoureth me, not he that pitieth me. *English*

7190. He is my friend who grinds at my mill [i.e., who is useful to me]. *English*

7191. He maun be a gude friend when ye dinna ken [do not know] his value. *Scottish*

7192. He never was a friend who has ceased to be one. *French*

7193. He that trusts a faithless friend has a good witness against him. *Spanish*

7194. He that would have many friends should try few of them. *Italian*

7195. He that's no my friend at a pinch is no my friend ava [at all]. *Scottish*

7196. He who has a good nest finds good friends. *Portuguese*

7197. He who is everybody's friend is either very poor or very rich. *Spanish*

7198. He who makes friends of all keeps none. *English*

7199. Hearts may gree though heads may differ. *Scottish*

7200. Hold a true friend with both thy hands. *Kanuri*

7201. I cannot be your friend and your flatterer, too. *American*

7202. I wad rather my friend should think me framet [strange] than fashious [troublesome]. *Scottish*

7203. If you bear with the faults of a friend, you make them your own. *Latin (Publilius Syrus)*

7204. In misfortune, what friend remains a friend. *Greek (Euripides)*

7205. In prosperous times, one has many friends; if fortune disappears, so do the friends. *Latin (Ovid)*

7206. In times of prosperity friends will be plenty, / In times of adversity, not one in twenty. *English*

7207. It is a difficult thing to replace true friends. *Latin (Seneca)*

7208. It is asked, is it not right to prefer friends to relatives? *Latin (Cicero)*

7209. It is better to have friends on the market than money in one's coffer. *Spanish*

7210. It is better to make one's friendships at home. *Greek*

7211. It is good to have friends, even in hell. *Spanish*

7212. It is more shameful to mistrust one's friends than to be deceived by them. *French (La Rochefoucauld)*

7213. It is not tint [lost] that is done to friends. *Scottish*

7214. It is the duty of friends to correct each other. *Latin*

7215. It's a friend that misses you. *Scottish*

7216. It's gude to hae friends baith in heaven and hell. *Scottish*

7217. It's poor friendship that needs to be constantly bought. *English*

7218. Just as yellow gold is tested in the fire, so is friendship to be tested by adversity. *Latin (Ovid)*

7219. Keep your ain fish-guts to your ain seamaws. (That is, save your leftovers for your friends.) *Scottish*

7220. Keep your friendships in repair. *American (Emerson)*

7221. Let him that is wretched and beggared try everybody, and then his friend. *Italian*

7222. Let me have no good thing unknown to a friend. *Greek*

7223. Let not the grass grow on the path of friendship. *American Indian*

7224. Life is partly what we make it, and partly what it is made by the friends we choose. *Chinese*

7225. Life without a friend is death with a vengeance. *English*

7226. Life without a friend is death without a witness. *English*

7227. Little intermeddling makes good friends. *Scottish*

7228. Loss of wealth is lamented with greater outcry than the loss of friends. *Latin (Juvenal)*

7229. Love your friend together with his fault. *Italian*

7230. Love your friends despite their faults. *American*

7231. Luve your freend, an' look to yoursel. *Scottish*

7232. Make new friends, but don't forget the old ones. *Yiddish*

7233. Many acquaintances, few friends. *Spanish*

7234. Many friends in general, one in special. *English*

7235. Many kinsfolk, few friends. *English*

7236. May God not prosper our friends that they forget us. *Spanish*

7237. My friend is he who helps me in time of need. *German*

7238. Nae man can be happy without a friend, nor be sure of him till he's unhappy. *Scottish*

7239. Never malign a friend. *Latin*

7240. No man can be happy without a friend, or be sure of his friend till he is unhappy. *English*

7241. Nothing can be purchased which is better than a true friend. *Latin*

7242. Nothing is more acceptable to a man, than a friend in time of need. *Latin (Plautus)*

7243. Nothing is so dangerous as an ignorant friend. *French*

7244. Now that I have a ewe and a lamb everybody says to me, "Good day, Peter." *Spanish*

7245. Of many friends there are few on whom a man can rely. *Latin (Plautus)*

7246. Offer not the right hand of friendship to everyone. *Latin*

7247. Old be your fish, your oil, your friend. *Italian*

7248. Old friends and old ways ought not to be disdained. *Danish*

7249. Old friends and old wine are best. *French*

7250. Old tunes are sweetest and old friends are surest. *American*

7251. One God, one wife, but many friends. *Dutch*

7252. One loyal friend is worth ten thousand relatives. *Greek (Euripides)*

7253. One should go invited to a friend in good fortune, and uninvited in misfortune. *Swedish*

7254. Our best friends are the source of our greatest sorrow. *French*

7255. Patched-up friendship seldom becomes whole again. *German*

7256. Poverty trieth friends. *English*

7257. Prove thy friend ere thou have need. *Latin*

7258. Real friends are few and far between. *American*

7259. Reconciled friendship is a wound ill salved. *Italian*

7260. Remember, man, and keep in mind, a faithful friend is hard to find. *Scottish*

7261. Short reckonings make long friends. *American*

7262. So long as fortune sits at the table friends sit there. *German*

7263. Strife and friendship allow of no excuse. *Greek*

7264. Sudden friendship is rarely formed without subsequent repentance. *Latin*

7265. Sudden friendship, sure repentance. *English*

7266. The best friends are in the purse. *German*

7267. The best mirror is an old friend. *Spanish*

7268. The best of friends must part. *English*

7269. The bird a nest, the spider a web, man friendship. *English (Blake)*

7270. The bread is eaten, the company departed. *Spanish*

7271. The fewer friends one has, the more one feels the value of friendship. *French*

7272. The friends of my friends are my friends. *French*

7273. The friends of the unfortunate live a long way off. *Latin*

7274. The friendship of superior men is as flavorless as water; the friendship of mean men, sweet has honey. *Chinese*

7275. The friendship of the great is fraternity with lions. *Italian*

7276. The friendship that can come to an end, never really began. *Latin (Publilius Syrus)*

7277. The image of friendship is truth. *Arabic*

7278. The name of friend is common, but faith in friendship is rare. *Latin*

7279. The only gain from the friendship of the great is a fine dinner. *Latin (Juvenal)*

7280. The only way to have a friend is to be one. *American (Emerson)*

7281. The poor man is hated by his neighbor, but the rich hath many friends. *English*

7282. The purse-strings are the most common ties of friendship. *American*

7283. The tooth often bites the tongue, and yet they stay together. *German*

7284. The vulgar herd estimate friendship by its advantages. *Latin*

7285. There are three faithful friends — an old wife, an old dog, and ready money. *American (Franklin)*

7286. There is no friendship without freedom, no freedom without the friendship of brothers. *American*

7287. There's no living without friends. *Portuguese*

7288. They are rich who have friends. *Portuguese*

7289. They cease to be friends who dwell afar off. *Greek*

7290. They're fremit [strange] friends that canna be fashed [bothered]. *Scottish*

7291. Three things on earth are precious: knowledge, grain, and friendship. *Burmese*

7292. Time, which strengthens friendship, weakens love. *French*

7293. 'Tis great confidence in a friend to tell him your faults, greater to tell him his. *American (Franklin)*

7294. To a friend's house the road is never long. *Dutch*

7295. To a wedding wait to be invited; to a funeral go uninvited. *Irish*

7296. To have the same likes and dislikes, therein consists the firmest bond of friendship. *Latin (Sallust)*

7297. To lose a friend is the greatest of injuries. *Latin*

7298. To meet an old friend in a distant country is like the delight of rain after a long draught. *Chinese*

7299. True friendship is a plant of slow growth. *American*

7300. True love kyths [appears] in time of need. *Scottish*

7301. Try your friend before you have need of him. *French*

7302. Unless you bear with the fault of a friend, you betray your own. *Latin (Publilius Syrus)*

7303. Water your friendships as you water your flower-pots. *American*

7304. We can live without a brother, but not without a friend. *German*

7305. We die as often as we lose a friend. *Latin (Publilius Syrus)*

7306. We should behave to our friends as we would wish our friends to behave to us. *Greek*

7307. We'll meet ere hills meet. *Scottish*

7308. Weel's him and wae's him that has a bishop in his kin. *Scottish*

7309. When a friend asks, there is no "tomorrow." *Spanish*

7310. When a friend deals with a friend, let the bargain be clear and well penn'd, that they may continue friends to the end. *American (Franklin)*

7311. When a man's friend marries, all is over between them. *French*

7312. When fortune begins to frown, friends will be few. *Latin*

7313. When fortune is fickle, the faithful friend is found. *Latin*

7314. When friends meet, hearts warm. *Scottish*

7315. When good cheer is lacking, / Our friends will be packing. *English*

7316. When my friends are one-eyed, I look at their profile. *French (Joubert)*

7317. When there are friends there is wealth. *Latin*

7318. When there are two friends to one purse, one sings and the other weeps. *Spanish*

7319. When you are forming new friendships, cultivate the old. *Latin*

7320. Wheresoever you see your kindred, make much of your friends. *English*

7321. While the pot boils, friendship blooms. *German*

7322. Who finds himself without friends is like a body without a soul. *Italian*

7323. Without confidence there is no friendship. *Greek*

7324. Without friends no one would choose to live. *Greek*

7325. You are your best friend — to the end. *American*

7326. You betray your own failing if you cannot bear with the fault of a friend. *Latin (Publilius Syrus)*

7327. You can't live without friends — and quite often you can't live with them. *American*

7328. You cannot buy a friend. *Russian*

Frugality *see also* Economy; Miserliness; Money; Parsimony; Saving and Spending; Thrift

7329. Frugality embraces all the other virtues. *Latin*

7330. Frugality is a great revenue. *Latin*

7331. Frugality is a handsome income. *Latin*

7332. Frugality is an estate alone. *English*

7333. Frugality is misery in disguise. *Latin*

7334. Frugality is the mother of all virtues. *Latin*

7335. Frugality is the sure guardian of our virtues. *Brahman*

7336. Frugality when all is spent comes too late. *American*

Frustration

7337. The worst things: To be in bed and sleep not, to wait for one who comes not, to try to please and please not. *Egyptian*

Fullness *see also* Emptiness

7338. As full as an egg is of meat. *Italian*

Futility *see also* Waste of Time

7339. Don't try to draw water with a sieve. *American*

7340. He is washing the crow. *English*

7341. To wash the Ethiopian. *Latin*

7342. You talk to a deaf man. *Latin*

Future

7343. A day to come seems langer than a year that's gane. *Scottish*

7344. Fear of the future is worse than one's present fortune. *Latin*

7345. Fill your garners, harvest lasts not forever. *Latin*

7346. Full of misery is the mind anxious about the future. *Latin (Seneca)*

7347. He must be mad who builds upon the future. *French*

7348. He that fears not the future may enjoy the present. *English*

7349. He that waits for dead men's shoes may go long barefoot. *English*

7350. Hearken to the hinder-end, after comes not yet. *Scottish*

7351. Heav'n from all creatures hides the Book of Fate. *English (Pope)*

7352. If you take no care for the future, you will look back with sorrow for the present. *Chinese*

7353. It is better to have a hen tomorrow than an egg today. *American*

7354. Leave tomorrow till tomorrow. *English*

7355. No man can tell what the future may bring forth. *Greek*

7356. No one has any right to draw for himself upon the future. *Latin*

7357. The future becomes the present if we fight for it. *American*

7358. The future is a sealed book. *American*

7359. The future is near. *Lebanese*

7360. The future struggles that it may not become the past. *Latin (Publilius Syrus)*

7361. The man who has no future loses his grip on the present. *American*

7362. The provision of tomorrow belongs to tomorrow. *American*

7363. The wise god covers with the darkness of night the issues of the future. *Latin (Horace)*

7364. The wise man guards against the future as if it were the present. *Latin (Publilius Syrus)*

7365. Today must borrow nothing of tomorrow. *German*

7366. Tomorrow comes never. *English*

7367. Tomorrow is a long day. *German*

7368. Tomorrow is a new [or another] day. *American*

7369. Tomorrow is the pupil of today. *Latin*

7370. Tomorrow will be another day. *Spanish*

7371. Tomorrow's sun to thee may never rise. *English (Congreve)*

7372. We steal if we touch tomorrow. It is God's. *American (Beecher)*

7373. When all else is lost the future still remains. *American*

Gain(s) *see* Buying and Selling; Ill-Gotten Gains; Profit and Loss

Gambling *see also* Profit and Loss; Venture and Investment; Winning and Losing

7374. At play, anything may happen. *French*

7375. Cards are the bible of 52 leaves. *Dutch*

7376. Cards are the devil's prayer-book. *German*

7377. Ducks lay eggs; geese lay wagers. *American*

7378. Fools use bets for arguments. *American*

7379. Gaming gains a loss. *English (Byron)*

7380. Gaming is the child of avarice and the parent of despair. *French*

7381. Gaming is the mother of lies and perjuries. *Latin*

7382. Gaming, wine, and women, through which I have become a beggar. *Latin*

7383. Hazard is the very mother of lyings. *English (Chaucer)*

7384. Lest he should lose, the gambler ceases not to lose. *Latin*

7385. Losing money is begotten of winning. *Chinese*

7386. Nane but fools and knaves lay wagers. *Scottish*

7387. One begins by being a dupe and ends by being a rascal. *French*

7388. Put up or shut up. *American*

7389. Quit while you're ahead. *American*

7390. The best throw of the dice is to throw them away. *English*

7391. The better the gambler, the worse the man. *Latin*

7392. The devil invented dicing. *Latin (St. Augustine)*

7393. The devil leads him by the nose, / Who the dice too often throws. *English*

7394. The more skillful the gambler, the worse the man. *Latin*

7395. Who wins at lottery will share with the devil. *Polish*

7396. Young gambler, old beggar. *German*

Generalization

7397. All flesh is not venison. *English*

7398. Fraud lurks in loose generalities. *Latin*

Generations *see* Parents and Children; Youth and Old Age

Generosity *see also* Charity; Gifts and Giving; Philanthropy

7399. A generous action is its own reward. *English*

7400. Be just before you're generous. *English*

7401. Bounty, being free itself, thinks all others so. *American*

7402. Bounty receives part of its value from the manner in which it is bestowed. *American*

7403. Broad is the shadow of generosity. *Arabic*

7404. Generosity is catching: you are generous if your neighbor is generous. *American*

7405. Generosity is more charitable than wealth. *American*

7406. Generosity veils all faults. *Arabic*

7407. If you give the loan of your breeches don't cut off the buttons. *Irish*

7408. It is easy to be generous with another man's money. *English*

7409. Lavishness is not generosity. *English*

7410. Liberal enough of another man's leather. *Latin*

7411. Our generosity should never exceed our abilities. *American*

7412. Prodigal of the property of others, sparing of his own. *Latin (Cicero)*

7413. The best generosity is that which is quick. *Arabic*
7414. The generous is always just and the just is always generous. *American*
7415. The generous man receives more than he gives. *American*
7416. The tree with too many nests dies before the others. *Algerian*

Genius
7417. Doing what is impossible for talent is genius. *French*
7418. Genius is one part inspiration, and three parts perspiration. *American*
7419. Genius is one percent inspiration and ninety-nine percent perspiration. *American (Edison)*
7420. Genius is patience. *French (Buffon)*
7421. Genius without education is like silver in the mine. *American (Franklin)*
7422. The first and last thing required of genius is the love of truth. *German (Goethe)*
7423. The lamp of genius burns more brightly than the lamp of life. *German (Schiller)*
7424. The memory of genius is immortal. *Latin*
7425. The worship of genius never makes a man rich. *Latin (Petronius)*
7426. When Nature has work to be done, she creates a genius to do it. *American (Emerson)*

Gentility
7427. Gentility, sent to market, will not buy a peck of meal. *English*

Gentlemen
7428. A gentleman without a living is like a pudding without suet. *English*
7429. It's not the gay coat makes the gentleman. *English*
7430. The gentleman of honor, ragged sooner than patched. *Spanish (Cervantes)*
7431. What's a gentleman but his pleasure? *English*

Gentleness *see also* Mildness; Soft Words
7432. A gentle hand may lead the elephant with a hair. *Persian*
7433. A gentle horse should be sindle [seldom] spurred. *Scottish*
7434. Better make penitents by gentleness than hypocrites by severity. *American*
7435. Fair and softly goes far. *Spanish (Cervantes)*
7436. Fair and softly goes far in a day. *English*
7437. Fleying a bird is no the way to grip it. *Scottish*
7438. Gentle laws make happy people. *American*
7439. Gentleness and kindness conquer at last. *American*
7440. Gentleness corrects whatever is offensive in our manner. *American*
7441. Gentleness does more than violence. *French*
7442. Gently but firmly. *Latin*
7443. Gently, gently, goes far. *Portuguese*
7444. He is gentle that doth gentle deeds. *English (Chaucer)*
7445. Men love gentleness; dogs like food. *Chinese*
7446. Sairs [sores] shouldna be sair handled [i.e., should be delicately handled]. *Scottish*
7447. The gentle calf sucks all the cows. *Portuguese*
7448. The gentle ewe is sucked by every lamb. *Italian*
7449. There is great force hidden in a sweet command. *English*
7450. Use a sweet tongue, courtesy, and gentleness, and thou mayst manage to guide an elephant with a hair. *Persian (Sa'di)*
7451. Violence frustrates its own purpose; gentleness rarely fails. *American*

Gifts and Giving *see also* Charity; Generosity; Philanthropy
7452. A gi'en piece is soon eaten. *Scottish*
7453. A gift in season is a double favor to the needy. *Latin (Publilius Syrus)*
7454. A gift in time of need is most acceptable. *Latin (Ovid)*
7455. A gift long expected is sold [paid], not given. *English*
7456. A gift, with a kind countenance, is a double present. *English*
7457. A given horse should not be looked in the teeth. *Scottish*
7458. A giving hand, though foul, shall have fair praise. *American*
7459. A hand accustomed to take is far from giving. *Arabic*
7460. A man whose leg has been cut off does not value a present of shoes. *Chinese (Chuang Tzu)*
7461. A present looks for a present. *Russian*
7462. A small gift, but well-timed. *Latin*
7463. A white elephant. *English*
7464. Be careful to whom you give. *Latin*
7465. Better to buy than be given. *Japanese*
7466. Bounty has no bottom. *Latin*
7467. By giving comes forgiving. *French*
7468. Cast a bone in the devil's teeth. *English*
7469. Do not drink wine given to you; it will cost you more than if you had bought it. *Russian*
7470. Do not take anything easily obtained, and forthwith make it out to be unimportant. *Chinese*
7471. Do not trouble about the color of a gift horse. *Italian*
7472. Even the gods are conciliated by offerings. *Latin*
7473. Ever [i.e., always] receive a present with approbation. *Latin*
7474. Every good gift and every perfect gift is from above. *Bible*
7475. Evil the gift that takes away our liberty. *Italian*
7476. For a paltry gift, little thanks. *Latin*
7477. Giff-gaff [exchanging gifts] maks gude friends. *Scottish*
7478. Giff-gaff was a good man, but he is soon weary. *English*
7479. Gifts are as the givers. *German*
7480. Gifts are often [or sometimes] losses. *Italian*
7481. Gifts from enemies are dangerous. *English*
7482. Gifts should be handed, not hurled. *Danish*

7483. Give a clown your finger and he'll take your whole hand. *Italian*

7484. Give a clown your foot and he will take your hand. *Spanish*

7485. Give a loaf, and beg a shive. *English*

7486. Give a thing and take again, / And you shall ride in hell's wain. *English*

7487. Give is a good girl; but Take is bad, and she brings death. *Greek*

7488. Give to him who has. *American*

7489. Giving and keeping require brains. *Spanish*

7490. Giving calls for genius. *Latin*

7491. Giving is an honor, asking is a pain. *Spanish*

7492. Giving is dead nowadays, and restoring very sick. *English*

7493. Giving is fishing. *Italian*

7494. Giving is storing up for oneself. *Zulu*

7495. God loveth a cheerful giver. *Bible*

7496. Gratis is both cheapest and dearest. *Serbian*

7497. Hae, lad, rin [run], lad; that maks a willing lad. *Scottish*

7498. Hae [have, take] gars [makes] a deaf man hear. *Scottish*

7499. He doubles his gift that gies in time. *Scottish*

7500. He gives an egg to get a chicken. *Dutch*

7501. He gives double who gives unasking. *Arabic*

7502. He gives too late who waits to be asked. *Latin*

7503. He gives twice who gives quickly. *Latin*

7504. He giveth twice who giveth in a trice. *English*

7505. He sends his presents with a hook attached. *Latin*

7506. He that eats capon gets capon. *French*

7507. He that gives to be seen would never relieve a man in the dark. *English*

7508. He that has a goose will get a goose. *English*

7509. He who can give has many a good neighbor. *French*

7510. He who gives bread to others' dogs is barked at by his own. *Italian*

7511. He who gives quickly gives doubly. *German*

7512. He who gives to the public gives to no one. *Spanish*

7513. He who would take must give. *Spanish*

7514. He's free o' his fruits that wants an orchard. *Scottish*

7515. His presents conceal a baited hook. *Latin*

7516. I give that you may give. *Latin*

7517. I would rather buy than beg. *Latin*

7518. If he gies a duck he expects a goose. *Scottish*

7519. If one give thee a cow, run with a cord. *Scottish*

7520. If you accept nothing you have nothing to return. *American*

7521. If you receive an ox you must return a horse. [You should give more than you receive.] *Chinese*

7522. It is inexcusable to have remained long away, and return emptyhanded. *Latin*

7523. It is more blessed to give than to receive. *Bible*

7524. It is not much to give the leg to him that gave you the fowl. *Spanish*

7525. It is not right to take away gifts. *Greek (Plato)*

7526. Let your portal be wide to the giver. *Latin*

7527. Liberty is of more value than any gifts; and to receive gifts is to lose it. *Persian (Sa'di)*

7528. Little presents keep up friendships. *French*

7529. Look not a gift horse in the mouth. *English*

7530. Measure a man by what he gives as well as by what he does. *American*

7531. Muckle [many] gifts mak beggars bauld [bold]. *Scottish*

7532. Naething freer than a gift. *Scottish*

7533. Not he gives who likes, but who has. *Spanish*

7534. Nothing costs so much as what is given us. *English*

7535. People don't give black-puddings to one who kills no pigs. *Spanish*

7536. People give to the rich and take from the poor. *German*

7537. Present meat, minced fish and shrimps to a teacher. *Chinese*

7538. Presents from an enemy must be received with suspicion. *Latin*

7539. Presents more burdensome than profitable. *Latin*

7540. Return gift for gift. *Chinese*

7541. Rich gifts wax poor, when givers prove unkind. *English (Shakespeare)*

7542. She that taks a gift hersel she sells, she that gies ane does naething else. *Scottish*

7543. Sic as ye gie [such as you give], sic will ye get. *Scottish*

7544. Small favors conciliate, but great gifts make enemies. *Latin*

7545. Small gifts come from the heart; big gifts come from the purse. *Turkish*

7546. Sometimes it is better to give your apple away, than eat it yourself. *English*

7547. Suit the present to the receiver. *Chinese*

7548. Take gifts without a sigh; most men give to be paid. *Irish*

7549. The "throw-in" is more thought of than the bought. *Chinese*

7550. The best of all gifts is the good intention of the giver. *Latin*

7551. The gear that is gifted is never so sweet as the gear that is won. *Scottish*

7552. The gift-bringer always finds an open door. *American*

7553. The gifts of enemies are not gifts, and have no value. *Greek (Sophocles)*

7554. The giver makes the gift precious. *American*

7555. The good that can be given, cannot be removed. *Latin*

7556. The good will accompanying the gift is the best portion of it. *Latin*

7557. The hand that gives, gathers. *English*

7558. The hand that gives is higher than the hand that takes. *Turkish*

7559. The hand that gives is the hand that gets. *Gaelic*

7560. The man who gives you something has already taken something away from you. *Maltese*

7561. The wise man does not lay up treasure. The more he gives the more he has. *Chinese*

7562. There is no benefit in the gifts of a bad man. *Greek (Euripides)*

7563. They are welcome that bring. *Scottish*

7564. They give, to find a pretext for asking. *Latin*

7565. They that come wi' a gift dinna need to stand lang at the door. *Scottish*

7566. They who give have all things; they who withhold have nothing. *Hindi*

7567. They're a' gude that gies [all good who give]. *Scottish*

7568. Things that are truly given must not be taken away. *Greek*

7569. Those presents are the most acceptable which are enhanced by our regard for the donor. *Latin (Ovid)*

7570. Though he has to shut his door against creditors he borrows money to make presents. *Chinese*

7571. To carry an offering of a pig's head, and be unable to find the door of the temple. *Chinese*

7572. To give an apple where there is an orchard. *English*

7573. To give an egg to get an ox. *English*

7574. To give and keep there is need of wit. *English*

7575. To give is honor; to lose is grief. *Spanish*

7576. To give is the business of the rich. *German (Goethe)*

7577. To give quickly is a great virtue [or the best charity]. *Hindi*

7578. To give without cause is to bribe. *Chinese*

7579. To one who has a pie in the oven you may give a bit of your cake. *French*

7580. To receive a gift; to make a suitable return; and still feel dissatisfied. *Chinese*

7581. Vinegar given is better than honey sought [or bought]. *Arabic*

7582. Wha canna gie will little get. *Scottish*

7583. What is bought is cheaper than a gift. *Portuguese*

7584. What ye gie shines aye [always], what ye get smells ill next day. *Scottish*

7585. What you give is written in sand; what you take, with an iron hand. *German*

7586. What's given shines, what's receiv'd is rusty. *American (Franklin)*

7587. Whatever I have given I still possess. *Latin*

7588. When a trifling present is sent a long distance, the gift may be light but the intention is weighty. *Chinese*

7589. When the bearer of a trifling present to one at a great distance, be sure you do not lose it. *Chinese*

7590. Where they give they take. *Spanish*

7591. While you look at what is given, look also at the giver. *Latin*

7592. Who gives bread to others' dogs is often barked at by his own. *Italian*

7593. Who gives his children bread, and suffers want in old age, should be knocked dead with a club. *German*

7594. Who gives his goods before his death prepares himself for much suffering. *Italian*

7595. Who gives to me teaches me to give. *Dutch*

7596. Who gives what he has before he is dead, hit him on the forehead with a mallet. *Spanish*

7597. Whoever gives thee a bone would not wish to see thee dead. *Spanish*

7598. You double your gift if you give in time. *American*

7599. You will never grow howbackit [hump-backed] bearing your friends. *Scottish*

Give and Take *see also* Borrowing and Lending; Gifts and Giving; Reciprocity

7600. Give first to take. *Japanese*

Giving *see* Borrowing and Lending; Charity; Generosity; Gifts and Giving

Gloom

7601. Gloom and sadness are poisons to the soul. *American*

7602. He who is only just is stern; he who is only wise lives in gloom. *American*

Glory *see also* Fame

7603. Envy the companion of glory. *Latin*

7604. Glory drags all men captive at the wheel of her glittering car. *Latin*

7605. Glory is a mighty spur. *Latin*

7606. Glory is a poison, good to be taken in small doses. *American*

7607. Glory is never where virtue is not. *French*

7608. Glory is the fair child of peril. *American*

7609. Glory is the recompense of gallant actions. *French*

7610. Glory paid to our ashes comes too late. *Latin*

7611. Hasty glory goes out in a snuff. *English*

7612. He will have true glory who despises glory. *Latin*

7613. If glory comes after death, I am in no hurry. *Latin*

7614. It may be a fire — tomorrow it will be ashes. *Arabic*

7615. Like madness is the glory of his life. *English (Shakespeare)*

7616. Men are guided less by conscience than by glory. *American*

7617. No flowery road leads to glory. *French*

7618. Our greatest glory consists not in never falling, but in rising every time we fall. *American*

7619. So much greater is our thirst for glory than for virtue. *Latin (Juvenal)*

7620. The best are slandered, the worst are glorified. *American*

7621. The desire for glory is the torch of the mind. *American*

7622. The glory of good men is in their conscience and not in the mouths of men. *Latin*

7623. The glory of great men should be measured by the means they have used to acquire it. *French (La Rochefoucauld)*

7624. The paths of glory lead but to the grave. *English (Gray)*

7625. The smoke of glory is not worth the smoke of a pipe. *American*

7626. Thus passes away the glory of the world. [*Sic transit gloria mundi.*] *Latin*

7627. We rise in glory as we sink in pride. *English (Young)*

7628. When glory comes, memory departs. *French*

Gluttony *see also* Eating; Obesity

7629. A belly full of gluttony will never study willingly. *English*

7630. A cramm'd kite maks a crazy carcase. *Scottish*

7631. As the sow fills, the draff sours. *Scottish*

7632. Double charges rive [split] cannons. *Scottish*

7633. Gluttony kills more than the sword. *Latin*

7634. Gluttony makes the body sting as well as the pocket. *American*

7635. Gourmands make their grave with their teeth. *French*

7636. He that eats till he is sick must fast till he is well. *American*

7637. He that eats while he lasts will be the waur [worse] when he die. *Scottish*

7638. He who eats too much cannot sleep. *Sumerian*

7639. He who eats too much knows not how to eat. *French*

7640. He'll hae enough some day, when his mouth's fu' o' mools [clods of earth (i.e., when he is buried)]. *Scottish*

7641. His eye is bigger than his belly. *American*

7642. Hunger and thirst scarcely kill any, / But gluttony and drink kill a great many. *English*

7643. I saw few die of hunger; of eating—100,000. *American (Franklin)*

7644. Ingenious is gluttony. *Latin*

7645. Many fall by the sword, but more from gluttony. *Latin*

7646. Men dig their graves with their teeth. *English*

7647. Over-feeding has destroyed many more than hunger. *Latin*

7648. Surfeit has killed more than famine. *Greek*

7649. Surfeits slay more than swords. *English*

7650. The belly is chains to the hands and fetters to the feet. *American*

7651. The glutton digs his grave with his teeth. *English*

7652. The glutton has two stomachs to eat but no stomach for work. *American*

7653. The glutton is born merely for the purpose of digestion. *American*

7654. The glutton's god is his belly and his glory is his shame. *American*

7655. The houses stored with food are full of mice; the bodies of gluttons are full of diseases. *American*

7656. The more the glutton eats the greater his appetite. *American*

7657. The mouth is a little hole, but it can swallow house and roof. *Yiddish*

7658. There is death in the pot. *Bible*

7659. What a vile beast is the belly. *Greek*

7660. You may know a carpenter by his chips. [A Suffolk saying, applied to great eaters.] *English*

Goals *see also* Ambition; Ends and Means; Purpose

7661. Keep your eye upon the goal. *Latin*

God *see also* Church; Divine Assistance; Heaven; Man and God; Prayer; Religion; Self-Help

7662. A God all mercy is a God unjust. *English (Young)*

7663. A mighty fortress is our God. *German (Luther)*

7664. A sparrow cannot fall to the ground without God's notice. *American*

7665. Be warned: learn justice, and not to despise the gods. *Latin* (Vergil)

7666. Better deal with God than with his saints. *French*

7667. Better God than gold. *American*

7668. Danger past, God is forgotten. *Scottish*

7669. Day and night are one to God. *American*

7670. Do the likeliest, and God will do the best. *Scottish*

7671. Don't bargain with God. *Yiddish*

7672. Each for himself, God for all. *Yiddish*

7673. Every man for himsel', and God for us a'. *Scottish*

7674. Everyone in his own house and God in all men's. *Spanish*

7675. Everyone is as God made him and very often worse. *Spanish*

7676. Father and mother are kind, but God is kinder. *Danish*

7677. Fear God and keep His commandments. *Bible*

7678. God does not pay weekly, but he pays at the end. *Dutch*

7679. God dwells in an honest man's head. *Japanese*

7680. God gives a cursed cow short horns. *Italian*

7681. God gives almonds to some who have no teeth. *Spanish*

7682. God gives little folk small gifts. *Danish*

7683. God gives refuge from the word "I." *Tunisian*

7684. God giveth the shoulder according to the burden. *German*

7685. God hangs the greatest weights upon the smallest wires. *American*

7686. God has many names though he is only one being. *Greek*

7687. God is everywhere except where he has his delegate. *Italian*

7688. God is love. *Bible*

7689. God is no respecter of persons. *Bible*

7690. God is not seen; He is recognized by the mind. *Arabic*

7691. God is one; what He does, sees none [i.e., none sees]. *Yiddish*

7692. God is our refuge and our strength. *Bible*

7693. God is patient because eternal. *Latin (St. Augustine)*

7694. God is truth and light His shadow. *Greek (Plato)*

7695. God knows what He does. *Yiddish*

7696. God moves in a mysterious way / His wonders to perform. *English (Cowper)*

7697. God postpones; He does not overlook. *Turkish*

7698. God punishes with one hand and blesses with the other. *Yiddish*

7699. God saves the moon from the wolves. *French*

7700. God tempers the wind to the shorn lamb. *French*

7701. God's in his heaven— / All's right with the world. *English (R. Browning)*

7702. God's mill grinds slow but sure. *English*

7703. God's mouth knows not to utter falsehood. *Greek*

7704. How dark are all the ways of God to man! *Greek (Euripides)*

7705. If God did not exist it would be necessary to invent him. *French (Voltaire)*

7706. If God did not forgive, Paradise would be empty. *Arabic*

7707. If it's God's will, a broomstick can shoot. *Yiddish*

7708. Let that please man which has pleased God. *Latin*

7709. Man is planning while God has His own design. *Egyptian*

7710. Man proposes and God disposes. *Italian (Ariosto)*

7711. Not my will, but Thine, be done. *Bible*

7712. One who recovers from sickness forgets about God. *Ethiopian*

7713. The Eternal Being is forever if He is at all. *French*

7714. The grace o' God is gear [wealth] enough. *Scottish*

7715. The voice of the people is the voice of God. *Greek (Hesiod)*

7716. The ways of the gods are long, but in the end they are not without strength. *Greek (Euripides)*

7717. There is a God to punish and avenge. *German*

7718. There is no key to God's counsel chamber. *Danish*

7719. There's a divinity that shapes our ends, / Rough-hew them as we will. *English (Shakespeare)*

7720. There's Ane abune a' [One above all]. *Scottish*

7721. They never sought in vain that sought the Lord aright. *Scottish (Burns)*

7722. To the greater glory of God. *Latin*

7723. To will is ours, but not to execute. *American*

7724. What Heaven ordains, the wise with courage bear. *American*

7725. When God dawns He dawns for all. *Spanish*

7726. When God pleases, it rains in fair weather. *Spanish*

7727. Who spits against heaven it falls in his face. *English*

7728. Whom the gods love die young. *Greek (Menander)*

7729. Yield to divine power. *Latin*

7730. You cannot serve God and mammon. *English*

Golden Rule *see also* Conduct

7731. As you behave toward others, expect that others will behave to you. *Latin*

7732. Do as you would be done by. *American*

7733. Do good if you expect to receive it. *English*

7734. Do not do to others that which would anger you if others did it to you. *Greek (Isocrates)*

7735. Do unto others as you would have others do unto you. *Bible*

7736. Do unto others before they do unto you. *American*

7737. What is hateful to thyself, do not unto thy neighbor. *Talmud*

7738. What you do not want done to yourself, do not do to others. *Chinese (Confucius)*

Good *see also* Chastity; Good and Evil; Sin and Virtue; Women and Virtue

7739. A good heart is better than all the heads in the world. *English*

7740. A good man's pedigree is little hunted up. *Spanish*

7741. A's guid that God sends us. *Scottish*

7742. Be good and you will be lonesome. *American (Twain)*

7743. Concealed goodness is a sort of vice. *English*

7744. Good things are hard. *Greek*

7745. If you put good in, you can take good out. *Yiddish*

7746. In every good man a god doth dwell. *Latin*

7747. Rather be called good than fortunate. *Latin*

7748. Say not that the good are dead. *Greek*

7749. So good that he is good for nothing. *Italian*

7750. That which is good makes men good. *Latin*

7751. The good man makes others good. *Greek*

7752. The worth of good is not known except by experience. *Turkish*

7753. True goodness springs from a man's own heart. *Chinese*

7754. What is good is never plentiful. *Spanish*

Good and Bad *see also* Adversity; Affliction; Good and Evil; Sin and Sinners; Sin and Virtue

7755. A bad man in Zion City is a good man in Chicago. *American*

7756. A bad mother wishes for good children. *English*

7757. A good garden may have some weeds. *English*

7758. Bad never becomes good till something worse happens. *Danish*

7759. Better bad from good than good from bad. *Yiddish*

7760. Every bean hath its black. *English*

7761. Every light hath its shadow. *English*

7762. Good comes to better, and better to bad. *French*

7763. He deserves not the sweet that will not taste of the sour. *English*

7764. He that hath a good harvest may be content with some thistles. *English*

7765. If you wish to be good, first believe that you are bad. *Greek*

7766. If you would have the hen's egg you must bear with her cackling. *English*

7767. Ill blows the wind that profits nobody. *English (Shakespeare)*

7768. Many a good cow hath a bad calf. *German*

7769. No gains without pains. *English*

7770. No house but has its cross. *Dutch*

7771. No house without a mouse. *English*

7772. No house without a mouse; no throne without a thorn. *American*

7773. No life without pain. *French*

7774. No scene of mortal life but teems with mortal woe. *Scottish (Scott)*

7775. No sunshine but hath some shadow. *English*

7776. No sweet without some sweat. *English*

7777. One ill weed mars a whole pot of pottage. *English*

7778. Take the good with the bad, the sweet with the bitter. *American*

7779. That which is good for the back is bad for the head. *English*

7780. The bad flourish; the good die young. *American*

7781. The rose is often found near the nettle. *Latin (Ovid)*

7782. The way to heaven is to bless the good and to punish the bad. *Chinese*

7783. There are good and bad men, as there are valuable and worthless goods. *Chinese*

7784. There is no rose without thorns. *Polish*

7785. There is no wheat without chaff. *Latin*

7786. There is some soul of goodness in things evil. *English (Shakespeare)*

7787. There never was a good town but had a mire at one end of it. *English*

7788. They ne'er beuk [baked] a gude cake but may bake an ill. *Scottish*

7789. What is bad for one is good for another. *French*

7790. When the curry is good, the rice is half-cooked. *Malay*

7791. Without pains, no prize. *German*

7792. You must take the fat with the lean. *American*

Good and Evil *see also* Sin and Virtue

7793. A good man has more hope in his death than a wicked man in his life. *English*

7794. Abhor that which is evil; cleave to that which is good. *Bible*

7795. Evil things are neighbors to good. *Latin*

7796. Good things are mixed with evil, evil things with good. *Latin*

7797. He that helps the evil hurts the good. *Greek*

7798. In a world of scoundrels, the good man is forced to blush. *American*

7799. On the doer of good God sends down all blessings, and on the doer of evil he sends all calamities. *Chinese*

7800. One good man represses a hundred bad ones. *Chinese*

7801. The devil himself is good when he is pleased. *English*

7802. The end of good is an evil, and the end of evil is a good. *French (La Rochefoucauld)*

7803. The evil that men do lives after them; / The good is oft interred with their bones. *English (Shakespeare)*

7804. The good man doing good finds the day insufficient; the evil man doing evil likewise finds the day insufficient. *Chinese*

7805. The thorn engenders the rose and the rose engenders the thorn. *Arabic*

7806. There is no evil without some good [or that does not bring good]. *Polish*

7807. There is no good but contains some evil; no evil but contains some good. *Latin*

7808. There is some soul of goodness in things evil. *English (Shakespeare)*

7809. To a good man nothing that happens is evil. *Greek*

7810. Where God hath his church, the devil will have his chapel. *English*

7811. Where God builds a church the devil builds a chapel. *American*

7812. Where there is good, there is evil. *Japanese*

Good Breeding *see also* Heredity

7813. A man of high birth may be of low worth — and vice versa. *American*

7814. Birth is much: breeding is more. *English*

7815. Birth's gude, but breeding's better. *Scottish*

7816. Every man's no born wi' a siller spune in his mouth. *Scottish*

7817. Good blood cannot lie. *French*

7818. Great birth is a very poor dish at table. *American*

7819. Gude breeding and siller [silver] mak' our sons gentlemen. *Scottish*

7820. He is not well-bred that cannot bear ill-breeding in others. *American*

7821. High birth is a poor dish at table. *Italian*

7822. Meat feeds, claith cleeds [lit., cloth clothes], but breeding maks the man. *Scottish*

7823. Not with whom you are born, but with whom you are bred. *Spanish (Cervantes)*

7824. Well-fed, well-bred. *American*

7825. With fowls, the pedigree; with men, breeding. *Burmese*

Good Deeds *see also* Favors; Service

7826. A generous action is its own reward. *English*

7827. A good action is never lost. *Spanish (Calderon)*

7828. A good deed bears a blessing for its fruit. *American*

7829. A good man makes no noise over a good deed. *Greek*

7830. Be quick to do good. *Japanese*

7831. Do good and ask not for whom. *Yiddish*

7832. Do good and don't look back. *Dutch*

7833. Do good, and never mind to whom. *Italian*

7834. Do good by stealth and blush to find it fame. *English (Pope)*

7835. For one good deed a hundred ill deeds should be overlooked. *Chinese*

7836. Good actions are founded on intelligence, though a fool may blunder into proper conduct. *American*

7837. Good deeds are the language of the soul. *American*

7838. Good deeds cut off tongues. *Arabic*

7839. He who does a good deed does not ask permission to do it. *Tunisian*

7840. How far that little candle throws his beams! / So shines a good deed in a naughty world. *English (Shakespeare)*

7841. If you want to win, return good for evil. *American*

7842. Kings and cabbages perish but good deeds live on. *American*

7843. Let us not be weary in well-doing. *Bible*

7844. Men do not value a good deed unless it brings a reward. *Latin*

7845. Nobody enters his good deeds in his day-book. *Latin*

7846. One good deed dying tongueless / Slaughters a thousand waiting upon that. *English (Shakespeare)*

7847. The acts of this life are the destiny of the next. *Chinese*

7848. Your one good action excuses a dozen bad ones. *American*

Good Nature

7849. By good nature and kindness even fierce spirits become tractable. *Latin*

Good News *see* News

Good Will

7850. Good will is taken for the deed. *French*

7851. Good will is the best deed. *Yiddish*

7852. Good-will, like the wind, bloweth where it listeth. *American (Franklin)*

7853. Gudewill ne'er wants time to show itself. *Scottish*

7854. Gudewill should aye be taken in pairt payment. *Scottish*

7855. Let us not be weary in well-doing. *Bible*

Good Words *see also* Fair Words; Plain Talk; Smooth Words; Soft Words, Words; Words and Deeds

7856. A good word always finds its man. *German*

7857. A good word costs no more than a bad one. *American*

7858. A good word extinguishes more than a pail full of water. *Spanish*

7859. A good word for a bad one is worth much and costs little. *Italian*

7860. A good word removes anger. *Accra*

7861. A good word stills great anger. *German*

7862. A gude word is as easy said as an ill ane. *Scottish*

7863. A word fitly spoken is like apples of gold in pictures of silver. *Bible*

7864. Good words are like a string of pearls. *Chinese*

7865. Good words cool more than cold water. *English*

7866. Good words cost nothing. *Hungarian*

7867. Honorable words by the bushel. *Latin*

7868. How forcible are right words! *Bible*

7869. No stomach is satisfied by good words. *Norwegian*

7870. One good word can warm three winter months. *Japanese*

7871. Sincere words are not grand. *Chinese*

7872. The words of the good are like a staff in a slippery place. *Hebrew*

7873. The words of the wise are as goads. *Bible*

7874. Words which are simple but far-reaching are good words. *Chinese*

Gossip *see also* Hearsay; Rumor; Scandal

7875. Don't broadcast the defects of others; correct your own. *American*

7876. Go into the country and hear what the news is in town. *English*

7877. Gossip needs no carriage. *Russian*

7878. Gossips and lying go together. *English*

7879. Gossips drink and talk; frogs drink and squawk. *American*

7880. Gossips fall out and tell each other truths. *Spanish*

7881. He's my friend that speaks well of me behind my back. *English*

7882. If you kick one walnut in the sack, all the rest clatter. *Hungarian*

7883. In ower muckle clavering [in excessive gossiping, talking foolishly] truth is tint [lost]. *Scottish*

7884. It is no time to gossip with the dying. *Turkish*

7885. Once in people's mouths it is hard to get out of them. *American*

7886. One rooster wakens all the roosters in the village. *German*

7887. Please your kimmer [a female gossip] and ye'll easy guide your gossip. *Scottish*

7888. Put no faith in tale-bearers. *American*

7889. The opposite of gossip is often truth. *French*

7890. There is never much talk of a thing but there is some truth in it. *American*

7891. There is nothing that can't be made worse by telling. *Latin*

7892. Those who bring gossip will carry it. *American*

7893. Wagging tongues do no one good. *American*

7894. Whispering tongues can poison truth. *American*

7895. Who chatters to you will chatter of you. *American*

7896. Whoever gossips to you will gossip about you. *Spanish*

Government

7897. A government of laws and not of men. *American (J. Adams)*

7898. A hated government does not endure long. *Latin (Seneca)*

7899. A hundred years of tyranny is preferable to one night of anarchy. *Arabic*

7900. An oppressive government is more to be feared than a tiger. *Chinese*

7901. As the government, so the people. *Italian*

7902. Every country has the government it deserves. *French*

7903. Ill can rule the great that cannot reach the small. *English (Spenser)*

7904. Let's be jovial, fill our glasses; / Madness 'tis for us to think / How the world is ruled by asses, / And the wise are swayed by chink. *Irish*

7905. The good governor should have a broken leg and keep at home. *Spanish (Cervantes)*

7906. The whole of government consists in the art of being honest. *American (Jefferson)*

7907. The world is governed with little wisdom. *Italian*

Grace

7908. Grace is to the body what judgment is to the mind. *French (La Rochefoucauld)*

7909. Without grace beauty is an unbaited hook. *French*

7910. Ye have fallen from grace. *Bible*

Gradualness *see also* Size; Trifles

7911. By repeated blows even the oak is felled. *Latin*

7912. Constant dropping wears the stone. *Bible*

7913. Drop by drop the lake is drained. *English*

7914. Feather by feather the goose is plucked. *English*

7915. Hair and hair makes the carle's [old man's] head bare. *Scottish*

7916. Link by link the coat of mail is made. *French*

7917. Little by little a fly eats a dog's ear. *Accra*

7918. Little by little the bird builds its nest. *French*

7919. Little strokes fell great oaks. *English*

7920. One hair after the other makes the pumpkin bald. *Danish*

7921. Step by step, one goes a long way. *French*

7922. Word by word the great books are written. *French (Voltaire)*

Gratitude *see also* Favors; Ingratitude; Thanks

7923. Ae [one] gude turn deserves anither. *Scottish*

7924. Ae [one] gude turn may meet anither, an' it were at the brig o' London. *Scottish*

7925. Do good and don't look back [i.e., for thanks]. *Dutch*

7926. Don't overload gratitude; if you do, she'll kick. *American (Franklin)*

7927. Gratefulness is the poor man's payment. *English*

7928. Gratitude is a heavy burden. *Scottish*

7929. Gratitude is the sign of noble souls. *American*

7930. Gratitude preserves auld friendships and begets new. *Scottish*

7931. Gratitude takes three forms: a feeling in the heart, an expression in words, and a giving in return. *Arabic*

7932. Lambs have the grace to suck kneeling. *Chinese*

7933. Men who are grateful are usually good. *American*

7934. Next to ingratitude, the most painful thing to bear is gratitude. *American (Beecher)*

7935. No load is heavier than gratitude. *Turkish*

7936. Poor men are fain of little things. *Scottish*

7937. Set that doun on the backside o' your count-book. *Scottish*

7938. The man who is excessively grateful for a favor, is preparing for favors to come. *American*

7939. To the grateful man give more than he asks. *Latin*

7940. What soon grows old? Gratitude. *Greek*

Great and Small

7941. A river is enlarged by its tributaries. Gĩkũyũ

7942. An ant hole may collapse an embankment. *Japanese*

7943. Great engines turn on small pivots. *English*

7944. Great oaks from little acorns grow. *American*

7945. Great weights may hang on small wires. *English*

7946. Great without small makes a bad wall. *English*

7947. However big the whale may be, the tiny harpoon can rob him of life. *Malay*

7948. If a little tree grows in the shade of a larger tree, it will die small. *Senegalese*

7949. It is as easy to be great as to be small. *American (Emerson)*

7950. No man is so tall that he need never stretch and none so small that he need never stoop. *Danish*

7951. One flea cannot raise a coverlet. *Chinese*

7952. The great oak bears small fruit. *German*

7953. There could be no great ones if there were no little. *English*

Greatness

7954. And seekest thou great things for thyself? seek them not. *Bible*

7955. Desire of greatness is a godlike sin. *English (Dryden)*

7956. Goodness is not tied to greatness, but greatness to goodness. *Greek*

7957. Great actions speak great minds. *English (Fletcher)*

7958. Great and good are seldom the same man. *English*

7959. Great deeds are reserved for great men. *Spanish (Cervantes)*

7960. Great fish are caught in great waters. *German*

7961. Great folks' servants are aye mair saucy than themselves. *Scottish (Scott)*

7962. Great gifts are from great men. *English*

7963. Great marks are soonest hit. *English*

7964. Great men are not always wise. *Bible*

7965. Great men's servants think themselves great. *Latin (Juvenal)*

7966. Great men's sons seldom do well. *Latin*

7967. Great minds think alike. *English*

7968. Great ships require deep waters. *English*

7969. Great spenders are bad lenders. *English*

7970. Great trees give more shade than fruit. *Italian*

7971. Great wits come together. *French*

7972. Greatness knows itself. *English (Shakespeare)*

7973. He is great who confers the most benefits. *American (Emerson)*

7974. He is great whose faults can be numbered. *Hebrew*

7975. In the wide world men are numberless, but who is the great man? *Chinese*

7976. It is a rough road that leads to the heights of greatness. *Latin*

7977. Some are born great, some achieve greatness, and some have greatness thrust upon them. *English (Shakespeare)*

7978. The bigger they are, the harder they fall. *American*

7979. The greatest strokes make not the best music. *English*

7980. The loftiest towers rise from the ground. *Chinese*

7981. The world is like a steam bath; the higher you go, the more you sweat. *Polish*

7982. Those who follow that part of themselves which is great, are great men; those who follow that part which is little, are little men. *Chinese*

7983. Though a tree grow ever so high, the falling leaves return to the root. *Malay*

7984. To be great is to be misunderstood. *American (Emerson)*

7985. To be just in the administration of wealth shows the great man. *Chinese*

7986. Towers are measured by their shadows, and great men by their calumniators. *Chinese*

7987. With great men one must allow five to be an even number. *Germany*

Greed *see also* Avarice

7988. A bank-book is the greedy man's Bible. *American*

7989. A covetous man's penny is a stone. *English*

7990. A greedie man God hates. *Scottish*

7991. A greedy ee [eye] ne'er got a fu' wame [belly]. *Scottish*

7992. A greedy ee [eye] ne'er got a gude pennyworth. *Scottish*

7993. A man may buy gold too dear. *English*

7994. A poor man's roast and a rich man's death are sniffed far off. *Yiddish*

7995. Big mouthfuls often choke. *Italian*

7996. Don't run after the wild boar and lose the pig at home. *Chinese*

7997. Feed a pig and you'll have a hog. *American*

7998. Give the hog a finger and he'll take the whole hand. *American*

7999. Grasp all, lose all. *English*

8000. Grasp no more than thy hand will hold. *English*

8001. Greed and the eye can no man fill. *German*

8002. Greed is envy's eldest brither; / Scraggy wark they mak' thegither. *Scottish*

8003. Greedy folks have long arms. *Scottish*

8004. He can hide his meat and seek mair. *Scottish*

8005. He comes for drink, though draff be his errand. *Scottish*

8006. He is better with a rake than a fork. *English*

8007. He wants forever, who would more acquire. *English*

8008. He who grabs too much holds fast but little. *Spanish*

8009. He will see daylight through a little hole. *Scottish*

8010. He'll get enough ae [one] day when his mouth 's fu' o' mools [i.e., when he is buried]. *Scottish*

8011. It is not good to want and to have. *Scottish*

8012. It's hard for a greedy ee [eye] to hae a leal [honest] heart. *Scottish*

8013. Mickle hes [much have], wald aye have mair [would always have more]. *Scottish*

8014. Much would have more. *Italian*

8015. Much would have more, and lost all. *English*

8016. The belly overreaches the head. *French*

8017. The dog who goes to many weddings eats at none. *Mexican*

8018. The dust alone can fill the eye of man. *Arabic*

8019. The eye is bigger than the mouth. *Yiddish*

8020. The greedy man and the cook are sune friends. *Scottish*

8021. The greedy man and the gileynoar [cheat] are soon agreed. *Scottish*

8022. The magpie wants more than its tail can carry. *Hungarian*

8023. To greed, all nature is insufficient. *Latin (Seneca)*

8024. Want all, lose all. *Latin*

8025. What your ee [eye] sees your heart greens for. *Scottish*

8026. Who grasps at too much makes little secure. *French (Rabelais)*

8027. Who takes too much retains too little. *Latin*

8028. Who wants all loses all. *Italian*

8029. Who wants the last drop out of the can gets the lid on his nose. *Dutch*

8030. Ye loe a' ye see [love all you see], like Rab Roole when he's ree [half-drunk]. *Scottish*

8031. Your een's [eyes are] greedier than your guts. *Scottish*

Grief *see also* Death; Misfortune; Mourning

8032. A black dog is lying in the fireplace. *Lugbara*

8033. Away with grieving, only fit for women. *Latin*

8034. Everyone can master a grief but he that has it. *English (Shakespeare)*

8035. Great griefs are mute. *American*

8036. Great souls suffer in silence. *German (Schiller)*

8037. Grief diminishes when it has nothing to grow upon. *Latin (Publilius Syrus)*

8038. Grief flows away in tears. *Latin*

8039. Grief once told brings somewhat back of peace. *English (Morris)*

8040. Grief pent-up will burst the heart. *English*

8041. Grief should be the instructor of the wise. *English (Byron)*

8042. Grieving for misfortunes is adding gall to wormwood. *English*

8043. He grieves sincerely who grieves unseen. *Latin*

8044. He grieves sore who grieves alone. *French*

8045. He that conceals his grief finds no remedy for it. *Turkish*

8046. Her grief is real who grieves when no one is by. *Latin (Martius)*

8047. It is better to drink of deep griefs than to taste shallow pleasures. *English (Hazlitt)*

8048. It is folly to tear the hair in grief, as if sorrow could be cured by baldness. *Latin (Cicero)*

8049. Light griefs can speak, but deeper ones are dumb. *Latin*

8050. Little griefs make us tender; great ones make us hard. *French (Chénier)*

8051. My skin is cold. *Kanuri*

8052. New griefs awaken the old. *American*

8053. Of all the many ills common to all men, the greatest is grief. *Greek*

8054. Patch grief with proverbs. *American*

8055. Secret griefs are the sharpest. *American*

8056. Sorrow for a father six months, sorrow for a mother a year, sorrow for a wife until a second wife, sorrow for a son forever. *Hebrew*

8057. Suppressed grief suffocates. *Latin*

8058. The man of wisdom is a man of grief. *American*

8059. The only cure for grief is action. *American*

8060. There is a limit to grief but not to fear. *American*

8061. There is no grief which time does not lessen. *Latin*

8062. This grief will prove a blessing. *Latin*

8063. Those griefs burn most which gall in secret. *Latin (Seneca)*

8064. What the eye doesn't see the heart doesn't grieve over. *American*

8065. Wherein is life sweet to him who suffers grief? *Greek*

Grievance

8066. A bad man may have a good grievance. *American*

8067. A good grievance is better than a bad payment. *Spanish (Cervantes)*

8068. Men often bear little grievances with less courage than they do large misfortunes. *Greek (Aesop)*

Growth

8069. It is not easy to straighten in the oak the crook that grew in the sapling. *Gaelic*

8070. The shell must break before the bird can fly. *English (Tennyson)*

8071. Under his nose it's beginning to sprout; but in his head it hasn't even been sown. *Russian*

Grudges

8072. I will lay a stone at your door. [I will bear a grudge against you.] *English*

Guests *see also* Hospitality; Uninvited Guests; Visiting

8073. A great guest is always dear to a host. *Russian*

8074. A guest and a fish stink on the third day. *Spanish*

8075. A guest in the house, God in the house. *Polish*

8076. A guest sees more in an hour than the host in a year. *Polish*

8077. A guest's eye is sharpsighted. *Icelandic*

8078. A house filled with guests is eaten up. *Spanish*

8079. After three days men grow weary of a wench, a guest, and rainy weather. *American*

8080. An unbidden guest is worse than a Tartar. *Russian*

8081. An unbidden guest knoweth not where to sit. *English (Heywood)*

8082. Be the last to come and the first to go. *American*

8083. Better slight a guest than starve him. *Chinese*

8084. Do not ask a guest questions until he has been entertained three days. *Bedouin*

8085. Entertain guests, but do not detain them. *Chinese*

8086. Fiddlers' dogs and flies come to feasts unasked. *Scottish*

8087. Fish and guests smell at three days old. *Danish*

8088. Foster the guest that stays — further him that maun gang. *Scottish*

8089. Good guests come uninvited. *Yiddish*

8090. Guests should not forget to go home. *Swedish*

8091. Guests that come by daylight are best received. *English*

8092. He that's welcome fares weel. *Scottish*

8093. If a guest gets up early, he means to stay for the night. *Russian*

8094. Let the guest go before the storm bursts. *German*

8095. Mony gude-nights is laith to gang. *Scottish*

8096. One guest hates another, and the host both. *Montenegrin*

8097. Receive all guests that come, making no difference between relatives and strangers. *Chinese*

8098. Seven days is the length of a guest's life. *Burmese*

8099. The busy man has few idle visitors; to the boiling pot the flies come not. *American (Franklin)*

8100. The first day a guest, the third a pest. *American*

8101. The first day a man is a guest, the second a burden, the third a pest. *French*

8102. The guest should veil his eyes, eat what is offered, and not gossip. *Arabic*

8103. The host is happy when his guest has gone. *Chinese*

8104. The host is the prisoner of his guests. *Arabic*

8105. The unbidden guest is ever a pest. *German*

8106. Unbidden guests / Are often welcomest when they are gone. *English (Shakespeare)*

8107. Welcome the coming, speed the parting guest. *English (Pope)*

8108. Withdraw thy foot from thy neighbor's house; lest he be weary of thee, and so hate thee. *Bible*

Guile

8109. Butter wouldn't melt in his mouth. *American*

Guilt *see also* Complicity; Conscience; Denial

8110. Guilt is always jealous. *English*

8111. Guilt makes the bravest man a coward. *American*

8112. Guilty men see guilt written on the faces of saints. *American*

8113. He confesses his guilt who flies from his trial. *Latin*

8114. He declares himself guilty who justifies himself before accusation. *English*

8115. He that does you a very ill turn will never forgive you. *English*

8116. He who flees proves himself guilty. *Danish*

8117. He who is guilty believes all men speak ill of him. *Italian*

8118. Let every sheep hang by its own shanks. *American*

8119. Suspicion always haunts the guilty mind. *English (Shakespeare)*

8120. The cat shuts his eyes while he steals the cream. *English*

8121. The fox who flies proves himself guilty. *American*

8122. The guilt and not the gallows makes the shame (of evil-doers). *French*

8123. The guilty are alarmed and turn pale at the slightest thunder. *Latin (Juvenal)*

8124. The sting of a reproach is the truth of it. *English*

8125. The thief doth fear each bush an officer. *English (Shakespeare)*

8126. The truest jests sound worst in guilty ears. *English*

8127. The wicked flee when no man pursueth; but the righteous are bold as a lion. *Bible*

8128. The wicked hate vice in others. *American*

8129. Their hearts sweat with undivulged guilt. *Latin (Juvenal)*

8130. Those whom guilt stains it makes equal. *Latin*

8131. We hate the man whom we have wronged. *Latin*

8132. When it thunders the thief becomes honest. *Italian*

Gullibility *see also* Credulity; Naivete

8133. He will never prosper who readily believes. *Latin*

8134. If you are ready to believe, you are easy to deceive. *American*

8135. Let any man speak long enough, he will get believers. *American*

8136. To buy the cat in the bag. *German*

8137. To go for wool and return shorn. *English*

Habit *see also* Custom; Heredity; Reform

8138. A kindly aver [cart horse] will never make a good nag. *Scottish*

8139. A nail is driven out by another nail; habit is overcome by habit. *Latin*

8140. A sparrow will never forget to dance till it is a hundred years old. *Japanese*

8141. An old dog can't alter his way of barking. *English*

8142. Auld use and wont hings about the fire. *Scottish*

8143. Ca' a cow to the ha' [hall] and she'll rin to the byre [cow barn]. *Scottish*

8144. Continuance becomes usage. *Italian*

8145. Every man has his peculiar habit. *Latin*

8146. Great is the power of habit. *Latin*

8147. Habit always triumphs. *Arabic*

8148. Habit becomes second nature. *English*

8149. Habit gives readiness. *Latin*

8150. Habit, if not resisted, becomes necessity. *American*

8151. Habit in sinning takes away the sense of sin. *Latin*

8152. Habit is second nature. *French (Montaigne)*

8153. Habit is stronger than nature. *Latin*

8154. Habits are at first cobwebs and at last cables. *American*

8155. Habits, if not resisted, soon become necessity. *Latin*

8156. He's like the smith's dog, so weel used to the sparks that he'll no burn. *Scottish*

8157. How many unjust things are done from habit! *Latin (Terence)*

8158. How use doth breed a habit in a man! *English (Shakespeare)*

8159. Learn a bad habit, and ye'll ca' 't a custom. *Scottish*

8160. Learn the cat the road to the kirn [churn] and she'll aye be lickin. *Scottish*

8161. Learn you to an ill habit and ye'll ca 't custom. *Scottish*

8162. Like the smith's dog, sleep at the sound o' the hammer, and wauk [wake] at the crunshing o' teeth. *Scottish*

8163. Man is an animal of habits. *German*

8164. Men do more things through habit than through reason. *Latin*

8165. Men's natures are alike; it is their habits that carry them far apart. *Chinese*

8166. Nae [no] carrion will kill a craw [crow]. *Scottish*

8167. Nothing so needs reforming as other people's habits. *American (Twain)*

8168. The habit is not a trifle. *Greek*

8169. The habits of our youth accompany us in our old age. *Latin*

8170. 'Tis easier to prevent bad habits than to break them. *American (Franklin)*

8171. To change a habit is like death. *Spanish*

8172. Use establishes habit. *Latin*

8173. What we first learn we best ken [know]. *Scottish*

8174. When sinning becomes a habit we lose our sense of sin. *American*

8175. Who is strong? He that can conquer his bad habits. *American (Franklin)*

Handicaps *see also* Blindness; Limitations

8176. A bird cannot fly without wings. *French*

8177. A broken sleeve holdeth the arm back. *English*

8178. A cat in gloves will never catch a mouse. *Italian*

8179. A gloved cat was never a good mouser. *Scottish*

8180. A muzzled cat is no good mouser. *English*

Handsomeness *see also* Face

8181. A handsome shoe often pinches the foot. *French*

8182. Good-day spectacles, farewell girls. *French*

8183. Handsome is as handsome does. *English*

8184. Handsome is not what is handsome, but what pleases. *Yiddish*

8185. The handsomest flower is not the sweetest. *English*

Happiness *see also* Joy; Joy and Sorrow; Mirth and Sorrow; Unhappiness

8186. A happy heart is better than a full purse. *Italian*

8187. A happy life consists in tranquility of mind. *Latin*

8188. A great obstacle to happiness is to expect too much happiness. *French*

8189. A man's happiness is to do a man's true work. *Greek*

8190. A merry heart doeth good like a medicine. *Bible*

8191. A wee house weel filled, a wee piece land weel till'd, a wee wife weel will'd, will make a happy man. *Scottish*

8192. All happiness is in the mind. *American*

8193. As brisk as bottled ale. *Scottish*

8194. Call no man happy till he dies. *French*

8195. Happiness attracts envy as fly-paper attracts flies. *American*

8196. Happiness does away with ugliness. *French*

8197. Happiness invites envy. *Latin*

8198. Happiness is but a name. *Scottish (Burns)*

8199. Happiness is like a sunbeam, which the least shadow intercepts. *Chinese*

8200. Happiness is made to be shared. *French*

8201. Happiness is not steadfast but transient. *Greek (Euripides)*

8202. Happiness is the child of sweat. *Lugbara*

8203. Happiness passes everyone in life once. *German*

8204. Happiness takes no account of time. *English*

8205. Happy man, happy dole. *English*

8206. Happy man, happy kevel [lot]. *English*

8207. He is happy that knoweth not himself to be otherwise. *English*

8208. He is happy who knows his good fortune. *Chinese*

8209. He is not happy who does not think himself so. *Latin (Publilius Syrus)*

8210. He is not the happy man who seems so to others, but he who seems so to himself. *Latin (Seneca)*

8211. He that is of a merry heart hath a continual feast. *Bible*

8212. He's no the happiest man wha has maist [most] gear [money, property]. *Scottish*

8213. How bitter a thing it is to look into happiness through another man's eyes! *English (Shakespeare)*

8214. How to live happily, not luxuriously, is the question. *Latin*

8215. I had rather have a fool to make me merry than experience to make me sad. *American*

8216. If you want to be happy make yourself useful. *American*

8217. It's better to be happy than wise. *American*

8218. Laugh and lay 't doun again. *Scottish*

8219. Laugh at leisure, ye may greet [weep] ere night. *Scottish*

8220. Lightsome sangs mak merry gate. *Scottish*

8221. Nature gives all the chance for happiness, knew they but how to use it. *Latin*

8222. No man is happy who does not think himself so. *Latin (Publilius Syrus)*

8223. No one can be perfectly happy till all are happy. *English (Spencer)*

8224. One is never as happy or as unhappy as he thinks. *French (La Rochefoucauld)*

8225. Only at the end of a man's prosperous life dare we pronounce him happy. *Greek*

8226. Seil [happiness] ne'er comes till sorrow be awa. *Scottish*

8227. The hour of happiness which comes unexpectedly is the happiest. *Latin (Horace)*

8228. The man with peace of mind is blissfully happy. *American*

8229. The will of a man is his happiness. *German (Schiller)*

8230. There is no such thing as perfect happiness. *Latin (Ovid)*

8231. To the happy man no hour strikes. *German*

8232. When the heart within is filled with cheer and brightness, it is heaven's hall; when the heart is dark and gloomy, it is earth's prison. *Chinese*

8233. You're truly happy if you make others happy. *American*

Hardness

8234. Hard with hard makes not the stone wall. *Latin*

8235. Hardness ever of hardness is the mother. *American*

Harm

8236. Keep out of harm's way. *American*

8237. When the harm is done, it is useless to unstring the bow. *French*

Harshness

8238. Knock a carl [old man] and ding a carl, and that's the way to win a carl; kiss a carl and clap a carl, and that's the way to tine [lose] a carl. *Scottish*

Haste

8239. A hasty man is never lusty. *Scottish*

8240. A hasty man never wanteth woe. *English*

8241. A house in a hastrie [reckless haste] is downright wastrie [waste, prodigality]. *Scottish*

8242. A quick decision may speed you into disaster. *American*

8243. A wise man will not dispute with one that is hasty. *Persian (Sa'di)*

8244. As hasty as Hopkins, that came to jail overnight, and was hanged the next morning. *English*

8245. Aye [always] in a hurry, and aye ahint [behind]. *Scottish*

8246. Desire to have things done quickly prevents their being done thoroughly. *Chinese (Confucius)*

8247. Discreet stops make speedy journeys. *English*

8248. Do not hurry, do not flurry, / Nothing good is got by worry. *English*

8249. Do nothing hastily but catching of fleas. *English*

8250. Fast enough if well enough. *Latin*

8251. Fools' haste is nae speed. *Scottish*

8252. Good and quickly seldom meet. *English*

8253. Haste and wisdom are things far odd. *English*

8254. Haste comes late in the end. *German*

8255. Haste comes not alone. *English*

8256. Haste is ever the parent of failure. *Greek*

8257. Haste is not speed. *Dutch*

8258. Haste is of the devil. *Arabic*

8259. Haste is prodigal. *Dutch*

8260. Haste is slow. *Latin (Quintus Curtius)*

8261. Haste makes waste, waste want, want strife, / Betwixt the good man and his wife. *English*

8262. Haste maketh waste. *English*

8263. Haste manages all things badly. *Latin*

8264. Haste trips up its own heels. *English*

8265. Haste with leisure. *German*

8266. Hasten deliberately. *Greek*

8267. Hasten gently. *Latin*

8268. Hastiness is the beginning of wrath, and its end repentance. *English*

8269. Hasty climbers have sudden falls. *English*

8270. Hasty conclusions lead to speedy repentance. *Latin*

8271. Hasty gamesters oversee. *English*

8272. Hasty glory goes out in a snuff. *English*

8273. Hasty love is soon hot and soon cold. *English*

8274. Hasty men seldom want woe. *English*

8275. Hasty people will never make good midwives. *English*

8276. Hasty was hanged, but Speed-o-foot wan awa. *Scottish*

8277. Hasty word is seldom good. *Finnish*

8278. He hastens to repentance who hastily judges. *Latin*

8279. He hastit to his end, like a moth to a candle. *Scottish*

8280. He that goes too hastily along often stumbles on a fair road. *French*

8281. He that rides ere he be ready wants aye some o' his graith [harness]. *Scottish*

8282. He that walks too hastily, often stumbles in plain way. *English*

8283. He tires betimes that spurs too fast betimes. *English (Shakespeare)*

8284. He who does things too hastily does them the less effectually. *Latin*

8285. He who hastens too much stumbles and falls. *Latin*

8286. He who makes too much haste gains his end later. *Latin*

8287. Hurry, hurry has no blessing. *Swahili*

8288. Hurry is good only for catching flies. *Russian*

8289. In haste is regret, in slowness peace. *Tunisian*

8290. It is better to get one's clothes wet than to hurry. *Chinese*

8291. "Mair [more] haste the waur [worse] speed," quo' the tailor to the lang thread. *Scottish*

8292. Make haste slowly. *Latin*

8293. Make no more haste than good speed. *English*

8294. Make too much haste and pay the penalty. *Latin*

8295. Man is created of hastiness. *Koran*

8296. Most haste, worst speed. *Latin*

8297. Naething to be done in haste but gripping o' fleas. *Scottish*

8298. Nothing can be done both hastily and prudently. *Latin*

8299. Nothing good ever comes from haste. *Yiddish*

8300. Nothing in haste but catching fleas. *German*

8301. Quick and well-done do not agree. *Irish*

8302. Repentance follows hasty counsel. *Latin (Publilius Syrus)*

8303. Sober, neighbour! The night's but young yet. *Scottish*

8304. Stay a little, that we may make an end the sooner. *English (Bacon)*

8305. Sudden friendship's sure repentance. *Scottish*

8306. The hasty bitch brings forth blind whelps. *Latin*

8307. The hasty hand catches frogs for fish. *English*

8308. The hasty man never wanteth woe. *English*

8309. There's a het hurry when there's a hen to roast. *Scottish*

8310. Those who are quick in deciding are in danger of being mistaken. *Greek (Sophocles)*

8311. Three things only are done well in haste: Flying from the plague, escaping quarrels, and catching fleas. *Italian*

8312. To catch the monkey requires patience. *Senegalese*

8313. Too great haste leads us to error. *French*

8314. Too ready compliance is not to be trusted. *Chinese*

8315. Too swift arrives as tardy as too slow. *English (Shakespeare)*

8316. Unless we hasten, we shall be left behind. *Latin*

8317. Who pours water hastily into a bottle spills more than goes in. *Spanish*

8318. Ye cut before the point. *Scottish*

8319. Ye drive the plough before the owfen [oxen]. *Scottish*

8320. Ye hae sew'd that seam wi' a het needle and a burning thread. *Scottish*

8321. Ye was sae hungry ye couldna stay the grace. *Scottish*

8322. Ye're cawking [chalking] the claith [cloth] ere the wab [web] be in the loom. *Scottish*

Hate *see also* Love; Love and Hate

8323. A true man hates no one. *French*

8324. Cherish those hearts that hate thee. *English (Shakespeare)*

8325. Hate knows no age but death. *Latin*

8326. Hatred is a settled anger. *Latin*

8327. Hatred openly proclaimed loses its chance for vengeance. *Latin*

8328. Hatred renewed is worse than at first. *Italian*

8329. He who is hated by all cannot expect to live long. *French*

8330. In time we hate that which we often fear. *English (Shakespeare)*

8331. Let them hate me so long as they fear me. *Latin*

8332. Press not thy hatred too far. *Latin*

8333. Violent hatred sinks us below those we hate. *French*

8334. We fear the men we hate and hate the men we fear. *American*

8335. When a person hates you, he will beat your animals. *Oji*

8336. Whom men fear they hate, and whom they hate they wish dead. *Latin*

Haughtiness *see also* Arrogance

8337. The best manners are stained by haughtiness. *Latin (Claudius)*

Haves and Have-Nots

8338. He who is starving hates him who is eating. *African*

8339. He whose belly is full believes not him whose is empty. *English*

8340. It's ill speaking between a fu' man and a fasting. *Scottish*

8341. The hungry will not fall asleep because someone else has enough to eat. *African*

8342. The naked will always meet those who have no clothes. *Polish*

8343. Them as has, gets. *American*

8344. There are but two lineages in the world, Have-much and Have-little. *Spanish (Cervantes)*

8345. Wealth is best known by want. *English*

8346. When one eats and the other looks on, there is likely to be a fight. *Turkish*

Health *see also* **Diet; Exercise; Fitness**

8347. A healthy body is the guest-chamber of the soul; a sick, its prison. *English (Bacon)*

8348. A sound mind in a sound body. *Latin*

8349. After cheese comes nothing. *American*

8350. After dinner sleep awhile, after supper go to bed. *English*

8351. After fish, milk do not wish. *American (Franklin)*

8352. Better keep weel than make weel. *Scottish*

8353. Good health and good sense are two great blessings. *Latin*

8354. Guard the health both of body and of soul. *Greek*

8355. He destroys his health by laboring to preserve it. *Latin (Virgil)*

8356. He dies every day who lives a lingering life. *French*

8357. He that wants health wants everything. *French*

8358. He that would be healthy must wear his winter clothes in summer. *Spanish*

8359. He who has health is rich and does not know it. *Italian*

8360. He who has not health has nothing. *English*

8361. He who would live long avoids excesses. *American*

8362. Health and good estate of body are above all gold. *Bible*

8363. Health is not valued till sickness comes. *American*

8364. Health without money is half a malady. *Italian*

8365. I would rather be healthy than rich. *Latin*

8366. It is a grievous illness to preserve one's health by a regimen too strict. *French*

8367. Joy and Temperance and Repose / Slam the door in the doctor's nose. *American (Longfellow)*

8368. Keep the feet dry and the head warm, and for the rest live like a beast. *Italian*

8369. Life consists not merely in existing, but in enjoying health. *Latin (Martius)*

8370. Life is lifeless without health. *American*

8371. Next to sickness, health is sweet. *Welsh*

8372. Not to live, but to be healthy is life. *American*

8373. One foot is better than two crutches. *American*

8374. Rest, good cheer, and moderate diet are the three best doctors. *American*

8375. Rise at five, dine at nine; sup at five, to bed at nine. *French*

8376. Study sickness while you are well. *German*

8377. The beginning of health is to know the disease. *Spanish (Cervantes)*

8378. The best physicians are Dr. Diet, Dr. Quiet, and Dr. Merryman. *American*

8379. The head and the feet keep warm; / The rest will take no harm. *English*

8380. To the well man every day is a feast. *Turkish*

8381. When you are well keep as you are. *French*

Hearing *see* **Deafness; Eyes and Ears; Listening; Seeing and Hearing**

Hearsay *see also* **Gossip; Rumor; Scandal**

8382. Hearsay goes everywhere. *French*

8383. Hearsay is half lies. *Dutch*

8384. Hearsay is not equal to personal experience. *Chinese*

8385. One eyewitness is better than ten hearsays. *American*

8386. "People say" is often a great liar. *French*

8387. They say. What do they say? Let them say. *Greek*

8388. "They say" is half a lie. *American*

Heart *see also* **Courage; Understanding**

8389. A better heart makes a stronger arm. *German*

8390. A bushel of hearts is not worth one grain of rice. *Chinese*

8391. A wounded heart is hard to cure. *German (Goethe)*

8392. Eat not thy heart. *Greek*

8393. Everyone speaks well of his heart, but no one dares speak ill of his head. *French (La Rochefoucauld)*

8394. Fire in the heart sends smoke into the head. *German*

8395. Have you wealth or have you none; if you lose heart all is gone. *American*

8396. His heart lies quiet like limpid water. *Efik*

8397. It is as difficult to gauge a man's heart as it is to chop a duck's gizzard. *Chinese*

8398. Knit your hearts with an unslipping knot. *English (Shakespeare)*

8399. Man's heart controls everything. *Chinese*

8400. Only the heart without a stain knows perfect ease. *German*

8401. Set a stout heart to a stae brae [a steep hillside]. *Scottish*

8402. The head is always the dupe of the heart. *French (La Rochefoucauld)*

8403. The heart does not lie. *Dutch*

8404. The heart has reasons which reason does not know. *French (Pascal)*

8405. The heart is deceitful above all things, and desperately wicked. *Bible*

8406. The heart is half a prophet. *Yiddish*

8407. The heart is the hidden treasure of man. *Hebrew*

8408. The heart knoweth its own bitterness. *Bible*

8409. The heart must either become hardened or break. *French*

8410. The heart's testimony is stronger than a thousand witnesses. *Turkish*

8411. The mouth obeys poorly when the heart murmurs. *French (Voltaire)*

8412. What stronger breastplate than a heart untainted! *English (Shakespeare)*

8413. When the heart dares to speak, it needs no preparation. *German (Lessing)*

8414. When there is room in the heart there is room in the house. *Danish*

8415. Where your treasure is, there will your heart be also. *Bible*

8416. With most people the heart grows old with the body. *French*

8417. You can look in the eye, but not in the heart. *Yiddish*

Heaven

8418. Even the hen, when it drinks water, looks toward heaven. *Turkish*

8419. Great is the idleness which prevails in heaven. *Latin (Juvenal)*

8420. He who offends against Heaven has none to whom he can pray. *Chinese (Confucius)*

8421. Heaven is doing good from good will. *Swedish (Swedenborg)*

8422. Heaven is mine if God says amen. *Spanish*

8423. Heaven is not really high; the heart of man aspires higher and higher. *Chinese*

8424. Heaven is the widow's champion and defense. *English (Shakespeare)*

8425. Heaven lies about us in our infancy. *English (Wordsworth)*

8426. Heaven means to be one with God. *Chinese (Confucius)*

8427. Heaven protects the just. *Greek*

8428. It is harder work getting to hell than to heaven. *German*

8429. Men go laughing to heaven. *Dutch*

8430. No one can know the height of heaven without climbing mountains. *Chinese*

8431. The net of heaven has large meshes and yet nothing escapes it. *Chinese (Laotse)*

8432. The road to heaven is easy to find, but myriads of people refuse to follow it. *Chinese*

8433. The road to heaven is equally short wherever we die. *Danish*

8434. The sword of heaven is not in haste to smite, / Nor yet doth linger. *Italian (Dante)*

8435. There are many languages on earth, but one in heaven. *Latin*

8436. Whatever heaven ordains is best. *Greek*

8437. You may see heaven through a needle's eye. *Japanese*

Heedlessness *see also* Advice; Listening

8438. In at one ear and out at the other. *English*

8439. It is in vain to speak reason where it will never be heard. *English*

Heirs *see* Inheritance

Hell *see also* Devil; Heaven

8440. He who is in hell knows not what heaven is. *Italian*

8441. Hell is a circle about the unbelieving. *Koran*

8442. Hell is never full: there is always room for one more. *American*

8443. Hell is paved with good intentions and roofed with lost opportunities. *Portuguese*

8444. Hell is paved with monks' cowls, priests' drapery, and spike-helmets. *German*

8445. Hell is paved with the skulls of great scholars, and paled in with the bones of great men. *English*

8446. In hell there is no retention. *Spanish (Cervantes)*

8447. Not even hell can lay hands on the invincible. *Greek*

8448. One Hades receives all mortals alike. *Greek*

8449. The descent to hell is easy. *Latin (Virgil)*

8450. The road to hell is easy to travel. *Greek*

8451. The road to hell is paved with good intentions. *English*

8452. The way of sinners is made plain with stones, but at the end thereof is the pit of hell. *Bible*

8453. There is no redemption from hell. *English*

Help *see* Assistance; Collaboration; Cooperation; Unity

Heredity *see also* Good Breeding

8454. A bad crow makes a bad egg. *American*

8455. A chip of the old block. *English*

8456. A good cow may have an ill calf. *Scottish*

8457. A good whelp will not come of a bad dog. *Hebrew*

8458. A gude goose may hae [have] an ill gaislin'. *Scottish*

8459. A rose can come from a thorn, a thorn can come from a rose. *Arabic*

8460. A wild goose never reared a tame gosling. *Irish*

8461. An apple does not fall far from the apple tree. *American*

8462. An ill cow may hae a gude calf. *Scottish*

8463. As the tree is, so is the fruit. *German*

8464. As the twig is bent the tree's inclined. *American*

8465. Bad bird [or fowl, or crow], bad egg. *Latin*

8466. Better fed than bred. *Scottish*

8467. Blood falla [follows] vein. *Belizean Creole*

8468. Breed is stronger than pasture. *English*

8469. Dogs bark as they are bred. *Scottish*

8470. Egg-plants never grow on cucumber-vines. *Japanese*

8471. Even in animals there exists the spirit of their sires. *Latin (Horace)*

8472. From a bad crow a bad egg. *Greek (Sophocles)*

8473. Gawsie [plump, jolly] cow, gudely calf. *Scottish*

8474. He comes o' gude, he canna be ill. *Scottish*

8475. He that comes of a hen must scrape. *Italian*

8476. Like cowe, like calfe. *English*

8477. Like father, like son. *Latin*

8478. Many a good cow has a bad calf. *American*

8479. Of evil grain no good seed can come. *English*
8480. Plant the crab-tree where you will, it will never bear pippins. *English*
8481. Sic father, sic son. *Scottish*
8482. Such a father, such a son. *English*
8483. That which comes of a cat will catch mice. *English*
8484. The apple does not fall far from the tree. *Danish*
8485. The chip doesn't fly too far from the block. *Belizean Creole*
8486. The old cask tastes of what the new cask held. *Latin*
8487. The seed is in the fruit and the fruit in the seed. *American*
8488. The sins of the fathers are visited upon the children. *American*
8489. The stream will not rise above its source. *American*
8490. Trot mother, trot father, how can the foal amble? *Scottish*
8491. Well-fed, well-bred. *American*
8492. What's bred in the bone will never out of the flesh. *English*
8493. Ye was bred about the mill, ye hae mooped [impaired] a' your manners. *Scottish*
8494. You may suppress natural propensities by force, but they will be certain to reappear. *Latin (Horace)*

Heroes and Heroism

8495. A hero is only known in time of misfortune. *Hebrew*
8496. A man must be a hero to understand a hero. *American*
8497. Heroes are bred in lands where livelihood comes hard. *Greek*
8498. One murder makes a villain, millions a hero. *American*
8499. The hero is known on the battlefield. *Turkish*
8500. There are heroes in evil as well as in good. *French*
8501. To believe in the heroic makes heroes. *American*

Hesitation *see also* Delay; Indecision

8502. He who hesitates is lost. *American*
8503. The gods hate those who hesitate. *Greek*

Hiding *see* Concealment

Hindsight *see also* Past

8504. Beware of "Had I wist." *English*
8505. Everybody is wise after the event. *American*
8506. Everyone is wise afterward. *German*
8507. "Had I known" was a fool. *Latin*
8508. "Had I wist [known]," quo' the fool. *Scottish*
8509. Had I wist cometh too late. *English*
8510. Had I wist is a poor man. *German*
8511. Had I wystis a thyng it servys of nought. *English*
8512. Hindsight is better than foresight. *American*
8513. I have had is a poor man. *German*
8514. If our foresight were as good as our hindsight we would never make mistakes. *American*
8515. The next time you dance, know whom you take by the hand. *Scottish*
8516. When the damage is done everyone is wise. *Spanish*

Hinting *see* Subtlety

History *see also* Past

8517. Happy is the nation which has no history. *French*
8518. History is philosophy derived from examples. *Greek*
8519. History repeats itself. *American*

Home *see also* Family

8520. A coal-heaver is lord in his own house. *French*
8521. A dog is stout on his own dunghill. *French*
8522. A hearth of your own and a good wife are worth gold and pearls. *German*
8523. A hearth of your own is worth gold. *Danish*
8524. A man is a king in his own house. *Latin*
8525. A man without a home is a bird without a nest. *French*
8526. A prospering man should remain at home. *Latin*
8527. A swan in his own village, a crow in the next. *Tamil*
8528. An Englishman's house is his castle. *English*
8529. At home a hero, abroad a coward. *Tamil*
8530. At home a spider, abroad a tiger. *Telugu*
8531. At home an elephant, abroad a cat. *Tamil*
8532. Be it ever so humble, there's no place like home. *American (Payne)*
8533. Bullock at home, a cat abroad. *Tamil*
8534. Dry bread at home is better than roast meat abroad. *English (Herbert)*
8535. East and west, at home is best. *German*
8536. Every bird thinks its ain [own] nest best. *Scottish*
8537. Every cock crows best on his own dunghill. *French*
8538. Every cricket knows its own hearth. *Russian*
8539. Every dog is a lion at home. *Italian*
8540. Every man is a child in his own home. *Arabic*
8541. Every man is king in his own house. *French*
8542. Hame's a hamely word. *Scottish*
8543. He that hath no rest at home is in the world's hell. *Turkish*
8544. He that is far from home is near to harm. *Danish*
8545. Home is dear, home is best. *Greek*
8546. Home is home, though it be never so homely. *English*
8547. Home is where the heart is. *Latin*
8548. Home is where you hang your hat. *American*
8549. Home, my own home, tiny though thou be, to me thou seemest an abbey. *Spanish*
8550. Home-keeping youths have ever homely wits. *English (Shakespeare)*
8551. If you live long, no matter where, that place will be as good as the capital for you. *Japanese*
8552. In my own house I am king. *Spanish*
8553. It takes three children to make a home. *Kurdish*

8554. It's not much, but it's home. *American*

8555. My home, my mother's breast. *Spanish*

8556. My house, my house, though you be small, you are an abbey to me. *Italian*

8557. No stronger castle than a poor man's. *Serbian*

8558. Our own home surpasses every other. *Latin*

8559. The dog is a lion in his own house. *Persian*

8560. The fierce ox grows tame on a strange mound. *Portuguese*

8561. The frog cannot out of her bog. *English*

8562. The longest road out is the shortest road home. *Irish*

8563. The ox in a strange stall often casts a longing look toward the door. *Latin*

8564. The smoke of a man's own house is better than the fire of another's. *Spanish*

8565. The snail is as soon at its rest as the swallow. *Scottish*

8566. There is no place like home. *English*

8567. Tie me hand and foot, and throw me among my own. *Spanish*

8568. To every bird its nest is fair. *Italian*

8569. Where the nest and eggs are, the birds are near. *French*

8570. Who is happy should bide at home. *Greek*

8571. Whom God loves, his house is sweet to him. *Spanish*

Homeland *see also* Country

8572. Though it rain gold and silver in a foreign land and daggers and spears at home, yet it is better to be at home. *Malay*

Honesty *see also* Accuracy; Fair Dealing

8573. A clean mouth and an honest hand. *German*

8574. A clean mouth and an honest hand will take a man through any land. *American*

8575. A full heart lied never. *Scottish*

8576. A man never surfeits of too much honesty. *English*

8577. A nod o' honest men is enough. *Scottish*

8578. A thread will tie an honest man better than a rape [rope] will do a rogue. *Scottish*

8579. An honest good look covereth many faults. *English (Fuller)*

8580. An honest man does not make himself a dog for the sake of a bone. *Danish*

8581. An honest man's word is as good as the king's. *Danish*

8582. An honest man's word is his bond. *American*

8583. As honest a man as any in the cards, when the kings are out. *English*

8584. Better go to heaven in rags than to hell in embroidery. *English*

8585. Clean hands are better than full ones. *Latin*

8586. Don't measure your neighbor's honesty by your own. *American*

8587. God looks at the clean hands, not the full ones. *Latin (Publilius Syrus)*

8588. He is wise that is honest. *Italian*

8589. He is wiser than most men are that is honest. *English*

8590. He may be trusted wi' a house fu' o' unbored millstanes. *Scottish*

8591. He who tells the truth saves himself the trouble of swearing. *Yiddish*

8592. Honest men are easily humbugged. *English*

8593. Honestly is safely. *Latin*

8594. Honesty endures longest. *German*

8595. Honesty gives wings to strength. *Latin*

8596. Honesty hauds lang the gate. *Scottish*

8597. Honesty is like an icicle; if once it melts that is the end of it. *American*

8598. Honesty is praised and starves. *Latin (Juvenal)*

8599. Honesty isna pride. *Scottish*

8600. Honesty maketh rich, but she works slowly. *German*

8601. Honesty may be dear bought, but can ne'er be an ill-pennyworth. *Scottish*

8602. Honesty with poverty is better than ill-gotten wealth. *Latin*

8603. Honesty's the best policy. *Scottish*

8604. Integrity is better than charity. *Greek*

8605. It is annoying to be honest to no purpose. *Latin (Ovid)*

8606. Knavery may serve for a turn, but honesty is best at long run. *English*

8607. Lang leal [long honest], lang poor. *Scottish*

8608. Leal [honest] folk ne'er wanted gear [wealth, property]. *Scottish*

8609. Leal [honest] heart leed [lied] never. *Scottish*

8610. Naething's a man's truly but what he comes by duly. *Scottish*

8611. No legacy so rich as honesty. *English (Shakespeare)*

8612. None can be wise and safe but he that is honest. *English*

8613. Of all crafts, to be an honest man is the master craft. *English*

8614. One honest word is better than two oaths. *Turkish*

8615. The best investment for income is honesty. *German*

8616. The man who makes an honest living is at peace with his maker. *American*

8617. The most honest people are those who are too ignorant to know how to do wrong. *American*

8618. The name o' an honest man's muckle worth. *Scottish*

8619. The word o' an honest man's enough. *Scottish*

8620. The world is so much knave, that it holds honesty to be a vice and a folly. *American*

8621. There is always less money, less wisdom, and less honesty than people imagine. *Italian*

8622. They are all honest men, but my cloak is not to be found. *Spanish*

8623. Thrive by honesty or remain poor. *English*

8624. 'Tis hard (but glorious) to be poor and honest. *American (Franklin)*

8625. We are bound to be honest, but not to be rich. *English*

8626. Ye'll ne'er be auld wi' sae muckle honesty. *Scottish*

8627. Your looking-glass will tell you what none of your friends will. *English*

Honor *see also* Integrity

8628. A man of honor should never forget what he is because he sees what others are. *Spanish (Gracián)*
8629. A man without honor is worse than dead. *Spanish (Cervantes)*
8630. Among men of honor a word is a bond. *Italian*
8631. An honor won is surety for more. *French*
8632. Beauty's muck [dung] when honour's tint [lost]. *Scottish*
8633. Before honor is humility. *Bible*
8634. Better be without food than without honor. *Italian*
8635. Better die with honor than live with shame. *American*
8636. Better poor with honor than rich with shame. *English*
8637. Clean hands are better than full ones in the sight of God. *Latin (Publilius Syrus)*
8638. Eild [old age] should [or would] hae honour. *Scottish*
8639. Good men seek honor, middling men seek wealth and honor, base men seek wealth; honor itself is wealth to great men. *Sanskrit*
8640. He who loses honor can lose nothing else. *Latin (Publilius Syrus)*
8641. Honor follows him who flies from it. *Latin*
8642. Honor follows the unwilling. *Latin*
8643. Honor has a big shadow. *Swedish*
8644. Honor is not seemly for a fool. *Bible*
8645. Honor is on his tongue and ice under it. *Russian*
8646. Honor lies in the mane of a horse. *Arabic*
8647. Honor the tree that gives you shelter. *Danish*
8648. Honor's but an empty bubble. *English (Dryden)*
8649. Honor's onerous. *Latin*
8650. Honors change manners. *Latin*
8651. Honour and ease are seldom bedfellows. *English*
8652. Honour and profit lie not all in one sack. *English*
8653. Honour without profit is a ring on the finger. *English*
8654. If I lose mine honor, I lose myself. *English (Shakespeare)*
8655. It is no honor for an eagle to vanquish a dove. *Italian*
8656. Let honor be spotless. *Latin*
8657. Let us do what honor demands. *French*
8658. Lordships change manners. *Scottish*
8659. No man can restore honor and life. *German*
8660. Take honor from me and my life is done. *English (Shakespeare)*
8661. The king may give the honor, but you must make yourself honorable. *German*
8662. The post of honor is the post of danger. *Latin*
8663. Virtue is the road to honor. *American*
8664. What is honorable is fitting and what is fitting is honorable. *Latin*
8665. What is most honorable is also safest. *Latin*
8666. Where honor binds me, I must satisfy it. *French*
8667. Where honor ceaseth, there knowledge decreaseth. *English*
8668. Where the law lacks, honor should eke it out. *Danish*
8669. Where there is no honor there is no dishonor. *Portuguese*
8670. Where there is no shame, there is no honor. *German*
8671. Who loses honor can lose nothing else. *Latin*

Hope *see also* Consolation; Encouragement

8672. A good hope is better than a bad possession. *Spanish*
8673. A man may hope for anything while he has life. *Latin*
8674. A well-prepared mind hopes in adversity and fears in prosperity. *American*
8675. All things are to be hoped by a man as long as he is alive. *Latin (Seneca)*
8676. All things, says an ancient proverb, may be hoped by a man as long as he lives. *French*
8677. As long as there is breath there is hope. *Hindi*
8678. Better a good hope than a bad holding. *Spanish*
8679. Better live in hope than die in despair. *Scottish*
8680. Cease to hope and you will cease to fear. *Latin*
8681. Do not hope without despair, nor despair without hope. *Latin*
8682. Don't feed yourself on false hopes. *American*
8683. He dies from hunger who lives by hope. *American*
8684. He gains enough that loses a vain hope. *Italian*
8685. He is consumed by a vain hope. *Latin*
8686. He that lives in hope, danceth without a minstrel. *Spanish*
8687. He that lives on hope has a slim diet. *Scottish*
8688. He that lives on hope shall die fasting. *American*
8689. Hope and a red-rag, are baits for men and mackerel. *American (Franklin)*
8690. Hope deceives, enjoyment undeceives. *French*
8691. Hope deferred maketh the heart sick. *Bible*
8692. Hope hauds up the head. *Scottish*
8693. Hope is as cheap as despair. *English*
8694. Hope is a good breakfast but a bad supper. *English*
8695. Hope is a medicine every doctor can dispense without cost to his patient. *American*
8696. Hope is a waking man's dream. *Greek*
8697. Hope is but the dream of those that wake. *Greek*
8698. Hope is grief's best music. *English*
8699. Hope is my strength. *French*
8700. Hope is our only comfort in adversity. *Latin*
8701. Hope is sawin' while death is mawin'. *Scottish*
8702. Hope is the last thing that we lose. *Italian*
8703. Hope is the last thing to abandon the unfortunate. *Italian*
8704. Hope is the pillar of the world. *Kanuri*
8705. Hope is the poor man's bread. *English*
8706. Hope is the poor man's income. *Danish*

8707. Hope keeps the heart from breaking. *American*
8708. Hope makes the fool rich. *German*
8709. Hope springs eternal in the human breast. *English (Pope)*
8710. Hope stays with those who have nothing else. *Greek*
8711. Hope supports men in distress. *Latin*
8712. Hope, the mother of fools. *Polish*
8713. Hope to the end. *Bible*
8714. Hope well and have well. *English*
8715. Hopers go to hell. *Scottish*
8716. Hopes delayed hang the heart upon tenterhooks. *English*
8717. I do not buy hope with money. *Latin*
8718. If it werena [were not] for hope the heart wad [would] break. *Scottish*
8719. If you live on hope you have a slender diet. *American*
8720. In the kingdom of hope there is no winter. *Russian*
8721. It is hope which maintains most of mankind. *Greek (Sophocles)*
8722. It is hope which makes even the fettered miner live. *Latin (Ovid)*
8723. It is said that whilst there is life to a sick man there is hope. *Latin (Cicero)*
8724. It's good to hope, it's the waiting that spoils it. *Yiddish*
8725. Let the fearful be allowed to hope. *Latin*
8726. Many a hopeful man has hope beguiled. *Latin*
8727. Many fools graze in the meadow of hope. *Russian*
8728. Nane are sae weel but they hope to be better. *Scottish*
8729. Ne'er quit certainty for hope. *Scottish*
8730. Put aside trifling hopes. *Latin (Horace)*
8731. The hope of life returns with the sun. *Latin*
8732. The man without hope needs no antagonist: he beats himself. *American*
8733. The miserable have no other medicine, / But only hope. *English (Shakespeare)*
8734. There is hope in certainty but no certainty in hope. *American*
8735. There is hope in the living, but the dead are hopeless. *Greek*
8736. There is no disease like hope. *Indian*
8737. Those who are fed on hope do not live but hang on. *Latin*
8738. Too much hope deceiveth. *English*
8739. When the heart's past hope the face is past shame. *Scottish*
8740. While I breathe I hope. *Latin*

Hospitality *see also* Guests; Visiting

8741. A hearty hand to gie [give] a hungry meltith [a meal]. *Scottish*
8742. A merry host makes merry guests. *Dutch*
8743. A woeful hostess brooks not merry guests. *English (Shakespeare)*
8744. As you treat guests at home you will be treated abroad. *Chinese*
8745. At open doors dogs come in. *Scottish*
8746. Be not forgetful to entertain strangers: for thereby some have entertained angels unawares. *Bible*
8747. He that bids me to eat, wishes me to live. *Scottish*
8748. He who is not hospitable to an excellent guest will soon have none. *Chinese*
8749. He winna send you awa wi' a sair [sore] heart. *Scottish*
8750. In ordinary life you must be economical; when you invite guests you must be lavish in hospitality. *Chinese*
8751. It is easy to treat a guest well at first; but if he stays too long it is hard. *Chinese*
8752. It is more disgraceful to turn out a guest than not to admit him. *Latin*
8753. Long visits make hosts uncivil; when a poor man visits his relatives they treat him coolly. *Chinese*
8754. Open your door to the stranger and don't shut up your heart. *American*
8755. The farther ben the welcomer. *Scottish*
8756. The guest is not welcome to the guest, but both to the host. *Turkish*
8757. To dismiss a guest is a more ungracious act than not to admit him at all. *Latin (Ovid)*

Houses *see also* Home

8758. A house you call a house in vain / If no man it doth contain. *Welsh*

Housewives *see also* Husbands and Wives; Marriage

8759. A house well-furnished makes a good housewife. *American*
8760. Bare walls make giddy housewives. *English*
8761. Between a cross dog and a cross-eyed woman a house is well kept: he barks and she swings the broom. *American*
8762. Silk and velvet let the kitchen fire out. *German*
8763. The eye of the housewife makes the cat fat. *American*
8764. The fingers of the housewife do more than a yoke of oxen. *German*
8765. The ugliest girl makes the best housewife. *American*

Humanity

8766. He has no religion who has no humanity. *Arabic*
8767. Human blood is all of one color. *English*
8768. I am a man, and nothing relating to men is a matter of indifference to me. *Latin (Terence)*
8769. Long teeth and short teeth eat the same food. [All men are essentially the same.] *Oji*
8770. White or black, we are human. *Spanish*

Humiliation *see also* Embarrassment

8771. Better a quiet death than a public misfortune. *Spanish*
8772. It is bitter to be taught obedience after you have learned to rule. *Latin (Publilius Syrus)*

Humility *see also* Modesty

8773. A cypher and humility make the other figures and virtues of tenfold value. *American (Franklin)*

8774. A man is closer to God when he stops playing the lord. *American*

8775. A man's hat in his hand never did him ony harm. *Scottish*

8776. All the virtues spring from humility. *American*

8777. Declaiming against pride, is not always a sign of humility. *American (Franklin)*

8778. Humble things become the humble. *Latin*

8779. Humble thyself in all things. *German (Thomas à Kempis)*

8780. Humility falls neither far, nor heavily. *Latin (Publilius Syrus)*

8781. Humility is the foundation of all virtues. *Chinese (Confucius)*

8782. Humility often gains more than pride. *Italian*

8783. Make way for your betters. *Latin*

8784. Man was created on the sixth day so that he could not be boastful, since he came after the flea in the order of creation. *Palestinian*

8785. Modest humility is beauty's crown. *American*

8786. One may be humble out of pride. *French (Montaigne)*

8787. Proclaim not all thou knowest, all thou owest, all thou hast, nor all thou can'st. *American (Franklin)*

8788. Rather to bow than break is profitable; / Humility is a thing commendable. *French*

8789. The bending of the humble is the graceful droop of the branches laden with fruit. *Persian*

8790. The fuller the ear is of rice-grain, the lower it bends; empty of grain, it grows taller and taller. *Malay*

8791. The heaviest ear of corn is the one that lowliest bends its head. *Irish*

8792. The humble are in danger when the powerful disagree. *Latin*

8793. The humble man is like the earth which alike kisses the feet of the king and of the beggar. *Persian*

8794. The humble reap advantage; the haughty meet misfortune. *Chinese*

8795. The humble suffer from the folly of the great. *French (La Fontaine)*

8796. The more noble, the more humble. *English*

8797. There is no humiliation for humility. *French*

8798. Those who fly low are hurt least when they fall. *Chinese*

8799. Too humble is half proud. *Yiddish*

8800. Too much humility is pride. *German*

8801. Whosoever exalteth himself shall be abased; and he that humbleth himself shall be exalted. *Bible*

Humor *see also* Jests and Jesting; Laughter; Wit

8802. Humor, to a man, is like a feather pillow. It is filled with what is easy to get but gives great comfort. *Irish*

Hunger *see also* Appetite; Eating; Excess; Gluttony; Obesity

8803. A bagpipe will not lightly [i.e., easily] speak until his belly be full. *English*

8804. A barking stomach. *Latin*

8805. A blind man can see his mouth. *Irish*

8806. A fine cage won't feed the hungry bird. *American*

8807. A handful of rice is riches to a starving man. *Japanese*

8808. A hunger and a burst. *Scottish*

8809. A hungrie man sees far. *Scottish*

8810. A hungry ass eats any straw. *Italian*

8811. A hungry ass heeds not a blow. *Latin*

8812. A hungry belly hath no ears. *Latin (Cato the Elder)*

8813. A hungry dog fears not the stick. *Italian*

8814. A hungry dog is not afraid of a cudgelling. *English*

8815. A hungry dog will eat dirty pudding. *English*

8816. A hungry horse makes a clean manger. *French*

8817. A hungry louse bites sair [sore]. *Scottish*

8818. A hungry man discovers more than a hundred lawyers. *Spanish*

8819. A hungry man has aye [always] a lazy cook. *Scottish*

8820. A hungry man is an angry man. *English*

8821. A hungry man smells meat far. *Scottish*

8822. A hungry man will listen to nothing. *Latin*

8823. A hungry stamach is aye [always] craving. *Scottish*

8824. A hungry stomach has no ears. *French (La Fontaine)*

8825. A hungry stomach rarely despises rough food. *Latin (Horace)*

8826. A hungry wretch is half mad. *French*

8827. A jade eats as much as a good horse. *English*

8828. A man who wants bread is ready for anything. *French*

8829. A sharp stomach makes a short devotion. *American*

8830. A short grace is gude for hungry folk. *Scottish*

8831. A starving populace knows nothing of fear. *Latin*

8832. A wolf in his belly. *English*

8833. An empty stomach will not listen to anything. *Spanish*

8834. As hungry as a church mouse. *English*

8835. Brackish water is sweet in a dry land. *Portuguese*

8836. Do not run up against a hungry man. *Latin*

8837. Even Fuji is without beauty to one hungry and cold. *Japanese*

8838. For bread of fifteen days, hunger of three weeks. *Spanish*

8839. Gie a greedy dog a muckle bane [big bone]. *Scottish*

8840. Hang hunger and drown drouth. *Scottish*

8841. He thinks of everything who wants bread. *French*

8842. His wame [belly] thinks his wizzen's [throat's] cut. *Scottish*

8843. Horses kick each other only at an empty trough. *American*

8844. Hunger and cold betray a man to his enemies. *Spanish*

8845. Hunger changes beans into almonds. *Italian*

8846. Hunger drives the wolf out of the wood. *Italian*

8847. Hunger droppeth out of his nose. *English*

8848. Hunger eats through stone walls. *Dutch*

8849. Hunger eats through stone walls and builds barricades. *American*

8850. Hunger fetches the wolf out of the woods. *English*

8851. Hunger finds no fault with the cookery. *English*

8852. Hunger gives a relish even to raw beans. *Latin*

8853. Hunger is a bad adviser. *French*

8854. Hunger is good kitchen meat. *English*

8855. Hunger is hard for a heal [sound] maw. *English*

8856. Hunger is sharper than thorn. *English*

8857. Hunger is the best cook. *Polish*

8858. Hunger is the best pickle. *American (Franklin)*

8859. Hunger is the best sauce in the world. *Spanish (Cervantes)*

8860. Hunger is the best spice of food; thirst of drink. *Latin (Cicero)*

8861. Hunger is the instructor of many. *Greek*

8862. Hunger is the teacher of the arts and the bestower of invention. *Latin (Persius)*

8863. Hunger is violent, and will be fed. *Greek*

8864. Hunger knows no friend. *English*

8865. Hunger makes dinners; pastime suppers. *English*

8866. Hunger makes hard bones sweet beans. *English*

8867. Hunger makes raw beans relish well. *English*

8868. Hunger maketh harde bones softe. *English*

8869. Hunger makes raw beans sweet. *Dutch*

8870. Hunger never fails o' a gude cook. *Scottish*

8871. Hunger sets the dog a-hunting. *Italian*

8872. Hunger sharpens the understanding even in fools. *Latin*

8873. Hunger sweetens beans. *Latin*

8874. Hunger sweetens everything but itself. *Latin*

8875. Hunger teaches us many a lesson. *Latin*

8876. Hunger thou me and I'll harry [ruin] thee. *English*

8877. Hunger waits only eight days. *English*

8878. Hunger will break through stone walls, or anything except Suffolk cheese. *English*

8879. Hunger will break through stone walls. *English (Shakespeare)*

8880. Hunger [or appetite] is the best sauce. *English*

8881. Hunger's gude kitchen to a cauld potato, but a wet divot to the low [flame] of love. *Scottish*

8882. Hungry bellies have no ears. *Latin (Cato)*

8883. Hungry dogges will eate durty puddinges. *English*

8884. Hungry dogs are blythe o' bursten puddin. *Scottish*

8885. Hungry flies bite sore. *English*

8886. Hungry folk are soon angry. *Scottish*

8887. Hungry stewards wear many shoon [shoes]. *Scottish*

8888. If loaves of bread came down as hail, the gypsies' hunger would not fail. *Bulgarian*

8889. It is all very well to preach fasting with a full stomach. *Italian*

8890. It is better to satisfy our hunger than to be clothed in purple. *Latin*

8891. Lang fasting gathers wind. *Scottish*

8892. Lang lean maks hamald [poor] cattle. *Scottish*

8893. Men are like bagpipes: no sound comes from them till they're full. *Irish*

8894. Ne'er gie me my death in a toom [empty] dish. *Scottish*

8895. No bread is bad to the hungry. *American*

8896. Scart-the-cog [scratch-the-dish] wad sup mair [more]. *Scottish*

8897. Sharp sauce gies a gude taste to sweatmeats. *Scottish*

8898. She was so hungry she could not stay for the parson to say grace. *English*

8899. The belly is ungrateful — it always forgets we already gave it something. *Russian*

8900. The first dish is aye best eating. *Scottish*

8901. The full belly does not believe in hunger. *Italian*

8902. The full-fed sheep is frightened at her own tail. *Spanish*

8903. The hungry ass will eat any sort of straw. *Italian*

8904. The hungry sigh; the sated belch. *Russian*

8905. The hungry stomach despises not common food. *Latin*

8906. The song of the stomach is hard to bear. *Wolof*

8907. They that have no other meat, / Bread and butter are glad to eat. *English*

8908. To him who is stinted of food a boiled turnip will relish like a roast fowl. *Persian (Sa'di)*

8909. To hunger there is no bad bread. *French*

8910. Wae to the wame [belly] that has a wilfu' maister. *Scottish*

8911. When a Jew is hungry, he sings; a peasant beats his wife. *Yiddish*

8912. Who goes to bed supperless, all night tumbles and tosses. *English*

8913. Ye hae tint [lost] your ain stamach and found a tyke's. *Scottish*

Hunting

8914. A good hound hunts by kind. *French*

Husbands and Wives *see also* Marriage; Widows; Wives: Choosing a Wife

8915. A bad wife is the shipwreck of her husband. *German*

8916. A dead wife's the best goods in a man's house. *English*

8917. A dumb wife curses, not with her mouth, but with her hands. *Yiddish*

8918. A fresh-cut flower stuck in a donkey's head. [A pretty woman married to an ugly man.] *Chinese*

8919. A good wife and good name hath no mate in goods nor fame. *English*

8920. A good wife and health, is a man's best wealth. *English*

8921. A good wife is a good portion. *Bible*

8922. A good yeoman makes a good woman. *English*

8923. A grunting horse and a groaning wife seldom fail their master. *English*

8924. A gude man maks a gude wife. *Scottish*

8925. A handsome husband is common property. *American*

8926. A horse broken and a wife to break is a horse made and a wife to make. *Scottish*

8927. A house can't be kept without talk. *Irish*

8928. A husband must be deaf, and the wife blind, to have quietness. *English*

8929. A husband with one eye rather than one son. *Spanish*

8930. A husband's cuffs leave no mark. *Russian*

8931. A little house well filled, a little land well tilled, a little wife well willed, are great riches. *English*

8932. A man can only find real delight in one wife. *Hebrew*

8933. A man's best fortune, or his worst, is his wife. *English*

8934. A mill and a wife are always in want of something. *Italian*

8935. A prudent wife is from the Lord. *Bible*

8936. A quiet wife is mighty pretty. *American*

8937. A smoky chimney and a scolding wife are two bad companions. *American*

8938. A vicious wife and an untoward sow no laws can govern. *Chinese*

8939. A virtuous wife rules her husband by obeying him. *Latin*

8940. A virtuous woman is a crown to her husband. *Bible*

8941. A wife and a horse should not be loaned. *Yiddish*

8942. A wife can spill more with a thimble than a husband can draw with a pail. *German*

8943. A wife is good for the body but not for the soul. *Yiddish*

8944. A wife is like a giant. *Accra*

8945. A wife is not a guitar; you can't play on her and then hang her on the wall. *Russian*

8946. A wife knows enough, who knows the good man's breeks [trousers] from a weilycoat [petticoat]. *Scottish*

8947. A wife speaks and spurs. *Hebrew*

8948. A wife's long tongue is the flight of steps by which misfortunes enter the house. *Chinese*

8949. A wise man should never give his wife too much rein. *Latin*

8950. A young wife is an old man's post-horse to the grave. *German*

8951. A young wife should be in her house but a shadow and an echo. *Chinese*

8952. A' are guid [good] lasses, but where do a' the ill wives come frae [from]? *Scottish*

8953. All married women are not wives. *Japanese*

8954. An ill wife and a new-kindled candle should hae [have] their heads hadden [held, kept] down. *Scottish*

8955. An unscolded wife, like an uncut millstone, does not go easily. *Romanian*

8956. Auld wives were aye gude maidens. *Scottish*

8957. Bachelors' wives and auld maids' bairns [children] are aye weel bred. *Scottish*

8958. Be a good husband, and you will get a penny to spend, a penny to lend, and a penny for a friend. *English*

8959. Better a husband without love than a jealous husband. *Italian*

8960. Better be an old man's darling than a young man's slave. *American*

8961. But wives must be had, be they good or bad. *English*

8962. Caesar's wife must be above suspicion. *Latin*

8963. Don't trust a horse on the road or a wife at home. *Yiddish*

8964. Emperors are only husbands in wives' eyes. *English (Byron)*

8965. Empty rooms make giddy housewives. *French*

8966. Every evil, but not an evil wife. *Hebrew*

8967. Every man can guide an ill wife weel but him that has her. *Scottish*

8968. Every man can tame a shrew but he that hath her. *English*

8969. Every man has a good wife and a bad trade. *Italian*

8970. Every married man should think his wife the one good woman in the world. *Spanish*

8971. Fire, water, and a bad wife are three great evils. *German*

8972. Fleas and a girning [fretful] wife are waukrife [wakeful] bedfellows. *Scottish*

8973. "Gie [give] her her will, or she'll burst," quoth the gudeman when his wife was dinging him [kamed his head wi' the three-legged stool]. *Scottish*

8974. Gnaw the bone which is fallen to thy lot. *Hebrew*

8975. Grief for a dead wife lasts to the door. *Italian*

8976. Happy's the maid that's married to a mitherless son. *Scottish*

8977. He that has a wife has a maister. *Scottish*

8978. He that loseth his wife and a farthing hath great loss of his farthing. *Italian*

8979. He that takes a wife takes care. *American*

8980. He wha tells his wife a' [all] is but newly married. *Scottish*

8981. He who does not honor his wife dishonors himself. *Spanish*

8982. He who has a bonny wife needs mair [more] than twa een [two eyes]. *Scottish*

8983. He who is cursed with an ugly wife sees darkness when he lights the evening lamp. *Greek*

8984. His wife wore the breeches. *Latin*

8985. How gently glides the married life away, / When she who rules still seems but to obey. *English*

8986. Husband and wife in perfect accord are the music of the harp and lute. *Chinese*

8987. Husbands are in heaven whose wives chide not. *English*

8988. Husbands, love your wives, and be not bitter against them. *Bible*

8989. I won't let a wife lead me to the altar [i.e., dominate me]. *Latin (Martius)*

8990. If the hen does not prate, she will not lay. *East Anglian*

8991. If the husband drinks, half the house is on fire; if the wife drinks, the whole house is ablaze. *Russian*

8992. If the wife sins, the husband is not innocent. *Italian*

8993. If the wife wears the pants, the husband must rock the cradle. *Yiddish*

8994. If ye sell your purse to your wife gie [give] her your breeks [trousers] to the bargain. *Scottish*

8995. If you love your children, you will slap them sometimes; if you love your wife, you will leave her sometimes. *Malay*

8996. If your wife is little, stoop to her. *Hebrew*

8997. It is a silly flock where the ewe bears the bell. *Scottish*

8998. It is better to dwell in a corner of the housetop than with a brawling woman in a wide house. *Bible*

8999. It is cheaper to find a wife than to feed a wife. *American*

9000. It's a sweet sorrow to bury a nagging wife. *American*

9001. Let it be a husband though it be but a log. *Spanish*

9002. Let not the hen talk and the cock be silent. *French*

9003. Man's best possession is a sympathetic wife. *Greek (Euripides)*

9004. Mills and wives are aye wanting. *Scottish*

9005. My better half. *Latin*

9006. Nae [no] man can thrive unless his wife will let him. *Scottish*

9007. Ne'er was a wife weel pleased coming frae the mill but ane, and she brak her neck bane [bone]. *Scottish*

9008. Never have dealings with other men's wives. *Latin*

9009. Next to nae wife a gude wife is the best. *Scottish*

9010. No fellow is so poor that he has not a wife on his arm. *German*

9011. Saith Solomon the Wise, "A good wife's a great prize." *English*

9012. She broke her elbow at the church door. [She became lazy after being married.] *English*

9013. She has got the measure of his shoe. *Irish*

9014. She looketh well to the ways of her household, and eateth not the bread of idleness. *Bible*

9015. She stoops to conquer. *English*

9016. Silk and velvet put out the kitchen fire. *German*

9017. Sweet in the bed, and sweir [heavy, lazy] up in the morning, was never a good housewife. *Scottish*

9018. Take a wife's advice without asking for it. *Welsh*

9019. The bed that holds a wife is never free from wrangling. *Latin*

9020. The better the man, the less good will he get out of his wife. *Latin (Juvenal)*

9021. The bitterest morsel of human life is a bad wife. *Greek*

9022. The contentions of a wife are a continual dropping. *Bible*

9023. The cunning wife makes her husband her apron. *Spanish*

9024. The dead wife and the living sheep make a man rich. *German*

9025. The death o' his first wife made sic [such] a hole in his heart that a' the rest slippit easily through. *Scottish*

9026. The devil will take away everything but a bad wife. *Yiddish*

9027. The first wife is a broom; the second, a lady. *Spanish*

9028. The first wife is like a dog; the second, like a cat; the third, like a pig. *Yiddish*

9029. The foot on the cradle, and hand on the distaff, is the sign of a good housewife. *Spanish*

9030. The husband is the last to know the dishonor of his house. *Latin*

9031. The husband of an ugly wife is better blinded. *Persian*

9032. The more a husband loves his wife, the more he increases her whims. *Chinese*

9033. The more a wife loves her husband, the more she corrects his faults. *Chinese*

9034. The nobleman finds a wife easier than the peasant. *German*

9035. The old wife, if she do not serve for a pot, serves for a cover. *Spanish*

9036. The wife carries her husband on her face; the husband carries his wife on his linen. *Bulgarian*

9037. The wife has the labor-pains, and the husband celebrates the circumcision. *Yiddish*

9038. The wife is the keeper of her husband's soul. *Arabic*

9039. The wife is twice precious only; when led into the house, and when taken out of the house. *Russian*

9040. There's but ae gude wife in the warld, and ilka ane thinks he has her. *Scottish*

9041. Three things drive a man out of doors: Smoke, dropping water [or a leaky roof], and a shrew. *Italian*

9042. To be under the slipper. *German*

9043. To know the husband, observe the face of the wife. *Spanish*

9044. Two good days for a man in this life: when he weds, and when he buries his wife. *American*

9045. Under the sign of the cat's foot. [Said of a henpecked man.] *English*

9046. Wae's the wife that wants [lacks] a tongue but weel's the man that gets her. *Scottish*

9047. When the husband earns well, the wife spends well. *Dutch*

9048. When the tail rules, the head goes wrong. *Polish*

9049. When the wife is asleep, the basket is asleep also. *Hebrew*

9050. When the wife rules the house, the devil is the man-servant. *German*

9051. Where a wife wears the breeches, and a husband the apron, things don't go well. *Italian*

9052. Where a woman wears the breeches, she has a good right to them. *American*

9053. Where cobwebs are plenty, kisses are scarce. *English*

9054. Where the cup is broken by the mistress of the house, one hears no noise. *Kurdish*

9055. Who has a bad wife is poor in the midst of riches. *German*

9056. Whoso findeth a wife findeth a good thing. *Bible*

9057. Why does the bear dance? Because he has no wife. *Yiddish*

9058. Wife, from thy spouse each blemish hide, more than from all the world beside. *American*

9059. Wives and water mills are aye wanting. *Scottish*

9060. Wives are young men's mistresses, companions for middle age, and old men's nurses. *English (Bacon)*

9061. Wives maun be had, whether gude or bad. *Scottish*

9062. Wives maun hae their wills when they live, for they mak nane when they dee [die]. *Scottish*

9063. Wives may be merry and honest too. *English (Shakespeare)*

9064. Ye may drive the deil [devil] into a wife, but ye'll ne'er ding him oot o' her. *Scottish*

9065. Ye wad mak a gude wife—ye keep the grip ye get. *Scottish*

9066. You can't fill your belly with beauty. *Arabic*

9067. You [the (male) head of the family] say "I have," not "We have." *Oji*

Hypochondria

9068. An imaginary ailment is worse than a disease. *Yiddish*

Hypocrisy *see also* Appearance; Deception

9069. A bad man becomes worse when he apes a saint. *Latin (Publilius Syrus)*

9070. A devoted [or holy] face and a cat's claws. *Spanish*

9071. A false superior man, but a truly mean man. *Chinese*

9072. A honeyed tongue, a heart of gall. *French*

9073. A hypocrite, a makhala fruit; beautiful outside, bitter within; a tiger in a tulsi grove; outside smooth and painted, inside only straw. *Bengalese*

9074. A hypocrite is worse than a demon. *Tamil*

9075. A hypocrite pays tribute to God only that he may impose on men. *English*

9076. A man who gives a furtive glance and has a laughing face, hides in his heart a murderous sword. *Chinese*

9077. A mouth like a sweet melon; a heart like a bitter gourd. *Chinese*

9078. A mouth that prays, and a hand that kills. *Arabic*

9079. A terrible ascetic, an atrocious thief. *Tamil*

9080. A wolf without, a sheep within. *American*

9081. Before people, a superior man; in secret, a mean man. *Chinese*

9082. Better the world should know you as a sinner than God know you as a hypocrite. *Danish*

9083. Beware of the man of two faces. *Dutch*

9084. Carrion crows bewail the dead sheep and then eat them. *English*

9085. Crocodile's tears. *Latin*

9086. Crows weep for the dead lamb and then devour him. *American*

9087. Every vice has its virtue except hypocrisy. *American*

9088. Externally a sheep, internally a wolf. *Greek*

9089. God on his tongue and the devil in his heart. *English*

9090. He braks my head an' syne [then] puts on my hoo [hood]. *Scottish*

9091. He cries with one eye. *Zulu*

9092. He eats mutton in the East and dog's flesh in the West. *Chinese*

9093. He has meikle [much] prayer but little devotion. *Scottish*

9094. He has one face to God and another to the devil. *Scottish*

9095. He has the Bible on his lips but not in his heart. *Dutch*

9096. He is a wolf in a lamb's skin. *Scottish*

9097. He kicks with his hind feet, licks with his tongue. *Russian*

9098. He loves to the eye. *Efik*

9099. He rins wi' the hound an' hauds wi' the hare. *Scottish*

9100. He shows honey, he mixes poison. *Greek*

9101. He sits like a tiger withdrawing his claws. *Malayan*

9102. He tells lies by thousands and builds a temple. *Tamil*

9103. He that speaks me fair and loves me not, I'll speak him fair and trust him not. *English*

9104. He utters in his language something different from what he ponders in his mind. *Latin*

9105. He will gae to hell for the house profit. *Scottish*

9106. He's a causey [causeway] saint and a house deil [devil]. *Scottish*

9107. His mouth is as sweet as honey; his heart as venomous as a snake. *Chinese*

9108. Hypocrisy is a homage which vice pays to virtue. *French (La Rochefoucauld)*

9109. I hate a bad man saying what is good. *Greek*

9110. Like a lamp-stand, he lights others but not himself. *Chinese*

9111. Many kiss the hand they wish to see cut off. *Arabic*

9112. Mony ane [many a one] kisses the bairn [child] for love o' the nurse. *Scottish*

9113. Never carry two faces under one hood. *English*

9114. No man is a hypocrite in his pleasures. *English (Johnson)*

9115. No villain like the conscientious villain. *English*

9116. None make a greater show of sorrow than those who are most delighted. *Latin (Tacitus)*

9117. O what may a man within him hide, / Though angel on the outward side! *English (Shakespeare)*

9118. Often poison and gall are under the honeyed speech. *Danish*

9119. One mouth with two tongues. *Chinese*

9120. Outside he wears a sheepskin; inside he hides a wolf's heart. *Chinese*

9121. Rosary in hand, the devil at heart. *Portuguese*

9122. Saint abroad, a devil at home. *American*

9123. She pretends not to eat fish, but there are three on her leaf. *Bengalese*

9124. The attachment of the insincere, a razor's blade. *Bengalese*

9125. The heron is a saint as long as the fish is not in sight. *Bengalese*

9126. The hypocrite has the look of an archbishop and the heart of a miller. *Greek*
9127. The hypocrite's mask becomes his face; he can't pull it off. *American*
9128. The mouth of Buddha, the heart of a snake. *Chinese*
9129. The scoundrel must bear the burden of hypocrisy. *American*
9130. Those who daub both sides of the wall. *Latin*
9131. To clothe a wolf in priest's clothing. *Japanese*
9132. To cry with one eye and laugh with the other. *English*
9133. To fawn with the tail and bite with the mouth. *Spanish*
9134. To plant sugar-cane on the lips. *Malayan*
9135. To weep at the tomb of a stepmother. *Latin*
9136. Under his arms a Koran, he casts his eyes on a bullock. *Afghan*
9137. Water under the grass. *Chinese*
9138. What the mouth says, the heart may not feel. *French*
9139. When you grind your corn, give not the flour to the devil and the bran to God. *Italian*

Idealism

9140. The toe of the star-gazer is often stubbed. *Russian*

Ideas *see* Opinion; Thought

Identity *see also* Appearance; Deception; Judging; Nature

9141. By his claw you may know the lion. *Latin*
9142. Every chimney smells of smoke. *American*
9143. The ass is known by his ears. *Latin*
9144. Ye may wash aff dirt but never dun hide. *Scottish*

Idleness *see also* Bystanders; Inactivity; Laziness; Usefulness

9145. A busy man is plagued with one desire, but an idle one with a thousand. *American*
9146. A young man idle, an old man needy. *Italian*
9147. All sins come out of the house of idleness. *American*
9148. An idle brain's the deil's smiddy [the devil's workshop]. *Scottish*
9149. An idle head is a box for the wind. *English*
9150. An idle person is the devil's playfellow. *Arabic*
9151. An idle youth, a needy age. *English*
9152. An idle youth becomes in age a beggar. *Latin*
9153. Apollo's bow is not always bent. *Latin*
9154. Be ever engaged, so that whenever the devil calls he may find you occupied. *Latin (St. Jerome)*
9155. Better sit idle than work for nought. *Scottish*
9156. By doing nothing we learn to do ill [or evil]. *Latin*
9157. Doing nothing is doing ill. *English*
9158. Expect poison from the standing water. *English (Blake)*
9159. Go to the ant, thou sluggard; consider her ways, and be wise. *Bible*
9160. He is idle that might be better employed. *English*
9161. He that is busy is tempted but by one devil, he that is idle by a legion [or by a thousand]. *Italian*
9162. He who does nothing but sit and eat, will wear away a mountain of wealth. *Chinese*
9163. Idle bairns [children] are the devil's workhouses. *Scottish*
9164. Idle dogs worry sheep. *Scottish*
9165. Idle folks have the most labor. *English*
9166. Idle folks lack no excuses. *English*
9167. Idle men are the devil's playfellows. *English*
9168. Idle young, needly auld. *Scottish*
9169. Idleness and lust are bosom friends. *American*
9170. Idleness and pride tax with a heavier hand than kings and parliaments. *American (Franklin)*
9171. Idleness cannot support even the frugal life. *Greek*
9172. Idleness has poverty for wages. *German*
9173. Idleness induces caprice. *Latin (Lucan)*
9174. Idleness is ever the root of indecision. *Latin*
9175. Idleness is the father of all the vices. *Italian*
9176. Idleness is the greatest prodigality. *American (Franklin)*
9177. Idleness is the key of beggary. *English*
9178. Idleness is the mother of hunger of [the brother of theft]. *Dutch*
9179. Idleness is the mother of poverty. *English*
9180. Idleness is the refuge of weak minds and the holiday of fools. *American*
9181. Idleness is the root of all evil. *American*
9182. Idleness is the sepulchre of a living man. *Latin*
9183. Idleness is the shipwreck of chastity. *Latin*
9184. Idleness makes the fullest purse empty. *German*
9185. Idleness produces all vices. *Latin*
9186. Idleness ruins a man's constitution. *Latin (Ovid)*
9187. Idleness teacheth much evil. *Bible*
9188. Idleness turns the edge of wit. *English*
9189. Idleness wastes the sluggish body, as water is corrupted unless it moves. *Latin (Ovid)*
9190. If the brain sows not corn, it plants thistles. *English*
9191. If the devil catches a man idle he'll set him to work. *Scottish*
9192. It is better to do nothing, than to be doing nothing. *Latin*
9193. It is only idle people who can find time for everything. *French*
9194. Let the devil never find you unoccupied. *Latin*
9195. Men learn to do ill by doing nothing. *Latin (Cato)*
9196. No deity assists the idle. *Latin*
9197. Nothing kills like doing nothing. *Danish*
9198. Of idleness cometh no goodness. *English*
9199. Providence assists not the idle. *Latin*
9200. Rust eats iron. *American*
9201. Rust wastes more than use. *French*
9202. Satan finds some mischief still / For idle hands to do. *English (Watts)*
9203. The devil tempts all other men, but idle men tempt the devil. *Arabic*

9204. The dog in the kennel barks at his fleas; the dog that hunts does not feel them. *Chinese*
9205. The hardest work is to be idle. *Yiddish*
9206. The idle mind knows not what it wants. *Latin*
9207. The stable wears out a horse more than the road. *French*
9208. The vices of idleness are only to be shaken off by active employment. *Latin (Seneca)*
9209. There is more trouble in having nothing to do than in having much to do. *American*
9210. There's nane sae [none so] busy as him that has least to do. *Scottish*
9211. They do nothing laboriously. *Latin*
9212. Time is life, and when the idle man kills time, he kills himself. *American*
9213. To do nothing is in every man's power. *English (Johnson)*
9214. Trouble springs from idleness, and grievous toil from needless ease. *American (Franklin)*
9215. We have more idleness of mind than of body. *French*
9216. With the idle it is always holy day time. *Latin*
9217. Without business, debauchery. *English*
9218. Woe to the idle shepherd that leaveth the flock. *Bible*
9219. Worms are bred in a stagnant pool, evil thoughts in idleness. *Latin*
9220. You're idle if you might be better employed. *American*

Ignorance *see also* Experience; Ignorance; Learning

9221. A man without knowledge is like one that is dead. *English*
9222. A third of the world is desert locked up in the human brain. *Moroccan*
9223. Be not ignorant of anything in great matter or small. *Bible*
9224. Being ignorant is not so much a shame, as being unwilling to learn. *American (Franklin)*
9225. Better to be ignorant of a matter than half know it. *Latin (Publilius Syrus)*
9226. Children and fools have merry lives. *English*
9227. He that knows little often repeats it. *English*
9228. He who knows little soon sings it out. *Spanish*
9229. He who knows nothing doubts nothing. *Italian*
9230. He who knows only his side of the case knows little of that. *American*
9231. How can he discern good and bad manners who doesn't know right from wrong? *Chinese*
9232. I am not ashamed to confess that I am ignorant of what I do not know. *Latin (Cicero)*
9233. If a camel comes to the village of ignorant people, they all declare that their ancestor has risen from the dead. *Behar*
9234. Ignorance and conceit go hand in hand. *Hebrew*
9235. Ignorance and incuriosity are two very soft pillows. *French*
9236. Ignorance breeds impudence. *American*
9237. Ignorance is a feeble remedy for our ills. *Latin*
9238. Ignorance is a voluntary misfortune. *American*
9239. Ignorance is always ready to admire itself. *French (Boileau)*
9240. Ignorance is better than error, but the active fool is a holy terror. *American*
9241. Ignorance is Buddha. *Japanese*
9242. Ignorance is Buddha-like lenience. *Japanese*
9243. Ignorance is the womb of monsters. *American (Beecher)*
9244. In knowing nothing is the sweetest life. *Greek (Sophocles)*
9245. It is better to conceal one's knowledge than to reveal one's ignorance. *Spanish*
9246. It is discreditable to a man to be ignorant of that in which he is employed daily. *Latin*
9247. It is well to be ignorant of many things. *Latin*
9248. Like scratching one's head with a firebrand. *Telugu*
9249. Men's ignorance makes the priest's pot boil. *American*
9250. Mustn't tie up the hound with a string of sausages. *Louisiana Creole*
9251. Not to know is bad; not to wish to know is worse. *Nigerian*
9252. O thou monster, Ignorance, how deformed dost thou look! *English (Shakespeare)*
9253. The ignorant arise and seize Heaven itself. *Latin (St. Augustine)*
9254. The man who does not learn is dark, like one walking in the night. *Chinese*
9255. The wise are too smart to deny their ignorance. *American*
9256. There is no darkness but ignorance. *English (Shakespeare)*
9257. To know nothing is the happiest life. *Latin*
9258. What darkness there is in mortal minds! *Latin (Ovid)*
9259. What I [or you] don't know won't hurt me [or you]. *American*
9260. What you know avails nothing; what you do not know hinders much. *Latin (Cicero)*
9261. Whatever is unknown is magnified. *Latin*
9262. Where ignorance is bliss, / 'Tis folly to be wise. *English (Gray)*
9263. Wisdom is prevented by ignorance, and delusion is the result. *Bhagavad-Gita*

Ill-Gotten Gains *see also* Buying and Selling; Money; Profit and Loss

9264. An ill-wan penny will cast down a pound. *Scottish*
9265. Bad gains are true losses. *American (Franklin)*
9266. Better it is to have more profit and less honor. *French*
9267. Evil gain does not bring good luck. *Latin*
9268. Evil gotten, evil spent. *English*
9269. Gain not base gains; base gains are the same as losses. *Greek (Hesiod)*
9270. Get thy brass fair, and then it'll wear. *English*
9271. He that eats the king's goose shall be choked with the feathers. *English*

9272. Ill-got gear [wealth, property] ne'er prospered. *Scottish*

9273. Ill-gotten gain brings loss. *Greek (Euripides)*

9274. Ill-gotten goods do no good. *German*

9275. Ill-won gear is aye ill wared [guided]. *Scottish*

9276. Ill-won gear winna enrich the third heir. *Scottish*

9277. Ill-won, ill-spent. *German*

9278. Ill-gotten gains work evil. *Greek*

9279. Ill-gotten goods seldom [or never] prosper. *German*

9280. Ill-gotten, ill-spent. *French*

9281. Ill-gotten wealth never prospers. *French*

9282. King's venison is sooner eaten than digested. *English*

9283. More men come to doom / through dirty profits than are kept by them. *Greek (Sophocles)*

9284. Naething's a man's truly but what he comes by duly. *Scottish*

9285. No man should make a gain of another's ignorance. *Latin*

9286. They that deal wi' the deil [devil] get a dear pennyworth. *Scottish*

9287. Unjust gains may be sweet in the mouth, but will be bitter in the belly. *English*

9288. Wealth ill-got goes to naught. *French*

9289. Well-gotten wealth may lose itself, but ill-gotten loses its master, too. *Spanish (Cervantes)*

9290. What is got badly, goes badly. *Irish*

9291. What is got over the devil's back is spent under his belly. *English*

Ill Words

9292. Hard words break no bones. *English*

9293. Heat breaks no bones. *Russian*

9294. Ill-will never said well. *English*

9295. One ill word asketh another. *English*

9296. One ill word meets another, an it were at the bridge of London. *English*

Illness *see also* Disease; Hypochondria; Physicians; Remedies

9297. Cold and poverty cause every illness. *Arabic*

9298. The chamber of sickness is the temple of devotion. *English*

9299. To tell what wood the ship was made of. [To be seasick.] *English*

Imagination *see also* Fancy; Fantasy

9300. Imagination is the eye of the soul. *French (Joubert)*

9301. The locust flies with the wings of a falcon. *Saudi Arabian*

9302. We suffer more in imagination than in reality. *Latin (Seneca)*

Imitation *see also* Example

9303. A needy man is lost when he wishes to imitate a powerful man. *Latin*

9304. Blind copying killed the hare. *Acholi*

9305. Easy to look at, difficult to imitate. *Chinese*

9306. Everything in art is but a copy of nature. *Latin (Seneca)*

9307. If you pull one pig by the tail, all the rest squeak. *Dutch*

9308. Imitation is suicide. *American (Emerson)*

9309. Imitate the best, not the worst. *American*

9310. Imitation is the sincerest form of flattery. *American*

9311. Man is an imitative creature. *German*

9312. No man was ever great by imitation. *English (Johnson)*

9313. One dog barks because it sees something; a hundred dogs bark because they heard the first dog bark. *Chinese*

9314. One dog looks at a pump [or something] and a hundred dogs at him. *Chinese*

9315. One sheep follows another. *Hebrew*

9316. Small men imitate; great men originate. *American*

9317. The grape gains its purple tinge by looking at another grape. *Latin*

9318. The man who follows the crowd often follows his doom. *American*

9319. The poor man is ruined as soon as he begins to ape the rich. *Latin (Publilius Syrus)*

9320. There is much difference between imitating a good man, and counterfeiting him. *American (Franklin)*

9321. When one dog barks another dog barks forthwith. *Latin*

Immobility *see* Idleness; Inactivity; Motionlessness

Immortality *see also* Death; Life; Mortality; Transience

9322. God created man to be immortal. *Bible*

9323. If a man die, shall he live again. *Bible*

9324. My flesh shall rest in hope. *Bible*

Impartiality

9325. He is not good himself who speaks well of everybody alike. *English*

9326. Hear the other side. *Latin*

9327. In doing its office, the balance does not distinguish between gold and lead. *French*

9328. The tree casts its shade upon all, even upon the woodcutter. *Hindi*

Impatience *see also* Patience

9329. An egg today, no chicken tomorrow. *Arabic*

9330. He that would have a cake out of the wheat must tarry the grinding. *English (Shakespeare)*

9331. Hungry men think the cook lazy. *English*

9332. Patience does not always help; impatience never helps. *Russian*

Imperfection *see* Error(s); Faults

Impermanence *see* Change; Permanence; Transience

Impetuosity *see also* Deliberation; Forethought

9333. Give time and permit a short delay; impetuosity ruins everything. *Latin (Statius)*

Imposition

9334. Good men get imposed upon, as good horses get ridden. *Chinese*

Impossibility

9335. A deed that is done cannot be altered. *Danish*
9336. A toad propping a bedpost. *Chinese*
9337. I keep filling, but the basin has a hole in it. *Tunisian*
9338. It is a disease of the soul to be enamored of the impossible. *Greek*
9339. It is always the impossible that happens. *French*
9340. It is certain, because it is impossible. *Latin (Tertullian)*
9341. It's hard sailing where there's no wind. *English*
9342. It's hard to sail over the sea in an egg shell. *English*
9343. It's ill killing a crow with an empty sling. *English*
9344. No man can skin a stone. *American*
9345. No one is bound to do the impossible. *American*
9346. Not even a thousand men in armor can strip a naked man. *Turkish*
9347. Nothing is impossible to a willing heart [or mind]. *English*
9348. Nothing is so difficult but that man will accomplish it. *Latin (Horace)*
9349. One foot cannot stand on two boats. *Chinese*
9350. One leg cannot dance alone. *African*
9351. Only he who attempts the absurd is capable of achieving the impossible. *Spanish (Unamuno)*
9352. Put the impossible out of your mind. *American*
9353. Sooner could you hide an elephant under your armpit. *Latin*
9354. Sooner shall earth mount to heaven. *Latin*
9355. Sooner will a beetle make honey. *Latin*
9356. Sooner will the tamarisk bear apples. *Latin*
9357. Sooner will the wolf take the sheep for a wife. *Latin*
9358. Soreness of the eye is cured with the elbow. *Portuguese*
9359. That which never has been, never is, and never will be. *Latin (Ovid)*
9360. The impossible always happens. *American*
9361. The word "impossible" is not in my dictionary. *French (Napoleon I)*
9362. There is no obligation to attempt the impossible. *Latin*
9363. To a brave heart nothing is impossible. *French*
9364. To believe a thing impossible is to make it so. *French*
9365. To carry your water in a basket. *Belizean Creole*
9366. To catch the shower in a sieve. *Latin*
9367. To correct the Magnificat. [To alter what is already perfect.] *English*
9368. To fence in the cuckoo. [An allusion to efforts by the wise men of Gothan to prolong summer.] *English*
9369. To keep the moon safe from the wolves. *French (Rabelais)*
9370. To make two extremes meet. *English*
9371. To pound water in a mortar. *Latin*
9372. Two watermelons cannot be held under one arm. *Turkish*
9373. Water does not remain in a sieve. *Cheremis*
9374. When mules breed. *Latin*
9375. When the frog has hair. *English*
9376. When the Greek Calends come round. *Latin*
9377. When two Sundays meet. *English*
9378. With one arrow two birds are not struck. *Osmanli*
9379. You are looking for wings in a wolf. *Latin*
9380. You can't draw blood out of a stone. *American*
9381. You can't get blood out of a turnip. *American*
9382. You can't have it both ways. *American*
9383. You can't have your cake and eat it, too. *American*
9384. You can't make a silk purse out of a sow's ear. *American*
9385. You can't sell the cow and have the milk, too. *American*
9386. You cannot clap with one hand. *Chinese*
9387. You cannot drink and whistle at the same time. *Italian*
9388. You cannot make a crab walk straight. *Greek*
9389. You seek water from a stone. *Latin*
9390. You should never touch your eye but with your elbow. *English*

Impotence

9391. A bee without a sting makes no honey. *Dutch*
9392. Dogs' cries do not reach the skies. *Polish*
9393. Don't show your teeth if you can't bite. *English*
9394. Harmless lightning. *Latin*
9395. He that has nought can do nought. *French*
9396. Less malevolence, or more power to exercise it. *Latin*
9397. Who lacks armament should avoid argument. *Polish*

Improbability

9398. Mice care not to play with kittens. *English*
9399. Where we least think, there goeth the hare away. *English*

Improvement

9400. Better is better. *German*

Imprudence *see also* Common Sense; Folly; Fools; Prudence

9401. Aye taking out o' the meal-pock [sack], and never putting in't, soon comes to the bottom. *Scottish*
9402. Back to the draught is face to the grave. *Chinese*
9403. Burning a halfpenny candle seeking for a farthing. *Scottish*
9404. Great tochers [dowries, fortunes] makna aye [make not always] the greatest testaments. *Scottish*
9405. He that spends his gear [money] before he thrives will beg before he thinks. *Scottish*
9406. He who rouses a sleeping tiger runs the risk of harm. *Chinese*
9407. He who sits chatting about nothing loses his candle. *Chinese*

9408. If you plant a grove to rear tigers in, when grown, the tigers will injure you. *Chinese*

9409. To be careless in great matters and careful in small ones. *Chinese*

9410. To break the constable's head and take refuge with the sheriff. *Spanish*

9411. To lose the great for the small. *Chinese*

9412. To neglect the present and plan for the future. *Chinese*

9413. To overload a leaking ship. *Chinese*

9414. To pour oil on the flames. *Chinese*

9415. To present one's head to a shower of stones. *Chinese*

9416. What! give the lettuce in charge to the geese! *English*

9417. Ye hae brought the pack to the pins. *Scottish*

9418. Ye hae ower muckle [have too much] loose leather about your chafts [chops]. *Scottish*

9419. You give the wolf the wether to keep. *English*

Impudence

9420. Impudence is a goddess. *Greek*

Impulsiveness

9421. Impulse manages all things badly. *Latin*

9422. Reason is absent, when impulse rules. *Latin*

Impunity

9423. A wealthy man can err with impunity. *Latin*

9424. Great men's vices are accounted sacred. *English*

Inactivity *see also* Activity; Idleness; Laziness

9425. By doing nothing we learn to do ill. *English*

9426. Dun is in the mire. (Things are at a standstill.) *English (Chaucer)*

9427. Rust wastes more than use. *French*

9428. Stagnant water is worth less than running water. *French*

9429. Stagnant waters putrefy. *Latin*

9430. Standing pools gather filth. *English*

9431. Staunin dubs [standing puddles] gather dirt. *Scottish*

9432. Still water breeds vermin. *English*

Inadequacy *see* Insufficiency

Inappropriateness *see also* Appropriateness; Timeliness

9433. A brazier in summer, a fan in winter. *Chinese*

9434. A hen which crows and a girl who whistles bring the house bad luck. *French*

9435. A sword of lead in a scabbard of ivory. *Latin*

9436. A woman who talks like a man, and a hen which crows like a cock, are no good to anyone. *French*

9437. A Yule feast may be quat [done without] at Pasche [Easter]. *Scottish*

9438. An old woman dancing makes a great dust. *Latin*

9439. Bring not a bagpipe to a man in trouble. *English*

9440. They attend a funeral robed in white, and a wedding in mourning. *Latin*

9441. To dance out of time. *Latin*

9442. To put on the mask of a dancer when wearing the toga. *Latin*

Incentive *see* Motivation

Incompatibility

9443. Oil and water don't mix. *American*

Inconsistency *see also* Consistency

9444. Blind guides which strain at a gnat and swallow a camel. *Bible*

9445. The chameleon changes its color depending on the place. [Usually used in reference to one's principles.] *Lugbara*

Inconvenience

9446. A light inconvenience is to be borne. *Latin*

Indecision *see also* Future; Hesitation; Lateness; Procrastination; Timeliness; Today and Tomorrow; Vacillation

9447. A double-minded man is a post in the mud, swinging to and fro. *American*

9448. A man's mind is as changeable as the autumn sky. *Japanese*

9449. A person who sits between two chairs may easily fall down. *Russian*

9450. Between two stools one goes to the ground. *Latin*

9451. He acts like a donkey standing between two bales of hay. *American*

9452. He became an infidel hesitating between two mosques. *Turkish*

9453. He who considers too much will perform little. *German*

9454. He who stands hesitating between two churches returns without prayer. *American*

9455. How long halt ye between two opinions? *Bible*

9456. I am at war 'twixt will and will not. *English (Shakespeare)*

9457. In indecision itself grief is present. *Latin*

9458. Indecision is like the stepchild: if he doesn't wash his hands, he is called dirty; if he does, he is wasting the water. *Madagascan*

9459. My inclination first leads me in one direction, then in the opposite. *Latin*

9460. No man, having put his hand to the plow, and looking back, is fit for the kingdom of God. *Bible*

9461. No wind serves him who addresses his voyage to no certain port. *French (Montaigne)*

9462. The flood takes me in, and the ebb takes me out. *Efik*

9463. The question is yet before the court. *Latin*

9464. Through indecision opportunity is often lost. *Latin*

9465. To swim between two streams; to waver between two parties. *French*

9466. While standing he holds one opinion, while sitting another. *Latin*

Independence

9467. A little in your own pocket is better than much in another's purse. *Spanish*

9468. Follow your own bent, no matter what people say. *German*
9469. He travels fastest who travels alone. *English (Kipling)*
9470. I ne'er sat on your coat tail. *Scottish*
9471. I'm no every man's dog that whistles on me. *Scottish*
9472. I'm no obliged to simmer and winter it to you. *Scottish*
9473. Let each man have the wit to go his own way. *Latin*

Indifference

9474. A man can sleep on every hurt but his own. *Gaelic*
9475. A tooth inside another man's mouth does not hurt. *Russian*
9476. Any water in the desert. *Arabic*
9477. Apples, eggs and nuts, you may eat if a slut gives them to you. *Latin*
9478. As good be hanged for an old sheep as a young lamb. *English*
9479. As muckle [much] upwith, as muckle downwith. *Scottish*
9480. As soon dies the calf as the cow. *French*
9481. As soon goes the lamb [to the butcher] as the sheep. *Spanish*
9482. As soon goeth the young lamb's skin to the market as the old ewe's. *English*
9483. Come and welcome; go by, and no quarrel. *English*
9484. Come fish, come frog, all to the basket. *Spanish*
9485. Fight dog, fight bear, wha wins deil [devil] care. *Scottish*
9486. He is master of another man's life who is indifferent to his own. *American*
9487. I carena [care not] whether the tod [fox] worry the goose, or the goose worry the tod. *Scottish*
9488. I'm neither sma' drink thirsty nor greybread hungry. *Scottish*
9489. If ane winna [one will not] anither will — the morn's the market day. *Scottish*
9490. If ane winna [one will not] anither will — sae [so] are maidens married. *Scottish*
9491. If it happens, it happens; if it does not happen, what will happen? *Persian*
9492. If they come, they come not; and if they come not, they come. *English*
9493. Let ae deil [devil] ding anither. *Scottish*
9494. Little kent [known] the less cared for. *Scottish*
9495. No one limps because another is hurt. *Danish*
9496. One man's beard is burning; another goes to light a cigarette by it. *Marathi*
9497. The camel is drowning and the goat asks him the depth of the water. *Marathi*
9498. The dogs bark, but the caravan moves on. *Arabic*
9499. The moon does not heed the barking of dogs. *Latin*
9500. Thou art neither hot nor cold. *Bible*
9501. When another man suffers, a piece of wood suffers. *Arabic*
9502. When you live next to the cemetery, you cannot weep for everyone. *Russian*

Indignation

9503. To bite the lip. *Latin*

Indispensability *see also* Necessity; Value; Worth

9504. An indispensable thing never has much value. *Russian*
9505. There is no man necessary. *French*

Individuality

9506. Eagles flee [fly] alane, but sheep herd thegither. *Scottish*
9507. Every man can tout best on his ain horn. *Scottish*
9508. When two do the same thing, it is not the same thing after all. *Latin (Publilius Syrus)*
9509. You cannot put the same shoe on every foot. *Latin (Publilius Syrus)*

Indolence

9510. An indolent man draws his breath but does not eat. *American*
9511. Indolence breeds misery. *American*
9512. Indolence is the sleep of the mind. *French*
9513. Nothing is difficult; it is only we who are indolent. *American*

Indulgence

9514. An indulgent man is not a fool; a fool can't make allowances for others. *Chinese*

Industry *see also* Work and Workers

9515. A foul hand makes a clean hearthstane. *Scottish*
9516. All things are easy to industry, all things difficult to sloth. *English*
9517. All things are won by industry. *Greek*
9518. An industrious life is the best security for food in old age. *Latin*
9519. An industrious man is tempted by one devil, an idle one by seven. *American*
9520. God gives all things to industry. *American (Franklin)*
9521. Industry is the mother of good fortune. *Spanish (Cervantes)*
9522. Industry need not wish. *American*
9523. Industry pays debts, despair encreases them. *American (Franklin)*
9524. Nothing is impossible to industry. *Latin*
9525. The foot at the cradle and the hand at the reel is a sign that a woman means to do weel. *Scottish*
9526. The gods assist the industrious. *Latin*
9527. To be busy at something is a modest maid's holiday. *Spanish*
9528. When industry goes out at the door, poverty comes in at the window. *American*

Ineffectiveness *see also* Futility; Waste of Time

9529. An iron clamp to bean-curd. *Japanese*
9530. Driving a nail into bran. *Japanese*

9531. Like scratching your feet through your shoes. *Chinese*

9532. Water on a frog's face. *Japanese*

9533. You pour flames upon flames, water into the sea. *Latin (Ovid)*

9534. Your windmill dwindles into a nutcrack. *English*

Inefficiency *see also* Quality

9535. He that doth most at once doth least. *English*

Inequality *see also* Equality

9536. Men are by nature unequal. *American*

9537. The wise man marries his equal; the fool marries above or beneath him. *American*

9538. There are no unequals before natural law. *American*

Inevitability *see also* Gullibility; Naivete

9539. A bad penny always returns. *American*

9540. A bad thing never dies. *English*

9541. A creaking door hangs long on its hinges. *English*

9542. A jug that has been mended lasts 200 years. *Russian*

9543. A tree falls the way it leans. *Bulgarian*

9544. A useless pitcher does not get broken. *Latin*

9545. A weel-bred dog gaes oot [out] when he sees them preparing to kick him oot. *Scottish*

9546. A worthless vessel does not fall from the hand. *Latin*

9547. Blessings do not come in pairs; misfortunes never come singly. *Chinese*

9548. Creaking wagons are long in passing. *Dutch*

9549. Every day hath its night, every weal its woe. *American*

9550. He that bourds [plays] with cats maun count on scarts [scratches]. (Scottish)

9551. Ill vessels seldom miscarry. *English*

9552. Nettles are never frostbitten. *Slovenian*

9553. No matter how often a pitcher goes to the water, it is broken in the end. *Irish*

9554. No one can flee what must be. *Egyptian*

9555. No summer but has a winter. *American*

9556. Nought is never in danger. *English*

9557. One always knocks oneself on the sore place. *French*

9558. Some cow will bear some calf sometime. *Irish*

9559. The best-fitting clothes wear out fastest. *Slovakian*

9560. The bird flies, but always returns to earth. *Wolof*

9561. The bread never falls but on its buttered side. *English*

9562. The damaged cask is not easily broken. *Hungarian*

9563. The herb that can't be got is the one that brings relief. *Irish*

9564. The hidden stone finds the plough. *Estonian*

9565. The pitcher doth not go so often to the well, but it comes home broken at last. *English*

9566. The spot always falls on the best cloth. *Spanish*

9567. There is no good in arguing with the inevitable. *American (Lowell)*

9568. We may escape misfortune for a while, but the evil day will come. *Latin (Publilius Syrus)*

9569. What goes up must come down. *English*

9570. When rubles fall from Heaven, there is no sack; when there is a sack, rubles don't fall. *Russian*

9571. Where the iron goes, there goes also rust. *Portuguese*

9572. Wherever a man dwells, there will be a thornbush near his door. *English*

Inexperience *see also* Gullibility

9573. Many go out for wool and come home shorn. *American*

9574. No man is his craft's master the first day. *English*

9575. Seldom rides tynes [loses] the spurs. *Scottish*

9576. The Portuguese apprentice, who does not know how to sew, and wants to cut out. *Spanish*

Infatuation

9577. Infatuation precedes destruction. *Hindi*

Inference *see also* Appearance; Beauty; Deception; Identity; Judging; Probability; Seeming

9578. All are not cooks who carry long knives. *Dutch*

9579. All are not cooks who sport white caps and carry long knives. *American*

9580. All are not harpers, who hold the harp. *Latin*

9581. All are not hunters that blow the horn. *French*

9582. All are not maidens that wear fair hair. *Scottish*

9583. All are not princes who ride with the emperor. *Dutch*

9584. All are not saints that go to church. *Italian*

9585. All are not soldiers who go to the wars. *Portuguese*

9586. All are not thieves that dogs bark at. *English*

9587. All is not gold that glitters. *Latin*

9588. From one you can tell ten. *Korean*

9589. He doesna aye [doesn't always] ride when he saddles his horse. *Scottish*

9590. Look for the honey where you see the bee. *American*

9591. One crow does not make a winter. *German*

9592. One swallow alone does not make the summer. *Spanish (Cervantes)*

9593. One swallow does not make a spring. *Greek (Aristotle)*

9594. One swallow does not make a summer. *American*

9595. One swallow does not make a summer; neither does one fine day. *Greek (Aristotle)*

9596. One swallow makes not a spring nor one woodcock a winter. *English*

9597. Where there's smoke, there's fire. *American*

9598. You shall not hold as gold everything which glitters as gold, nor every beautiful apple to be good. *Latin*

Inferiority *see* Superiority and Inferiority

Infidelity (Marital) *see* Marriage and Infidelity; Women and Trustworthiness

Influence

9599. A cock has great influence on his own dunghill. *Latin (Publilius Syrus)*

9600. Branches may be trained, but not the trunk. *Latin*

9601. Each man, in corrupting others, corrupts himself. *Latin*

9602. Every hair makes its shadow on the ground. *Spanish*

9603. It is easy to set a cask a rolling [i.e., to influence a fool]. *Latin*

9604. Like master, like man. *English*

9605. Like mistress, like maid. *Latin*

9606. Like priest, like people. *English*

9607. Like prince, like people. *Latin*

9608. One man yawning makes another yawn, too. *Latin*

9609. Swine, women, and bees cannot be turned. *English*

9610. The madness of one makes many mad. *Latin*

Ingratiation

9611. He is looking out for a fig. [Alluding to Athenian nobles who sought to win the favor of peasants on the approach of the fig season.] *Latin*

9612. He that is kinder than he was wont hath a design upon thee. *English*

9613. Please all, and you will please none. *Greek (Aesop)*

9614. When the fox wants to catch geese, he wags his tail. *English*

Ingratitude *see also* Gratitude; Thanks

9615. A thankless man never does a thankful deed. *Danish*

9616. After crossing the river the boatman gets a cuff. *Tamil*

9617. All things are ungrateful; it is nothing to have conferred a favor. *Latin*

9618. An ungrateful man is a tub full of holes. *Latin*

9619. As soon as you have drunk you turn your back upon the spring. *English*

9620. Be not ungrateful to your old friend. *Hebrew*

9621. Bring up a raven and it will pick out your eyes. *German*

9622. Buy a thief frae the widdie [from the gallows] and he'll help to hang ye. *Scottish*

9623. Do good to a knave, and pray God he requite thee not. *Danish*

9624. Do not cut down the tree that gives you shade. *Arabic*

9625. Don't bite the hand that feeds you. *American*

9626. Don't pick a wasp out of a cream-jug. *English*

9627. Earth produces nothing worse than an ungrateful man. *Latin*

9628. Eaten bread is soon forgotten. *Spanish*

9629. Gie a beggar a bed and he'll pay you wi' a louse. *Scottish*

9630. Give assistance, and receive thanks lighter than a feather: injure a man, and his wrath will be like lead. *Latin (Plautus)*

9631. God deprives him of bread who likes not his drink. *English*

9632. Good fortune forgets father and mother. *Spanish*

9633. Gratitude is the least of virtues, ingratitude the worst of vices. *English*

9634. He has brought up a bird to pick out his own eyes. *English*

9635. He that keeps another man's dog shall have nothing left him but the line. *English*

9636. He that you seat upon your shoulder will often try to get upon your head. *Danish*

9637. Hell is crowded with ungrateful wretches. *English*

9638. How quickly is a kindness forgotten! *Latin*

9639. How sharper than a serpent's tooth it is / To have a thankless child! *English (Shakespeare)*

9640. I put a date in his mouth, and he puts a stick in my eye. *Tunisian*

9641. I taught you to swim, and now you'd drown me. *English*

9642. Ingratitude is the child [or daughter] of pride. *Spanish*

9643. Ingratitude is the mother of every vice. *French*

9644. Ingratitude is the world's reward. *German*

9645. It is an evil thing to serve the ungrateful. *Latin*

9646. It is an ill guest that never drinks to his host. *English*

9647. It's a' tint [lost] that's dune to [i.e., for] auld folk and bairns [children]. *Scottish*

9648. Most people return small favors, acknowledge middling ones, and repay great ones with ingratitude. *American (Franklin)*

9649. Nothing is more easily blotted out than a good turn. *English*

9650. One finds few ingrates as long as he is capable of bestowing favors. *French (La Rochefoucauld)*

9651. One ungrateful man injures all who need assistance. *Latin (Publilius Syrus)*

9652. Put a snake in your bosom, and when it is warm it will sting you. *English*

9653. Put anither man's bairn [child] in your bosom and he'll creep oot at your sleeve. *Scottish*

9654. Save a thief from the gallows and he will hang you for it. *French*

9655. Save a thief from the gallows and he'll be the first to cut your throat. *English*

9656. Sore cravers are aye ill payers. *Scottish*

9657. Take an evil-doer from the gallows and he will put you there. *French*

9658. Take down a horse-thief from the gallows and he'll hang you with his own rope. *American*

9659. Thank 'ee for nothing. *English*

9660. The axe goes to the wood from which it borrowed its helve. *English*

9661. The sword has forgotten the smith that forged it. *English*

9662. The wicked are always ungrateful. *Spanish*

9663. They whom I benefit injure me most. *Latin (Sappho)*

9664. To do good to the ungrateful is to throw rose-water into the sea. *English*

9665. To look a gift horse in the mouth. *Latin*

9666. We find many ungrateful men; and we create more. *Latin*

9667. What you do for an ungrateful man is thrown away. *Latin (Seneca)*

9668. When gude cheer is lacking, friends go a-packing. *Scottish*

9669. When I had thatched his house, he would have hurled me from the roof. *English*

9670. You love a nothing when you love an ingrate. *Latin*

Inheritance

9671. Happy are the children whose fathers are damned [i.e., whose fathers were wealthy]. *French*

9672. Happy for the son when the dad gaes to the deil [i.e., whose father was wealthy]. *Scottish*

9673. He comes for the inheritance, and has to pay the funeral expenses. *Yiddish*

9674. He pulls with a long rope that waits for another's death. *French*

9675. He should wear iron shoon that bides his neighbour's death. *Scottish*

9676. He who inherits a penny is expected to spend a dollar. *German*

9677. It is ill waiting for dead men's shoes. *English*

9678. Land was never lost for want of an heir. *English*

9679. Look not out for dead men's shoes. *English*

9680. Many heirs make small portions. *German*

9681. The grief of an heir is only masked laughter. *Latin (Publilius Syrus)*

9682. The next heir is always suspected and hated. *Latin*

9683. Trust not to an inheritance; the produce of one's hands is sufficient. *Yoruba*

Initiative

9684. He is like the devil's valet; he does more than he is told. *French*

Injury *see also* Affront; Insult; Offense

9685. A green wound is soon healed. *English*

9686. A worthy man forgets past injuries. *Greek*

9687. A wound never heals so well but that the scar can be seen. *Danish*

9688. Ane [one] is no sae [not so] soon heal'd as hurt. *Scottish*

9689. Even when the wound is healed the scar remains. *Latin*

9690. Everyone suffers wrongs for which there is no remedy. *American (Howe)*

9691. Folks often injure all they fear and hate all they injure. *American*

9692. For ill do well, / Then fear not hell. *English*

9693. He who is pleased, forgets his cause of pleasure; he who is grieved remembers his cause of grief. *Latin*

9694. How bitter it is when you have sown benefits to reap injuries! *Latin*

9695. Injuries destroy affection. *Latin*

9696. Injuries may be forgiven, but not forgotten. *Greek (Aesop)*

9697. Injury is to be measured by malice. *English*

9698. Injury serves as a lesson. *Latin*

9699. It is a proof of nobility of mind to despise injuries. *Latin (Seneca)*

9700. It is better to receive than to do an injury. *Latin*

9701. It is easy to hurt; it is hard to cure. *German*

9702. It's better to suffer an injury than to commit one. *American*

9703. No one is injured except by himself. *Latin*

9704. Since I wronged you, I have never liked you. *Spanish*

9705. The best remedy for an injury is to forget it. *American*

9706. The injured never forgets. It is the offender who forgets. *Zulu*

9707. The injuries we do and those we suffer are seldom weighed in the same scale. *Greek*

9708. The remedy for injuries is to forget them. *Latin*

9709. Those whom men have injured they despise. *Latin (Seneca)*

9710. 'Tis better to suffer wrong than do it. *English*

9711. To meditate an injury is to commit one. *Latin (Seneca)*

9712. We are more mindful of injuries than benefits. *American*

9713. You invite future injuries if you revive past ones. *American*

Injustice *see also* Justice; Law; Might and Right

9714. Censure pardons the ravens but rebukes the doves. *Latin (Juvenal)*

9715. Injustice all around is justice. *Persian*

9716. Injustice in the end produces independence. *French (Voltaire)*

9717. No one is hanged who has money in his pocket. *Russian*

9718. One man may steal a horse while another may not look over the hedge. *English*

9719. Pigeons are taken when crows fly at pleasure. *English*

9720. Rigid justice is the greatest injustice. *English*

9721. That trial is not fair where affection is judge. *English*

9722. The frost hurts not weeds. *English*

9723. The worst pig often gets the best pear. *English*

9724. To do injustice is more disgraceful than to suffer it. *Greek (Plato)*

9725. When innocence trembles, it condemns the judge. *Latin (Publilius Syrus)*

Innocence *see also* Chastity; Purity

9726. A heart unspotted is not easily daunted. *English (Shakespeare)*

9727. A mind conscious of innocence laughs at rumor. *Latin*

9728. An innocent man needs no loud-speaker: his life speaks for itself. *American*

9729. He who is free from fever fears not to eat watermelons. [An innocent man fears nothing.] *Chinese*

9730. Innocence breeds confidence. *American*

9731. No protection is so sure as that of innocence. *Latin*
9732. True innocence is ashamed of nothing. *Russian*
9733. We become innocent when we are unfortunate. *French*
9734. When the hand is clean, / It needs no screen. *English*
9735. When the wolf is king innocence is no protection for the lambs. *American*

Innovation *see also* **Change; Invention; Newness; Novelty**
9736. Every innovation startles us more by its novelty than it benefits us by its utility. *Latin*
9737. It is easy to add to inventions. *Latin*

Inquiry *see* **Asking**

Inquisitiveness *see also* **Asking; Curiosity; Questions; Questions and Answers**
9738. An inquisitive man is always ill-natured. *Latin*
9739. Shun an inquisitive man; he is invariably a telltale. *Latin (Horace)*

Insanity *see* **Madness**

Insatiability *see also* **Appetite; Excess; Sufficiency**
9740. Women, priests and poultry are never satisfied. *Italian*

Insecurity
9741. He lives in a fool's paradise. *American*

Insight *see* **Understanding**

Insignificance
9742. Not worth the snap of a finger. *Latin*
9743. Our insignificance is often the cause of our safety. *Greek (Aesop)*

Insincerity *see also* **Sincerity**
9744. When the cat mourns for the mouse, you need not take her too seriously. *Japanese*
9745. When the fox preaches, look out, poultry. *Italian*
9746. When the tod [fox] preaches, take tent o' the lambs. *Scottish*

Insolence *see also* **Arrogance**
9747. Insolence is pride with her mask pulled off. *English*
9748. The greater the fool, the greater his insolence. *Latin*
9749. The insolent are never without wounds. *Turkish*

Inspiration
9750. Inspiration cannot be commanded. *French*

Instability
9751. Men with soft heads and hard hearts love change the most. *American*
9752. Unstable as water, you shall not excel. *American*

Instinct *see also* **Reason; Reason and Understanding**
9753. By a divine instinct men's minds mistrust ensuing dangers. *English (Shakespeare)*
9754. Drive a cow to the ha' and she'll run to the byre. *Scottish*
9755. Instinct is untaught ability. *English*
9756. Let him make use of instinct who cannot make use of reason. *Latin*
9757. We heed no instincts but our own. *French*

Insufficiency *see also* **Sufficiency**
9758. A broken sack will hold no corn. *English*
9759. A feeble dart short of its mark. *Latin (Juvenal)*
9760. A mad bull is not to be tied up with a packthread. *English*
9761. A rope of sand. *English*
9762. He has nothing who has not enough. *French*
9763. It is folly to bolt a door with a boiled carrot. *English*
9764. That is a bad bridge which is shorter than the stream. *German*
9765. The poor have little,— beggars none; / The rich too much — enough not one. *American (Franklin)*
9766. There is never enough where nothing is left. *Italian*
9767. There is not enough if there is nothing over. *Italian*
9768. To be good enough you must be too good. *French*
9769. To bind a dog with the gut of a lamb. *Latin*
9770. Too much is not enough. *French*
9771. You cannot drive a windmill with a pair of bellows. *American*

Insult *see also* **Affront; Injury; Offense**
9772. A decent man won't insult me, a heel can't. *American*
9773. An injury is much sooner forgiven than an insult. *English*
9774. He who allows himself to be insulted deserves to be. *French*
9775. If you speak insults, you shall also hear them. *Latin*
9776. Insult begets insult as bugs beget bugs. *American*
9777. Insults should be well avenged or well endured. *Spanish*
9778. It is often better to see an insult than to avenge it. *Latin*
9779. To add insult to injury. *Latin*

Integrity *see also* **Honor**
9780. He won't buy soy with money intended for vinegar. *Chinese*
9781. Integrity is praised and starves. *Latin (Juvenal)*

Intelligence
9782. A nod of the head is enough for an intelligent man. *Chinese*
9783. All things are slaves to intelligence. *Greek*
9784. An intelligent man needs but few words; a good drum doesn't require hard beating. *Chinese*
9785. Crows are smart enough not to peck out each other's eyes. *American*
9786. He's mair buirdly [strongly made] i' the back than i' the brain. *Scottish*

9787. Many complain of their looks, but none of their brains. *Yiddish*

9788. The less wit a man has, the less he kens [understands] the want o't. *Scottish*

9789. To know how many five are. *Spanish*

Intemperance

9790. Intemperance is the doctor's wet nurse. *English*

9791. Intemperance is the physician's provider. *Latin (Publilius Syrus)*

Intensity

9792. A heavy shower is soon over. *American*

9793. For violent fires soon burn out themselves. *English (Shakespeare)*

9794. Small showers last long, but sudden storms are short. *English (Shakespeare)*

9795. That which is violent never lasts long. *Latin*

9796. The more light a torch gives, the shorter it lasts. *English*

9797. The more violent the storm the sooner it is over. *Latin*

Intention *see also* Motivation; Will

9798. A joyous heart spins the hemp. *Serbian*

9799. A thing done perforce is not worth a rush. *Italian*

9800. As he thinketh in his heart, so is he. *Bible*

9801. Chalk is no shears. [Marking the cloth is one thing, cutting it is another.] *Scottish*

9802. Good intentions are solaces in misfortune. *Latin*

9803. Good intentions may result in great evil. *Egyptian*

9804. He sins not, who is not wilfully a sinner. *Latin (Seneca)*

9805. Heaven always favors good desires. *Spanish*

9806. Heaven favors good intentions. *Spanish (Cervantes)*

9807. Hell is full of good intentions. *Spanish*

9808. Hell is paved with good intentions. *French*

9809. High heaven will not forget the man with good intent. *Chinese*

9810. It was intended to be a vase, it has turned out a pot. *Latin (Horace)*

9811. It's the intention that makes an action good or bad. *American*

9812. Lang mint [intended], little dint [done]. *Scottish*

9813. Man punishes the action, but God the intention. *English*

9814. Mere intentions are not to be esteemed as actions. *Latin*

9815. Minting [intending, proposing] gets no bairns [children]. *Scottish*

9816. No man does as much work today as he is going to do tomorrow. *American*

9817. One man may lead the horse to the water, but fifty can't make him drink. *English*

9818. Ossing [intending] comes to bossing [botching]. *English*

9819. Our outward actions reveal our hidden intentions. *Latin*

9820. Take away the motive and the sin is taken away. *Spanish (Cervantes)*

9821. Take the will for the deed. *English*

9822. The act itself does not constitute a crime, unless the intent be criminal. *Latin*

9823. The way to perdition is paved with good intentions. *German*

9824. To aim is not enough; we must hit. *German*

9825. We are remembered by our good actions, not by our good intentions. *American*

Interference *see also* Meddling

9826. Allow the sick man to furnish his own perspiration. *Chinese*

9827. Don't speak to the man at the helm. *English*

Intimacy

9828. A man knows his companion in a long journey and a little inn. *English*

9829. It is a foolish sheep that makes the wolf his confessor. *Italian*

Intolerance

9830. Intolerance is the child of ignorance. *American*

Invention *see also* Innovation; Newness

9831. God hath made man upright; but they have sought out many inventions. *Bible*

9832. If it is not true, it is very well invented. *Italian*

9833. Invention breeds invention. *American (Emerson)*

Invitation

9834. Don't be afraid of inviting too many guests; one goose will be sufficient for them all. *Chinese*

9835. When you invite guests don't invite ladies. If you do, fifty invited may mean a hundred. [They will probably bring children.] *Chinese*

Irrelevance

9836. A scarecrow in a garden of cucumbers keepeth nothing. *Bible*

9837. He giveth one knock on the hoop, and another on the barrel. *Italian*

9838. I speak of garlic, you reply about onions. *Latin*

9839. I talk of cheese, you of chalk. *Latin*

Irrevocableness

9840. A deed that is done cannot be altered. *Danish*

9841. A statement once let loose cannot be caught by four horses. *Japanese*

9842. A word and a stone once let go cannot be recalled [or called back]. *English*

9843. A word spoken is past recalling. *American*

9844. An army that has crossed the river can't turn back. *African*

9845. Four things are not to be recalled: a word spoken, an arrow discharged, a divine decree, and past time. *Arabic*

9846. Grieve not for that which is irreparably lost. *Latin*

9847. No use crying [or Don't grieve, or Don't cry] over spilt milk. *English*

9848. That should be long considered which can be decided but once. *Latin*

9849. The arrow that has left the bow never returns. *Persian*

9850. Time and words can't be recalled. *English*

9851. Time flies, and what is past is done. *German (Goethe)*

9852. What is done is done for this time. *Spanish*

9853. What is done, is done: / Spend not the time in tears, but seek for justice. *English (Ford)*

9854. What's done can't be mended. *Latin (Terence)*

9855. What's done can't be undone. *English (Shakespeare)*

9856. What's gone and what's past help / Should be past grief. *English (Shakespeare)*

9857. Who draws his sword against the prince must throw away the scabbard. *English*

9858. You cannot unscramble eggs. *American*

Irritability *see also* Sensitivity

9859. A galled horse will not endure the comb. *English*

9860. As cross as nine highways. *English*

Isolation

9861. The lone sheep's in danger of the wolf. *English*

Jealousy *see also* Envy; Women and Jealousy

9862. Beggar is jealous of beggar, and poet of poet. *Greek*

9863. He who is not jealous is an ass. *Lebanese*

9864. It is the green-eyed monster which doth mock the meat it feeds on. *English (Shakespeare)*

9865. Jealousy is a pain which seeks what causes pain. *German*

9866. Jealousy is cruel as the grave. *Bible*

9867. Jealousy is nourished by doubt. *French*

9868. Jealousy is the greatest evil. *American*

9869. Nae faut [no fault], but she sets her bannet ower weel. *Scottish*

9870. There's aye [always] ill-will amang cadgers. *Scottish*

Jests and Jesting *see also* Humor; Laughter; Wit

9871. A jest is half a truth. *Yiddish*

9872. A jest loses its point when the jester laughs himself. *German*

9873. A jest that comes too near the truth leaves a sting behind. *Latin*

9874. A jest [or joke] driven too far brings home hate. *English*

9875. A sooth bourd [true jest] is nae [no] bourd. *Scottish*

9876. A true jest is an evil jest, as the Fleming says. *English (Chaucer)*

9877. All in the way of a joke the wolf goes to the ass. *Spanish*

9878. Better lose a jest than a friend. *English*

9879. Bitter jests poison friendship. *Scottish*

9880. Bourdna [jest not] wi' bawty [a dog], lest he bite ye. *Scottish*

9881. Bourdna [jest not] wi' my ee, nor wi' mine honour. *Scottish*

9882. Don't carry a joke too far. *American*

9883. Drop the jest when it pleases most. *Italian*

9884. Gie o'er when the play is gude. *Scottish*

9885. He makes a foe, who makes a jest. *American (Franklin)*

9886. He that jokes confesses. *Italian*

9887. He that would jest must take a jest, else to let it alone were best. *Dutch*

9888. It is not good jesting with God, death, or the devil. *Arabic*

9889. It's nae play when ane [one] laughs and anither greets [weeps]. *Scottish*

9890. It's past joking when the head's off. *Scottish*

9891. Jest not with the eye, or with religion. *Spanish*

9892. Jest with an ass and he will flap you in the face with his tail. *English*

9893. Jest with your equals. *Welsh*

9894. Jest with your equals: a fool can't take a joke. *American*

9895. Jesting costs money. *Spanish*

9896. Jests spare no one. *French*

9897. Jests that give pain are no jests. *Spanish*

9898. Joke at leisure; ye kenna [know not] wha may jibe yoursel. *Scottish*

9899. Joke went out and brought home his fellow, and they began a quarrel. *American*

9900. Jokes that carry injury with them are never agreeable. *Latin*

9901. Joking must have its proper limits. *Latin (Cicero)*

9902. Lang sporting turns aft to earnest. *Scottish*

9903. Leave a jest when it pleases you best. *Scottish*

9904. Leave jesting whiles it pleaseth, lest it turn to earnest. *English*

9905. Let the jests be without anything vile about them. *Latin*

9906. Long jesting was never good. *English*

9907. Many a friend was lost through a joke, but none was ever gained so. *Czech*

9908. Many a true word has been spoken in jest. *American*

9909. Mony a true tale's tauld in jest. *Scottish*

9910. Mows [jests] may come to earnest. *Scottish*

9911. Rather spill [spoil] your joke than tine [lose] your freend. *Scottish*

9912. Rather spoil your joke than roil your wife. *American*

9913. Said in sport, meant in earnest. *German*

9914. The worst jests are the true ones. *French*

9915. The would-be wits and can't-be gentlemen. *English (Byron)*

9916. True jests breed bad blood. *American*

9917. What seems a joke is very often the truth. *Italian*

9918. When the demand is a jest, the fittest answer is a scoff. *Greek*

9919. When your jest is at its best — let it rest. *American*

9920. Witticisms which hurt are never welcome. *Latin*

Joint Ownership *see also* Shared Authority; Shared Responsibility

9921. A dog out of two yards never gets anything to eat. *Estonian*

9922. A field held in common is always ravaged by the bears. *Russian*
9923. A joint pot does not boil. *Irish*
9924. A pig that has two owners is sure to die of hunger. *English*
9925. A shared pot doesn't boil. *Omani*
9926. Cow of many—well milked and badly fed. *Spanish*
9927. If two men keep a horse, it is thin; if two families keep a boat, it leaks. *Chinese*
9928. That is neglected by all which is possessed by all. *Latin*
9929. The ass that is common property is always the worst saddled. *English*
9930. The donkey that belongs to many is the first to be eaten by wolves. *Silesian*
9931. The man who owns one ear of the camel has a right to make it kneel. *Lebanese*

Jokes *see* Jests and Jesting

Joy *see also* Happiness; Joy and Sorrow; Mirth and Sorrow

9932. A joy that's shared is a joy made double. *English*
9933. Joy is like the ague; one good day between two bad ones. *Danish*
9934. Joys do not abide, but take wing and fly away. *Latin*
9935. Sweets with sweets war not, joy delights in joy. *English (Shakespeare)*
9936. The future joy makes the past and the present bearable. *American*
9937. The souls in hell dream of the joys of heaven. *American*
9938. There's no joy in anything unless we share it. *American*
9939. There's not a joy the world can give like that it takes away. *English (Byron)*

Joy and Sorrow *see also* Happiness; Joy; Mirth and Sorrow; Unhappiness

9940. A joyous evening often leads to a sorrowful morning. *Dutch*
9941. After sorrow, joy. *Latin*
9942. All the joys in the world can't take one gray hair out of our heads. *American*
9943. Brief is sorrow, and endless is joy. *German (Schiller)*
9944. Forever the latter end of joy is woe. *English (Chaucer)*
9945. Great joys weep, great sorrows laugh. *French*
9946. If you laugh today, you will cry tomorrow. *English*
9947. It is heaven's will for sorrow to follow joy. *Latin*
9948. Joy surfeited turns to sorrow. *Latin*
9949. The holy days of joy are the vigils of sorrow. *English*
9950. There's no joy without alloy: grief is mixed with the keenest bliss. *American*
9951. When joy is in the parlor, sorrow is at the kitchen sink. *American*

Judges *see also* Judging; Judgment

9952. A corrupt judge weighs truth badly. *Latin*
9953. Fear not the law, but the judge. *Russian*
9954. God help the sheep when the wolf is judge. *Danish*
9955. He who has his father for the judge, goes into court with an easy mind. *Spanish*
9956. He who is a judge between two friends loses one of them. *French*
9957. If the judge be your accuser, may God be your help. *Turkish*
9958. Judges should have two ears—both alike. *German*
9959. Jurists are bad Christians. *German*
9960. That money is well lost which the guilty man gives to the judge. *Latin*
9961. The best judge knows the least. *American*
9962. The duty of the judge is to administer justice, but his practice is to delay it. *French*
9963. The judge is condemned when the guilty is acquitted. *Latin*
9964. The law is loosened when the judge grows tenderhearted. *Latin*
9965. The magistrate is a speaking law, but the law is a silent magistrate. *Latin*
9966. The upright judge condemns the crime, but does not hate the criminal. *Latin*
9967. Thieves for their robbery have authority / When judges steal themselves. *English (Shakespeare)*
9968. Truth is straight but judges are crooked. *Russian*
9969. When a judge puts on his robe, he puts off his relations to any. *American*

Judging *see also* Appearance; Beauty; Clothes; Criticism; Fault-Finding; Inference; Judgment; Prejudice

9970. At a distance from home a man is judged by what he wears; near home he is judged by what he is. *Chinese*
9971. Bonnie feathers dinna aye [do not always] mak bonnie birds. *Scottish*
9972. Do not measure another's coat on your own body. *Malay*
9973. Don't hear one and judge two. *Greek*
9974. Don't judge a book by its cover. *American*
9975. Don't judge a man's actions at first sight; give them a second look. *American*
9976. Don't judge a tree by its bark. *French*
9977. Don't judge any man until you have walked two moons in his moccasins. *American Indian*
9978. Don't judge by appearances. *American*
9979. Don't judge men or things at first sight. *American*
9980. Don't judge of men's wealth or piety, by their Sunday appearances. *American (Franklin)*
9981. Every man judges of others by himself. *Latin*
9982. From the straws in the air we judge of the wind. *English*
9983. He hath a good judgment that relieth not wholly on his own. *English (Fuller)*
9984. He hears but half who hears one side only. *Greek*
9985. He'll kythe [appear] in his ain [own] colours yet. *Scottish*

9986. Hear all parties. *Scottish*
9987. Hear the other side. *Latin*
9988. If Jack's in love, he's no judge of Jill's beauty. *American (Franklin)*
9989. If you judge between two sweethearts you'll lose both. *American*
9990. Judge men by their deeds, not by their creeds. *American*
9991. Judge not of a ship as she lies on the stocks. *English*
9992. Judge not, that ye be not judged. *Bible*
9993. Judge not the tree by its bark. *French*
9994. Judge of a tree by its fruit, not by its leaves. *Latin (Phaedrus)*
9995. Judge one banana rotten and you judge the whole bunch. *American*
9996. Men judge the affairs of others better than their own. *Latin*
9997. No one should be a judge in his own cause. *Latin*
9998. No one so hard upon the poor as the pauper who has got into power. *American*
9999. None judge so wrong as those who think amiss. *English (Pope)*
10000. Out of thine own mouth will I judge thee. *English*
10001. Well to judge depends on well to hear. *Italian*
10002. When you judge others you condemn yourself. *American*
10003. Who judges others condemns himself. *Italian*
10004. Wise men appreciate all men, for they see the good in each and know how hard it is to make anything good. *Spanish (Gracián)*
10005. You can't judge of the horse by the harness. *American*
10006. You cannot judge men by their looks; you cannot measure the sea with a peck measure. *Chinese*
10007. You cannot judge of the wine by the barrel. *American*
10008. You measure everyone's corn by your own bushel. *English*
10009. You must look at the pig and not at the trough. *American*

Judgment *see also* Judges; Judging; Prejudice

10010. All wholesale judgments are imperfect. *French*
10011. Blind men should judge no colors. *Latin*
10012. Haste in judgment is criminal. *Latin*
10013. He hath a good judgment that relieth not wholly on his own. *English*
10014. Next to excellence is the appreciation of it. *English (Thackeray)*
10015. Of judgment everyone has a stock on hand for sale. *Italian*
10016. Plenty of memory and little judgment. *French*
10017. Rightness of judgment is bitterness to the heart. *Greek (Euripides)*
10018. Strength without judgment falls by its own weight. *Latin*
10019. The judgment of man is fallible. *Latin*
10020. 'Tis with our judgments as our watches, none / Go just alike, yet each believes his own. *English (Pope)*
10021. To him of good judgment, the sound of a gnat suffices. *Turkish*
10022. We believe our own judgments as we believe our own watches, whether they are fast or slow. *American*

Justice *see also* Balance; Fairness; Injustice; Law; Lawsuits; Lawyers; Loopholes

10023. A' law is no justice. *Scottish*
10024. Anytime is the proper time for justice. *Greek*
10025. As soon as Justice returns, the golden age returns. *Latin (Virgil)*
10026. Even, it [justice] is like the sun on a flat plain; uneven, it strikes like the sun on a thicket. *Malay*
10027. Every place is safe for him who lives in justice. *Greek*
10028. Everyone is glad to see a knave caught in his own trap. *English*
10029. Everyone loves justice in the affairs of another. *Italian*
10030. He made a pit and digged it, and has fallen into the ditch which he made. *English*
10031. He who spares the bad seeks to corrupt the good. *Latin*
10032. If all men were just, there would be no need of valor. *Greek*
10033. It is sheer folly to expect justice from the unprincipled. *Latin*
10034. Justice again our guide. *Latin*
10035. Justice, but not for my own house. *Spanish*
10036. Justice, even if slow, is sure. *Greek*
10037. Justice hath a nose of wax. *German*
10038. Justice is half religion. *Turkish*
10039. Justice is the queen of virtues. *Latin*
10040. Justice is the right of the weakest. *French (Joubert)*
10041. Justice is truth in action. *French (Joubert)*
10042. Justice pleaseth few in their own house. *English*
10043. Justice prepared at a price is sold at a price. *Latin*
10044. Justice shines by its own light. *Latin*
10045. Justice will not condemn even the devil himself wrongfully. *English*
10046. Justice wrangs nae man [wrongs no man]. *Scottish*
10047. Let justice be done, though the heavens fall. *Latin*
10048. One hour in doing justice is worth a hundred in prayer. *Arabic*
10049. Rats and conquerors must expect no mercy in misfortune. *English*
10050. Sparing justice feeds iniquity. *English (Shakespeare)*
10051. The bare right is almost injustice. *Irish*
10052. The just hand is a precious ointment. *Latin*
10053. There should be no sword in the hand of justice. *Latin*
10054. To everyone his own is but justice. *French*

Killing *see also* Crime and Criminals; Murder

10055. Dying is more honorable than killing. *Latin (Seneca)*

10056. Human blood is heavy; the man that has shed it cannot run away. *African*

10057. Thou shalt not kill. *Bible*

Kindness

10058. A forced kindness deserves no thanks. *American*

10059. A fu' [full] heart is aye [always] kind. *Scottish*

10060. A kindness bestowed on the good is never thrown away. *Latin*

10061. A man may be kind, yet gie little o' his gear [wealth, property]. *Scottish*

10062. A word of kindness is better than a fat pie. *Russian*

10063. Be kind to animals. *American*

10064. He suffocates me with kindness. *Latin*

10065. Kindness begets kindness. *Latin (Cicero)*

10066. Kindness breaks no bones. *German*

10067. Kindness cannot be bought. *Scottish*

10068. Kindness comes o' will; it canna be cost [bought]. *Scottish*

10069. Kindness consists in loving people more than they deserve. *French (Joubert)*

10070. Kindness is a bed to sleep on. *Hausa*

10071. Kindness is ever the begetter of kindness. *Greek*

10072. Kindness is like cress-feed; it grows fast. *Scottish*

10073. Kindness is more binding than a loan. *Chinese*

10074. Kindness is not to be repented of. *Greek (Theophrastus)*

10075. Kindness is worth more than beauty. *French*

10076. Kindness lies not aye [always] in ane [one] side of the house. *Scottish*

10077. Kindness o'ercomes a dislike. *Scottish*

10078. Kindness, so far as we can return it, is agreeable. *Latin (Tacitus)*

10079. Kindness to the good is a better investment than kindness to the rich. *Latin*

10080. Kindness to the just is never lost, but kindness to the wicked is unkindness to yourself. *American*

10081. Kindness will creep where it canna gang [go]. *Scottish*

10082. Kindnesses, like grain, increase by sowing. *English*

10083. Never forget a kindness. *American*

10084. No thanks attach to a kindness long deferred. *Latin (Ovid)*

10085. Nothing grows old sooner than a kindness. *French*

10086. Nothing is so popular as kindness. *Latin*

10087. Persistent kindness conquers the ill-disposed. *Latin*

10088. The heart benevolent and kind / The most resembles God. *Scottish (Burns)*

10089. To kindness from thy heart be kinder still: / To cruelty be hard against thy will. *Welsh*

10090. Unfading are the gardens of kindness. *Greek*

10091. Unkindness has no remedy at law. *English*

Kings and Rulers

10092. A change of rulers is the joy of fools. *Romanian*

10093. A dead king is not a man less. *French*

10094. A king is he who has no fear, and desires naught. *Latin*

10095. A king without subjects is no king. *Wolof*

10096. A king's cheese goes half away in parings [i.e., half of his revenues are gone before they enter his coffers]. *English*

10097. Dreadful is the wrath of kings. *Greek (Homer)*

10098. Every monarch is subject to a mightier one. *Latin*

10099. Every ruler is harsh whose rule is new. *Greek (Aeschylus)*

10100. He that is hated of his subjects cannot be counted a king. *Scottish*

10101. He who is to be a good ruler must first have been ruled. *Greek*

10102. He who would rule must hear and be deaf, see and be blind. *German*

10103. Iron hand in velvet glove. *French*

10104. It is absurd that he who does not know how to govern himself should govern others. *Latin*

10105. King hae [have] lang hands. *Scottish*

10106. Kings and bears oft worry their keepers. *Scottish*

10107. Kings are kittle [difficult] cattle to shae [shoe] behint. *Scottish*

10108. Kings are out of play. *Scottish*

10109. Kings hae long lugs [ears]. *Scottish*

10110. Kings have long hands. *Latin*

10111. Kings play the fool, and the people suffer for it. *Latin (Horace)*

10112. Let the ruler be slow in punishing, swift in rewarding. *Latin*

10113. "Must" is for the king to say [or is a king's word]. *English*

10114. No ruler sins as long as he is a ruler. *Greek*

10115. Nothing becomes a king so much as justice. *Greek*

10116. On alien soil, kingship stands not sure. *Latin (Seneca)*

10117. Only with a new ruler do you realize the value of the old. *Burmese*

10118. Princes have long hands and many ears. *German*

10119. Stolen scepters are held in anxious hands. *Latin (Seneca)*

10120. The czar is far but his hands are long. *Cheremis*

10121. The desire to rule is stronger than all the other passions. *Latin*

10122. The halls of kings are full of men, but void of friends. *Latin (Seneca)*

10123. The king can do no wrong. *Latin*

10124. The king cannot deceive or be deceived. *Latin*

10125. The king is dead. Long live the king! *French*

10126. The king never dies. *Latin*

10127. The king of good fellows is appointed for the queen of beggars. *English (Fuller)*

10128. The king reigns, but does not govern. *Polish*

10129. The king's leavings are better than the lord's bounty. *Spanish (Cervantes)*

10130. The king's word is more than another man's oath. *English*

10131. The right divine [of kings] to govern wrong. *English (Pope)*

10132. The subject's love is the king's best guard. *English*

10133. The virtue of kings consists in justice. *French*

10134. To love the king is not bad, but a king who loves you is better. *Wolof*

10135. Unjust rule never endures. *Latin*

10136. When kings are building, draymen have something to do. *German*

Kinship *see also* Family; Relationship; Relatives

10137. Beasts of like kind will spare those of kindred spots. *Latin (Juvenal)*

10138. Dog won't eat dog. *English*

10139. He goes safely to trial whose father is the judge. *Spanish*

10140. 'Tis a hard winter when one wolf eats another. *English*

Kissing

10141. A kiss for the child is as good as a kiss for its mother. *Yiddish*

10142. A lisping lass is good to kiss. *English*

10143. Don't kiss a homely maid — she'll brag about it. *Yiddish*

10144. Gin a body kiss a body, / Need a body cry? *Scottish (Burns)*

10145. Kiss and be kind, the fiddler is blind. *Scottish*

10146. Kisses are the messengers of love. *Danish*

10147. Kissing goes by favor. *English*

10148. Kissing is cried doun since the shaking o' hands. *Scottish*

10149. Many kiss the child for love of the nurse. *Latin*

10150. The hawk kissed the hen — up to the last feather. *Russian*

10151. The kisses of an enemy are deceitful. *Bible*

10152. Ye're black about the mou' for want o' kissing. *Scottish*

Knowledge *see also* Experience; Ignorance; Learning

10153. A handful of knowledge is worth a bushelful of learning. *American*

10154. A learned man has always riches in himself. *Latin*

10155. A little knowledge is a dangerous thing. *English (Pope)*

10156. A man is but what he knoweth. *English (Bacon)*

10157. A man of knowledge increaseth strength. *Bible*

10158. A man of knowledge like a rich soil, feeds / If not a world of corn, a world of weeds. *American (Franklin)*

10159. All that we know is that we know nothing. *American*

10160. All wish to know, but none to pay the fee. *Latin*

10161. An investment in knowledge pays the best interest. *American (Franklin)*

10162. Better ignorance than half-knowledge. *Latin*

10163. Bright enough in the dark, dull in time of day. [Schooled in useless knowledge, ignorant of everything else.] *Latin*

10164. Concealed knowledge is buried treasure. *American*

10165. He knows how mony beans maks five. *Scottish*

10166. He that increaseth knowledge increaseth sorrow. *Bible*

10167. He who does not know one thing knows another. *Kenyan*

10168. He who knows has many cares. *German*

10169. Hidden knowledge differs little from ignorance. *Latin (Horace)*

10170. Increase your knowledge and you increase your griefs. *American*

10171. It is better to know something about everything than all about one thing. *French (Pascal)*

10172. It is not permitted us to know all. *Latin*

10173. Knowledge finds its price. *French*

10174. Knowledge indeed is better even than great valor. *Greek (Theognis)*

10175. Knowledge is a treasure, but practice is the key to it. *English*

10176. Knowledge is folly except [i.e., unless] grace guide it. *English*

10177. Knowledge is madness if good sense does not direct it. *Spanish*

10178. Knowledge is power. *Latin*

10179. Knowledge is the wing wherewith we fly to heaven. *English (Shakespeare)*

10180. Knowledge puffeth up, but charity edifieth. *Bible*

10181. Knowledge without practice makes but half an artist. *English*

10182. Let him who knows how ring the bells. *Spanish*

10183. Money spent on the brain is never spent in vain. *American*

10184. Only one good: knowledge; only one evil: ignorance. *Greek*

10185. Profess not the knowledge thou hast not. *Bible*

10186. The fool gets nothing from the Book of Knowledge, not even the knowledge that he is a fool. *American*

10187. The fox knew too much: that's how he lost his tail. *American*

10188. The ladder of knowledge reaches beyond the ladder of life. *Arabic*

10189. The raft of knowledge ferries the worst sinner to safety. *Bhagavad-Gita*

10190. The wealth of the mind is the only true wealth. *Greek*

10191. The wise know most and say the least. *American*

10192. There are no national frontiers to learning. *Japanese*

10193. There are two that are never satisfied: he who seeks after learning and he who seeks after wealth. *Arabic*

10194. There is a certain wonderful sweetness and delight in knowledge. *Latin*

10195. There is not a gem in every rock, no pearl in every elephant, nor sandlewood in every forest, nor erudition in every place. *Burmese*

10196. 'Tis not knowing much, but what is useful, that makes a wise man. *English*

10197. To be proud of knowledge is to be blind with light. *American (Franklin)*

10198. To know everything is to know nothing. *Italian*

10199. To know one's ignorance is the best part of knowledge. *Chinese*

10200. To seek to know is to seek to doubt. *French*

10201. We don't know when we're well off. *American*

10202. Who knows most believes least. *Italian*

10203. Who knows most forgives most. *Italian*

10204. Without knowledge there is no sin or sinner. *American*

10205. Your knowing a thing is nothing, unless another knows you know it. *Latin (Persius)*

Labor *see* Work and Workers

Lack *see also* Insufficiency

10206. For want of a nail a shoe is lost. *Spanish*

Land

10207. The land a man knows is his mother. *Spanish*

10208. Who buys land buys war. *Italian*

Language *see also* Speaking; Words

10209. Custom is the most certain mistress of language. *English (Jonson)*

10210. Don't be frightened at high-sounding words. *Latin*

10211. Even silence itself has its prayers and its language. *American*

10212. He who is ignorant of foreign languages knows not his own. *German (Goethe)*

10213. Language is the dress of thought. *English (Johnson)*

10214. Language was the immediate gift of God. *American (Webster)*

10215. Men's language is as their lives. *Latin (Seneca)*

10216. That is not good language that all understand not. *American*

10217. Write with the learned but speak with the vulgar. *English*

Last *see also* Lateness; Order; Punctuality

10218. He that comes last makes all fast. *English*

10219. It's the last one whom the dogs attack. *Yiddish*

10220. The hindmost dog may catch the hare. *English*

10221. The last best, like to gude wives' daughters. *Scottish*

10222. The last one must shut the door. *Italian*

10223. The last suitor wins the maid. *English*

10224. The last to arrive are the best loved. *French*

Lateness *see also* Last; Punctuality; Timeliness

10225. A courtesy much entreated is half recompensed. *English*

10226. A little late is much too late. *German*

10227. After death the doctor. *French*

10228. After death the medicine. *French*

10229. After death, the prescription. *Korean*

10230. After meat comes mustard. *English*

10231. After the carriage is broken, many offer themselves to show the road. *Turkish*

10232. After the rain, there's no need for an umbrella. *Bulgarian*

10233. After the vintage, baskets. *Spanish*

10234. After the wedding, we don't need music. *Tartar*

10235. An empty purse makes a man wise, but too late. *American*

10236. Better late than never. *Latin*

10237. Better late thrive than never do weel. *Scottish*

10238. Bones for those who come late. *Latin*

10239. Caution comes too late when we are in the midst of evils. *Latin (Seneca)*

10240. Come late, come right. *Hindi*

10241. For the last comer the bones. *French*

10242. Glory comes too late when we are nought but ashes. *Latin (Martius)*

10243. God keep you from "It is too late." *Spanish*

10244. Good, that comes too late, is good as nothing. *English*

10245. He has done like the Perugian, who, when his head was broken, ran home for his helmet. *Italian*

10246. He who comes late must eat what is left. *Yiddish*

10247. It is late but not too late. *English*

10248. It is too late to grieve when the chance has passed. *English*

10249. It's nae [no] time to stoop when the head's aff. *Scottish*

10250. It's never too late. *American*

10251. It's never too late to mend. *English*

10252. It's ower late to lout when the head's got a clout. *Scottish*

10253. It's too late for the bird to scream when it is caught. *French*

10254. It's too late to cast anchor when the ship's on the rocks. *English*

10255. It's too late to come with water when the house has burned down. *Danish*

10256. It's too late to cover the well when the child has drowned. *Danish*

10257. It's too late to learn how to box when you're in the ring. *American*

10258. It's too late to lock the stable door when the horses have gone. *French*

10259. It's too late to spare when the bottom is bare. *American*

10260. Late fruit keeps well. *German*

10261. Late repentance is seldom true. *English*

10262. Plenty of words when the cause is lost. *Italian*

10263. Saving comes too late when you get to the bottom. *Latin (Seneca)*
10264. The bird cries out too late when it is taken. *French*
10265. The cage is ready but the bird is flown. *American*
10266. The fire engines arrive after the house has burned down. *German*
10267. The fool grows wise after the evil has come upon him. *Latin*
10268. The gladiator having entered the lists is seeking advice. *Latin*
10269. The last comers are often the masters. *French*
10270. The mill does not grind with the water that's past. *French*
10271. The nest is made but the bird is dead. *American*
10272. The way to good conduct is never too late. *Latin (Seneca)*
10273. Time has a forelock, but is bald behind. *Latin*
10274. 'Tis never too late to mend. *English*
10275. 'Tis too late to spare, / When the bottom is bare. *English*
10276. To bring out the implements of war, when the battle is over. *Latin*
10277. To cut a stick when the fight is over. *Japanese*
10278. To stop the hole after the mischief is done. *Spanish*
10279. Too late do I take up the shield after the wound. *Latin (Ovid)*
10280. Too late to grieve when the chance is past. *English*
10281. When a thing is lost people take advice. *French*
10282. When his head is broken, he puts on his helmet. *Italian*
10283. When the battle is over you make your appearance. *Latin*
10284. When the calf is drowned, they cover the well. *Dutch*
10285. When the calf is stolen, the peasant mends the stall. *German*
10286. When the corn is eaten, the silly body builds the dyke. *Gaelic*
10287. When the fool has made up his mind, the market has gone by. *Spanish*
10288. When the friar's beaten, then comes James. *English*
10289. When the horse is starved, you bring him oats. *English*
10290. When the mischief is done, the door is shut. *Latin (Juvenal)*
10291. When the wine runs to waste in the cellar, he mends the cask. *German*
10292. When your armor is on, it is too late to retreat. *Latin (Juvenal)*
10293. When your money is spent, you cut off wine; when growing old, you turn to the classics. *Chinese*
10294. Who comes late is ill-lodged. *Italian*
10295. Who doesn't come at the right time must take what is left. *American*
10296. Who rises late must trot all day. *French*
10297. Ye rin [run] for the spurtle [a short stick for stirring porridge] when the pat's boiling ower. *Scottish*
10298. You anoint the dead man with salve. *Latin*
10299. You come too late for the fair. *English*
10300. You have come too late for the feast. *Latin*
10301. You plead after sentence is given. *English*

Latitude

10302. Wide will wear, but tight [or narrow] will tear. *English*

Laughter *see also* Humor

10303. A laugh is worth a hundred groans in any market. *American*
10304. All things are cause for either laughter or weeping. *Latin*
10305. As the crackling of thorns under a pot, so is the laughter of a fool. *Bible*
10306. Better the last smile than the first laughter. *English*
10307. By much laughter you detect the fool. *Latin*
10308. Even in laughter the heart is sorrowful; and the end of mirth is heaviness. *Bible*
10309. Give winners leave to laugh, for if you do not they'll take it. *English*
10310. He chastises manners with a laugh. *Latin*
10311. He is not laughed at that laughs at himself first. *English*
10312. He laugheth that winneth. *English*
10313. He laughs ill that laughs himself to death. *English*
10314. He laughs well who laughs last. *French*
10315. He that laughs alane will make sport in company. *Scottish*
10316. He that laughs at his ain jokes spoils the sport o' them. *Scottish*
10317. He who laughs last laughs best. *English*
10318. He who laughs on Friday will weep on Saturday. *French*
10319. He who loves to laugh has teeth that are white. *Russian*
10320. He who tickles himself may laugh when he pleases. *German*
10321. He will laugh best who will laugh last. *French*
10322. If you laugh at your ain sport the company will laugh at you. *Scottish*
10323. If you take a cat to church, the folks are going to laugh. *American*
10324. Ill-timed laughter is a dangerous evil. *Greek*
10325. It is not mere laughter which proves a mind at ease. *French*
10326. Laugh and grow fat. *English*
10327. Laugh and the world laughs with you; weep, and you weep alone. *American*
10328. Laugh if you are wise. *Latin*
10329. Laughter abounds in the mouths of fools. *Latin*
10330. Laughter comes of itself; so does weeping. *Yiddish*
10331. Laughter is the hiccup of a fool. *English*
10332. Laughter leaves us doubly serious shortly after. *English (Byron)*

10333. Laughter makes good blood. *Italian*
10334. Let people laugh, as long as I am warm. *Spanish*
10335. Let us not be laughing-stocks to other men's humors. *English (Shakespeare)*
10336. Men show their characters in what they think laughable. *German (Goethe)*
10337. No one is sadder than he who laughs too much. *German*
10338. Nothing is more ill-timed than an ill-timed laugh. *Latin (Martius)*
10339. That day is lost on which one has not laughed. *French*
10340. The excess of mirth leads to tears. *Latin*
10341. The fool will laugh though there be nothing to laugh at. *Greek*
10342. The gods have not granted to mortals laughter without tears. *Greek*
10343. The loud laugh betrays the vacant mind. *American*
10344. The merchant who loses cannot laugh. *French*
10345. The more fools, the more laughter. *English*
10346. The price of a laugh is too high, if it is raised at the expense of propriety. *Latin*
10347. The winners laugh, the losers weep. *American*
10348. They laugh aye that winnes. *Scottish*
10349. They laugh till they cry. *English*
10350. To condemn by a cutting laugh comes readily to all. *Latin*
10351. To laugh in one's face and cut one's throat. *English*
10352. We must laugh before we are happy, lest we die before we laugh at all. *French*
10353. What is viler than to be laughed at? *Latin*
10354. When you laugh, all see; when you weep, no one. *Yiddish*
10355. Who laughs too much may have an aching heart. *Italian*

Lavishness *see* Extravagance

Law *see also* Injustice; Justice; Lawsuits; Lawyers; Loopholes

10356. A friend in court is worth a penny in a man's purse. *English*
10357. A friend in court makes the trial short. *American*
10358. A multiplicity of laws and of physicians in a country is equally a sign of its bad condition. *Italian*
10359. A rotten case abides no handling. *English (Shakespeare)*
10360. All things by law. *Greek*
10361. All things obey fixed laws. *Greek*
10362. Arms and laws do not flourish together. *Latin*
10363. Bad laws are the worst sort of tyranny. *American*
10364. Better have no laws at all than in prodigious numbers. *French (Montaigne)*
10365. Better no law than laws not enforced. *American*
10366. Crooks obey the law at the end of a nightstick. *American*
10367. Draco made his laws not with ink, but with blood. *Greek*
10368. Extreme law, extreme injustice. *Latin*
10369. Good laws are the offspring of bad actions. *Latin (Macrobius)*
10370. He that loes [loves] law will soon get his fill o't. *Scottish*
10371. Ignorance of the law excuses no one. *Latin*
10372. In a thousand pounds of law there is not an ounce of love. *French*
10373. In a very corrupt state there are very many laws. *Latin (Tacitus)*
10374. Law cannot persuade where it cannot punish. *English*
10375. Law is a deadly distemper amang friends. *Scottish*
10376. Law is founded not on theory but on nature. *Latin*
10377. Law is king. *Scottish*
10378. Law is the safest helmet. *Latin*
10379. Law is the tyrant of mankind. *Greek*
10380. Law licks up a'. *Scottish*
10381. Law-makers should not be law-breakers. *Scottish*
10382. Laws are dumb in the midst of arms. *Latin*
10383. Laws are made to be evaded. *American*
10384. Laws are not made for the good. *Greek*
10385. Laws are useful to those who have; vexatious to those who have not. *French*
10386. Laws catch flies and let hornets go. *American*
10387. Laws go as kings like. *Spanish*
10388. Laws have wax noses. *French*
10389. Laws too gentle are seldom obeyed; too severe, seldom executed. *American (Franklin)*
10390. Laws were made that the stronger might not in all things have his way. *Latin*
10391. Laws were made to be broken. *American*
10392. Laws without penalties are bells without clappers. *Czech*
10393. Legality kills us. *French*
10394. Let the force of arms give place to law and justice. *Latin (Cicero)*
10395. New laws, new deceit. *German*
10396. New laws, new monkey-business. *American*
10397. New lords, new laws. *English*
10398. Of what use are laws nullified by immorality? *Latin*
10399. So many lands, so many laws. *Latin*
10400. So many laws argue so many sins. *English (Milton)*
10401. Strict law is often great injustice. *Latin (Cicero)*
10402. The atrocity of a law prevents its execution. *French*
10403. The brain may devise laws for the blood, but a hot temper leaps o'er a cold decree. *English (Shakespeare)*
10404. The clatter of arms drowns the voice of the law. *French (Montaigne)*
10405. The law is good, if a man use it lawfully. *Bible*
10406. The law often allows what honor forbids. *French*

10407. The law that codifies evil is the essence of lawlessness. *American*
10408. The laws obey custom. *Latin*
10409. The letter killeth, but the spirit giveth life. *Bible*
10410. The man who does no wrong needs no law. *Greek*
10411. The more by law the less by right. *Danish*
10412. The more law, the less right [or justice]. *German*
10413. The more laws, the more offenders. *Latin*
10414. The prince is not above the laws. *Latin*
10415. There's no worse torture than the torture of laws. *English (Bacon)*
10416. To violate the law is the same crime in the emperor as in the subject. *Chinese*
10417. War, hunting and law are as full of trouble as of pleasure. *English*
10418. When a law is made, the way of craftiness is discovered. *Italian*
10419. When there's no law, there's no bread. *American (Franklin)*
10420. Where drums speak, laws are dumb. *Latin (Cicero)*
10421. Where is there any book of the law so clear to each man as that written in his heart? *Russian (Tolstoy)*
10422. Where law can do no right, / Let it be lawful that law bar no wrong. *English (Shakespeare)*
10423. Where law ends, tyranny begins. *American*

Lawsuits *see also* Injustice; Justice; Law; Lawyers; Might and Right

10424. A lawsuit is civil war. *German*
10425. A lean compromise is better than a fat lawsuit. *Italian*
10426. Agree, for the law is costly. *English*
10427. By lawsuits no one has become rich. *German*
10428. Go not to law, because the musician keeps false time with his foot. *Latin*
10429. He goes to law for a sheep and loses his cow. *German*
10430. Law's costly; tak a pint an' 'gree. *Scottish*
10431. Lawsuits are gulfs. *French*
10432. Lawsuits consume time, and money, and rest, and friends. *English*
10433. "Mine" and "Thine" is the source of all lawsuits. *Dutch*
10434. Some go to law for the wagging of a straw. *American*
10435. The nobleman is always in the right when the peasant sues. *Russian*
10436. The worst of law is that one lawsuit breeds twenty. *Spanish*

Lawyers *see also* Injustice; Justice; Law; Lawsuits

10437. A good lawyer, a bad neighbor. *French*
10438. A lawyer and a cart-wheel must be greased. *German*
10439. A lawyer never goes to law himself. *Italian*
10440. A lawyer's advice is expensive, but it'll cost you more if you consult yourself. *American*
10441. A peasant between two lawyers is like a fish between two cats. *Spanish*
10442. Lawyers and painters can soon change white to black. *Danish*
10443. Lawyers' houses are built on the heads of fools. *French*
10444. One may steal nothing but a lawyer's purse. *French*
10445. The good have no need of an advocate. *Greek*
10446. The lawyer's pouch is a mouth of hell. *French*
10447. They let out on hire their passions and eloquence. *Latin (Martius)*
10448. Three Philadelphia lawyers are a match for the devil. *American*
10449. Until hell is full no lawyer will be saved. *French*
10450. "Virtue in the middle," said the Devil, when he sat down between two lawyers. *Danish*
10451. Woe unto you, lawyers! for ye have stolen away the key of knowledge. *Bible*

Laziness *see also* Idleness

10452. A lazy boy and a warm bed are difficult to part. *Danish*
10453. A lazy girl and a warm bed are hard to separate. *American*
10454. A lazy man should be sent for the Angel of Death. *Yiddish*
10455. A lazy man works twice. *Norwegian*
10456. A lazy messenger finds many excuses. *Yiddish*
10457. A life of leisure, and a life of laziness, are two things. *English*
10458. A slothfu' hand maks a slim fortune. *Scottish*
10459. A slothful man is a beggar's brother. *Scottish*
10460. An indolent man draws his breath but does not live. *Latin*
10461. As lazy as Ludlam's dog that leaned his head against the wall to bark. *English*
10462. Better wear [i.e., wear out] shoon [shoes] than sheets. *Scottish*
10463. Blame is the lazy man's wages. *Danish*
10464. Drowsiness shall clothe a man with rags. *Bible*
10465. For eating he has two stomachs, but for work, one. *American*
10466. For the slothful it is always a holiday. *Latin*
10467. Go to the ant, thou sluggard; consider her ways, and be wise. *Bible*
10468. He that sleeps in harvest is a son that causes shame. *American*
10469. He who does nothing but sit and eat, will wear away a mountain of wealth. *Chinese*
10470. He who shuns labor labors doubly. *American*
10471. He's willing to swallow but too lazy to chew. *Russian*
10472. It costs the devil little trouble to catch a lazy man. *German*
10473. It's a sorry ass that will not bear his own burden. *American*
10474. Laziness has no boosters but many pals. *American*
10475. Laziness is like a greyhound when it chases the hare of excuse. *Russian*

10476. Laziness is the devil's pillow. *Danish*

10477. Laziness travels so slowly that Poverty soon overtakes him. *American (Franklin)*

10478. Lazy youth maks lousy age. *Scottish*

10479. No dullard but must lazy be; / Nor lazy, but a sinner he. *Welsh*

10480. No one has become immortal by sloth. *Latin*

10481. Nothing falls into the mouth of a sleeping fox. *Hungarian*

10482. Shirk work and you will want bread. *Latin*

10483. Sloth is the mother of poverty. *English*

10484. Sloth must breed a scab. *English*

10485. Slouthe bringeth in alle wo. *English*

10486. That shameful siren, sloth, is ever to be avoided. *Latin (Horace)*

10487. The lazy are always wanting to do something. *French (Vauvenargues)*

10488. The way of a slothful man is as a hedge of thorns. *Latin*

10489. They must hunger in frost who will not work in heat. *English*

10490. To the lazy every day is a holiday. *Turkish*

10491. We excuse our sloth under pretext of difficulty. *Latin*

10492. What use is a good head if the legs won't carry it? *Yiddish*

10493. When the fox is asleep, nothing falls into his mouth. *French*

Leaders and Leadership *see also* Authority; Government; Kings and Rulers; Master and Man; Obedience; Shared Authority; Women in Authority

10494. A good leader makes a good follower. *Latin*

10495. A good leader produces a good soldier. *Latin*

10496. An army of stags led by a lion would be more formidable than one of lions led by a stag. *Latin*

10497. Anyone can hold the helm when the sea is calm. *Latin (Publilius Syrus)*

10498. As the master is, so is the shop. *Polish*

10499. Command shows the man. *Greek*

10500. He does not command well who has not obeyed command. *Latin*

10501. He that most curteisly commandeth, to him men most obeyen. *English*

10502. He who has never learned to obey cannot be a good commander. *Greek (Aristotle)*

10503. In calm weather everyone is captain. *Maltese*

10504. It is an absurdity that he should rule others who cannot command himself. *Latin*

10505. It's an ill battle where the devil carries the colours. *English*

10506. It's an ill procession where the devil holds the candle. *English*

10507. Many captains and the ship goes to the rocks. *Japanese*

10508. No fat charioteer; no lazy person as manager. *Latin*

10509. The highest trees have the most reason to dread the thunder. *French*

10510. The superior man is easy to serve and difficult to please. *Chinese (Confucius)*

10511. Through obedience learn to command. *Greek*

10512. Unless the water is deep [i.e., unless the leader is great], the fish will not gather in a school. *Korean*

10513. When one sheep leads the way, the rest follow. *American*

10514. Who is foremost leads the flock. *German (Schiller)*

10515. Who knows not to obey knows not to command. *French*

Learned Fools *see also* Fools and Folly

10516. A fool, unless he knows *Latin*, is never a great fool. *Spanish*

10517. A learned blockhead is a greater blockhead than an ignorant one. *American (Franklin)*

10518. A learned fool is a greater fool than an ignorant fool. *French (Molière)*

10519. He's a fool that cannot conceal his wisdom. *American (Franklin)*

10520. Jack has studied in order to be a fool. *French*

10521. Learned fools are the greatest fools. *French*

10522. None can play the fool as well as a wise man. *English*

10523. There is no fool like an educated fool. *American*

Learning *see also* Experience; Knowledge; Learned Fools; Scholars and Scholarship

10524. A handful of life is better than a bushel of learning. *Scottish*

10525. A single day among the learned lasts longer than the longest life of the ignorant. *Latin (Seneca)*

10526. All pursuits are mean in comparison with that of learning. *Chinese*

10527. An infant learns to walk by crawling. *American*

10528. How many perish in the earth through vain learning! *German (Thomas à Kempis)*

10529. How vain is learning unless intelligence go with it. *Greek (Stobaeus)*

10530. If you love learning you shall be learned. *Greek*

10531. It is never too late to learn. *Latin*

10532. It takes ten pounds of common sense to carry one pound of learning. *Persian*

10533. Learn young, learn fair; learn auld [old], learn mair [more]. *Scottish*

10534. Learning colors a man more than vermilion or black does. *Chinese*

10535. Learning is a treasure which follows its owner everywhere. *Chinese*

10536. Learning is better than house or land. *Irish*

10537. Learning is far more precious than gold. *Chinese*

10538. Learning makes a good man better and a bad man worse. *American*

10539. Learning teacheth more in one year than experience in twenty. *English (Ascham)*

10540. Learning which does not daily advance will daily decrease. *Chinese*

10541. Learning without thought is labor lost; thought without learning is dangerous. *Chinese*

10542. Learnt young, done old. *German*
10543. Men of learning are plain men. *American*
10544. Most things are easy to learn, but hard to master. *Chinese*
10545. Much learning does not teach understanding. *Greek (Heraclitus)*
10546. Much learning doth make thee mad. *Bible*
10547. Of learned fools I have seen ten times ten; of unlearned wise men I have seen a hundred. *American*
10548. Of what use is learning without understanding? *French*
10549. Soon learned, soon forgotten. *American*
10550. The learned pig did not learn its letters in a day. *American*
10551. The learning of books that you do not make your own wisdom is money in the hands of another in time of need. *Sanskrit*
10552. The older you grow the more you learn. *American*
10553. There is no royal road to learning. *Greek (Euclid)*
10554. 'Tis harder to unlearn than to learn. *American*
10555. We learn from the mistakes of others. *American*
10556. We live and learn. *American*
10557. We live and learn; we learn and live. *American*
10558. What we have to learn to do we learn by doing. *Greek*
10559. You must assimilate what you learn. *Chinese*
10560. You must learn to crawl before you can walk. *American*
10561. You're never too old to learn. *American*

Leaving *see also* Absence; Friends and Friendship; Love

10562. He can ill rin [run] that canna gang [go]. *Scottish*
10563. He gangs [goes] awa in an ill time that ne'er comes back again. *Scottish*
10564. He has gane without takin' his leave. *Scottish*

Leftovers

10565. Cats eat what hussies spare. *Scottish*
10566. There is little for the rake to get after the bissome [broom]. *Scottish*
10567. There's little for the rake after the shool [shovel]. *Scottish*
10568. There's never eneugh where nought leaves. *English*
10569. What the goodwife spares the cat eats. *English*

Legality *see* Law

Leisure *see also* Ease; Rest

10570. He enjoys true leisure who has time to improve his soul's estate. *American (Thoreau)*
10571. He has not leisure even to scratch his ears. *Latin*
10572. He was never less at leisure than when at leisure. *Latin*
10573. He who knows not how to employ his leisure hath more cares on his mind than the busiest of busy men. *Latin*
10574. Leisure breeds lust. *Chinese*
10575. Leisure is the best of all possessions. *Greek*
10576. Leisure nourishes the body and the mind. *Latin*
10577. Leisure with dignity. *Latin*
10578. Leisure without study is death. *Latin*
10579. Take away Leisure, and Cupid's bow is broken. *Latin (Ovid)*
10580. The busiest men have the most leisure. *American*
10581. The indolent but delightful condition of doing nothing. *Latin (Pliny)*

Lending *see* Borrowing and Lending

Leniency *see* Forgiveness; Pardon and Leniency; Punishment

Libel *see also* Slander

10582. The greater the truth the greater the libel. *English*

Liberality *see also* Generosity

10583. He that lets his wife go to every feast, and his horse drink at every water, shall neither have good wife nor good horse. *Italian*
10584. Our liberality should not exceed our ability. *Latin (Cicero)*
10585. The liberal soul shall be made fat. *Bible*

Liberty *see* Freedom and Liberty

Lies and Lying *see also* Boasting; Exaggeration; Lying and Stealing; Slander; Truth and Falsehood

10586. A false report rides fast. *American*
10587. A fu' heart never lee'd [lied]. *Scottish*
10588. A great lie is the best. *American*
10589. A great talker, a great liar. *French*
10590. A half truth is the blackest lie. *American*
10591. A liar believes no one. *Yiddish*
10592. A liar in youth — a thief in old age. *Yiddish*
10593. A liar is an economist of the truth. *Scottish*
10594. A liar is like a deaf-mute — both do not tell the truth. *Yiddish*
10595. A liar is sooner caught than a cripple. *Italian*
10596. A liar needs a good memory. *Latin*
10597. A liar will not be believed even when he speaks the truth. *Greek (Aesop)*
10598. A lie always needs a truth for a handle to it. *English*
10599. A lie begets a lie. *English*
10600. A lie can go around the world while the truth is getting its britches on. *American*
10601. A lie has no legs to stand on but it gets places. *American*
10602. A lie has short legs. *Spanish*
10603. A lie has short legs; truth overtakes it. *Dutch*
10604. A lie may sometimes be more helpful than one's maternal uncle. *Korean*
10605. A lie stands on one leg, truth on two. *English*

10606. A lie travels round the world while truth is putting on her boots. *English*

10607. A little truth makes the whole lie pass. *Italian*

10608. A vaunter and a liar are the same thing. *English*

10609. A white lie is harmless; so is a necessary one. *American*

10610. An untruthful man is like untempered steel; an untruthful woman is like rotten grass and tangled hemp. *Chinese*

10611. Better the feet slip than the tongue. *Italian*

10612. Birds are entangled by their feet and men by their tongues. *English*

10613. Curses never put men in hearses, but lying tongues have dug many graves. *American*

10614. Falsehood is a red apple rotten at the core. *American*

10615. Falsehood is the darkness of faith. *Persian*

10616. Falsehood, like a nettle, stings those who meddle with it. *English*

10617. Fause [false] folk should hae mony witnesses. *Scottish*

10618. Fausehood [falsehood] maks ne'er a fair hinder-end. *Scottish*

10619. Figures never lie, but liars can figure. *American*

10620. Frost and fausehood hae baith a dirty wa' gang. *Scottish*

10621. Great talkers are commonly liars. *German*

10622. He can lee as weel as a dog can lick a dish. *Scottish*

10623. He never lies but when the holly's green. [He lies all the time.] *Scottish*

10624. He wad gar you trow [would make you believe] that the mune's made o' green cheese. *Scottish*

10625. He who lied yesterday will not be believed tomorrow. *Russian*

10626. I said in my haste, all men are liars. *Bible*

10627. I wish you were laird o' your word. *Scottish*

10628. I'll no tell a lee for scant o' news. *Scottish*

10629. If a lee could hae chokit you, ye wad hae been dead langsyne [long ago]. *Scottish*

10630. If lying paid a tax it would pay the national debt. *American*

10631. If you believe a lie it's truth as far as you are concerned. *American*

10632. If you lie and eat fish at the same time, you might swallow a bone. *Costa Rican*

10633. It is a low thing to lie; truth becomes the well-born man. *Latin*

10634. It's a sin to lee on the deil. *Scottish*

10635. It's as true as Biglam's cat crew and the cock rocked the cradle. *Scottish*

10636. Lee for him and he'll swear for you. *Scottish*

10637. Leears should hae gude memories. *Scottish*

10638. Leein' rides on debt's back. *Scottish*

10639. Liars and gossips are Siamese twins. *American*

10640. Liars are always most disposed to swear. *Italian*

10641. Liars are not believed when they speak the truth. *American*

10642. Liars begin by imposing on others, and end by deceiving themselves. *English (Bacon)*

10643. Liars end by deceiving themselves. *American*

10644. Liars have short wings. *English*

10645. Liars need good memories to cover up their lies, but people who tell the truth need remember little. *American*

10646. Liars pay the penalty of their own misdeeds. *Latin (Phaedrus)*

10647. Lies and *Latin* go round the world. *Danish*

10648. Lies beget lies and give birth to generations of liars. *American*

10649. Lies have short legs. *German*

10650. Lies, however numerous, will be caught by truth when it rises up. *Wolof*

10651. Lying is the first step to the prison gates. *American*

10652. Lying is weakness; truth is health. *Arabic*

10653. Lying like a dentist. *French*

10654. Lying pays no tax. *Portuguese*

10655. Lying rides on debt's back. *American*

10656. Nothing can overtake an untruth if it has a minute's start. *American*

10657. O what a goodly outside falsehood hath! *English (Shakespeare)*

10658. O what a tangled web we weave, / When first we practice to deceive. *Scottish (Scott)*

10659. Old men and far travellers may lie by authority. *English*

10660. One falsehood leads to another. *English*

10661. One falsehood spoils a thousand truths. *Ashanti*

10662. One lie draws ten after it. *Italian*

10663. One lie makes many. *English*

10664. Painters and poets have leave to lie. *Scottish*

10665. Show me a liar, and I'll show you a thief. *French*

10666. Snake, he ain't got no friend; neither the long-tongued liar. *American*

10667. Tell a lie and find the truth. *English*

10668. The bigger the lie the more it is believed. *American*

10669. The liar is caught faster than a lame dog. *Hungarian*

10670. The liar never believes the truth even when he tells it himself. *American*

10671. The mouth that lies slays the soul. *Bible*

10672. The small lie is disguised, the Big Lie passes as truth without a mask. *American*

10673. Though a thing has been false a hundred years it cannot become true. *German*

10674. To hide one lie, a thousand lies are needed. *Telugu*

10675. To lie faster than a dog can lick a dish. *English*

10676. To lie faster than a horse trots. *Belizean Creole*

10677. To tell a lie is the beginning of a thief. *Japanese*

10678. Trust not a man who lies for you, for he may lie to you. *Arabic*

10679. Truth ill-timed is as bad as a lie. *American*

10680. Wad ye gar us trow [would you have us believe] that the mune's made o' green cheese, or that spade shafts bear plooms [plums]? *Scottish*

10681. We know how to speak many things which are false as if they were true, and we know, when we choose, how to wrap up truth in fable. *Greek*

10682. Ye didna lick your lips since ye lee'd last. *Scottish*

Life *see also* Death; Longevity; Mortality; Transience

10683. A blossom full of promise is life's joy that never comes to fruit. *American*

10684. A live ass is worth more than a dead doctor. *Italian*

10685. A living dog is better than a dead lion. *Bible*

10686. A living mouse is better than a dead lion. *Russian*

10687. A man cannot live on air. *French*

10688. A man should live only so long as he can support himself. *Yiddish*

10689. A short life is long enough for living well. *Latin*

10690. A short life—and a merry one. *American*

10691. Actions from youth, advice from the middle-aged, prayers from the aged. *Latin (Hesiod)*

10692. After the coffin lid is closed a man's life can be evaluated. *Chinese*

10693. All the world's a stage. *Latin*

10694. As an infant, man is wrapped in his mother's womb; grown up, he is wrapped in custom; dead, he is wrapped in earth. *Malay*

10695. As leaves on the trees is the life of man. *Greek (Homer)*

10696. As long as the Fates permit, live cheerfully. *Latin*

10697. As long as you live, keep learning how to live. *Latin*

10698. As the life is, so is its end. *Latin*

10699. As you live on, you live to see everything. *Yiddish*

10700. Bad lives come to bad ends. *American*

10701. Be happy while ye'er leevin [living], / For ye'er a lang time deid. *Scottish*

10702. Better live poor than die rich. *American*

10703. Better to live well than long. *American*

10704. Birth is the messenger of death. *Arabic*

10705. Blessed be nothing. ["Expresses the transcendentalism of common life"—Emerson.] *American (Emerson)*

10706. Breathing is not living. *American*

10707. Choose the best life, habit will make it pleasant. *Greek*

10708. Day by day passes until the last stands behind the door. *Bosnian*

10709. Don't live on the borrowed opinions of other men. *American*

10710. Each day that fate adds to your life, put down as so much gain. *Latin (Horace)*

10711. For men on earth 'tis best never to be born at all. *Greek (Homer)*

10712. Good or bad, we must all live. *Italian*

10713. He does not live more who lives longer. *Russian*

10714. He is master of another's life who slights his own. *Italian*

10715. He is not worthy of life that causes not life in another. *Latin*

10716. He that will have no trouble in this world must not be born in it. *English*

10717. He who lives a long life must pass through much evil. *Spanish*

10718. He who lives for no one does not necessarily live for himself. *Latin*

10719. I wept when I was born, and every day shows why. *English*

10720. It is a misery to be born, a punishment to live, and a trouble to die. *Latin*

10721. It is better to live well than to live long. *American*

10722. It is easy to live—hard to die. *Yiddish*

10723. It is good for us to be here. *Bible*

10724. It is not life unless you are at ease. *French*

10725. Let us live then and be glad, / While young life's before us. *Latin*

10726. Life ain't all beer and skittles. *American (Sam Slick)*

10727. Life can only be understood backwards; but it must be lived forwards. *Danish (Kierkegaard)*

10728. Life holds more disappointment than satisfaction. *Greek*

10729. Life is a fortress unknown to all of us. *French*

10730. Life is a game played with marked cards. *American*

10731. Life is a kind of sleep: old men sleep longest. *French*

10732. Life is but a dewdrop on the lotus leaf. *Indian (Tagore)*

10733. Life is downhill, not uphill. *Russian*

10734. Life is given to us to be used. *Latin*

10735. Life is half spent before one knows what life is. *French*

10736. Life is just one damned thing after another. *American*

10737. Life is like an onion, which one peels crying. *French*

10738. Life is like the moon; now dark, now full. *Polish*

10739. Life is long if it is full. *Latin*

10740. Life is more like wrestling than dancing. *Greek (Marcus Aurelius)*

10741. Life is nearer every day to death. *Latin*

10742. Life is short and full of blisters. *American*

10743. Life is short, but its ills make it seem long. *Latin (Publilius Syrus)*

10744. Life is short to the fortunate, long to the unfortunate. *Greek (Homer)*

10745. Life is subject to ups and downs. *American*

10746. Life is sweet. *Greek*

10747. Life is the greatest bargain; we get it for nothing. *Yiddish*

10748. Life is too short to waste time on trifles. *American*

10749. Life lieth not in living, but in liking. *English*
10750. Live and learn. *Italian*
10751. Live and let live. *German*
10752. Live as if you were going to die tomorrow. *Latin*
10753. Live, not die. [Life is to be lived.] *Polish*
10754. Live righteously; you shall die righteously. *Latin*
10755. Live today, forget the past. *Greek*
10756. Live your own life, for you will die your own death. *Latin*
10757. Look at the end [of life]. *Greek*
10758. Man has been lent, not given, to life. *Latin*
10759. Man that is born of woman is of few days, and full of trouble. *Bible*
10760. Man's life is a sojourn in a strange land. *Latin*
10761. Man's life on earth is a warfare. *Bible*
10762. Men are sleeping, and when they die, they wake. *Koran*
10763. Most men employ the earlier part of life to make the other part miserable. *French*
10764. Nature has given man no better than shortness of life. *Latin*
10765. No one has died miserably who has lived well. *Latin*
10766. Not life itself, but living ill, is evil. *Greek*
10767. Nothing in life is certain for men, children of a day. *Greek*
10768. O Life! thou art a galling load, / Along a rough, a weary road. *Scottish (Burns)*
10769. Oh, life, how long to the wretched, how short to the happy! *Latin*
10770. One half of the world knows not how the other half lives. *French (Rabelais)*
10771. One wants to live and cannot; another can and will not. *Yiddish*
10772. Our days on the earth are as a shadow. *Bible*
10773. Praise day at night and life at end. *Greek*
10774. Quick with the quick, and dead with the dead. *Italian*
10775. Sadness and gladness succeed each other. *English*
10776. That long and cruel malady called life. *French*
10777. The days of our years are three-score and ten. *Bible*
10778. The dead to the grave and the living to the loaf. *Spanish*
10779. The hour which gives us life begins to take it away. *Latin*
10780. The life of man is a winter's day, and a winter's way. *English*
10781. The life of man is the plaything of Fortune. *Greek*
10782. The life of man, solitary, poor, nasty, brutish, and short. *English (Hobbes)*
10783. The lot of man: to suffer and to die. *Greek*
10784. The web of our life is of mingled yarn, good and ill together. *English (Shakespeare)*
10785. The world is a stage; each plays his part and receives his portion. *Dutch*
10786. The worst life is better than the best death. *Yiddish*
10787. There is ay life for a living man. *Scottish*
10788. They live ill who are always beginning to live. *Greek*
10789. They live ill who think they will live forever. *Latin*
10790. To live at ease is not to live. *Latin*
10791. To live is Christ, and to die is gain. *Bible*
10792. Today let me live well; none knows what may be tomorrow. *Greek*
10793. Tomorrow you will live? Today itself is too late; the wise lived yesterday. *Latin (Martial)*
10794. Until death it is all life. *Spanish (Cervantes)*
10795. We are always beginning to live, but are never living. *Latin*
10796. We are born crying, live complaining, and die disappointed. *English*
10797. We are born; we die. *Latin*
10798. We break up life into little bits and fritter them away. *Latin*
10799. We live, not as we wish, but as we can. *Greek*
10800. Wherever the human wretch goes there will be famine. *Hindi*
10801. While life lasts let us enjoy it. *Latin*
10802. Who lives will see. *French*
10803. You may laugh if you're a slave, you are dumb within the grave. *Bulgarian*

Light

10804. A lamp unto my feet, and a light unto my path. *Bible*
10805. And God said, Let there be light: and there was light. *Bible*
10806. Dry light is ever the best. *Greek*
10807. Every light is not the sun. *French*
10808. Light is sown for the righteous. *Bible*
10809. The light is nought for sore eyes. *English*
10810. To a diseased eye the light is annoying. *French*
10811. To light a lamp in the house is like the flowering of the lotus on the lake. *Kashmiri*
10812. Walk while ye have the light, lest darkness come upon you. *Bible*
10813. Where there is much light, the shadows are deepest. *German*

Lightning

10814. It is vain to look for a defense against lightning. *Latin*
10815. Lightning never strikes twice in the same place. *English*

Likeness *see* Affinity; Similarity

Limitations *see also* Handicaps

10816. A bull does not enjoy fame in two herds. *Rhodesian*
10817. A good marksman may miss. *English*
10818. A life without love, a year without summer. *Swedish*
10819. All keys hang not on one girdle. *English*
10820. Be sure to keep an eye out for what you can swallow—and also for what can swallow you. *Telugu*

10821. Cut your coat according to your cloth. *English*

10822. Everyone stretches his leg according to his coverlet. *Spanish*

10823. Fit your stocking to your foot. *French*

10824. He that may not as he wad [would], maun do as he may. *Scottish*

10825. He would fain fly but he wants feathers. *English*

10826. If thou hast not a capon, feed on an onion. *English*

10827. If we cannot do what we want, we must do what we can. *Latin (Terence)*

10828. If you cannot drive an ox, drive a donkey. *Latin*

10829. Let him play the second fiddle who can't play the first. *Latin (Cicero)*

10830. Let him sing to the flute, who cannot sing to the harp. *Latin (Cicero)*

10831. Men cease to interest us when we find their limitations. *American*

10832. No living man all things can. *English*

10833. No man can climb out beyond the limitations of his own character. *American*

10834. No man can do nothing and no man can do everything. *German*

10835. No man is capable of undertaking all things. *English*

10836. One can only do so much. *American*

10837. One who cannot pick up an ant and wants to pick up an elephant will someday see his folly. *Jabo*

10838. Souters [cobblers] shouldna gae ayont [beyond] their last. *Scottish*

10839. Stretch your arm no farther than your sleeve. *English*

10840. Stretch your legs according to your coverlet. *English*

10841. The dog has four paws, but it is not able to go four different ways. *Martinique Creole*

10842. The frog enjoys itself in water, but not in hot water. *African*

10843. Trees don't grow into the skies. *American*

10844. We cannot all of us do everything. *Latin*

10845. We commonly think that we can do no more than we are able. *Latin (Seneca)*

10846. We must draw the line somewhere. *English*

10847. Who cannot play should not touch the instrument. *Dutch*

Listening *see also* Advice; Alertness; Eavesdropping; Hearing; Heedlessness

10848. A man of sense talks little and listens much. *American*

10849. A pair of good ears will drink dry an hundred tongues. *American (Franklin)*

10850. Ears-hard [i.e., unwilling to listen], children go to market twice. *Belizean Creole*

10851. From listening comes wisdom, and from speaking repentance. *Italian*

10852. He that speaks, sows; he that hears, reaps. *English*

10853. Listeners hear no good of themselves. *English*

10854. The wisest person is the one who listens. Gĩkũyũ

10855. To listen well is a second inheritance. *Latin (Publilius Syrus)*

Literalness

10856. The verse will halt if the tongue's too true. *Burmese*

Loneliness *see also* Isolation

10857. The four corners of the room are the guests of the lonely man. *Russian*

10858. The lonely man is at home everywhere. *Russian*

Long Life *see* Longevity

Longevity

10859. As lang lives the merry man as the sad. *Scottish*

10860. As long lives a merry heart as a sad. *English*

10861. As long lives the merry man as the wretch for all the craft he can. *Scottish*

10862. He liveth long that liveth well. *American*

10863. Long life has long misery. *American*

10864. Medicine can prolong life, but death will seize the doctor, too. *American*

10865. Of the five happinesses, long life is the greatest. *Chinese*

10866. The longer we live the more strange sights we see. *Scottish*

10867. They seldom live well who think they shall live long. *English*

10868. They that live longest must go farthest for wood. *English*

10869. Three things contribute to a long life: A large house, an obedient wife and a swift horse. *Arabic*

10870. To go slowly and to live a long time are two brothers. *Dutch*

10871. We ought not care for living a long life, but for living a sufficient life. *Latin (Seneca)*

10872. Who lives long knows what pain is. *French*

10873. Who lives longest sees much evil. *Spanish*

Loopholes *see also* Injustice; Law

10874. Every law has a loophole. *Scottish*

10875. There is no law without a loophole for him who can find it. *German*

Loquaciousness *see also* Brevity; Conversation; Silence; Speaking

10876. A fool uttereth all his mind. *Bible*

10877. A fool's voice is known by a multitude of words. *English*

10878. A greater chatterbox than a raven. *Latin*

10879. A talkative fellow is like an unbraced drum: he beats a wise man out of his wits. *American*

10880. Asses that bray most eat least. *English*

10881. Blab is not cheer; froth is not beer. *American*

10882. Every time he opens his mouth he puts his foot in it. *American*

10883. Folks who have little business are very great talkers. *French*

10884. Great talkers are like leaky pitchers; everything runs out of them. *American*

10885. He that is a blab is a scab. *English*

10886. In chatter a river, in understanding but a single drop. *Latin*

10887. In many words, the truth goes by. *American*

10888. Many speak much who cannot speak well. *American*

10889. Much speaking and lying are cousins. *German*

10890. Much talk will produce errors. *Burmese*

10891. No fool can be silent at a feast. *American*

10892. The loquacity of fools is a lecture to the wise. *American*

10893. The shallowest persons are the most loquacious. *American*

10894. There are braying men in the world as well as braying asses. *American*

10895. They talk most who have the least to say. *American*

10896. Too much scratching pains, too much talking plagues. *French*

Loss *see also* **Defeat; Mourning; Surrender**

10897. A little loss frightens, a great one tames. *Spanish*

10898. A loss of which we are ignorant is no loss. *Latin (Publilius Syrus)*

10899. A man suffers death himself as often as he loses those dear to him. *Latin (Publilius Syrus)*

10900. A man who marries twice is a two-time loser. *American*

10901. A's tint that's put into a riven dish. [All's lost that's put into a broken dish.] *Scottish*

10902. After one loss come many. *French*

10903. Better lose the anchor than the whole ship. *Dutch*

10904. Better lose the saddle than the horse. *Italian*

10905. Fear not the loss of the bell more than the loss of the steeple. *American*

10906. For a tint [lost] thing care na [not]. *Scottish*

10907. Greedy folks are hard losers. *American*

10908. He ne'er tint [lost] a cow that grat [wept] for a groat. *Scottish*

10909. If you have not lost a thing, you have it. *Greek*

10910. If you have nothing, you lose nothing. *American*

10911. Ignorant men / Don't know what good they hold in their hands until / They've flung it away. *Greek (Sophocles)*

10912. Let us not throw the rope after the bucket. *Spanish*

10913. Lose a leg rather than your life. *American*

10914. Lose an hour in the morning and you'll be all day hunting for it. *English*

10915. Lost happiness never returns. *American*

10916. Never grieve over spilt milk. *English*

10917. No weeping for shed milk. *English*

10918. Nothing stings us so bitterly as the loss of money. *Latin (Livy)*

10919. One day unfolds it and one day destroys it. *Latin (Ausonius)*

10920. Praising what is lost makes the remembrance dear. *English (Shakespeare)*

10921. Quick come, quick go. *English*

10922. Seek not the rose which is once lost. *Latin*

10923. That which is worth taking is worth returning. *American*

10924. The ass does not know the value of his tail till he has lost it. *Italian*

10925. The cow that was stolen used to give four pails of milk. *Hungarian*

10926. The fish that got away always seems bigger. *Korean*

10927. The knife that was lost had a golden haft. *Uzbek*

10928. The loss which is unknown is no loss at all. *Latin*

10929. The shepherd would rather lose the wool than the sheep. *American*

10930. The time ye're pu'in' [pulling] runts ye're no setting kail. *Scottish*

10931. The water spilled from a tray never returns to it. *American*

10932. To fear the loss of the bell more than the loss of the steeple. *English*

10933. Trivial losses often prove great gains. *Latin (Ovid)*

10934. We always return to our first loves. *American*

10935. We do not care about what we have, but we cry when it is lost. *Russian*

10936. We do not know what is good until we have lost it. *Spanish (Cervantes)*

10937. We don't know a good thing till we've lost it. *French*

10938. We learn the value of things more in their loss than in their enjoyment. *Latin*

10939. We ne'er ken [know] the worth o' water till the well gae [goes] dry. *Scottish*

10940. We only appreciate the comforts of life in their loss. *Latin (Plautus)*

10941. What is lost in the fire must be sought in the ashes. *Dutch*

10942. When the wolf is slain the lambs do not mourn their loss. *American*

10943. Wine poured out is not wine swallowed. *French*

10944. You never miss the water till the well runs dry. *American*

Love *see also* **Absence; Love and Blindness; Love and Duration; Love and Envy; Love and Friendship; Love and Hate; Love and Jealousy; Love Concealed; Love, Renewal of; Lovers' Quarrels**

10945. A credulous thing is love. *Latin (Ovid)*

10946. A fence between makes love more keen. *German*

10947. A life without love, a year without summer. *Swedish*

10948. A lover should be regarded as a person demented. *Latin*

10949. A pennyweight o' love is worth a pound o' law. *English*

10950. A tocher's [dowry's] nae word in a true lover's parle. *Scottish*

10951. All love is vanquished by a succeeding love. *Latin*

10952. As the cat loves mustard. *English*

10953. As the devil loves holy-water. *English*

10954. As the wolf loves the lamb. *Latin*

10955. Be mine; I will be thine. *Latin*

10956. Better a dinner of herbs where love is, than a stalled ox and hatred therewith. *Bible*

10957. But one always returns to his first love. *French*

10958. By beating love decays. *French*

10959. Can a mouse fall in love with a cat? *English*

10960. Cauld [cold] grows the love that kindles ower het [hot]. *Scottish*

10961. Change everything except your loves. *French (Voltaire)*

10962. Delicacy is to love what grace is to beauty. *French*

10963. Dogs, birds, arms, and loves, for one pleasure a thousand pains. *French*

10964. Dry bread is better with love than fried chicken with fear and trembling. *American*

10965. Even Jupiter himself cannot be in love and wise at the same time. *Latin*

10966. Everybody loves a lover. *American*

10967. Fair chieve [comes] all where love trucks [bargains]. *English*

10968. Fanned fires and forced love ne'er did weel. *Scottish*

10969. Follow love and it will flee; flee love and it will follow thee. *English*

10970. For what may we lovers not hope. *Latin (Virgil)*

10971. Forced love does not last. *English*

10972. Forced love, like fanned fire, will never whet your desire. *American*

10973. Gray and green made the worst medley. *English*

10974. Habit causes love. *Latin*

10975. He loves bacon well that licks the swine-sty door. *English*

10976. He loves mutton well that eats the wool. *English*

10977. He loves roast meat well that licks the spit. *English*

10978. He who falls in love meets a worse fate than he who leaps from a rock. *Latin*

10979. He who has love in his heart has spurs in his sides. *Italian*

10980. He who loves well never forgets. *Irish*

10981. He's a fool that's fond. *English*

10982. How wretched is the man who loves! *Latin*

10983. Hunting, hawking, paramours, for ane [one] joy a hundred displeasures. *Scottish*

10984. I cannot get on with you, or without you. *Latin*

10985. If she was my wife I wad mak a queen o' her. *Scottish*

10986. If you are in love, fly to the mountain. *Turkish*

10987. In love, pain and pleasure are at strife. *Latin*

10988. In the spring a young man's fancy lightly turns to thoughts of love. *English (Tennyson)*

10989. In their first passions, women love the lover, and in the others they love love. *French (La Rochefoucauld)*

10990. In time comes she [or he] whom God sends. *English*

10991. Insidious love glides into defenseless breasts. *Latin*

10992. It is hard to keep flax from the lowe [fire]. *Scottish*

10993. It is not reason that governs love. *French*

10994. It's as difficult to win love as to wrap salt in pine-needles. *American*

10995. It's love that makes the world go 'round. *French*

10996. Knowledge and love together agree not. *Italian*

10997. Let every lover be pale; that is the color that suits him. *Latin*

10998. Let him not be a lover who has no courage. *Italian*

10999. Let no man think he is loved by any when he loves none. *Greek*

11000. Listlessness and silence denote the lover. *Latin*

11001. Love a thing aye [always] full of busy dread. *English (Chaucer)*

11002. Love abounds in honey and poison. *Latin*

11003. Love and dignity do not dwell together. *Latin (Ovid)*

11004. Love and lairdship like nae marrows [no rivals]. *Scottish*

11005. Love and lordship hate companions. *American (Franklin)*

11006. Love asks faith, and faith asks firmness. *Italian*

11007. Love begets love. *Latin*

11008. Love begets love as confidence begets confidence. *American*

11009. Love begins with love. *French*

11010. Love can make any place agreeable. *Arabic*

11011. Love cannot be bought or sold; its only price is love. *English*

11012. Love comes in at the windows and goes out at the doors. *English*

11013. Love conquers all things. *Latin (Virgil)*

11014. Love demands faith, and faith steadfastness. *Latin*

11015. Love does much, money does all. *French*

11016. Love does not depend upon our will. *French*

11017. Love doesn't do for age. *German*

11018. Love enters man through his eyes, woman through her ears. *Polish*

11019. Love fears no danger. *German*

11020. Love finds an altar for forbidden fires. *English (Pope)*

11021. Love grows with obstacles. *English*

11022. Love has na [not] luck. *Scottish*

11023. Love has nae [no] law. *Scottish*

11024. Love is a credulous thing. *Latin*

11025. Love is a kind of warfare. *Latin*

11026. Love is an egoism of two. *French*

11027. Love is an excuse for its own faults. *Italian*

11028. Love is as warm amang cottars [among cottagers] as courtiers. *Scottish*
11029. Love is commenced at the mind's bidding, but is not cast off by it. *Latin (Publilius Syrus)*
11030. Love is faithless. *Latin*
11031. Love is he that alle thing may bind. *English (Chaucer)*
11032. Love is like a shuttlecock. *Latin*
11033. Love is master of all arts. *Italian*
11034. Love is of sae mickle [so much] might, / That it all paines makis light. *Scottish (Barbour)*
11035. Love is smoke raised with the fume of sighs. *English (Shakespeare)*
11036. Love is strong as death. *Bible*
11037. Love is stronger than death. *French*
11038. Love is the child of illusion, and the parent of disillusion. *Spanish (Unamuno)*
11039. Love is the fruit of love. *Latin*
11040. Love is the fulfilling of the law. *Bible*
11041. Love is the maker of suspicions. *Italian*
11042. Love is the same in all people. *Latin (Virgil)*
11043. Love is the touchstone of virtue. *French*
11044. Love is the very price at which love is to be bought. *Italian*
11045. Love is too young to know what conscience is. *English (Shakespeare)*
11046. Love is very fruitful both of honey and gall. *Latin (Plautus)*
11047. Love keeps his revels where there are but twain. *English (Shakespeare)*
11048. Love knows no measure. *Italian*
11049. Love knows no obstacles and grows with them. *American*
11050. Love knows not labor. *Italian*
11051. Love lessens woman's delicacy and increases man's. *German (Richter)*
11052. Love levels all men down — and up — to the human. *American*
11053. Love lives in cottages as well as in courts. *English*
11054. Love made the world. *Latin*
11055. Love makes all equal. *Italian*
11056. Love makes clever hands. *Scottish*
11057. Love makes passion, but money makes marriage. *French*
11058. Love must be fostered with soft words. *Latin*
11059. Love often gets the better of reason. *French*
11060. Love, resistless in battle. *Greek*
11061. Love rules his kingdom without a sword. *Italian*
11062. Love rules without law. *Italian*
11063. Love subdues all but the ruffian's heart. *French*
11064. Love teaches asses to dance. *French*
11065. Love that is forced does not last. *Dutch*
11066. Love warms more than a thousand fires. *Italian*
11067. Love without return is like a question without an answer. *English*
11068. Love your friend and look to yoursel. *Scottish*
11069. Love's anger is fuel to love. *German*
11070. Lover, lunatic. *Latin*
11071. Lovers derive their pleasures from their misfortunes. *Greek*
11072. Lovers live by love as larks by leeks. *English*
11073. Lovers remember all things. *Latin (Ovid)*
11074. Lovers' oaths enter not the ears of the gods. *Greek*
11075. Man is fire, woman tow, and the devil comes and blows. *Spanish*
11076. Man loves only once. *German*
11077. Man's love is of man's life a thing apart, / 'Tis woman's whole existence. *English (Byron)*
11078. Many waters cannot quench love, neither can the floods drown it. *Bible*
11079. May and December never agree. *English*
11080. Men have died from time to time, and worms have eaten them, but not for love. *English (Shakespeare)*
11081. Nae [no] curb will tame love. *Scottish*
11082. Never seemed a prison fair or a mistress foul. *French*
11083. No folly to being in love. *Welsh*
11084. No love without bread and wine. *French*
11085. Old love does not rust. *German*
11086. Old love is little worth when new is more preferred. *English (Spenser)*
11087. One can't choose when one is going to love. *Norwegian*
11088. Only a wise man knows how to love. *Latin*
11089. Pains of love be sweeter far / Than all other pleasures are. *English (Dryden)*
11090. She's a drap o' my dearest blude. *Scottish*
11091. Slighted love is sair to bide [painful to endure]. *Scottish*
11092. Speak low, if you speak love. *English (Shakespeare)*
11093. Spice a dish with love, and it pleases every palate. *Latin*
11094. The course of true love did never run smooth. *English (Shakespeare)*
11095. The less my hope, the hotter my love. *Latin*
11096. The lover's soul dwells in the body of another. *Latin*
11097. The man who loves is easy of belief. *Latin*
11098. The pleasures of love are enhanced by injuries. *Latin*
11099. The sight of lovers feedeth those in love. *English (Shakespeare)*
11100. The woman we love will always be in the right. *French*
11101. There are as many pangs in love as shells upon the shore. *Latin*
11102. There are many who would never have been in love, if they had never heard love spoken of. *French (La Rochefoucauld)*
11103. There is love for none except him whom fortune favors. *Latin*
11104. There is no fear in love; but perfect love casteth out fear. *Bible*
11105. There is no living in love without suffering. *Latin*
11106. They love too much that die for love. *English*

11107. They that lie doun [fall sick] for love should rise up for hunger. *Scottish*

11108. They who love most are least set by. *English*

11109. Thy love to me was wonderful, passing the love of women. *Bible*

11110. 'Tis better to have loved and lost / Than never to have loved at all. *English (Tennyson)*

11111. 'Tis impossible to love and be wise. *English*

11112. 'Tis unseemly for the old man to love. *Latin*

11113. To be able to say how much you love is to love but little. *Italian*

11114. To be loved, be lovable. *Latin (Ovid)*

11115. To love and be wise is scarcely given to a god. *Latin*

11116. To love and to be wise is impossible. *Spanish*

11117. To love as the cat loves mustard. *English*

11118. To love is a pleasure of youth, a sin in old age. *Latin*

11119. To love is to choose. *French*

11120. True love is aye blate [always bashful]. *Scottish*

11121. True love is the ripe fruit of a lifetime. *French (Lamartine)*

11122. True love kythes [appears] in time o' need. *Scottish*

11123. True love never grows hoary [or gray]. *Italian*

11124. True love's the waft o' love, but it whiles comes through a sorrowfu' shuttle. *Scottish*

11125. Two souls in one, two hearts into one heart. *Latin*

11126. Venus lends deaf ears to love's deceits. *Latin*

11127. We learn only from those we love. *German (Goethe)*

11128. What is there that love will not achieve? *Latin*

11129. What limit is there in love? *Latin*

11130. Whatsoever love commands, it is not safe to despise. *Latin*

11131. When love cools, our faults are seen. *Scottish*

11132. When love is satisfied all charm is gone. *French*

11133. When misfortune enters the house, love flies out. *German*

11134. When we love, it is the heart that judges. *French*

11135. Where love is the case, / The doctor's an ass. *English*

11136. Where love is, there is the eye. *Italian*

11137. Where the love is, thither turns the eye. *Latin*

11138. Who can deceive a lover? *Latin*

11139. Who can give law to lovers? *Latin*

11140. Who loves believes, who loves fears. *Italian*

11141. Who loves Jack loves his dog. *French*

11142. Who would be loved must love. *Italian*

11143. Whom we love best to them we can say least. *English*

11144. With all thy faults, I love thee still. *English (Cowper)*

11145. Without bread and wine, Venus will starve. *Latin*

11146. Without Ceres and Bacchus, Venus freezes. *Latin*

11147. Without love, without sense. *Welsh*

11148. Ye're bonny enough to them that loe [love] ye, and ower bonny to them that loe ye and canna get ye. *Scottish*

11149. You must anger a lover if you wish him to love. *Latin*

Love and Blindness

11150. Blind are the eyes of love. *Egyptian*

11151. Blind love mistakes a harelip for a dimple. *American*

11152. Everyone is blind when maddened by love. *Latin*

11153. He who loves a one-eyed girl thinks that one-eyed girls are beautiful. *Latin*

11154. He, whose mistress squints, says she ogles. *English*

11155. If a man falls in love with a frog, he thinks his frog a very Diana. *Latin*

11156. Love can beauties spy / In what seem faults to every common eye. *English (Gay)*

11157. Love has nae [no] lack, be the dame e'er sae [so] black. *Scottish*

11158. Love is blind all day and may not see. *English (Chaucer)*

11159. Love is blind but sees afar. *Italian*

11160. Nobody's sweetheart is ugly. *Dutch*

11161. One's sweetheart is never ugly. *French*

11162. People in love think that other people's eyes are out. *Spanish*

11163. The lover's eye sees a Hsi Shih [the embodiment of loveliness in *Chinese* tradition]. *Chinese*

11164. Where love fails we espy all faults. *English*

11165. Who can blind a lover's eyes? *Latin (Virgil)*

Love and Duration

11166. He is not a lover who does not love forever. *Greek*

11167. It's gane [gone], the thing I lo'ed you for. *Scottish*

11168. Love kills happiness; happiness kills love. *Spanish*

11169. Love makes time pass; time makes love pass. *French*

11170. Love never dies of starvation, but often of indigestion. *French*

11171. Luve me lightly, luve me lang [long]. *Scottish*

11172. There is no such thing as eternal love. *French*

Love and Envy

11173. Love speaks nae [no] ill; envy thinks nae gude [no good]. *Scottish*

Love and Friendship

11174. A friend always loves, but he who loves is not always a friend. *Latin (Seneca)*

11175. Friendship is a prodigal, but love is a miser. *French*

11176. Friendship is ever serviceable; love at times is also hurtful. *Latin (Seneca)*

11177. Love and friendship exclude each other. *French*

11178. Most friendship is feigning, most loving mere folly. *English (Shakespeare)*

Love and Hate *see also* Hate; Love

11179. A woman either loves or hates; there is no third course. *Latin*

11180. Hatred stirreth up strife: but love covereth all sins. *Bible*

11181. He loves me for a little that hates me for nought. *Scottish*

11182. If God gives reason to hate, he also gives reason to love. *Wolof*

11183. Love and hate are blood relations. *German*

11184. Love takes hearts by storm, hatred by a long siege. *Russian*

11185. People love without reason, and without reason they hate. *French (Regnard)*

11186. The greatest hate springs from the greatest love. *American*

11187. Who love too much, hate in the same extreme. *Greek*

Love and Jealousy

11188. A loving man, a jealous man. *Italian*

11189. A loving man, a jealous woman. *Italian*

11190. It is better to have a husband without love than with jealousy. *Italian*

11191. Love and jealousy are sindle sindry [seldom separated]. *Scottish*

11192. Love being jealous makes a good eye look asquint. *English*

11193. Love expels jealousy. *French*

11194. Love gives for guerdon jealousy and broken faith. *Italian*

11195. Love is never without jealousy. *Latin*

11196. Love is the maker of suspicions. *Italian*

11197. Where there is no jealousy there is no love. *German*

Love at First Sight

11198. To see her is to love her. *English*

11199. Who ever lov'd, that lov'd not at first sight? *English (Marlowe)*

Love Concealed

11200. If ye loe [love] me let it kythe [be seen]. *Scottish*

11201. Love, a cough, and gall cannot be hid. *French*

11202. Love, a cough, and the itch cannot be hid. *Italian*

11203. Love, a cough, the itch, and the stomach cannot be hid. *Venetian*

11204. Love and a red rose can't be hid. *English (Holcroft)*

11205. Love and a sneeze cannot be hid. *English*

11206. Love and light winna hide. *Scottish*

11207. Love and murder will out. *English (Congreve)*

11208. Love and poverty are hard to hide. *English*

11209. Love and smoke cannot be hid. *French*

11210. Love knows hidden paths. *German*

11211. Love, smoke and a cough cannot be hid. *French*

11212. Nature and love cannot be hid. *English*

11213. Poverty and love are hard to hide. *Danish*

11214. Though ye tether time and tide, love and light ye canna hide. *Scottish*

11215. True love endures no concealment. *Spanish*

11216. Two things a man cannot hide: that he is drunk, and that he is in love. *Greek*

Love, Renewal of

11217. Cold broth hot again, that loved I never; / Old love renew'd again, that loved I ever. *English*

11218. For nothing grows again more easily than love. *Latin (Seneca)*

11219. Old loves and old brands kindle at all seasons. *French*

11220. Old pottage is sooner heated than new made. *English*

11221. One always returns to one's first love. *French*

11222. The falling out of lovers is the renewal of love. *Latin*

Lovers' Quarrels *see also* Love, Renewal of

11223. A lover's quarrel is short-lived. *Greek*

11224. By biting and scratching cats and dogs come together. *English*

11225. Love's quarrels oft in pleasing concord end. *English*

11226. Quarrels enhance the pleasures of love. *Latin*

11227. The quarrels of lovers lead but to the renewal of love. *Latin (Terence)*

11228. Those who like each other peck at each other. *Polish*

Loyalty *see also* Divided Loyalty

11229. Loyalty is the holiest good in the human heart. *Latin*

11230. Loyalty is worth more than money. *French*

11231. The best way to keep loyalty in a man's heart is to keep money in his purse. *Irish*

11232. The dog bites not his master. *Osmanli*

Luck *see also* Fortune; Misfortune

11233. A grain of good luck is better than an ass-load of skill. *Persian*

11234. A handful of luck is better than a sackful of wisdom. *German*

11235. A little wit ser's [serves] a lucky man. *Scottish*

11236. A lucky dog is rarer than a white crow. *Latin*

11237. A lucky man needs little counsel. *Scottish*

11238. A man does not seek his luck; luck seeks its man. *Turkish*

11239. A meeting in the sunlight is lucky and a burying in the rain. *Irish*

11240. A unlucky man's cart is eithly coup'd. *Scottish*

11241. Against a lucky man even a god has little power. *Latin (Publilius Syrus)*

11242. All is luck or ill-luck in this world. *American*

11243. An ounce of luck is better than a pound of wisdom. *English*

11244. An ounce of luck is worth a pound of wisdom. *French*

11245. An unlucky fish tak's bad bait. *Scottish*

11246. As for luck, wait in your bed. *Japanese*

11247. Bad luck, bad credit. *German*

11248. Bad luck often brings good luck. *German*

11249. Better an ounce of luck than a hundredweight of wisdom. *Polish*

11250. Better an ounce of luck than a pound of gold. *Polish*

11251. Better be born lucky than wise. *Italian*

11252. Better be lucky born than a rich man's son. *English*

11253. Better be the lucky man than the lucky man's son. *Scottish*

11254. Do not be born good or handsome, but be born lucky. *Russian*

11255. Even the street dog has his lucky days. *Japanese*

11256. Fair eyes, unlucky hands. *Greek*

11257. For him who is lucky even the cock lays eggs. *Russian*

11258. For luck one does not need wisdom. *Yiddish*

11259. Give a man luck and throw him into the sea. *English*

11260. God is a father; luck, a stepfather. *Yiddish*

11261. God send you luck, my son, and little wit will serve your turn. *Spanish*

11262. Good luck comes by cuffing. *English*

11263. Good luck comes by elbowing. *Spanish*

11264. Good luck is better than early rising. *Irish*

11265. Good luck is not sold in the market. *Persian*

11266. Good luck lasts not forever. *Latin*

11267. Half an ounce of luck is better than a pound of sense. *German*

11268. He that has luck leads the bride to church. *Dutch*

11269. He that is afraid of bad luck, will never know good. *Russian*

11270. He that would have good luck in horses must kiss the parson's wife. *English*

11271. He who has bad luck hazards boldly. *Spanish*

11272. He who is lucky passes for a wise man. *Italian*

11273. He who is not lucky, let him not go a-fishing. *English*

11274. If an unlucky man becomes a cultivator, either his oxen die or there is a want of rain. *Hindi*

11275. If an unlucky person goes to the river he makes it smoke. *Persian*

11276. If it is to be luck, the bull may as well calve as the cow. *Danish*

11277. If luck comes to you, offer him a chair. *Yiddish*

11278. If luck comes, who comes not? If luck comes not, who comes? *Chinese*

11279. If luck is your way, your ox calves. *Yiddish*

11280. Ill luck comes by pounds and goes away by ounces. *Italian*

11281. Ill luck enters by arms full, and departs by inches. *Spanish*

11282. Ill luck is worse than found money. *English*

11283. In bad luck, hold out; in good luck, hold in. *German*

11284. It is better not to be born at all than to be born luckless. *Yiddish*

11285. It is better that luck seek the man than man seek luck. *Yiddish*

11286. It is better to be born lucky than rich. *English*

11287. It is lucky to see a wolf; it is also lucky not to see one. *Persian*

11288. It was my luck, my leddy, and I canna get by 't. *Scottish*

11289. It's best to let saut water tak its ain gate; luck never came o' crossing it. *Scottish*

11290. Labor without luck helps not. *German*

11291. Luck alone does not help a man, if the man does not help along. *Yiddish*

11292. Luck can never come of a half-drowned man or a half-hanged one. *Scottish*

11293. Luck comes and wisdom follows. *Polish*

11294. Luck follows the hopeful, ill luck the fearful. *German*

11295. Luck for the fools and chance for the ugly. *English*

11296. Luck gives many too much, but no one enough. *German*

11297. Luck has but a slender anchorage. *Danish*

11298. Luck has much for many but enough for no one. *Danish*

11299. Luck is better than a hundred marks. *Danish*

11300. Luck is for the few, death for the many. *German*

11301. Luck meets the fool but he seizes it not. *German*

11302. Luck never made a man wise. *Latin (Seneca)*

11303. Luck perhaps visits the fool, but does not sit down with him. *German*

11304. Luck seeks those who flee, and flees those who seek it. *German*

11305. Luck stops at the door and inquires whether prudence is within. *Danish*

11306. Luck will carry a man across the brook if he is not too lazy to leap. *Danish*

11307. Mair [more] by luck than gude [good] guiding. *Scottish*

11308. More unlucky than a dog in church. *Italian*

11309. My right eye itches; some good luck is near. *Greek*

11310. Ne'er luck when a priest is on board. *Scottish*

11311. Nothing seems worse to a man than his death, and yet it may be the height of his good luck. *Irish*

11312. The de'il's bairns [devil's children] hae aye [have always] their daddy's luck. *Scottish*

11313. The feet of mendicants drive away ill luck. *Persian*

11314. The gods delight in odd numbers. *Latin*

11315. The happy [lucky] man canna be harried. *Scottish*

11316. The honester man, the worse luck. *English*

11317. The lucky man waits for prosperity; the unlucky man gives a blind leap. *Irish*

11318. The lucky man's bitch litters pigs. *Spanish*

11319. The more knave, the better luck. *Danish*

11320. The worse knave, the better luck. *English*

11321. The worse service, the better luck. *Dutch*

11322. There is no one luckier than he who thinks himself so. *German*

11323. To a lucky man every land is a fatherland. *Latin*

11324. To have luck needs little wit. *Italian*

11325. What's worse than ill luck? *English*

11326. When good luck comes to thee, take it in. *Spanish*

11327. When ill luck falls asleep, let nobody wake her. *Spanish*

11328. When luck is wanting, diligence is useless. *Spanish*

11329. Who has luck needs no understanding. *German*

11330. Who has luck plays well with bad cards. *German*

11331. Who has luck warms himself without fire and grinds without wind or water. *German*

11332. Who has no ill luck grows tired of good. *Spanish*

11333. Without luck, it is better not to be born. *Yiddish*

11334. You can't seek Lady Luck; Lady Luck seeks you. *American*

Lust *see also* Passion(s)

11335. Lust is the oldest lion of them all. *Italian*

Lying and Stealing *see also* Forbidden Fruit; Stealing; Thieves

11336. He who lies, steals. *German*

11337. Lying and stealing live next door to each other. *American*

Madness

11338. As mad as a March hare. *English*

11339. Every madman thinks all other men mad. *Latin*

11340. Madness in great ones must not go unwatched. *English (Shakespeare)*

11341. The different sorts of madness are innumerable. *Arabic*

11342. Though this be madness, yet there is method in it. *English (Shakespeare)*

11343. We are all mad at some time or other. *Latin*

11344. Who then is sane? He who is not a fool. *Latin*

11345. Whom the gods would destroy they first make mad. *Greek*

11346. With the mad it is necessary to be mad. *Latin*

Maidens

11347. A maiden's heart is a dark forest. *Russian*

11348. A' are gude lasses, but where do a' the ill wives come frae? *Scottish*

11349. Auld [old] wives were aye gude [always good] maidens. *Scottish*

11350. Butter and burn trouts are kittle [difficult] meat for maidens. *Scottish*

11351. Cats and carlins [old women] sit in the sun, but fair maidens sit within. *Scottish*

11352. Fair maidens wear nae [no] purses. *Scottish*

11353. Glass and a maid are ever in danger. *Italian*

11354. He must have keen eyes that would know a maid at sight. *German*

11355. If a maid marries an old man, she becomes a young widow. *Yiddish*

11356. Judge a maid at the kneading trough and not in a dance. *Danish*

11357. Lasses are like lamb legs — they'll neither saut [salt] nor keep. *Scottish*

11358. Maidens should be meek until they be married. *Scottish*

11359. Maidens should be mild and meek, quick to hear, and slow to speak. *Scottish*

11360. Maidens should be mim [prim and proper] till they're married, and then they may burn kirks [churches]. *Scottish*

11361. Maidens want naething [nothing] but a man, and then they want a'thing [everything]. *Scottish*

11362. Maidens' tochers [dowreys] and ministers' stipends are aye [always] less than ca'd. *Scottish*

11363. Marry off a maid, or she'll marry herself off. *Yiddish*

11364. Mealy mou'd [mouthed] maidens stand lang [long] at the mill. *Scottish*

11365. The virtuous maid and the broken leg must stay at home. *Spanish*

11366. They rin [run] fast that deils [devils] and lasses drive. *Scottish*

11367. When maidens sue, men give like gods. *English (Shakespeare)*

11368. Ye're a maiden marrowless [without equal]. *Scottish*

Maintenance

11369. It is easier to build two chimneys than to keep one in fuel. *American (Franklin)*

11370. It is easier to build two chimneys than to maintain one. *English*

11371. It is easy to open a shop, but hard to keep it open. *Chinese*

11372. It's easier to big lums [build chimneys] than to keep them reeking [smoking]. *Scottish*

11373. Wise care keeps what it has gained. *German*

Makeshifts

11374. A good shift may serve long, but it will not serve ever. *English*

Malice

11375. Bear no malice. *Latin*

11376. He that keeps malice harbors a viper in his heart. *English*

11377. He who digs out malicious talk disturbs his own peace. *Latin*

11378. Malice bears down truth. *English (Shakespeare)*

11379. Malice drinks its own poison. *English*

11380. Malice feeds on the living. *Latin*

11381. Malice is ay mindfu'. *Scottish*

11382. Malice is blind. *Latin*

11383. Malice is cunning. *Latin*

11384. Malice tells what it sees, but not the causes. *Latin*

11385. More malice than matter. *English*

11386. The malevolent have hidden teeth. *Latin*

11387. The malice of one man quickly becomes the ill word of all. *Latin*

Man *see also* Man and God; People

11388. A man is not known till he comes to honor. *Dutch*

11389. A man is one who is faithful to his word. *Spanish*

11390. A man's a man for a' that. *Scottish (Burns)*

11391. A man's a man, though he hath but a hose on 's head. *English*

11392. A spectacle unto the earth, and to angels. *Bible*

11393. All men are bad, and in their badness reign. *English (Shakespeare)*

11394. Even though he's a pig, he's still a man. *Russian*

11395. Every man is as God made him — and often worse. *Spanish*

11396. Forget not that you are a man. *Latin*

11397. God made him, and therefore let him pass for a man. *English (Shakespeare)*

11398. He is a man who acts like a man. *Danish*

11399. Man carries his superiority inside, animals theirs outside. *Russian*

11400. Man has a wild beast within him. *German*

11401. Man is a little soul carrying around a corpse. *Greek*

11402. Man is a reasoning animal. *Latin*

11403. Man is dearer to the gods than he is to himself. *Latin*

11404. Man is the measure of all things. *Greek (Protagoras)*

11405. Man is the only animal that blushes. Or needs to. *American (Twain)*

11406. Man is to man a wolf. *Latin*

11407. Man to man is a god. *Greek*

11408. Man was made by the gods for them to try and play withal. *Greek*

11409. Man's inhumanity to man / Makes countless thousands mourn. *Scottish (Burns)*

11410. Men and beasts are all alike. *Chinese*

11411. Men are but children of a larger growth. *English (Dryden)*

11412. Most men are bad. *Greek*

11413. Nothing is more wretched or more proud than man. *Latin*

11414. The fool of fate — man. *Greek*

11415. The noble man is only God's image. *German*

11416. Though men are brothers their pockets are not sisters. *Turkish*

11417. Though men were made of one metal, yet they were not cast all in the same mould. *Scottish*

11418. We are dust and shadow. *Latin (Horace)*

11419. What dwarfs men are! *Latin*

Man and God *see also* God; Man

11420. Give to God what is God's; unto man, what is man's. *Yiddish*

11421. God guards the guarded [i.e., those who take care of themselves]. *Polish*

11422. God has given; God has taken away. *Yiddish*

11423. God is the guardian of a blind man's wife. *Hindi*

11424. God leads a man along the road he would go. *Yiddish*

11425. God ne'er measures men by inches. *Scottish*

11426. God often visits us, but most of the time we are not at home. *French*

11427. God send ye mair [more] sense and me mair siller [silver]. *Scottish*

11428. God send ye the warld ye bode, and that's neither scant nor want. *Scottish*

11429. God sends fools fortunes. *Scottish*

11430. God sends nothing but what can be borne. *Italian*

11431. God shapes the back for the burden. *Scottish*

11432. God will know His own. *French*

11433. Hae [have] God, hae a'[all]. *Scottish*

11434. He is poor that God hates. *Scottish*

11435. He is rich indeed whom God loves. *French*

11436. He who has known God reverences Him. *Latin*

11437. If God be with us, who shall stand against us? *Bible*

11438. If God lived on earth, men would break His windows. *Yiddish*

11439. Man doth what he can, and God what he will. *English*

11440. Man rides and God holds the reins. *Yiddish*

11441. Man shoots but God carries the bullet. *Polish*

11442. Most men forget God all day, and ask Him to remember them at night. *American*

11443. No one against God except God Himself. *Latin*

11444. That man is to be feared who fears not God. *Turkish*

11445. The fear of the Lord is the beginning of wisdom. *Bible*

11446. The servant of God has a good master. *French (Pascal)*

11447. They're weel guided that God guides. *Scottish*

11448. We are because God is. *Swedish (Swedenborg)*

11449. We are full of sins, and Thou O God art an ocean of mercy. *Persian*

11450. We do nothing without the leave of God. *Latin*

11451. We must obey God rather than men. *American*

11452. When it is God's will to plague a man, a mouse can bite him to death. *Dutch*

11453. While we meditate one thing, God determines another. *Hindi*

11454. Whom God loves he punishes. *Yiddish*

11455. Whom the Lord loveth He chasteneth. *Bible*

11456. Whom God will help nae man can hinder. *Scottish*

Man and Nature

11457. "Sail!" quoth the king; "Hold!" saith the wind. *English*

11458. Having seen animals alive, one cannot bear to see them die; having heard their dying cries, one cannot bear to eat their flesh. *Chinese (Mencius)*

11459. Wherever nature does least, man does most. *American*

Management *see also* Business and Commerce; Master and Man

11460. Good management is better than good income. *English*

11461. If you have money to throw away, set on workmen and don't stand by. *Italian*

11462. Not to oversee workmen, is to leave your purse open. *English*

11463. One cannot manage too many affairs: like pumpkins in the water, one pops up while you try to hold down the other. *Chinese*

11464. One eye of the master sees more than four of the servants. *English*

11465. That business does not prosper which you transact with the eyes of others. *Latin*

11466. The foot of the owner is the best manure for his land. *English*

Manners *see also* Civility; Courtesy; Golden Rule; Politeness

11467. A man without manners speaks perversely; an ox without strength drags the harrow crosswise. *Chinese*

11468. As are the times, so are the manners. *Spanish*

11469. As manseless [ill-mannered] as a tinkler's messan [mongrel dog]. *Scottish*

11470. Degenerate manners grow apace. *Latin*

11471. Don't shake hands too eagerly. *Greek*

11472. Everyone's manners make his fortune. *Latin*

11473. Good advice may be given, but not good manners. *Turkish*

11474. Good manners are made up of petty sacrifices. *American*

11475. He has nae mair mense [no more manners] than a miller's horse. *Scottish*

11476. If ye had as little money as ye had manners, ye would be the poorest man o' a' your kin. *Scottish*

11477. Manners are more than meat, and morals more than manners. *American*

11478. Manners make often fortunes. *English*

11479. Manners make the man. *American*

11480. Meat feeds, and claith cleeds [cloth clothes], but manners mak a man. *Scottish*

11481. Meat is gude [good], but mense [good manners] is better. *Scottish*

11482. Office changes manners. *Spanish*

11483. Other times, other manners. *French*

11484. Suit your manners to the man. *Latin*

11485. The man may be bad while his manners are not. *Chinese*

11486. The society of good women is the foundation of good manners. *German (Goethe)*

11487. Things which are unbecoming are unsafe. *Latin*

11488. Vulgarity of manners defiles fine garments more than mud. *Latin (Plautus)*

11489. What times! What manners! *Latin (Cicero)*

11490. Ye hae gude [have good] manners, but ye dinna [do not] bear them about wi' ye. *Scottish*

11491. You know good manners but you use but few. *English*

March

11492. A load of March dust is worth a ducat. *German*

11493. A dry March never begs its bread. *English*

Marriage *see also* Dowries; Faithfulness; Husbands and Wives; Marriage and Infidelity; Women's Advice; Women and Trustworthiness; Women's Work

11494. A dish o' married love right soon grows cauld [cold], and dosens [settles down, cools] down to nane as folk grow auld [old]. *Scottish*

11495. A handsome wife brings no fortune. *Spanish*

11496. A hawk's marriage: the hen is the better bird. *French*

11497. A house wi' a reek and a wife wi' a reerd [scolding noise] will sune mak a man run to the door. *Scottish*

11498. A kiss and a drink of water is a tasteless breakfast. *American*

11499. A maid marries to please her parents; a widow pleases herself. *Chinese*

11500. A man canna wive and thrive the same year. *Scottish*

11501. A man may woo where he will, but must wed where he's wierd [i.e., where he is fated to wed]. *Scottish*

11502. A man must ask his wife's leave to thrive. *English*

11503. A raggit coat was ne'er a mote in a man's marriage. *Scottish*

11504. A shotgun marriage won't last longer than the honeymoon. *American*

11505. A state of wedlock, a state of woe. *German*

11506. A wife's long tongue is the staircase by which misfortunes ascend to the house. *Chinese*

11507. A young man married is a young man marr'd. *English (Shakespeare)*

11508. Always say "no," and you will never be married. *French*

11509. An impudent face never marries. *German*

11510. And they two shall be one flesh. *Bible*

11511. As your wedding ring wears, so do your cares. *English*

11512. Before you marry, be sure of a house wherein to tarry. *Italian*

11513. Better be half hanged than ill-wed. *English*

11514. Better hand loose than an ill tethering. *Scottish*

11515. Bone of my bones, and flesh of my flesh. *Bible*

11516. Choose such a man as you can love. *Latin*

11517. Death and marriage break term-day. *Scottish*

11518. Don't praise marriage on the third day, but after the third year. *Russian*

11519. Early marriage, long love. *German*

11520. Either marry very young or turn monk very young. *Greek*

11521. Everyone sings as he has the gift, and marries as he has the luck. *Portuguese*

11522. For a wife and a horse go to your neighbor. *Italian*

11523. For a young man, not yet; for an old man, never at all. *Greek*

11524. Good wives and good plantations are made by good husbands. *American (Franklin)*

11525. Grief for a dead wife lasts to the door. *Italian*

11526. Hasty marriages seldom turn out well. *German*

11527. He got his mother's malison [curse] that day he was married. *Scottish*

11528. He has faut [fault] o' a wife that marries mam's pet. *Scottish*

11529. He that goes far to marry will deceive or be deceived. *Spanish*

11530. He that has a wife has strife. *French*

11531. He that loseth his wife and a farthing hath a great loss of his farthing. *Italian*

11532. He that marries a beggar eats muckle [much] dirt. *Scottish*

11533. He that marries a beggar gets a louse for a tocher [dowry]. *Scottish*

11534. He that marries a widow and two dochters [daughters] has three back doors to his house. *Scottish*

11535. He that marries before he's wise will dee [die] ere he thrive. *Scottish*

11536. He that marries for love has good nights and bad days. *French*

11537. He that marries for money earns it. *American*

11538. He that marries or [i.e., before] he be wise will die or [before] he thrive. *Scottish*

11539. He that takes a wife takes care. *American (Franklin)*

11540. He that will not be ruled by his own dame must be ruled by his step-dame. *English*

11541. He that will not hear motherhead shall bear step-motherhead. *English*

11542. He that's needy when he is married, shall be rich when he is buried. *English*

11543. He wha marries for love, without money, hath merry nights and sorry days. *Scottish*

11544. He who is about to marry is on his way to repentance. *Greek*

11545. He who marries a beauty marries trouble. *Yoruba*

11546. He who marries a widow will often have a dead man's head thrown in his dish. *Spanish*

11547. He who marries early makes no mistake. *Osmanli*

11548. He who marries early will leave a widow. *Osmanli*

11549. He who marries ill is long in becoming widowed. *Spanish*

11550. He who marrieth does well, but he who marrieth not, better. *English*

11551. He's a fool that marries at Yule; for when the bairn's to bear [the child is to be born] the corn's to shear. *Scottish*

11552. Honest men marry soon, wise men never. *English*

11553. Humble wedlock is better than proud virginity. *Latin (St. Augustine)*

11554. I do not want a shoe larger than my foot. [Don't marry above yourself.] *Babylonian Talmud*

11555. I had nae [no] mind I was married, my bridal was sae feckless. *Scottish*

11556. I never married and I wish my father never had. *Greek*

11557. If heaven wants to rain, or your mother marry again, nothing can prevent them. *Chinese*

11558. If marriages are made in heaven, you [or some] had few friends there. *English*

11559. If the hen crows instead of the cock, there will be no peace in the farmyard. *Japanese*

11560. If the hen does not prate, she will not lay. *East Anglian*

11561. If you marry a beautiful blonde, you marry trouble. *American*

11562. If you would wed fitly, wed in your station. *Latin*

11563. In buying a horse and taking a wife, shut your eyes and commend yourself to God. *Italian*

11564. In marriage and in death the devil contrives to play a role. *French*

11565. In the house where there are cobwebs the girls don't marry. *Spanish*

11566. In the rich woman's house she commands always, and he never. *Spanish*

11567. Is the gude [good] or ill choice o' a gude or ill wife. *Scottish*

11568. It goes ill with the house when the hen sings and the cock is silent. *Spanish*

11569. It is a sad house where the hen crows louder than the cock. *Italian*

11570. It is a shame to a man to be refused by a woman, left by a boat, or thrown by a mare. *Gaelic*

11571. It is a silly flock where the ewe bears the bell. *Scottish*

11572. It is better to marry than to burn. *Bible*

11573. It is easier to build two hearths than always to have a fire on one. *German*

11574. It is good to marry late or never. *English*

11575. It is hard to wive and thrive both in a year. *English*

11576. It is not beauty that bewitches bridegrooms but nobleness. *Greek*

11577. It's lang ere [long before] four bare legs gather heat in a bed. *Scottish*

11578. Keep your eyes wide open before marriage, half shut afterwards. *American (Franklin)*

11579. Let everyone marry an equal. *Spanish (Cervantes)*

11580. Let like mate with like. *Greek*

11581. Like blood, like good, and like age, make the happiest marriage. *English*

11582. Love is often a fruit of marriage. *French*

11583. Maids want nothing but husbands, but when they have them want everything. *English*

11584. Make haste when you are purchasing a field, but be slow in marrying. *Hebrew*

11585. Make your plans for the year at its beginning; correct your wife from the first day. *Japanese*

11586. Marriage and hanging gae [go] by destiny. *Scottish*

11587. Marriage is a covered dish. *Swiss*

11588. Marriage is a lottery in which men stake their liberty and women their happiness. *French*

11589. Marriage is an evil—but a necessary evil. *Greek*

11590. Marriage is heaven or [or and] hell. *German*

11591. Marriage is honorable in all. *Bible*

11592. Marriage is honourable, but housekeeping's a shrew. *English*

11593. Marriage is like a castle under siege — those within want to get out, those outside want to get in. *Arabic*

11594. Marriage is of three kinds — marriage for beauty, for convenience, and for money. *Arabic*

11595. Marriage is the worst punishment. *Russian*

11596. Marriage makes or mars a man. *Italian*

11597. Marriage, marriage, it sounds good but tastes bad. *Portuguese*

11598. Marriages are all happy; it's having breakfast together that causes all the trouble. *Irish*

11599. Marriages are made in heaven and completed [or consummated] on earth. *French*

11600. Marriages are made in heaven. *English*

11601. Marriages are not as they are made, but as they turn out. *Italian*

11602. Marriages are written in heaven. *French*

11603. Married folk are like rats in a trap — fain to get ithers in, but fain to be out themsels. *Scottish*

11604. Married in haste we may repent at leisure. *English (Congreve)*

11605. Marry a person in your own rank in life. *Latin*

11606. Marry a widow before she leave mourning. *English*

11607. Marry abune [above] your match and get a maister. *Scottish*

11608. Marry first and love will follow. *English*

11609. Marry for love and work for siller [silver]. *Scottish*

11610. Marry in haste and repent at leisure. *Greek*

11611. Marry in haste, repent at leisure. *Scottish (Scott)*

11612. Marry, in preference to all other women, one who dwells near thee. *Greek (Hesiod)*

11613. Marry late or never. *American*

11614. Marry, marry, and what about the housekeeping? *Portuguese*

11615. Marry over the mixon [dung hill], and you will know who and what she is. *German*

11616. Marry the daughter only after knowing the mother. *Hindi*

11617. Marrying early and getting up early are not regretted. *Zyryan*

11618. Men under forty are too young to marry, and if they're over forty they're too old. *American*

11619. Mind, not body, makes marriage lasting. *Latin*

11620. Mony [many] fair promises at the marriage making, but few at the tocher [dowry] paying. *Scottish*

11621. "Mother, what sort of a thing is marriage?" "Daughter, it is spinning, bearing children, and weeping." *Spanish*

11622. Nae [no] man can thrive unless his wife will let him. *Scottish*

11623. Ne'er marry a penniless maiden that's proud o' her pedigree. *Scottish*

11624. Ne'er seek a wife till ye hae [have] a house and a fire burning. *Scottish*

11625. Ne'er seek a wife till ye ken [know] what to do with her. *Scottish*

11626. No one marries but repents. *French*

11627. No pot so ugly as not to find a cover. *Italian*

11628. Observe the mother and take the daughter. *Turkish*

11629. One year of joy, another of comfort, and all the rest of content. *English*

11630. Pray for one hour before going to war, for two before going to sea, for three before going to be married. *Indian*

11631. She has given them green stockings. [She has married before her elder sisters, making them envious.] *Scottish*

11632. Take a wife's advice without asking for it. *Welsh*

11633. Take no woman for a wife in whom you cannot find a flaw. *Gaelic*

11634. The bacon of paradise for the married man that has not repented. *Spanish*

11635. The day you marry, you either kill yourself or save yourself. *Spanish*

11636. The first bond of society is marriage. *Latin*

11637. The good or ill hap of a good or ill life, is the good or ill choice of a good or ill wife. *American (Franklin)*

11638. The gray mare is the better horse. *English*

11639. The man who marries for money works hard for it. *Yiddish*

11640. The marriage ceremony takes only an hour, but its troubles last a lifetime. *Yiddish*

11641. The married are blessed, the single twice-blessed. *American*

11642. The married man must turn his staff into a stake. *English*

11643. The old man who is married bids death to the feast. *German*

11644. The wife is the keeper of her husband's conscience as well as his soul. *American*

11645. There are mair [more] married than gude [good] househauders. *Scottish*

11646. There are many fair words in the marriage making, but few in the portion paying. *Scottish*

11647. There as my heart is set, there will I wive. *English (Chaucer)*

11648. There is nothing worse always about the house than what a man is. *Welsh*

11649. There will be discord in the home if the distaff rules. *French*

11650. There'll be white blackbirds before an unwilling woman ties the knot. *Irish*

11651. There's but ae gude [one good] wife in the country, and ilka [each] man thinks he's got her. *Scottish*

11652. Therefore shall a man leave his father and mother, and shall cleave unto his wife. *Bible*

11653. Though women are angels, yet wedlock's the devil. *English (Byron)*

11654. Thrice ill-starred is he who marries when he is poor. *Greek*

11655. 'Tis time to yoke when the cart comes to the capples [horses]. *English*

11656. To marry once is a duty, twice a folly, thrice is madness. *Dutch*

11657. Waes [woe to] the wife that wants the tongue, but weel's the man that gets her. *Scottish*

11658. We wedded men live in sorrow and care. *English (Chaucer)*

11659. Wedding and ill wintering tame baith [both] man and beast. *Scottish*

11660. Weddings and magistracy are arranged by heaven. *Italian*

11661. Wedlock is a padlock. *English*

11662. Wedlock is like a place besieged; those within wish to get out, those without wish to get in. *Arabic*

11663. Wedlock rides in the saddle, and repentance on the croup. *French*

11664. What else goes wrong for a woman — except her marriage? *Greek (Euripides)*

11665. What therefore God hath joined together, let not man put asunder. *Bible*

11666. When an old man marries a young wife, he becomes young and she becomes old. *Yiddish*

11667. When the gudeman drinks to the gudewife, a' wad be weel; when the gudewife drinks to the gudeman, a's weel. *Scottish*

11668. Who marries a widow with three children marries four thieves. *Danish*

11669. Who marries between the sickle and scythe will never thrive. *English*

11670. Who marries changes [i.e., a man's bad habits will change after he is married]. *Polish*

11671. Who marries for love without money, hath good nights and sorry days. *Italian*

11672. Who weds ere he be wise, shall die ere he thrive. *English*

11673. "Why so flushed? I want to get married.— Why so pale? I am married." *Russian*

11674. Women when they marry buy a cat in a bag. *French*

11675. You have tied a knot with your tongue you cannot undo with your teeth. *English*

11676. You will live life more easily if you have not a wife to maintain. *Greek*

11677. You will marry and grow tame. *Spanish*

11678. Your wife and your nag get from a neighbor. *Italian*

Marriage and Infidelity *see also* Women and Trustworthiness

11679. A faithless wife is the shipwreck of a home. *Latin*

11680. He who can't do any better goes to bed with his wife. *Spanish*

11681. If a man is unfaithful to his wife, it's like spitting from a house into the street; but if a woman is unfaithful to her husband, it's like spitting from the street into the house. *American*

11682. If I had relied on you, O husband, we would never have had children. *Moroccan*

11683. If the wife sins, the husband is equally guilty. *American*

11684. In marriage cheat who can. *French*

11685. The chain of wedlock is so heavy that it takes three to carry it. *American*

11686. The cheating wife doubts the chastity of all women. *American*

11687. Where there's marriage without love, / there will be love without marriage. *American (Franklin)*

Martyrs and Martyrdom

11688. It is the cause, not the death, that makes the martyr. *French*

11689. When a man goes to a house knowing there is plague in it, he does not die a martyr. *Arabic*

11690. When genius is punished, its fame is exalted. *Latin (Tacitus)*

Master and Man *see also* Subordinates

11691. A gude greive [good overseer] is better than an ill worker. *Scottish*

11692. A lion does not cultivate; he hinders the cultivators. Akkadian

11693. As guid may houd the stirrup as he that loups on. *Scottish*

11694. Early maister, lang knave [i.e., servant]. *Scottish*

11695. Early master, soon knave. *Scottish*

11696. Every man has his master. *American*

11697. If all get into the palanquin, who will be the bearers? *Hindi*

11698. If I am master, and you are master, who will drive the asses? *Arabic*

11699. If I am the mistress and you are the young lady, who will sweep the house? *Spanish*

11700. If the abbot sings well the novice is not far behind him [or soon gets in harmony with him]. *Spanish (Cervantes)*

11701. If you are a lady, and I am a lady, who will put the sow out? *Spanish*

11702. If you eat his rice you must obey him. *Chinese*

11703. It is the blood of the soldier that makes the general [or captain] great. *Italian*

11704. It is the clerk that makes the justice. *English*

11705. It is the master that shames me, not the servitude. *Latin*

11706. Let no man be the servant of another, who can be his own master. *Latin*

11707. Masters, give unto your servants that which is just and equal. *Bible*

11708. We can't all be masters. *American*

Maturity *see also* Aging

11709. A ragged colt may make a good horse. *English*

11710. An unhappy lad may make a good man. *English*

11711. Early ripe, early rotten. *English*

11712. Strong meat belongeth to them that are of full age. *Bible*

11713. The most unruly students prove the most pious teachers. *German*

11714. There is no crop worse than fruit that never ripens. *American*

11715. To leave the nuts. [To put away childish things.] *Latin*

11716. When the pear is ripe, it falls. *American*

Meaning

11717. An old dog never yelps in vain. *French*

11718. It is time to look out when the old dog barks. *Latin*

11719. One ought to take heed of the bark of an old dog. *French*

Meanness

11720. Meanness is the parent of insolence. *American (Franklin)*

Means *see* **Cause and Effect; Ends and Means**

Measurement

11721. Don't measure other people's corn by your own bushel. *American*

11722. Don't measure yourself; it will make you die. *American*

11723. Measure yourself by your own foot. *Latin*

11724. When the measure is full it runs over. *American*

11725. You can't measure the whole world with your own yardstick. *Yiddish*

Meddling *see also* **Interference**

11726. A nose with three nostrils expels too much air. *Chinese*

11727. Dinna meddle wi' the deil and the laird's bairns. *Scottish*

11728. Dirty-nosed folk always want to wipe other folks' noses. *French*

11729. Don't scald your tongue in other people's broth. *English*

11730. Don't stick your nose where you've put no penny. *Polish*

11731. Don't taste every man's soup—you'll burn your mouth. *American*

11732. Every fool will be meddling. *Bible*

11733. Having no business of his own to attend to, he busies himself with the affairs of others. *Latin (Horace)*

11734. He has licket the butter aff my bread. *Scottish*

11735. He knows enough who knows how to mind his own business. *American*

11736. He that mindeth not his own business shall never be trusted with mine. *American*

11737. He who tastes every man's broth sometimes burns his mouth. *Danish*

11738. It's ill meddling between the bark and the rind. *Scottish*

11739. Let-a-be [let alone] for let-a-be. *Scottish*

11740. Let every man mind his own business. *Spanish*

11741. Little meddling maks fair pairting. *Scottish*

11742. Mind your own business. *English*

11743. Never thrust your sickle into another's corn. *Latin*

11744. O' little meddling comes muckle care. *Scottish*

11745. Put not your hand between the bark and the tree. *American*

11746. Sweep before your own door. *English*

11747. Sweep under your own mats. *German*

11748. Walk on your own lands. *English*

Medicine *see also* **Physicians; Remedies**

11749. By medicine life may be prolonged, yet death / Will seize the doctor, too. *English (Shakespeare)*

11750. By opposites opposites are cured. *Greek*

11751. It is medicine, not scenery, for which a sick man must go searching. *Latin (Seneca)*

11752. It is part of the cure to wish to be cured. *Latin*

11753. Meet the malady on its way. *Latin*

11754. No one tries desperate remedies at first. *Latin*

11755. Not even medicines can master incurable diseases. *Latin*

11756. Nothing hinders a cure so much as frequent change of medicine. *Latin*

11757. Starve the measles and nourish the smallpox. *Chinese*

11758. Strongest maladies need strongest remedies. *French*

Mediocrity

11759. Mediocrity is praised in all cases. *French*

11760. Mediocrity is safest. *Latin*

Meekness *see also* **Submission**

11761. Blessed are the meek: for they shall inherit the earth. *Bible*

11762. He that makes himself a sheep shall be eaten by the wolf. *American*

11763. He that makes himself dirt is trod on by the swine. *American*

11764. He who makes a mouse of himself will be eaten by the cats. *German*

11765. He who makes himself a dove is eaten by the hawk. *Italian*

11766. He who makes himself honey will be eaten by the bees. *American*

11767. Make thyself a sheep, and the wolf is ready. *Russian*

11768. Make yourself a lamb, and the wolf will eat you. *French*

11769. Make yourself an ass, and you'll have every man's sack on your back. *German*

11770. The gentle ewe is sucked by every lamb. *Italian*

11771. The meek are terrible in their wrath. *American*

11772. They can be meek that have no other cause. *English (Shakespeare)*

11773. Who lets one sit on his shoulders will soon have him sit on his head. *German*

Melancholy

11774. He is a fool that is not melancholy once a day. *English*

11775. Melancholy is the pleasure of being sad. *French*

11776. Melancholy men are the most witty. *Greek*

Memory *see also* **Remembering**

11777. A good memory is not equal to pale ink. *Chinese*

11778. How sweet to remember the trouble that is past! *Greek*

11779. Memory is a falcon, that, if it be caught, is not

held; affection is a sparrow's nest, that, if it be crushed, is not made. *Osmanli*

11780. Memory is the treasurer of the mind. *English*

11781. Memory is the treasury and guardian of all things. *Latin*

11782. Memory is the watchman of the brain. *American*

11783. Memory, like women, is usually unfaithful. *Spanish*

11784. No greater grief than to remember days / Of joy when misery is at hand. *Italian (Dante)*

11785. No man has a bad memory for pretty faces. *American*

11786. Our memory is always at fault, never our judgment. *American*

11787. Pleasant is the recollection of dangers past. *Latin (Cicero)*

11788. That which was bitter to endure may be sweet to remember. *English*

11789. The memory of a great love is kept green forever. *American*

11790. The memory of happiness makes misery woeful. *English*

11791. The remembrance of past pleasures adds to present sorrows. *Latin*

11792. This is truth the poet sings, / That a sorrow's crown of sorrows is remembering happier things. *English (Tennyson)*

11793. To be able to enjoy one's past life is to live twice. *Latin (Martial)*

11794. Twice does he live who can enjoy the remembrance of the past. *Latin (Ovid)*

11795. We may with advantage at times forget what we know. *Latin (Publilius Syrus)*

11796. What was hard to bear is sweet to remember. *Portuguese*

Men *see* Man; Man and God; People

Men and Women *see also* Courtship; Husbands and Wives; Wives: Choosing a Wife; Womanizing; Women

11797. A dog is wiser than a woman; he does not bark at his master. *Russian*

11798. A man of straw is worth a woman of gold. *English*

11799. A man should walk behind a lion rather than behind a woman. *Hebrew*

11800. A man's virtue is considered an endowment; a woman's want of endowment is considered a virtue. *Chinese*

11801. A woman is flax, man is fire, the devil comes and blows the bellows. *Italian*

11802. A woman's word is wind in the wind, a man's word is rock in the wall. *Moroccan*

11803. Adam must have Eve to blame for his faults. *Italian*

11804. All women can be caught; spread but your nets. *Latin*

11805. Change of women makes bald knaves. *English*

11806. Even if a woman's candlestick is cast in gold, still it is the man who must supply the candle. *Turkish*

11807. He suffers long who does a woman wrong. *Polish*

11808. He that does not love a woman sucked a cow. *Spanish*

11809. He who can avoid women, let him avoid them. *Latin (Plautus)*

11810. Man and woman, fire and chaff. *Latin*

11811. Man is of fire, woman of tow; the devil comes and blows. *French*

11812. Man is the head, but woman turns it. *American*

11813. Men make laws; women make manners. *French*

11814. No man is less than any woman. *Arabic*

11815. Obedience to women leads to Hell. *Tunisian*

11816. The devil can outwit one man; a woman can outwit ten. *Russian*

11817. The father to his desk, the mother to her dishes. *American*

11818. The proof of gold is fire; the proof of woman, gold; the proof of man, a woman. *American*

11819. Three kinds of men can't understand women: young men, old men, and middle-aged men. *American*

11820. Unmarried, a woman obeys her father; married, her husband. *Chinese*

11821. When a girl falls she always lands on her back. *Yiddish*

11822. When petticoats woo, breeks [trousers] come speed. *Scottish*

11823. When the hen gaes [goes] to the cock the birds may get a knock. *Scottish*

11824. When the man's fire, and the wife's tow, / In comes the deil [devil] and blaws it in a lowe [blaze]. *Scottish*

11825. When two agree in their desire, / One sparke will set them both on fire. *English (Quarles)*

11826. Who is the man that was never fooled by a woman? *German*

11827. Woman brings to man the greatest blessing and the greatest plague. *Greek*

11828. Woman is man's confusion. *Latin*

11829. Women and dogs set men together by the ears. *English*

11830. Women can accomplish all, because they rule the persons who govern all. *French*

Merchants *see* Business and Commerce

Mercy *see also* Forgiveness; Leniency

11831. Be merciful to those who show mercy. *American*

11832. Blessed are the merciful: for they shall obtain mercy. *Bible*

11833. Clemency is the support of justice. *Russian*

11834. Don't kick a man when he's down. *American*

11835. It is an honorable thing to be merciful to the vanquished. *Latin (Statius)*

11836. It's safer to err on the side of mercy. *American*

11837. Mercy is better than vengeance. *Greek*

11838. Mercy often gives death instead of life. *Latin*

11839. Mercy surpasses justice. *English (Chaucer)*

11840. Mercy sways the brave. *Greek*
11841. Mercy to the criminal may be cruelty to the people. *Arabic*
11842. Nothing emboldens sin as much as mercy. *American*
11843. Sweet mercy is nobility's true badge. *English (Shakespeare)*
11844. The brave are merciful; cowards do not dare to forgive their enemies. *American*
11845. The quality of mercy is not strain'd. *English (Shakespeare)*

Merit *see also* Desert; Winning and Losing

11846. Don't pin medals on yourself; let others recognize your merit. *American*
11847. First deserve and then desire. *English*
11848. It is a good dog that can catch anything. *English*
11849. It is a good horse that never stumbles, / And a good wife that never grumbles. *English*
11850. Let him bear the palm [or prize] who has deserved it. *Latin*
11851. Men are rare. *French*
11852. Merit consists in action. *Latin*
11853. Merit is sure to rise to the surface. *American*
11854. Merit lives from man to man. *American*
11855. Nature makes merit and fortune uses it. *French*
11856. Some things are good, some middling, more bad. *Latin (Martius)*
11857. The test of merit is success. *Latin*
11858. True merit is like a river: the deeper it is the less noise it makes. *American*

Messengers *see also* News

11859. Though the senders be ten thousand times wrong, it is not the messenger's fault. *Chinese*

Method *see also* Ends and Means

11860. Better one safe way than a hundred on which you cannot reckon. *Greek (Aesop)*
11861. It is often better to go by a circuitous than by a direct path. *Latin*
11862. Little by little does the trick. *Greek (Aesop)*
11863. Look for a tough wedge for a tough log. *Latin (Publilius Syrus)*
11864. There's method in my [or his or her] madness. *American*

Might and Right *see also* Injustice; Justice; Law

11865. A handful of might is better than a sackful of right. *German*
11866. Might and right govern everything; might till right is ready. *French*
11867. Might is not always right. *Dutch*
11868. Might is right. *Greek (Plato)*
11869. Might overcomes right. *English*
11870. The reason of the strongest is always the best. *French (La Fontaine)*
11871. The stronger is most in the right. *Russian*
11872. The strongest has right. *German*
11873. There is no arguing with a large fist. *American*
11874. There is no argument like that of the stick. *Spanish*
11875. Where might is master, justice is servant. *German*
11876. Where there is no might, right loses itself. *Portuguese*

Mildness *see also* Gentleness; Soft Words

11877. Mildness governs more than anger. *English*

Mind

11878. A golden mind stoops not to show of dross. *English (Shakespeare)*
11879. A good mind possesses the kingdom. *American*
11880. A mind diseased cannot bear anything harsh. *American*
11881. A noble mind is free to all men. *Latin*
11882. A sick mind cannot endure any harshness. *Latin*
11883. A wise man will be master of his mind; a fool, its slave. *Latin*
11884. An undisturbed mind is the best salve for a!iction. *Latin*
11885. Anxious minds quake with both hope and fear. *Latin*
11886. He who has peace of mind has conquered an empire. *American*
11887. It is good to rub and polish our minds against those of others. *French (Montaigne)*
11888. It is the mind that ennobles, not the blood. *German*
11889. Light minds are pleased with trifles. *Latin*
11890. Mad tenants move into a vacant mind. *American*
11891. Mind is ever the ruler of the universe. *Greek (Plato)*
11892. Mind is the great lever of all things. *American*
11893. Mind moves matter. *Latin*
11894. Mind unemployed is mind unenjoyed. *American*
11895. Small minds are lured by trifles. *American*
11896. The mind alone cannot be exiled. *Latin (Ovid)*
11897. The mind is playful when unburdened. *American*
11898. The mind is the man. *Latin*
11899. The most perfect mind is a dry light. *Greek*
11900. To relax the mind is to lose it. *Latin*
11901. To the trapped mind the world has no exits. *American*
11902. Vacant minds are open to all suggestions. *Chinese*

Mind and Body

11903. A feeble body enfeebles the mind. *French*
11904. A sound mind in a sound body. *Latin*
11905. Bodies without minds are like statues in the marketplace. *Greek*
11906. However broken down is the spirit's shrine, the spirit is there all the same. *Nigerian*
11907. Pain of mind is worse than pain of body. *Latin*

11908. The contagion of a sick mind affects the body. *Latin*

11909. The mind ill at ease, the body suffers also. *Latin (Ovid)*

11910. The sickness of the body may be a medicine for the mind. *American*

11911. We employ the mind to rule, the body to serve. *Latin*

11912. When the head acheth, all the body is the worse. *English*

Miracles

11913. Even miracles become boring in the end. *Russian*

11914. Let the miracle be wrought, though it be by the devil. *Spanish*

11915. Little saints also perform miracles. *Danish*

11916. The Mother of God appears to fools. *Spanish*

11917. The sheik's miracles are those of his own telling. *Turkish*

11918. Things that are mysterious are not necessarily miracles. *German*

11919. To him who does not believe in them there are no miracles. *French*

Mirrors

11920. An ugly maid hates the mirror. *Yiddish*

11921. The mirror reflects all objects without being sullied. *Chinese*

Mirth *see also* Joy and Sorrow; Mirth and Sorrow

11922. A cent of mirth is worth a dollar of grief. *American*

11923. A merry heart doeth good like a medicine. *Bible*

11924. A pennyworth of mirth is worth a pound of sorrow. *English*

11925. Always merry is seldom rich. *German*

11926. Mirth cannot move a soul in agony. *English (Shakespeare)*

11927. Mirth is hard to feign when the mind is sad. *Latin*

11928. Mirth is the medicine of life; it cures its ills and calms its strife. *American*

11929. Mirth must be indulged in to prepare the mind for more serious matters. *Latin*

11930. Mirth prolongs life. *American*

Mirth and Sorrow *see also* Joy and Sorrow

11931. Sorrow is the bitter pill in every cup of mirth. *American*

11932. The end of mirth is the beginning of sorrow. *Dutch*

11933. Unseasonable mirth turns to sorrow. *Spanish*

Mischief

11934. A little mischief is a little too much. *American*

11935. As fu' o' mischief as an egg's fu' o' meat. *Scottish*

11936. He has hay upon his horn. *Latin (Horace)*

11937. He prepares evil for himself who plots mischief for others. *Latin*

11938. He that mischief hatcheth, mischief catcheth. *English (Fuller)*

11939. Mischief comes by the pound and goes by the ounce. *American*

11940. The mair [more] mischief the better sport. *Scottish*

11941. The mother o' mischief is nae [no] bigger than a gnat wing. *Scottish*

11942. When you plot mischief for others you're preparing trouble for yourself. *American*

11943. You can find money for mischief when you can't find any for a meal. *American*

Miserliness *see also* Economy; Money; Parsimony; Saving and Spending; Thrift; Wealth

11944. A goose cannot graze after him. *English*

11945. A miser puts his back and his belly into his pocket. *English*

11946. A miserly father has a thriftless son. *English*

11947. A miser's money takes the place of wisdom. *Dutch*

11948. He even begrudges the water with which he washes. *Latin*

11949. He will not lose the parings of his nails. *English*

11950. It's folly to live poor to dee [die] rich. *Scottish*

11951. Misers lose twice. *Polish*

11952. Misers' money goes twice to market. *Spanish*

11953. Nothing gets into the closed fist; "Nor out of it," said the miser. *Gaelic*

11954. The miser and the pig are of no use until dead. *French*

11955. The miser does spoil his coat by scanting a little cloth. *English (Shakespeare)*

11956. The miser is as much in want of what he has as of what he has not. *Latin*

11957. The miser is ever in want. *Latin (Horace)*

11958. The miser's teeth are frozen together by greed. *Russian*

11959. The money of the miser is coming out of the earth when he is himself going into it. *Persian (Sa'di)*

11960. The prodigal robs his heir, the miser himself. *English*

11961. The rich miser and the fat goat are good after they are dead. *Yiddish*

11962. The wolf is sometimes satisfied, the miser never. *German*

11963. Those who make a fortune by being miserly will not enjoy it long. *Chinese*

11964. To ask a miser for a handout is like begging a naked man to give you his clothes. *American*

11965. To beg of the miser is to dig a trench in the sea. *Turkish*

11966. Water will not slip through the miser's grasp. *Malay*

11967. What greater evil could you wish a miser, than long life? *Latin (Publilius Syrus)*

11968. What he has is of no more use to the miser than that which he has not. *Latin (Publilius Syrus)*

Misery *see also* Suffering; Wretchedness

11969. A man is twice miserable when he fears his misery before it comes. *American*

11970. Fate finds for every man / His share of misery. *Greek (Euripides)*

11971. It is easy to mock the miserable. *Latin*

11972. Misery acquaints a man with strange bedfellows. *English (Shakespeare)*

11973. Misery is but the shadow of happiness; happiness is but the cloak of misery. *Chinese (Laotse)*

11974. Misery loves company. *American*

11975. Misery makes strange bedfellows. *American*

11976. Sacred even to gods is misery. *Greek*

11977. The miseries of the virtuous are the scandal of the good. *Latin*

Misfortune *see also* Luck

11978. A misfortune and a friar are seldom alone. *Italian*

11979. A pestilence follows a famine. *Latin*

11980. After losing, one loses roundly. *French*

11981. All bite the bitten dog. *Portuguese*

11982. An unlucky man's cart is eith [easily] tumbled [upset]. *Scottish*

11983. Another man's misfortunes hang by a hair. *Spanish (Cervantes)*

11984. Another's misfortune does not cure my pain. *Portuguese*

11985. Bad luck is fertile. *Russian*

11986. Better twa skaiths [two injuries] than ae [one] sorrow. *Scottish*

11987. Blessed is the misfortune which comes alone. *Italian*

11988. By speaking of our misfortunes we often relieve them. *French*

11989. Come what may, all bad fortune is to be conquered by endurance. *Latin (Virgil)*

11990. Do not rejoice over another's misfortune. *Polish*

11991. Even a misfortune may prove useful in three years. *Japanese*

11992. Even an ass will not fall twice in the same quicksand. *English*

11993. Every path hath a puddle. *English*

11994. Flying from the bull, I fell into the river. *Spanish*

11995. Fortune is never satisfied with bringing one sorrow. *Latin (Publilius Syrus)*

11996. Fortune may rob us of our wealth, not of our courage. *Latin (Seneca)*

11997. Fortune rarely brings good or evil singly. *English*

11998. From smoke to flame. *Latin*

11999. Gane [gone] is the goose that laid the muckle [big] egg. *Scottish*

12000. He blames Neptune unjustly who twice suffers shipwreck. *Latin (Publilius Syrus)*

12001. He falls on his back and breaks his nose. *French*

12002. He ran away from the wolf only to meet the bear. *Russian*

12003. He that has ill luck gets ill usage. *French*

12004. He that is born under a threepenny planet will never be worth a groat. *Irish*

12005. He that's down, down with him. *English*

12006. He who cannot bear misfortune, is not worthy of good fortune. *French*

12007. He who cannot bear misfortune is truly unfortunate. *Greek*

12008. He who is the cause of his own misfortune may bewail it himself. *Italian*

12009. He who stumbles twice over one stone deserves to break his shins. *English*

12010. He would break his neck upon a straw. *Italian*

12011. He would drown in a spoonful of water. *Italian*

12012. He's cowpet [overturned] the crans [iron rods for supporting the pot while on the fire]. *Scottish*

12013. Him that falls all the world run over. *German*

12014. I broke my leg, perhaps for my good. *Spanish*

12015. If a man's gaun doun the brae, ilka ane gies him a jundie. [When a man is going downhill, everyone gives him a push.] *Scottish*

12016. If fortune turns against you, even jelly breaks your tooth. *Persian*

12017. If I peddle salt, it rains; if I peddle flour, the wind blows. *Japanese*

12018. If I went to sea I should find it dry. *Italian*

12019. If I were to trade in winding-sheets no one would die. *Arabic*

12020. If it isn't one thing, it's another. *American*

12021. If it was raining soup, he would be out with a fork. *American*

12022. If my beard is burnt, others try to light their pipes at it. *Turkish*

12023. If my father had made me a hatter, men would have been born without heads. *Irish*

12024. If the wind blows it enters at every crevice. *Arabic*

12025. If there were no clouds we should not enjoy the sun. *English*

12026. Ignorance of one's misfortunes is clear gain. *Greek (Euripides)*

12027. Ill comes upon waur's back [upon the back of worse]. *Scottish*

12028. In avoiding one evil we fall into another, if we use not discretion. *Latin (Horace)*

12029. In flying from one enemy you encounter another. *Latin*

12030. Into each life some rain must fall. *American (Longfellow)*

12031. It is better to try to forget your troubles than to speak of them. *French*

12032. It is the nature of mortals to kick a man when he is down. *Greek*

12033. It never rains but it pours. *English*

12034. It's a man's job to bear misfortune lightly. *American*

12035. Knock a man down and kick him for falling. *English*

12036. Maggots breed in his salt-box. *Basque*

12037. Misfortune comes in bunches. *American*

12038. Misfortune comes on horseback and goes away on foot. *French*

12039. Misfortune comes to all men and most women. *Chinese*

12040. Misfortune does not always come to injure. *Italian*

12041. Misfortune is a good teacher. *German*

12042. Misfortune is friendless. *Greek*

12043. Misfortune is good for something. *French*

12044. Misfortune is not that which can be avoided, but that which cannot. *Chinese*

12045. Misfortune never comes without his retinue. *German (Heine)*

12046. Misfortune sometimes comes as a blessing in disguise. *American*

12047. Misfortunes come by forties. *Welsh*

12048. Misfortunes come unsent for. *Latin*

12049. Misfortunes make friends. *Latin*

12050. Misfortunes make happiness more sweet when it comes. *Latin*

12051. Misfortunes make strange bedfellows. *English*

12052. Misfortunes never come singly. *English*

12053. Misfortunes seldom come alone. *American*

12054. Misfortunes tell us what fortune is. *English*

12055. Misfortunes that can't be avoided must be sweetened. *English*

12056. Misfortunes when asleep are not to be awakened. *English*

12057. Nae [no] butter will stick to my bread. *Scottish*

12058. No weeping for shed milk. *English*

12059. Nothing is bad if we understand it right. *German*

12060. Of ane [one] ill comes many. *Scottish*

12061. Often bad fortune does not lead to harm. *Italian*

12062. Often out of a great evil a great good is born. *Italian*

12063. One ill calls another. *Italian*

12064. One misfortune draws on another. *French*

12065. One misfortune is the eve of another. *Italian*

12066. One misfortune is the vigil of another. *Italian*

12067. Out of the frying pan and into the fire. *English*

12068. Out of the smoke into the smother. *English (Shakespeare)*

12069. See that in avoiding cinders you step not on burning coals. *Latin*

12070. Some innocents 'scape not the thunderbolt. *English (Shakespeare)*

12071. That's waur [worse] and mair o 't [more of it]. *Scottish*

12072. The custom of Lorris: the beaten pay the fine. *French*

12073. The darkness of night is more certain than the light of day. *Russian*

12074. The ill-clad to windward. *French*

12075. The man born to misfortune will fall on his back and fracture his nose. *American*

12076. The misfortunes to which we are accustomed affect us less deeply. *Latin*

12077. The more we work, the more we shall be downtrodden. *French*

12078. The whip that's lost always had a golden handle. *Chinese*

12079. There is none misfortune cannot reach. *Greek*

12080. There ne'er was an ill that couldna be waur [worse]. *Scottish*

12081. To err again on the same string. *Latin*

12082. To fall from the frying pan into the burning coals. *Italian*

12083. To go from Ceca to Mecca, and from bad to worse. *Spanish (Cervantes)*

12084. To hit a policeman over the head and then to take refuge with the sheriff. *Spanish*

12085. To jump into the water to escape the rain. *French*

12086. To leap from the frying pan and throw oneself into the coals. *French*

12087. To stumble twice over the same stone. *English*

12088. We all have sufficient strength to bear other people's misfortunes. *French (La Rochefoucauld)*

12089. We can always bear our neighbors' misfortunes. *American*

12090. Wealth softens and misfortune wears out. *Arabic*

12091. Welcome, Misfortune, if thou comest alone. *Spanish*

12092. Well comes evil if it comes alone. *Spanish (Cervantes)*

12093. What ye win at that ye may lick aff a het [hot] girdle [griddle]. *Scottish*

12094. What you fear happens sooner than what you hope. *Latin*

12095. When fortune deserts us, our friends are nowhere. *Latin*

12096. When the tree is down, everybody gathers wood. *Latin*

12097. Wherever a man dwells, he shall be sure to have a thorn-bush near his door. *English*

12098. While avoiding the smoke I have fallen into the flame. *Latin*

12099. Whither goest thou, Misfortune? To where there is more. *Spanish*

12100. Whither goest thou, Sorrow? Whither I am wont. *Spanish*

12101. Who has no misfortune is fortunate enough. *German*

12102. Ye hae [have] come in time to tine [lose] a darg [a day's work]. *Scottish*

12103. Ye hae [have] miss'd that, as ye did your mither's blessing. *Scottish*

12104. Ye're ane [one] o' snawba's bairn [snowball's child] time. *Scottish*

Mistake(s) *see* Error(s)

Misunderstanding

12105. Ill hearing maks wrang rehearsing. *Scottish*

12106. Misunderstanding brings lies to town. *English*

12107. No one would talk much in society if he only knew how often he misunderstood others. *American*

Mixed Blessing

12108. Well's him and wooes [woe's] him that has a bishop in his kin. *Scottish*

Mobs

12109. A mob is a monster with many hands and no brains. *American*

12110. Mobs in their emotions are much like children, / subject to the same tantrums and fits of fury. *Greek (Euripides)*

12111. The mob has many heads but no brains. *English*

12112. The rabble are not influenced by reason, but blind impulse. *Latin*

12113. Who builds on the mob builds on sand. *Italian*

Mockery

12114. Hanging's stretching; mocking's catching. *English*

12115. If you mock the lame you will go so yourself. *English*

12116. It is never becoming to mock the miserable. *French*

12117. Mockery is often poverty of wit. *French*

12118. Point not the mockery behind the grand pasha's back. *Turkish*

12119. There are many sooth [true] words spoken in bourding [mockery]. *Scottish*

Moderation *see also* **Limitations; Longevity; Self-Denial; Self-Discipline; Temperance**

12120. A middle course is the safest. *Latin*

12121. According to the arm be the blood-letting. *French*

12122. Better leave than lack. *English*

12123. Butter spoils no mean and moderation no cause. *Danish*

12124. Can we ever have too much of a good thing? *Spanish*

12125. Cold water to hot water; hot water to cold water. *Telugu*

12126. Don't bite off more than you can chew. *American*

12127. Drink moderately, love moderately, live moderately: everything in moderation. *English*

12128. Every virtue is but halfway between two vices. *Latin*

12129. Extreme justice is the extreme of injury. *American*

12130. He drinks even water by measure. *Latin*

12131. He that commences many things finishes few. *American*

12132. He that eats but ae [one] dish seldom needs the doctor. *Scottish*

12133. He that is rich need not live sparingly, and he that can live sparingly need not be rich. *American (Franklin)*

12134. He that runs fast will not run long. *English*

12135. Hooly and fairly men ride far journeys. *Scottish*

12136. How many things I can do without! *Greek (Socrates)*

12137. Keep within compass and you may be sure, / That you will not suffer what others endure. *English*

12138. Let everyone stretch his leg according to his coverlet. *Spanish*

12139. Live not beyond your means. *Latin*

12140. Measure is a merry mean. *English*

12141. Measure is treasure. *Scottish*

12142. Meat and measure mak [make] a man wise. *Scottish*

12143. Men live better on little. *Latin*

12144. Moderate measures succeed best. *Latin*

12145. Moderate riches will carry you; if you have more, you must carry them. *American*

12146. Moderation in all things. *American*

12147. Moderation is best. *Greek*

12148. Moderation is the inseparable companion of wisdom, but with genius it has not even a nodding acquaintance. *American*

12149. Moderation is the silken string running through the pearl chain of all virtues. *American*

12150. Ne'er use the taws [a leather whip used by schoolmasters] when a gloom [frown] will do. *Scottish*

12151. Never overdrive the best horse alive. *American*

12152. Only moderation gives charm to life. *German*

12153. Slow and steady wins the race. *American*

12154. Soft fire makes sweet malt. *English*

12155. Stretch your arm no further than your sleeve will reach. *English*

12156. Take-it-easy and Live-long are brothers. *German*

12157. The best things pall in time. *American*

12158. The golden rule in life is moderation in all things. *Latin*

12159. The heart is great which shows moderation in the midst of prosperity. *Latin (Seneca)*

12160. The wise man sets bounds even to his innocent desires. *Latin (Juvenal)*

12161. There are only 24 hours in the day. *American*

12162. There is a medium in all things. *Latin (Horace)*

12163. There is no such gain as to be sparing with what you have. *Latin*

12164. There's a measure in a' things, even in kail [broth] supping. *Scottish*

12165. Things that are moderate last a long while. *Latin*

12166. Things which are moderate are sure. *Latin*

12167. To go half-way and stop. *Chinese*

12168. To rise at five, dine at nine, sup at five, go to bed at nine — make a man live to ninety-nine. *French*

12169. To rise at six, eat at ten, sup at six, go to bed at ten — make a man live years ten times ten. *French*

12170. Too hot to last. *English*

12171. True happiness springs from moderation. *German*

12172. Virtue is found in the mean. *American*

12173. Virtue lies in moderation. *Latin*

12174. Who wishes to travel far spares his steed. *French*

Modesty *see also* **Humility**

12175. And Modesty, who, when she goes, / Is gone for ever. *English (Landor)*

12176. Don't hide your light under a bushel. *American*
12177. Everything that is exquisite hides itself. *French*
12178. He who has one order would like to hang it on his forehead; he who has ten, buttons his coat over them. *Russian*
12179. He who speaks without modesty will find it difficult to make his words good. *Chinese (Confucius)*
12180. Loquacity storms the ear, but modesty takes the heart. *English*
12181. Majesty knows modesty. *Irish*
12182. Modest dogs miss much meat. *American*
12183. Modesty becomes a virgin but it's a vice in a widow. *American*
12184. Modesty becomes a young man. *Latin*
12185. Modesty cannot be taught; it must be born. *Latin*
12186. Modesty forbids what the law does not. *Latin*
12187. Modesty is a quality in a lover more praised by the woman than liked. *American*
12188. Modesty is an ornament, yet people get on better without it. *German*
12189. Modesty is like the snow: when it melts it is gone forever. *American*
12190. Modesty is the citadel of beauty and of virtue. *Greek*
12191. Modesty is the light of faith. *Turkish*
12192. Modesty is the sweet song-bird which no open cage door can tempt to flight. *American*
12193. Modesty is useless to a man who is in want. *Latin*
12194. Modesty, once lost, never returns. *Latin (Publilius Syrus)*
12195. Modesty should accompany youth. *Latin (Plautus)*
12196. Modesty, when she goes, is gone forever. *American*
12197. The higher our position the more modestly should we behave. *Latin (Cicero)*
12198. When modesty has once perished, it will never revive. *Latin (Seneca)*
12199. Without modesty beauty is ungraceful and wit detestable. *American*

Money *see also* Buying and Selling; Ill-Gotten Gains; Miserliness; Payment; Poverty; Profit and Loss; Rich and Poor; Saving and Spending; Venture and Investment; Wealth

12200. A man hath no more than he hath good of. *Scottish*
12201. A string of cash can but reach to one's heels. *Chinese*
12202. All money is clean — even if it's dirty. *American*
12203. All things are obedient to money. *English*
12204. An ass loaded with gold climbs to the top of a castle. *English*
12205. Bad money always comes back. *American*
12206. Be the business never so painful, you may have it done for money. *English*
12207. Beauty is potent, but money is omnipotent. *English*
12208. Between smith and smith no money passes. *Spanish*
12209. Blessed is the man who has both mind and money, for he employs the latter well. *Greek (Menander)*
12210. Don't spoil the ship for a halfpenny-worth of tar. *English*
12211. Don't suppose that you know a man till you come to divide a spoil with him. *Gaelic*
12212. Ell and tell [ready money] is good merchandise. *Scottish*
12213. Eloquence avails nothing against the voice of gold. *Latin*
12214. Get money; honor is good if you can afford it. *American*
12215. Give me money, not advice. *Portuguese*
12216. God makes, and apparel shapes, but it's money that finishes the man. *English*
12217. God send us siller [silver], for they're little thought o' that want [i.e., lack] it. *Scottish*
12218. Gold goes worse than formerly. *French*
12219. Gold in the purse drives away melancholy. *German*
12220. Gold may be dear cost. *Scottish*
12221. Hand in gear [money, property] helps weel. *Scottish*
12222. He that has money may choose a husband for his daughter. *Spanish*
12223. He that is of the opinion that money will do everything may well be suspected of doing everything for money. *American*
12224. He that tines [loses] his siller [silver] is thought to hae tint [have lost] his wit. *Scottish*
12225. Help me to money and I'll help myself to friends. *English*
12226. I wot [know] well how the world wags, he is most loved that has the most bags. *English*
12227. If a man's money be white, his face may be black. *Turkish*
12228. If money be not thy servant, it will be thy master. *Italian*
12229. If one would know how much a ducat is worth, seek to borrow one. *Spanish*
12230. If the walls were adamant, gold would take the town. *English*
12231. It's a rare thing for siller [silver] to lack a maister. *Scottish*
12232. Lack of money is trouble without equal. *French*
12233. Love can do much, gold can do everything. *German*
12234. Love does much, money does all. *French*
12235. Make money, by fair means if you can; if not, by any means. *Latin (Horace)*
12236. Make money your servant, not your master. *American*
12237. Mention money, and the world is silent. *German*
12238. Money alone sets all the world in motion. *Latin (Publilius Syrus)*
12239. Money amassed with excessive care chokes many. *Latin*

12240. Money answereth all things. *Bible*
12241. Money buys sugar. *Yiddish*
12242. Money controls even the orders of hell. *Japanese*
12243. Money controls the battle and not the strong arm. *Portuguese*
12244. Money does not get hanged. *German*
12245. Money doesn't grow on trees. *American*
12246. Money has no smell. *Latin*
12247. Money has wings. *French*
12248. Money is a bottomless sea, in which honor, conscience and truth may be drowned. *American*
12249. Money is a good servant but a poor guide. *Polish*
12250. Money is a good soldier, and will on. *English (Shakespeare)*
12251. Money is aye [always] welcome, were it even in a dirty clout. *Scottish*
12252. Money is better than my lord's letter. *Scottish*
12253. Money is both blood and life to men. *Latin*
12254. Money is brother to money. *Italian*
12255. Money is like the muck midden [dunghill]; it does nae gude [no good] till it be spread. *Scottish*
12256. Money is needed both by monk and dervish. *Turkish*
12257. Money is only lost through want of money. *French*
12258. Money is the man. *German*
12259. Money is the measure of all things. *Portuguese*
12260. Money is the ruling spirit of all things. *Latin*
12261. Money is the sinew of love as well as of war. *English*
12262. Money is the sinews of affairs [or war]. *Greek*
12263. Money is the soul of business. *German*
12264. Money makes dogs dance. *French*
12265. Money makes strangers. *Japanese*
12266. Money makes the man. *Greek*
12267. Money makes the mare to go. *English*
12268. Money maks a man free ilka whar [everywhere]. *Scottish*
12269. Money maks the mear [mare] to go whether she has legs or no. *Scottish*
12270. Money never comes out of season. *French*
12271. Money often unmakes the man who makes it. *American*
12272. Money recommends a man everywhere. *American*
12273. Money soothes more than the words of a cavalier. *Spanish*
12274. Money talks. *French*
12275. Money will do anything. *American*
12276. Money will make the pot boil, though the devil should pour water on the fire. *American*
12277. Money's the wise man's religion. *Greek (Euripides)*
12278. Moyen [influence] does muckle [much], but money does mair [more]. *Scottish*
12279. Much on earth, little in heaven. *American*
12280. Muck and money gae thegither. *Scottish*
12281. My money, your money, let us go to the tavern. *Portuguese*
12282. Nae [no] friend like the penny. *Scottish*
12283. Ne'er let your gear owergang [master] ye. *Scottish*
12284. No lock will hold against the power of gold. *English*
12285. Nothing but money is sweeter than honey. *American*
12286. Nothing is man's truly but that he comes by duly. *English*
12287. Nothing is so secure as that money will not defeat it. *Latin (Cicero)*
12288. Nothing more eloquent than ready money. *French*
12289. One handful of money is stronger than two handfuls of truth. *Danish*
12290. Public money is like holy water: everyone helps himself to it. *Italian*
12291. Put not your trust in money but your money in trust. *American*
12292. Ready money can put anything in stock. *Chinese*
12293. Ready money is ready medicine. *American*
12294. Ready money will away. *English*
12295. The abundance of money ruins youth. *English*
12296. The best foundation in the world is money. *Spanish*
12297. The devil of money has the better end of the staff. *Spanish*
12298. The golden key opens every door. *English*
12299. The love of money grows as money itself grows. *Latin*
12300. The love of money is the root of all evil. *Bible*
12301. There is no companion like the penny. *Spanish*
12302. There is no fortune so strong that money cannot take it. *Latin*
12303. To disregard money, on suitable occasions, is often a great profit. *Latin (Terence)*
12304. To know the price of money one must be compelled to borrow some. *French*
12305. What is infamy, so long as our money is safe. *Latin*
12306. When gold argues the cause, eloquence is impotent. *Latin (Publilius Syrus)*
12307. When gold speaks, every tongue is silent. *Italian*
12308. When I had money in my purse, I had food in my mouth. *Danish*
12309. When money spaks, the truth keeps silent. *Russian*
12310. When reason rules, money is a blessing. *Latin (Publilius Syrus)*
12311. Where gold avails, argument fails. *English*
12312. Where you have lost money, there you must look for it. *Yiddish*
12313. Who has, is. *Italian*
12314. Who has not, is not. *Italian*
12315. With money in your pocket, you are wise and you are handsome and you sing well, too. *Yiddish*
12316. Without money all things are in vain. *Latin*
12317. You may speak with your gold and make other tongues silent. *English*

Morality *see also* Conduct; Virtue

12318. A full gut supports moral precepts. *Burmese*

12319. Manners are more than meat, and morals more than manners. *American*

12320. No man's religion ever survived his morals. *English*

12321. Not the whiteness of years but of morals is to be praised. *Latin*

12322. There are many religions, but only one morality. *American*

12323. Veracity is the heart of morality. *American*

Morning *see also* Earliness; Early Rising

12324. All the speed is in the morning. *English*

12325. An hour in the morning is worth two in the evening. *American*

12326. He who does not rise with the sun does not enjoy the day. *Spanish*

12327. The morning is wiser than the evening. *Russian*

12328. The morning [or morning hour] has gold in its mouth. *Dutch*

Mortality *see also* Change; Death; Life; Transience

12329. A generation is like a swift horse passing a crevice. *Chinese*

12330. A hundred years hence we shall all be bald. *Spanish*

12331. All men are mortal. *American*

12332. All, soon or late, are doom'd that path to tread. *Greek (Homer)*

12333. All that belongs to mortals is mortal. *Greek*

12334. All things are born of earth; all things earth takes again. *Greek*

12335. As for man, his days are as grass: as a flower of the field, so he flourisheth. *Bible*

12336. As soon dies the calf as the cow. *French*

12337. As wave follows wave, so new men take old men's places. *Chinese*

12338. Birth is the messenger of death. *Arabic*

12339. Black death summons all things under the sway of its law. *Latin*

12340. Death devours lambs as well as sheep. *Spanish*

12341. Death is a debt we must all pay. *Greek*

12342. Death is common to all. *Latin*

12343. Death keeps no calendar. *American*

12344. Death spares neither pope nor beggar. *Italian*

12345. Eat, drink, and be merry, for tomorrow we die. *American*

12346. Every door may be shut but death's door. *American*

12347. Few have luck; all have death. *Danish*

12348. For dust thou art, and unto dust shalt thou return. *Bible*

12349. From the day of your birth you begin to die as well as to live. *French*

12350. Here today and gone tomorrow. *American*

12351. Lak! Lak! cries the stork, and his days are gone. *Turkish*

12352. Let us eat and drink; for tomorrow we shall die. *Bible*

12353. Life is a light before the wind. *Japanese*

12354. Man is a bubble. *Greek*

12355. Man is but breath and shadow. *Greek (Epictetus)*

12356. Man's life is like a candle in the wind or hoarfrost on the tiles. *Chinese*

12357. Men live like birds together in a wood; when the time comes each takes his flight. *Chinese*

12358. No one can escape death. *Latin*

12359. Nothing is so sure as death. *American*

12360. Remember that thou art mortal. *Greek*

12361. Remember the end. *Greek*

12362. Remember you must die. [Memento mori.] *Latin*

12363. Rome can give no dispensation from death. *French*

12364. Summer lasts not forever; seasons succeed each other. *Latin (Cicero)*

12365. The coffin is the brother of the cradle. *German*

12366. The days being finished [i.e., if it is one's time to die], there is no medicine. *Kanuri*

12367. The fall of a leaf is a whisper of the living. *Russian*

12368. The greatest king must at last go to bed with a shovel. *English*

12369. The oldest man that ever lived died at last. *Gaelic*

12370. The timid and the brave alike must die. *Latin*

12371. The whole earth is a sepulchre for famous men. *Greek*

12372. The young may — the old must. *Yiddish*

12373. There grows not the herb, which can protect against the power of death. *Latin*

12374. There is a remedy for everything except death. *Spanish*

12375. There is no medicine against death. *Latin*

12376. There's no dying by proxy. *French*

12377. They that live longest must die at last. *American*

12378. Today we mourn; tomorrow we are mourned. *American*

12379. We are but of yesterday, and know nothing, because our days upon earth are a shadow. *Bible*

12380. We think all men mortal but ourselves. *American*

12381. What belongs to nature lasts to the grave. *Italian*

12382. What is sucked in with mother's milk runs out in the shroud. *Spanish*

12383. When death knocks at your door you must answer. *American*

12384. When we take off our boots today, who can tell that we shall wear them tomorrow? *Chinese*

12385. Xerxes the great did die, and so must you and I. *American*

12386. Young folk may dee, auld folk maun dee. *Scottish*

Mothers and Daughters *see also* Heredity; Wives: Choosing a Wife

12387. If the mare have a bald face the filly will have a blaze. *English*

12388. The daughter of a good mother will be the mother of a good daughter. *American*

Mothers and Motherhood *see also* Mothers and Daughters; Mothers and Sons; Parents and Children

12389. A child without a father is half an orphan; without a mother, a whole orphan. *Finnish*

12390. A mother does not hear the music of the dance when her children cry. *German*

12391. A mother needs a large apron to cover her children's faults. *English*

12392. A mother's love will draw [or dash] up from the depths of the sea. *Russian*

12393. Better the child should cry than the mother sigh. *Danish*

12394. Children are the anchors that hold a mother to life. *Greek*

12395. Dear is the home where a mother dwells. *Polish*

12396. Every beetle is a gazelle in the eyes of its mother. *Moorish*

12397. Every mother's child is handsome. *German*

12398. God could not be everywhere and therefore he made mothers. *Hebrew*

12399. He that wipes the child's nose kisseth the mother's cheek. *German*

12400. Her children arise and call her blessed. *Bible*

12401. It is not the mother who bears but who rears the child. *Polish*

12402. Mother's love is ever in its spring. *French*

12403. Mother's truth keeps constant youth. *German*

12404. No mother has a homely child. *Yiddish*

12405. One mother can satisfy ten children, but ten children not one mother. *Yiddish*

12406. Quickly too'd [toothed], and quickly go, / Quickly will thy mother have mo'. *English*

12407. The good mother saith not, will you, but gives. *Italian*

12408. The mither's breath is aye [ever] sweet. *Scottish*

12409. The mother is a matchless beast. *Scottish*

12410. The owl thinks all her young ones beauties. *American*

12411. There is no bad mother or good death. *Yiddish*

12412. There is no mother like the mother that bore us. *Spanish*

12413. They are scarce of news that speak ill of their mother. *Irish*

12414. "What bird so white as mine?" says the crow. *English*

12415. Where the goat leaps, there leaps the kid which sucks her. *Spanish*

12416. Where yet was found a mother / Who'd give her booby for another? *English (Gay)*

12417. Who takes the child by the hand, takes the mother by the heart. *German*

Mothers and Sons *see also* Heredity; Mothers and Motherhood; Parents and Children; Sons

12418. A motherless son is a fish in low water. *Burmese*

12419. A son who marries gives his wife a contract and his mother a divorce. *Yiddish*

12420. Good wombs have born bad sons. *English (Shakespeare)*

12421. Men are what their mothers make them. *American*

12422. There is no friend to a man like his mother. *Osmanli*

12423. When a boy's foot is broken, he finds his mother's yard. *Jamaican*

12424. Your husband is what you make of him; your son is how you raise him. *Arabic*

Mothers-in-Law *see also* Daughters-in-Law; Sons-in-Law

12425. A mother-in-law is a fever, a sister-in-law is a poisonous serpent. *Lebanese*

12426. A mother-in-law is cold iron fallen to earth. *Arabic*

12427. As long as I was a daughter-in-law I never had a good mother-in-law, and as long as I was a mother-in-law I never had a good daughter-in-law. *Spanish*

12428. Give up all hope of peace so long as your mother-in-law lives. *Latin*

12429. Happy is she who marries the son of a dead mother. *English*

12430. If my mother-in-law dies, I will fetch somebody to flay her. *Portuguese*

12431. Of all the ould [old] women that ever I saw, / Sweet bad luck to my mother-in-law. *Irish*

12432. She is well married who has neither mother-in-law nor sister-in-law. *Spanish*

12433. The best mother-in-law is she on whose gown the geese feed. *German*

12434. The cask full, the mother-in-law drunk. *Spanish*

12435. The husband's mother is the wife's devil. *Dutch*

12436. The mother-in-law forgets that she was a daughter-in-law. *Spanish*

12437. There is no good mother-in-law but she that wears a green gown [i.e., that is covered with the turf in a cemetery]. *German*

Motion and Motionlessness *see also* Activity

12438. A millstone does not become moss-grown. *German*

12439. A rolling stone does not produce seaweed. *Greek*

12440. A rolling stone gathers no moss. *Latin*

12441. A setting hen loses her breast feathers. *English*

12442. A setting hen never gets fat. *English*

12443. A tethered sheep soon starves. *English*

12444. The marble stone on which men often tread seldom gathers moss. *English*

12445. Who stands still in the mud sticks in it. *Chinese*

12446. You can stand still in a flowing stream, but not in the world of mankind. *Japanese*

Motionlessness *see* Idleness; Inactivity; Motion and Motionlessness

Motivation *see also* Incentive; Willingness

12447. A fast horse does not want [i.e., need] the spur. *Portuguese*

12448. A good horse has no need of the spur. *Italian*

12449. A good horse often wants [i.e., needs] a good spur. *English*

12450. A good horse should be seldom spurred. *English*

12451. Be the horse good or bad, always wear your spurs. *Italian*

12452. Do not spur a free horse. *English*

12453. Eith to learn the cat to the kirn. [It's easy to teach the cat the way to the churn.] *Scottish*

12454. Fodder is the best whip. *Hungarian*

12455. It is ill to spur a flying horse. *English*

12456. It is the bridle and spur that makes a good horse. *English*

12457. One whip is good enough for a good horse, for a bad one, not a thousand. *Russian*

12458. Spur not a willing horse. *Spanish*

12459. The beast which goes well never wants someone to try him. *Spanish*

12460. The horse that pulls best is most whipped. *Italian*

Motive *see* Motivation

Mourning *see also* Death; Grief

12461. Him who is dead honor with remembrance, not with tears. *Latin*

12462. Make little weeping for the dead, for he is at rest. *Bible*

12463. We mourn the dead best by continuing their good works. *American*

Murder *see also* Crime and Criminals; Killing

12464. Many who do not murder would like the power to do it. *Latin*

12465. The act of murder is the act of madness. *American*

12466. The guilt of murder is the same; whether the victim be renowned or obscure. *Latin*

Music

12467. A song will outlive sermons. *American*

12468. Even the fear of death is dispelled by music. *Latin*

12469. Give me the making of the songs of a people, I care not who makes their laws. *American*

12470. Heard melodies are sweet, but those unheard / Are sweeter. *English (Keats)*

12471. Music does not fill the stomach. *French*

12472. Music hath charms to soothe the savage breast. *English (Congreve)*

12473. Music induces more madness in many than wine. *Latin*

12474. Music is the best cure for a sorrowing mind. *Latin*

12475. Music is the handmaid of divinity. *Latin*

12476. Music is the key to the female heart. *American*

12477. Music is the medicine of a troubled mind. *Latin*

12478. Music washes away from the soul the dust of everyday life. *American*

12479. No man who loves music can be wholly evil. *American*

12480. Where there is music there can be nothing bad. *Spanish (Cervantes)*

12481. Where there's music there can be no mischief. *Spanish*

Mutability *see also* Change; Life; Transience; Vicissitudes

12482. Change yourself and fortune will change you. *American*

12483. Today wed, tomorrow dead. *American*

Mystery

12484. There is mystery in the meanest trade. *English*

Naivete *see* Credulity; Gullibility; Ignorance; Innocence

12485. He who does not open his eyes must open his purse. *German*

12486. The good man is the last to know what's wrong at home. *Latin*

Nakedness

12487. More naked than a post. *Latin*

12488. More naked than an egg. *Latin*

12489. More naked than the cast-off skin of a serpent. *Latin*

12490. Naked was I born, naked I am, I neither win nor lose. *Spanish*

Name-Calling *see also* Fault-Finding

12491. One donkey calls another longears. *Spanish*

12492. The fool says to the fool: You are a fool. *African*

12493. The frying-pan says to the kettle, "Avaunt, black brows." *English*

12494. The pot calls the kettle black. *American*

Names

12495. Don't name your child before it is born. *Yiddish*

12496. What signifies knowing the names, if you know not the natures of things? *American (Franklin)*

12497. What's in a name? that which we call a rose / By any other name would smell as sweet. *English (Shakespeare)*

12498. When a tiger dies it leaves its skin; when a man dies he leaves his name. *Japanese*

Nations

12499. The ruin of a nation begins in the homes of its people. *Ashanti*

Nature *see also* Human Nature; Nature (=Essential Character); Nature and Nurture; Unchangeableness

12500. All nature exists in the very smallest things. *Latin*

12501. Everything unnatural is imperfect. *French*

12502. It is kind father to him. *Scottish*

12503. Nature does not proceed by leaps. *Latin*

12504. Nature does nothing in vain. *Latin*

12505. Nature forms us for ourselves, not for others. *French*

12506. Nature is the true law. *English*

12507. Nature makes women to be won, and men to win. *American*

12508. Never does Nature say one thing and Wisdom another. *Latin*

12509. One touch of nature makes the whole world kin. *English (Shakespeare)*

12510. The physician cures, nature makes well. *Latin*

12511. The truth of nature lies hidden in mines and caverns. *Greek*

12512. Things which are of nature are not a cause of disgrace. *Latin*

12513. What is natural is never disgraceful. *Greek*

Nature (=Essential Character) *see also* Character; Identity

12514. A crow is never the whiter for washing herself often. *Scottish*

12515. A wolf remains a wolf even if it has not devoured your sheep. *Mongolian*

12516. Drive away nature, and back it comes at a gallop. *French*

12517. Drive nature out the door and it will return by the window. *American*

12518. Everyone follows the inclination of his own nature. *Latin*

12519. It is hard to change nature. *Latin*

12520. Live according to nature. *Latin*

12521. No matter how much you feed a wolf he will always return to the forest. *Russian*

12522. Pound the water and it is still water. *Arabic*

12523. Set a frog on a golden stool, and off it hops again into the pool. *German*

12524. The son of an ass brays twice a day. *Spanish*

12525. The wolf changes his coat, but not his nature. *Latin*

12526. The wolf loses his teeth but not his inclinations. *Spanish*

12527. Though you cast out nature with a fork, it will still return. *Latin (Horace)*

12528. What is born of a cat will catch mice. *Italian*

12529. What is born of a hen will scrape. *Italian*

12530. Whatever the bee sucks turns to honey, and whatever the wasp sucks turns to venom. *Portuguese*

Nature and Nurture

12531. A dog's tail, even after 40 years of stretching, will come out crooked. *Tunisian*

12532. Crooked by nature is never made straight by education. *English*

12533. Nature is stronger than education. *French*

12534. Nature passes nurture. *Scottish*

12535. You will never make a crab walk straight forward. *Greek (Aristophanes)*

Nearness *see also* Distance

12536. Far water does not put out near fire. *Italian*

12537. Harry Chuck ne'er slew a man till he cam nigh him. *Scottish*

12538. Near the kirk [church], but far frae [from] grace. *Scottish*

12539. Near the monastery, last at mass. *French*

12540. Nearer the bone, sweeter the flesh. *English*

12541. Nearer the rock, the sweeter the grass. *Scottish*

12542. Nearest the king, nearest the widdy [the rope or gallows]. *Scottish*

12543. The nearest, the dearest. *German*

12544. The smoke of our own country is brighter than fire abroad. *Latin*

12545. The tunic is nearer than the frock. *Latin*

12546. We suffer by our proximity. [We receive a blow meant for another.] *Latin (Ovid)*

Neatness

12547. A place for everything, and everything in its place. *American*

12548. As neat as a pin. *American*

12549. As neat as a ninepence. *English*

Necessity *see also* Desperation

12550. A bird cannot fly without wings. *French*

12551. A blind man has nae [no] need o' a looking-glass. *Scottish*

12552. A blind man's wife needs nae [no] painting. *Scottish*

12553. A man driven by necessity does as much as thirty. *Spanish*

12554. A man must plough with such oxen as he hath. *English*

12555. A naked man maun rin [must run]. *Scottish*

12556. A wise man never refuses anything to necessity. *Latin (Publilius Syrus)*

12557. Apple blossoms are beautiful, but dumplings are better. *Japanese*

12558. Bad is want which is born of plenty. *Latin*

12559. Even the gods do not fight against necessity. *Greek*

12560. Every act of necessity is disagreeable. *Greek*

12561. Everyone must speak of his wants, be he where he will. *Spanish*

12562. Everything goes to him who does not want it. *French*

12563. For want of a nail the shoe is lost; for want of a shoe the horse is lost; for want of a horse the rider is lost. *American (Franklin)*

12564. He is not in want who has no desires. *Latin*

12565. He made virtue of necessity. *French (Rabelais)*

12566. He maun lout [must stoop] that has a laigh [low] door. *Scottish*

12567. He needs maun rin [run] that the deil [devil] drives. *Scottish*

12568. He that may not as he would mon [must] do as he may. *Scottish*

12569. He that wants the kernel must crack the nut. *French*

12570. He who has diarrhea looks for the bush. Gĩkũyũ

12571. He who has no mother sucks his grandmother. *Wolof*

12572. He's no nice but needfu'. *Scottish*

12573. If you can't get what you want, you must want what you get. *Yiddish*
12574. It is better to satisfy our hunger than to be clothed in purple. *Latin*
12575. It is wretched business to be digging a well just as thirst is mastering you. *American*
12576. Make a virtue of necessity. *Latin*
12577. Maun-do [must-do] is a fell fallow. *Scottish*
12578. Must is a hard nut. *German*
12579. My poverty, but not my will consents. *English (Shakespeare)*
12580. Necessity and opportunity may make a coward valiant. *English*
12581. Necessity breaks iron. *Dutch*
12582. Necessity can turn any weapon to advantage. *Latin (Publilius Syrus)*
12583. Necessity has a greater power than duty. *American*
12584. Necessity has its own rules. *Egyptian*
12585. Necessity has no holidays. *Latin*
12586. Necessity has no law. *Greek*
12587. Necessity is a good teacher. *American*
12588. Necessity is a hard master. *American*
12589. Necessity is a stubborn thing. *Greek (Euripides)*
12590. Necessity is a tremendous weapon. *Latin (Seneca)*
12591. Necessity is a violent school-mistress. *French*
12592. Necessity is the argument of tyrants; it is the creed of slaves. *American*
12593. Necessity is the mistress of art. *Latin*
12594. Necessity is the mother of invention. *Latin*
12595. Necessity knows no shame. *Latin*
12596. Necessity makes even the timid brave. *Latin (Sallust)*
12597. Necessity makes strange bed-fellows. *American*
12598. Necessity never made a good bargain. *American (Franklin)*
12599. Necessity recognizes no law. *Latin*
12600. Necessity sharpens industry. *American*
12601. Necessity teaches all things. *German*
12602. Necessity teaches art. *German*
12603. Necessity turns a lion into a fox. *Persian*
12604. Necessity will teach a man, however stupid, to be wise. *Greek*
12605. Nede has na peer. *English (Chaucer)*
12606. Need breaks iron; poverty breaks locks. *Yiddish*
12607. Need gars [makes] naked men rin [run], and sorrow gars wabsters [weavers] spin. *Scottish*
12608. Need has ne law. *Scottish*
12609. Need makes the old wife trot. *Danish*
12610. Need makes virtue. *Scottish*
12611. Need maks a man o' craft. *Scottish*
12612. Need maks greed. *Scottish*
12613. Need maks the naked quean [lass] spin. *Scottish*
12614. Need maks virtue. *Scottish*
12615. Need sharpens the brain. *Yiddish*
12616. Need teaches things unlawful. *Latin*
12617. Needs must when the devil drives. *English*
12618. Nothing is grievous which necessity enjoins. *Latin*
12619. Of need make virtue. *Scottish*
12620. Put a coward to his mettle, and he'll fight the deil [devil]. *Scottish*
12621. Sic [such] things maun [must] be if we sell ale. *Scottish*
12622. Stern is the visage of necessity. *German (Schiller)*
12623. The cow [or goat] must browse where she is tied. *French*
12624. The force of necessity is irresistible. *Greek (Aeschylus)*
12625. Them that canna [cannot] get a peck maun [must] put up wi' a stimpart [a fourth of a peck]. *Scottish*
12626. Them that canna [cannot] ride maun shank it [must walk]. *Scottish*
12627. There is no virtue like necessity. *English (Shakespeare)*
12628. There's muckle [much] ado when dominies [schoolmasters] ride. *Scottish*
12629. Thirst teaches us the value of water. *Russian*
12630. Those who want much are always much in want. *Latin*
12631. To have no wants is divine. *Greek (Socrates)*
12632. To maken vertue of necessitie. *English (Chaucer)*
12633. Want is the mother of industry. *American*
12634. Want makes strife between man and wife. *American*
12635. Want too oft betrays the tongue to lies. *Greek*
12636. Want will be your master. *American*
12637. We all must bow to necessity. *American*
12638. We give necessity the praise of virtue. *Latin*
12639. We make allowance for necessity. *Latin (Cicero)*
12640. What is a workman without his tools? *English*
12641. When a' fruits fail, welcome haws [the fruit of the hawthorn]. *Scottish*
12642. When the arrow is on the string, it must go. *Chinese*
12643. When the buck's bound there he may bleat. *Scottish*
12644. When the cork is drawn, the wine must be drunk. *French*
12645. When you come to an impasse, there will be a way through. *Korean*
12646. Where necessity speaks it demands. *Russian*
12647. You cannot escape necessities; but you can conquer them. *Latin*

Need *see* Necessity

Neglect

12648. A fertile field, when neglected, will produce nothing but weeds and thorns. *American*
12649. A lean dog shames its master. *Japanese*
12650. A little neglect may breed great mischief. *American*
12651. Cobblers' children are worst shod. *English*

12652. Fire, if neglected, will soon gain strength. *Latin (Horace)*
12653. Great negligence is a fault; gross fault is a fraud. *American*
12654. Gross negligence is equal to intentional wrong. *American*
12655. He that repairs not a part, builds all. *English*
12656. Ill weeds grow apace. *English*
12657. It is said that the wife of the mat-maker died on the bare ground. *Tamil*
12658. Kame sindle [comb seldom], kame sair. [Combing is painful if neglected.] *Scottish*
12659. Nip the briar in the bud. *English*
12660. Nothing is easy to the negligent. *American*
12661. Present neglect makes future regret. *American*
12662. Shoemakers are always the worst shod. *French*
12663. Slight not what is near through aiming at what is far. *Greek (Euripides)*
12664. The foot of the lamp is the worst lighted. *Chinese*
12665. The potter eats out of a broken dish. Kafir
12666. The smith's mare and the cobbler's wife are always the worst shod. *American*
12667. The tailor's wife is worst clad. *American*
12668. Trouble neglected becomes more troublesome. *Chinese*
12669. When the smith's wife wants a nail, she must buy it at the shopkeeper's. *German*
12670. Who goes more bare / Than the shoemaker's wife and the smith's mare? *English*

Neighbors

12671. A bad neighbor brings bad luck. *Latin*
12672. A Christian neighbor is better than a brother five miles away. *Welsh*
12673. A good bird selects the tree on which it wishes to rest. *Chinese*
12674. A good neighbor is a precious thing. *American*
12675. A hedge between keeps friendship green. *English*
12676. A hedge is a good thing between neighbors' gardens. *German*
12677. A monkey never watches his own tail; he watches his neighbor's. *American*
12678. A quarrel in a neighbor's house is refreshing. *Tamil*
12679. Better a good neighbor than a bad relative. *Yiddish*
12680. Better a neighbor that is near than a brother far off. *American*
12681. Better good neighbors near, than relatives at a distance. *Chinese*
12682. Better is a near neighbor than a distant cousin. *Italian*
12683. Better my neighbor should think me fremit [strange] than fashous [bothersome]. *Scottish*
12684. Distance from people is great booty. *Arabic*
12685. Distant water will not quench a fire that is near; distant relations are not so good as near neighbors. *Chinese*
12686. Every man's neighbor is his looking-glass. *English*
12687. Folks like the truth that hits their neighbor. *American*
12688. He who has a good neighbor has a good morning. *Italian*
12689. If you want the truth about a man, talk to his neighbors. *Chinese*
12690. It is not as thy mother says, but as thy neighbors say. *Hebrew*
12691. Live in harmony with your neighbors. *Chinese*
12692. Love thy neighbor. *Greek (Thales)*
12693. Love your neighbor, but do not pull down the hedge. *German*
12694. Love your neighbor, but don't let him in your house. *Maltese*
12695. Mix with the neighbors, and you learn what's doing in your own house. *Yiddish*
12696. My neighbor's hen lays more eggs than mine. *Spanish*
12697. Neighbor's right, God's right. *Turkish*
12698. Neighbors are good when they are neighborly. *American*
12699. No man tells the truth about himself; only his neighbors do. *American*
12700. No one is rich enough to do without a neighbor. *American*
12701. No one's house is so big that he does not need good neighbors. *Swedish*
12702. On a journey you need good company; at home you need good neighbors. *Chinese*
12703. Possessed of a neighbor's knowledge. *Chinese*
12704. The bad neighbor gives a needle without thread. *Spanish*
12705. Thou shalt love thy neighbor as thyself. *Bible*
12706. To be on good terms with one's neighbor is as good as finding a treasure. *Chinese*
12707. We are nearer neighbors to ourselves than whiteness to snow. *French*
12708. We can live without our friends, but not without our neighbors. *English*
12709. What my neighbor eats does my stomach no good. *Spanish*
12710. You must ask your neighbours if you shall live in peace. *English*
12711. You never had neighbors as good as boundary fences. *Irish*

Nephews

12712. Him to whom God gave no sons the Devil gives nephews. *Spanish*

Nerve *see also* Courage

12713. He who loses money, loses much; he who loses a friend loses more; he who loses his nerve, loses all. *American*

Newness *see also* Innovation; Invention; Novelty; Variety

12714. A new bissome [broom] soupes [sweeps] clean. *Scottish*
12715. A new broom is good for three days. *Italian*

12716. A new broom sweeps clean. *German*

12717. A new broom sweeps the room well. *Italian*

12718. A new servant will catch a deer. *Hindi*

12719. A novice always behaves with propriety. *Latin (Martius)*

12720. All that is new is fine. *French*

12721. Everything new meets with resistance. *Russian*

12722. New songs are eagerly sung. *American*

12723. New things are most looked at. *English*

12724. Nothing is invented and perfected at the same time. *Latin*

12725. Nothing is so new, as what has been long forgotten. *German*

12726. One always hangs up a new sieve. *Estonian*

12727. There is nothing new but what has grown old [or what has been forgotten]. *German*

12728. There is nothing new [or no new thing] under the sun. *Bible*

News *see also* Gossip; Hearsay; Messengers; Rumor; Scandal

12729. As cold water to a thirsty stone, so is good news from a far country. *Bible*

12730. Bad news is always true. *Spanish*

12731. Bad news is the first to arrive. *Italian*

12732. Bad news travels fast. *American*

12733. Before good news goes out the door, bad news is known a thousand miles away. *Chinese*

12734. Do not buy either the moon or the news, for in the end they will both come out. *Syrian*

12735. False news is a good omen. *Lebanese*

12736. For evil news rides post, while good news baits. *English (Milton)*

12737. Good news is reported, but bad news flies. *Spanish*

12738. He comes to the door too quickly who brings bad news. *French*

12739. He comes too early who brings bad news. *German*

12740. He knocks boldly who brings good news. *Italian*

12741. He that brings good news knocks hard. *Danish*

12742. He was scant o' news that tauld his feyther [father] was hangit [hanged]. *Scottish*

12743. Ill news are aye ower [too often] true. *Scottish*

12744. Ill news [or bad news] hath wings. *English*

12745. No news is good news. *German*

12746. Nowadays truth is the greatest news. *English*

12747. The goodness of news half lies in the hearer's ear. *American*

12748. When the messenger is slow, the news is good. *Moorish*

12749. When the rich man is pricked by a thorn the whole city knows; when the poor man is bitten by a snake the event is unrecorded. *Lebanese*

12750. Whenever everybody tends to his own business, news is scarce. *American*

Night *see also* Bed; Sleep

12751. At night there is no such thing as an ugly woman. *Latin (Ovid)*

12752. By night comes counsel to the wise. *Greek*

12753. Darkness and night are mothers of thought. *English*

12754. In night there is counsel. *Greek*

12755. Night bears dark children. *Arabic*

12756. Night has [or gives] counsel. *French*

12757. Night is a pregnancy. *Turkish*

12758. Night is the mother of counsel. *Latin*

12759. Night is the mother of thoughts. *Italian*

12760. Night is the queen of shades. *Wolof*

12761. Pondering over many things by night. *Latin*

12762. Take thy thoughts to bed with thee, for the morning is wiser than the evening. *Russian*

12763. The best advice is found on the pillow. *Danish*

12764. The night is long to one kept awake by pain. *French*

12765. The night is no man's friend. *German*

12766. The night rinses what the day has soaped. *Swiss*

12767. Three hundred things at night, and nothing in the morning. *Serbian*

12768. What I take from my nights I add to my days. *French*

Nobility

12769. A noble deed never dies. *American*

12770. Born to consume the fruits of the earth. *Latin*

12771. He is noble that hath noble conditions. *English*

12772. Nobility constrains us. *French*

12773. Nobility is nothing but ancient riches, and money is the world's idol. *English*

12774. Nobility of conduct is a greater recommendation than nobility of birth. *Latin*

12775. The nobly born must nobly meet their fate. *Greek*

12776. There is a rank of mind as well as of birth. *American*

12777. 'Tis only noble to be good. *American*

12778. True nobility is exempt from fear. *English (Shakespeare)*

12779. Virtue, not pedigree, should characterize nobility. *American*

12780. Who does right is born sufficiently noble. *American*

Noise *see also* Complaint

12781. He that loves noise must buy a pig. *Spanish*

12782. I do not like noise unless I make it myself. *French*

12783. The bleating lamb loses his dinner. *French*

12784. The full cask makes no noise. *English*

12785. The lowest spoke in the wheel rattles most. *American*

12786. The noisiest drum has nothing in it but air. *American*

12787. Too many cocks spoil the night. *Arabic*

Nonsense

12788. A little nonsense now and then / Is relish'd by the best of men. *English*

12789. As charms are nonsense, nonsense is a charm. *American*

12790. Nonsense can be defended only by nonsense. *American*

12791. Nonsense, when earnest, is often mistaken for sense. *American*

Nostalgia *see also* **Past**

12792. The next day is never so good as the day before. *Latin (Publilius Syrus)*

Nothing and Nothingness

12793. He goes safely who has nothing. *French*

12794. Nobody don't never get nothing for nothing, nowhere, no time, nohow. *American*

12795. Nothing can be made of nothing. *Latin*

12796. The king loses his rent where there is nothing to take. *French*

12797. The man who is everything is nothing. *American*

12798. There's nothing new, and there's nothing true, and it don't signify. *Cornish*

12799. Where nothing is to be had, [even] the king must lose his right. *English*

Novelty *see also* **Change; Innovation; Invention; Newness; Variety**

12800. A duck will not always dabble in the same gutter. *English*

12801. A nice new nothing to hang on my sleeve. *English*

12802. Ever something new, seldom something good. *German*

12803. Man naturally yearns for novelty. *Latin (Pliny)*

12804. Men love novelty most of all. *American*

12805. Men will do anything for novelty. *American*

12806. New churches and new taverns are seldom empty. *American*

12807. New dishes beget new appetites. *English*

12808. New meat begets a new appetite. *French*

12809. Nothing can be said which has not been said already. *Latin*

12810. Novelty always appears handsome. *Latin*

12811. Novelty in all things is charming. *Latin (Ovid)*

12812. Novelty is the great parent of pleasure. *American*

12813. The novelty of noon is out of date by night. *American*

12814. 'Tis novelty that sets the people a-gaping. *American*

Nudity *see* **Nakedness**

Number *see also* **Counting**

12815. The mair [more] the merrier; the fewer, better cheer. *Scottish*

Oaths *see also* **Promises; Swearing; Women and Trustworthiness; Words and Deeds**

12816. A true word needs no oath. *Turkish*

12817. An unlawful oath is better broken than kept. *English*

12818. As false as dicers' oaths. *English (Shakespeare)*

12819. Children are to be deceived with comfits and men with oaths. *Greek*

12820. Eggs and oaths are easily broken. *Danish*

12821. It is a great sin to swear unto sin, / But greater sin to keep a sinful oath. *English (Shakespeare)*

12822. Oaths are but words, and words but wind. *English*

12823. Oaths are not surety for the man, but the man for the oaths. *Greek*

Obedience *see also* **Child-Rearing; Children and Childhood; Discipline; Discipline and Women; Parents and Children**

12824. Disobedience is the father of insolence. *Yoruba*

12825. Disobedience will drink water with his hand tied to his neck. [One who is determined to disobey will find a way.] *Yoruba*

12826. Give obedience where 'tis truly owed. *English (Shakespeare)*

12827. Learn to obey before you command. *Greek (Solon)*

12828. Let them obey that know not how to rule. *English (Shakespeare)*

12829. No one can rule except one who can be ruled. *Latin*

12830. Obedience is better than politeness. *Chinese*

12831. Obedience is the mother of happiness. *Latin*

12832. Obedience is the mother of success, the wife of safety. *Greek (Aeschylus)*

12833. Obedience is yielded more readily to one who commands gently. *Latin (Seneca)*

12834. Speak when ye're spoken to, do what ye're bidden, / Come when ye're ca'd, an' ye'll no be chidden. *Scottish*

12835. Speak when ye're spoken to, / Drink when ye're drucken to. *Scottish*

12836. Speak when you're spoken to; come when you're called. *English*

12837. The dog that minds not your whistle is good for nothing. *American*

12838. The widow gave orders to her cat and the cat gave them to its tail. *American*

12839. Unbychid [unbidden], unbain [disobedient]. *Scottish*

12840. What the law demands, give of your own free will. *Latin*

Obesity *see also* **Eating; Gluttony**

12841. A fat belly does not produce a fine sense. *Latin*

12842. A fat paunch never bred a subtle mind. *Greek*

12843. A gross belly does not produce a refined mind. *Greek*

12844. A horse grown fat kicks. *Italian*

12845. Fat head, lean brains. *Italian*

12846. Who drives fat oxen should himself be fat. *English (Johnson)*

12847. Women, melons and cheese should be chosen by weight. *Spanish*

Objection

12848. To hunt for a knot in a rush which has no knots. [To raise unnecessary objections.] *Latin*

Obligation *see also* **Borrowing and Lending; Bribery; Debt; Duty; Favors; Gifts and Giving; Good Deeds**

12849. Be not unmindful of obligations conferred. *Latin*

12850. Begging a courtesy is selling liberty. *English*

12851. Do a man a good deed and he'll never forgive you. *Scottish*

12852. Do not drink wine given to you; it will cost you more than if you had bought it. *Russian*

12853. Eat the present, and break the dish [in which it was brought]. [The dish would remind one of the obligation.] *Arabic*

12854. Excess of obligations may lose a friend. *English*

12855. If he gies [gives] a duck he expects a goose. *Scottish*

12856. Man is the slave of beneficence. *Arabic*

12857. That is the bitterness of a gift, that it deprives us of our liberty. *English*

12858. To give without cause is to bribe. *Chinese*

12859. To place yourself under an obligation is to sell your liberty. *Latin*

12860. When a friend asketh, there is no tomorrow. *Spanish*

Obscurantism

12861. Obscurity often brings safety. *Greek (Aesop)*

Observation *see* **Bystanders**

Obstacles

12862. A low hedge is easily leapt over. *English*

12863. A narrow neck keeps the bottle from being emptied in one swig. *Irish*

12864. Obstacles increase desire. *French*

Obstinacy

12865. He can never be good that is not obstinate. *American*

12866. It is the frog going to the back of the hut. *Zulu*

12867. Obstinacy is most positive when it is most in the wrong. *American*

12868. Obstinacy is the strength of the weak. *American*

12869. The deeper we are in error the more angry we are. *American*

12870. The foolhardy learn from the flow of blood. *Zulu*

12871. The obstinate man does not hold opinions; his opinions hold him. *American*

Odds *see also* **Possibility; Probability**

12872. Not even Hercules himself could resist such odds. *Latin*

12873. One man must not fight with two. *Latin*

Offense *see also* **Affront; Injury; Insult**

12874. A man may cause his own dog to bite him. *English*

12875. A true friend never offends. *American*

12876. He who offends writes in sand; he who is offended, in marble. *Italian*

12877. Naething [nothing] is ill said if its nae [not] ill ta'en. *Scottish*

12878. Neither give offense to others, nor take offense from them. *Latin*

12879. No word is ill-spoken if it be not ill-taken. *American*

12880. That is well spoken that is well taken. *English*

Office *see also* **Authority**

12881. A bad man in office is a mischief to the public. *American*

12882. All offices are greasy [i.e., something sticks to them]. *Danish*

12883. An honest official has no fat subordinates. *American*

12884. For faut [fault] o' wise men fules [fools] sit on binks [benches]. *Scottish*

12885. For want of good men they made my father alcalde. *Spanish*

12886. He cannot keep a good course who serves without reward. *Italian*

12887. He who manages other people's wealth does not go supperless to bed. *Italian*

12888. Office tests the man. *Latin*

12889. Office will show the man. *Greek*

12890. Office without pay [or with inadequate pay] makes thieves. *German*

12891. Public office is a public trust. *American*

12892. The magistrate and the office discover [i.e., reveal] the man. *French (Rabelais)*

12893. The office teaches the man. *German*

12894. They that buy an office must sell something. *American*

12895. To whom God gives an office he gives understanding also. *German*

Old Age *see also* **Age; Aging; Maturity; Youth; Youth and Old Age**

12896. A graceful and honorable old age is the childhood of immortality. *Latin (Pindar)*

12897. A man is as old as he feels; a woman as old as she looks. *American*

12898. A man is as old as his arteries. *French*

12899. Age breeds aches. *American*

12900. Age does not give sense, it only makes one go slowly. *Finnish*

12901. Age is a bad [or sorry] traveling companion. *Danish*

12902. Age is like love; it cannot be hid. *English (Dekker)*

12903. Age is rarely despised but when it is contemptible. *English (Johnson)*

12904. Age lacks kindness, as dry weather dew. *Chinese*

12905. Age that lessens the enjoyment of life, increases our desire of living. *English (Goldsmith)*

12906. Aged men are virtuous. *Chinese*

12907. All would live long, but none would be old. *American (Franklin)*

12908. An auld [old] hound bites sicker [sure]. *Scottish*

12909. An old ape hath an old eye. *English*

12910. An old ass is never good. *French*

12911. An old bird is not taken with a new net. *Italian*

12912. An old broom is better than a new one. *Accra-West Africa*

12913. An old cat laps as much as a young kitten. *English*

12914. An old dog does not bark at nothing. *Zyryan*

12915. An old dog will learn no tricks. *English*

12916. An old duck is hard to pluck. *American*

12917. An old establishment never wants customers. *American*

12918. An old goat is never the more reverend for his beard. *English*

12919. An old lion is better than a young ass. *Latin*

12920. An old man and a yellow pearl are worthless. *Chinese*

12921. An old man at school is a contemptible and ridiculous object. *Latin (Seneca)*

12922. An old man has the almanac in his body. *Italian*

12923. An old man in the house is a good sign. *American (Franklin)*

12924. An old man is a bed full of bones. *English*

12925. An old man is twice a child. *English (Shakespeare)*

12926. An old man loved is winter with flowers. *German*

12927. An old man's saying is rarely untrue. *Danish*

12928. An old tree is hard to straighten. *French*

12929. As a man grows older, he grows colder. *Yiddish*

12930. As ginger and cinnamon age, their flavor becomes richer. *Chinese*

12931. At seventy, a man is a candle in the wind; at eighty, hoar-frost on the tiles. *Chinese*

12932. Auld [old] men are twice bairns [children]. *Scottish*

12933. Auld [old] sparrows are ill [difficult] to tame. *Scottish*

12934. Auld [old] stots [bulls, oxen] have stiff horns. *Scottish*

12935. Be old betimes, if you wish your old age to last. *Latin*

12936. Be old when young, if you would be young when old. *English*

12937. Bees touch no fading flowers. *English*

12938. Better die ten years too soon, than spend those years in poverty. *Chinese*

12939. Branches may be made straight, but not an old trunk. *Arabic*

12940. Care keeps his watch in every old man's eye. *English (Shakespeare)*

12941. Do not beat men of seventy, nor curse those of eighty. *Chinese*

12942. Dying while young is a boon in old age. *Yiddish*

12943. Eild [age] should [or would] hae [have] honour. *Scottish*

12944. Every man desires to live long, but no man would be old. *Irish (Swift)*

12945. Experience eases old age. *Greek (Euripides)*

12946. Fear increasing age, for it does not come without companions. *Latin*

12947. Few people know how to be old. *French (La Rochefoucauld)*

12948. Gray hairs are death's blossoms. *German*

12949. He is old and cold and ill to lie by. *Scottish*

12950. He who does not wish to become old may hang himself when young. *German*

12951. He who won't listen to aged men will do foolish things. *Chinese*

12952. He who won't take an old man's advice, will one day become a beggar. *Chinese*

12953. He wrongs not an old man that steals his supper from him. *Spanish*

12954. He's ower auld [too old] a cat to draw a strae [straw] before. *Scottish*

12955. Hoary hairs are death's messengers. *Arabic*

12956. How rare to find old age and happiness in one! *Latin (Seneca)*

12957. I won't laugh at another for having grown old, for that will assuredly happen to me. *Chinese*

12958. If a family has an old person in it, it possesses a jewel. *Chinese*

12959. If deferential to experienced old men, in trouble you can rely on them. *Chinese*

12960. If you lie upon roses when young, you will lie upon thorns when old. *English*

12961. Impartial justice may be expected from the aged; they won't forgive even great men. *Chinese*

12962. In an old stove the devil makes the fire. *Polish*

12963. It is always in season for the old to learn. *Greek (Aeschylus)*

12964. It is difficult to teach an old dog to bark. *German*

12965. It is ill teaching an old dog to keep still. *Danish*

12966. It's lang or Like-to-dee fills the Kirkyard. *Scottish*

12967. It's the life of an auld [old] hat to be weel cockit. *Scottish*

12968. Life is most delightful when it is on the downward slope. *Latin (Seneca)*

12969. Life protracted is protracted woe. *English (Johnson)*

12970. Little may an auld horse do if he maunna nicher [may not neigh]. *Scottish*

12971. Look for the old so as to learn the new. *American*

12972. Man grows old but his heart doesn't; a family may be poor but still do noble acts. *Chinese*

12973. Many a good drop of broth may come out of an old pot. *American*

12974. Many annoyances surround an aged man. *Latin*

12975. Many foxes grow gray, but few grow old. *American (Franklin)*

12976. Men of seventy have always been rare. *Chinese*

12977. Move an old tree and it will wither to death. *American*

12978. Nae fules [no fools] like auld [old] fules. *Scottish*

12979. Nature abhors the old. *American (Emerson)*

12980. Never do good to an old man. *Greek*

12981. No one is so old as to think he cannot live one more year. *Latin (Seneca)*

12982. Nobody loves life like an old man. *Greek (Sophocles)*

12983. Nothing is less worthy of honor than an old man who has no other evidence of having lived long except his age. *Latin (Seneca)*

12984. Old age and happiness seldom go together. *Latin (Seneca)*

12985. Old age and the wear of time teach many things. *Greek (Sophocles)*

12986. Old age comes uncalled. *German*

12987. Old age creeps on us ere we think it nigh. *English (Dryden)*

12988. Old age has disgraces of its own; do not add to them the shame of vice. *Latin (Cato)*

12989. Old age is a disease. *Latin (Terence)*

12990. Old age is a heavy burden to men. *Latin*

12991. Old age is a malady of which one dies. *German*

12992. Old age is a tyrant who forbids, upon pain of death, all the pleasures of youth. *French (La Rochefoucauld)*

12993. Old age is an incurable disease. *Latin (Seneca)*

12994. Old age is dreary solitude. *Greek (Plato)*

12995. Old age is more to be feared than death. *Latin (Juvenal)*

12996. Old age is not so fiery as youth, but when once provoked cannot be appeased. *English*

12997. Old age is the harbor of all ills. *Greek (Bion)*

12998. Old age makes us wiser and more foolish. *French*

13299. Old age plants more wrinkles in the mind than in the face. *French (Montaigne)*

13000. Old birds are hard to pluck. *German*

13001. Old camels carry young camels' skins to the market. *Hebrew*

13002. Old cattle breed not. *French*

13003. Old churches have dim windows. *German*

13004. Old foxes want no tutors. *English*

13005. Old men are twice children. *Greek*

13006. Old oxen have stiff horns. *Danish*

13007. Old people see best in the distance. *German*

13008. Old pigs have hard snouts. *German*

13009. Old trees are hollow inside; old men see things clearly. *Chinese*

13010. Old trees have withered tops. *American*

13011. Old trees must not be transplanted. *German*

13012. Old wood, old friends, old wine and old authors are best. *Spanish (Alonzo of Aragon)*

13013. Old young and old long. *English*

13014. Remove an auld [old] tree and it'll wither. *Scottish*

13015. Slowly and imperceptibly old age comes creeping on. *Latin*

13016. The aged come for new year congratulations, but each succeeding year is worse than the former. *Chinese*

13017. The almond tree is in flower. *Hebrew*

13018. The autumn of beauty is still beautiful. *Latin*

13019. The beauty of old men is the gray head. *Bible*

13020. The cat became blind yet still was hankering after mice. *Arabic*

13021. The child sees little, but the old man, sitting on the ground, sees everything. *Wolof*

13022. The evening crowns the day. *English*

13023. The more thy years, the nearer thy grave. *English*

13024. The old man who dances furnishes the devil fine sport. *German*

13025. The old man's staff is a knocker at death's door. *Spanish*

13026. The old parrot does not mind the stick. *Latin*

13027. The old pipe gives the sweetest smoke. *Irish*

13028. The older the fiddle the sweeter the tune. *Irish*

13029. The sun is still beautiful, though ready to set. *English*

13030. The young like dress; the aged food. *Chinese*

13031. There is no fool like an old fool. *English*

13032. There is nothing like newness in clothes; nothing like age in man. *Chinese*

13033. 'Tis late e'er an old man comes to know he is old. *English*

13034. 'Tis worse to rouse an old woman than a dog. *Greek*

13035. To live long is to outlive much. *American*

13036. Water never dries up in an old river. *American*

13037. We become wiser as we grow older. *Latin*

13038. We do not count a man's years, until he has nothing else to count. *American (Emerson)*

13039. We get too soon old, and too late smart. *American*

13040. We grow old, but who grows wise? *German (Goethe)*

13041. We remember riding on bamboos as boys, and lo! we are white-headed old men. *Chinese*

13042. What else is an old man but voice and shadow? *Greek (Euripides)*

13043. When an old dog barks, then look out. *Latin*

13044. When an old man cannot drink, prepare his grave. *Spanish*

13045. When an old man will not drink, look for him in another world. *Italian*

13046. When bees are old they yield no honey. *English*

13047. When old men are not upright, they teach their sons to be rogues. *Chinese*

13048. When the age is in, the wit is out. *English (Shakespeare)*

13049. When the old dog barks he giveth counsel. *English*

13050. When the roses are gone, nothing is left but the thorn. *Latin (Ovid)*

13051. When the teeth fall out the tongue wags loose. *Chinese*

13052. White hairs are not only on old men; we see them also on the young. *Chinese*

13053. Who steals an old man's supper, does him no harm. *Spanish*

13054. With the ancient is wisdom; and in length of days understanding. *Bible*

13055. You can be as old as Methuselah and still be a fool. *American*

13056. You can't teach an old dog new tricks. *American*

13057. You must be old early if you wish to be old late. *Latin*

13058. Young people do not believe the words of the aged. *Chinese*

Omens *see also* Future; Inference; Prophecy; Prediction

13059. An April shower is a jewel without price. *Arabic*

13060. Certain signs are the forerunners of certain events. *Latin (Cicero)*

13061. Every cloud engenders not a storm. *English (Shakespeare)*

13062. Good omens come from the mouths of children. *Arabic*

13063. It's a bad sign when a man in a sweat shivers. *Latin (Plautus)*

13064. The galley is in a bad way when the corsair promises masses and candles. *Spanish*

13065. Winds in March, bad harvests in April. *Arabic*

Onesidedness

13066. A Montgomery division—all on one side, nothing on the other. *French*

13067. One man's story is no story; hear both sides. *Japanese*

Opinion *see also* People

13068. A man's own opinion is never wrong. *Italian*

13069. Different men have different opinions; / Some like apples, some onions. *English*

13070. Different people have different opinions. *American*

13071. Do not cut your donkey's tail in a crowd—one will say "It is too long," another "Too short." *Osmanli*

13072. He who lives after nature, shall never be poor; after opinion, shall never be rich. *American*

13073. It is difference of opinion that makes horse-races. *American (Twain)*

13074. Many men, many minds. *American*

13075. Men are tormented by their own opinions of things, and not by the things themselves. *Greek*

13076. Nobody has a right to have opinions, but only knowledge. *American*

13077. One man thinks one thing best, another another. *Latin*

13078. Opinion in good men is but knowledge in the making. *English (Milton)*

13079. Opinion is the mistress of fools. *English*

13080. Opinion is the queen of the world. *French (Pascal)*

13081. Opinion's but a fool, that makes us scan / The outward habit by the inward man. *English (Shakespeare)*

13082. Opinions are like fashions, beautiful when new, ugly when discarded. *French*

13083. Popular opinion is the greatest lie in the world. *American*

13084. Singularity in right hath ruined many; happy those who are convinced of the general opinion. *American*

13085. So many heads, so many minds. *Italian*

13086. So many men, so many minds. *English*

13087. So many men, so many opinions. *Latin (Terence)*

13088. Some men are just as sure of the truth of their opinions as are others of what they know. *Greek (Aristotle)*

13089. That man is best who considers everything for himself. *Greek*

13090. That must be true which all men say. *American*

13091. That's but ae [one] doctor's opinion. *Scottish*

13092. The clash of opinion brings sparks of light. *French*

13093. The man is a fool who when asked for his candid opinion gives it. *American*

13094. The opinions of men who think are always growing and changing, like living children. *American*

13095. Those who never retract their opinions love themselves more than they love truth. *French*

13096. We think very few people sensible, except those who are of our opinion. *American*

13097. Wind puffs up empty bladders; opinion, fools. *Greek*

Opportunity *see also* Delay; Deliberation; Futility; Procrastination; Temptation; Timeliness; Waste of Time

13098. A dog in the kitchen desires no company. *French*

13099. A man must make his opportunity as oft as find it. *English (Bacon)*

13100. A man who misses his chance, and a monkey who misses his branch, cannot be helped. *Hindi*

13101. A thief makes an opportunity. *Dutch*

13102. A wise man turns chance into good fortune. *English*

13103. A wise man will make more opportunities than he finds. *English (Bacon)*

13104. A wool-seller knows a wool-buyer. *English*

13105. An opportunity is found with difficulty and easily lost. *Latin*

13106. Be like the ant in the days of summer. *Arabic*

13107. Catch the opportunity while it lasts, and rely not on what the morrow may bring. *Latin (Horace)*

13108. Christmas comes but once a year. *American*

13109. Every dog has his day, and every man his hour. *American*

13110. Gather flowers while the morning sun lasts. *Latin*

13111. Gather ye rosebuds while ye may, / Old time is still a-flying. *English (Herrick)*

13112. Gie [give] him a hole and he'll find a pin. *Scottish*

13113. Gie [give] him tow [rope] enough and he'll hang himsel. *Scottish*

13114. Give a rogue an inch and he'll take an ell. *Dutch*

13115. Give me a seat and I'll make room to lie down. *Spanish*

13116. Go West, young man. *American*

13117. Grind with every wind. *English*

13118. He is not thirsty who will not drink water. *French*

13119. He that lets his fish escape, may cast his net often yet never catch it again. *English*

13120. He that will not when he may, / When he would he shall have nay. *English (Burton)*

13121. He who seizes the right moment is the right man. *German (Goethe)*

13122. He who waits for chance may wait a year. *Yoruba*

13123. He who waits till an opportunity occurs may wait forever. *Latin*

13124. He who will not when he may, may not when he will. *Latin*

13125. Hell is paved with good intentions and roofed with lost opportunities. *Portuguese*

13126. If the badger leaves his hole the tod [fox] will creep into it. *Scottish*

13127. If you give him a foot he will take four. *French*

13128. If you give him one inch he takes a piece as long as your arm. *French*

13129. It is easy to rob an orchard when none keeps it. *English*

13130. It is good fishing in troubled waters. *French*

13131. Know your opportunity. *Greek (Pittacus)*

13132. Lamps out, the turban vanishes. *Hindi*

13133. Let us snatch our opportunity from the day. *Latin (Horace)*

13134. Look to the main chance. *English*

13135. Make haste about it if it is a good thing. *Japanese*

13136. Make hay while the sun shines. *English*

13137. Never refuse a good offer. *Latin*

13138. No fishing to fishing in the sea. *English*

13139. "No, thank you," has lost many a good butter-cake. *English*

13140. Not the mouse is the thief, but the hole in the wall. *Yiddish*

13141. On the fall of an oak every man gathers wood. *Greek*

13142. Opportunities do not wait. *American*

13143. Opportunities, like eggs, come one at a time. *American*

13144. Opportunities pass like clouds. *Syrian*

13145. Opportunity is a god. *Greek*

13146. Opportunity is the cream of time. *English*

13147. Pluck with a quick hand the fruit before you. *Latin (Ovid)*

13148. Recognize your opportunity. *Latin*

13149. Rights are forfeited by disuse. *Latin*

13150. Set a beggar on horseback and he will gallop. *Dutch*

13151. Set a beggar on horseback and he'll ride to the devil. *English*

13152. Slaves would be tyrants if the chance were theirs. *French*

13153. Swiftly running water is a good place to catch fish. *Chinese*

13154. Take hold of a good minute. *English*

13155. Take time in time ere time be tint [lost]. *Scottish*

13156. Take time when time is, for time will away. *English*

13157. The cat is absent, and the mice dance. *Greek*

13158. The cat is honest when the meat is out of her reach. *American*

13159. The fisherman fishes in troubled waters. *Portuguese*

13160. The gods cannot help a man who ignores opportunity. *Chinese*

13161. The good time only comes once. *Italian*

13162. The hole invites the thief. *English*

13163. The opportunity is often lost by deliberating. *American*

13164. The opportunity of a lifetime is seldom so labeled. *American*

13165. The opportunity that God sends does not wake up him who is asleep. *Senegalese*

13166. The tree is no sooner down, but everyone runs for his hatchet. *American*

13167. The wise make tools of whatever comes to hand. *American*

13168. There is a tide in the affairs of men / Which taken at the flood leads on to fortune. *English (Shakespeare)*

13169. Time and tide for nae [no] man bide. *Scottish*

13170. Turn the mill while there is sugar-cane. *Hindi*

13171. Two dogs strive for a bone, and the third runs away with it. *English*

13172. Warm yourself while the fire burns. *German*

13173. We must take the current when it serves, / Or lose our ventures. *English (Shakespeare)*

13174. Well wots [knows] the mouse / The cat's out of the house. *Scottish*

13175. When a beggar gets on horseback the devil cannot outride him. *German*

13176. When fair occasion calls, 'tis fatal to delay. *Latin*

13177. When fortune smiles on thee, take the advantage. *English*

13178. When one door closes, another opens. *Spanish (Cervantes)*

13179. When one door is shut a thousand are opened. *Hindi*

13180. When one door shuts, a hundred open. *Spanish*

13181. When the cat is away the mice will play. *Latin*

13182. When the cat is not in the house, the mice [or rats] dance. *Italian*

13183. When the cat sleeps the mice play. *Dutch*

13184. When the cat's away, it is jubilee with the mice. *Dutch*

13185. When the cat's gone, the mice grow saucy. *English*

13186. When the king is away, the queen is free to act as she likes. *Behar*

13187. When the ox stumbles, all whet their knives. *Yiddish*

13188. When the snake is old, the frog will tease him. *Persian*

13189. When the wind is fair it is time to hoist your sail. *American*

13190. When you will, they won't; when you won't, they will. *Latin (Terence)*

13191. Where the cat is not, the mice are awake. *French*

13192. Where the dam is lowest the water first flows over. *Dutch*

13193. Where the dyke is lowest men go over. *English*

13194. Where the dyke's laighest [lowest] it's easiest loupit [leaped]. *Scottish*

13195. Where there are no dogs the fox is a king. *Italian*

13196. Where there is no tiger, the hare behaves like a lord. *Korean*

13197. While I am speaking, the opportunity is lost. *Latin (Ovid)*

13198. While the dogs are snarling at each other, the wolf devours the sheep. *French*

13199. While the shoe is on thy foot, tread upon the thorns. *Hebrew*

13200. While we discuss matters, the opportunity passes by. *Latin*

13201. While we stop to think, we often miss our opportunity. *Latin (Publilius Syrus)*

13202. Whilst we deliberate how to begin a thing, it grows too late to begin it. *Latin (Quintilian)*

13203. Wickedness and malice only require an opportunity. *Latin*

13204. Winnow while there is wind. *Hindi*

13205. You are a man among the geese when the gander is away. *American*

Opposites

13206. In avoiding one vice fools rush into the opposite extreme. *Latin (Horace)*

13207. When you have abandoned a thing, beware of its opposite. *Arabic*

Oppression

13208. He that oppresseth the poor reproacheth his maker. *Bible*

13209. Oppression will mak a wise man wud [mad]. *Scottish*

Optimism *see also* Encouragement; Hope

13210. A good soldier talks of success, not of failure. *Greek*

13211. As the devil said to Noah, "It's bound to clear up." *English*

13212. Bear with evil, and expect good. *English*

13213. Endure the present, and watch for better things. *Latin (Virgil)*

13214. God's in his Heaven—/ All's right with the world. *English (R. Browning)*

13215. He expects the larks will fall ready roasted in his mouth. *American*

13216. If the sky falls we shall catch larks. *American*

13217. Many have come to port after a great storm. *American*

13218. There is no devil in the world we go through. *Japanese*

13219. There is still sunshine on the wall. *Spanish*

Oratory *see also* Speech

13220. A good orator is the worst man. *Latin*

13221. A man becomes an orator; he is born eloquent. *French*

13222. An orator without judgment is a horse without a bridle. *American*

13223. An orator's virtue is to speak the truth. *Greek*

13224. Despise not a rustic orator. *Greek*

13225. He is a good orator who convinces himself. *American*

13226. Many persons think they are wise, when they are only windy. *American*

13227. Meat is more than carving, and truth is more than oratory. *American*

13228. Orators are driven by their weakness to noise, as lame men take to horses. *Latin (Cicero)*

Order *see also* Method

13229. All is soon ready in an orderly house. *American*

13230. Before preceding, one must reach. *Wolof*

13231. Everything is good in its place. *American*

13232. Horns grow not before the head. *Wolof*

13233. Let all things be done decently and in order. *Bible*

13234. Let all your things have their place; let each part of your business have its time. *American*

13235. Never put the plow before the oxen. *American*

13236. Order is Heaven's first law. *English (Pope)*

13237. Set thine house in order. *Bible*

13238. What is not understood [explained] by what is less understood. [That is, to compound confusion.] *Latin*

13239. Working without a plan is sailing without a compass. *American*

13240. Working without method, like a pig's tail, goes all day and does nothing. *American*

Originality *see also* Novelty

13241. It is no easy matter to say commonplace things in an original way. *Latin (Horace)*

Ornament

13242. A buckle is a great addition to an old shoe. *Irish*

Ostentatiousness

13243. Great doings at Gregory's; heated the oven twice for a custard. *English*

Others

13244. None knows the weight of another's burden. *English*

Outcome *see also* Cause and Effect; End

13245. A bad day never has a good night. *American*

13246. A great villain, a great fall. *French*

13247. A thing may be sweet to the taste and prove sour to the digestion. *American*

13248. A tree is known by its fruit. *English*

13249. All is well ended, if the suit be won. *English (Shakespeare)*

13250. All shall be well, and Jack shall have Jill. *English*

13251. All's lost that's put in a riven dish. *English*

13252. As a man lives, so shall he die; / As a tree falls, so shall it lie. *Bible*

13253. As you make your bed, so you must lie on it. *American*

13254. By flying, men often rush into the midst of calamities. *Latin (Livy)*

13255. Digging for a worm, up rose a snake. *Bengalese*

13256. Don't saw off the branch you're sitting on. *American*

13257. Each man reaps his own reward. *American*

13258. Every light has its shadow. *American*

13259. Evils follow each other. *Latin*

13260. From a pure fountain pure water flows. *Latin*

13261. From little one comes to great. *French*

13262. Gather thistles, expect prickles. *English*

13263. He is not the master who starts but he who finishes. *Polish*

13264. He that makes his bed ill lies thereon. *English*

13265. He that strikes with the sword shall be beaten with the scabbard. *English*

13266. He who crosses the sea is wet. *Wolof*

13267. He who plays with a cat must expect scratches. *Algerian*

13268. If the wind does not blow, the leaves do not move. *Cheremis*

13269. If you give your milk to the cat you must drink water out of the sink. *American*

13270. If you sing before breakfast, you'll cry before night. *American*

13271. If you submit to one wrong you bring on another. *American*

13272. If you want the hen's egg, you must put up with her cackling. *English*

13273. In making a god, an ape turned up. *Bengalese*

13274. It's pity fair weather should do any harm. *English*

13275. Joy and sorrow are next-door neighbors. *English*

13276. Little children, little sorrows; big children, big sorrows. *Danish*

13277. Little rogues easily become great ones. *American (Franklin)*

13278. Much bran and little meal. *English*

13279. Much bruit, little fruit. *English*

13280. Much cry and little wool said the the fool as he sheared a pig. *German*

13281. Much outcry, little outcome. *Greek (Aesop)*

13282. Muckle din [much noise] and little 'oo, / As the deil [devil] said when he clippit the sow. *Scottish*

13283. Muddy springs will have muddy streams. *American*

13284. No bees, no honey; no work, no money. *American*

13285. No corn without chaff. *Dutch*

13286. Nothing down, nothing up. *English*

13287. O' ae ill [of one ill] come mony. *Scottish*

13288. Of ill debtors men take oaths. *Scottish*

13289. Of nothing comes nothing. *American*

13290. Sorrow follows pleasure. *Latin (Juvenal)*

13291. Still water breeds worms. *Italian*

13292. The act is judged of by the event. *Latin (Ovid)*

13293. The end praises [or crowns] the deed. *Polish*

13294. The evening crowns the day. *English*

13295. The groat is ill saved that shames the master. *Scottish*

13296. The honey is sweet, but the bee stings. *American*

13297. The horses were fighting each other, but it was the donkey who got kicked. *Arabic*

13298. The mountain labored and gave birth to a mouse. *American*

13299. The proof of the pudding is in the eating. *English*

13300. The work praises the artist. *German*

13301. The work proves the workman. *Latin*

13302. There is no wheat without chaff. *Latin*

13303. There's no catching trout with dry breeches. *Portuguese*

13304. They are as good cats who scare the mice away as those who devour them. *German*

13305. They had never an ill day that had a good evening. *Scottish*

13306. Thou hast dived deep and brought up a potsherd. *Hebrew*

13307. 'Tis not the fight that crowns us, but the end. *English (Herrick)*

13308. To get out of the rain under the spout. *English*

13309. Vipers breed vipers. *American*

13310. Whatever you undertake, think of the end. *American*

13311. When buffaloes battle, the grass gets trampled. *Laotian*

13312. When elephants battle, ants perish. *Cambodian*

13313. When elephants fight, the mousedeer between them is killed. *Malay*

13314. When lizards eat pepper, it is the frog that perspires. Ghanaian

13315. When the chimney smokes, the meal is being cooked. *American*

13316. When the craw flees [crow flies], her tail follows. *Scottish*

13317. When the good man is frae hame [(away) from home], the tablecloth's tint [lost]. *Scottish*

13318. When the goodman's from home, the goodwife's table is soon spread. *English*

13319. When the gudeman's awa' the board cloth's tint; / When the gudewife's awa' the keys are tint. *Scottish*

13320. When the head suffers every limb sympathizes with it. *Spanish*

13321. When the pat's fu' it will boil over. *Scottish*

13322. When the shepherd strays the sheep stray. *American*

13323. When work troubles the head it troubles all the limbs. *Latin*

13324. When you see Pákpattan cloth you will rejoice; when you wash it you will weep. *Punjabi*

13325. Where light is, there shadow is. *American*

13326. Where the carcass is, the eagles will be gathered together. *English*

13327. Where the honey is, there are the bees. *Latin*

13328. Who deals in dirt has foul fingers. *American*

13329. Who wants the last drop out of the can gets the lid on his nose. *Dutch*

13330. You may take spoilt herrings of bad debtors. *Danish*

Overconfidence *see also* Arrogance; Confidence

13331. Better to be despised for too anxious apprehensions than ruined by too confident a security. *English (Burke)*

13332. Danger breeds best on too much confidence. *French (Corneille)*

13333. Good swimmers are oftenest drowned. *English*

13334. How fortune brings to earth the oversure! *Latin (Petrarch)*

13335. Let him that thinketh he standeth take heed lest he fall. *Bible*

Oversimplification

13336. More belongs to riding than a pair of boots. *English*

13337. There belongs more than whistling to going to plough. *English*

Ownership *see* Joint Ownership; Property

Pacifism *see also* Peace

13338. If a donkey bray at you, don't bray at him. *English (Herbert)*

13339. Whosoever shall smite thee on the right cheek, turn to him the other also. *Bible*

Pain *see also* Pain and Pleasure

13340. Comb sindle [seldom], comb sore. *Scottish*

13341. Every pain, but not heart pain; / Every ache, but not headache. *Hebrew*

13342. Great pains cause us to forget the small ones. *German*

13343. He preaches patience that never knew pain. *American*

13344. Naething [nothing] is got without pains but dirt and lang [long] nails. *Scottish*

13345. No matter which finger you bite, it will hurt. *Russian*

13346. Pain compels all things. *Latin (Seneca)*

13347. Pain will force even the truthful to speak falsely. *Latin (Publilius Syrus)*

13348. The hand often travels to the part where the pain is. *Latin*

13349. The tongue ever turns to the aching tooth. *English*

13350. There is no pain so great that time will not soften. *American*

13351. Where a man feels pain he lays his hand. *Dutch*

Pain and Pleasure *see also* Pain

13352. A man of pleasure is a man of pains. *English (Young)*

13353. After pleasant scratching comes unpleasant smarting. *Danish*

13354. After your fling, watch for the sting. *English*

13355. An hour of pain is as long as a day of pleasure. *English*

13356. Danger and delight grow on one stock. *English*

13357. "For my own pleasure," as the man said when he struck his wife. *English*

13358. From the cradle to the tomb, / Not all gladness, not all gloom. *English*

13359. He ate the food and then the food ate him. *Zulu*

13360. No pleasure without pain. *American*

13361. No sunshine but hath some shadow. *English*

13362. Pain mingles with pleasure. *Latin*

13363. Pain past is pleasure. *English*

13364. Pain wastes the body; pleasures the understanding. *American*

13365. Pains are the wages of ill pleasures. *American*

13366. Pleasure bought with pain does harm. *Latin (Horace)*

13367. Pleasure is the source of pain; pain is the source of pleasure. *American*

13368. Pleasure often comes from pain. *Latin*

13369. Pleasure purchased by pain is injurious. *American*

13370. Pleasure will be followed by pain. *Japanese*

13371. Sweet is pleasure after pain. *English (Dryden)*

13372. Sweet is the pleasure that springs from another's pain. *Latin (Ovid)*

13373. The honest man takes pains, and then enjoys pleasures; the knave takes pleasure, and then suffers pain. *American*

13374. There is a pleasure akin to pain. *Greek*

Pardon *see also* Forgiveness

13375. He invites future injuries who rewards past ones. *English*

13376. He that spares the bad injures the good. *English*

13377. He who forbids not sin when he may, commands it. *Latin (Seneca)*

13378. He who overlooks a fault, invites the commission of another. *Latin*

13379. He who spares the wicked injures the good. *Latin (Publilius Syrus)*

13380. He who spares vice wrongs virtue. *English*

13381. It is more noble to pardon than to punish. *Arabic*

13382. Know all and you will pardon all. *Greek*

13383. Misplaced leniency is an offense against society. *American*

13384. Mistakes are to be pardoned. *Latin*

13385. One pardons in the degree that one loves. *French (La Rochefoucauld)*

13386. Pardon is the choicest flower of victory. *Arabic*

13387. Pardon one offense, and you encourage the commission of many. *Latin (Publilius Syrus)*

13388. Pardoning the bad, is injuring the good. *English*
13389. The offender never pardons. *Italian*
13390. There are faults we would fain pardon. *Latin (Horace)*
13391. Too much lenity makes robbers bold. *English (Shakespeare)*
13392. Who does not punish evil invites it. *German*
13393. Whoever has his foe at his mercy, and does not kill him, is his own enemy. *Persian (Sa'di)*

Parenthood *see* Daughters; Fathers and Sons; Heredity; Mothers and Daughters; Mothers and Motherhood; Mothers and Sons; Sons; Stepparents

Parents and Children *see also* Children and Childhood; Child-Rearing; Daughters; Fathers and Daughters; Fathers and Sons; Heredity; Mothers and Daughters; Mothers and Motherhood; Mothers and Sons; Sons; Stepparents

13394. A baby girl is the beauty of cows. [A suitor may one day offer cattle for her hand in marriage.] *Lugbara*
13395. A black hen may bring forth white eggs. *English*
13396. A colt is worth nothing unless he breaks his cord. *French*
13397. A father and mother can do without their children, but children cannot do without their father and mother. *Chinese*
13398. A noggen [rough] mother's better than a gowden [complacent] father. *English*
13399. As the old birds sing, so the young ones twitter. *German*
13400. Aye [always] tak' care what ye do afore the bairns [children]. *Scottish*
13401. Children are a torment and nothing more. *Russian*
13402. Children are certain sorrow, but uncertain joy. *Danish*
13403. Children are poor men's riches, certain cares, but uncertain comforts. *English*
13404. Children are poor men's riches. *Danish*
13405. Children bring with them innumerable cares. *Latin*
13406. Children pick up words as chickens peas. *American*
13407. Children suck the mother when they are young, and the father when they are old. *English*
13408. Children, when they are little, make parents fools; when great, mad. *English*
13409. Everything is dear to its parent. *Greek (Sophocles)*
13410. Honor the gods, reverence parents. *Greek*
13411. If our child squints, our neighbor's child has a cast in both eyes. *Livonian*
13412. If the child does not cry, the mother does not understand it. *Russian*
13413. If you wish your children to have a quiet life, let them always be a little hungry and cold. *Chinese*
13414. Little children and headaches, great children and heartaches. *Italian*
13415. Little children are little sorrows, but great joys. *Italian*
13416. Little pitchers have long ears. *English*
13417. Married life without children is as the day deprived of the sun's rays. *Latin*
13418. No ape but swears he has the finest children. *German*
13419. No fathers or mothers think their children ugly. *Spanish*
13420. One is always somebody's child, and that is a comfort. *French*
13421. Our neighbor's children are always the worst. *German*
13422. Parents can give everything but common sense. *Yiddish*
13423. Respect the counsel of your parents. *American*
13424. Revere your parents. *Latin*
13425. Soot is the child of smoke. *Lugbara*
13426. Strangers forgive, parents forget. *Bulgarian*
13427. The ardor of parental affection consumes the heart with its fire. *Arabic*
13428. The baby that was thoughtlessly got must be patiently bred. *Welsh*
13429. The child names the father; the mother knows him. *Livonian*
13430. The child that is no child leave upon the waters and let him swim. *Hebrew*
13431. [The child] who does not listen to father and mother will listen to a dog's hide [i.e., a whip]. *Polish*
13432. The children of heroes are causes of trouble. *Greek*
13433. The egg is wiser than the hen. [Said sarcastically.] *Polish*
13434. The errors of parents the gods turn to the undoing of their children. *Greek (Euripides)*
13435. The fine pullet shows its excellence from the egg. *Arabic*
13436. The hand that rocks the cradle rules the world. *American*
13437. The virtue of parents is a great dowry. *Latin (Horace)*
13438. Waly, waly! bairns are bonny; / One's enough, and twa's [two's] too mony. *Scottish*
13439. We never know the love of our parents for us till we have become parents. *American (Beecher)*
13440. What children hear at home soon flies abroad. *English*
13441. What the child hears at the fire is soon known at the minster. *French*
13442. What the parents spin the children must reel. *German*
13443. When children are married, cares are increased. *Portuguese*
13444. Who has no children does not know what love is. *Latin (Petrarch)*

Parsimony *see also* Frugality; Miserliness; Thrift

13445. He counts his ha'penny gude siller [silver]. *Scottish*

13446. He cuts awfu' near the wood. *Scottish*

13447. He hid a bodle [an ancient Scottish coin valued at one-sixth of the English penny] and thought it a hoard. *Scottish*

13448. He left his siller in his ither pocket. *Scottish*

13449. He would gang a mile to flit [to remove from one house to another] a sow. *Scottish*

13450. He would rake hell for a bodle. *Scottish*

13451. He would skin a louse for the tallow o't. *Scottish*

13452. He'd skin a louse, and send the hide and fat to market. *English*

13453. He'll gang tae [go to] hell for house profit. *Scottish*

13454. If he binds his pock [sack] she'll sit doun on't. *Scottish*

13455. It's an ill kitchen that keeps the bread awa [away, out of sight]. *Scottish*

13456. Ye'll follow him lang ere he let five shillings fa'. *Scottish*

Parting *see also* Absence; Friends and Friendship; Love

13457. Little intermeddling makes fair parting. *English*

13458. The hours of parting are the warmest. *French*

13459. To part is to die a little. *French*

13460. There's careless parting between the mare and the cart. *English*

13461. "There's sma' sorrow at our pairting," as the auld mear [old mare] said to the broken cart. *Scottish (Scott)*

Partnership *see* Shared Authority

Parts and Wholes *see also* Alternatives

13462. As if a group of blind men were feeling an elephant and describing it. *Korean*

13463. Better give the wool than the sheep. *Italian*

13464. Every great thing only consists of many small particles united. *Latin*

13465. Goose, and gander, and gosling, / Are three sounds, but one thing. *English*

Passion(s) *see also* Feeling; Lust

13466. A man in a passion rides a horse that runs away with him. *English*

13467. All passions are extinguished with old age. *French*

13468. All the passions are sisters. *French*

13469. Govern your passions, or they will govern you. *Latin*

13470. Great passions are incurable diseases: the very remedies make them worse. *German (Goethe)*

13471. Hat luve [hot love] an' hasty vengeance. *Scottish*

13472. He that overcomes his passions, overcomes his greatest enemies. *American*

13473. He's a wise man that leads passion by the bridle. *English*

13474. Hot love soon cold. *English*

13475. It is a harder lot to be a slave to one's passion than to tyrants. *Greek*

13476. No man can guess in cold blood what he may do in a passion. *American*

13477. None can be free who is a slave to his passions. *Greek*

13478. Passions are good servants and bad masters. *Greek*

13479. Plenty destroys passion. *Latin*

13480. Serving one's own passions is the greatest slavery. *English*

13481. The passions are like fire and water, good servants but bad masters. *American*

13482. The passions are merely different kinds of self-love. *French (La Rochefoucauld)*

13483. The passions are only orators who always persuade. *French (La Rochefoucauld)*

13484. The vicious obey their passions as slaves do their masters. *Greek*

13485. What Reason weaves is by Passion undone. *English (Pope)*

13486. When passion entereth at the fore-gate, wisdom goes out at the postern. *English*

13487. When the heart is afire some sparks will fly out at the mouth. *English*

13488. When the passions become masters, they are vices. *French (Pascal)*

13489. Where passion is high, there reason is low. *American*

Past *see also* Nostalgia

13490. A sponge for the past, a rose for the present, a kiss for the future. *Arabic*

13491. Can a mill go with the water that's past? *English*

13492. Consider the past and you will know the future. *Chinese*

13493. From what has taken place we infer what is about to happen. *Latin*

13494. He that would know what shall be must consider what hath been. *English*

13495. It is as good as second life to be able to look back upon our past life with pleasure. *Latin (Martius)*

13496. Men moralize among ruins. *American*

13497. No man can call again yesterday. *American*

13498. No one thinks of the snow that fell last year. *Swedish*

13499. Nothing is certain except the past. *Latin*

13500. Study the past if you would divine the future. *Chinese (Confucius)*

13501. The best prophet of the future is the past. *English (Byron)*

13502. The golden age was never the present age. *English*

13503. The man who abandons his past is lost. *Egyptian*

13504. The mind still longs for what it has missed, and loses itself in the contemplation of the past. *Latin (Petronius)*

13505. There is no retracing our steps. *Latin (Horace)*

13506. Troy is a thing of the past. *Latin*

13507. Waste not fresh tears over old griefs. *Greek (Euripides)*

13508. We praise old times, but show no curiosity about modern events. *Latin (Tacitus)*

13509. What hath been hath been. *Spanish*

13510. What is past, even the fool knows. *Greek*

13511. When the times you complain of are gone you will weep for them. *Arabic*

Patience *see also* **Accumulation; Gradualness; Haste; Slowness**

13512. A hour's patience will procure a long period of rest. *Arabic*

13513. A moment's patience is a comfort for ten years. *Greek*

13514. A patient person will cook a stone and drink its broth. *Hausa*

13515. A poor man without patience is like a lamp without oil. *American*

13516. Abused patience turns to fury. *English*

13517. All comes right for him who can wait. *French*

13518. All commend patience, but none can endure to suffer. *English*

13519. An ounce of patience is worth a pound of brains. *Dutch*

13520. At the bottom of patience there is heaven. *Kanuri*

13521. Be patient toward all men. *Bible*

13522. Bear and blame not what you cannot change. *American*

13523. Beware of vinegar made of sweet wine. *English*

13524. Bide weel, betide weel. *Scottish*

13525. Don't try to push the river. It flows by itself. *Polish*

13526. Dree [suffer, endure] out the inch when ye have thol'd [suffered] the span. *Scottish*

13527. Every misfortune is subdued by patience. *Latin*

13528. Everything comes in time to him that can wait. *American*

13529. Give time to time. *Italian*

13530. Have patience, and endure. *Latin*

13531. Have patience, cossack, thou wilt come to be a hetman. *Russian*

13532. He that can be patient finds his foe at his feet. *Dutch*

13533. He that can have patience can have what he will. *American (Franklin)*

13534. He that has patience has fat thrushes for a farthing. *English*

13535. He that has patience may compass anything. *French*

13536. He that weel bides weel betides. *Scottish*

13537. He who does not tire, tires adversity. *French*

13538. He who endures with patience is a conqueror. *Latin*

13539. He who has patience may accomplish anything. *French (Rabelais)*

13540. How poor are they that have not patience. *English (Shakespeare)*

13541. If you can't go through evil, you will never live to enjoy the good. *Yiddish*

13542. If you wait, there will come nectar-like fair weather. *Japanese*

13543. It's an ill turn that patience winna owercome. *Scottish*

13544. It's enough to make a parson swear, or a quaker kick his mother. *English*

13545. One cannot do everything in one day. *French*

13546. Paris was not made in one day. *French*

13547. Patience accomplishes its object while hurry speeds to its ruin. *Persian (Sa'di)*

13548. Patience and diligence, like faith, remove mountains. *American (Penn)*

13549. Patience and posset drink cure all maladies. *English*

13550. Patience, and the mulberry leaf becomes a silk gown. *Chinese*

13551. Patience conquers. *English (Chaucer)*

13552. Patience devours the devil. *German*

13553. Patience excels learning. *Dutch*

13554. Patience in market, is worth pounds in a year. *American (Franklin)*

13555. Patience is a bitter plant but it has sweet fruit. *German*

13556. Patience is a flower that grows not in every garden. *English*

13557. "Patience is a good plant but it doesn't grow in my garden," said the hangman. *German*

13558. Patience is a good nag, but she'll bolt. *English*

13559. Patience is a plaster for all sores. *English*

13560. Patience is a tree whose root is bitter, but its fruit very sweet. *Persian*

13561. Patience is a virtue. *English (Chaucer)*

13562. Patience is the art of hoping. *French*

13563. Patience is the best of dispositions; he who possesses patience possesses all things. *Yoruba*

13564. Patience is the door of joy. *German*

13565. Patience is the greatest prayer. *Hindi*

13566. Patience is the key to Paradise. *Persian*

13567. Patience is the remedy for every misfortune. *Latin (Publilius Syrus)*

13568. Patience is the virtue of asses. *French*

13569. Patience lightens what sorrow cannot heal. *Latin (Horace)*

13570. Patience overtaxed turns to rage. *Latin*

13571. Patience passes science. *French*

13572. Patience perforce is a medicine for a mad dog. *English*

13573. Patience pierces the rock. *American*

13574. Patience provoked often turns to fury. *Latin*

13575. Patience revels in misfortunes. *Latin (Lucan)*

13576. Patience, time, and money overcome everything. *Italian*

13577. Patience wears out stones. *American*

13578. Patience wi' poverty is a man's best remedy. *Scottish*

13579. Patience with poverty is all a poor man's remedy. *English*

13580. Patience! and shu!e the cards! *Spanish (Cervantes)*

13581. Patient men win the day. *English (Chaucer)*

13582. Patient waiters are no losers. *English*

13583. Rome was not built in a day. *American*

13584. Sit down and dangle your legs, and you will see your revenge. *Italian*

13585. Take time: much may be gained by patience. *Latin (Ovid)*

13586. The patient conquer [or overcome]. *Latin*

13587. The remedy for hard times is to have patience. *Arabic*

13588. The wedding will not be over, and the grocer will not die. *Tunisian*

13589. The world is his who has patience. *Italian*

13590. Though patience be a tired mare, yet she will plod. *English (Shakespeare)*

13591. To wait and be patient soothes many a pang. *Danish*

13592. Vengeance with patience becomes wine. *Turkish*

13593. Verjuice with patience becomes wine, and the mulberry leaf becomes satin. *Turkish*

13594. We shall sooner have the fowl by hatching the egg than by smashing it. *American (Lincoln)*

13595. What can't be alter'd must be borne, not blamed. *English*

13596. What cannot be removed, becomes lighter through patience. *Latin*

13597. Whoever has no patience has no wisdom. *Persian (Sa'di)*

13598. With patience and time the mulberry becomes a silk gown. *Spanish*

13599. Ye have heard of the patience of Job. *Bible*

13600. Zamora was not conquered in an hour. *Spanish (Cervantes)*

Patriotism *see also* Citizens and Citizenship; Country

13601. A good citizen owes his life to his country. *Russian*

13602. A patriot is a fool in ev'ry age. *English (Pope)*

13603. He dies a glorious death who dies for his country. *Greek*

13604. He serves me most who serves his country best. *Greek*

13605. It is sweet and glorious to die for one's native land. *Latin*

13606. Patriotism is the last refuge of a scoundrel. *English (Johnson)*

13607. When a nation is filled with strife, then do patriots flourish. *Chinese*

Payment *see also* Buying and Selling; Debt

13608. A good paymaster needs no surety. *Spanish*

13609. Ance payit, never cravit. [Once paid, never minded.] *Scottish*

13610. Corn him well, he'll work the better. *Scottish*

13611. Good demander, bad payer. *Yiddish*

13612. He need say nothing about the score who pays nothing. *French*

13613. He that cannot pay, let him pray. *English*

13614. He that payeth beforehand shall have his work ill done. *English*

13615. He that pays last ne'er pays twice. *Scottish*

13616. He who pays the piper may call the tune. *English*

13617. If you would have your work ill-done pay beforehand. *American*

13618. Misreckoning is no payment. *English*

13619. Nae [no] penny, nae pardon. *Scottish*

13620. Never give the skin when you can pay with the wool. *German*

13621. No penny, no paternoster. *English*

13622. Of pence misreckoned no thanks and no good proceeds. *French*

13623. Pay as you go. *American*

13624. Pay-before-hand's never weel fer'd. *Scottish*

13625. Pay me that thou owest. *Bible*

13626. Pay what you owe, and what you're worth you'll know. *Spanish*

13627. Payment in advance is evil payment. *Spanish*

13628. Sair cravers are aye ill payers. *Scottish*

13629. Soon paid is well paid. *American*

13630. Sweet's the wine but sour's the payment. *Irish*

13631. The money paid, the work delayed. *Spanish*

13632. There's ae day o' reckoning and anither day o' payment. *Scottish*

13633. When wages are paid, the arms are broken. *Spanish (Cervantes)*

13634. Who cannot pay with his purse, must pay with his skin. *German*

13635. Who cannot pay with money, must pay with his body. *Latin*

13636. Who wants his work ill done, let him pay beforehand. *Italian*

13637. Wrong compt [count] is na payment. *Scottish*

Peace *see also* War; War and Peace

13638. A cake eaten in peace is better than two in trouble. *Danish*

13639. A disarmed peace is weak. *American*

13640. Better a lean peace than a fat victory. *English*

13641. Better beans and bacon in peace than cakes and ale in fear. *Greek (Aesop)*

13642. Better keep peace than make peace. *American*

13643. Blessed are the peacemakers. *Bible*

13644. He only truly lives who lives in peace. *American*

13645. He who wants to live in peace should not disturb it. *Danish*

13646. Hear, see, and hold your peace, if you would live in peace. *Italian*

13647. Honorable peace becomes men, fierce anger belongs to beasts. *Latin (Ovid)*

13648. How beautiful upon the mountains are the feet of him that bringeth good tidings, that publisheth peace. *Bible*

13649. In His will is our peace. *Italian (Dante)*

13650. No man can live at peace unless his neighbor lets him. *American*

13651. No one can have peace longer than his neighbor pleases. *Dutch*

13652. Peace and a little. *French*

13653. Peace and patience and death with penitence. *Spanish*

13654. Peace at any price. *French*

13655. Peace flourishes when reason rules. *American*

13656. Peace is liberty in tranquillity. *Latin*

13657. Peace is more valuable than gold. *Finnish*

13658. Peace is the father of friendship. *Yoruba*

13659. Peace is the most profitable of things. *Greek*
13660. Peace without truth is poison. *German*
13661. The cudgel brings peace. *French*
13662. The peace of God which passeth all understanding. *Bible*
13663. The sheep who talks peace with a wolf will soon be mutton. *American*
13664. When a man finds no peace within himself, it is useless to seek it elsewhere. *French*
13665. Where there is peace there is blessing. *Yiddish*

Penitence *see also* **Repentance**
13666. By penitence the / Eternal's wrath's appeas'd. *English (Shakespeare)*
13667. No power can absolve the impenitent. *Italian (Dante)*

People *see also* **Mobs; Opinion**
13668. It is easy to go over to the crowd. *Latin*
13669. No doubt but ye are the people, and wisdom shall die with you. *Bible*
13670. No man who depends upon the caprice of the ignorant rabble can be accounted great. *Latin (Cicero)*
13671. Nothing is so uncertain as the judgments of the mob. *Latin*
13672. The fickle mob. *Latin*
13673. The mob tramples on the coward. *Latin*
13674. The people — docile to the yoke. *Latin*
13675. The views of the mob are neither bad nor good. *Latin*
13676. The voice of the people is the voice of God. [Vox populi, vox Dei.] *Latin (Alcuin)*
13677. The well-being of the people shall be the highest law. *Latin*
13678. Trust not the many-minded populace. *Greek*
13679. To perceive things in the germ is intelligence. *Chinese (Laotse)*

Perfection *see also* **Ability; Error(s); Faults; Skill; Superiority; Superiority and Inferiority**
13680. A man perfect to the finger tips. *Latin*
13681. Be ye therefore perfect, even as your Father which is in heaven is perfect. *Bible*
13682. Better a diamond with a flaw than a pebble without. *Chinese*
13683. He who has nothing but virtues is not much better than he who has nothing but faults. *Swedish*
13684. Nobody's perfect. *American*
13685. Trifles make perfection, but perfection is no trifle. *Italian (Michelangelo)*
13686. We shall never have friends, if we expect to find them without fault. *English*

Permanence *see* **Change; Unchangeableness**

Perseverance *see also* **Accumulation; Gradualness; Patience; Pertinacity; Repetition**
13687. After a bad harvest sow again. *Latin (Seneca)*
13688. An oak is not felled at one blow. *Spanish*
13689. By perseverance the Greeks reached Troy. *Latin*
13690. By repeated blows even the oak is felled. *Latin*
13691. Constant dropping wears the stone. *Latin*
13692. Daddy Tortoise goes slow, but he gets to the goal while Daddy Deer is asleep. *Louisianian Creole*
13693. Do what ye ought, and come what can; think o' ease, but work on. *Scottish*
13694. Drop by drop the sea is drained. *English*
13695. Dropping water makes the rock hollow, not by force, but by constant action. *Latin*
13696. For a just man falleth seven times and riseth up again. *Bible*
13697. God is with those who persevere. *Arabic*
13698. He conquers who sticks in his saddle. *Italian*
13699. He who shoots often hits at last. *American*
13700. If at first you don't succeed, try, try again. *American*
13701. If you can't fly, crawl. *American*
13702. In time a mouse will gnaw through a cable. *German*
13703. Lick by lick the cow ate the grindstone. *American*
13704. Like a tailor's needle, say: "I go through." *American*
13705. Little by little the cotton thread becomes a loincloth. *African*
13706. Many strokes overthrow the tallest oaks. *English (Lyly)*
13707. No tree falls at the first stroke. *German*
13708. Perseverance kills the game. *Spanish*
13709. Persevere, and preserve yourself for better days. *Latin*
13710. Plaister thick and some will stick. *Scottish*
13711. Raindrops will hollow a stone. *Korean*
13712. Seek till you find, and you'll not lose your labour. *English*
13713. Step after step the ladder is ascended. *American*
13714. Step by step climbs the hill. *Scottish*
13715. Step by step one ascends the staircase. *Turkish*
13716. Step by step one gets to Rome. *Italian*
13717. The toughest skin holds longest out. *English*
13718. The tree doesna fa' at the first strake. *Scottish*
13719. There's nae [no] iron sae [so] hard but rust will fret it; there's nae claith [cloth] sae fine but moths will eat it. *Scottish*
13720. To persevere, trusting in what hopes he has, is courage in a man. *Greek (Euripides)*
13721. Victory belongs to the most persevering. *American*
13722. Who hangs on, wins. *American*
13723. With time a mulberry leaf becomes satin. *Chinese*
13724. With time and straw meddlers ripen. *French*

Perspective *see also* **Distance**
13725. A dog has a good look at the bishop. *French*
13726. A lamb is as dear to the poor man as an ox to the rich. *American*
13727. A ship should not be judged from the land. *Italian*
13728. Ae [one] half o' the world doesna ken [does not know] how the ither half lives. *Scottish*

13729. All others are ill, but over the water and over the hill. [Ref. to the appeal of things distant.] *Scottish*

13730. Death to the wolf is life to the lambs. *Latin*

13731. Distance lends enchantment. *American*

13732. Every field looks green from a distance — even a cemetery. *American*

13733. Far awa' fowls hae fair feathers. *Scottish*

13734. He measures another by himself. *Dutch*

13735. He measures others by his own yard. *Italian*

13736. He that has one sheep in the flock will like all the rest better for it. *Scottish*

13737. He that never eats flesh thinks harrigals [the heart, liver, etc., of a sheep] a feast. *Scottish*

13738. If you were in my situation, you would think otherwise. *Latin*

13739. Men in the game are blind to what men looking on see clearly. *Chinese*

13740. No man ever thought his own too much. *German*

13741. O wad some power the giftie gie us / To see oursels as ithers see us. *Scottish (Burns)*

13742. On painting and fighting look afar off. *English*

13743. One half of the world laughs at the other half. *German*

13744. Perhaps the day may come when we shall remember these sufferings with joy. *Latin (Virgil)*

13745. The bat hanging upside down laughs at the topsy-turvy world. *Japanese*

13746. The crow thinks her own bird fairest. *English*

13747. The frog that has not seen the sea thinks the well a fine stretch of water. *Japanese*

13748. The grass is greener on the other side of the fence. *American*

13749. The other side of the road always looks cleanest. *American*

13750. The wolf knows what the ill beast thinks. *French*

13751. There is pleasure in hardship heard about. *Greek (Euripides)*

13752. They never saw great dainties that think haggis a feast. *Scottish*

13753. Things from afar please us the more. *Latin*

13754. Though you seat the frog on a golden stool, / He'll soon jump off, and into the pool. *English*

13755. To a frog in a well heaven is only a sieve in size. *American*

13756. To measure another by your own yard. *English*

13757. To see it rain is better than to be in it. *English*

13758. To the raven her own chick is white. *Irish*

13759. We admire things which deceive us from a distance. *Latin*

13760. We see not our own backs. *Latin (Catullus)*

13761. What is true to the master is false to the slave; what is true to the good man is false to the knave. *American*

13762. Ye shape my shoon [shoes] by your ain shackled [deformed] feet. *Scottish*

13763. Your neighbor's burden is always light. *American*

Persuasion *see also* **Soft Words**

13764. By long forbearance is a prince persuaded. *Bible*

13765. Contrivance is better than force. *French*

13766. If the horn cannot be twisted, the ear can. *Malay*

13767. If you cannot make a man think as you do, make him do as you think. *American*

13768. Machination is worth more than force. *French (Rabelais)*

13769. Milking yields milk, pressure yields blood. *Moroccan*

13770. More persuasive than the Sirens. *Latin*

13771. The persuasion of a friend is a strong thing. *Greek (Homer)*

13772. Win by persuasion, not by force. *Latin*

13773. Would you persuade, speak of interest, not of reason. *American (Franklin)*

Pertinacity *see also* **Perseverance**

13774. The provoking pertinacity of a fly. *Latin*

Perversity

13775. All things can corrupt perverted minds. *Latin*

Pessimism *see also* **Optimism**

13776. A pensive soul feeds upon nothing but bitters. *American*

13777. He that hopes no good fears no ill. *English*

13778. Our birth is nothing but our death begun. *American*

13779. Say no ill of the year till it is past. *American*

Pettiness

13780. A bucket full of water does not splash about, only a bucket half-full splashes. *Malay*

13781. They fight with tweezers, not swords. *Latin*

Philanthropy *see also* **Charity; Generosity; Gifts and Giving**

13782. He that plants trees lo'es [loves] ithers beside himsel. *Scottish*

Physicians

13783. A good surgeon must have an eagle's eye, a lion's heart, a lady's hand. *English*

13784. A man who is his own doctor has a fool for his patient. *American*

13785. A new doctor, a new grave-digger. *German*

13786. A physician is nothing but a consoler of the mind. *Latin*

13787. An ignorant doctor is no better than a murderer. *Chinese*

13788. Do not dwell in a city whose governor is a physician. *Hebrew*

13789. Doctors' faults are covered with earth and rich men's with money. *American*

13790. Every doctor thinks his pills the best. *German*

13791. Every man at thirty is either a fool or a physician. *Latin*

13792. From the physician and lawyer keep not the truth hidden. *Italian*

13793. Generals pray for wars and doctors for diseases. *American*

13794. God heals, and the doctor takes the fees. *American (Franklin)*

13795. Happy the doctor who is called in at the end of the disease. *French*

13796. He is a fool that makes his physician his heir. *Latin*

13797. Honor a physician before thou hast need of him. *Hebrew*

13798. If the doctor cures, the sun sees it; if he kills, the earth hides it. *American*

13799. In fleeing diseases you fall into the hands of doctors. *Latin*

13800. More danger from the physician than from the disease. *Latin*

13801. No good doctor ever takes physic. *Italian*

13802. Only a fool will make a doctor his heir. *Russian*

13803. Physician, heal thyself. *Bible*

13804. Physicians' faults are covered with earth. *English*

13805. Rich men's faults are covered with money and physicians' with earth. *English*

13806. The best surgeon is he that hath been hacked himself. *English*

13807. The city is in a bad case, whose physician has the gout. *Hebrew*

13808. The doctor cannot prescribe by letter; he must feel the pulse. *Latin*

13809. The doctor is often more to be feared than the disease. *French*

13810. The physician takes the fee, but God sends the cure. *German*

13811. The physician who accepts no fee is worth no fee. *Hebrew*

13812. There is no better surgeon than one with many scars. *Spanish*

Pictures

13813. A picture is a poem wanting [i.e., lacking] words. *Latin*

Piety *see also* God; Man and God; Religion

13814. Fear God, and your enemies will fear you. *American (Franklin)*

13815. Fear him who does not fear God. *Arabic*

13816. No piety delays the wrinkles. *Latin*

13817. Piety is the foundation of all virtues. *Latin*

13818. Set your affection on things above, not on things of the earth. *Bible*

13819. Tears of man for fear of God are the lustre of the eye. *Arabic*

13820. The best way to see divine light is to put out thy own candle. *English*

13821. True piety elevates the spirit, ennobles the heart and strengthens the courage. *American*

Pity

13822. Better cause envy than pity. *French*

13823. For pity runneth soon in gentle heart. *English (Chaucer)*

13824. He that hath pity on the poor lendeth to the Lord. *Bible*

13825. He that pities another minds [or remembers] himsel. *Scottish*

13826. He who would have others pity him must pity others. *Yiddish*

13827. It is better to be envied than pitied. *Greek (Herodotus)*

13828. Pity and need make all flesh kin. *American*

13829. Pity melts the mind to love. *American*

13830. Pity the conquered: you might be beaten yourself someday. *American*

13831. The best cure for sorrow is to pity somebody. *American*

13832. We all have enough strength to bear the misfortunes of others. *French (La Rochefoucauld)*

13833. With opposing warriors, he who has pity conquers. *Chinese*

Place

13834. Each man has his own place. *Latin*

13835. It is not the places that grace men, but men the places. *Greek*

13836. Nothing is more annoying than a low man in a high place. *Latin*

13837. One place is everywhere, everywhere is nowhere. *Persian*

13838. The place is dignified by the doer's deed. *English (Shakespeare)*

Plagiarism

13839. Perish those who said our good things before us. *Latin*

Plain Dealing

13840. Plain dealing is a jewel, but they that wear it are out of fashion. *English*

13841. Plain dealing's a jewel, but they that use it die beggars. *English*

Plain Living

13842. Four things impair the strength of man: sin, journeying, fasting and royalty. *Palestinian Talmud*

13843. Give me neither poverty nor riches; feed me with food convenient for me. *Bible*

13844. Plain living is nothing but voluntary poverty. *Latin (Seneca)*

Plain Talk

13845. A common word is always correct. *Polish*

13846. An honest tale speeds best being plainly told. *English (Shakespeare)*

13847. We call figs figs and a hoe a hoe. *Latin*

Plans and Planning

13848. Amid a multitude of projects, no plan is devised. *Latin (Publilius Syrus)*

13849. Do not plan for ventures before finishing what's at hand. *Greek (Euripides)*

13850. Do not think too far ahead lest you fall close by. *Arabic*

13851. It is a bad plan that admits of no modification. *Latin (Publilius Syrus)*

13852. Make plans for the year in spring; make plans for the day in the early morning. *Chinese*

13853. The best-laid plans o' mice an' men / Gang aft agley. *Scottish (Burns)*

Play *see also* **Winning and Losing**

13854. Even play has ended in fierce strife and anger. *Latin (Horace)*

13855. He plays best who wins. *French*

13856. It is not an art to play, but it is a very good art to leave off play. *Italian*

13857. Lang sports turn to earnest. *Scottish*

13858. Play's gude, while it is play. *English*

13859. The less play the better. *Scottish*

13860. There are toys for all ages. *English*

13861. They play till they quarrel. *English*

Pleasure *see also* **Pain; Pain and Pleasure; Pleasure-Seeking**

13862. A safe pleasure is a tame pleasure. *Latin (Ovid)*

13863. A wise man resists pleasures; a fool is a slave to them. *Greek*

13864. Better be jocund with the fruitful grape / Than sadden after none, or bitter, fruit. *Persian (Omar Khayyám)*

13865. Consider not pleasures as they come but as they go. *Greek*

13866. Each is attracted to some special pleasure. *Latin*

13867. Flee the pleasure that will bite tomorrow. *American*

13868. Fly pleasure and it will follow thee. *English*

13869. It is novelty that gives zest to pleasure. *Latin*

13870. No pleasure endures unseasoned by variety. *Latin (Publilius Syrus)*

13871. Never pleasure without repentance. *English*

13872. Nothing is ever long which gives endless pleasure. *Latin*

13873. Pleasure has a sting in its tail. *English*

13874. Pleasure is frail like a dewdrop; while it laughs, it dries. *Indian (Tagore)*

13875. Pleasure is none if not diversified. *English (Donne)*

13876. Pleasure is the bait of evil. *Latin*

13877. Pleasure is the greatest incentive to vice. *Greek*

13878. Pleasure's a sin, and sometimes sin's a pleasure. *English (Byron)*

13879. Pleasures are transient, honors are immortal. *Greek*

13880. Short pleasure, long lament. *French*

13881. The human mind runs downhill from toil to pleasure. *Latin*

13882. There is no pleasure unalloyed. *Latin*

Pleasure-Seeking *see also* **Pain; Pain and Pleasure; Pleasure**

13883. If you long for pleasure, you must labor hard to get it. *Chinese*

13884. Maids are drawn to pleasure as moths to the flame. *American*

13885. Many a man thinks he is buying pleasure, when he is really selling himself a slave to it. *American (Franklin)*

13886. Many seek good nights and lose good days. *Dutch*

13887. One cannot both feast and become rich. *Ashanti*

13888. Short pleasure is soon the parent of sorrow. *Latin*

Plenty *see* **Abundance**

Poets and Poetry

13889. A poet is born, not made. *Latin*

13890. He does not write whose verses no one reads. *Latin*

13891. It costs less to keep a lion than a poet: the poet's belly is more capacious. *Latin (Juvenal)*

13892. It is not good to be the poet of a village. *German*

13893. Those err who follow the poets. *Koran*

13894. To a poet even a rush may be vocal. *Turkish*

Point of View *see* **Distance; Perspective**

Pointlessness *see also* **Futility; Impossibility**

13895. Cultivate not a barren soil. *Latin*

13896. Don't throw pearls before swine. *American*

13897. Enchantments to Egypt. *English*

13898. Fir trees to Norway. *English*

13899. Gae [go] shoe the geese. *Scottish*

13900. Hard by a river he digs a well. *Latin*

13901. Indulgences to Rome. *English*

13902. Is it necessary to add acid to the lemon? *Hindi*

13903. It is folly to waste labor about trifles. *Latin (Martius)*

13904. It is in vain to look for yesterday's fish in the house of the otter. *Hindi*

13905. It is not good to teach a fish to swim. *French*

13906. It's like carrying coals to Newcastle. *English*

13907. Let the drunkard alone, and he will fall of himself. *Hebrew*

13908. Never bray at an ass. *American*

13909. Owls to Athens. *Latin*

13910. Pepper to Hindustan. *English*

13911. Puff not against the wind. *English*

13912. The woman is angry with the market, but the market doesn't know it. *Polish*

13913. To add water to the ocean. *Latin*

13914. To carry fir trees to Norway. *Dutch*

13915. To carry leaves to the wood. *French*

13916. To carry oil to the city of olives. *Hebrew*

13917. To carry water to the river [or to the sea]. *Dutch*

13918. To carry wood to the forest. *Latin (Horace)*

13919. To sell shells to those who come from St. Michel. *French*

13920. To swim a river with a bridge close by. *English*

13921. To wash an ass's head is loss of suds. *French*

13922. What is the use of running when we are not on the right road? *German*

13923. What's the use of putting honey in an ass's mouth? *English*

13924. You are carrying owls to Athens. *Latin*

13925. You are importing pepper into Hindustan. *Hindi*

13926. You cast water in the Thames. *English*

13927. You count the waves. [You labor in vain.] *Latin*

Policy

13928. Deny it—but do it. *American*

13929. He knows which side of his bread is buttered. *American*

13930. Molasses catches more flies than vinegar. *American*

Politeness *see also* Courtesy; Golden Rule; Manners

13931. As charity covers a multitude of sins before God, so does politeness among men. *American*

13932. Behave towards everyone as if receiving a great guest. *American*

13933. Even a well-bred dog makes hosts of friends. *American*

13934. Excessive politeness covers deceit. *Chinese*

13935. Hat in hand goes through the land. *German*

13936. Politeness gains the confidence of princes. *Chinese*

13937. Politeness is what warmth is to wax. *German*

13938. Politeness smooths wrinkles. *French*

13939. Reason, virtue, benevolence and goodness are not brought to perfection without politeness. *Chinese*

13940. Too much politeness is a form of cunning. *American*

13941. True politeness consists in treating others just as you love to be treated yourself. *American*

13942. Truly polite is always polite. *American*

13943. With politeness, one can go anywhere in the world; without politeness it is difficult to take the smallest step. *Chinese*

Politics and Politicians *see also* Office

13944. A man who takes up politics is a man trying to climb into the garbage can. *Lebanese*

13945. He never sought to stem the current. [Said of a politician who follows public opinion.] *Latin (Juvenal)*

13946. He that puts on a public gown must put off a private person. *English*

13947. It is better to herd cattle than rule men. *Arabic*

13948. Man is a political animal. *Greek (Aristotle)*

13949. Old politicians chew on wisdom past. *English (Pope)*

13950. Politics—a rotten egg; if broken open, it stinks. *Russian*

13951. The best qualities for a minister [of state] are justice, thorough investigation, wise determination, firmness and secrecy. *Sanskrit*

13952. There is no religion in politics. *Lebanese*

13953. When the sheikh dies his alliances die with him. *Arabic*

Pomposity

13954. He speaks like a prent book. *Scottish*

13955. He spoke as if every word would lift a dish. *Scottish*

13956. He struts like a craw in the gutter. *Scottish*

13957. He's as stiff as if he had swallowed the poker. *Scottish*

Popularity *see also* Opinion

13958. A beauty acclaimed from eight directions. *Japanese*

13959. He had need rise betimes that would please everybody. *English*

13960. He labors in vain who attempts to please everybody. *Latin*

13961. He that has many friends has no friends. *Greek (Aesop)*

13962. He that would please all and himself, too, / Undertakes what he cannot do. *English*

13963. Jupiter himself cannot please everybody. *Latin*

13964. No man can like all, or be liked by all. *English*

13965. One cannot please all the world and his father. *French*

13966. Popularity is glory in copper pieces. *French*

13967. Sound conviction should influence us rather than public opinion. *Latin (Cicero)*

13968. The love of popularity holds you in a vice. *Latin (Juvenal)*

13969. The popularity of a bad man is as treacherous as himself. *Latin*

13970. When Fortune favors us, Popularity bears her company. *Latin*

13971. When one has a good table, he is always right. *French*

13972. Woe unto you, when all men shall speak well of you! *Bible*

Portent *see* Omens

Position *see* Rank

Possession *see also* Alternatives; Compromise; Property

13973. All possessions of mortals are mortal. *Latin*

13974. As having nothing, and yet possessing all things. *Bible*

13975. Better haud [hold] by a hair nor [than] draw by a tether. *Scottish*

13976. Better say, "Here it is," than "Here it was." *Scottish*

13977. Better to have than wish. *English*

13978. Blessed are those who possess. *Latin*

13979. Everything goes to him who wants nothing. *French*

13980. Father's having and mother's having is not like having oneself. *Chinese*

13981. Great possessions are great cares. *American*

13982. He is a good man who is a man of goods. *French*

13983. Him that is in possession God helps. *Italian*

13984. I carry all my possessions with me. *Greek*

13985. I'll not change a cottage in possession for a kingdom in reversion. *English*

13986. Is it not lawful for me to do what I will with mine own? *Bible*

13987. It's no[t] "What is she?" but "What has she?" *Scottish*

13988. Let ne'er your gear [wealth, property, goods] owergang ye. *Scottish*

13989. Mine is better than ours. *American (Franklin)*

13990. Much will have more. *English*

13991. Naething is a man's truly, / But what he cometh by duly. *Scottish*

13992. One bird in the hand is worth four in the air. *Latin*

13993. Possession is as good as title. *French*

13994. Possession is eleven points o' the law. *Scottish*

13995. Possession is nine points of the law. *American*

13996. Possession is the grave of pleasure. *English*

13997. Possession is worth an ill charter. *Scottish*

13998. So much as you have, so much are you sure of. *Spanish*

13999. To each his own. *Latin*

14000. To have may be taken from us; to have had, never. *Latin*

14001. Unto everyone which hath shall be given. *Bible*

14002. What is not ours charms more than our own. *Latin*

14003. What is thine own hold as thine own. *Latin*

14004. What you have, hold. *Latin*

14005. What's yours is mine, and what's mine's my ain [own]. *Scottish*

14006. When all men have what belongs to them it cannot be much. *American*

14007. Who has but one lamb makes it fat. *French*

14008. Who has the hilt has the blade. *Welsh*

14009. Who holds an eel by the tail may well say that it is not his. *French*

14010. You are judged of by what you possess. *Latin (Horace)*

14011. You can never consider that as your own which can be changed. *Latin*

14012. You can't take it with you. *American*

14013. You must leave your possessions behind, when God summons. *Yiddish*

Possibility *see also* Certainty; Hope; Impossibility; Odds; Probability

14014. Every maybe hath a may not be. *Scottish*

14015. He has not lost all that has one cast left. French

14016. Nothing is impossible to a willing heart [or mind]. *English*

14017. The buke [book] o' "May-be's" is very braid [broad; i.e., thick]. *Scottish*

Posterity

14018. Posterity pays for the sins of their fathers. *Latin*

Postponement *see also* Delay; Future; Lateness; Opportunity; Procrastination; Timeliness; Today and Tomorrow

14019. Defer not till tomorrow what may be done today. *English*

14020. Evening is speedier than morning [i.e., tomorrow morning]. *Irish*

14021. If there is anything disagreeable to do, do it tomorrow. *Japanese*

14022. If you have time, don't wait for time. *American (Franklin)*

14023. If you wait till tomorrow have no fear of mishap. *Osmanli*

14024. Never put off till tomorrow what you can do today. *German*

14025. Omittance is no quittance. *English (Shakespeare)*

14026. Postponed is not abandoned. *German*

14027. That which is deferred is not abandoned. *Latin*

14028. To put off is not to let off. *German*

14029. What is postponed is not lost. *French*

14030. What you want to say, say it tomorrow. *Japanese*

Potential

14031. All soils are not fertile. *Latin (Cicero)*

14032. One that promised better things. *Latin*

14033. Stretch your foot to the length of your blanket. *Persian*

Poverty *see also* Beggars and Begging; Money; Rich and Poor; Scholars and Scholarship; Wealth

14034. A house fu' o' folk and a purse wi' three fardins in' the corner o't dinna [do not] sort weel thegither. *Scottish*

14035. A light purse is a heavy curse. *American (Franklin)*

14036. A light purse maks a heavy heart. *Scottish*

14037. A poor man has few acquaintances. *Danish*

14038. A poor man has no friend. *Oji*

14039. A poor man is all plans. *Spanish*

14040. A poor man is fain o' little. *Scottish*

14041. A poor man is hungry after eating. *Portuguese*

14042. A poor man is not believed, though he speak the truth. *Greek*

14043. A poor man maks a poor marriage. *Scottish*

14044. A poor man's table is soon spread. *English*

14045. A proud mind and a puir [poor] purse gree ill thegither. *Scottish*

14046. A sillerless man [a man without silver] gangs fast through the market. *Scottish*

14047. A toom [empty] purse maks a blate [bashful] merchant. *Scottish*

14048. Alas for the son whose father goes to heaven [i.e., whose father dies poor]. [The idea is that rich men go elsewhere.] *Portuguese*

14049. All the days of the poor are evil. *Hebrew*

14050. An empty hand, an empty prayer. *French*

14051. An empty purse frightens away friends. *English*

14052. As poor as a kirk [church] mouse. *Scottish*

14053. As poor as a sheep new shorn. *English*

14054. As poor as Job. *English*

14055. As poor as Job's turkey that had but one feather in its tail. *American*

14056. As poor as Job's turkey that had to lean against a fence to gobble. *American*

14057. Better an empty purse than an empty head. *German*

14058. Better be poor than wicked. *American*

14059. Bless be ye poor: for yours is the kingdom of God. *Bible*

14060. Eild [old age] and poortith [poverty] 's fair to thole [endure]. *Scottish*

14061. Eild [old age] and poortith [poverty] are a fair burden for ae [one] back. *Scottish*
14062. Everyone likes to wipe his shoes on poverty. *German*
14063. For one poor person there are a hundred indigent. *American (Franklin)*
14064. For puir [poor] folk they seldom ring. *Scottish*
14065. Fortune takes least from him to whom she has given least. *Latin*
14066. From poverty to wealth is a troublesome journey, but the way back is easy. *Japanese*
14067. Hard fare maks hungry bellies. *Scottish*
14068. He bears poverty very ill, who is ashamed of it. *English*
14069. He had not twopence to rub on a tombstone. *English*
14070. He has a cauld [cold] coal to blaw [blow] at. *Scottish*
14071. He has not even a clod of earth left to cover his remains. *Latin*
14072. He hasna [has not] a bauchle [old shoe] to swear by. *Scottish*
14073. He hasna [has not] a hail nail to claw him wi'. *Scottish*
14074. He is not poor that hath not much, but he that craves much. *English*
14075. He is poor but proud. *American*
14076. He is too poor to buy a rope to hang himself. *German*
14077. He is very thoughtful who has no bread. *French*
14078. He that has no money might as well be buried in a rice tub with his mouth sewn up. *Chinese*
14079. He that is poor, all his kindred scorn him; he that is rich, all are kind to him. *English*
14080. He that was born under a three-halfpenny planet shall never be worth twopence. *English*
14081. He who has made a fair compact with poverty is rich. *Latin*
14082. He who has no bread has no authority. *Turkish*
14083. He who has no money in his purse, should have honey on his tongue. *French*
14084. He who has nothing fears nothing. *American*
14085. He'll get the poor man's answer — No. *Scottish*
14086. He's as bare as the birk [birch] at Yule. *Scottish*
14087. He's cooling and supping. *Scottish*
14088. His wit gat [got] wings and wad hae [would have] flown, but pinching poortith [poverty] held him down. *Scottish*
14089. Honest poverty is thinly sewn. *French*
14090. If thou be poor, thy brother hateth thee. *English (Chaucer)*
14091. It is a bad thing to be poor, and seem poor. *English*
14092. It is easier to praise poverty than to bear it. *American*
14093. It is natural for a poor man to count his flock. *Latin*
14094. It [poverty] is cunning: it catches even a fox. *German*
14095. It's a poor family that has neither a whore nor a thief in it. *American*
14096. Let the gown be gray, so long as virtue's whole. *Polish*
14097. Money is very slow to come where there is poverty. *Latin*
14098. Naked [i.e., poor] as a Turkish saint. *Polish*
14099. No one lives so poor as he is born. *Latin*
14100. Not he who has little, but he who wishes for more, is poor. *Latin*
14101. Nothing is more luckless than a poor man. *Greek*
14102. Penniless souls maun [must] pine in purgatory. *Scottish*
14103. Poor and proud. *Latin (Juvenal)*
14104. Poor as a church mouse. *Spanish*
14105. Poor folk are fain [glad] of little. [Because they have little hope of obtaining it.] *Scottish*
14106. Poor folk fare the best. *English*
14107. Poor folk hae [have] neither ony [any] kindred nor freends. *Scottish*
14108. Poor folks are contented with duck-soup. *American*
14109. Poor folks must be glad of pottage. *English*
14110. Poor folks' friends soon misken [overlook, neglect] them. *Scottish*
14111. Poor fowk [folk] are soon pish't on. *Scottish*
14112. Poor men do penance for rich men's sins. *Italian*
14113. Poor men, they say, hesna [have no] souls. *Scottish*
14114. Poor men's reasons are not heard. *English*
14115. Poor men's tables are soon spread. *English*
14116. Poor without debt is better than a prince. *Turkish*
14117. Poortha [poverty] is a pain, but no disgrace. *Scottish*
14118. Poortith is better than pride. *Scottish*
14119. Poortith takes away pith. *Scottish*
14120. Poortith wi' patience is less painfu'. *Scottish*
14121. Poortith's pain, but nae [no] disgrace. *Scottish*
14122. Poverty and hunger have many learned disciples. *German*
14123. Poverty and sloth are brothers. *Yiddish*
14124. Poverty is a hateful blessing. *Latin*
14125. Poverty is a shirt of fire. *Turkish*
14126. Poverty is a sort of leprosy. *French*
14127. Poverty is death in another form. *Latin*
14128. Poverty is hateful good. *English*
14129. Poverty is no crime. *English*
14130. Poverty is no disgrace, but it is no great honor, either. *Yiddish*
14131. Poverty is no sin, but it is a branch of roguery. *Spanish*
14132. Poverty is no sin, but it is terribly inconvenient. *American*
14133. Poverty is no sin, but twice as bad. *Russian*
14134. Poverty is no vice, but it is a sort of leprosy. *French*

14135. Poverty is not perversity. *Spanish*

14136. Poverty is not sin; all the same, it is better to hide it. *French*

14137. Poverty is the daughter of laziness. *German*

14138. Poverty is the heritage of poverty. *Russian*

14139. Poverty is the mother of all the arts. *Scottish*

14140. Poverty is the mother of crime. *Latin*

14141. Poverty is the mother of health. *English*

14142. Poverty is the sixth sense. *German*

14143. Poverty is wisdom. *Arabic*

14144. Poverty makes a man mean. *Latin*

14145. Poverty makes the heart blind. *Arabic*

14146. Poverty parteth fellowship [or friends]. *English*

14147. Poverty parts good company, and is an enemy to virtue. *Scottish*

14148. Poverty shows us who are our friends and who our enemies. *Latin*

14149. Poverty turns a free man into a slave. *Oji*

14150. Poverty which keeps under a great people, is a heavy and unbearable evil. *Latin*

14151. Poverty—the mother of manhood. *Latin*

14152. Poverty—the mother of temperance. *Greek*

14153. Remember to bear patiently the burden of poverty. *Latin*

14154. Slow rises worth by poverty depressed. *English (Johnson)*

14155. The best that can happen to a poor man is that ae bairn dee [one child die] and the rest follow. *Scottish*

14156. The body is well, but the purse is sick. *Latin*

14157. The destruction of the poor is their poverty. *Bible*

14158. The devil wipes his breech [or tail] with poor folks' pride. *English*

14159. The drunkard and the glutton come to poverty, and drowsiness clothes a man with rags. *English*

14160. The first place poverty lies down on, is the face. *Yiddish*

14161. The gods protect the poor. *Greek*

14162. The life of the poor is the curse of the heart. *Bible*

14163. The man who has lost his purse will go wherever you wish. *Latin*

14164. The penniless traveler may sing before thieves. *Latin*

14165. The poor is hated even of his own neighbors. *Bible*

14166. The poor man has his crop destroyed by hail every year. *Spanish*

14167. The poor man is aye [always] put to the warst. *Scottish*

14168. The poor man is despised everywhere. *Latin*

14169. The poor man pays for all. *English*

14170. The poor man's debt makes a great noise. *English (Fuller)*

14171. The poor man's shilling is but a penny. *English*

14172. The poor sing free throughout the world. *German*

14173. The poor sleep soundly. *Japanese*

14174. The poor, wishing to imitate the powerful, perish. *Latin*

14175. The poor ye always have with you. *Bible*

14176. The poorest man in the world is he who has nothing but money. *American*

14177. The sun is the cloak of the poor. *Arabic*

14178. The traveler with empty pockets may laugh in the bandit's face. *American*

14179. The wind blows in a poor man's eyes. *Polish*

14180. Their rise is one of difficulty, whose merits are impeded by poverty. *Latin (Juvenal)*

14181. There are many things which ragged men dare not say. *Latin*

14182. There are none poor but such as God hates. *English*

14183. There's nothing agrees worse / Than a proud mind and a beggar's purse. *English*

14184. They hae nae [have no] need o' a canny cook that hae but ae [have but one] egg to their dinner. *Scottish*

14185. To be poor and seem poor is the very devil. *English*

14186. To have nothing is not poverty. *Latin*

14187. Toom [empty] stalls mak biting horses. *Scottish*

14188. Want o' warld's gear [worldly goods] aften sunders fond hearts. *Scottish*

14189. We do not praise poverty, but him whom poverty cannot bend. *Latin*

14190. We will do anything for the poor man except get off his back. *Russian (Tolstoy)*

14191. What the poor need is less advice and more helping hands. *American*

14192. When poverty comes in at the door, love flies out at the window. *Scottish*

14193. When we want, friends are scant. *Scottish*

14194. When ye are poor naebody kens ye [nobody knows you], when ye are rich a' body [everybody] lends ye. *Scottish*

14195. Who doth sing so merry a note / As he that cannot change a groat? *English*

14196. Whoso stoppeth his ear at the cry of the poor, shall cry himself and not be heard. *Hebrew*

14197. Without a fine coat, but a good soul. *Polish*

Power *see also* Authority; Kings; Shared Authority

14198. Better be the head o' the commons than the tail o' the gentry. *Scottish*

14199. Deny a strong man his due, and he will take all he can get. *Latin (Lucan)*

14200. For sovereign power all laws are broken. *Spanish*

14201. Hares can gambol over the body of a dead lion. *Latin (Publilius Syrus)*

14202. He has got the heavy end of him. *Scottish*

14203. He has gotten the whip hand o' him. *Scottish*

14204. It is better to be the head of a mouse than the tail of a lion. *Spanish*

14205. Lust of power is the strongest of all passions. *Latin*

14206. Mickle [much] power—mickle [many] enemies. *Scottish*

14207. Money controls the battle and not the strong arm. *Portuguese*

14208. Not surpassing in crafty measures, but in the power of arms. *Latin*

14209. One lie in the sultan's head provides an obstacle for twenty truths. *Arabic*

14210. Power acquired by guilt was never used for a good purpose. *Latin*

14211. Power can achieve more by gentle means than by violence. *Latin*

14212. Power goes before talent. *Danish*

14213. Power on my head, or the raven on my corpse. *Turkish*

14214. Power passes to the best from the inferior. *Latin*

14215. Power won by crime no one ever yet turned to a good purpose. *Latin (Tacitus)*

14216. Sodgers [soldiers], fire and water soon mak room for themsels. *Scottish*

14217. Speak softly and carry a big stick. *American*

14218. The eagle suffers little birds to sing. *English (Shakespeare)*

14219. The fox's wiles will never enter the lion's head. *English*

14220. The highest power may be lost by misrule. *Latin*

14221. The love of dominion is the most engrossing passion. *Latin (Tacitus)*

14222. The powers that be are ordained by God. *Bible*

14223. Though they don't want to kill anybody, they like to have the power to do so. *Latin (Juvenal)*

14224. Who can do as he pleases, commands when he entreats. *French*

14225. Who is too powerful seeks power beyond his power. *Latin*

Powerlessness *see* Impotence

Practicality *see also* Purpose; Use; Usefulness; Value; Work and Workers; Worth; Worthlessness

14226. Cultivate a rice-field rather than make verses. *Japanese*

14227. Hay is more acceptable to an ass than gold. *Latin*

14228. I will keep no more cats than will catch mice. *English*

Practice *see also* Experience; Repetition

14229. A surgeon tries his experiments on the heads of orphans. *Latin*

14230. By writing we [or you] learn to write. *Latin*

14231. No man is his craft's master the first day. *English*

14232. Not knowledge, but practice. *Greek*

14233. Practice can do all things. *Latin*

14234. Practice is better than theory. *Latin*

14235. Practice is everything. *Greek*

14236. Practice is the best master. *Latin*

14237. Practice makes perfect. *Latin*

14238. Practice makes the master. *German*

14239. Practice not your art [i.e., if you do not practice your art], and 'twill soon depart. *English*

14240. Practice well if you would excel. *Chinese*

14241. The barber learns his trade on the orphan's chin. *Arabic*

14242. The surgeon [or barber] practices on the orphan's head. *Arabic*

14243. Try your skill in gilt first, and then in gold. *English*

14244. Use makes the craftsman. *German*

14245. Use maks perfyteness. *Scottish*

14246. Use of hand is father of lear [learning]. *Scottish*

14247. Work makes the workman. *Latin*

Praise *see also* Applause; Appreciation; Approval; Honor

14248. A chuck under the chin is worth two kisses. *English*

14249. A man commends himself in praising that which he loves. *Latin*

14250. A part of a man's praise may be told in his presence; the whole, in his absence. *Hebrew*

14251. A puff of wind and popular praise weigh alike. *English*

14252. An honest man is hurt by praise unjustly bestowed. *French*

14253. Be sparing in praising, and more so in blaming. *Latin*

14254. Damn with faint praise. *English (Pope)*

14255. Every cook praises his own soup. *American*

14256. Every man likes his own praise best. *American*

14257. Every potter praises his own pot. *American*

14258. Funeral sermon — lying sermon. *German*

14259. He wants worth who dares not praise a foe. *English (Dryden)*

14260. He who praises himself must have bad neighbors. *Yiddish*

14261. He who praises himself will soon find someone to deride him. *Latin*

14262. Honorable mention encourages science, and merit is fostered by praise. *Latin (Cicero)*

14263. I am pleased to be praised by one whom everyone praises. *Latin*

14264. I praise loudly, I blame softly. *Russian*

14265. If thou wouldst have praise, die. *Welsh*

14266. If you would reap praise you must sow the seeds, gentle words and useful deeds. *American (Franklin)*

14267. It is a disgrace to be praised by those who deserve no praise. *Latin*

14268. It is a kind of encumbrance to be overmuch praised. *Greek*

14269. It is discreditable to be praised by the undeserving. *Latin*

14270. It is not befitting to praise yourself— but it does no harm. *Yiddish*

14271. Let every man praise the bridge he goes over. *English*

14272. Men praise themselves to save praising others. *American*

14273. Never praise your cider or your horse. *American (Franklin)*

14274. One has only to die to be praised. *German*

14275. Our praises are our wages. *English (Shakespeare)*

14276. Praise a maid in the morning, and weather in the evening. *Italian*

14277. Praise is the hire of virtue. *English*

14278. Praise little, dispraise less. *American (Franklin)*

14279. Praise makes good men better and bad men worse. *English*

14280. Praise undeserved is satire in disguise. *English*

14281. Praise undeserved is scandal in disguise. *American*

14282. Praise yourself, Basket, for I want to sell you. *Spanish*

14283. Praises from an enemy imply real merit. *English*

14284. Self-praise is half slander. *American*

14285. Self-praise is no recommendation. *American*

14286. Some things are better praised by silence than by remark. *Latin*

14287. The most pleasing of all sounds — that of your own praise. *Greek*

14288. The praise of fools is censure in disguise. *English*

14289. The refusal of praise is a wish to be praised twice. *French (La Rochefoucauld)*

14290. The three dearest of things: Hen's eggs, pork and old women's praise. *Gaelic*

14291. They praise what they do not understand. *Latin*

14292. To be praised is to be ruined. Gɨkʉyʉ

14293. To give instruction in the form of praise. *Latin*

14294. To throw a blot on a man's reputation by praising him. *Latin (Cicero)*

14295. Unless new praise arises, even the old is lost. *Latin*

14296. Usually we praise only to be praised. *French (La Rochefoucauld)*

14297. We are all imbued with the love of praise. *Latin*

14298. When all praised the peacock's tail, the birds cried, "Look at his legs, and what a voice!" *Japanese*

Prayer *see also* Divine Assistance; God; Man and God; Self-Help; Self-Reliance

14299. A god, when angry, is moved by the voice of prayer. *Latin*

14300. A grateful thought toward Heaven is a complete prayer. *German*

14301. A short prayer enters heaven. *Latin*

14302. Affliction teaches a wicked man to pray, prosperity never. *American*

14303. All things, whatsoever ye ask in prayer, ye shall receive. *Bible*

14304. Ask, and it shall be given you; seek and ye shall find; knock, and it shall be opened unto you. *Bible*

14305. Beware the weapons of the weak [i.e., their prayers.] *Arabic*

14306. Do not pray for yourself: you do not know what will help you. *Greek*

14307. Fear drives to praying. *Latin*

14308. He has mickle [much] prayer, but little devotion. *Scottish*

14309. If you pray for another, you will be helped yourself. *Yiddish*

14310. Long tarries destiny, but comes to those who pray. *Greek*

14311. Much praying, but no piety. *English*

14312. Necessity teaches how to pray. *American*

14313. Nightly prayer makes the day to shine. *Arabic*

14314. None can pray well but he that lives well. *English*

14315. Nothing costs so much as what is bought by prayers. *Latin (Seneca)*

14316. Pray and work. *Latin*

14317. Prayer is the pillow of religion. *Arabic*

14318. Prayer is the voice of faith. *American*

14319. Prayer should be the key of the day and the lock of the night. *English*

14320. Prayers go up and blessings come down. *Yiddish*

14321. Prayers travel faster when said in unison. *Latin*

14322. The fewer the words the better the prayer. *German*

14323. The prayer of a dog does not reach heaven. *Spanish*

14324. The prayer of faith shall save the sick. *Bible*

14325. To join the hands [in prayer] is well; to open them [in work] is better. *French*

14326. Watch and pray. *Bible*

14327. Who prays without trust cannot hope to have his prayers answered. *French*

14328. Your Father knoweth what things ye have need of, before you ask Him. *Bible*

Preachers and Preaching *see also* Example; Priests

14329. He preaches well that lives well. *Spanish (Cervantes)*

14330. It is bad preaching to deaf ears. *German*

14331. It is easy preaching to the fasting with a full belly. *Italian*

14332. More vacant pulpits would more converts make. *English (Dryden)*

14333. Practice yourself what you preach. *Latin*

14334. There are many preachers who don't hear themselves. *German*

Precaution *see also* Carefulness; Caution; Common Sense; Preparedness; Watchfulness

14335. A curst cur must be tied short. *English*

14336. A fall hurts not those who fly low. *Chinese*

14337. A fidging [skittish] mare should be weel girthed. *Scottish*

14338. A mouse relies not solely on one hole. *Latin (Plautus)*

14339. A thief does not always thieve, but be always on your guard against him. *Russian*

14340. Admire a little ship, but put your cargo in a big one. *Greek (Hesiod)*

14341. Always be provided against danger and rebellion. *Chinese*

14342. An ill-willie [bad-tempered] cow should have short horns. *English*

14343. Better is a turn of the key than a friar's conscience. *Spanish*

14344. Blow first and sip afterwards. *American*

14345. Good watch prevents misfortune. *English*

14346. Grin when ye bind, and laugh when ye loose. *Scottish*

14347. Harm watch, harm catch. *English*

14348. He should hae [have] a lang-shafted spune that sups kail wi' the deil [devil]. *Scottish*

14349. He that looks na ere he loup [not before he leaps], will fa' ere he wit [knows] o' himsel'. *Scottish*

14350. He who enjoys favors should be prepared for reverses; he who lives in security should think of possible danger. *Chinese*

14351. If you use a walking stick you will not fall; if you take counsel you will not err. *Chinese*

14352. If your head is made of wax don't work in the sun. *American*

14353. It is best to trust to two anchors. *Latin*

14354. Lock the stable door before the horse is stolen. *American*

14355. Never play with a mad dog. *American*

14356. Never venture out of your depth till you can swim. *American*

14357. Never wade in unknown waters. *American*

14358. Stand away from a horse's heels. *Latin*

14359. State all the conditions first. *Chinese*

14360. Take care before you leap. *Italian*

14361. Take heed lest you stumble. *Latin (Horace)*

14362. Test the danger by the Carians [mercenaries]. *Latin*

14363. The mouse that only trusts to one poor hole, / Can never be a mouse of any soul. *English*

14364. The rat which has but one hole is soon caught. *English*

14365. There's no need to fear the wind if your haystacks are tied down. *Irish*

14366. When you know there are tigers on the hills, don't go there. *Chinese*

14367. Who goes for a day in the forest should take bread for a week. *Czech*

14368. Who hath a wolf for his mate, needs a dog for his man. *Italian*

14369. Who sees not the bottom, let him not pass the water. *Italian*

Precedent

14370. As well to create good precedents as to follow them. *English (Bacon)*

14371. The more ancient the abuse the more sacred it is. *French (Voltaire)*

Precision *see also* Accuracy

14372. You have hit the nail on the head. *English*

14373. You have hit the point exactly. *Latin*

Precocity

14374. He dies before he is old who is wise before his day. *American*

14375. It early pricks that will be a thorn. *English*

14376. Precocious youth is a sign of premature death. *Latin*

14377. Soon crooks the tree / That good gambrel would be. *English*

14378. The real nettle will sting early. *Latin*

14379. What ripens fast does not last. *American*

Prediction *see also* Future; Omens; Prophecy

14380. Freits [predictions] follow those who look to them. *Scottish*

14381. He is the best diviner who conjectures well. *Greek (Euripides)*

Preference *see also* Alternatives; Choice; Taste

14382. A frog would leap from a throne of gold into a puddle. *Latin (Publilius Syrus)*

14383. A sow prefers bran to roses. *French*

14384. Every man rejoices in his peculiar study. *Latin*

14385. One does well what one likes most. *Japanese*

14386. Our ain reek's [own smoke's] better than ither folk's fire. *Scottish*

14387. The pig prefers mud to clean water. *Latin*

14388. There are as many preferences as there are men. *Latin (Horace)*

14389. "Wae worth ill company," quo' the daw o' Camnethan. *Scottish*

Prejudice *see also* Appearance; Beauty; Clothes; Inference; Judges; Judging; Judgment

14390. A runaway monk never spoke in praise of his monastery. *Italian*

14391. All looks yellow to the jaundiced eye. *American*

14392. Drive out prejudices by the door, they will come back by the window. *French*

14393. He that is an enemy of the bride does not speak well of the wedding. *Spanish*

14394. It is never too late to give up our prejudices. *American (Thoreau)*

14395. Never let the prejudice of the eye determine the heart. *American*

14396. Opinions grounded on prejudice are always sustained with the greatest violence. *American*

14397. Prejudice is the child of ignorance. *Latin*

14398. Prejudice is the reason of fools. *American*

14399. When the judgment is weak the prejudice is strong. *American*

14400. When we destroy an old prejudice we have need of a new one. *American*

Prematureness *see also* Earliness

14401. Ane [one] may bind the sack before it's fu'. *Scottish*

14402. Boast not thyself of tomorrow; for thou knowest not what a day may bring forth. *Bible*

14403. Boil not the pap before the child is born. *English*

14404. Call me not "olive" till you see me gathered. *Spanish*

14405. Call not a surgeon before you are wounded. *English*

14406. Cry no herring till you have it in the net. *Dutch*

14407. Cry not out before you are hurt. *English*

14408. Dinna [do not] gut your fish till ye've catched them. *Scottish*

14409. Dinna [do not] lift me before I fa'. *Scottish*

14410. Do not bless the fish until you land it. *Irish*

14411. Do not climb the hill until you get to it. *English*

14412. Do not sell the hide before you have caught the fox [or bear]. *Danish*

14413. Don't boast when you set out, but when you get there. *Russian*

14414. Don't count your chickens before they're hatched. *American*

14415. Don't cry "Hey!" till you are over the ditch. *German*

14416. Don't cry fish before they're caught. *English*

14417. Don't cry fried fish before they are caught. *Italian*

14418. Don't cry till you are out of the wood. *English*

14419. Don't give the lie until you are ready with your blow. *Irish*

14420. Don't kick till ye're spurred. *Irish*

14421. Don't sell the bird on the bough. *Italian*

14422. Don't sell the skin till you have caught the fox. *Danish*

14423. Don't sing triumph before the victory. *Greek*

14424. Don't snap your fingers at the dogs before you are out of the village. *English*

14425. Don't try to fly before you have wings. *French*

14426. Don't try to run before you can walk. *English*

14427. Draw not thy bow before thy arrow be fixed. *English*

14428. Drive not a second nail till the first be clinched. *English*

14429. Gut nae [no] fish till ye get them. *Scottish*

14430. Having heard talk about a bath, he undressed in the street. *Arabic*

14431. It is ill prizing of green barley. *Scottish*

14432. It is not fish until it is on the bank. *Irish*

14433. It's lang [long] or ye need cry "Schew!" to an egg. *Scottish*

14434. Let not the praise be before the victory. *Greek*

14435. Make not the sauce till you have caught the fish. *American*

14436. Never ask pardon before you are accused. *English*

14437. Never boil your rabbit till you've got him. *American*

14438. Never fry a fish till it's caught. *American*

14439. Never howl till you are bit. *Irish*

14440. Praise a fair day at night. *German*

14441. Praise not the day before night. *English*

14442. Ruse [praise] the fair day at een [in the evening]. *Scottish*

14443. Sell not the bear's skin before you have caught him. *English*

14444. Sing not of triumph before the victory. *Latin*

14445. Sometimes the canoe sinks before it reaches shore. *Cameroonian*

14446. Soon ripe soon rotten. *English (Heywood)*

14447. Sune enough to cry "chick" when it's out o' the shell. *Scottish*

14448. Take not the antidote before the poison. *Latin*

14449. That which prematurely arrives at perfection soon perishes. *Latin (Quintilian)*

14450. The baby is not yet born, and you say his nose is like his grandfather's. *Punjabi*

14451. To swallow gudgeons ere they're catched / And count their chickens ere they're hatched. *English (Butler)*

14452. Unlaid eggs are uncertain chickens. *German*

14453. Wait till night before saying it has been a fine day. *French*

14454. You are like the eels of Melun; you cry out before you are skinned. *French (Rabelais)*

14455. You must not sell the bearskin before the bear is killed. *German*

14456. You should praise a fine day when it is night. *German*

Preparedness *see also* Common Sense; Defense; Precaution; Prudence

14457. A forewarned man is worth two. *Spanish*

14458. A good knight is not at a loss for a lance. *Italian*

14459. A man prepared has half fought the battle. *Spanish (Cervantes)*

14460. A man that is warned is half armed. *English*

14461. Being prepared beforehand is better than after-thought. *Kanuri*

14462. Collect at leisure to use in haste. *Chinese*

14463. Fore-talk spares after-talk. *English*

14464. Forewarned, forearmed; to be prepared is half the victory. *Spanish*

14465. Have an umbrella ready before you get wet. *American*

14466. He who is not prepared today, will be less so tomorrow. *Latin*

14467. If you wish for peace, prepare for war. *Latin*

14468. In a narrow passage be prepared for a dagger. *Chinese*

14469. In fine weather carry an umbrella; though not hungry take provisions with you. *Chinese*

14470. In summer make a sledge, in winter a carriage. *Estonian*

14471. In times of peace we should think of war. *Latin*

14472. It is better to be always prepared than to suffer once. *Latin*

14473. It is not enough for a man to know how to ride; he must know how to fall. *Mexican*

14474. Keep your powder dry. *American*

14475. Prepare for calamity not yet in bud. *Chinese*

14476. Provision in season maks a bein [comfortable] house. *Scottish*

14477. Rear sons for old age; and store grain against famine. *Chinese*

14478. She's a sairy mouse that has but ae [one] hole. *Scottish*

14479. The beggar provides for a rainy day. *Chinese*

14480. The blow falls more lightly when it is anticipated. *Latin*

14481. The dam must be made before the flood comes. *Hindi*

14482. The wise man avoids evil by anticipating it. *Latin (Publilius Syrus)*

14483. Though the sun shines, leave not your cloak at home. *Spanish*

14484. To fear the worst oft cures the worse. *English (Shakespeare)*

14485. When the wolf comes into your mind prepare a stick for him. *Arabic*

14486. When you travel by boat be prepared for a ducking. *Chinese*

14487. Where there is previous preparation there will be no calamity. *Chinese*

14488. Who carries a sword, carries peace. *French*

14489. You must step back to make the better leap. *American*

Present *see also* **Future; Past; Postponement; Procrastination; Today and Tomorrow**

14490. Each day provides its own gifts. *Latin (Martial)*

14491. If you are lucky today count it as a gain. *American*

14492. Past, and to come, seems best; things present, worst. *English (Shakespeare)*

14493. Seize today [or the day], trust tomorrow as little as possible. [Carpe diem.] *Latin (Horace)*

14494. The present alone can make no man wretched. *Latin*

14495. There is no time like the present. *American*

14496. Today is yesterday's pupil. *English*

14497. Today's egg is better than tomorrow's hen. *Turkish*

14498. When a [free] woman enters service, she is called a slave. [What matters is what you are, not what you were.] *Oji*

Presumption

14499. A beardless boy would teach old men! *Latin*

14500. Give the hen a place to roost and she'll say, "I'll be higher yet." *Polish*

14501. He that knows least commonly presumes most. *English*

14502. Jack Sprat would teach his grandame. *English*

14503. Presumption first blinds a man, then sets him a running. *American (Franklin)*

14504. Shall the gosling teach the goose to swim? *English*

14505. Teach your father to get children. *English*

14506. Teach your grandam to spin. *English*

14507. Teach your grandame to grope her ducks [or to sup sour milk]. *English*

14508. Teach your grandame to suck eggs. *English*

14509. The fool would teach the learned. *Latin*

14510. The goslings would lead the geese to grass. *French*

Pretense

14511. He is a mock sportsman who slings a dead rat in his girdle. *Chinese*

14512. He's nae [not] so daft as he lets on. *Scottish*

14513. Pretending to be deaf and dumb; no truth but falsehood. *Chinese*

14514. The mask of pretense often becomes reality. *American*

14515. To snore with wakeful nose. [To pretend to be asleep.] *Latin (Juvenal)*

14516. When a beggar is out at night, it is all a pretense of being busy. *Chinese*

Pretension *see also* **Affectation**

14517. A' Stuarts are no sib to the king. *Scottish*

14518. All kinds of wood burn silently except thorns, which crackle and call out, "We, too, are wood." *Talmud*

14519. Begin with another's to end with your own. *Spanish (Gracián)*

14520. Doctor Luther's shoes will not fit every village priest. *German*

14521. Every ass thinks himself worthy to stand with the king's horses. *English*

14522. He that is a donkey, and believes himself a deer, finds out his mistake at the leaping of the ditch. *Italian*

14523. I ask your pardon, coach; I thought you were a wheelbarrow when I stumbled over you. *Irish*

14524. It is some way from Peter to Peter. *Spanish*

14525. Many talk of Robin Hood that never shot his bow. *English*

14526. Nothing is lasting that is feigned. *English*

14527. Sparrows who emulate peacocks are likely to break a thigh. *Burmese*

14528. The best pilots stand on shore. *Dutch*

14529. The crow that pretends to be a cormorant gets drowned. *Japanese*

14530. The frog tried to look as big as the elephant, and burst. *African*

14531. They came to shoe the horses of the pasha; the beetle then stretched out its leg. *Arabic*

14532. "We hounds slew the hare," quoth the messan [lapdog]. *Scottish*

14533. When the bad imitate the good, there is no knowing what mischief is intended. *Latin (Publilius Syrus)*

Pretext

14534. Friday pretexts are not fasting. *Spanish*

14535. He that would hang his dog, gives out first that he is mad. *English*

14536. If a man wants to thrash his wife, let him ask her for drink in the sunshine. *Spanish*

14537. If you want a pretense [i.e., pretext] to whip a dog, it is enough to say he ate up the frying-pan. *American*

14538. If you want to flog your dog, say he ate the poker. *Spanish*

14539. On a little pretext the wolf seizes the sheep. *French*

14540. Pretexts are not wanting when one wishes to use them. *Italian*

14541. The wolf never wants a pretext against the lamb. *English*

Prevention

14542. An ounce of prevention is worth a pound of cure. *American*

14543. Better keep the deil [deil] out than hae [have] to put him out. *Scottish*

14544. Better keep the deil [devil] without the door than drive him out o' the house. *Scottish*

14545. Better skaiths [injuries] saved than mends made. *Scottish*

14546. Check disease in its approach. *Latin (Persius)*

14547. Hang him that has nae [no] shift, and hang him that has ower mony [too many]. *Scottish*

14548. It is better to ward off than to cure disease. *Chinese*

14549. It is easier to prevent ill habits than to break them. *English*

14550. Justice is exercised in the proper prevention, rather than in the severe punishment, of crime. *Latin*

14551. One must pay Health its tithes. *Irish*

14552. One sword keeps another in the scabbard. *English*

14553. Pervidin's perventin'. [Providing is preventing.] *English*

14554. Prevention is better than cure. *Latin*

Pride *see also* **Appearance; Conceit; Vanity**

14555. A proud heart in a poor breast has muckle dolour [much sorrow] to dree [suffer, endure]. *Scottish*

14556. A proud man is always a foolish man. *American*

14557. A proud mind and a poor purse are ill-met. *American*

14558. A proud woman brings distress on her family. *American*

14559. An avenging god pursues the proud. *Latin*

14560. Are they no a bonny pair?—as the devil said to his hoofs. *Scottish*

14561. As pride increases, fortune declines. *American (Franklin)*

14562. Bastard brood are aye [always] proud. *Scottish*

14563. Being on his own dunghill makes the dog proud. *French*

14564. But yesterday out of the shell, today he despises it. *Turkish*

14565. Deil [devil] stick pride—my dog died o't. *Scottish*

14566. Every craw thinks his ain [own] bird whitest. *Scottish*

14567. Every man thinks his ain [own] craw blackest. *Scottish*

14568. God is the enemy of the proud. *Turkish*

14569. Great merit is coy, as well as great pride. *American (Franklin)*

14570. He carries his nose in the air. *Hungarian*

14571. He gaes [goes] awa' wi' born head. *Scottish*

14572. He maks meikle [much] o' his painted sheets. *Scottish*

14573. He spills unspoken to. *Scottish*

14574. He struts as proudly as a peacock. *American*

14575. He who is on horseback no longer knows his own father. *Russian*

14576. He who swells up in prosperity will sink in adversity. *American*

14577. He'll gang [go] mad on a horse wha's proud on a pownie. *Scottish*

14578. He's a proud beggar that maks his ain awmous [his own alms]. *Scottish*

14579. If wishes were horses beggars would ride, and a' the warld be drowned in pride. *Scottish*

14580. Ingratitude is the child of pride. *Spanish*

14581. It is pride, not nature, that craves much. *American*

14582. Mair [more] pride nor [than] pith. *Scottish*

14583. Peacock, look at your legs. *German*

14584. Poor and proud, fie, fie. *English*

14585. Pride and conceit were the original sin of man. *French*

14586. Pride and gout are seldom cur'd throughout. *American (Franklin)*

14587. Pride and grace ne'er dwell in ae [one] place. *Scottish*

14588. Pride breakfasted with Plenty, dined with Poverty, and supped with Infamy. *American (Franklin)*

14589. Pride dines upon vanity, sups on contempt. *American (Franklin)*

14590. Pride gets into the coach, and shame mounts behind. *American (Franklin)*

14591. Pride goeth before destruction, and an haughty spirit before a fall. *Bible*

14592. Pride has no beauty. *Lugbara*

14593. Pride in prosperity turns to misery in adversity. *American*

14594. Pride is as loud a beggar as want, and a great deal more saucy. *American*

14595. Pride is innate in beauty, and haughtiness is the companion of the fair. *Latin (Ovid)*

14596. Pride is the mask of one's own faults. *Hebrew*

14597. Pride joined with many virtues chokes them all. *English*

14598. Pride never leaves his master till he gets a fa'. *Scottish*

14599. Pride often apes humility. *American*

14600. Pride often borrows the cloak of humility. *American*

14601. Pride, perceiving humility honorable, often borrows her cloak. *English*

14602. Pride prinks her brow for the deil [devil] to pouse [despoil]. *Scottish*

14603. Pride that dined with vanity supped with poverty. *English*

14604. Pride will have a fall. *English*

14605. Pride's an ill horse to ride. *Scottish*

14606. Pride's chickens have bonny feathers but bony bodies. *Scottish*

14607. Proud men in their feasts become fools. *Latin*

14608. Providence crushes pride. *Latin*

14609. Send your gentle blude to the market and see what it will buy. *Scottish*

14610. Small men never think they are small; great men never know they are great. *Chinese*

14611. Some ane [someone] has tauld [told] her she was bonnie. *Scottish*

14612. The dorty [proud] dame may fa' [fall] in the dirt. *Scottish*

14613. The haughty hawk winna [will not] stoop to carrion. *Scottish*

14614. The higher the hill, the lower the grass. *American*

14615. The highest tree has the greatest fall. *American*

14616. The nobler the blood the less the pride. *American*

14617. The owl of ignorance lays the egg of pride. *American*

14618. The proud hate pride — in others. *American (Franklin)*

14619. The proudest nettle grows on a midden [dung hill]. *Scottish*

14620. There is no pride like that of a beggar grown rich. *American*

14621. To be proud of virtue, is to poison yourself with the antidote. *American (Franklin)*

14622. Two coins in a bag make more noise than a hundred. *Talmud*

14623. When a proud man hears another praised, he thinks himself injured. *English*

14624. When pride cometh, then cometh shame. *Bible*

14625. When pride is in the saddle, mischief is on the crupper. *French*

14626. When pride's in the van begging's in the rear. *Scottish*

14627. When we succeed our pride betrays us. *American*

14628. Ye kenna [don't know] what may cool your kail yet. *Scottish*

14629. You a lady, I a lady, who will put the sow out of doors? *Spanish*

Priests *see also* Preachers and Preaching

14630. Give the priest a drink, for the clerk is thirsty. *Italian*

14631. Priests pay each other no tithes. *German*

14632. Priests pray for enemies but princes kill. *English (Shakespeare)*

14633. That priest is a fool who decries his relics. *Italian*

14634. The priest should live by the altar. *French*

14635. The quarreling of priests is the devil's jubilee. *German*

14636. What village priest would not like to be pope? *French*

14637. When the priest visits you, do not rejoice; he will soon begin to beg. *Russian*

Principles

14638. Better to be poisoned in one's blood, than to be poisoned in one's principles. *American*

14639. Expedients are for the hour, but principles are for the ages. *American (Beecher)*

14640. In politics a man must learn to rise above principle. *American*

14641. Men must have righteous principles in the first place, and then they will not fail to perform virtuous actions. *American*

14642. Men of principle are sure to be bold, but those who are bold may not always be men of principle. *Chinese (Confucius)*

14643. Principle is a passion for truth and right. *American*

14644. Principles last forever; but special rules pass away with the things and conditions to which they refer. *American*

14645. Principles, like brave soldiers, are undisturbed and stand fast. *American*

Printing

14646. The printing press is the mother of errors. *American*

Priority *see also* Last; Order

14647. Before eating, open the mouth. *Wolof*

14648. Before shooting, one must aim. *Wolof*

14649. Blow first, and sip afterwards. *English*

14650. First come, first served. *American*

14651. First come to the mill, first grind. *English*

14652. First think of food, then of clothing. *Chinese*

14653. First Venetian, then Christian. *Venetian*

14654. Go ahead of others, and you will have the upper hand. *Japanese*

14655. He that comes first to the hill may sit where he will. *Scottish*

14656. He that's first up's no aye [always] first ser'd. *Scottish*

14657. He who comes first grinds first. *Spanish*

14658. He who has come to the mill first does not grind last. *Latin*

14659. He who is born the first, has the most of ragged clothes. [In Africa the younger children get the best clothes.] *Wolof*

14660. He who is first in time has the prior right. *Latin*

14661. Let the best horse leap the hedge first. *English*

14662. Say before they say. *Polish*

14663. The first go in front. *French*

14664. The first is most right. *Russian*

14665. The first, the better. *Polish*

14666. The foremost dog catcheth the hare. *English*

14667. Who comes first to the mill ought to have the first grinding. *French*

14668. Whoso that first to mille comth, first grint. *English (Chaucer)*

Probability *see also* Certainty; Odds; Possibility

14669. A thousand probabilities do not make one truth. *English*

14670. Always suspect that which seems probable. *French*

14671. "Like[ly] to die" fills not the kirkyard. *Scottish*

14672. The wise man is guided by probabilities. *Latin (Cicero)*

Problems

14673. The bride is tall, and the doorway is short. *Tunisian*

Procrastination *see also* Delay; Future; Lateness; Opportunity; Postponement; Timeliness; Today and Tomorrow

14674. Afterward does not exist. *Lugbara*

14675. An auld [old] horse may die waiting for the grass. *Scottish*

14676. Avoid delays: procrastination always does harm. *Latin (Lucan)*

14677. By and by never comes. *Latin*

14678. Delays have dangerous ends. *English*

14679. It will be the last word o' his testament. *Scottish*

14680. It's time enough to mak my bed when I'm gaun to lie doun. *Scottish*

14681. Man is ambitious by nature, but water flows downward. *Chinese*

14682. No one has ever seen tomorrow. *English*

14683. One of these days is none of these days. *American*

14684. Procrastination is the thief of time. *English (Young)*

14685. Tarry [being picky] lang brings little hame. *Scottish*

14686. The procrastinating man is ever struggling with ruin. *Greek*

14687. Tomorrow is often the busiest day of the week. *Spanish*

14688. Two anons and a by-and-by is an hour-and-a-half. *English*

14689. What may be done at any time will be done at nae time. *Scottish*

14690. When God says today, the devil says tomorrow. *German*

14691. While we are postponing, life speeds by. *Latin*

14692. Ye fyke [trifle] it awa, like auld [old] wives baking. *Scottish*

Prodigal Son

14693. A miserly father makes a prodigal son. *American*

14694. A returning prodigal is not to be exchanged for gold. *Chinese*

Productivity *see* Accomplishment; Usefulness; Work and Workers

Proficiency *see also* Skill

14695. Better be proficient in one art than a smatterer in a hundred. *Japanese*

Profit *see* Buying and Selling; Ill-Gotten Gains; Money; Profit and Loss

Profit and Loss *see also* Buying and Selling; Ill-Gotten Gains; Money

14696. Better to sell for small profits than to fail in business. *Chinese*

14697. Cut your losses and let your profits run. *American*

14698. Eith [easy] pains and little gains soon mak a man weary. *Scottish*

14699. Everyone fastens where there is gain. *English*

14700. Forgotten pains when follow gains. *Scottish*

14701. Great profits, great risks. *Chinese*

14702. Great winnings mak wark easy. *Scottish*

14703. He is no merchant who always gains. *Dutch*

14704. He plans less for profit than for quick returns, who will buy a thing for three and sell it for two. *Chinese*

14705. He sings for joy who makes a profit easily. *Chinese*

14706. He who flees loss flees profit. *Arabic*

14707. In the empire there are only two busy men — Messrs. Gain and Reputation. *Chinese*

14708. Love of gain turns wise men into fools. *Chinese*

14709. No great loss but some small profit. *American*

14710. One man's loss is another man's gain. *Latin*

14711. One man's profit is another man's loss. *American*

14712. Pain is forgotten where gain comes. *English*

14713. Quick returns mak rich merchants. *Scottish*

14714. Rather lose honorably than gain basely. *Latin*

14715. Share equally in profit and loss. *Chinese*

14716. Small and frequent gains are better than large ones and seldom. *German*

14717. Small gains bring in wealth. *Dutch*

14718. Small profits and heavy expenses mean a life of ceaseless activity. *Chinese*

14719. Small profits are sweet. *Danish*

14720. Small profits on large capital are after all great; big profits on small capital are after all only small. *Chinese*

14721. The greatest burdens are no the maist gainfu' [not the most profitable]. *Scottish*

14722. The merchant who gains not, loseth. *English*

14723. The smell of profit is clean / And sweet, whatever the source. *Latin (Juvenal)*

14724. To amass an immense fortune, a man must know how to make a profit. *Chinese*

14725. To gain without another's loss is impossible. *Latin*

14726. To run from east to west for profits no bigger than a pinhead. *Chinese*

14727. We'll bear wi' the stink when it brings in the clink [money]. *Scottish*

14728. What's gairly gathered is roundly spent. *Scottish*

14729. What's nane o' my profit will be nane o' my peril. *Scottish*

14730. When gain is in view, think of righteousness. *Chinese*

14731. Who will rise early if no profit is to be made? *Chinese*

Profligacy *see* Intemperance; Pleasure-Seeking; Saving and Spending

Profundity *see also* Shallowness

14732. Smooth runs the water where the brook is deep. *English (Shakespeare)*

Progress *see also* Advancement

14733. Change isn't necessarily progress. *American*

14734. He who moves not forward goes backward. *Latin*

14735. When the blind man carries the lame man, both go forward. *American*

Prohibition

14736. There is pain in prohibition. *Irish*

Promises *see also* Oaths; Swearing; Women and Trustworthiness; Words and Deeds

14737. A man's word is his honor. *Danish*

14738. A promise is a debt. *American*

14739. A promise is a promise, though you make it in the dark of the moon. *American*

14740. A promise makes a fool rejoice. *Polish*

14741. A promised dollar is not worth half. *German*

14742. All promises are either broken or kept. *English*

14743. An Englishman's word is his bond. *English*

14744. An honest man's word is as good as the king's. *Portuguese*

14745. An honest man's word is as good as his bond. *English*

14746. Be slow to make a promise but swift to keep it. *American*

14747. Better break your word than do worse in keeping it. *English*

14748. Better deny at once than promise long. *Danish*

14749. Bihest [promise] is dette [debt]. *English (Chaucer)*

14750. Buffaloes are held by cords, man by his words. *Malay*

14751. Fair hechts [promises] mak fools fain [glad]. *Scottish*

14752. Fair promises bind fools. *Italian*

14753. He is poor indeed that can promise nothing. *English*

14754. He that promises too much, means nothing. *English*

14755. He who gave his word gave his neck. *Tunisian*

14756. He who has a wide mouth has a narrow heart. *Hebrew*

14757. He who lightly asserts will seldom keep his word. *Chinese*

14758. He who promises runs into debt. *Spanish*

14759. He's poor that canna promise. *Scottish*

14760. In the land of promise a man may die of hunger. *Danish*

14761. Many promises impair confidence. *Latin*

14762. Men are bound by words, bulls' horns by ropes. *Latin*

14763. Men's vows are women's traitors. *English (Shakespeare)*

14764. My word is my bond. *English*

14765. Neither promise wax to the saint, nor cakes to the child. *Greek*

14766. Never promise a poor man, and never owe a rich one. *Brazilian*

14767. No greater promisers than those who have nothing to give. *American*

14768. Promises are like pie-crust; they are made to be broken. *American*

14769. Promises don't fill the belly. *American*

14770. Promises won't butter any bread. *American*

14771. Promising is not giving, but it contents fools. *Portuguese*

14772. Promising makes debt. *German*

14773. Take heed, girl, of the promise of a man, for it will run like a crab. *Spanish*

14774. The more you promise, the less you will have to deliver. *American*

14775. The righteous promise little and perform much; the wicked promise much and perform not even a little. *Hebrew*

14776. The word of an unstable man is a bundle of water. *American*

14777. Things promised are things due. *French*

14778. To promise and give nothing is a comfort to a fool. *English*

14779. To promise is ae [one] thing, to keep it's anither. *Scottish*

14780. To promise — a thing of the lord; to fulfill — a thing of the slave. *Russian*

14781. Vows made in storms are forgot in calms. *English*

14782. We make large promises to avoid making small presents. *French*

14783. We will do it. [I.e., Consider it done.] *German*

14784. Who makes hasty promises forgets them quickly. *Japanese*

14785. Who makes no promises has none to perform. *German*

14786. Ye maun be auld [must be old] ere ye pay sic [such] a gude wad [would — i.e., a pledge or promise]. *Scottish*

14787. Ye should be a king of your word. *Scottish*

14788. You can't live on promises. *American*

14789. Your surety wants a surety. *Hebrew*

Promptness *see also* Punctuality; Timeliness

14790. Disease is soon shaken / By physic soon taken. *English*

Proof *see also* Evidence; Judging

14791. Do not judge of the ship while it is on the stocks. *Italian*

14792. He that proves too much proves nothing. *American*

14793. It will be seen in the frying of the eggs. *Spanish (Cervantes)*

14794. Never try to prove what nobody doubts. *American*

14795. Proof rather than argument. *Japanese*

14796. Prove all things; hold fast that which is good. *Bible*

14797. That which proves too much proves nothing. *French*

14798. The event proves the act. *Latin*

14799. The proof of the pudding is not in chewing the bag. *American*

14800. Who proves too much proves nothing. *French*

Property *see also* Possession

14801. A house built and a garden to grow never brought what they cost. *Scottish*

14802. He that hath nothing is frightened at nothing. *English*

14803. He who tells you to give away your property deserves your thanks. *Wolof*

14804. If ye hae [have] little gear [property], ye hae the less care. *Scottish*

14805. In vain does a man possess property if he makes no use of it. *Latin*

14806. "Mine" and "Thine" is the source of all lawsuits. *Dutch*

14807. Mony ane [many a one] for land taks a fool by the hand. *Scottish*

14808. Property is the prop of life. *Kanuri*

14809. The best friend is an acre of land. *Welsh*

14810. The man without property looks upon property as theft. *American*

Prophecy *see also* Future; Omens; Prediction

14811. A prophet is not without honor, save in his own country, and in his own house. *Bible*

14812. Beware of false prophets, which come to you in sheep's clothing but inwardly they are ravening wolves. *Bible*

14813. God has granted to every people a prophet in his own tongue. *Koran*

14814. It is surprising that an augur can see an augur without smiling. *Latin*

14815. Make me a prophet and I will make you rich. *Italian*

14816. No man is a prophet in his own country. *American*

Propriety *see also* Conduct

14817. If you cannot conduct yourself with propriety, give place to those who can. *Latin (Horace)*

14818. Propriety rules the superior man; law rules the mean man. *Chinese*

Prosperity *see also* Prosperity and Adversity

14819. All claim kindred with the prosperous. *Latin*

14820. In prosperity no altars smoke. *Italian*

14821. It is not easy to bear prosperity unru!ed. *Latin (Ovid)*

14822. Our hearts run riot in prosperity. *Latin (Ovid)*

14823. Prosperity destroys fools and endangers the wise. *American*

14824. Prosperity forgets father and mother. *Spanish*

14825. Prosperity has many friends. *Latin*

14826. Prosperity is a feeble reed. *French*

14827. Prosperity is like a tender mother, but blind, who spoils her children. *English*

14828. Prosperity is nurse to ill-temper. *Latin*

14829. Prosperity makes few friends. *French*

14830. Prosperity tries your virtue more than calamity. *American*

14831. Prosperity's the very bond of love. *English (Shakespeare)*

14832. That city cannot prosper when an ox is sold for less than fish. *American*

14833. The habitual living in prosperity is most injurious. *Latin (Publilius Syrus)*

14834. The prosperity of fools shall destroy them. *American*

14835. The prosperous man is never sure that he is loved for himself. *Latin*

14836. There never was a banquet so sumptuous but someone dined poorly at it. *French*

14837. They who prosper take on airs of vanity. *Greek (Aeschylus)*

14838. When prosperity smiles, beware of its guiles. *Dutch*

Prosperity and Adversity *see also* Prosperity

14839. A man is insensible to the relish of prosperity till he has tasted adversity. *Persian (Sa'di)*

14840. Adversity is easier borne than prosperity forgot. *English*

14841. Adversity reveals genius, prosperity hides it. *Latin (Horace)*

14842. Be moderate in prosperity, prudent in adversity. *Greek (Periander)*

14843. From fortune to misfortune is but a step; from misfortune to fortune is a long way. *Yiddish*

14844. In prosperity look out for squalls. *Latin*

14845. In prosperity think of adversity. *American*

14846. In prosperity you may count on many friends: if the sky becomes overcast you will be alone. *Latin (Ovid)*

14847. In the day of prosperity, adversity is forgotten and in the day of adversity, prosperity is not remembered. *Bible*

14848. In the day of prosperity be joyful, but in the day of adversity consider. *Bible*

14849. In time of a!iction, a vow; in the time of prosperity, an inundation [or increase of wickedness]. *Hebrew*

14850. In time of prosperity consider how you will bear adversity. *Latin*

14851. In time of prosperity, friends will be plenty; in time of adversity, not one in twenty. *American*

14852. Prosperity doth best discover [i.e., expose or reveal] vice, but adversity doth best discover virtue. *English (Bacon)*

14853. Prosperity has no power over adversity. *Latin (Publilius Syrus)*

14854. Prosperity is a great teacher; adversity is a greater. *English (Hazlitt)*

14855. Prosperity makes [or gains] friends, adversity tries them. *Latin (Publilius Syrus)*

14856. Prosperity proves the fortunate, adversity, the great. *Latin*

14857. The virtue of prosperity is temperance; the virtue of adversity is fortitude. *English (Bacon)*

14858. When prosperity was well mounted, she let go the bridle, and soon came tumbling out of the saddle. *American (Franklin)*

Prostitution

14859. A whore and a buffoon fare ill in their old age. *Spanish*

14860. He who has one foot in a brothel has another in a hospital. *Spanish*

14861. Spit in a whore's face, and she'll say it's raining. *Yiddish*

14862. Water in a jar does not become sour milk, and a whore does not repent. *Arabic*

Protection

14863. Pull down your hat on the wind side. *American*

Providence *see also* **Divine Assistance; Man and God**

14864. All is in vain unless Providence is with us. *Latin*

14865. Let the morn come and the meat wi't. *Scottish*

14866. The ways of the gods are full of providence. *Greek*

14867. We must follow, not force, Providence. *American*

14868. Whatever befalls is just and right, and therefore not unendurable. *American*

Proximity *see* **Nearness**

Prudence *see also* **Caution; Common Sense; Folly; Fools and Foolishness; Imprudence; Precaution**

14869. A grain of prudence is worth a pound of craft. *American*

14870. A prudent man does not make the goat his gardener. *Hungarian*

14871. A Scottish man is ay [always] wise behind the hand. *Scottish*

14872. Abandon not your old clothes till you get your new. *American*

14873. As the wind blaws seek your beild [shelter]. *Scottish*

14874. Aye [always] tak the fee when the tear's in the ee. *Scottish*

14875. Be cautious as to what you say of men, and to whom you speak it. *Latin (Horace)*

14876. Be it better, be it worse, be ruled by him that has the purse. *Scottish*

14877. Be on the safe side. *American*

14878. Bear wealth weel, poortith [poverty] will bear itsel. *Scottish*

14879. Best to be aff wi' the auld [old] love before we be on wi' the new. *Scottish*

14880. Better an auld [old] man's darling than a young man's warling [worldling]. *Scottish*

14881. Better eat gray bread in your mouth than in your age. *Scottish*

14882. Better haud wi' the hounds than rin [run] wi' the hare. *Scottish*

14883. Better keep the devil at the door than turn him out of the house. *Scottish*

14884. Better kiss a knave than cast oot wi' him. *Scottish*

14885. Better master ane [one] than fight wi' ten. *Scottish*

14886. Better wade back mid-water than gang forward and be drowned. *Scottish*

14887. Bind the sack ere it be fu'. *Scottish*

14888. Call the bear "Uncle" until you are safe over the bridge. *Turkish*

14889. Castna [cast not] out the dowed [dirty] water till ye get the clean. *Scottish*

14890. Chance fights ever on the side of the prudent. *Greek*

14891. Colts by falling and lads by losing grow prudent. *Spanish*

14892. Court not companionship with tigers. *Latin*

14893. Cross the stream where it is ebbest. *English*

14894. Dame, deem warily—ye watna [know not] wha wytes [blames] yoursel. *Scottish*

14895. Dinna touch him on the sair [sore] heel. *Scottish*

14896. Do not disturb an evil which is well buried. *Latin*

14897. Do not provoke lions. *Latin*

14898. Do not speak of secret matters in a field that is full of little hills. *Hebrew*

14899. Don't argue with your bread and butter. *American*

14900. Don't borrow from the newly rich, don't visit the newly wed. *Malay*

14901. Don't carry [or put] all your eggs in one basket. *English*

14902. Don't eat anything poisonous, and don't break the law. *Chinese*

14903. Don't whistle until you're out of the woods. *American*

14904. Fair gae [go] they, fair come they, and aye [always] their heels hindmost. *Scottish*

14905. Fire is gude for the fireside. *Scottish*

14906. Fools must not be sent to deliver eggs. *Welsh*

14907. Gie ne'er the wolf the wedder to keep. *Scottish*

14908. Give every man thine ear, but few thy voice. *English (Shakespeare)*

14909. Good fortune ever fights on the side of prudence. *Greek*

14910. Good men carry their hearts on their tongues; prudent men carry their tongues in their hearts. *Turkish*

14911. Great good nature, without prudence, is a great misfortune. *American (Franklin)*

14912. Hang not all your bells upon one horse. *English*

14913. Have a care how you irritate the wasps. *Latin*

14914. Have more strings to thy bow than one. *Latin*

14915. Have more than thou showest, / Speak less than thou knowest. *English (Shakespeare)*

14916. Have not all your eggs in one nest. *English*

14917. He does not go wrong who goes to a good inn. *French*

14918. He gies nae whitings without banes. *Scottish*

14919. He hears wi' his heels, as the geese do in hairst [harvest]. *Scottish*

14920. He is free from danger who is on guard, even when he is safe. *Latin*

14921. He lay in his scabbard, as mony a gude sword's done. *Scottish*

14922. He sits fu' close [or still] that has a riven breech [or riven breeks (trousers)]. *Scottish*

14923. He that gropes in the dark finds that [i.e., that which] he would not. *English*

14924. He that has horns in his bosom needna put them on his head. *Scottish*

14925. He that hath a head of wax must not walk in the sun. *English*

14926. He that maks friends fear'd o' his wit should be fear'd o' their memories. *Scottish*

14927. He that saveth his dinner will have the more for his supper. *English*

14928. He that speaks without care shall remember with sorrow. *English*

14929. He that's scant o' wind shouldna meddle wi' the chanter [piper]. *Scottish*

14930. He who cannot conceal his sentiments, knows not how to live. *Latin*

14931. He who separates men who are fighting should not strike them. *Wolof*

14932. He who wants a rose must respect the thorn. *Persian*

14933. He'll rather turn than burn. *Scottish*

14934. He'll wag as the bush wags. *Scottish*

14935. Heat not a furnace for your foe so hot / That it do singe yourself. *English (Shakespeare)*

14936. I prefer silent prudence to loquacious folly. *Latin (Cicero)*

14937. I'd rather have them say "There he goes" than "Here he lies." *American*

14938. I'll ne'er dirty the bannet [bonnet] I' gaun to put on. *Scottish*

14939. I'll ne'er keep a cow when I can get milk sae cheap. *Scottish*

14940. If the bull would throw thee, lie down. *Wolof*

14941. If the hen had not cackled, we should not know she had laid an egg. *English*

14942. If the snake cares to live, it doesn't journey upon the high-road. *French Guyana Creole*

14943. If thou canst not see the bottom, wade not. *English*

14944. If thy heart fails thee, climb not at all. *English*

14945. If you talk to wolves, have a club handy. *Arabic*

14946. If you would like to beat the dog, look well to its master's face. *Burmese*

14947. In childhood be modest, in youth temperate, in manhood just, in old age prudent. *American*

14948. Innocence itself sometimes hath need of a mask. *English*

14949. It is folly to punish your neighbor by fire when you live next door. *Latin (Publilius Syrus)*

14950. It is well to have two strings in one bow. *French*

14951. It is well to moor your bark with two anchors. *Latin (Publilius Syrus)*

14952. It's better sheltering under an auld [old] hedge than under a new planted wood. *Scottish*

14953. It's better to sup wi' a cutty [a short spoon] than want a spune. *Scottish*

14954. It's hard to sit in Rome and strive wi' the pope. *Scottish*

14955. It's ill to say it's wrang when my lord says it's right. *Scottish*

14956. Jouk [stoop to avoid a blow], and let the jaw gang by. *Scottish*

14957. Keep the staff in your ain hand. *Scottish*

14958. Keep your back from the fire and don't mix your liquors. *Irish*

14959. Keep your mouth shut and your een [eyes] open. *Scottish*

14960. Keep your tongue a prisoner and your body will gang free. *Scottish*

14961. Keep your tongue within your teeth. *Scottish*

14962. Lay the head o' the sow to the tail o' the gryce. *Scottish*

14963. Least said is soonest mended. *Scottish*

14964. Leave aff while the play's gude. *Scottish*

14965. Leave the court ere the court leave you. *Scottish*

14966. Let aye the bell'd wether break the snaw [snow]. *Scottish*

14967. Let by-ganes be by-ganes. *Scottish*

14968. Let that flee [fly] stick to the wa'. *Scottish*

14969. Let your purse be your master. *English*

14970. Like the wife wi' the mony dochters [many daughters], the best's aye hindmost. *Scottish*

14971. Little boats must keep the shore; / Larger ships may venture more. *English*

14972. Little said is soon mended; little gear [money] is soon spended. *Scottish*

14973. Little wats [knows] the ill-willy [ill-willed] wife what a dinner may haud in. *Scottish*

14974. Look before you leap. *Spanish*

14975. Love is without prudence and anger without counsel. *American*

14976. Mak ae [one] pair o' legs worth twa [two] pair o' hands. *Scottish*

14977. Mak friends o' fremit folk [strangers]. *Scottish*

14978. Mak nae [no] orts [that which is rejected, set aside] o' gude hay. *Scottish*

14979. Mind thysel, the world will mind the lave [rest]. *Scottish*

14980. Ne'er put a sword in a wudman's [madman's] hand. *Scottish*

14981. Ne'er spend gude siller [silver] looking for bad. *Scottish*

14982. Ne'er strive against the stream. *Scottish*

14983. Ne'er tell your fae [foe] when your fit [foot] sleeps. *Scottish*

14984. Never ask directions of an innkeeper. *Turkish*

14985. Never cut what you can untie. *Portuguese*

14986. Never sit where someone can tell you to move. *Arabic*

14987. No one tests the depth of a river with both feet. *Ashanti*

14988. No wise man stands behind an ass when he kicks. *Latin (Terence)*

14989. One mustn't put the tow too near the fire. *French*

14990. Prudence availeth more than strength. *Latin*

14991. Prudence in action avails more than wisdom in conception. *Latin (Cicero)*

14992. Prudence is always in season. *French*

14993. Prudence is sometimes stretched too far, until it blocks the road of progress. *Chinese*

14994. Prudence is the charioteer of all virtues. *Latin*

14995. Prudence is the first thing to desert the wretched. *Latin*

14996. Prudence should be winning when thrift is spinning. *Scottish*

14997. Put by for a rainy day. *American*

14998. Put nae [no] force against the flail. *Scottish*
14999. Raise no more spirits than you can conjure down. *English*
15000. Reckon up your winning at your bedstock. *Scottish*
15001. Save yoursel frae the deil [from the devil] and the laird's bairns [children]. *Scottish*
15002. Speak little, speak the truth; spend little, pay cash. *German*
15003. Speaking the truth is useful to the hearer, harmful to the speaker. *German*
15004. Tak nae mair [take no more] on your back nor ye're able to bear. *Scottish*
15005. Take heed is a good rede. *English*
15006. Take heed of an ox before, an ass behind, and a monk on all sides. *Spanish*
15007. Take heed of enemies reconciled, and of meat twice boiled. *Spanish*
15008. Take heed you find not that [i.e., that which] you do not seek. *English*
15009. Take your meal wi' ye and your brose [a dish of oatmeal and boiling water] will be the thicker. *Scottish*
15010. Tell not all you know, believe not all you hear, do not all you are able. *Italian*
15011. Tell your business, and leave the devil alone to do it for you. *Italian*
15012. That's my gude [good] that does me gude. *Scottish*
15013. The chickens don't brag about chicken soup. *Martinique Creole*
15014. The day has eyne [eyes], the night has ears. *Scottish*
15015. The farthest way aboot is aft the nearest way hame. *Scottish*
15016. The prudent man looketh well to his going. *Bible*
15017. The prudent seldom err. *Chinese*
15018. The tod [fox] keeps aye [always] his ain [own] hole clean. *Scottish*
15019. They ne'er gie wi' the spit but they gat wi' the ladle. *Scottish*
15020. They should kiss the gudewife that wad win the gudeman. *Scottish*
15021. Though your dog be tame, do not bite him on the lip. *Portuguese*
15022. Till you are across the river, beware how you insult the mother alligator. *Haitian Creole*
15023. To name the rope in the house of one who has been hanged. *Spanish (Cervantes)*
15024. Trust not your all in one ship. *Latin*
15025. Use another's foot to kick a dog. *Chinese*
15026. Venture not all in one bottom [i.e., boat]. *American*
15027. Venture not all your eggs in one basket. *Spanish*
15028. Wake not a sleeping lion. *American*
15029. We accomplish more by prudence than by force. *Latin*
15030. We cannot prevent birds from flying over our heads, but we can prevent them from nesting in our hair. *Swiss*
15031. Weel won corn should be housed eye the morn. *Scottish*
15032. When the water reaches the upper deck, follow the rats. *American*
15033. Who fears all snares falls into none. *Latin*
15034. Why walk into the sea when it rages? *Hebrew*
15035. Wide lugs [ears] and a short tongue are best. *Scottish*
15036. With great lords it is not good to eat cherries. *German*
15037. You must not let your mousetrap smell of cheese. *English*

Public Opinion *see* Opinion

Public Service *see also* Government; Office

15038. He who serves the public hath but a scurvy master. *English*
15039. Who serves the public has a bad master. *Italian*
15040. Who serves the public serves a fickle master. *Dutch*

Punctuality

15041. Better be an hour too early than a minute too late. *American*
15042. Better late than never, but better still, never late. *American*
15043. Better three hours too soon than a minute too late. *English (Shakespeare)*
15044. Men count up the faults of those who keep them waiting. *French*
15045. Punctuality is the politeness of kings. *French*
15046. Punctuality is the soul of business. *American*

Punishment and Retribution *see also* Child-Rearing; Crime and Criminals; Desert; Discipline; Discipline and Women; Inevitability; Law; Leniency; Obedience; Pardon; Retaliation; Revenge; Women and Revenge

15047. A man may kill another in jest, and be hanged in earnest. *American*
15048. Care must be taken that the punishment does not exceed the offense. *Latin (Cicero)*
15049. Chastisement may be deferred, but it is not put off forever. *Italian*
15050. Criminals are punished that others may be amended. *Italian*
15051. Curses, like chickens, always come home to roost. *English*
15052. Disgrace does not lie in the punishment, but in the crime. *Italian*
15053. Every man's sin falls on his own head. *Latin*
15054. Every sin carries its own punishment. *American*
15055. Foxes find themselves at last at the furrier's. *French*
15056. God permits the wicked; but not forever. *English*
15057. Great thieves hang petty thieves. *French*
15058. Hang a dog on a crab-tree, and he'll never love verjuice. *English*

15059. Hang a thief when he is young, and he'll no steal when he is old. *Scottish*

15060. Hang him that hath no shifts. *English*

15061. Harm set, harm get. *American*

15062. He falls into the pit who leads another to it. *American*

15063. He prepares evil for himself who plots mischief for others. *Latin*

15064. He that diggeth a pit shall fall into it. *Bible*

15065. He that has no money must pay with his skin. *German*

15066. He that is to die by the gallows may dance on the river. *Italian*

15067. He that slays shall be slain. *Scottish*

15068. He who sows evil reaps remorse. *Arabic*

15069. Heat not a furnace for your foe so hot / That it doth singe yourself. *English (Shakespeare)*

15070. If he has no gear to tine, he has shins to pine. [If he is unable to pay his fine, he will be put in the stocks.] *Scottish*

15071. If you give a blow you must be able to take one. *American*

15072. It is cruelty to the innocent not to punish the guilty. *American*

15073. Let the punishment be equal with the offense. *Latin*

15074. Let the ruler be slow to punish, swift to reward. *Latin*

15075. Let them fall into the snare which they have laid. *Latin*

15076. Let those who have deserved their punishment bear it patiently. *Latin*

15077. Many without punishment, none without sin. *English*

15078. Neglect will kill an injury sooner than revenge. *English*

15079. No mad dog runs seven years. *Dutch*

15080. One day brings the punishment which many days demand. *Latin*

15081. Pay him wi' his ain coin. *Scottish*

15082. Petty thieves are hanged; people take off their hats to great ones. *German*

15083. Providence may delay, but punishment will come at length. *Latin*

15084. Prudence will punish to prevent crime, not to avenge it. *Latin (Seneca)*

15085. Punishment awaits all offenses. *Latin*

15086. Punishment comes slowly, but it comes. *American*

15087. Punishment follows close on the heels of crime. *Latin (Horace)*

15088. Punishment is a cripple, but it arrives. *Spanish*

15089. Punishment rights no wrongs, but it deters a hundred others. *Arabic*

15090. Retribution is sure to come to him who does wrong. *American*

15091. Sins against heaven may be left to heaven. *Latin*

15092. Swift is heaven's retribution. *American*

15093. The cow may want her tail yet. *Scottish*

15094. The fox is taken when he comes to take. *American*

15095. The gallows was made for the unlucky. *Spanish*

15096. The gallows will have its own at last. *English*

15097. The king may come in the cadger's [beggar's] gate. *Scottish*

15098. The mills of the gods grind slowly, but they grind exceeding small. *Greek*

15099. The public has more interest in the punishment of an injury than he who receives it. *American*

15100. The punishment should fit the crime. *American*

15101. The water will ne'er waur the woodie. [He that deserves to be hanged will never drown.] *Scottish*

15102. There never was the worse use made of a man than hanging him. *Irish*

15103. There's a day coming that'll show wha's blackest. *Scottish*

15104. They have sown the wind, and they shall reap the whirlwind. *Bible*

15105. Those who sow injustice reap hate and vengeance. *American*

15106. To clip his wings. *Latin*

15107. To cut his comb off. *English*

15108. To take him down a peg. *English*

15109. Whatsoever a man soweth, that shall he also reap. *Bible*

15110. Who punishes one threatens a hundred. *French*

15111. Who sows ill reaps ill. *American*

15112. Whoso sheddeth man's blood, by man shall his blood be shed. *Bible*

15113. Ye'll get your gear [money, goods, property], and they'll get the widdie [be hanged] that stole't. *Scottish*

15114. You are guilty of a crime when you do not punish crime. *Latin*

Puns

15115. Who makes a pun will pick a pocket. *English*

Purity

15116. Blessed are the pure in heart: for they shall see God. *Bible*

15117. Have not only clean hands, but clean minds. *Greek*

15118. His heart cannot be pure whose tongue is not clean. *American*

15119. In an ermine spots are soon discovered. *English*

15120. The stream is always pure at its source. *French*

15121. To the pure all things are pure. *Latin*

15122. Unto the pure all things are pure. *Bible*

Purpose *see also* Intention; Motivation

15123. All meat's to be eaten, all maids to be wed. *English*

15124. If you love not the noise of bells, why pull the ropes? *American*

15125. It's for her own good that the cat purrs. *Irish*

15126. Pursue worthy aims. *Greek*

15127. When a man does not know what harbor he is making for, no wind is the right wind. *Latin*

Purposelessness *see also* **Futility; Impossibility**

15128. He has worked for the King of Prussia. [He has worked in vain.] *French*

15129. What need has a blind man of a looking glass? *Latin*

15130. What's the good of a sundial in the shade? *English*

Quality *see also* **Ability; Dexterity; Excellence; Perfection; Skill; Superiority; Superiority and Inferiority**

15131. A carrion kite will never make a good hawk. *Scottish*

15132. A good drum does not need hard striking. *Japanese*

15133. As good never a whit as never the better. *English*

15134. Better a diamond with a flaw than a pebble without. *Chinese*

15135. Better a wit bought than two for nought. *Scottish*

15136. Better is better. *German*

15137. Better is the enemy of well. *Italian*

15138. Cheap meat is for dogs. *Polish*

15139. Do your turn weel, and nane [none] will speir [ask] what time ye took. *Scottish*

15140. Even though naked, quality will show itself. *Philippine*

15141. Good wine needs no bush. *English*

15142. He's the best spoke o' your wheel. *Scottish*

15143. Ill ware is never cheap. *English*

15144. Make good cheese, if you make little. *American*

15145. One never has a good bargain with bad ware. *French*

15146. Soon enough if well enough. *English*

15147. The nearer the bone the sweeter the flesh. *English*

15148. Though good be good, yet better is better [or yet better carries it]. *English*

Quantity *see also* **Abundance; Excess; Sufficiency**

15149. Quality, without quantity, is little thought of. *Scottish*

Quarreling *see also* **Argument; Contention; Discord; Dispute; Fighting; Stress and Strain; Strife**

15150. A quarrelsome disposition makes few friends. *American*

15151. A quarrelsome man has no good neighbors. *American (Franklin)*

15152. A toolying [fighting] tike comes limping hame. *Scottish*

15153. An old quarrel is easily renewed. *American*

15154. Avoid quarrels caused by wine. *Latin*

15155. Even the ladle and the cooking pot collide. *Malay*

15156. From one quarrel comes a hundred sins. *American*

15157. God blesses peace and curses quarrels. *Spanish*

15158. He is scattering the ashes of the fireplace. *Hawaiian*

15159. He that crabs [quarrels] without cause, should mease [grow calm] without amends. *Scottish*

15160. He that passeth by, and meddleth with strife belonging not to him, is like one that taketh a dog by the ears. *English*

15161. He who cannot hold his peace will never live at ease. *American*

15162. He would fain rip up auld sairs [old wounds]. *Scottish*

15163. Interfere not in the quarrels of others. *Latin*

15164. It is the buyer who profits from the fight of two shopkeepers. *Korean*

15165. It takes two to make a quarrel. *Greek*

15166. It will aye [always] be a dirty dub [puddle] between them. *Scottish*

15167. It's ill to quarrel wi' a misrid [entangled, confused] warld. *Scottish*

15168. Make sure to be in with your equals if you're going to fall out with your superiors. *Yiddish*

15169. Most bitter are the quarrels of brothers. *Latin*

15170. Never quarrel with your bread and butter. *American*

15171. Old wounds bleed easily. *German*

15172. One who would quarrel about goat's wool. *Latin*

15173. One word draws another. *Italian*

15174. Quarrel and strife make short life. *Swedish*

15175. Quarrel makes agreement more precious. *Latin*

15176. Quarreling is the weapon of the weak. *American*

15177. Quarrels are easily begun, but with difficulty ended. *American*

15178. Quarrels do not last long if the wrong is only on one side. *French*

15179. Quarrelsome dogs get dirty coats. *English*

15180. Robbers quarrel and robbers are discovered. *French*

15181. The quarrels of friends are the opportunities of foes. *Greek (Aesop)*

15182. The second word makes the quarrel. *Japanese*

15183. They are twice as much friends together as they were before quarreling. *Latin (Plautus)*

15184. They quarrel about an egg and let the hen fly. *German*

15185. Thieves quarrel, and the thefts are discovered. *Spanish*

15186. Those, who in quarrels interpose, / Must often wipe a bloody nose. *English (Gay)*

15187. To quarrel with his little finger. *English*

15188. Two buttocks cannot avoid friction. Chitonga

15189. When knaves fall out, true men come by their goods. *English*

15190. When one will not, two cannot quarrel. *English*

15191. When two quarrel, both are to blame. *Dutch*

15192. When two quarrel, the third rejoices. *Spanish*

15193. Wranglers never want words. *English*

Questions *see also* **Answers; Asking; Denial; Questions and Answers; Refusal; Response**

15194. Avoid a questioner, for he is also a tattler. *Latin (Horace)*

15195. He who questions nothing learns nothing. *American*

15196. No question is settled until it is settled right. *American*

15197. To beg the question. *Greek*

15198. To question a wise man is the beginning of wisdom. *German*

Questions and Answers *see also* **Answers; Asking; Denial; Refusal; Response**

15199. A fool can ask more questions than seven wise men can answer. *American*

15200. A thrawn [obstinate] question should hae a thrawart [cross-tempered] answer. *Scottish*

15201. Ask me no questions and I'll tell you no lies. *English (Goldsmith)*

15202. Every question has its answer. *American*

15203. Hard questions must have hard answers. *Greek*

15204. He who asks questions cannot avoid the answers. *Cameroonian*

15205. It isn't very intelligent to find answers to questions which are unanswerable. *French (Fontenelle)*

15206. It is not every question that deserves an answer. *Latin*

15207. Make a slow answer to a hasty question. *American*

15208. Never answer a question until it is asked. *American*

15209. 'Tis not every question that deserves an answer. *American*

15210. To a man full of questions make no answer at all. *American*

15211. Who asks many questions gets many answers. *German*

Quiet *see also* **Brevity; Silence**

15212. A quiet tongue shows a wise head. *English*

15213. Better is a dry morsel, and quietness therewith, than a house full of sacrifices with strife. *Bible*

15214. In quietness and confidence shall be your strength. *Bible*

15215. Quietness is best. *Scottish*

15216. Sometimes quiet is an unquiet thing. *Latin*

15217. Study to be quiet. *Bible*

15218. The highest degree of earthly happiness is quiet. *American*

Rank

15219. A cat may look on a king. *English*

15220. Better in the dust than crawl near the throne. *German*

15221. Even workhouses have their aristocracy. *English*

15222. Look down if you would know how high you stand. *Yiddish*

15223. Surely men of low degree are vanity, and men of high degree are a lie. *Bible*

15224. The higher an ape mounts, the more he shows of his breech. *English*

Rashness

15225. A rash man provokes trouble, but is no match for it when it comes. *Chinese*

15226. He sets a' on six an' seven. *Scottish*

15227. If you leap into a well, Providence is not bound to fetch you out. *English*

15228. It is difficult to be strong and not rash. *Japanese*

15229. Rashness is not always fortunate. *Latin*

15230. Reflection ensures safety, but rashness is followed by regrets. *American*

Reading *see* **Books and Reading**

Reality *see also* **Appearance; Perception; Seeming**

15231. As you see a thing, so take it. *French*

15232. Take the world as it is, not as it ought to be. *German*

Reason *see also* **Cause and Effect; Causes; Excuses; Feeling**

15233. A man without reason is a beast in season. *English*

15234. Be led by reason. *Greek*

15235. Better to die than to turn your back on reason. *Chinese*

15236. Don't marry without love, but don't love without reason. *American*

15237. Good reasons must of force give place to better. *English (Shakespeare)*

15238. Hear reason, or she'll make you feel her. *American (Franklin)*

15239. If you will not hear Reason, she will surely rap your knuckles. *American (Franklin)*

15240. If you wish to subject all things to yourself, subject yourself to reason. *Latin*

15241. It is the instinct of understanding to contradict reason. *German*

15242. Nothing can be lasting when reason does not rule. *Latin*

15243. Reason binds the man. *Scottish*

15244. Reason does not come before years. *German*

15245. Reason is not measured by size or height. *Greek*

15246. Reason lies between the spur and the bridle. *English*

15247. Reason will not act in vain. *Chinese*

15248. Reason — the choicest gift bestowed by heaven. *Greek*

15249. Reason — the light and lamp of life. *Latin*

15250. There's reason in roasting of eggs. *English*

15251. 'Tis in vain to speak reason where 'twill not be heard. *English*

15252. Unto the good, their reason ever is a good. *Greek*

15253. We have not enough strength to follow reason absolutely. *French (La Rochefoucauld)*

15254. We often say things because we can say them well, rather than because they are sound and reasonable. *American*

15255. What is now reason was formerly impulse. *Latin*

15256. When force pushes on, reason draws back. *Japanese*

15257. Who wants to beat his dog finds plenty of sticks. *French*

Rebellion *see also* **Desperation; Opposition; Resistance**

15258. A cat that is locked up may change into a lion. *Dutch*

15259. A man may provoke his own dog to bite him. *English*

15260. Who draws his sword against the prince must throw away the scabbard. *English*

Rebuke *see also* **Reproof**

15261. Open rebuke is better than secret hatred. *American*

15262. Open rebuke is better than secret love. *Bible*

15263. Rebukes ought not to have a grain more salt than sugar. *English*

Recidivism *see also* **Repetition**

15264. A dog returned to his vomit. [Returning to bad habits.] *Latin*

15265. The sow that was washed is turned to her wallowing in the mire. *English*

Reciprocity

15266. A Roland for an Oliver. *English*

15267. Ae [one] hand winna [will not] wash the ither [other] for nought. *Scottish*

15268. Do not go to his house if he does not come to yours. *Tunisian*

15269. Give me fire, and I will give you a light. *Arabic*

15270. Hand washes hand, leg supports leg. *Polish*

15271. If you say hard things you must expect to hear them in return. *Latin (Plautus)*

15272. It is but fair that he who requires indulgence for his own offences should grant it to others. *Latin*

15273. Mules help to scratch each other. [The bad speak well of each other.] *Latin*

15274. Mutual assistance in despair will make this ugly world more fair. *American*

15275. Old men rub one another. *Latin*

15276. One ass scratches the other. *Latin*

15277. One barber shaves another. *French*

15278. One good turn deserves another. *Latin*

15279. One hand washes the other, and the two wash the face. *Dutch*

15280. One hand washes the other. *Greek*

15281. One kindness is the price of another. *English*

15282. One kindness requires another. *French*

15283. One shrewd turn asks another. *English*

15284. Open hand makes open hand. *English*

15285. Roll my log and I'll roll yours. *American*

15286. Rub the back of one who rubs you. *Greek*

15287. Scraitch me and I'll scraitch thee. *Scottish*

15288. Scratch my back and I'll scratch yours. *Latin*

15289. That which I receive, that I return. *Latin*

15290. The sort of thing you say is the thing that will be said to you. *Greek (Homer)*

15291. Trim my beard, and I will trim your top-knot. *English*

15292. We give and take in turn. *Latin*

15293. Who gives pleasure requires pleasure. *French*

15294. Who gives, teaches a return. *English*

15295. You amuse my child, and I'll take care of your old father. *Hindi*

15296. You scratch my back, and I'll scratch yours. *American*

15297. You tickle me, and I'll tickle you. *American*

Recklessness *see also* **Fools and Folly**

15298. Fearless of death, the pigeon feeds among the hawks. *Yoruba*

Recognition

15299. A thief knows a thief, as a wolf knows a wolf. *American*

15300. One beetle recognizes another. *Irish*

15301. One rogue knows another. *American*

15302. Takes one to know one. *American*

15303. The angels know each other. *Irish*

15304. Thief knows thief, and wolf knows wolf. *Latin*

Reconciliation

15305. Beware of enemies reconciled and of meat twice boiled. *American*

15306. Love-quarrels oft in pleasing concord end. *English (Milton)*

Reconsideration *see also* **Advice**

15307. Second thoughts are best. *English (Dryden)*

15308. Second thoughts are certainly wiser. *Greek (Euripides)*

15309. Take a woman's first advice and not the second. *French*

Reflection *see also* **Deliberation**

15310. A wise man reflects and then speaks; a fool speaks and then reflects on his silly remarks. *American*

Reform *see also* **Amendment**

15311. Chasten thy son while there is hope. *English*

15312. Him who reforms, God assists. *Spanish*

15313. If you try to cleanse others, you will waste away in the process, like soap. *Madagascan*

15314. In vain will you fly from one vice if in your wilfulness you embrace another. *Latin (Horace)*

15315. It's no easy to straucht [straighten] in the oak the crook that grew in the sapling. *Scottish*

15316. Never came reformation in a flood. *English (Shakespeare)*

15317. Never too late to tread the path of honesty. *Latin*

15318. No matter how far you have gone on a wrong road, turn back. *Turkish*

15319. To change the course we have begun for the better. *Latin (Virgil)*

15320. To turn over a new leaf. *English*

15321. Vices which have grown with us are with difficulty cut away. *Latin*

15322. What was and is not, should not be entered in the register [i.e., if a man has changed, don't hold his past actions against him]. *Polish*

Refusal *see also* **Denial; Resistance; Response; Soft Words; Women Saying No**

15323. A prompt refusal has in part the grace of a favor granted. *Latin*

15324. A reason for refusing is never wanting to the miser. *Latin*

15325. Handsomely asked, handsomely refused. *French*

15326. He who refuses nothing will soon have nothing to refuse. *Latin*

15327. It is kindness to refuse immediately what you intend to delay. *Latin*

15328. "No" has the same number of letters as "si." *Spanish*

15329. "No" is a good answer when given in time. *Danish*

15330. One "no" averts seventy evils. *Indian*

15331. The prompter the refusal, the less the disappointment. *Latin (Publilius Syrus)*

15332. To refuse graciously is half to grant a favor. *American*

15333. Who gives a doubtful hope, refuses. *Latin*

15334. Who refuses courteously grants half our suit. *Latin*

15335. Who refuses, muses. *French*

Regret

15336. Don't cry over spilled milk. *American*

15337. He'll never rue but ance [once], and that'll be a' his life. *Scottish*

15338. The first half of life is spent in longing for the second; the second in regretting the first. *American*

Rejection

15339. Thou art weighed in the balance and found wanting. *Bible*

Relationship *see* **Relatives**

Relatives

15340. A little more than kin, and less than kind. *English (Shakespeare)*

15341. A lot of relatives, a lot of trouble. *American*

15342. A stranger who is kind is a relative; an unkind relative is a stranger. *American*

15343. All are kin to the fortunate. *Greek*

15344. Curse on account with relatives. *Spanish*

15345. Folk canna help a' their kin. *Scottish*

15346. Hatched in the same nest. *Latin (Horace)*

15347. He who interferes with the quarrels of relations must pass through life without a friend. *American*

15348. Hunt the wolf with a brother-in-law, the bear with a brother [who is more trustworthy]. *Polish*

15349. If you love your wife, you must love her relatives. *Yiddish*

15350. It is a piece of luck to have relatives scarce. *Greek*

15351. Let us have florins and we shall find cousins. *Italian*

15352. Money has no blood relations. *American*

15353. Mony [many] kinsfolk, but few friends. *Scottish*

15354. Mony aunts, mony emes [uncles], mony kin, but few friends. *Scottish*

15355. Much kindred, much trouble. *French*

15356. One is never betrayed except by one's kindred. *French*

15357. Poverty has no relations. *Italian*

15358. Relations [i.e., relatives] are only for visits and not for living with. *Livonian*

15359. Relationship compels. *Greek (Aeschylus)*

15360. Relatives are friends from bitter necessity. *American*

15361. Relatives are scorpions. *Tunisian*

15362. Relatives wish for good relatives; neighbors wish for good neighbors. *Chinese*

15363. The malice of relatives is like a scorpion's sting. *Egyptian*

15364. The unfortunate have no relatives. *Latin*

15365. There ne'er was a poor man in his kin. *Scottish*

15366. Visit your aunt, but not every day; and call at your brother's but not every night. *American*

15367. We may choose our friends, but God sends us our relatives. *American*

15368. With a relative eat and drink, but transact no business with him. *American*

15369. You recognize your relatives when they get rich. *Yiddish*

15370. Your family may chew you, but they will not swallow you. *Arabic*

Relativity *see also* **Perspective**

15371. A giant among pigmies. *English*

15372. A triton among minnows. *English*

15373. Bad is never good until worse happens. *Danish*

15374. Happy are one-eyed men in the country of the blind. *Latin*

15375. He is a giant who has many dwarfs about him. *Yiddish*

15376. In Blindman's land your one-eyed man's a god. *English*

15377. In the ant's house the dew is a flood. *Persian*

15378. In the land of the naked, people are ashamed of clothes. *Livonian*

15379. Rubbish is only matter out of place. *American*

15380. Sables feel proud in the absence of ermine. *American*

15381. Show him death, and he'll be content with fever. *Persian*

15382. When the moon is not full, the stars shine more brightly. Buganda

Relaxation *see* **Leisure; Rest**

Reliability

15383. A cracked bell can never sound well. *English*

15384. A madman and a fool are no witnesses. *American*

Relief *see* **Consolation; Encouragement**

Religion *see also* **Church; Divine Assistance; God; Man and God; Prayer; Self-Help**

15385. A man without religion is like a horse without a bridle. *Latin*

15386. A profitable religion never wants proselytes. *Italian*

15387. A religious life is a struggle and not a hymn. *French*

15388. A woman without religion, a flower without perfume. *German*

15389. Many have quarrel'd about religion, that never practiced it. *American (Franklin)*

15390. Nature teaches us to love our friends, but religion our enemies. *English*

15391. Religion is the best armor in the world, but the worst cloak. *English*

15392. Talking against religion is unchaining a tyger; the beast let loose may worry his deliverer. *American (Franklin)*

15393. The truest temples are fixed in the heart. *American*

Reluctance *see* Unwillingness; Willingness

Remedies *see also* Ends and Means; Medicine

15394. A bitter drug oft brings relief. *Latin (Ovid)*

15395. A desperate disease must have a desperate cure. *American*

15396. A disease known is half cured. *American*

15397. A doubtful remedy is better than none. *Latin*

15398. A leaky ship needs muckle [much] pumping. *Scottish*

15399. A thousand ills require a thousand cures. *Latin (Ovid)*

15400. After bale cometh boote [remedy]. *English*

15401. All sorrows are good [or are less] with bread. *Spanish (Cervantes)*

15402. Better use medicines at the outset than at the last moment. *Latin (Publilius Syrus)*

15403. Bitter pills may have wholesome effects. *English*

15404. Burn not your house to fright away the mice. *English*

15405. Cure the disease, and kill the patient. *American*

15406. Desperate diseases must have desperate cures. *Latin*

15407. Different sores must have different salves. *English*

15408. Diseases, desperate grown, / By desperate appliance are reliev'd, / Or not at all. *English (Shakespeare)*

15409. Early, not late remedies are the most effective. *Latin*

15410. Extreme remedies are never the first to be resorted to. *Latin (Seneca)*

15411. Feed a cold and starve a fever. *American*

15412. For a stubborn ass a stubborn driver. *English*

15413. His sickness increases from the remedies applied to cure it. *Latin (Virgil)*

15414. How readily do men at ease prescribe to those sick at heart. *American*

15415. If there be no remedy, why worry? *Spanish*

15416. In poison there is physic. *English (Shakespeare)*

15417. It's ill healing an old sore. *English*

15418. Knotty timber requires sharp wedges. *English*

15419. Like cures like. *Latin*

15420. Music helps not the toothache. *English*

15421. No cure, no pay. *Chinese*

15422. One is not so soon healed as hurt. *English*

15423. One poison is cured by another. *Latin*

15424. Our remedies oft in ourselves do lie, / Which we ascribe to heaven. *English (Shakespeare)*

15425. Poison quells poison. *English*

15426. Some remedies are worse than the dangers. *Latin*

15427. The cure may be waur [worse] than the disease. *Scottish*

15428. The patient's bed is his best medicine. *American*

15429. The poor are cured by work, the rich by the doctor. *Polish*

15430. The purse of the patient protracts his cure. *German*

15431. The remedy is worse than the disease. *English*

15432. The rose blooms near the nettle; the remedy is not far from the disease, though it's often hard to find. *American*

15433. The sick soul must cure itself. *American*

15434. There are some remedies worse than the disease. *Latin (Publilius Syrus)*

15435. There is a remedy for everything, could men find it. *English*

15436. There is a remedy for everything except death. *French*

15437. There is help for all, except for the dead. *Danish*

15438. There is no remedy for death and taxes. *American*

15439. There is remedy for all things except stark dead. *Scottish*

15440. There's a salve for every sore. *English*

15441. To cure everyone with the same ointment. *Latin*

15442. What butter and whiskey will not cure there's no cure for. *Irish*

15443. What cures Sancho makes Martha sick. *Spanish*

15444. When remedies are needed, sighing is of no avail. *Italian*

Remembering *see also* Memory

15445. That is pleasant to remember which was hard to endure. *Italian*

15446. We have all forgotten more than we remember. *American*

Reminders *see also* Remembering

15447. A good Jew needs no reminder; to a bad Jew it is of no use. *Yiddish*

15448. Remind a man of what he remembers, and you will make him forget. *Latin (Plautus)*

Remorse

15449. Remorse is the echo of a lost virtue. *American*

Repair *see also* Amendment

15450. A jug that has been mended lasts 200 years. *Russian*

15451. It's a bad sack will abide no mending. *American*

Repentance *see also* Penitence

15452. A noble mind disdains not to repent. *Greek*

15453. All criminals turn preachers when they are under the gallows. *Italian*

15454. Better rue sit than rue flit. *Scottish*

15455. Fast comes the arrow, faster comes revenge, but fastest comes repentance. *Persian*

15456. From short pleasure long repentance. *American*

15457. He who repents his sins is almost innocent. *Latin*

15458. He who repents of his fault is almost guiltless. *Latin (Seneca)*

15459. If I hae done amiss I'll mak amends. *Scottish*

15460. If ye do wrang, mak amends. *Scottish*

15461. It's never too late to repent. *English*

15462. Joy shall be in heaven over one sinner that repenteth. *Bible*

15463. Late repentance is rarely sincere. *Latin*

15464. Repentance costs dear. *French*

15465. Repentance drives from the soul the elements of its corruption. *American*

15466. Repentance is the May of the virtues. *Chinese*

15467. Repentant tears wash out the stain of guilt. *Latin*

15468. Some refuse roast meat, and afterwards long for the smoke of it. *Italian*

15469. That may be soon done which brings long repentance. *American*

15470. The madness is short, repentance long. *German*

15471. The sinning is the best part of repentence. *Arabic*

15472. The stone will never melt, and the whore will never repent. *Tunisian*

Repetition *see also* Recidivism

15473. A good song is none the worse for being sung twice. *American*

15474. A good tale is none the worse for being twice told. *English*

15475. A good thing can be twice, nay, even thrice spoken. *Latin*

15476. Better twice measured than once wrong. *Danish*

15477. Commit a sin thrice and you will think it allowable. *Hebrew*

15478. Could everything be done twice, everything would be done better. *German*

15479. Do nothing twice over. *Latin (Cicero)*

15480. He makes himself ridiculous who is forever repeating the same mistake. *Latin (Horace)*

15481. I cannot rethresh the sorghum that is already threshed. *Zulu*

15482. If things were done twice all would be wise. *American*

15483. It is folly to sing twice to a deaf man. *English*

15484. It's no use boiling your cabbage twice. *Irish*

15485. Oft ettle [aim, attempt], whiles hit. *Scottish*

15486. Often shooting hits the mark. *English*

15487. Once does not count. *American*

15488. Shooting often hits the mark. *German*

15489. That is never too often repeated which is never sufficiently learned. *Latin (Seneca)*

15490. Things always thrive at thrice. *American*

15491. Well done, twice done. *English*

15492. What happens twice will happen thrice. *Japanese*

15493. Who is there that, shooting all day long, does not sometimes hit the mark? *Latin (Cicero)*

Reproaches

15494. Reproach, the most strong, / Redresses no wrong. *Welsh*

15495. Reproaches are as soap to the heart. *Syrian*

Reproof *see also* Rebuke

15496. A smart reproof is better than smooth deceit. *American*

15497. He that sharply chides is the most ready to pardon. *English*

15498. Reproof never does a wise man harm. *American*

15499. Reprove not a scorner, lest he hate thee; rebuke a wise man, and he will love thee. *Bible*

15500. Reprove others but correct yourself. *American*

15501. Reprove thy friend privately, commend him publicly. *American*

15502. Who reproves the lame must go upright. *Danish*

Reputation *see also* Accusation; Character; Slander

15503. A good name covers theft. *German*

15504. A good name endureth forever. *Bible*

15505. A good name is better than oil. *Dutch*

15506. A good name is better than precious ointment. *Bible*

15507. A good name is like sweet-smelling ointment. *Latin*

15508. A good name is rather to be chosen than great riches. *Bible*

15509. A good name is the fruit of life. *Arabic*

15510. A good name is worth more than a golden girdle. *French*

15511. A good name keeps its luster in the dark. *English*

15512. A good name lost is hard to regain. *American*

15513. A good reputation covers a multitude of sins. *American*

15514. A good reputation goes far; a bad one farther. *Montenegrin*

15515. A gude name is sooner tint [lost] than won. *Scottish*

15516. A man had better die than lose his good name. *Turkish*

15517. An honorable reputation is a sacred patrimony. *Latin*

15518. At every word, a reputation dies. *Welsh*

15519. Be the same thiung that ye wa'd be ca'd. *Scottish*

15520. Better a gude fame than a gude face. *Scottish*
15521. Better tine [lose] life since tint [lost] is gude fame. *Scottish*
15522. Credit lost is like a broken looking-glass. *English*
15523. Get a good name and go to sleep. *Spanish*
15524. Get a good name, and you may lie a-bed. *French*
15525. Get the word o' soon rising and ye may lie in bed a' day. *Scottish*
15526. Give a dog an ill name, and you may as well hang him. *English*
15527. Glass, china, and reputation, are easily crack'd, and never well mended. *American (Franklin)*
15528. Good ale needs not a wisp [i.e., does not need to be advertised]. *Scottish*
15529. Good repute is like the cypress: once cut, it never puts forth leaf again. *Italian*
15530. Good wine needs no bush [i.e., no advertising]. *Latin*
15531. Good wine needs no crier. *Spanish*
15532. Good wine praises itself. *Dutch*
15533. Good wine sells itself. *German*
15534. Have regard for your name, since it will remain for you longer than a great store of gold. *Bible*
15535. He that fa's in a gutter, the langer he lies the dirtier he is. *Scottish*
15536. He that hath an ill name is half hanged. *English*
15537. He that hath lost his credit, is dead to the world. *English*
15538. He that is evil deemed is half hanged. *Scottish*
15539. He who has the reputation of getting up in the morning can sleep until dinner-time. *French*
15540. He who is known for an early riser may lie abed till noon. *Yiddish*
15541. If a man hath lost his good name, how shall he in future gain his living? *Latin (Publilius Syrus)*
15542. If one's name be up, he may lie in bed. *English*
15543. If you have a bad name you are half-hanged. *American*
15544. It is true what all men say. *American*
15545. Life is for one generation; a good name is forever. *Japanese*
15546. Men's evil manners live in brass, / Their virtues we write in water. *English (Shakespeare)*
15547. No ruins are so irreparable as those of reputation. *American*
15548. Once in folks' mouths, hardly ever well out of them again. *German*
15549. One may better steal a horse than another look over the hedge. *English*
15550. Read not my blemishes in the world's report. *English (Shakespeare)*
15551. Reputation is commonly measured by the acre. *English*
15552. Reputation is the life of the mind as breath is the life of the body. *Latin*
15553. Reputation is what you are in the light; character is what you are in the dark. *American*
15554. Reputation serves to virtue as light does to a picture. *American*
15555. Saleable wine needs no bush [i.e., no advertising]. *Latin*
15556. Take away my good name, take away my life. *English*
15557. The brighter the moon, the more the dog howls. *American*
15558. The evil wound is cured, but not the evil name. *English*
15559. The good name is better than anything else. *Hungarian*
15560. The greater a man's reputation, the greater the criticism. *American*
15561. The lion is not half so fierce as he's painted. *American*
15562. There is no reputation so clear but a slander may stain it. *English*
15563. Those who are once found to be bad are presumed to be so forever. *Latin*
15564. To an upright man a good reputation is the greatest inheritance. *Latin (Publilius Syrus)*
15565. To good wine no sign. *French*
15566. Try to deserve the reputation you enjoy. *Latin*
15567. Vendible wine needs no ivy hung up [i.e., no advertising]. *Latin*
15568. We believe not a liar, even when he is speaking the truth. *Latin (Cicero)*
15569. Who has a bad name is half hanged. *Italian*
15570. Wish rather to be well spoken of than to be rich. *Greek (Menander)*
15571. Your own deeds will long be baptized on you. *Irish*

Request *see* Asking

Rescue
15572. Bones snatched from the mouth of a hungry dog. *Latin*
15573. To snatch the lamb from the wolf. *Latin*

Resemblance *see* Similarity

Resentment
15574. Men are as resentful as they are grateful. *American*

Resignation *see* Acceptance; Submission

Resistance *see* Desperation; Opposition; Rebellion

Resolution *see also* Commitment; Decision; Determination; Perseverance
15575. A resolute man cares nothing about difficulties. *American*
15576. Be resolved and the thing is done. *Chinese*
15577. He who resolves suddenly repents at leisure. *English*
15578. Strike with the sword and rest in its shadow. *Arabic*
15579. Without resolution a man must make his living by the sweat of his brow. *Chinese*

Respect *see also* **Reputation**

15580. A man is respected according to how well he dresses. *Arabic*

15581. If the laird slight the lady, so will all the kitchen boys. *Scottish*

15582. If you bow at all, bow low. *Chinese*

15583. Respect a man, he will do the more. *English*

15584. Respect is greater from a distance. *Latin*

15585. Respect is mutual. *Zulu*

Response *see also* **Answer; Denial; Refusal; Retaliation; Soft Words**

15586. Answer a fool according to his folly. *Bible*

15587. No reply is best. *Scottish*

15588. Not every word wants an answer. *Italian*

15589. The second blow makes the fray. *English (Bacon)*

Responsibility *see also* **Blame; Cause and Effect; Guilt; Shared Responsibility**

15590. Bad things never have owners. *Belizean Creole*

15591. Everybody's business is nobody's business. *English*

15592. He that becomes responsible pays. *French*

15593. He who ate the nuts must sweep away the shells. *German*

15594. Intoxication is not the wine's fault, but the man's. *Chinese*

15595. That which a man causes to be done by another he does himself. *Latin*

15596. Who commits the fault must drink it. *French*

15597. Wite [blame] yourself if your wife be with bairn [child]. *Scottish*

15598. You have cooked the broth, now spoon it out. *Russian*

Rest *see also* **Ease; Leisure; Stress and Strain; Weariness**

15599. A field that has rested gives a bountiful crop. *Latin*

15600. Absence of occupation is not rest. *American*

15601. God has given us this repose. *Latin*

15602. He that can take rest is greater than he that can take cities. *American*

15603. "If I rest, I rust," it says. *German*

15604. "If I rest, then I rust," says the key. *German*

15605. In a long work sleep may be naturally expected. *Latin (Horace)*

15606. In the hum of the market there is money, but under the cherry tree there is rest. *American*

15607. Men tire themselves in pursuit of rest. *American*

15608. No rest is worth anything except the rest that is earned. *American*

15609. Nothing can exist long without occasional rest. *Latin*

15610. Relaxation should at times be given to the mind, the better to fit it for toil when resumed. *Latin (Phaedrus)*

15611. Rest awhile and run a mile. *French*

15612. Rest breeds rust. *German*

15613. Rest comes from unrest and unrest from rest. *American*

15614. Rest is for the dead. *American*

15615. Rest is the sweet sauce of labor. *American*

15616. Rest is won only by work. *Turkish*

15617. Straining breaks the bow, relaxation the mind. *Latin (Publilius Syrus)*

15618. The fertile field becomes sterile without rest. *Spanish*

15619. Too much rest itself becomes a pain. *Greek*

15620. Want of rest is worse than want of wealth. *American*

Restraint *see also* **Abstinence; Common Sense; Moderation; Prudence; Self-Denial; Self-Discipline; Temperance**

15621. A mischievous cur must be tied short. *American*

15622. Between the bridle and the spur consists reason. *Italian*

15623. He rules easier wi' a saugh [willow] wand than wi' a sharp brand. *Scottish*

15624. Little sticks kindle the fire; great ones put it out. *English*

15625. Ne'er draw your dirk [knife] when a dunt [a blow] will do. *Scottish*

15626. Ne'er use the taws [a leather whip used by schoolmasters] when a gloom [frown] will do. *Scottish*

15627. One at a time is good fishing. *Scottish*

15628. Reserve the master-blow. *English*

15629. Speaking sweetly does not flay the tongue. *Italian*

15630. Stretch your legs according to your coverlet. *English*

15631. Strike as ye feed, and that's but soberly. *Scottish*

15632. The king goes as far as he dares, not as far as he desires. *Spanish*

15633. The Scot will not fight till he sees his own blood. *English*

15634. The sheep should be shorn and not flayed. *French*

15635. There are three classes of people one must not provoke: officials, customers and widows. *American*

Result *see* **Cause and Effect; End; Outcome**

Retaliation *see also* **Retribution; Revenge; Women and Revenge**

15636. A man may cause his own dog to bite him. *English*

15637. A stick has two ends. *Polish*

15638. And with what measure ye mete, it shall be measured to you again. *Bible*

15639. Claw me, and I'll claw thee. *English*

15640. Claw my elbow and I'll claw thy breech. *English*

15641. Eye for eye, tooth for tooth, hand for hand, foot for foot. *Bible*

15642. He who returns the first blow begins the quarrel. *English*

15643. I gave him the plague, he gave me pneumonia. *Maltese*

15644. If someone steps on your foot, step on his neck. *Lebanese*

15645. If you make your wife an ass, she will make you an ox. *American*

15646. Ka me, ka thee. *Scottish*

15647. Tickle me, Bobby, and I'll tickle you. / Scratch my breech, and I'll claw your elbow. *English*

Reticence *see* Brevity; Quiet; Silence

Retreat

15648. Always wise men go aback for to leap the further. *French*

15649. Better a fair pair of heels than a halter. *English*

15650. Better to turn back than to lose your way. *Russian*

15651. Flying from the bull he fell into the river. *Spanish*

15652. Flying men often meet their fate. *Latin*

15653. For a fleeing enemy make a golden bridge. *Spanish*

15654. Go back a little to leap the further. *French*

15655. He fightith wele that fleith faste. *English*

15656. He that fights and runs away, / Will live to fight another day. *English (Butler)*

15657. He that flies may fight another day. *Latin*

15658. He who runs away and escapes is clever. *Wolof*

15659. It is better to fly than to remain in disgrace. *Latin*

15660. It is better to run back than to run wrong. *Latin*

15661. It is better to turn back than to get lost [or go astray]. *Russian*

15662. It is better to turn back than to persevere in an evil course. *Latin*

15663. Of the thirty-six strategies, there is none better than retreat. *Korean*

15664. Of the thirty-six tricks, flight is the best. *Japanese*

15665. One must step back to make a better leap. *French*

15666. To run away is not glorious, but very healthy. *Russian*

15667. Well fight that well flight. *English*

15668. When the mouse laughs at the cat, there is a hole nearby. *Nigerian*

Retribution *see* Punishment and Retribution; Retaliation; Revenge; Women and Revenge

Revelation

15669. Don't tell all you know nor do all you can. *American*

15670. Nothing comes fairer to light than what has been lang [long] hidden. *Scottish*

15671. The cat's oot o' the pock [bag]. *Scottish*

Revelry *see also* Drinking and Drunkenness; Womanizing

15672. Wine and wenches empty men's purses. *English*

15673. Wine and women bring misery. *Latin (Martius)*

15674. Women, money and wine have their pleasure and their poison. *French*

Revenge *see also* Women and Revenge

15675. Blood cannot be washed out with blood. *Persian*

15676. Blood washes away blood. *Arabic*

15677. Don't avenge every insult—you'll have no time to do anything else. *American*

15678. Forgetting of a wrong is a mild revenge. *English*

15679. Forgiveness is better than revenge. *Greek*

15680. Have ye him on the hip. *English (Heywood)*

15681. He is a great fool who forgets himself to feed another. *Spanish*

15682. He that will revenge every wrong, the longer he lives, the less he will have. *English*

15683. Heat not a furnace for your foe so hot / That it do singe yourself. *English (Shakespeare)*

15684. If I had revenged all wrong, / I had not worn my skirts so long. *English (Ray)*

15685. If you want to be revenged, hold your tongue. *Spanish*

15686. It costs more to revenge injuries than to bear them. *American*

15687. It is but the weak and little mind that rejoices in revenge. *Latin (Juvenal)*

15688. It is worse to do than to revenge an injury. *English*

15689. Living well is the best revenge. *English (Herbert)*

15690. Men are more prone to revenge injuries than to requite kindnesses. *English*

15691. Neglect kills injuries; revenge increases them. *American (Franklin)*

15692. No revenge is more honorable than the one not taken. *Spanish*

15693. Recompense injury with justice, and recompense kindness with kindness. *Chinese (Confucius)*

15694. Revenge in cold blood is the devil's own act and deed. *English*

15695. Revenge is a confession of pain. *Latin*

15696. Revenge is a dish that should be eaten cold. *English*

15697. Revenge is a luscious fruit which you must leave to ripen. *French*

15698. Revenge is a mouthful for a god. *Italian*

15699. Revenge is sweeter far than flowing honey. *Greek*

15700. Revenge is sweeter than life itself. *Latin (Juvenal)*

15701. Revenge of an hundred years old hath still its sucking teeth. *English*

15702. Swift vengeance waits on wrong. *Greek*

15703. The best means of destroying an enemy is to make him your friend. *American*

15704. The man who does not take revenge is the nephew of an ass. *Sudanese*

15705. The noblest vengeance is to forgive. *English*

15706. The revenge of an idiot is without mercy. *English*

15707. There is small revenge in words, but words may be greatly revenged. *American*

15708. Tit for tat. *English*

15709. To be avenged on an enemy is to obtain a second life. *Latin*

15710. To forget a wrong is the best revenge. *Italian*

15711. Vengeance erases shame. *Arabic*

15712. Vengeance has no foresight. *French*

15713. Vengeance is mine; I will repay, saith the Lord. *Bible*

15714. Vengeance is slow, but stern. *Latin*

15715. Vengeance is the pleasure of the gods. *French*

15716. Vengeance lies open to patient craft. *Latin*

15717. Vengeance should always pursue crime. *Arabic*

15718. Where vice is, vengeance follows. *English*

15719. Where villany goes before, vengeance follows after. *English*

15720. Who has patience sees his revenge. *American*

Reward *see also* Accomplishment

15721. Nae [no] swat, nae sweet. *Scottish*

15722. Take away her rewards, and who will ever clasp naked Virtue to his bosom? *Latin (Juvenal)*

15723. The deed is everything, the glory naught. *German (Goethe)*

15724. The prize is not without dust. *Latin*

15725. The reward of a thing rightly done is to have done it. *Latin*

15726. There is sufficient reward in the mere consciousness of a good action. *Latin (Cicero)*

15727. Who does well shall not be without his reward. *Arabic*

Rich and Poor *see also* Haves and Have-Nots; Money; Poverty; Wealth

15728. A rich man thinks of the future, a poor man thinks of the present. *Chinese*

15729. Bear wealth; poverty will bear itself. *Scottish*

15730. God help the poor; the rich can help themselves. *Scottish*

15731. God help the rich, for the poor can beg. *Scottish*

15732. He who has wealth has many cares; he who has none can sleep soundly. *Chinese*

15733. I prefer a man without money, to money without a man. *Greek*

15734. If our wealth commands us, we are poor indeed. *American*

15735. If poor, do not murmur, and if rich do not boast; for neither wealth nor poverty is abiding. *Chinese*

15736. If poor, don't cheat; if rich, don't presume. *Chinese*

15737. If poor, don't lose your self-reliance; if rich, don't act the fool. *Chinese*

15738. If the poor man associates with the rich, the poor man will soon have no trousers to wear. [He will spend more than he can afford to spend.] *Chinese*

15739. If you are poor, distinguish yourself by your virtues; if rich, by your good deeds. *French*

15740. If you have money, take a seat; if not, stand on your feet. *German*

15741. It is better to endure poverty than the arrogance of the rich. *Greek*

15742. Just as it's bad to be rich, it's no joy to be a pauper either. *Dutch*

15743. Men honor the well-to-do; dogs bite the ill-dressed. *Chinese*

15744. Painless poverty is better than embittered wealth. *Greek*

15745. Poor folk seek meat for their stamacks, and rich folk stamacks for their meat. *Scottish*

15746. Poor men go to heaven as soon as rich. *English*

15747. Poverty is not happiness, and riches are not disgrace. *German*

15748. Poverty is safe; riches, exposed to danger. *Latin*

15749. Rich men feel misfortunes that fly over poor men's heads. *English*

15750. Rich men read books; poor men rear pigs. *Chinese*

15751. Riches run after the rich, and poverty runs after the poor. *Russian*

15752. Riches — sin before God; poverty — sin before men. *Russian*

15753. The dainties of the great are the tears of the poor. *English*

15754. The jungle may hide the fragrant orchid, and a thatched roof may cover a future monarch. *Chinese*

15755. The pleasures of the rich are bought with the tears of the poor. *English*

15756. The poor do penance for the sins of the rich. *Italian*

15757. The poor enjoy the favor of the rich; the rich, the favor of heaven. *Chinese*

15758. The poor man is ruined as soon as he begins to ape the rich. *Latin (Publilius Syrus)*

15759. The poor man must walk to get meat for his stomach, the rich man to get a stomach for his meat. *American*

15760. The poor man seeks food, the rich man appetite. *American*

15761. The poor must dance as the rich pipe. *German*

15762. The poor sing, the rich listen. *Russian*

15763. The pride of the rich makes the labors of the poor. *American*

15764. The rich get richer and the poor get babies [or pregnant, or children]. *American*

15765. The rich have many well-to-do friends; the poor have few associates. *Chinese*

15766. The rich would have to eat money, but luckily the poor provide food. *Russian*

15767. Though poverty may bring sorrow, riches create restlessness. *Danish*

15768. With money you are a dragon; with no money, a worm. *Chinese*

Ridicule *see also* Mockery; Scorn

15769. A fear of becoming ridiculous is the best guide in life and will save one from all sorts of scrapes. *American*

15770. A wise man may look ridiculous in the company of fools. *American*

15771. Ridicule dishonors more than dishonor. *French (La Rochefoucauld)*

15772. The blind man is laughing at the bald-head. *Persian*

15773. The dread of ridicule extinguishes originality in its birth. *American*

15774. There is but one step from the sublime to the ridiculous. *French*

15775. Who are serious in ridiculous things, will be ridiculous in serious affairs. *Latin*

Right *see also* Good and Bad; Right and Wrong; Wrong

15776. A fool must now and then be right by chance. *English (Cowper)*

15777. As right as rain. *American*

15778. I will go forward against thousands and tens of thousands [i.e., because I believe that I am right]. *Chinese (Mencius)*

15779. It is praiseworthy to do what is right, not what is lawful. *Latin*

15780. Nothing can be great which is not right. *American*

15781. Richt wrangs nae man. [Right wrongs no man.] *Scottish*

15782. Right goes before might. *German*

15783. Right is better than law. *Greek*

15784. Right is with the strongest. *German*

15785. Right on our side, doubt not of victory. *American*

15786. Right or wrong, it's our house up to the roof. *Spanish*

15787. Whatever is, is right. *English (Pope)*

15788. Whatever is, is right. *Greek*

15789. Where force prevails, right perishes. *Spanish*

Right and Wrong *see also* Good and Bad; Good and Evil; Right; Sin and Sinners; Sin and Virtue; Wrong

15790. Better to be wrong with everyone than right by yourself. *Moorish*

15791. Better to do right without thanks, than wrong without punishment. *Latin*

15792. Better to limp upon the right way than to ride upon the wrong. *American*

15793. I see the right and approve it, yet I follow the wrong. *Latin (Ovid)*

15794. If you keep insisting you're right, you're wrong. *Yiddish*

15795. Many love to praise right and do wrong. *English*

15796. Protest long enough that you are right, and you will be wrong. *Yiddish*

15797. There is as much in knowing how not to do wrong as there is in knowing how to do right. *American*

15798. When everyone is wrong, everyone is right. *French*

Risk *see also* Boldness; Chance; Future; Venture and Investment

15799. A chair unsound / Soon finds the ground. *English*

15800. Cockroach eber so drunk, him no walk past fowl yard. *Haitian Creole*

15801. Do not entrust your all to one vessel. *Latin*

15802. Doubtful the die, and dire the cast. *English*

15803. Even a good swimmer is not safe from all chance of drowning. *French*

15804. He that bites on every weed must needs light on poison. *English*

15805. He that is far from his gear [goods] is near his skaith [injury]. *Scottish*

15806. He that nought nassayeth, nought nacheveth. *English (Chaucer)*

15807. He that runs in the dark may well stumble. *English*

15808. If the fire is near the tow, the Devil comes along and blows. *Spanish*

15809. It is better to risk than to delay overmuch. *American*

15810. It is necessary to risk something. *American*

15811. Risk is a noble thing. *Russian*

15812. So long cometh the pot to the water that it cometh to home broke. *French*

15813. Swift risks are often attended with precipitate falls. *American*

15814. The cockroach is never silly enough to approach the door of the henhouse. *Martinique Creole*

15815. The goose goes so often to the kitchen that at last she is fastened to the spit. *Danish*

15816. The pitcher goes so often to the fountain that it gets broken. *Spanish (Cervantes)*

15817. The pitcher which goes often to the fountain loses either its handle or its spout. *Spanish*

15818. Those who wade in unknown waters will be sure to be drowned. *English*

15819. To be between the hammer and the anvil. *French*

15820. To lean against a tottering wall. *Latin*

15821. Unhardy [unventuresome] is unsely [unlucky]. *English (Chaucer)*

15822. When cockroach make dance, him no ax fowl. *Haitian Creole*

15823. When thy neighbor's house doth burn, be careful of thine own. *English*

15824. Who perisheth in needless danger is the devil's martyr. *English*

15825. You attack a horned animal. *Latin*

15826. You play with edged tools. *English*

Rivalry *see also* Competition; Shared Authority

15827. Heaven cannot brook two suns, nor earth two masters. *Greek*

15828. Two cocks in one yard do not agree. *American*

Rogues

15829. A face shaped like the petals of the lotus; a voice as cool as sandal; a heart like a pair of scissors, and excessive humility — these are the signs of a rogue. *Sanskrit*

15830. A rogue is as soft as cotton; a fool as hard as iron. *Chinese*

15831. If you pity rogues you are no great friend of honest men. *American*

15832. It is easier to fill a rogue's belly than his eyes. *Danish*

15833. No rogue like the godly rogue. *English*

15834. Nobody calls himself a rogue. *American*

15835. One rogue does not betray another. *American*

15836. One rogue is usher to another. *Greek*

15837. When a rogue kisses you, count your teeth. *Hebrew*

15838. When rogues fall out, honest men come by their own. *American*

Routine *see* Habit

Rudeness

15839. An ungracious man is like a story told at the wrong time. *Bible*

15840. He who says what he likes shall hear what he does not like. *English*

15841. Rudeness will repel when courtesy would attract friends. *American*

Ruin

15842. Going to ruin is silent work. *Gaelic*

15843. One man's wealth is often many men's ruin. *American*

15844. Ruin is most fatal when it begins at the bottom. *American*

15845. When a man lays the foundation of his own ruin, others will build on it. *American*

Rulers *see* Kings and Rulers

Rules

15846. No rule is so general, which admits not some exception. *English (Burton)*

15847. Submit to the rule you yourself laid down. *Latin*

15848. There is no rule which does not fail. *French*

15849. There is no useful rule [or no general rule] without an exception. *English*

Rumor *see also* Gossip; Hearsay; Scandal

15850. In calamity any rumor is believed. *Latin*

15851. Rumor doth double, like the voice and echo, / The number of the fear'd. *English (Shakespeare)*

15852. There is nothing among men swifter than rumor. *Latin*

Sacred and Profane

15853. You mix what is sacred with what is profane. *Latin*

Sacrifice *see also* Self-Sacrifice

15854. A hook is weel tint [lost] to catch a salmon. *Scottish*

15855. "Every little helps to lighten the freight," said the captain, as he threw his wife overboard. *Dutch*

Safety *see also* Carefulness; Caution; Common Sense; Precaution; Prudence; Watchfulness

15856. Be wary then; best safety lies in fear. *English (Shakespeare)*

15857. He is safe from danger who is on guard even when safe. *Latin*

15858. He that's secure is not safe. *American*

15859. He who goes the lowest builds the safest. *American*

15860. It is better to be safe than sorry. *American*

15861. Out of this nettle, danger, we pluck this flower, safety. *English (Shakespeare)*

15862. Safety lies in the middle course. *Latin*

15863. The only safety for the conquered is to expect no safety. *Latin*

15864. The way to be safe is never to feel secure. *English*

15865. There is nothing like being on the safe side. *Latin*

15866. What is safe is distasteful; in rashness there is hope. *Latin*

Salvation

15867. Salvation is from God only. *Latin*

15868. Strait is the gate, and narrow is the way, which leadeth unto life, and few there be that find it. *Bible*

15869. The fearless man is his own salvation. *American*

15870. The knowledge of sin is the beginning of salvation. *Latin*

Sarcasm

15871. Sarcasm is the language of the devil. *American*

15872. Sarcasm poisons reproof. *American*

Satiety *see* Excess; Satisfaction; Sufficiency

Satire

15873. It is hard to abstain from writing satire. *Latin (Juvenal)*

Satisfaction *see also* Adequacy; Sufficiency

15874. A full belly neither fights nor flies well. *Scottish*

15875. The poor are rich when they are satisfied. *American*

Saving and Spending *see also* Buying and Selling; Frugality; Miserliness; Parsimony; Payment; Profit and Loss; Thrift; Use; Venture and Investment

15876. A fat kitchen has poverty for a neighbor. *Italian*

15877. A niggard spends as much as a generous man. *French*

15878. A penny hain'd [saved] 's a penny clear, and a preen a-day 's a groat a-year. *Scottish*

15879. A penny hain'd [saved] 's a penny gained. *Scottish*

15880. A penny in my purse will gar me drink when my friends winna. *Scottish*

15881. A penny in the purse is a gude companion. *Scottish*

15882. A penny in the purse is better than a friend at court. *English*

15883. A penny in the purse is better than a crown spent. *Scottish*

15884. A penny is sometimes better spent than spared. *English*

15885. A penny saved is a penny earned. *American*
15886. A penny saved is a penny got. *English*
15887. A penny saved is twopence got. *English*
15888. A penny spared is twice got. *English*
15889. A poor man's shilling is but a penny. *English*
15890. A shilling spent idly by a fool, may be picked up by a wiser man. *American (Franklin)*
15891. Add pence to pence / For wealth comes hence. *English*
15892. At a good bargain bethink you. *Italian*
15893. Better is rule than rent. *French*
15894. Better spared than ill-spent. *Scottish*
15895. Better spent than spared. *American*
15896. Beware of little expenses; a small leak will sink a ship. *American*
15897. By always taking out and never putting in, the bottom is soon reached. *Spanish*
15898. Cheap bargains are dear. *Spanish*
15899. E'ening [evening] orts [that which is rejected or thrown aside] are gude morning's fodder. *Scottish*
15900. Frae savin' comes havin'. *Scottish*
15901. Get and save, and thou wilt have. *Scottish*
15902. Get weel and keep weel. *Scottish*
15903. Get what you can, and keep what you hae [have], that's the way to get rich. *Scottish*
15904. Good is the farthing which saves the penny. *French*
15905. Hain'd gear [money saved] helps weel. *Scottish*
15906. He can make a wine-cellar out of a raisin. *Lebanese*
15907. He that gets his gear before his wit will be short while master of it. *Scottish*
15908. He that hains [saves] his dinner will hae the mair [will have the more] to his supper. *Scottish*
15909. He that spends more than he is worth, spins a rope for his own neck. *French*
15910. He that will not stoop for a point shall never be worth a point. *English*
15911. He that winna lout and lift a preen [pin] will ne'er be worth a groat. *Scottish*
15912. He wha mair than he's worth doth spend, aiblins [perhaps] a rape [rope] his life will end. *Scottish*
15913. He who eats and puts something by, spreads the table twice. *Spanish*
15914. He, who more than he is worth doth spend, / E'en makes a rope, his life to end. *English*
15915. He who would save should begin with his mouth. *American*
15916. If you spend a thing you cannot have it. *Latin*
15917. If you would be wealthy, think of saving as well as of getting. *American*
15918. In spending lies the advantage. *American*
15919. It is easier to make money than to keep it. *Yiddish*
15920. It's too late to spare, / When the bottom is bare. *English*
15921. It's weel won that's aff the wame [off the belly]. *Scottish*
15922. Keep something for a fair [or sair] fit [foot]. [Hold on to something you might need.] *Scottish*
15923. Keeping is harder than winning. *American*
15924. Ken [know] when to spend and when to spare, and ye needna be busy, and ye'll ne'er be bare. *Scottish*
15925. Lay your wame [belly] to your winning. *Scottish*
15926. Let your purse be your master. *English*
15927. Live according to your income. *Latin (Persius)*
15928. Making money is like digging with a needle; spending it is like water soaking into sand. *Chinese*
15929. Men make the money and women save it. *Italian*
15930. Money burns a hole in the pocket. *American*
15931. Money is flat and meant to be piled up. *Scottish*
15932. Money is like an arm and a leg: use it or lose it. *American*
15933. Money is like an eel in the hand. *Welsh*
15934. Money is like promises, easier made than kept. *American*
15935. Money is round, and rolls away. *Italian*
15936. Much worth never cost little. *Spanish*
15937. One cannot have a good pennyworth of bad ware. *French*
15938. Penny and penny laid up will be many. *English*
15939. Penny is penny's brother. *German*
15940. Placks [two bodles, one-third of the English penny] and bawbees [halfpennies] grow pounds. *Scottish*
15941. Prepare in youth for your old age. *Yiddish*
15942. Put by for a rainy day. *English*
15943. Put twa [two] pennies in a purse and they'll creep thegither. *Scottish*
15944. Put your hand quickly to your hat and slowly to your purse. *Danish*
15945. Put your hand twice to your bonnet for once to your pouch. *Scottish*
15946. Riches are like muck which stinks in a heap, but spread abroad makes the earth fruitful. *English*
15947. Save something for the man that rides on the white horse. *English*
15948. Saving is getting. *American*
15949. Saving is the first gain. *Italian*
15950. Spare weel and hae weel. *Scottish*
15951. Spare when ye're young; and spend when ye're auld. *Scottish*
15952. Spend one sou less than the clear gain. *French*
15953. Spending is quick, it is earning that is slow. *Russian*
15954. Store is no sore. *French*
15955. Take care of the halfpence and pence, and the shillings and pounds will take care of themselves. *American (Franklin)*
15956. Take care of the pence, and the pounds will take care of themselves. *English*
15957. That man's purse will never be bare / Who knows when to buy, to spend, and to spare. *German*
15958. The proverb of the three S's: spend, spend profusely, and spare. *English*
15959. There is more art in saving than in gaining. *German*

15960. There is no way to make money so certain as to save what you have. *Latin*

15961. There was a wife that kept her supper for her breakfast, an' she was dead or day. *Scottish*

15962. They buy gude cheap that bring naething home. *Scottish*

15963. Through not spending enough we spend too much. *Spanish*

15964. To achieve alchemy with the teeth. [To save money by eating less.] *French*

15965. To hain [save] is to hae [have]. *Scottish*

15966. To spend much and gain little is the sure road to ruin. *German*

15967. Wha burns rags will want a winding sheet. *Scottish*

15968. What is not needed is dear at a farthing. *English*

15969. What winna mak a pat [pot] may mak a pat lid. *Scottish*

15970. What you don't store up in this world, you can't take with you to a future world. *Yiddish*

15971. What you save is, later, like something found. *Yiddish*

15972. Who heeds not a penny / Shall never have any. *Scottish*

15973. Who more than he is worth doth spend, / He maketh a rope his life to end. *English*

15974. Who spends more than he should, shall not have to spend when he would. *English (Fuller)*

15975. Who saves, saves for the cat. *Italian*

15976. Winter finds out what Summer lays up. *English*

15977. Winter is summer's heir. *English*

15978. You must spend money, if you wish to make money. *Latin*

Saying and Doing *see* Boasting; Promises; Threat(s); Words and Deeds

Scandal *see also* Reputation; Rumor; Slander

15979. A lie has no legs, but a scandal has wings. *English*

15980. Every one that repeats it, adds something to the scandal. *American*

15981. Fame lies down, but ill fame runs abroad. *Russian*

15982. Foul linen should be washed at home. *American*

15983. In scandal as well as robbery, the receiver is as bad as the thief. *American*

15984. It is at home, not in public, one washes his dirty linen. *French*

15985. Nothing moves more quickly than scandal. *Latin (Livy)*

15986. Scandal's the sweetener of a female feast. *English (Cowper)*

15987. Tell it not in Gath, publish it not in the streets of Askelon. *Bible*

15988. Who is always looking for mud generally finds it. *American*

Scarcity

15989. Scarce things are prized. *Latin*

15990. The best things are worst to come by. *English*

Scholars and Scholarship

15991. A scholar has usually three maladies—poverty, pride and the itch. *American*

15992. Every good scholar is not a good schoolmaster. *American*

15993. Great scholars are not the shrewdest men. *American*

15994. He who would know all, grows old soon. *Yiddish*

15995. In learning, length of study does not count; the most intelligent becomes master. *Chinese*

15996. Scholars are not classified by age; the intelligent take precedence. *Chinese*

15997. Scholarship knows no national boundary. *Korean*

15998. The greatest scholars are not the wisest men. *Latin*

15999. The ink of a scholar is more sacred than the blood of the martyr. *Arabic*

16000. The scholar who cherishes the love of comfort is not fit to be deemed a scholar. *Chinese (Confucius)*

16001. Who robs a scholar, robs twenty men. [Because much of what a scholar possesses is borrowed.] *English*

Scolding

16002. He scolds most that can hurt the least. *American*

Scorn

16003. Scorn at first makes after-love the more. *English (Shakespeare)*

16004. Scorn comes commonly wi' skaith [injury]. *Scottish*

16005. Scornfu' dogs eat dirty puddins. *Scottish*

16006. Scorning is catching. *English*

16007. Ye hae [have] got baith [both] the skaith [injury] and the scorn. *Scottish*

Seasons *see also* Spring; Summer; Winter

16008. When the heavenly river [i.e., Milky Way] flows diagonally across the sky, put on your wadded clothes. *Chinese*

16009. When the Milky Way divides [the sky], bring out your thin garments. *Chinese*

Secrets and Secrecy *see also* Women and Secrets; Women and Trustworthiness

16010. A healthy ear can endure sick words. *Senegalese*

16011. A secret between two is a secret of God; a secret between three is a secret of everybody's. *Spanish*

16012. A secret fire is discovered by the smoke. *Catalan*

16013. A secret is like a dove: when it leaves my hand it takes wing. *Yemeni*

16014. A secret is your blood; let it out too often and you die. *Arabic*

16015. A secret is your slave if you keep it, your master if you lose it. *Arabic*

16016. After nine months the secret comes out. *Yiddish*

16017. Betray not a secret even though racked by wine or wrath. *Latin (Horace)*

16018. Beware of a door that has too many keys. *American*

16019. Confide a secret to a dumb man and it will make him speak. *Livonian*

16020. Confidence is the only bond of friendship. *Latin (Publilius Syrus)*

16021. Do not tell your secrets behind a wall or a hedge. *Spanish*

16022. Eggs are close things, but the chicks come out at last. *Chinese*

16023. Give up the smallest part of a secret, and the rest is no longer in your power. *German*

16024. He that communicates his secret to another makes himself that other's slave. *Spanish (Gracián)*

16025. He who keeps his own secret avoids much mischief. *Spanish*

16026. He who revealeth his secret, maketh himself a slave. *Arabic*

16027. Hills see, walls hear. *Spanish*

16028. If one knows, it is a secret; if two, it is public. *Hindi*

16029. If possible, don't tell your secrets to your friend. *Persian*

16030. If you wish another to keep your secret, first keep it yourself. *Latin*

16031. If you would keep your secret from an enemy, tell it not to a friend. *American (Franklin)*

16032. It is wise not to seek a secret and honest not to reveal it. *American (Franklin)*

16033. Leave to concealment what has long been concealed. *Latin*

16034. Let the shirt next to your skin not know what's within. *French*

16035. Love, pain and money cannot be kept secret. They soon betray themselves. *Spanish*

16036. None are so fond of secrets as those who do not mean to keep them. *American*

16037. Nothing is so burdensome as a secret. *French*

16038. One hand doesn't know what the other hand is up to. *American*

16039. Secrecy is the seal of speech. *Greek*

16040. Secrecy is the soul of all great designs. *American*

16041. Sooner will men hold fire in their mouths than keep a secret. *Latin*

16042. Tell your friend your secret and he will set his foot on your throat. *Spanish*

16043. Tell your secret to your servant and you make him your master. *American*

16044. The forest has ears, the field has eyes. *German*

16045. The secret of two is God's secret — the secret of three is all the world's. *French*

16046. There is a skeleton in every house. *Italian*

16047. Thieves quarrel, and thefts are discovered. *Spanish*

16048. Three can keep a secret when twa [two] are awa [away]. *Scottish*

16049. Three may keep a secret, if two of them are dead. *American (Franklin)*

16050. Three things cannot be kept secret: love, pregnancy and riding a camel. *Arabic*

16051. Thy secret is thy prisoner; if thou let it go, thou art a prisoner to it. *Hebrew*

16052. To whom thy secret thou dost tell, to him thy freedom thou dost sell. *American (Franklin)*

16053. To whom you reveal your secret you surrender your liberty [or freedom]. *Spanish*

16054. To whom you tell your secrets, to him you resign your liberty. *Portuguese*

16055. Two may keep counsel when the third's away. *English (Shakespeare)*

16056. Under the rose. *Latin*

16057. We confide our secret through friendship, but it escapes through love. *French*

16058. What is whispered in the ear is often heard a hundred miles off. *Chinese*

16059. What three know, every creature knows. *Spanish*

16060. When a secret is revealed, it is the fault of the man who confided it. *French*

16061. When the cook and the butler fall out we shall know what is become of the butter. *Dutch*

16062. Would you know secrets? Look for them in grief or pleasure. *English*

16063. You are to be pitied when you have to conceal what you wish to tell. *Latin*

16064. You ought not to tell the secret of your heart to any but a friend. *Persian*

Security *see also* Carefulness; Caution; Precaution; Preparedness; Safety; Watchfulness

16065. A lock is meant only for honest men. *Yiddish*

16066. Neither armies nor treasures are the safeguards of a state, but friends. *American*

Seduction *see also* Men and Women; Women Saying No

16067. A woman that loves to be at the window is a bunch of grapes on the highway. *English*

16068. Had we but world enough, and time, / This coyness, lady, were no crime. *English (Marvell)*

16069. Venus yields to caresses, not to compulsion. *Latin (Publilius Syrus)*

Seeing and Hearing *see also* Alertness; Eyes and Ears; Listening; Watchfulness

16070. Deny, but what thou seest believe. *Wolof*

16071. I see much, but I say little and do less. *English*

16072. Men trust their ears less than their eyes. *Latin (Herodotus)*

16073. One eyewitness is better than ten hearsays. *Latin (Plautus)*

16074. Seeing excites to knowing. *Wolof*

16075. Seeing is believing. *English*

16076. Seeing produces knowing. *Wolof*

16077. Seeing's beliving a' the warld o'er. *Scottish*

16078. The eyes are always children. *French*

16079. The eyes believe themselves, the ears other people. *English*

16080. To hear a hundred times is not so good as to see once. *Japanese*
16081. We should trust our eyes more than our ears. *Latin*
16082. What one hears is doubtful; what one sees is certain. *Chinese*
16083. What the eyes see the heart believes. *German*
16084. What we hear strikes the mind with less force than what we see. *Latin*
16085. Where the eye sees it saw not, the heart will think it thought not. *Scottish*
16086. Who sees with the eye believes with the heart. *Italian*
16087. Who sees with the eye of another is as blind as a mole. *German*
16088. Words are but wind, but seein's believin'. *Scottish*

Seeking
16089. Seek, and ye shall find; knock, and it shall be opened unto you. *Bible*
16090. Those who seek cake lose their bread. *Yiddish*
16091. Who seeks what he should not, finds what he would not. *German*

Seeming *see also* **Deception; Identity**
16092. Be content to seem what you really are. *Latin (Martial)*
16093. How little do they see what is, who frame their hasty judgments upon that which seems. *English (Southey)*
16094. Men are valued not for what they are, but for what they seem to be. *English (Bulwer-Lytton)*
16095. Seem not greater than thou art. *Latin*
16096. Things are not always what they seem. *Latin (Phaedrus)*
16097. Things are not as they are, but as they seem. *Italian*
16098. Things are seldom what they seem, / Skim milk masquerades as cream. *English (Gilbert)*
16099. What is not seen is as if it was not. Even the right does not receive proper consideration if it does not seem right. *Latin* (Gracian)

Self-Confidence *see also* **Arrogance; Confidence**
16100. Self-confidence first, money second, personal appearance third. *Japanese*

Self-Deception
16101. To deceive one's self is very easy. *English*
16102. What camel ever saw its own hump? *Arabic*
16103. What you see in the mirror is not in the mirror. *German*
16104. Who has deceiv'd thee so oft as thy self? *English*

Self-Defense
16105. Self-defense is nature's eldest law. *English (Dryden)*

Self-Denial *see also* **Abstinence; Limitations; Moderation; Self-Discipline; Temperance**
16106. The more a man denies himself, the more he will receive from the gods. *Latin (Horace)*

Self-Determination *see also* **Self-Reliance**
16107. Every man is the architect of his own fortune. *Latin (Sallust)*
16108. Every man is the son of his own works. *Spanish*

Self-Discipline
16109. Beware of no man more than thyself. *American*
16110. Govern yourself and you can govern the world. *Chinese*
16111. He conquers twice who conquers himself in victory. *Latin*
16112. He has wit at will, that with angry heart can hold him still. *Scottish*
16113. He is indeed a conqueror who conquers himself. *Latin*
16114. He is most powerful who governs himself. *Latin (Seneca)*
16115. He that is master of himself will soon be master of others. *English*
16116. He who conquers others is strong; / He who conquers himself is mighty. *Chinese (Laotse)*
16117. He who gets the better of an irascible temperament conquers his worst enemy. *Latin (Publilius Syrus)*
16118. He's a fool that forgets himsel. *Scottish*
16119. I am myself my own commander. *Latin*
16120. Keep yourself within yourself. *English (Shakespeare)*
16121. Rule lust, temper tongue and bridle the belly. *English*
16122. The greatest power of ruling consists in the exercise of self-control. *Latin (Seneca)*
16123. The superior man, though cold, does not shiver. *Chinese*
16124. Who cannot rule himself can never rule a state. *American*

Self-Esteem *see also* **Self-Respect; Self-Worth**
16125. A man's worth is as he esteems himself. *French*
16126. A prudent traveler never disparages his own country. *American*
16127. What you think of yourself is much more important than what others think of you. *Latin*
16128. Who does not esteem himself will gain esteem. *Italian*

Self-Help *see also* **Divine Assistance; God; Man and God; Prayer; Self-Reliance**
16129. God says, "Get up," [and then,] "Let me help you." *Hausa*

Self-Importance *see also* **Pride; Vanity**
16130. A fly before his own eye is bigger than an elephant in the next field. *English*
16131. Every cock is proud on his own dunghill. *English*
16132. Everyone thinks that all the bells echo his own thoughts. *German*
16133. He does not think milk-and-water of himself. *English*

16134. He does not think small beer of himself. *English*

16135. The big drum only sounds well from afar. *Persian*

16136. The crow that pretends to be a cormorant gets drowned. *Japanese*

16137. The pebble in the brook secretly thinks itself a precious stone. *Japanese*

16138. The priest forgets he was a clerk. *English*

16139. The turtle lays thousands of eggs without anyone knowing, but when the hen lays an egg, the whole country is informed. *Malay*

16140. The world will end when I die. *Egyptian*

16141. To have a good opinion of himself. *Latin*

16142. We hounds killed the hare, quoth the lapdog. *English*

16143. We would rather speak badly of ourselves than not talk about ourselves at all. *French (La Rochefoucauld)*

16144. When a beggar gets on horseback the devil cannot outride him. *German*

16145. When a clown is on a mule, he remembers neither God nor the world. *Spanish*

16146. When the slave is freed he thinks himself a nobleman. *African*

16147. When they came to shoe the horses, the beetle stretched out his leg. *English*

Self-Injury *see also* Self-Sacrifice; Perverseness

16148. A hair shirt does not always render those chaste who wear it. *French (Montaigne)*

16149. A man's worst enemy can't wish him what he thinks up for himself. *Yiddish*

16150. Don't heat a furnace for your foe so hot that it will singe yourself. *American*

16151. Every man is his own worst enemy. *Latin*

16152. Everyone carries his enemy in his breast. *Danish*

16153. God defend me from myself! *Spanish*

16154. He is most cheated who cheats himself. *Danish*

16155. He is sairest dung [hardest hit] when his awn wand dings [hits] him. *Scottish*

16156. He that's cheated twice by the same man is an accomplice with the cheater. *English*

16157. He's sairest dung that paid wi' his ain wand. *Scottish*

16158. He's well worth [deserving of] sorrow that buys it wi' his ain siller. *Scottish*

16159. If he has no other burden, he'll take up a load of stones. *Malay*

16160. Liberate me from that bad fellow, myself. *Latin*

16161. No man has a worse friend than he brings with him from home. *English*

16162. Troubles hurt the most / when they prove self-inflicted. *Greek (Sophocles)*

16163. We are the authors of our own disasters. *Latin*

16164. We often give our enemies the means for our own destruction. *Greek (Aesop)*

Self-Interest *see also* Selfishness

16165. A cock is crouse [courageous] in his own midding [on his own dunghill]. *Scottish*

16166. A dealer in rubbish sounds the praises of rubbish. *Latin*

16167. A man's aye crousest [keenest, most courageous] in his ain [own] cause. *Scottish*

16168. A shepherd strikes not his sheep. *Wolof*

16169. A turkey never voted for an early Christmas. *Irish*

16170. At the kinges court, my brother, / Eche man for himself. *English (Chaucer)*

16171. Before healing others, heal thyself. *Wolof*

16172. Close sits my shirt, but closer my skin. *English*

16173. Each man skins his own turnip. *Polish*

16174. Every cock scratches towards himself. *English*

16175. Every cow licks her own calf. *Serbian*

16176. Every man for himself. *Scottish*

16177. Every man is most skillful in his own business. *Arabic*

16178. Every man looks well after his own interests. *Latin*

16179. Every miller draws water to his own mill. *English*

16180. Every miller wad weise [beguile, attract] the water to his ain mill. *Scottish*

16181. Every old woman blows under her own kettle. *Serbian*

16182. Every peddler praises his needles. *Spanish*

16183. Every person for his own skin. *Turkish*

16184. Every potter praises his pot, and all the more if it is cracked. *Spanish*

16185. Every prophet prays for his own soul. *Kurdish*

16186. Everyone has his hands turned toward himself. *Polish*

16187. Everyone is eloquent in his own cause. *Latin*

16188. Everyone pulls the blanket to his side of the bed. *Lebanese*

16189. Everyone rakes the embers to his own cake. *Arabic*

16190. Everyone rakes the fire under his own pot. *English*

16191. Everyone says, "I have right on my side." *French*

16192. Everyone to his own business, and the cows will be well looked after. *French*

16193. He does not lose his alms who gives it to his pig. *French*

16194. He is a fool that will forget himself. *English (Chaucer)*

16195. I myself am nearest myself. *Latin (Terence)*

16196. I today, you tomorrow. *Latin*

16197. If it's not your worry, don't hurry. *Polish*

16198. If you have lost your nose, put your hand before the place. *Italian*

16199. If your neighbor's beard is on fire, pour water on your own. *Martinique Creole*

16200. In the King's Court everyone is for himself. *French*

16201. It's an ill bird that bewrays its own nest. *English*

16202. Keep your ain [own] grease for your ain cairtwheels. *Scottish*

16203. Let each be careful to look after his own coat and hat. *Chinese*

16204. Let every fox take care of his own tail. *English*

16205. "Let us agree not to step on each other's feet," said the cock to the horse. *English*

16206. Men are blind in their own cause. *Scottish*

16207. My teeth are closer to me than my relatives. *Spanish*

16208. My tunic is nearer to me than my mantle. *Latin*

16209. Near is my petticoat but nearer is my smock. *English*

16210. No one is second to himself. *Latin*

16211. Number one is the first house in the row. *English*

16212. People say "one" before they say "two." *Accra*

16213. People should wash their foul linen at home. *French (Napoleon I)*

16214. Self is the first object of charity. *Latin*

16215. Self's the man. *Dutch*

16216. Ser' [serve] yoursel and your friends will think the mair [more] o' ye. *Scottish*

16217. Shame fa' them that think shame to do themsels a gude turn. *Scottish*

16218. That which should feed our children ought not be given to dogs. *Latin*

16219. The auld [old] fisher's rule — every man for his ain [own] hand. *Scottish*

16220. The crow does not louse the buffalo to clean him, but to feed herself. *Bulgarian*

16221. The laundress washeth her own smock first. *English*

16222. The miller ne'er got better moulter [toll] than he took wi' his ain [own] hands. *Scottish*

16223. The mirror shows everyone his best friend. *Yiddish*

16224. The tod [fox] ne'er sped better than when he gaed his ain [went on his own] errand. *Scottish*

16225. The world is ruled by interest alone. *German*

16226. There is no elbow that bends outward. *Chinese*

16227. There is no need to blow what does not burn you. *Danish*

16228. 'Tis a mad priest who blasphemes his relics. *Italian*

16229. What is gude [good] to give is gude to keep. *Scottish*

16230. When the next house is on fire, 'tis high time to look to your own. *English*

16231. When your companions get drunk and fight, / Take up your hat, and wish them good night. *English*

16232. When your neighbour's house is in danger tak tent [take care, look to] o' your ain [own]. *Scottish*

16233. Ye drew not so well when my mare was in the mire. *Scottish*

16234. Ye'll no sell your hens on a rainy day. *Scottish*

Selfishness *see also* Priority; Self-Interest

16235. A hired horse never tired. *Scottish*

16236. He who lives for himself is truly dead to others. *Latin (Publilius Syrus)*

16237. He would not lend his knife to the devil to stab himself. *Italian*

16238. No man is more cheated than the selfish man. *American (Beecher)*

16239. Sel [i.e., selfishness], sel, has half filled hell. *Scottish*

16240. The man who lives for himself doesn't deserve to live. *American*

Self-Knowledge

16241. Every man is best known to himself. *English*

16242. Every man kens [knows] best where his ain sair [sore] lies. *Scottish*

16243. Every man kens [knows] best where his ain shae [shoe] binds him. *Scottish*

16244. Full wise is he that can himselven [himself] know. *English (Chaucer)*

16245. He that knoweth himself best, esteemeth himself least. *English*

16246. I know myself better than any doctor can. *Latin (Ovid)*

16247. I wot weel [know well] where my ain [own] shoe binds me. *Scottish*

16248. In another's, yes, but in his own eye he sees no dirt. *Burmese*

16249. Ken [know] yoursel an' your neebours winna misken you. *Scottish*

16250. Know then thyself, presume not God to scan; / The proper study of mankind is Man. *English (Pope)*

16251. Know thyself better than he does who speaks of thee. *Wolof*

16252. Know thyself. *Greek*

16253. Knowledge of yourself will preserve you from vanity. *Spanish*

16254. Let him tak his fling and he'll find oot his ain [own] weight. *Scottish*

16255. Live within yourself, and you will discover how small a stock there is. *Latin*

16256. Lose all, but find yourself. *American*

16257. No one on earth is difficult to manage; all that is necessary is to examine oneself thoroughly. *Chinese*

16258. Observe all men; thyself most. *American (Franklin)*

16259. Search others for their virtues, thyself for thy vices. *American (Franklin)*

16260. The sages are diminished by half; self-scrutinizing men are all gone. *Chinese*

16261. There are three things extreamly hard: steel, a diamond and to know one's self. *American (Franklin)*

16262. We know what we are, but know not what we may be. *English (Shakespeare)*

16263. Who knows himself knows others; for heart can be compared with heart. *Chinese*

16264. Whoso knoweth himself shall find the kingdom of heaven. *Greek*

Selflessness

16265. The diligent husbandman sows trees, of which he himself will never see the fruit. *Latin (Cicero)*

Self-Love

16266. Every living creature loves itself. *Latin (Cicero)*

16267. He is in love with himself, and need fear no rival. *Latin (Cicero)*

16268. Many will hate you if you love yourself. *Latin*

16269. No one loves another more than he loves himself. *Latin*
16270. O' a' flatterers, self-love is the greatest. *Scottish*
16271. Of all mankind each loves himself the best. *American*
16272. Offended self-love never forgives. *French*
16273. Self-love is a mote in every man's eye. *English*
16274. Self-love is the greatest of all flatterers. *French (La Rochefoucauld)*
16275. Self-love makes one blind. *German*

Self-Neglect *see also* Neglect
16276. Among wonderful things is a sore-eyed person who is an oculist. *Arabic*
16277. Physician, heal thyself. *English*
16278. We can catch rats for other people, but not even a mouse for ourselves. *German*

Self-Praise *see also* Boasting; Praise
16279. A man would scarcely have any pleasure if he never flattered himself. *French*
16280. He that praiseth himself spattereth himself. *English*
16281. If no one flatters you, you flatter yourself. *American*
16282. Let another man praise thee, not thine own mouth. *English*
16283. Praise yourself boldly; something will stick. *Latin*
16284. Self-exaltation is the fool's paradise. *English*
16285. Self-praise is nae [no] honour. *Scottish*
16286. Self-praise is odious. *Latin*
16287. Self-praise and self-dispraise are equally absurd. *Greek*
16288. Self-praise comes aye [always] stinking ben [inwards]. *Scottish*
16289. Self-praise disgraces. *Spanish (Cervantes)*
16290. Self-praise is no recommendation. *Latin*
16291. Self-praise smells, friend's praise halts. *German*
16292. The salt will not say of itself, "I have a pleasant taste." *Oji*
16293. There is no such flatterer as is a man's self. *English (Bacon)*
16294. When you die, your trumpeter will be buried. *American*
16295. Who praises himself fouls himself. *Italian*

Self-Preservation *see* Desperation

Self-Reliance *see also* Divine Assistance; God; Man and God; Prayer; Self-Help
16296. Better do it than wish it done. *Scottish*
16297. Can do is easily carried about wi' ane [one]. *Scottish*
16298. Every man for himself. *Latin*
16299. Every man for his ain [own] hand, as Henry Wynd fought. *Scottish*
16300. Every man must go to the mill with his own sack. *English*
16301. Every man must skin his own skunk. *American*
16302. For that thou canst do thyself, rely not on another. *English*
16303. Give orders and leave it and no more will be done. *Portuguese*
16304. Haud [hold] the hank in your ain [own] hand. *Scottish*
16305. He is strong that can knock a man down; he is stronger who can lift himself up. *French*
16306. He must serve himself that has no servant. *English (Chaucer)*
16307. He that by the plough would thrive, / Himself must either hold or drive. *English*
16308. He that performs his own errand, saves his messenger's hire. *Danish*
16309. He who depends on himself will attain the greatest happiness. *Chinese*
16310. He's a wise man that can tak care o' himsel'. *Scottish*
16311. I hae muckle [have much] to do and few to do for me. *Scottish*
16312. If you want a thing done right, do it yourself. *American*
16313. If you want good service, serve yourself. *Spanish*
16314. If you want your business weel done, do't yoursel. *Scottish*
16315. If you wish a thing done, go; if not, send. *English*
16316. Ilka [every] bird maun [must] hatch its ain [own] egg. *Scottish*
16317. Ilka [every] blade o' grass keps [catches] its ane [own] drap o' dew. *Scottish*
16318. "I'll go myself," and "I'll see to it," are two good servants in a countryman's farm. *Danish*
16319. Let every man carry his own sack to the mill. *French*
16320. Let every man skin his own skunk. *American*
16321. Let every peddler carry his own pack [or burden]. *English*
16322. Let every tub stand on its own bottom. *English*
16323. Let him ride his ain [own] horse wi' his ain hauding [own holding]. *Scottish*
16324. Let him tak a spring on his ain [own] fiddle. *Scottish*
16325. Let him that has a mouth not say to another, "Blow." *Spanish*
16326. Let him that owns the cow take her by the tail. *Scottish*
16327. Let him that's cauld blaw the ingle [fire]. *Scottish*
16328. Let ilka ane [everyone] soop [sweep] before their ain door. *Scottish*
16329. Let ilka [each] cock fight his ain battle. *Scottish*
16330. Let ilka [every] herring hing [hang] by his ain [own] head. *Scottish*
16331. Let ilka [every] man soop [sweep] the ice wi' his ain besom [broom]. *Scottish*
16332. Let ilka [every] sheep hang by its ain [own] shank. *Scottish*
16333. Let ilka [every] tub stand on its ain [own] bottom. *Scottish*

16334. Lippen [trust] to me, but look to yoursel'. *Scottish*
16335. Look after your own needs. *Hausa*
16336. Never expect your friends to do for you that which you can yourself accomplish. *Latin*
16337. Never trust to another what you can do yourself. *American*
16338. One is never so well served as by oneself. *French*
16339. Only the tent pitched by your own hands will stand. *Arabic*
16340. Paddle your own canoe. *American*
16341. Self do, self have. *English*
16342. Self done, well done. *American*
16343. Self is the man. *German*
16344. Tak your will, your wise enough. *Scottish*
16345. There is a great difference between "go" and "gaw" [let us go]. *East Anglian*
16346. Tie up your camel as best you can, and then trust it to Providence. *Arabic*
16347. Trust not to another for what you can do yourself. *English*
16348. What you cannot arrange for yourself will not be arranged for you. *Arabic*
16349. What you do yourself is half done. *American*
16350. Who goes himself wishes it; who sends someone else, does not care. *Italian*
16351. Who wants a thing done quickly and well, let him do it himself. *Italian*
16352. Who wants to be ill served, let him keep plenty of servants. *Italian*
16353. Ye maun [must] redd [put in order] your ain [own] ravelled clue [a ball of worsted]. *Scottish*
16354. You must scratch your own head with your own nails. *Arabic*

Self-Respect *see also* Self-Esteem; Self-Worth

16355. Respect yourself most of all. *Greek*
16356. Self-respect is the corner-stone of virtue. *English*

Self-Restraint *see also* Self-Discipline

16357. He is twice a conqueror, who can restrain himself in the hour of triumph. *Latin (Publilius Syrus)*
16358. He that is slow to anger is better than the mighty, and he that ruleth his spirit than he that taketh a city. *English*
16359. It is the duty of a good shepherd to shear, not to skin his sheep. *Latin (Suetonius)*
16360. It is the duty of a good sportsman to kill game freely, but not to kill all. *Latin*
16361. Leave the chicken in its feathers. *Hausa*
16362. Shear the sheep but don't flay them. *English*
16363. The orange that is too hard squeezed yields a bitter juice. *English*
16364. There is nothing better than self-restraint. *Chinese (Laotse)*

Self-Sacrifice *see also* Sacrifice; Selflessness

16365. Drown not thyself to save a drowning man. *English*
16366. Greater love hath no man than this, that a man lay down his life for his friends. *Bible*
16367. Sacrifice not thy heart upon every altar. *English*
16368. To lay down one's life for the truth. *Latin (Juvenal)*

Self-Sufficiency *see also* Self-Interest; Self-Reliance

16369. The humble receive advantage; the self-sufficient provoke loss. *Chinese*

Self-Worth

16370. Everyone gives himself credit for more brains than he has and less money. *Italian*
16371. So much is a man worth as he esteems himself. *French (Rabelais)*

Sense *see also* Carefulness; Common Sense; Prudence

16372. Better sense in the head than cents in the pocket. *American*
16373. Borrowed sense is of no use. *Yiddish*
16374. God send you mair [more] sense and me mair siller [more silver]. *Scottish*
16375. It is hard to talk sense, but harder to find listeners if you do. *American*
16376. Nonsense charms the multitude; plain sense is despised. *American*
16377. Science is madness if good sense does not cure it. *Spanish*
16378. Where sense is wanting, everything is wanting. *American (Franklin)*

Sensitivity *see also* Irritability

16379. A galled horse will not endure the comb. *English*
16380. A scabby head fears the comb. *Dutch*
16381. A scurfy person does not love the comb. *Italian*
16382. A scurvy horse does not like to be combed. *French*
16383. The scabbed head loesna [loves not] the kame [comb]. *Scottish*
16384. To touch a sore place. *Latin*
16385. Touch a galled horse and he will fling. *Dutch*
16386. Touch a galled horse on the back and he'll kick [or wince]. *English*

Sensuality

16387. Sensuality is the grave of the soul. *American*

Separation *see* Absence; Leaving; Parting

Sequence *see also* Cause and Effect; Last; Order; Priority

16388. As proud come behind as go before. *English*
16389. Horns grow not before the head. *Wolof*
16390. The frog calls for rain; rain comes. *Efik*

Servants and Servitude *see also* Master and Man; Slavery

16391. A fat housekeeper makes lean executors. *Scottish*

16392. As the master is, so is his dog. *American*
16393. As with the servant, so with his master. *Bible*
16394. Do not be too ready to believe a wife complaining of servants. *Latin*
16395. Do not stuff your servant with bread, and he won't ask for cheese. *Spanish*
16396. Every great house is full of saucy servants. *Latin*
16397. If the servant grows rich and the master poor, they are both good for nothing. *German*
16398. Pay your servant before his sweat dries. *Arabic*
16399. Slaves of the rich are slaves indeed. *Latin*
16400. So many servants, so many enemies. *Latin*
16401. Starve your dog and it will follow you. *Arabic*
16402. The lazy servant takes eight steps to avoid one. *Spanish*
16403. The master in his own house is always a guest of his servants. *Turkish*
16404. The servant wench that has a mother in town swoons seven times a day. *Spanish*
16405. The tongue of a bad servant is his worst part. *Latin*
16406. The truest report comes from a man's servants. *Latin*
16407. There's nae gude [no good] in speaking ill o' the laird within his ain [own] bounds. *Scottish*
16408. Well done, thou good and faithful servant. *Bible*
16409. Who wishes to be ill-served, let him keep many servants. *Italian*

Service *see also* Favors; Good Deeds; Kindness; Servants and Servitude

16410. A service done to the unwilling is no service. *Latin*
16411. He merits no thanks that does a kindness for his own end. *English*
16412. He who serves is not free. *Spanish*
16413. He who serves is preserved. *Latin*
16414. Proffered service stinks. *Latin*
16415. Serve like a serf or fly like a deer. *French*
16416. To oblige persons often costs little and helps much. *Spanish (Gracián)*
16417. Unwilling service earns no thanks. *Danish*

Servility

16418. If the king saith at noonday, "It is night," you are to say, "Behold the moon and stars!" *Chinese*
16419. When the monkey reigns dance before him. *Egyptian*

Shallowness *see also* Profundity

16420. Shallow waters make most din. *Scottish*

Shame *see also* Accusation; Blame; Conscience; Guilt

16421. A shameless man is ready for anything. *Chinese*
16422. Do not carry your shame to the top of a mountain. *Arabic*
16423. Give your friend cause to blush, and you will be likely to lose him. *Latin (Publilius Syrus)*
16424. Having been poor is no shame, but being ashamed of it, is. *American (Franklin)*
16425. He that fears no shame, comes to no honor. *Dutch*
16426. He that has no shame has no conscience. *American*
16427. He that shames [his neighbor] shall be shent [shamed]. *Scottish*
16428. Hide your shame in your house. *Arabic*
16429. I count him lost who is lost to shame. *Latin*
16430. If it were not for shame, there would be no honest women. *Arabic*
16431. It is a shame to be shameless. *Latin*
16432. It is easier to bear shame than annoyance. *Latin*
16433. It is false shame that covers unhealed wounds. *Latin*
16434. None but the shamefaced lose. *French*
16435. On shameful things shame everywhere attends. *Greek*
16436. Shame is shame, whether you think so or not. *Latin*
16437. Shame is worse than death. *Russian*
16438. Shame lasts longer than poverty. *Dutch*
16439. Shame once gone does not return. *Latin*
16440. Shame take him that shame thinketh. *French*
16441. The eyes are the abode of shame. *Greek*
16442. The skin of his face is as thick as a city wall. *Chinese*
16443. The worthy may be blamed but never shamed. *Scottish*
16444. There is hope of salvation where there is shame. *Latin*
16445. There is no shame but thinking makes it so. *Greek*
16446. Who has no shame, all the world is his own. *Italian*
16447. Who has no shame before men, has no fear of God. *Yiddish*

Shared Authority *see also* Leaders and Leadership

16448. A partnership with the powerful is never safe. *Latin*
16449. A ship with two captains will sink. *Egyptian*
16450. All power is impatient of a partner. *Latin*
16451. Authority issuing from one is strong, issuing from two is weak. *Chinese*
16452. Ower mony [too many] greives [overseers, stewards, factors] hinder the wark. *Scottish*
16453. The highest seat will not hold two. *Latin*
16454. The swallows say partnerships are bad. *Polish*
16455. Too many chiefs and not enough Indians. *American*
16456. Two captains sink the ship. *Turkish*
16457. Two rams cannot drink from the same calabash. *Yoruba*
16458. Two swords cannot fit in one scabbard; two sultans cannot rule at the same time. *Omani*
16459. When two ride the same horse one must ride behind. *English*
16460. Your partner is your opponent. *Egyptian*

Shared Misfortune *see also* **Community; Encouragement; Hope; Indifference; Neighbors; Sympathy**

16461. Companions in misfortune. *English*

16462. Company in distress makes less trouble. *French*

16463. It is a solace to the miserable to have a companion in their grief. *Latin*

16464. Society in shipwreck is a comfort to all. *Latin (Publilius Syrus)*

16465. Those who suffer from the same illness pity each other. *Korean*

16466. To be in the same hospital. *Latin*

16467. Two in distress makes sorrow the less. *English*

16468. Where there are two, one cannot be wretched, and one not. *Greek (Euripides)*

Shared Responsibility *see also* **Joint Ownership**

16469. Every man's man had a man, and that made the Treve [a castle in Scotland] fall. *Scottish*

16470. Mony [many] cooks ne'er made gude kail [broth]. *Scottish*

16471. Ower mony [too many] cooks spoil the broth. *Scottish*

16472. There is no one to sweep a common hall. *Chinese*

16473. When there are two midwives, the baby's head is misshapen. *Persian*

16474. With seven nurses the child loses its eye. *Russian*

Sharing *see also* **Cohabitation; Divided Loyalty; Joint Ownership; Possession; Shared Authority; Shared Misfortune; Shared Responsibility**

16475. A thing is bigger for being shared. *Gaelic*

16476. All who would win / Must share it. Happiness was born a twin. *English (Byron)*

16477. He who shares has the worst share. *English*

16478. Men eat through other men. *Zulu*

16479. Share and share alike. *American*

16480. Share and share alike — some all and some never a whit. *English*

16481. That's the best gown that gaes [goes] up and doun the house. *Scottish*

16482. We can enjoy nothing without someone to share the pleasure. *Latin*

16483. What's yours is mine, and what's mine's my ain [own]. *Scottish*

16484. When the orphan was asked whether he had enough, he said, "If you had given to me as you gave to your [own] child, I should have had enough." *Oji*

Shortcuts

16485. Better go about than fall into the ditch. *English*

16486. Short cuts are long ways around. *Latin*

16487. The farthest way about is the nearest way home. *English*

Shrewdness

16488. He is of Spoleto. [He is "a sharp blade."] *Italian*

16489. He is Yorkshire. [He is shrewd.] *English*

16490. He's as sharp as if he lived on Tewkesbury mustard. *English*

Shrews *see also* **Husbands and Wives; Wives**

16491. Everyone can tame a shrew but him that has her. *American*

Sickness

16492. An ailing woman lives forever. *Spanish*

16493. Every invalid is a physician. *Irish*

16494. Had he not been visited by sickness, he would have perished utterly. *Latin*

16495. He is in great danger who being sick thinks himself well. *American*

16496. If you would live in health, be old early. *Spanish*

16497. In time of sickness the soul collects itself anew. *Latin*

16498. Sickly body, sickly mind. *German*

16499. Sickness comes in haste and goes at leisure. *American*

16500. Sickness comes on horseback and departs on foot. *Dutch*

16501. Sickness is every man's master. *Danish*

16502. Sickness shows us what we are. *Latin*

16503. The sick man is free to say all. *Italian*

Silence *see also* **Brevity; Quiet**

16504. A hadden [held, kept] tongue maks a slabbered [besmeared] mouth. *Scottish*

16505. A sage thing is timely silence, and better than any speech. *Greek (Plutarch)*

16506. A shut mouth incurs no debt. *Welsh*

16507. A shut mouth keeps one from strife. *American*

16508. A silent man's words are not brought into court. *Danish*

16509. A silent mouth is sweet to hear. *Irish*

16510. A still sow eats a' the draff. *Scottish*

16511. A still tongue maketh a wise head. *English*

16512. A wise head keeps a still tongue. *American*

16513. All things except silence bring repentance. *Greek*

16514. Amyclae was undone by silence. *Latin*

16515. Be checked for silence, but never taxed for speech. *English (Shakespeare)*

16516. Be silent and pass for a philosopher. *American*

16517. Be silent, or say something that is better than silence. *Greek*

16518. Better say nothing than nothing to the purpose. *English*

16519. Better silence than ill speech. *Swedish*

16520. Better silent like a fool than talk like a fool. *German*

16521. Between you and the lang day be't. *Scottish*

16522. Beware the silent dog. *Arabic*

16523. By talking too loud the jaw becomes swelled. *Louisiana Creole*

16524. Deep rivers move in silence [or with silent majesty]; shallow brooks are noisy. *English*

16525. Deep vengeance is the daughter of deep silence. *Italian (Alfieri)*

16526. Dit [fill up, close] your mouth wi' your meat. *Scottish*

16527. Do not give an opinion until it is asked for. *Latin*

16528. Do you wish people to think well of you? Don't speak. *French*

16529. Dumb dogs and still waters are dangerous. *German*

16530. Dummie canna lee [lie]. *Scottish*

16531. Even if words were jewels, silence would be preferable. *Maltese*

16532. Flies cannot enter a closed mouth. *Moroccan*

16533. From his silence a man's consent is inferred. *Latin*

16534. God rights him that keeps silence. *Persian*

16535. Have a care of a silent dog and still water. *English*

16536. He consents enough who does not say a word. *French*

16537. He kens [knows] muckle [much] wha kens when to speak, but far mair [more] wha kens when to haud [hold] his tongue. *Scottish*

16538. He knows enough that knows how to hold his peace. *Italian*

16539. He knows enough who knows how to live and be silent. *French*

16540. He that hath knowledge spareth his words. *Bible*

16541. He that hears much and speaks not at all / Shall be welcome both in bower and hall. *English*

16542. He that is silent, gathers stones. *English*

16543. He that knows nothing knows enough if he knows how to be silent. *Italian*

16544. He that speaks doth sow, he that holds his peace doth reap. *Italian*

16545. He's silly that spares for ilka [every] speech. *Scottish*

16546. Hear all, say nothing. *Latin*

16547. Hear, see, and be silent, if you wish to live in peace. *Latin*

16548. Him that speaks not, God hears not. *Spanish*

16549. If a word be worth one shekel, silence is worth two. *Hebrew*

16550. If the crow could feed in silence, he would have more meat and less quarreling. *Latin*

16551. If the fish had not opened its mouth, it would not have been caught. *Mexican*

16552. If the mouth is shut, flies do not enter. *Spanish*

16553. If you can't say something nice, don't say anything at all. *American*

16554. In silence God brings all to pass. *Greek*

16555. In the company of strangers silence is safe. *American*

16556. It is better to say nothing than not enough. *Latin*

16557. It is but a small merit to observe silence, but it is a grave fault to speak of matters on which we should be silent. *Latin (Ovid)*

16558. It is sad when men have neither wit to speak, nor judgment to hold their tongues. *French*

16559. It is the part of a wise man sometimes to be silent. *Latin*

16560. It's a virtue above all virtues to keep the tongue behind the teeth. *Polish*

16561. Keep shut the door of thy mouth even from the wife of thy bosom. *Hebrew*

16562. Keep silence, or say something better than silence. *German*

16563. Keep your breath to cool your own crowdie [or parriteh, porridge]. *Scottish*

16564. Let a fool hold his tongue and he will pass for a sage. *Latin (Publilius Syrus)*

16565. Let not the tongue say what the head shall pay for. *Spanish*

16566. Let thy speech be better than silence, or be silent. *Greek (Dionysius the Elder)*

16567. Many a fool might pass for a wise man if he would only keep his mouth shut. *English*

16568. More silent than a statue. *Latin*

16569. Nae [no] plea is best. *Scottish*

16570. Ne'er let on, but laugh in your ain [own] sleeve. *Scottish*

16571. Never was a mewing cat a good mouser. *English*

16572. No one betrays himself by silence. *German*

16573. No wisdom like silence. *Greek*

16574. Put your thoom [thumb] upon that. *Scottish*

16575. Silence and reflection cause dejection. *American*

16576. Silence and thought hurt nae [no] man. *Scottish*

16577. Silence answers much. *Dutch*

16578. Silence does not make mistakes. *Hindi*

16579. Silence doth seldom harm. *English*

16580. Silence gives consent. *Latin*

16581. Silence grips [catches] the mouse. *Scottish*

16582. Silence has been the loss of many friendships. *Latin*

16583. Silence is a friend that will never betray. *Chinese (Confucius)*

16584. Silence is a healing of all ailments. *Hebrew*

16585. Silence is also speech. *Yiddish*

16586. Silence is confession. *Italian*

16587. Silence is gain to many of mankind. *Greek*

16588. Silence is man's chief learning. *Greek*

16589. Silence is safest for one who distrusts himself. *French*

16590. Silence is taught by life's misfortune. *Latin*

16591. Silence is the cloak of ignorance. *Arabic*

16592. Silence is the fittest reply to folly. *American*

16593. Silence is the ornament of the ignorant. *Sanskrit*

16594. Silence is the sweet medicine of the heart. *Sanskrit*

16595. Silence is the virtue of a fool. *American*

16596. Silence is the wit of fools. *French*

16597. Silence is true wisdom's best reply. *Greek*

16598. Silence is wisdom and gets a man friends. *English*

16599. Silence is wisdom, but the man who practices it is seldom seen. *Arabic*

16600. Silence is wisdom, when speaking is folly. *English*

16601. Silence never betrays. *Irish*

16602. Silence never makes mistakes. *Hindi*

16603. Silence speaks. *Hausa*

16604. Silence was never written down. *Italian*

16605. Silent people are dangerous. *French*

16606. Some people's silence is worse than swearing. *Russian*

16607. Spare to speak and spare to need. *American*

16608. Spare your breath to cool your pottage. *English*

16609. Speech is oft repented, silence never. *Danish*

16610. Speech is silver, silence is golden. *Scottish* (Carlyle)

16611. Sure is the reward of silence. *Latin*

16612. Talking comes by nature, silence of understanding. *German*

16613. The deepest rivers flow with the least sound. *Latin (Quintus Curtius)*

16614. The fool is wise according as he holds his tongue. *French*

16615. The reward of silence is certain. *Latin*

16616. The sheep that bleats is strangled by the wolf. *Italian*

16617. The silence of the people is a warning for the king. *French*

16618. The silence often of pure innocence / Persuades, when speaking fails. *English (Shakespeare)*

16619. The silent countenance often speaks with expressive eloquence. *Latin (Ovid)*

16620. The silent dog is the first to bite. *German*

16621. The stillest humors are always the worst. *English*

16622. The stillest tongue can be the truest friend. *Greek (Euripides)*

16623. The tree of silence bears the fruit of peace. *Arabic*

16624. There are voice and words in a silent look. *Latin*

16625. There is a time to speak and a time to be silent. *American*

16626. There is a time when nothing should be said, there is a time when some things may be said, but there is indeed no time in which everything can be said. *Latin*

16627. There is no shame in keeping silent if you have nothing to say. *Russian*

16628. There's twa [two] things in my mind, and that's the least o' them. *Scottish*

16629. 'Tis a good word that can better a good silence. *Dutch*

16630. 'Tis easier to know how to speak than how to be silent. *English*

16631. To have been silent never does harm, but to have spoken does. *Latin*

16632. To silence another, first be silent yourself. *Latin*

16633. Were fools silent they would pass for wise. *Dutch*

16634. When silent men speak they speak to the purpose. *English*

16635. Who holds his peace and gathers stones will find a time to throw them. *American*

16636. Who is silent is held to consent. *Latin*

16637. Who is silent is strong. *Latin*

16638. Who keeps silent, consents. *American*

16639. Who knows most keeps silence most. *Spanish*

16640. Who speaks, sows; who keeps silence, reaps. *Italian*

16641. Words uttered are my masters; of words suppressed I am theirs. *Arabic*

Similarity *see also* **Affinity**

16642. As is the mother, so is her daughter. *Bible*

16643. As like as bees. *Latin*

16644. As like as eggs. *English (Shakespeare)*

16645. As like as two peas. *French*

16646. As the abbot sings the monk replies. *Spanish*

16647. Asses have a remarkable resemblance to each other. *American*

16648. At night all cats are gray. *Spanish (Cervantes)*

16649. "Crooked carlin!" quoth the cripple to his wife. *Scottish*

16650. "God help the fool!" said the idiot. *English*

16651. If you have known one, you have known them all. *Latin*

16652. If you've seen one, you've seen them all. *English*

16653. Let beggar match with beggar. *English*

16654. Like author, like book. *English*

16655. Like blude, like gude, like age, / Make the happy marriage. *Scottish*

16656. Like king, like law; like law, like people. *Portuguese*

16657. Like lip, like lettuce. *Latin*

16658. Like master, like man. *Latin*

16659. Like mistress, like waiting women. *Latin (Cicero)*

16660. Like people, like priest. *Latin*

16661. Like pot, like cover. *Dutch*

16662. Likeness is the mother of love. *English*

16663. More like than egg to egg. *Latin*

16664. Nothing similar is the same. *Latin*

16665. One ass nicknames another Longears. *German*

16666. One beast easily recognizes another. *Latin*

16667. Said the raven to the crow, "Get out of that, blackamoor." *Spanish*

16668. Similarity is the mother of friendship. *Greek*

16669. Six of one and half-a-dozen of the other. *American*

16670. Such a father, such a son. *English*

16671. Such a king, such a people. *Latin*

16672. Such a saint, such an offering. *English*

16673. Sympathy of manners maketh conjunction of minds. *English*

16674. The kiln calls the oven burnt house. *English*

16675. The pan says to the pot, "Keep off, or you'll smutch me." *Italian*

16676. The pot calls the kettle black bottom. *English*

16677. The same in green. [That is, "six of one, half a dozen of the other."] *German*

16678. The shovel makes sport of the poker. *French*

16679. The smith and his penny are both black. *English*

16680. There was never a cake but it had a make [mate]. *Scottish*

16681. They agree like bells; they want nothing but hanging. *English*

16682. They agree like London clocks. *English*

16683. They're both tarred with the same brush. *American*

16684. Those who resemble each other assemble with each other. *French*

Simplicity

16685. Blissful are the simple, for they shall have much peace. *Latin*

16686. Less is more. *English (R. Browning)*

16687. Nature hangs out a sign of simplicity in the face of a fool. *American*

16688. Nothing is more foolish than to dabble in too many things. *Latin*

16689. The girl is more inviting who smells of wild thyme than she who smells of musk. *Latin*

16690. The great artist is the simplifier. *Swiss (Amiel)*

16691. The greatest luxury is simplicity. *Kurdish*

16692. The simple man's the beggar's brither. Scottish

16693. Ye breed o' the gowk [simpleton], ye hae [have] ne'er a rhyme but ane [one]. *Scottish*

Simultaneity *see also* Divided Interest

16694. A man cannot spin and reel at the same time. *English*

16695. A man cannot whistle and drink at the same time. *Danish*

16696. Don't embark in two boats, for you'll be spilt and thrown on your back. *American*

16697. He who follows two hares loses both. *Latin*

16698. It is difficult to whistle and drink at the same time. *Latin (Plautus)*

16699. Nae man can baith [both] sup and blaw [blow] at once [or at the same time]. *Scottish*

16700. One cannot hunt eels and hares at the same time. *German*

16701. To stand on two boats at once. *Chinese*

16702. You can't be in two places at the same time. *American*

16703. You can't ride two horses at the same time. *American*

Sin *see also* Sin and Sinners

16704. A man does not sin by commission only, but often by omission. *Latin (Marcus Aurelius)*

16705. A man more sinned against than sinning. *English (Shakespeare)*

16706. A sin concealed needs two forgivings. *American*

16707. All that defiles comes from within. *Greek*

16708. Be sure your sin will find you out. *Bible*

16709. Every man has his besetting sin. *American*

16710. Few love to hear the sins they love to act. *American*

16711. Fools make a mock of sin. *Bible*

16712. For a fresh sin a fresh penance. *Spanish*

16713. God hardens the hearts of sinners. *French*

16714. He does not cleanse himself of his sins who denies them. *Latin*

16715. He does not sin who sins without intent. *Latin*

16716. He that is without sin among you, let him cast the first stone. *Bible*

16717. He who does not forbid sin when he can, encourages it. *Latin*

16718. It is more wicked to love a sin than to commit one. *Latin*

16719. One does not sin with the mind, but with the will. *Russian*

16720. Sin and sorrow are inseparable. *American*

16721. Sin can be well-guarded, but cannot be free from anxiety. *Latin*

16722. Sin is not hurtful because it is forbidden, but it is forbidden because it is hurtful. *American (Franklin)*

16723. Sin is the seed and death is the harvest. *American*

16724. Sin writes histories; goodness is silent. *German (Goethe)*

16725. Some rise by sin, and some by virtue fall. *English (Shakespeare)*

16726. The gods visit the sins of the fathers upon the children. *Greek*

16727. The longer thread of life we spin, / The more occasion still to sin. *English (Herrick)*

16728. The righteous sometimes pay for the sins of others. *Spanish*

16729. The sins committed by many pass unpunished. *Latin*

16730. The son pays the father's debt of sin. *Chinese*

16731. The wages of sin is death. *Bible*

16732. The way of transgressors is hard. *Bible*

16733. There is a sin of omission as well as of commission. *Greek*

16734. There is no death without sin. *Hebrew*

16735. Who is not ashamed of his sins, sins double. *German*

Sin and Sinners

16736. Condemn the fault, but not the actor of it. *English (Shakespeare)*

16737. Preserve the guns, but destroy the gunners. *English*

16738. War with vices, but peace with individuals. *Latin*

Sin and Virtue *see also* Good and Evil

16739. Man's twal [twelve] is no sae gude's a deil's dizzen [not so good as a devil's dozen]. *Scottish*

16740. Many who have gold in the house are looking for copper outside. *Russian*

16741. One limps toward God, one leaps toward the devil. *Danish*

16742. To sin one rushes, to virtue one crawls. *German*

Sincerity *see also* Candor; Forthrightness; Frankness; Insincerity

16743. Mouth and heart should never part. *American*

16744. Sincerity gives wings to power. *Latin*

16745. The pen of the tongue should be dipped in the ink of the heart. *English*

16746. What comes from the heart goes to the heart. *German*

Single-Mindedness *see also* **Ambition; Aspiration; Commitment; Purpose**

16747. When you are at sea, keep clear of the land. *Latin (Publilius Syrus)*

Size *see also* **Accumulation; Cause and Effect; Ends and Means; Insignificance; Shortness; Trifles**

16748. A lion may be beholden to a mouse. *English*

16749. A little bird wants but a little nest. *English*

16750. A little man fells a great oak. *French*

16751. A little man may cast a large shadow. *French*

16752. A little stone overturns a great cart. *English*

16753. A mote may choke a man. *English*

16754. A needle is as valuable as a heap of iron bars. *Efik*

16755. A short horse is soon curried. *English*

16756. A short man needs no stool to give a great lubber a box on the ear. *English*

16757. A small cloud may hide both sun and moon. *Danish*

16758. A small coin in a big jar makes a great noise. *Hebrew*

16759. A small heart hath small desires. *English*

16760. A small pack becomes a small pedlar. *English*

16761. Alexander the Great was but of small stature. *Latin*

16762. At a little fountain one drinks first. *French*

16763. Even a hair casts a shadow. *Latin*

16764. Even a smallest spark shines brightly in darkness. *Latin*

16765. Good things come in small packages. *American*

16766. He tint [lost] never a cow that grat [wept] for a needle. *Scottish*

16767. He who neglects the small things, loses the greater. *Latin*

16768. It doesn't depend on size, or a cow would catch a rabbit. *American*

16769. Little and good. *Hebrew*

16770. Little bird, little nest. *Spanish*

16771. Little brooks make great rivers. *American*

16772. Little fish are fish. *Dutch*

16773. Little folk are soon angry. *Scottish*

16774. Little heads may contain much learning. *French*

16775. Little potatoes are hard to peel. *American*

16776. Little strokes fell great oaks. *English*

16777. Little things are pretty. *English*

16778. Little toads are also poisonous. *American*

16779. No tree so small but it can cast a shade. *English*

16780. No viper so little but hath its venom. *English*

16781. Sma' fish are better than nane [none]. *Scottish*

16782. Small axes fell great trees. *German*

16783. Small rain lays a great wind. *French*

16784. Small rain lays great dust. *English*

16785. Small talk is sufficient for little men. *American*

16786. Small things become the small. *Latin (Horace)*

16787. Small things befit a small man. *Latin*

16788. Small things have their own peculiar charm. *Latin*

16789. Small things make base men proud. *English (Shakespeare)*

16790. That little which is good fills the trencher. *English*

16791. The biggest horse is no aye [not always] the best traveller. *Scottish*

16792. The biggest nuts are the empty ones. *Moroccan*

16793. The gods give small things to the small. *Greek*

16794. The peony, though large, is useless; the date blossom, though small, yields fruit. *Chinese*

16795. The smallest boy often carries the biggest fiddle. *American*

16796. The smallest fishes bite the fastest. *American*

16797. There is grace in small things. *Greek*

16798. There is no bush so small as to be without shade. *French*

16799. Tread on a worm and it will turn. *English*

16800. Wisdom fails to go through the whole system of a big man. *Japanese*

Skepticism

16801. An ass will deny more in an hour than a hundred philosophers will prove in a year. *American*

Skill *see also* **Ability; Dexterity; Excellence; Perfection; Proficiency; Strength and Skill; Superiority; Superiority and Inferiority**

16802. He who has an art has everywhere a part. *Italian*

16803. Pith's gude [skill is good] at a' [all] play but threading o' needles. *Scottish*

16804. Skill and assurance are an invincible couple. *American*

16805. Skill is nae [no] burden. *Scottish*

16806. There's skill in gruel making. *Scottish*

16807. Well to work and make a fire, / It doth care and skill require. *English*

Slander *see also* **Accusation; Calumny; Gossip; Reputation; Rumor; Scandal**

16808. A generous heart repairs a slanderous tongue. *Greek (Homer)*

16809. A slander that is raised is ill to fell. *English*

16810. A tongue prone to slander is the proof of a depraved mind. *Latin (Publilius Syrus)*

16811. Destruction and spite are received with eager ears. *Latin*

16812. Half the world delights in slander, and the other half in believing it. *French*

16813. He that flings dirt at another dirtieth himself most. *English*

16814. He that praises publicly will slander privately. *American*

16815. He that repeateth a matter separateth very friends. *Bible*

16816. He that strikes with his tongue must ward with his head. *French*

16817. He who slanders his neighbor makes a rod for himself. *American*

16818. I hate the man who builds his name / On ruins of another's fame. *English (Gay)*

16819. If the ball does not stick to the wall, it will at least leave a mark. *English*

16820. If you slander a dead man, you stab him in the grave. *American*

16821. It flies gently, but wounds deeply. *Latin*

16822. Never make your ear the grave of another's good name. *American*

16823. No wool is so white that the dye can't make it black. *American*

16824. One must have a clean mouth to slander. *Welsh*

16825. Slander always finds an easy entrance to ignoble minds. *Latin*

16826. Slander expired at a good woman's door. *American*

16827. Slander is canine eloquence. *Latin*

16828. Slander leaves a scar behind it. *Latin*

16829. Slander leaves a score behind it. *English*

16830. Slander, like coal, will either dirty your hand or burn it. *Russian*

16831. Slander lives upon succession, / Forever housed where it gets possession. *English (Shakespeare)*

16832. Slander slays three persons: the speaker, the spoken to, and the spoken of. *Hebrew*

16833. Slanderers are the devil's bellows, to blow up contention. *English*

16834. Speak no ill of a friend, nor even of an enemy. *Greek*

16835. The poison of asps is under their lips. *English*

16836. The slanderer brings disgrace on one, like leprosy which attacks one on the point of the nose. *Yoruba*

16837. The tongue breaketh bone, though itself hath none. *American*

16838. The way to close the mouth of a slanderer is to treat him with contempt. *American*

16839. The whisperer's tongue is worse than serpent's venom. *Latin*

16840. The wounds of the tongue cut deeper than the wounds of the sword. *Arabic*

16841. There is no remedy against the bite of a secret slanderer. *Latin*

16842. There is no sufficient recompense for an unjust slander. *English*

16843. There is nothing to choose between bad tongues and wicked ears. *Danish*

16844. We slander through vanity more often than through malice. *French (La Rochefoucauld)*

16845. When men speak ill of you, live so that no one will believe them. *American*

16846. Whispered words are heard afar. *Chinese*

16847. Who throws mud at another soils his own hands. *American*

16848. Whoso wants to kill his dog has but to charge him with madness. *Spanish*

16849. You make no repute for yourself when you publish another's secret fault. *Persian*

Slavery *see also* Freedom and Slavery

16850. Account not that work slavery that brings in penny savory. *American*

16851. As the slave departs the man returns. *American*

16852. Better the devil's than a woman's slave. *American*

16853. He that is one man's slave is free from none. *American*

16854. Slavery enchains a few; more enchain themselves. *Latin*

16855. Slavery is a weed that grows in every soil. *American*

16856. The foulest death rather than the fairest slavery. *Latin*

16857. The sign of slavery is to have a price and to be bought for it. *American*

Sleep *see also* Bed; Night

16858. As you are rocked to sleep so do you sleep. *Yiddish*

16859. Bed is a medicine. *Italian*

16860. Blessed are the sleepy, for they shall soon drop off. *German*

16861. Blessings on him that first invented sleep. *Spanish (Cervantes)*

16862. Even the one-eyed man must sleep. *Yiddish*

16863. Everyone will sleep as he makes his bed. *American*

16864. Five hours of sleep a traveler, seven a scholar, eight a merchant, and eleven a knave. *Italian*

16865. Go to bed with the lamb and rise with the lark. *English*

16866. He sleeps enough who does nothing. *French*

16867. He sleeps well who knows not that he sleeps ill. *Latin*

16868. He that thinks in his bed has a day without a night. *Scottish*

16869. He who sleeps catches no fish. *Italian*

16870. He who sleeps late has short days. *Yiddish*

16871. He who sleeps much learns little. *Spanish*

16872. He who sleeps wants no dinner. *French*

16873. I sleep for myself; I work for I know not whom. *Italian*

16874. It is not fitting for a man of counsel to sleep the whole night through. *Greek*

16875. Let your midday sleep be short or none at all. *Latin*

16876. No one when asleep is good for anything. *Greek*

16877. One hour's sleep before midnight is worth two hours after. *German*

16878. Seven hours of sleep is enough for the young and the aged. *Latin*

16879. Six hours for a man, seven for a woman, eight for a fool. *Latin*

16880. Sleep after dining is not good. *Latin*

16881. Sleep anticipates his brother, Death. *Greek*

16882. Sleep is all important. *Latin*

16883. Sleep is the best cure for waking troubles. *Spanish*

16884. Sleep is the only medicine that gives ease. *Greek*

16885. Sleep makes the darkness brief. *Latin*

16886. Sleep, to be truly enjoyed, must be interrupted. *German*

16887. Sleep to the sick is half health. *German*

16888. Sleep vanishes before the house of care. *Latin*

16889. Sweer [unwillingly] to bed, an' sweer up i' the morning. *Scottish*

16890. The net of the sleeper catches fish. *Greek*

16891. The sleep of a laboring man is sweet. *Bible*

16892. The sleeping fox catches no poultry. *English*

16893. The slumberers are the prey of the wakeful. *American*

16894. There will be sleeping enough in the grave. *American (Franklin)*

16895. To sleep is to feast. *Persian*

16896. When I go to bed I leave my troubles in my clothes. *Dutch*

16897. While we are asleep, we are all equal. *Spanish*

16898. Who goes fasting to bed will sleep but lightly. *Dutch*

16899. You are always best when asleep. *American*

16900. You can sleep on both ears [i.e., in security]. *Latin*

Slowness *see also* Accumulation; Gradualness; Method; Weariness

16901. A snail's gallop. *English*

16902. Good is never done better than when it takes effect slowly. *French*

16903. Slow and sure like Pedley's mare. *English*

16904. Slow and sure. *German*

16905. Slow at meat, slow at work. *English*

16906. Slow fire makes a sweet malt. *English*

16907. Slowly but safely. *Latin*

16908. Snail's pace. *Latin (Plautus)*

16909. The best fruits are slowest in ripening. *Scottish*

16910. The race is not always to the swift. *English*

16911. The slower you go the quicker you'll get there. *Yiddish*

16912. The swift are overtaken by the slow. *Latin*

Smallness *see also* Insignificance; Shortness; Size; Trifles

16913. A little stone may upset a large cart. *American*

16914. The red pepper, though small, is hot. *Korean*

Smiling

16915. A cup must be bitter that a smile will not sweeten. *American*

16916. A smile is a light in the window of a face which shows that the heart is at home. *American*

16917. A smile recures the wounding of a frown. *English (Shakespeare)*

16918. Better the last smile than the first laughter. *English*

16919. There's daggers in men's smiles. *English (Shakespeare)*

Smooth Words *see also* Fair Words; Good Words; Soft Words

16920. He that hasna siller [has not silver] in his purse should hae [have] silk on his tongue. *Scottish*

16921. Smooth words do not flay the tongue. *Italian*

16922. Smooth words make smooth ways. *English*

Sneers

16923. A sneer cannot be answered. *American*

16924. A sneer is the weapon of the weak. *American*

16925. Sneers are poor weapons at best. *American*

16926. Who can refute a sneer? *English (Paley)*

16927. Without sneering, teach the rest to sneer. *English (Pope)*

Society

16928. Custom and convention govern society. *Greek*

16929. Man is a social animal. *Latin*

16930. Society is as ancient as the world. *French*

16931. The wise man flees society for fear of being bored. *French*

16932. You are ushered in according to your dress; shown out according to your brains. *Yiddish*

Soft Words *see also* Answers; Fair Words; Gentleness; Good Words; Mildness; Persuasion; Response; Smooth Words; Sweetness

16933. A honey-comb in the mouth of a lion. *Latin*

16934. A kindly word cools anger. *Scottish*

16935. A soft answer bids a Furioso to put up his sword. *English*

16936. A soft speech has its poison. *Latin*

16937. He subdues their rising passion and soothes their anger by soft remonstrance. *Latin (Virgil)*

16938. He that can reply to an angry man is too hard for him. *English*

16939. Rebuke with soft words and hard arguments. *American*

16940. Soft speeches injure not the mouth of the speaker. *Latin*

16941. Soft words, and hard arguments. *English*

16942. Soft words are hard arguments. *Irish*

16943. Soft words break no bones. *English*

16944. Soft words butter no parsnips but they won't harden the heart of the cabbage either. *Irish*

16945. Soft words do not flay the tongue. *French*

16946. Soft words hurt not the mouth. *English*

16947. Soft words open iron gates. *Bulgarian*

16948. Soft words scald not the tongue. *English*

16949. The force of anger is broken by a soft answer. *Latin*

16950. Use soft words and hard arguments. *American*

16951. With soft words, one may talk a serpent out of its hole. *Iranian*

Soldiers

16952. A beaten soldier fears a reed. *Japanese*

16953. A soldier, fire, and water soon make room for themselves. *Italian*

16954. A young soldier, an old beggar. *German*

16955. It is the blood of the soldier that makes the general great. *Italian*

16956. No faith and no honor in men who follow camps. *Latin*

16957. The soldiers fight, and the kings are heroes. *Hebrew*

16958. The soup makes the soldier. *Spanish*

16959. The warrior lives an honorable life even in poverty. *American*

16960. To a soldier there is nothing left of a man after death but a corpse. *Latin*

16961. What makes the real general, is to have clean hands. *Greek*

Solitude *see also* **Companions and Companionship; Company; Isolation**

16962. A bad person is better than an empty house. *Accra*

16963. A man if he lives alone is either a god or a demon. *Latin*

16964. A solitary man is either a brute or an angel. *Italian*

16965. A wise man is never less alone than when he is alone. *American*

16966. Happy is the mole which moves underground and sees not the world. *Zulu*

16967. I am never less alone than when alone. *Latin*

16968. If you would live innocently, seek solitude. *Latin (Publilius Syrus)*

16969. It is not good that the man should be alone. *Bible*

16970. One man is no man. *Latin*

16971. One would not be alone even in Paradise. *Italian*

16972. Solitude dulls the thought; too much company dissipates it. *American*

16973. Solitude is sometimes the best society. *American*

16974. Solitude is the nest of thoughts. *Kurdish*

16975. Solitude is the nurse of wisdom. *English*

16976. Solitude is within us. *French*

16977. The eagle flies alone. *American*

16978. The earth is a beehive; we all enter by the same door but live in different cells. *African*

16979. The pine stands afar and whispers to its own forest. *Russian*

16980. There was never a scabby sheep in a flock that didn't like to have a comrade. *Irish*

16981. There's safety in solitude. *Persian (Sa'di)*

16982. Who could be happy and alone or good? *English (Byron)*

16983. Woe to him that is alone when he falleth. *Bible*

16984. You will be melancholy, if you are solitary. *Latin (Ovid)*

Sons *see also* **Fathers and Sons; Mothers and Sons; Parents and Children**

16985. A good son is the light of the family. *American*

16986. A lame mule and a stupid son have to endure everything. *Spanish*

16987. A miser's son is a spendthrift. *American*

16988. A son is a son until he takes a wife. *Estonian*

16989. A wise son maketh a glad father: but a foolish son is the heaviness of his mother. *Bible*

16990. Everyone calls his son his son, whether he has talents or not. *Chinese (Confucius)*

16991. One son is no son, two sons is no son, but three sons is a son. *Russian*

16992. Preachers' sons always turn out badly. *American*

16993. 'Tis a happy thing / To be the father unto many sons. *English (Shakespeare)*

16994. To your son, a good name and a trade. *Spanish*

16995. Who has no son has no satisfaction. *American*

Sons and Daughters *see also* **Parents and Children**

16996. He begat a mourner [or a weeper (i.e., a daughter] and a gravedigger [a son]. *Yoruba*

Sons-in-Law *see also* **Mothers-in-Law**

16997. After your daughter is married you can always find sons-in-law a-plenty. *French*

16998. He who has gold can choose his son-in-law. *German*

16999. I can see by my daughter's face when the devil takes hold of my son-in-law. *Italian*

17000. The son-in-law's sack is never full. *Danish*

17001. To a son-in-law and a hog you need not show the way but once. *Spanish*

Sorrow *see also* **Encouragement; Hopes; Joy and Sorrow; Mirth and Sorrow; Shared Misfortune**

17002. A day of sorrow is longer than a month of joy. *Chinese*

17003. A fated sorrow may be lightened with words. *Latin*

17004. A sorrowfu' heart's aye [always] dry. *Scottish*

17005. All sorrows are good [or are less] with bread. *Spanish (Cervantes)*

17006. And last, the crown of a' [all] my grief. *Scottish (Burns)*

17007. Dolour [sorrow] pays nae [no] debts. *Scottish*

17008. Doul [sorrow, woe] and an ill life soon mak [make] an auld [old] wife. *Scottish*

17009. He gains enough who loses sorrow. *French*

17010. He's weel worthy o' sorrow that buys it wi' his ain siller [own silver]. *Scottish*

17011. Let ne'er sorrow come sae [so] near your heart. *Scottish*

17012. My hair is grey, but not with years. *English (Byron)*

17013. O' a' [of all] sorrow, a fu' [full] sorrow's the best. *Scottish*

17014. Rejoice not in another's sorrow. *Turkish*

17015. Sing away sorrow. *Spanish*

17016. Small sorrows speak; great ones are silent. *Latin*

17017. Sorrow and ill weather come unsent for. *English*

17018. Sorrow brings on premature old age. *Latin*

17019. Sorrow dwells on the confines of pleasure. *Latin*

17020. Sorrow hath killed many, and there is no profit therein. *Bible*
17021. Sorrow is dry. *Irish*
17022. Sorrow is good for nothing but sin. *English*
17023. Sorrow is laughter's daughter. *American*
17024. Sorrow is like a precious treasure, shown only to friends. *African*
17025. Sorrow is soon enough when it comes. *Scottish*
17026. Sorrow is to the soul what the worm is to wood. *Turkish*
17027. Sorrow kills not, but it blights. *Russian*
17028. Sorrow will pay no debt. *English*
17029. Sorrows come uninvited. *Latin*
17030. Stained / With grief, that's beauty's canker. *English (Shakespeare)*
17031. The finishing stroke of all sorrow. *Latin (Juvenal)*
17032. There is no day without sorrow. *Latin*
17033. There's aye [always] sorrow at somebody's door. *Scottish*
17034. When sorrow is asleep wake it not. *English*
17035. When sorrows come, they come not single spies, / But in battalions. *English (Shakespeare)*
17036. When the heart's fu' [full] the tongue canna [cannot] speak. *Scottish*

Soul

17037. For what is a man profited, if he shall gain the whole world, and lose his own soul? *Bible*
17038. It is more necessary to cure the soul than the body. *Greek*
17039. Money lost, nothing lost; courage lost, much lost; honor lost, more lost; soul lost, all lost. *Dutch*
17040. The soul alone renders us noble. *Latin*
17041. There is a divinity within our breast. *Latin*

Sour Grapes

17042. As the fox says of the mulberries when he cannot get them. *French*
17043. "Fie upon heps [berries]," quoth the fox, because he could not reach them. *English*
17044. He whose mouth is out of taste says the wine is flat. *French (Montaigne)*
17045. It is easy to despise what you cannot get. *Greek (Aesop)*
17046. Sour grapes can ne'er make sweet wine. *English*
17047. "Sour grapes," said the fox when he could not reach them. *English*
17048. The fathers have eaten sour grapes and set the children's teeth on edge. *Syrian*

Space

17049. In space comes grace. *Scottish*
17050. The mind loves free space. *Russian*

Speaking *see also* Brevity; Conversation; Loquaciousness; Oratory; Silence

17051. A closed mouth catches no flies. *American*
17052. A fool might be counted wise if he kept his mouth shut. *American*
17053. A fool's heart dances on his lips. *English*
17054. A great talker never wants for enemies. *Chinese*
17055. A house can't be kept without talk. *Irish*
17056. A knavish speech sleeps in a foolish ear. *English (Shakespeare)*
17057. A long tongue is the sign of a short hand. *Scottish*
17058. A man is hid under his tongue. *Arabic (Ali Ibn-abi-Talib)*
17059. A man's character is revealed by his speech. *Greek*
17060. A nasty tongue is worse than a wicked hand. *Yiddish*
17061. After the devil is painted on the walls he finally appears in person. *French*
17062. An unguarded speech reveals the truth. *Latin*
17063. As the man, so is his speech. *Danish*
17064. Do not talk Arabic in the house of a Moor. *Spanish*
17065. Even the most timid man can deliver a bold speech. *Latin*
17066. Every time the sheep bleats it loseth a mouthful. *English*
17067. Evil comes by talking of it. *Gaelic*
17068. Give ear to that man who has four ears. *Latin*
17069. He is with a sharp mouth. [He talks fast.] *Mpangwe*
17070. He must have leave to speak that cannot hold his tongue. *Scottish*
17071. He that cannot speak cannot keep silence. *Latin*
17072. He that is worth anything is talked about. *Estonian*
17073. He that says what he should not, hears what he would not. *Latin*
17074. He that speaks much, is much mistaken. *American (Franklin)*
17075. He that speaks the thing he shouldna [should not] will hear the thing he wouldna [would not]. *Scottish*
17076. He that talks much errs much. *English*
17077. He who talks much cannot always talk well. *Italian*
17078. He who talks much is sometimes right. *Spanish*
17079. If a' your hums and haws were hams and haggises, the parish needna [need not] fear a dearth. *Scottish*
17080. It is always the worst wheel that creaks. *Italian*
17081. It is better to guard speech than to guard wealth. *Greek*
17082. Let people talk and dogs bark. *German*
17083. Let your speech be always with grace, seasoned with salt. *Bible*
17084. Let your talk be worthy of belief. *Latin*
17085. Man's speech is like his life. *Greek*
17086. Mild speech enchains the heart. *Arabic*
17087. More have repented speech than silence. *English*
17088. Much talk, much foolishness. *Hebrew*
17089. Muckle [much] spoken pairt [part] spilt. *Scottish*

17090. One speaks little when vanity does not make one speak. *French (La Rochefoucauld)*

17091. Out of the abundance of the heart the mouth speaketh. *Bible*

17092. Pleasant words are the food of love. *Latin (Ovid)*

17093. Save your breath to cool your porridge. *American*

17094. Silence is not always a sign of wisdom, but babbling is ever a folly. *American (Franklin)*

17095. Speak after the manner of men. *Bible*

17096. Speak o' the deil [devil] and he'll appear. *Scottish*

17097. Speech is the picture of the mind. *English*

17098. Spoken is spoken, you cannot wipe it out with a sponge. *German*

17099. Such as the man is, such will be his discourse. *English*

17100. Talk is but talk, but 'tis money buys lands. *English*

17101. Talk much and err much. *Spanish*

17102. Talk of the absent and he will appear. *Arabic*

17103. Talk of the wolf and behold his skin. *Portuguese*

17104. Talking of love is making it. *English*

17105. The dumbness in the eyes of animals is more touching than the speech of men, but the dumbness in the speech of men is more agonizing than the eyes of animals. *Hindi*

17106. The smooth speeches of the wicked are full of treachery. *Latin*

17107. The talk of the lips tendeth only to penury. *Bible*

17108. The talker sows, the listener reaps. *Italian*

17109. The tongue is a person of skill, dwelling in the same place with the teeth. *Efik*

17110. The tongue kills man and the tongue saves man. *Oji*

17111. The tongue may mount an elephant, or put the head in peril. *Hindi*

17112. The virtue of the mouth healeth all it toucheth. *Italian*

17113. The word flies out a sparrow and comes back an ox. *Polish*

17114. They who are thirsty drink in silence. *Latin*

17115. Think before you speak. *English*

17116. This is idle talk. *Latin*

17117. Though the speaker be a fool, let the hearer be wise. *Spanish*

17118. To speak much is one thing, to speak well, another. *Greek*

17119. Two great talkers will not travel far together. *Spanish*

17120. Use your mouth according to your purse. *French*

17121. When all men speak, na [no] man hears. *Scottish*

17122. When you mention the wolf, then he comes. *German*

17123. When you talk of the devil you will hear his bones rattle. *Dutch*

17124. Where there is least heart there is most tongue. *Italian*

17125. Wisely and with measure deal out words and treasure. *Polish*

17126. You may judge of a man by his remarks. *Latin*

17127. You talk like a book. *French*

17128. Your tongue gangs [goes] like a lamb's tail. *Scottish*

17129. Your tongue rins aye [runs always] before your wit. *Scottish*

Specialization and Generalization

17130. To taste many things bespeaks but a poor appetite. *Latin (Seneca)*

Spending *see also* Economy; Saving and Spending; Thrift

17131. A farthing saved is twice earned. *Italian*

17132. In hard times the wise man cuts his expenses; the foolish spendthrift cuts his throat. *American*

17133. Ken [know] when to spend, and when to spare, / And when to buy, and you'll ne'er be bare. *Scottish*

Spite

17134. A spiteful cur must be tied short. *French*

17135. Don't cut off your nose to spite your face. *American*

17136. He'd take one of his own eyes out, only to take both of yours. *Yiddish*

Spring

17137. In spring heat returns to the bones. *Latin*

17138. In spring time, the only pretty ring time. *English (Shakespeare)*

17139. When beans are in flower, fools are in full strength. *French*

Stasis *see* Idleness; Immobility; Inactivity; Motionlessness

Stature

17140. A man stands as high as he places himself. *American*

Stealing *see also* Crime and Criminals; Forbidden Fruit; Lying and Stealing; Temptation

17141. A cutpurse is a sure trade, for he hath ready money when his work is done. *English*

17142. A thief is an inferior man, but in cleverness surpasses the superior man. *Chinese*

17143. Don't steal if you can't conceal. *American*

17144. He gangs early to steal that cannot say na. *Scottish*

17145. He that steals a preen [pin] will steal a better thing. *Scottish*

17146. He that steals an egg will steal an ox. *English*

17147. He that steals can hide, too. *Scottish*

17148. He that steals gold is put in prison; he that steals land is made a king. *Japanese*

17149. He that will steal an ounce will steal a pound. *American*

17150. He who steals once is never to be trusted. *Spanish*

17151. It is a sin to steal a pin. *English*
17152. Little thieves are hung but big ones escape. *American*
17153. Not the mouse is the thief, but the hole in the wall. *Yiddish*
17154. One who steals a pin will steal anything. *American*
17155. Stolen wool does not warm long. *German*
17156. Take a wife from near, but steal from afar. *Czech*
17157. The arms of a thief are long. *Lugbara*
17158. The stolen ox sometimes puts his head out of the stall. *Latin (Publilius Syrus)*
17159. Theft and poison are sisters. *Lugbara*
17160. They are both thieves alike, the receiver and the man who steals. *Greek (Phocylides)*
17161. Thieves will be with us till Judgment Day. *American*
17162. Who steals a calf steals a cow. *German*
17163. Who steals once is ever a thief. *German*

Stepmothers *see* **Stepparents**

Stepparents
17164. A different mother [i.e., a stepmother] is the intestines of a porcupine [i.e., very bitter]. *Lugbara*
17165. A stepmother has a hard hand. *Danish*
17166. The child who gets a stepmother also gets a stepfather. *Greek*
17167. There are as many good stepmothers as white ravens. *German*

Stinginess *see also* **Miserliness; Selfishness**
17168. A rich man who is stingy is the worst pauper. *Yiddish*
17169. A stingy man is always poor. *French*
17170. He hath left his purse in his other breeks [pants]. *Scottish*
17171. He wouldn't give you the paring of his nails. *American*
17172. If you're not stingy you're not wealthy, and if you're not wealthy, you're not stingy. *American*

Storytelling
17173. There is much good sleep in an old story. *German*

Strain *see* **Stress and Strain**

Strangers
17174. All strangers are related to each other. *Arabic*
17175. The stranger has no friend, unless it be a stranger. *Persian (Sa'di)*
17176. When you shake hands with a stranger, count your fingers. *Persian*

Strength *see also* **Strength and Skill**
17177. As thy days, so shall thy strength be. *Bible*
17178. Be strong, and quit [i.e., acquit] yourselves like men. *Bible*
17179. He is strong that can knock a man down; he is stronger who can lift himself up. *French*
17180. He who has great strength should use it lightly. *Latin*
17181. It is excellent to have a giant's strength, / But it is tyrannous to use it like a giant. *English (Shakespeare)*
17182. Let your strength be the law of justice. *Bible*
17183. Make it strong with strength [i.e., very strong]. *Mpangwe*
17184. Pith [strength] is gude in all plays. *Scottish*
17185. Such strength as a man has he should use. *Latin*
17186. The stronger always wins. *Latin*
17187. They that wait on the Lord shall renew their strength. *Bible*

Strength and Skill *see also* **Skill; Strength**
17188. As much by strength as by skill. *Latin*
17189. Skill is stronger than strength. *French*
17190. Skill surpasses force. *French*
17191. Skill will enable us to succeed in that which sheer force could not accomplish. *Latin*
17192. Stickin' gangsna [goes not] by strength, but by the right use o' the gully [a large pocket knife]. *Scottish*

Stress and Strain *see also* **Argument; Contention; Discord; Dispute; Fighting; Quarreling; Strife**
17193. A bow long bent at length waxeth weak. *English*
17194. The bow too tensely strung is easily broken. *Latin (Publilius Syrus)*

Strife see also Argument; Contention; Discord; Dispute; Fighting; Quarreling; Stress and Strain
17195. Avoid strife when you can; never seek it. *Latin*
17196. Happy the man who keeps out of strife. *Latin*
17197. Life means strife. *German*
17198. Strife begets strife. *Latin*
17199. Strife never begets a gentle child. *Yoruba*

Study *see also* **Learning; Scholars and Scholarship**
17200. By eating, we overcome hunger; by study, ignorance. *Chinese*
17201. Do your best to make a full meal; exert your energies to the utmost for study. *Chinese*
17202. Every character must be chewed to get out its juice. *Chinese*
17203. Every man rejoices in his peculiar study. *Latin*
17204. Good students resemble workers in hard wood. *Chinese*
17205. He who neglects to study diligently in youth, will, when white-headed, repent that he put it off until too late. *Chinese*
17206. If a man does not study, he will not know how to do what is right. *Chinese*
17207. If study be neglected in youth, what will you do in old age? *Chinese*
17208. In all learning there is profit. *Chinese*
17209. Knowledge comes by study, ignorance follows its neglect. *Chinese*
17210. No pleasure equals the pleasure of study. *Chinese*

17211. One who is studious, though a peasant's son, may become a prince; a prince's son by neglecting study may become an ordinary person. *Chinese*

17212. Rich families have no need to buy fertile fields; and study is sure to yield its thousand measures of grain. *Chinese*

17213. Some study shows the need of more. *Chinese*

17214. Studies grow into habits. *Latin*

17215. Study goes on like a flowing stream. *Chinese*

17216. Study much and you will avoid vulgarity. *Chinese*

17217. Study thoroughly and think deeply. *Chinese*

17218. The more we study the more we discover our ignorance. *American*

17219. Those who do not study the past and the present are only horses and oxen in clothes. *Chinese*

17220. Three day's neglect of study makes one's conversation dull. *Chinese*

17221. Three years' reading is not so good as hearing the explanation. *Chinese*

17222. To live in peace there is no necessity to rear lofty halls; study naturally reveals its house of gold. *Chinese*

17223. To spend too much time in studies is sloth. *English (Bacon)*

17224. You may study to old age and yet have things to learn. *Chinese*

Stupidity

17225. A dumb man wins nae [no] law. *Scottish*

17226. A stupid man will be somebody's lap-dog. *Chinese*

17227. Against stupidity the gods themselves contend in vain. *German (Schiller)*

17228. An ox remains an ox, even if it goes to Vienna. *Hungarian*

17229. Bore as one will, the gimlet will not enter. *Chinese*

17230. Dumb folks get no lands. *English*

17231. Dumbie winna [or canna] lee [lie]. *Scottish*

17232. He has eyes but can't recognize gold inlaid with jade. *Chinese*

17233. He is like a camel, preferring heavy weights to light ones. *Chinese*

17234. He studies to no purpose; all he can do is keep accounts. *Chinese*

17235. He that makes himself an ass must not take it ill if men ride him. *English*

17236. He who deals with a blockhead will need much brain. *Spanish*

17237. Nature delights in punishing stupid people. *American (Emerson)*

17238. One who has not yet opened his eyes. *Chinese*

17239. Send you to the sea and ye'll no get saut [salt] water. *Scottish*

17240. The fault rests with the gods who have made us stupid. *French*

17241. The more stupid the more happy. *Chinese*

17242. Thick enough for soup. *Chinese*

17243. When a finger points at the moon, the imbecile looks at the finger. *Chinese*

17244. Who has not a head should have legs. *Italian*

17245. Who sits in a well to observe the sky does not see very much. [An ignorant man's sphere of observation is limited.] *Chinese*

17246. Whom God teaches not, man cannot. *Gaelic*

17247. Ye canna [cannot] see the wood for trees. *Scottish*

17248. Ye gae [go] far about seeking the nearest. *Scottish*

17249. Ye hae nae mair [have no more] sense than a sooking turkey. *Scottish*

17250. Ye'll neither dee [die] for your wit nor be drown'd for a warlock. *Scottish*

17251. Ye're like the man that sought his horse and him on its back. *Scottish*

17252. You can't blow up a fire through a rolling pin. *Chinese*

Style

17253. The style proclaims the man. *Latin*

Submission *see also* Acceptance; Resignation

17254. By submitting to an old insult you invite a new one. *Latin*

17255. Make yourself an ass, and you'll have every man's sack on your shoulders. *English*

17256. Submission to one wrong brings on another. *Latin*

Subordinates *see also* Divided Loyalty; Master and Man; Servants and Servitude; Slavery

17257. It is better to have to do with God than with his saints. *French*

17258. Never deal with the man when you can deal with the master. *English*

Subtlety

17259. He is from Chateaudun; he understands a hint. *French*

Success *see also* Success and Failure

17260. A successful man loses no reputation. *English*

17261. A thief passes for a gentleman when stealing has made him rich. *English*

17262. Audacity fathers success; good luck mothers it. *American*

17263. Either do not attempt it, or succeed. *Latin*

17264. Every man has the right to be conceited until he is successful. *American*

17265. Everything is subservient to success. *French*

17266. He may laugh that wins. *Scottish*

17267. In success be moderate. *American*

17268. It is a bad action that success cannot justify. *English*

17269. Nothing succeeds like success. *French*

17270. Singing and dancing alone will not advance one in the world. *American*

17271. Success alters our manners. *Latin*

17272. Success consecrates the foulest crimes. *English*

17273. Success gives the character of honesty to some classes of wickedness. *Latin (Seneca)*

17274. Success has many friends. *Greek*

17275. Success has ruined many a man. *American*

17276. Success in crime always invites to worse deeds. *Latin*

17277. Success in men's eyes is God, and more than God. *Greek*

17278. Success is the child of audacity. *American*

17279. Success is the gift of heaven. *Greek*

17280. Success is the reward of toil. *Greek*

17281. Success leads to insolence. *Latin*

17282. Success makes a fool seem wise. *English*

17283. Success makes fools admired, makes villains honest. *American*

17284. Success makes success as money makes money. *American*

17285. Success often costs more than it is worth. *American*

17286. Success soon palls. *American*

17287. Successful villainy is called virtue. *Latin (Seneca)*

17288. That's a tee'd ba' [ball]. [Tee = the goal in curling, quoits, etc.] *Scottish*

17289. The race is not to the swift, nor the battle to the strong. *Bible*

17290. The true touchstone of desert—success. *English (Byron)*

17291. The worst use that can be made of success is to boast of it. *American*

17292. They craw [crow] crouse [courageous, lively] that craw last. *Scottish*

17293. We never know when we have succeeded best. *Spanish (Unamuno)*

Success and Failure *see also* Success

17294. Affairs which depend on many seldom succeed. *American*

17295. Failure teaches success. *American*

17296. Failures are the pillars of success. *Welsh*

17297. He will either make a spoon or spoil a horn. [He will be either a success or a failure. The reference is to the process of making horn-spoons. The result was either a spoon or a ruined horn.] *Scottish*

17298. One may sooner fall than rise. *English*

17299. Success at first often undoes men at last. *American*

17300. Success has brought many to destruction. *Latin (Phaedrus)*

17301. Success has ruined many a man. *American*

17302. The stronger always succeeds; the weakest goes to the wall. *American*

17303. The surest way not to fail is to determine to succeed. *American*

Suddenness

17304. Suddenly as a storm. *Latin*

Suffering

17305. Crosses are ladders that lead to heaven—but few of us want to climb. *American*

17306. Even the fool knows when he has suffered. *Greek (Hesiod)*

17307. Experience purchased by suffering teaches wisdom. *Latin*

17308. He that lives long suffers much. *Spanish*

17309. He who suffers conquers. *Latin*

17310. He who suffers much will know much. *Greek*

17311. How great the sufferings we endure. *Latin*

17312. Many suffer for what they cannot help. *French*

17313. Of suffrance comth ease. *English (Heywood)*

17314. Present sufferings seem greater than those we dread. *Latin*

17315. Suffer in order to know; toil in order to have. *Spanish*

17316. Sufferance is the badge of all our tribe. *English (Shakespeare)*

17317. Suffering is common to all; life is a wheel, and good fortune is unstable. *Greek (Phocylides)*

17318. Suffering is teaching. *Greek (Aeschylus)*

17319. Suffering, when it climbs highest, lasts not long. *Greek*

17320. The soul that suffers is stronger than the soul that rejoices. *English (E. Shepard)*

17321. The sufferer becomes a chatterer. *Turkish*

17322. To every one his own cross is heaviest. *American*

17323. We by our sufferings learn to prize our bliss. *English (Dryden)*

17324. When another man suffers, a piece of wood suffers. *Arabic*

17325. When we suffer a great loss we must bear our cross. *American*

Sufficiency *see also* Abundance; Quantity; Satisfaction

17326. A bird can roost on but one branch. *Chinese*

17327. A few things are abundantly sufficient for the moderate. *Latin*

17328. A mouse can drink no more than its fill from a river. *Chinese*

17329. Bread and cheese is gude to eat when folk can get nae ither [no other] meat. *Scottish*

17330. Enough and to spare. *Latin*

17331. Enough is as good as a feast. *Greek*

17332. Enough is enough for the wise. *Greek*

17333. Enough is enough of bread and cheese. *English*

17334. Enough is enough. *American*

17335. Enough is great riches. *American*

17336. Enough of a good thing is plenty. *American*

17337. Folk should never ask for mair [more] than they can mak a gude use o'. *Scottish*

17338. Half enough is half fill. *Scottish*

17339. Hap an' a ha'penny is world's gear [wealth, property, goods] enough. *Scottish*

17340. Happy is the man to whom nature has given a sufficiency with even a sparing hand. *Latin*

17341. He is rich enough who does not want. *Italian*

17342. His eye is full. [He possesses every object of his desire.] *Arabic*

17343. Leave well enough alone. *American*

17344. Let him who has enough ask for nothing more. *Latin*

17345. Let not the shoe be larger than the foot. *Greek*

17346. Many men toil hard to earn a loaf when a slice is sufficient. *Dutch*

17347. No man is so rich as to say, "I have enough!" *Latin*

17348. Nothing will content him who is not content with a little. *Greek*

17349. Of enough men leave. *English*

17350. One stone is sufficient to frighten a thousand crows. *Turkish*

17351. Too much spoileth; too little is nothing. *English*

17352. What suffices is enough. *Latin*

17353. When the belly is full, the bones would have rest. *Scottish*

Suitability *see also* **Appropriateness; Ends and Means**

17354. A velvet saddle doesn't fit on the back of a jackass. *American*

17355. All things are not equally suitable to all men. *Latin (Propertius)*

17356. Be not a baker if your head be o' butter. *Scottish*

17357. Cut your coat according to your cloth. *Scottish*

17358. Send not for a hatchet to break open an egg with. *English*

17359. That suit is best that fits me. *English*

Summer

17360. Wide is the carpet of summer. *Arabic*

Superiority *see also* **Superiority and Inferiority**

17361. An equal combination of elegance and plainness is the fashion of the superior man. *Chinese*

17362. He burns us by his brightness. *Latin (Horace)*

17363. Not to be loquacious in liquor marks the true superior man. *Chinese*

17364. The superior man avoids intoxicated people. *Chinese*

17365. The superior man cultivates himself, not his appetite. *Chinese*

17366. The superior man is flavorless as water [i.e., reserved], but his friendship is strengthened by time. *Chinese*

17367. The superior man's life is at the service of heaven. *Chinese*

17368. There are plenty of men, but few superior men. *Chinese*

17369. There is nothing noble about being superior to some other man. The true nobility is in being superior to your previous self. *Hindi*

17370. When an affair is finished, men recognize the superior man. *Chinese*

Superiority and Inferiority *see also* **Inferiors and Inferiority; Superiors and Superiority**

17371. A man with a big head is a superior man; a man with big feet is an mean man. *Chinese*

17372. He is a true superior man who gives charcoal in snowy weather; the inferior man adds flowers to embroidery. *Chinese*

17373. Right influences the superior man; profit, the inferior. *Chinese*

17374. The friendship of superior men is as flavorless as water; the friendship of inferior men, sweet as honey. *Chinese*

17375. The superior man commands respect and yet keeps humble; the inferior man resents being avoided. *Chinese*

17376. The superior man doesn't remember the faults of inferior men. *Chinese*

17377. The superior man eats but to taste flavors; the inferior man gorges himself to death and is not satisfied. *Chinese*

17378. The superior man improves, the inferior man deteriorates. *Chinese*

17379. The superior man is able to bear with others; the inferior man cherishes an envious spirit. *Chinese*

17380. The superior man is conversant with his duty toward his neighbor; the inferior man is conversant with self-interest. *Chinese*

17381. The superior man loves men with a desire for their good; the inferior man simply indulges their weaknesses. *Chinese*

17382. The superior man, though poor, still entertains benevolence; the inferior man uses his wealth to oppress others. *Chinese*

17383. The superior man's heart is liberal and indulgent; the inferior man's heart is selfish and stingy. *Chinese*

17384. Though the wolf be lean, he can contend with a goat. *Wolof*

17385. What the superior man seeks is in himself. What the inferior man seeks is in others. *Chinese (Confucius)*

Superstition

17386. Better be dumb than superstitious. *English (Jonson)*

17387. In all superstition wise men follow fools. *English (Bacon)*

17388. Of all pests the most pestilent is superstition. *Latin*

17389. Sickness and sorrows come and go, but a superstitious soul hath no rest. *English (Burton)*

17390. Superstition destroys peace of mind. *Latin*

17391. Superstition obeys vanity as a son obeys his father. *Greek (Socrates)*

Surprise

17392. A man surprised is half beaten. *English*

Surrender *see also* **Defeat; Yielding**

17393. Never give up the ship. *American*

Suspicion *see also* **Distrust; Doubt**

17394. A crook thinks every man is a crook. *American*

17395. A suspicious mind sees everything on the dark side. *Latin*

17396. Avoid suspicion. *Chinese*

17397. He that has suspicion is rarely at fault. *Italian*

17398. He that is at fault is suspected. *Italian*

17399. Ill-doers, ill-deemers. *English*

17400. Suspicion begets suspicion. *Latin (Publilius Syrus)*

17401. Suspicion breeds phantoms. *Japanese*

17402. Suspicion follows closest on mistrust. *German*

17403. Suspicion is no less an enemy to virtue than to happiness. *English (Johnson)*

17404. Suspicion is the company of mean souls. *American (Paine)*

17405. Suspicion is the poison of friendship. *French*

17406. Suspicion raises hobgoblins in the dark. *Japanese*

17407. The hawk suspects the snare, and the pike the covered hook. *Latin*

17408. The losing side is full of suspicion. *Latin*

17409. Those who are conscious of their own iniquity, suspect others. *Latin*

17410. Whose nature is so far from doing harms, / That he suspects none. *English (Shakespeare)*

Swearing *see also* Cursing; Oaths; Promises; Women and Trustworthiness

17411. He'll swear through an inch board. *English*

17412. He's swearing even when he says nothing. *Russian*

17413. My tongue has sworn it, but my mind is unsworn. *Greek*

17414. There is nothing hard inside the olive; nothing hard outside the nut. [A man who will make a statement that is patently false will swear to anything.] *Latin (Horace)*

17415. To swear is unbecoming to a man of sense. *Latin*

Sweetness *see also* Soft Words

17416. Honey catches more flies than vinegar. *Danish*

17417. More flies are taken with a drop of honey than a tun of vinegar. *English*

17418. Sugared words prove bitter. *Spanish*

Sycophancy *see also* Flattery; Servility

17419. Sycophants scratch pimples for a livelihood. *Telugu*

Sympathy *see also* Indifference; Shared Misfortune

17420. A tear dries quickly, especially when it is shed for the troubles of others. *Latin (Cicero)*

17421. Do not rejoice at my grief, for when mine is old, yours will be new. *Spanish*

17422. If you can't help your friend with money, help him at least with a sigh. *Yiddish*

17423. Rejoice with them that do rejoice, and weep with them that weep. *Bible*

17424. The comforter's head never aches. *Italian*

17425. The groin hurts in sympathy with the sore. *Zulu*

17426. The sorrow of a widow is known to her widowed friend. *Korean*

Tact *see also* Discretion

17427. A bridle for the tongue is a necessary piece of furniture. *English*

17428. A tactless man is like an axe on an embroidery frame. *Malay*

17429. Dinna speak o' a rape [rope] to a chiel [child] whase father was hanged. *Scottish*

17430. Do not limp before the lame. *French*

17431. Do not mention a rope in the house of a thief. *Portuguese*

17432. Do not remind people of their infirmities. *American*

17433. Do not talk of color to the blind. *Turkish*

17434. It is cruel to refer to those things which cause sorrow. *Latin*

17435. It is not right to speak of a rope in presence of one who has been hanged. *French*

17436. Name not a rope in his house that hanged himself. *English*

17437. Never speak of a rope in the house of one who was hanged. *Italian*

17438. Social tact is making your company feel at home, even though you wish they were. *American*

17439. Some people have tact, others tell the truth. *American*

17440. You should never speak of rope in the family of one who has been hanged. *French*

Talent *see also* Ability; Dexterity; Excellence; Quality; Skill; Superiority; Superiority and Inferiority; Talent and Virtue

17441. A man of talent is short-lived. *Japanese*

17442. Great talent has always a little madness mixed up with it. *Latin (Seneca)*

17443. Great talents mature late. *Japanese*

17444. Half his talents are natural; the other half are acquired. *Chinese*

17445. Hide not your talents, they for use were made. / What's a Sun-dial in the Shade? *American (Franklin)*

17446. Often the greatest talent lies in obscurity. *Latin (Plautus)*

17447. The more talents, the more they will be developed. *Chinese*

17448. Till perseverance it doth wed, / Talent has a barren bed. *Welsh*

Talent and Virtue *see also* Talent

17449. He whose virtues exceed his talents is the superior man; he whose talents exceed his virtues is the inferior man. *Chinese*

17450. Talent without virtue is like silver without a master. *Chinese*

Talk *see* Brevity; Conversation; Loquaciousness; Silence; Speaking

Talkativeness *see* Loquaciousness

Tardiness *see* Lateness

Taste *see also* Opinion; Preference

17451. Ae [one] man's breath is anither man's death. *Scottish*

17452. Ae [one] man's meat is anither man's poison. *Scottish*

17453. All feet tread not in one shoe. *English*

17454. All men do not admire and love the same objects. *Latin (Horace)*

17455. Different men like different things. *Latin*

17456. Different pursuits suit different ages. *Latin*

17457. Every man to his taste, as the man said when he kissed his cow. *Scottish*

17458. Everyone to his liking. *English*

17459. Everyone to his own taste. *French*
17460. Ilka [every] man as he likes — I'm for the cook. *Scottish*
17461. Ilka [every] man buckles his belt his ain gait [own way]. *Scottish*
17462. It is as common for men to change their taste as it is uncommon for them to change their inclination. *American*
17463. Men lose their tempers in defending their tastes. *American (Emerson)*
17464. Men of different tastes have different pursuits. *Latin (Cicero)*
17465. No disputing about taste. *Latin*
17466. One man's meat is another's poison. *American*
17467. Some prefer turnips and others pears. *American*
17468. Tastes differ. *American*
17469. There are as many tastes as there are men. *Latin*
17470. There is no accounting for taste. *Latin*
17471. To a depraved taste sweet is bitter. *Spanish*
17472. Whether sugar be white or black, it preserves its proper taste. *Turkish*

Taxes

17473. Taxes and gruel will continually grow thicker. *Hindi*

Teachers and Teaching *see also* Education; Knowledge; Learning; Scholars and Scholarship

17474. A teacher is better than two books. *German*
17475. A teacher should be sparing of his smile. *American*
17476. A young branch takes on all the bends that one gives it. *Chinese*
17477. An inferior master makes a stupid pupil. *Chinese*
17478. Give a man a fish, and you feed him for a day. Teach a man to fish, and you feed him for a lifetime. *Chinese*
17479. He is either dead or teaching school. *Greek*
17480. He teacheth ill who teacheth all. *English*
17481. If you employ a teacher, employ one with a reputation. *Chinese*
17482. It is good to be taught even by an enemy. *Latin (Ovid)*
17483. It is impossible to be worse off than a teacher. *Chinese*
17484. Teaching others teacheth yourself. *English*
17485. Teaching should be full of ideas, not stuffed with facts. *American*
17486. The same dish cooked over and over again wears out the irksome life of the teacher. *Latin (Juvenal)*
17487. The same persons telling to the same people the same things about the same things. *Greek*
17488. The secret of life is to hear lessons, and not to teach them. *American*
17489. The teaching makes the difficulty. *Latin (Quintilian)*
17490. The tree must be bent while it is young. *German*
17491. Those having torches will pass them on to others. *Greek*
17492. Thraw [twist] the wand while it is green. *Scottish*
17493. To educate without rigor shows the teacher's indolence. *Chinese*
17494. To know how to suggest is the art of teaching. *American*
17495. Train up a child in the way he should go: and when he is old he will not depart from it. *Bible*
17496. We learn by teaching. *Latin*
17497. When a rich man becomes poor he becomes a teacher. *Chinese*
17498. When the teacher is strict, his instruction will be respected. *Chinese*
17499. Who chooses to be his own teacher has a fool as his pupil. *German*
17500. Who teaches me for a day is my father for life. *Chinese*
17501. Who teacheth, often learns himself. *English*
17502. You can't teach an old dog new tricks. *English*
17503. You will learn by teaching. *Latin*

Tears *see* Crying; Women and Tears

Teasing

17504. They that tease each other, love each other. *German*

Temper *see also* Anger

17505. All music jars when the soul's out of tune. *Spanish (Cervantes)*
17506. Govern your temper, which will rule you unless kept in subjection. *Latin (Horace)*
17507. He called me scabbed because I will not call him scald. *Scottish*
17508. He has his head near his cap. [He is quick-tempered.] *French*
17509. He has swallowed a flee [fly]. *Scottish*
17510. He who loses his temper is in the wrong. *French*
17511. It would be a pity to hae [have] spoilt twa [two] houses wi' them. *Scottish*
17512. Short temper causes losses. *Japanese*
17513. Want of temper is want of pluck. *English*

Temperance *see also* Abstinence; Moderation

17514. Be temperate in wine, in eating, girls, and cloth, or the gout will seize you and plague you both. *American (Franklin)*
17515. Eat not to dulness; drink not to elevation. *American (Franklin)*
17516. Temperance consists in forgoing bodily pleasures. *Latin*
17517. Temperance is the best medicine. *Latin*

Temptation *see also* Opportunity

17518. A bad padlock invites a picklock. *American*
17519. A hole tempts the thief. *Spanish*
17520. An open box tempts an honest man. *Dutch*
17521. At an open chest the righteous sin. *French*
17522. Between a holy man and a holy woman place a stone wall. *Spanish*

17523. Blessed is the man that endureth temptation. *Bible*
17524. Devils soonest tempt, resembling spirits of light. *American*
17525. Fishes follow the bait. *English*
17526. Great possessions and great want of them, are both strong temptations. *American*
17527. He that shows his purse bribes the thief. *Scottish*
17528. He who avoids the temptation avoids the sin. *Spanish*
17529. How oft the sight of means to do ill deeds / Makes ill deeds done. *English (Shakespeare)*
17530. If sinners entice thee, consent thou not. *Bible*
17531. If the eye did not see, the hand would not steal. *Yiddish*
17532. If the eye do not admire, the heart will not desire. *Italian*
17533. If you keep your safe open don't complain if your office-boy turns crook. *American*
17534. It's good to be without vices, but it is not good to be without temptations. *American*
17535. Keep yourself from opportunities, and God will keep you from sin. *Italian*
17536. May God defend me from myself. *French*
17537. No man has learned the art of life till he has been well tempted. *American*
17538. Shut your door and you will make your neighbor good. *Spanish*
17539. Temptations, like misfortunes, are sent to test our moral strength. *American*
17540. The devil hath power / To assume a pleasing shape. *English (Shakespeare)*
17541. The fish does not go after the hook, but after the bait. *Czech*
17542. The fish follow the bait. *English*
17543. The heron's a saint when there are no fish about. *Japanese*
17544. The key to my girdle keeps me good and my neighbor, too. *Spanish*
17545. The open door tempts a saint. *English*
17546. The success of the wicked tempts many to sin. *Latin (Phaedrus)*
17547. Though the bird may fly over your head, let it not make its nest in your hair. *Danish*
17548. We can resist everything except temptation. *American*
17549. When gold comes near, it glistens. *Oji*
17550. Where a chest lieth open, a righteous man may sin. *English*

Thanks *see also* Gratitude; Favors

17551. In everything give thanks. *Bible*
17552. Thanks are justly due for boons unbought. *Latin*
17553. You can't put thanks into your pocket. *American*

Theft *see* Stealing

Thieves *see* Stealing

Thinking

17554. A penny for your thoughts. *American*
17555. First thoughts are not always the best. *Italian*
17556. Good thoughts, even if forgotten, do not perish. *Latin*
17557. Great thoughts come from the heart. *French*
17558. Have no depraved thoughts. *Chinese (Confucius)*
17559. He that never thinks will ne'er be wise. *Scottish*
17560. Life is thought. *Greek*
17561. Man is only miserable so far as he thinks himself so. *Italian*
17562. Men suffer from thinking more than from anything else. *Russian (Tolstoy)*
17563. Second thoughts are wisest. *Greek*
17564. The less people think the more they talk. *French*
17565. The man who doesn't know how to think doesn't know how to live. *Arabic*
17566. The profound thinker always suspects that he is superficial. *American*
17567. There are two classes of thinkers: the shallow ones who fall short of the truth and the abstruse ones who go beyond it. *American*
17568. Thinkers are as scarce as gold. *American*
17569. Thinking is not knowing. *Portuguese*
17570. Those who dare to think by themselves can make others think with them. *American*
17571. Though he says nothing, he pays it with thinking, like the Welshman's jackdaw. *English*
17572. Thought is free. *Latin*
17573. Thoughts are mightier than strength of hand. *Greek*
17574. Thoughts are toll-free but not hell-free. *German*
17575. To live is to think. *Latin*
17576. To think is to converse with oneself. *Spanish*

Thirst

17577. The thirsty drink in silence. *Greek*
17578. Thirst makes wine out of water. *German*
17579. Who has no thirst has no business at the fountain. *Dutch*
17580. You look at what I drink and not at my thirst. *Spanish*

Thoroughness

17581. Many hounds are the death of the hare. *American*
17582. What you are doing do thoroughly. *Latin*
17583. Whatever is worth doing at all is worth doing well. *American*

Thought *see* Ideas; Thinking; Thought and Action; Thought and Language; Words and Deeds

Thought and Action *see also* Deliberation

17584. Act quickly, think slowly. *Greek*
17585. Deliberate slowly, execute quickly. *English*
17586. Deliberate with caution, but act with decision. *English (Colton)*
17587. Imitate the snail in deliberation, the bird in execution. *Latin*

17588. The end of man is action, and not thought. *English (Carlyle)*

17589. Thinking does not matter, but doing. *Italian*

17590. Who is never done thinking, never begins doing. *Italian*

17591. You'll never plough a field by turning it over in your mind. *Irish*

Thought and Language

17592. Ane [one] may think that daurna [dare not] speak. *Scottish*

17593. First think, and then speak. *American*

17594. It is easy for men to say one thing and think another. *Latin*

17595. Speaking, though speechless, exercises dominion over the mind. *Latin*

17596. Speech both conceals and reveals the thoughts of men. *Latin*

17597. Speech is the picture of the mind. *English*

17598. Speech was given to man to disguise his thoughts. *English*

17599. Think mair [more] than ye say. *Scottish*

17600. Think much, speak little, write less. *French*

17601. What the heart thinketh the tongue speaketh. *English*

Threat(s) *see also* Words and Deeds

17602. A blow threatened was never well given. *Italian*

17603. A dog which barks much is never good at hunting. *Portuguese*

17604. A dog which bites does not bark in vain. *Italian*

17605. A loaded gun frightens one, an unloaded gun frightens two. *Bulgarian*

17606. A man does not die of threats. *Dutch*

17607. A shor'd [threatened] tree stands lang. *Scottish*

17608. A white eye [i.e., a look of hatred or ill will] does not kill a bird. *Oji*

17609. Beware of a silent dog and still water. *Latin*

17610. David did not slay Goliath with words. *Icelandic*

17611. Fleying [frightening] a bird is no the way to grip it. *Scottish*

17612. Hares are not caught with beat of drum. *French*

17613. He that shows his teeth has no skill in biting. *French*

17614. He that threatens, warns. *German*

17615. He that threatens wastes his anger. *Portuguese*

17616. He threatens many that hath injured one. *English (Jonson)*

17617. He threatens who is afraid. *English*

17618. He who injures one man threatens many. *Latin (Publilius Syrus)*

17619. His bark is worse than his bite. *Scottish*

17620. I'll gar ye claw [claw you] where it's no yeuky [itchy]. *Scottish*

17621. I'll gar [make] him draw his belt to his ribs. *Scottish*

17622. I'll gar [make] his ain [own] garters bind his ain hose. *Scottish*

17623. I'll gie ye a sarkfu' [shirtfull] o' sair [sore] banes [bones]. *Scottish*

17624. I'll mak the mantle meet for the man. *Scottish*

17625. I'll pay you, and put naething in your pouch. *Scottish*

17626. I'll put daur [dare] ahint [behind] the door, and do't. *Scottish*

17627. If you can't bite, don't show your teeth. *Yiddish*

17628. It is easy to threaten a bull from the window. *American*

17629. It's lang ere Like-to-dee [die] fills the kirkyaird [churchyard]. *Scottish*

17630. It's lang ere the deil [devil] dees [dies] at the dykeside. *Scottish*

17631. Lang mint, little dint. [A blow long aimed or threatened has little force.] *Scottish*

17632. Longer lives he that is threatened than he that is hanged. *Italian*

17633. Many a one threatens while he quakes for fear. *English*

17634. More are threatened than are stabbed. *Spanish*

17635. Ne'er shaw your teeth unless ye can bite. *Scottish*

17636. No one dies of threats. *Dutch*

17637. Not all threateners fight. *Dutch*

17638. Play carl [old man] wi' me again if ye daur [dare]. *Scottish*

17639. Shor'd [threatened] folk live lang, an' so may him ye ken [know] o'. *Scottish*

17640. Some threaten who are afraid. *French*

17641. The cat's curse hurts the mice less than her bite. *Livonian*

17642. The dog barks, but the caravan passes. *Turkish*

17643. The dog's bark is not might, but fright. *Madagascan*

17644. The excommunicated person eats bread very well. *French*

17645. The greatest barkers bite not sorest. *English*

17646. The threatener loses the opportunity of vengeance. *Spanish*

17647. The way to catch a bird is no to fling your bonnet at her. *Scottish*

17648. Threatened folk, too, eat bread. *Portuguese*

17649. Threatened folks live the longest: they take numerous precautions. *American*

17650. Threatened men live, and men beheaded die. *French*

17651. Threatened men [or folks] live long. *English*

17652. Threateners do not fight. *Dutch*

17653. Threats are arms for the threatened. *Italian*

17654. Timid dogs bark worse than they bite. *Latin*

17655. To freemen threats are impotent. *Latin*

17656. What matters the barking of the dog that does not bite? *German*

17657. When she doesna scold the shores. *Scottish*

17658. Who cares naught for death cares naught for threats. *French*

17659. Who threatens warns. *German*

17660. Ye daur [dare] weel, but ye downa [cannot]. *Scottish*

17661. Ye yirr and yowl, ye bark, but daurna [dare not] bite. *Scottish*

Thrift *see also* Economy; Frugality; Miserliness; Parsimony; Saving and Spending

17662. By crookedness, not thrift, people grow rich. *Polish*

17663. By thrift and work people grow rich. *Polish*

17664. Grain to grain and there'll be a measure. *Polish*

17665. He that borrows and bigs, maks feasts and thigs, drinks an's no dry — nane o' these three are thrifty. *Scottish*

17666. Penny to penny and you'll buy a hen. *Polish*

17667. Thrift and he are at fray. *English*

17668. Thrift begins at the mouth of the sack. *Welsh*

17669. Thrift is a gude revenue. *Scottish*

17670. Thrift is better than an annuity. *English*

17671. Thrift is the philosopher's stone. *English*

Time *see also* Change; Delay; Postponement; Procrastination; Transience

17672. A foot of jade is of no value; an inch of time should be highly prized. *Chinese*

17673. A hundred years is not long, but never is a great deal. *French*

17674. A time to love, and a time to wed, and a time to rest. *Greek*

17675. Ae [one] hour in the morning is worth twa [two] at night. *Scottish*

17676. All in good time. *Spanish*

17677. All our sweetest hours fly fastest. *Latin (Virgil)*

17678. All the treasures of earth cannot bring back one lost moment. *French*

17679. An inch of time cannot be bought by an inch of gold. *Chinese*

17680. Anytime means no time. *English*

17681. Be ruled by time, the wisest counsellor of all. *Greek*

17682. Belyve [by and bye] is twa [two] hours and a-half. *Scottish*

17683. By time all things are produced and judged. *Greek (Gregory Nazianzen)*

17684. Day by day passes until the last stands behind the door. *Bosnian*

17685. Employ thy time well, if thou meanest to gain leisure. *American (Franklin)*

17686. Enjoy in happiness the pleasures which each hour brings with it. *Latin*

17687. Even as we speak, envious Time has fled. *Latin (Horace)*

17688. Ever aging Time teaches all things. *Greek (Aeschylus)*

17689. Every day in thy life is a leaf in thy history. *English*

17690. For long is not for ever. *German*

17691. For the just, Time is the best of champions. *Greek*

17692. Good things require time. *American*

17693. Handle the pudding while it's hot. *English*

17694. He that gains time gains all things. *American*

17695. He that neglects time, time will neglect. *English*

17696. If the time doesn't suit you, suit yourself to the time. *Turkish*

17697. Imperceptibly the hours glide on, and beguile us as they pass. *Latin (Ovid)*

17698. In time even a bear can be taught to dance. *Yiddish*

17699. In time the savage bull doth bear the yoke. *English (Shakespeare)*

17700. Length of time rots a stone. *Latin*

17701. Let time, that makes you homely, make you sage. *American*

17702. Life like an empty dream flits by. *American (Longfellow)*

17703. Little and often make a heap in time. *American*

17704. Man cannot buy time. *German*

17705. Nae [no] man can tether time nor tide. *Scottish (Burns)*

17706. Never is a lang [long] term. *Scottish*

17707. Nothing is ours except time. *Latin (Seneca)*

17708. Nothing is so dear and precious as time. *French*

17709. Other times, other names. *American*

17710. Our time is a very shadow that passeth away. *Bible*

17711. Place no faith in time. *Moroccan*

17712. Since thou are not sure of a minute, throw not away an hour. *American (Franklin)*

17713. Tak time ere time be tint [lost]. *Scottish*

17714. Take time by the forelock — for she is bald behind. *Greek*

17715. Take time by the forelock. *American*

17716. The clock does not strike for the happy. *German (Schiller)*

17717. The happier the time, the more quickly it passes. *Latin*

17718. The hour is passing. *Latin*

17719. The inconstant hour flies on double wings. *Latin (Horace)*

17720. The passing hour is sometimes a mother, sometimes a stepmother. *Latin*

17721. The shortest day is too long to waste. *American*

17722. The stream of time glides on smoothly. *Latin*

17723. The swiftness of time is infinite, which is the more evident to those who look back on what has past. *Latin (Seneca)*

17724. The wisest thing is time, for it brings everything to light. *Greek*

17725. There is no appeal from time past. *Italian*

17726. There is no bridle that can curb the flying days. *Latin*

17727. There is nothing more precious nor [than] time. *Scottish*

17728. There's a time to gley and a time to look straught. *Scottish*

17729. Thus years glide by. *Latin*

17730. Time and I against any two. *Spanish*
17731. Time, and not medicine, cures the sick. *Spanish*
17732. Time and straw ripen medlars. *English*
17733. Time and thinking tame the strongest grief. *English*
17734. Time and tide wait for no man. *English*
17735. Time bides na man. *Scottish*
17736. Time brings everything to those who can wait for it. *American*
17737. Time brings everything. *Greek*
17738. Time brings roses. *Dutch*
17739. Time changes the oak tree into a coffin. *American*
17740. Time covers and uncovers. *German*
17741. Time cures a!iction. *Latin*
17742. Time destroys all things. *French* (Rabelais)
17743. Time devours all things. *English*
17744. Time discloses all things. *English*
17745. Time dissolves all things, and makes them old. *Greek (Aristotle)*
17746. Time does not bow to you; you must bow to time. *Russian*
17747. Time dresses the greatest wounds. *American*
17748. Time, ebb, and flood wait for no man. *German*
17749. "Time enough" lost the ducks. *English*
17750. Time fleeth away without delay. *English*
17751. Time flies, eternity waits. *Polish*
17752. Time flies like an arrow, and time lost never returns. *American*
17753. Time flies like an arrow, days and months as a shuttle. *Chinese*
17754. Time flies like an arrow. *Japanese*
17755. Time flies never to be recalled. *Latin (Virgil)*
17756. Time flies with hasty step. *Latin*
17757. Time flies. [Tempus fugit.] *Latin*
17758. Time flieth away / without delay. *English*
17759. Time hath turned white sugar to white salt. *English*
17760. Time heals all. *German*
17761. Time is a file that wears and makes no noise. *American*
17762. Time is a gentle deity. *Greek (Sophocles)*
17763. Time is a hard taskmaster. *American*
17764. Time is a noiseless file. *Italian*
17765. Time is a river of passing events — a rushing torrent. *Greek*
17766. Time is a true friend to sorrow. *American*
17767. Time is an herb that cures all diseases. *American (Franklin)*
17768. Time is anger's medicine. *English*
17769. Time is fickle. *English*
17770. Time is God's, not ours. *Dutch*
17771. Time is longer than a sausage. *Maltese*
17772. Time is man's equal. *German*
17773. Time is money. *Greek*
17774. Time is not tied to a post like a horse to a manger. *Danish*
17775. Time is the best counsellor. *Greek*
17776. Time is the best healer. *Yiddish*
17777. Time is the discoverer of all things. *Spanish (Cervantes)*
17778. Time is the great teacher. *Greek (Aeschylus)*
17779. Time is the greatest innovator. *Latin*
17780. Time is the herald of truth. *Latin*
17781. Time is the one loan that no one can repay. *Latin*
17782. Time is the rider that breaks [i.e., breaks in] youth. *English*
17783. Time is the soul of business. *Latin*
17784. Time is the soul of the world. *Greek*
17785. Time is the sovereign physician of our passions. *French*
17786. Time is, time was, and time is past. *English*
17787. Time makes hay. *German*
17788. Time reveals all things. *Latin*
17789. Time rides on the back of a mare. *Arabic*
17790. Time ripens all things. *Spanish*
17791. Time rolls his ceaseless course. *Scottish (Scott)*
17792. Time rolls on, and we grow old with silent years. *Latin (Ovid)*
17793. Time rolls swiftly ahead, and rolls us with it. *Latin*
17794. Time softens animosity. *English*
17795. Time softens grief. *Latin*
17796. Time stands with impartial law. *Latin*
17797. Time stoops to no man's lure. *French (Swinburne)*
17798. Time subdues all things. *Arabic*
17799. Time that devours all things. *Latin*
17800. Time tries a', as winter tries the kail [colewort]. *Scottish*
17801. Time tries all things. *English*
17802. Time tries the truth. *English*
17803. Time undermines us. *English*
17804. Time waits for no man. *American*
17805. Time will bring healing. *Greek*
17806. Time will show. *American*
17807. Time will soften. *Greek (Euripides)*
17808. Time works wonders. *German*
17809. To things immortal, Time can do no wrong. *English (Cowley)*
17810. Today is the elder brother of tomorrow, and a heavy dew is the elder brother of the rain. *African*
17811. Wait for good luck in your sleep. *American*
17812. We take no note of time / But from its loss. *English (Young)*
17813. What is there that injurious time does not lessen? *Latin*
17814. What reason and endeavor cannot bring about, often time will. *English*
17815. Whilst time permits, live happy in the midst of pleasures; live mindful also that your time is short. *Latin (Horace)*

Time, Wasting *see* Waste of Time

Timeliness *see also* Delay; Deliberation; Lateness; Opportunity; Procrastination

17816. A stone thrown at the right time is better than gold given at the wrong time. *Persian*
17817. A windy day is not the day for thatching. *Irish*

17818. All hours are not ripe. *French*

17819. Beat out the iron while it is hot. *Arabic*

17820. Chasten thy son while there is hope. *English*

17821. Counsel is irksome when the matter is past remedy. *English*

17822. Everything has its season. *Latin*

17823. Everything has its time, and sae [so] has a rippling kame [comb]. *Scottish*

17824. Everything has its time. *American*

17825. He is the wisest man who does everything at the proper time. *Latin (Ovid)*

17826. It is a small thing to run; we must start at the right moment. *French*

17827. It is always time to do well. *French*

17828. It will happen in its time, it will go in its time. *Hindi*

17829. Know your time. *Latin*

17830. Make a cart in winter, a sledge in summer. *Cheremis*

17831. Never cross a bridge until you come to it. *American*

17832. Nip sin in the bud. *English*

17833. Now or never. *Latin*

17834. One cannot shoe a running horse. *Dutch*

17835. Strike while the iron is hot. *German*

17836. The chameleon says, "Speed is good, and slowness is good." *Oji*

17837. The day of the storm is not the time for thatching. *Irish*

17838. There is a season for all things. *Latin*

17839. There is a time for all things. *Bible*

17840. There is a time to fish and a time to dry nets. *Chinese*

17841. There is a time to wink as well as to see. *English*

17842. Timeliness is best in all matters. *Greek (Hesiod)*

17843. To beat the dog before the lion. [To do a thing at the wrong time.] *French*

17844. To every thing there is a season, and a time to every purpose under the heaven. *Bible*

17845. Unseasonable kindness gets no thanks. *English*

17846. Untimeous [untimely] spurring spoils the steed. *Scottish*

17847. When the iron is hot, strike. *English*

17848. When the play is best, it is best to leave. *Scottish*

17849. When thy daughter's chance comes, wait not her father's coming from the market. *Spanish*

17850. You must look for grass on the top of the oak tree. [When the tree is in leaf.] *English*

Timidity *see also* Bashfulness

17851. A bleet [or blate: timid] cat makes a proud mouse. *Scottish*

17852. Faint-hearted men never erect a trophy. *Greek*

17853. Great empires are not maintained by timidity. *Latin (Tacitus)*

17854. He cannot say boh [or shooh] to a goose. *English*

17855. He who is afraid of every nettle must not walk through the tall grass. *American*

17856. He who is afraid of every nettle should not piss in the grass. *English*

17857. If you spit in a timid man's eye, he says, "It's raining." *American*

17858. It is easy to frighten a bull from the window. *Italian*

17859. The most timorous animals are hardest to train. *Greek*

17860. The timid man calls himself cautious; the sordid man, thrifty. *Latin*

17861. The timid see dangers which do not exist. *Latin*

17862. Timid dogs bark most. *American*

17863. To fly, when no one pursues us. *Latin*

17864. Who timidly requests invites refusal. *Latin*

Today *see* Present; Today and Tomorrow

Today and Tomorrow *see also* Future; Present

17865. Don't worry today about what you're going to eat tomorrow. *American*

17866. Enjoy the present moment and don't grieve for tomorrow. *American*

17867. Now is now; and Yule's in winter. *Scottish*

17868. One today is worth ten tomorrows. *German*

17869. So enjoy the pleasures of the hour as not to spoil those that are to follow. *Latin (Seneca)*

17870. Today is worth two tomorrows. *American*

17871. What's lost today may be won tomorrow. *Spanish*

Tolerance *see also* Forbearance

17872. Other country, other customs. *Polish*

17873. Wink at small faults. *English*

17874. Go into the country and hear what the news is in town. *English*

17875. God made the country and man made the town. *English (Cowper)*

Trade *see also* Business and Commerce

17876. A trade is a shield against poverty. *Yiddish*

17877. "Every man to his ain [own] trade," quo' the browster [brewer] to the bishop. *Scottish*

17878. Every man to his trade. *English*

17879. Every trade has its ways. *Chinese*

17880. Everyone finds fault with his own trade. *Italian*

17881. He that brings not up his son to some trade makes him a thief. *Hebrew*

17882. He that hath a trade hath an estate, and he that hath a calling hath an office of profit and honor. *American*

17883. He who has a trade may travel through the world. *Spanish*

17884. Let every man practice the trade which he best understands. *Latin (Cicero)*

17885. There is roguery in all trades but our own. *American*

17886. Who has a trade may go anywhere. *Spanish*

Traitors *see also* Betrayal; Treachery; Treason

17887. The successful traitor becomes a hero. *American*

Transience *see also* **Beauty; Change; Changeableness; Life; Love; Mortality; Time; Youth and Old Age**

17888. All that's bright must fade. *English (Moore)*
17889. Here today, gone tomorrow. *American*
17890. Human life is as ephemeral as the may-fly's. *Japanese*
17891. It is all one a hundred years hence. *English*
17892. So ends all earthly glory. *Latin*
17893. The love of a woman and a bottle of wine / Are sweet for a season, but last for a time. *English*
17894. The morning sun never lasts a day. *English*
17895. The moth whirls and whirls, and is then consumed by fire. *Tunisian*
17896. The thistle's blossoms last but a moment. *American*
17897. There is no security in either time or money. *Tunisian*
17898. Today a king, tomorrow nothing. *French*
17899. What a day may bring a day may take away. *English*

Transparency

17900. You dance in a net and think that nobody sees you. *English*

Travel

17901. A man need not go away from home for instruction. *Latin*
17902. A traveler should have a hog's nose, a deer's legs, and an ass's back. *American (Franklin)*
17903. A wise traveler never despises his own country. *Italian*
17904. Away from home you can tell as many lies as you wish. *Arabic*
17905. Every journey is a little piece of Hell. *Tunisian*
17906. Half-way is twelve miles when you have fourteen miles to go. *Spanish*
17907. He that travels much knows much. *English*
17908. He that would travel much, should eat little. *American (Franklin)*
17909. He travels safest in the dark night who travels lightest. *Spanish*
17910. He who never leaves his country is full of prejudices. *Italian*
17911. He who takes the wrong road must make his journey again. *Spanish*
17912. If a goose flies across the sea, there comes back a quack-quack. *German*
17913. If an ass goes traveling, he'll not come home a horse. *English*
17914. In going abroad we change the climate, not our dispositions. *Latin (Horace)*
17915. Leave thy home, O youth, and seek out alien shores. *Latin (Petronius)*
17916. On a long journey even a straw is heavy. *Italian*
17917. Only with travel can a man ripen. *Persian*
17918. See one mountain, one sea, one river—and see all. *Greek*
17919. Send a fool to France and a fool he'll come back. *Scottish*
17920. The crow went traveling abroad and came home just as black. *English*
17921. The heaviest baggage for a traveler is an empty purse. *English*
17922. The traveler without money will sing before the robber. *Latin*
17923. They change their sky, not their soul, who run beyond the sea. *Latin (Horace)*
17924. Travel broadens the mind. *American*
17925. Trees often transplanted seldom prosper. *Dutch*
17926. Who goes and returns makes a good journey. *French*

Treachery *see also* **Betrayal; Traitors; Treason**

17927. Always stroke the head you wish to cut off. *Arabic*
17928. It is time to fear when tyrants seem to kiss. *American*
17929. Men are oftener treacherous through weakness than design. *American*
17930. Punic faith. *Latin*
17931. There is no knife that cuts so sharply and with such poisoned blade as treachery. *American*
17932. Treachery, in the end, betrays itself. *Latin*
17933. Treachery lurks in honeyed words. *Danish*
17934. Treachery will eventually betray itself. *Latin*

Treason *see also* **Betrayal; Traitors; Treachery**

17935. A traitor is a coward. *Turkish*
17936. Kings love the treason, but not the traitor. *English*
17937. The treason is loved, but the traitor is hated. *Italian*
17938. Traitor's words ne'er yet hurt honest cause. *Scottish*
17939. Traitors are hated even by those whom they prefer. *Latin (Tacitus)*
17940. Treason is never successful; for when it is successful, men do not call it treason. *American*

Trees

17941. A twig in time becomes a tree. *Latin*
17942. A young tree bends; an old one breaks. *Yiddish*
17943. Good fruit never comes from a bad tree. *Portuguese*
17944. He is a fool who looks at the fruit of a tree and does not measure its height. *Latin*
17945. He that plants trees loves others besides himself. *English*
17946. High trees give more shade than fruit. *Dutch*
17947. The forest is the poor man's overcoat. *American*
17948. The tree is known by his fruit. *Bible*
17949. The tree is not to be judged by its bark. *Italian*

Trickery

17950. Every monkey has his tricks. *American*
17951. The fox barks not when he would steal the chickens. *American*

17952. The fox praises the cheese out of the crow's mouth. *American*

Trifles *see also* Cause and Effect; Ends and Means; Insignificance; Size

17953. Frivolous minds are won by trifles. *Latin*

17954. Great businesses turn on a little pin. *American*

17955. He that condemneth small things, will perish by little and little. *Bible*

17956. It is bad to contend about trifles. *Latin*

17957. It is degrading to make difficulties of trifles. *Latin*

17958. It's a shame to eat the cow and worry on the tail. *Scottish*

17959. Letna [let not] the plough stand to kill a mouse. *Scottish*

17960. Men are led by trifles. *French*

17961. Men trip not on mountains but on molehills. *Chinese*

17962. Men trip not on mountains but on stones. *Hindi*

17963. One cloud is enough to eclipse all the sun. *English*

17964. Practice yourself in little things. *Greek*

17965. The eagle does not catch flies. *Latin*

17966. The eagle does not make war against frogs. *Italian*

17967. The elephant does not feel a flea-bite. *American*

17968. Those who apply themselves too much to little things usually become incapable of great ones. *French (La Rochefoucauld)*

17969. To excite waves in a ladle. *Latin (Cicero)*

17970. To give importance to trifling matters. *Latin (Horace)*

17971. Trifles console us because trifles distress us. *French (Pascal)*

17972. Trifles often lead to serious results. *Latin*

17973. We are tortured to death by pin-point wounds. *French*

17974. Win us with honest trifles, to betray us / In deepest consequence. *English (Shakespeare)*

17975. Your mind's aye [always] chasing mice. *Scottish*

Trouble

17976. Man is born unto trouble, as the sparks fly upward. *Bible*

17977. Trouble looks for trouble. *Zyryan*

Trust *see also* Belief; Credibility; Distrust; Faith

17978. Do not believe those who praise you. *Latin*

17979. Don't trust a horse's heel or a dog's tooth. *American*

17980. Don't trust a new friend or an old enemy. *American*

17981. Don't trust others, but don't trust yourself either. *Arabic*

17982. Don't trust people too much—or too little. *American*

17983. Even reckoning keeps [or makes] good friends. *Dutch*

17984. False in one respect, never trustworthy. *Latin*

17985. From those I trust, God guard me; from those I mistrust, I will guard myself. *Italian*

17986. God save me from him in whom I trust [or confide in]. *French*

17987. He may be trusted with a house full of millstones. *American*

17988. He who trusts to the promises of others is often deceived. *Latin*

17989. In God we trust; all other, cash. *American*

17990. It is an equal failing to trust everybody, and to trust nobody. *English*

17991. It's a vice to trust all, and equally a vice to trust none. *Latin (Seneca)*

17992. Love all, trust a few. *English (Shakespeare)*

17993. None are deceived, but they that confide. *American (Franklin)*

17994. None is deceived but he who trusts. *Italian*

17995. Put not your trust in princes. *Bible*

17996. Remember to distrust. *Greek*

17997. Sudden friendship, sure repentance. *English*

17998. Sudden trust brings sudden repentance. *English*

17999. Swim on, and don't trust. *French*

18000. Take a horse by his bridle and a man by his word. *Dutch*

18001. Take a man by his word and a cow by her horn. *Scottish*

18002. These three things cannot be trusted: a boat, a horse and a woman. *Zyryan*

18003. To trust yourself is good; not to trust yourself is better. *Italian*

18004. Trust, beware whom. *English*

18005. Trust, but not too much. *German*

18006. Trust is dead, ill payment kill'd it. *Italian*

18007. Trust is the mother of deceit. *English*

18008. Trust makes way for treachery. *English*

18009. Trust no man until you have consumed a peck of salt with him. *Latin*

18010. Trust not a horse on the road and a wife at home. *Yiddish*

18011. Trust not a horse's heel, nor a dog's tooth. *English*

18012. Trust not a new friend nor an old enemy. *English*

18013. Trust not him that hath once broken faith. *English (Shakespeare)*

18014. Trust, observe, but [be careful] whom. *German*

18015. Trust thyself only, and another shall not betray thee. *English*

18016. Trust was a good man, Trust-not was a better. *Italian*

18017. Trust-well rides away with the horse. *German*

18018. We live by reposing trust in each other. *Latin (Pliny)*

18019. Who mistrusts most should be trusted least. *Greek*

Truth *see also* Belief; Credibility; Faith; Falsehood; Lies and Lying; Trust; Truth and Falsehood

18020. A leal [true, honest, faithful] heart never lied. *Scottish*

18021. A needle wrapped in a rag will be found in the end. *Vietnamese*

18022. All truth is not to be told at all times. *English*

18023. All will come out in the washing. *Spanish*

18024. Antiquity is not always a mark of verity. *English*

18025. Better to suffer for the truth than be rewarded for a lie. *Swedish*

18026. Buy the truth and sell it not. *Bible*

18027. Children and drunkards speak the truth. *Danish*

18028. Children and fools are diviners. *French*

18029. Children and fools cannot lie. *English*

18030. Children and fools tell the truth. *German*

18031. Craft must be at charge for clothes, but truth can go naked. *American (Franklin)*

18032. Daylight will peep through a sma' hole. *Scottish*

18033. Even from a crooked chimney the smoke rises straight. *Turkish*

18034. Every truth has two sides; it is well to look at both, before we commit ourselves to either. *Greek (Aesop)*

18035. Great is truth and strongest of all. *Bible*

18036. He that speaks the truth must have one foot in the stirrup. *Turkish*

18037. He who would speak the truth must keep a sharp lookout. *Italian*

18038. In the end truth will out. *English (Shakespeare)*

18039. In the mountains of truth you never climb in vain. *German (Nietzsche)*

18040. In too much disputing the truth is lost. *French*

18041. In truth is right. *Turkish*

18042. Individuals may perish; but truth is eternal. *French*

18043. It is right to yield to the truth. *Latin*

18044. It is truth that makes a man angry. *Italian*

18045. It may be true what some men say, it maun [must] be true what a' [all] men say. *Scottish*

18046. It takes many shovelfuls of earth to bury the truth. *German*

18047. It will be seen in the frying of the eggs. *Spanish (Cervantes)*

18048. It would be wrong to put friendship before truth. *Greek (Aristotle)*

18049. It's possible if true. *French*

18050. It's strange, but true: for truth is always strange. *English*

18051. My gossips dislike me because I tell them the truth. *Spanish*

18052. Nature has buried truth at the bottom of the sea. *Greek*

18053. Never argue for victory but for verity. *American*

18054. No good without truth. *Wolof*

18055. No man has seen pure truth. *Greek*

18056. No man was ever harmed by truth. *Greek*

18057. No one was ever ruined by speaking the truth. *Hindi*

18058. Nothing is truer than the truth. *Latin*

18059. Nowadays truth is news. *Scottish*

18060. Nowadays truth is the greatest news. *English*

18061. While you live, tell truth, and shame the devil. *English (Shakespeare)*

18062. Oil and truth will get uppermost at last. *English*

18063. One must not say all that is true. *German*

18064. Out of the mouths of babes and drunks comes the truth. *American*

18065. Pushing any truth out very far, you are met by a counter-truth. *American (Beecher)*

18066. Ridicule is the test of truth. *American*

18067. Simple is the language of truth. *Latin (Seneca)*

18068. Some truths are not for all men at all times. *French*

18069. Speak the truth and shame the devil. *Italian*

18070. Speaking the truth is useful to the hearer, harmful to the speaker. *German*

18071. Strike the table and the scissors will speak out. *Polish*

18072. That is true which all men say. *English*

18073. The credit got by a lie lasts only till the truth comes out. *English*

18074. The crime was committed in the bush, but it is now talked about on the highway. *Samoan*

18075. The most useful truths are the plainest. *American*

18076. The tail of the fox will show no matter how hard he tries to hide it. *Hungarian*

18077. The truth hurts. *American*

18078. The truth is always green. *Spanish*

18079. The truth is always the strongest argument. *Greek (Sophocles)*

18080. The truth is bitter to fools. *Greek*

18081. The truth may be told, even about one's own father. *Yiddish*

18082. The truth may stretch but will not break. *Spanish*

18083. The voice of truth is easily known. *Wolof*

18084. The words of truth are always paradoxical. *Chinese (Laotse)*

18085. There is always less money, less wisdom, and less honesty than people imagine. *Italian*

18086. There is no proverb which is not true. *Spanish (Cervantes)*

18087. There is no standard for truth; we cannot even agree on the meaning of words. *American*

18088. There's never much talk of a thing but there's some truth in it. *Italian*

18089. Though malice may darken truth, it cannot put it out. *English*

18090. Time will reveal the truth. *Colombian*

18091. To define a truth is to limit its scope. *American*

18092. To fool the world, tell the truth. *German (Bismarck)*

18093. To utter great truths is no easier than to lie. *Russian*

18094. To withhold truth is to bury gold. *Danish*

18095. True blue will never stain. *American*

18096. Truth alone wounds. *French*

18097. Truth and honesty keep the crown o' the causey [i.e, march boldly down the middle of the road]. *Scottish*

18098. Truth and oil always come to the surface [or top]. *Spanish*

18099. Truth and roses have thorns about them. *American*

18100. Truth before peace. *Spanish (Unamuno)*

18101. Truth breeds hatred. *Greek*

18102. Truth, by whomsoever spoken, is from God. *Latin*

18103. Truth conquers all things. *Latin*

18104. Truth does not always seem true. *French*

18105. Truth fears no colors. *English*

18106. Truth finds foes, where it makes none. *English*

18107. Truth has a handsome face but tattered clothes. *German*

18108. Truth hates delays. *Latin*

18109. Truth hath always a fast bottom. *English*

18110. Truth is better than gold. *Arabic*

18111. Truth is great and will prevail. *Latin*

18112. Truth is green. *English*

18113. Truth is heavy; few therefore can bear it. *Hebrew*

18114. Truth is mighty and will prevail. *Bible*

18115. Truth is often attended with danger. *Latin*

18116. Truth is often eclipsed but never extinguished. *Latin*

18117. Truth is the daughter of God. *Spanish*

18118. Truth is the daughter of Time. *Latin*

18119. Truth is the gate of justice. *Osmanli*

18120. Truth is the only thing which wounds. *French*

18121. Truth is the pleasantest of sounds. *Greek (Plato)*

18122. Truth is the salt of mankind. *Arabic*

18123. Truth is the spring of heroic virtue. *American*

18124. Truth is too heavy for most people to bear. *American*

18125. Truth is truth to the end of reckoning. *English*

18126. Truth is victim of its own simplicity. *Arabic*

18127. Truth lies at the bottom of a well. *Greek*

18128. Truth may be blamed, but it shall never be shamed. *English*

18129. Truth may be smothered but not extinguished. *German*

18130. Truth may be suppressed, but not strangled. *German*

18131. Truth may languish but can never perish. *Italian*

18132. Truth never grows old. *American*

18133. Truth seeks no corner. *Latin*

18134. Truth should not always be revealed. *English*

18135. Truth sometimes comes out of the devil's mouth. *American*

18136. Truth speaks in a language that is simple and direct. *American*

18137. Truth will aye [always] stand without a prop. *Scottish*

18138. Truth will be uppermost, one time or other. *English*

18139. Truth will out. *American*

18140. Truth will prevail. *American*

18141. Truth [or Truth flows] in wine. (In vino veritas.) *Latin*

18142. Truth's best ornament is nakedness. *English*

18143. Two things the traveler easily forgets, his umbrella and the truth. *American*

18144. We know the truth not only by the reason but also by the heart. *French (Pascal)*

18145. What a' body [everybody] says maun [must] be true. *Scottish*

18146. What is true by lamplight is not always true by sunlight. *French*

18147. Where the tongue slips, it speaks the truth. *Irish*

18148. Wine in, truth out. *American*

18149. Ye shall know the truth, and the truth shall make you free. *Bible*

Truth and Falsehood *see also* Fact and Fiction

18150. A half truth is a whole lie. *Yiddish*

18151. A lie that is half a truth is ever the blackest of lies. *English (Tennyson)*

18152. Better suffer for truth than prosper by falsehood. *Danish*

18153. Better to suffer for the truth than be rewarded for a lie. *Swedish*

18154. Everyone loves the truth, but not everyone tells it. *Yiddish*

18155. Falsehood is often rocked by truth, but she soon outgrows her cradle, and discards her nurse. *English (Colton)*

18156. Falsehood, though it seems profitable, will hurt you; truth, though it seems hurtful, will profit you. *Arabic*

18157. Falsehoods border on truths. *Latin (Cicero)*

18158. He who does not speak the whole truth is a traitor to truth. *Latin*

18159. It is ungentlemanly to lie; truthfulness becomes the gentleman. *Latin*

18160. Man is ice for truth, fire for falsehood. *French (La Fontaine)*

18161. People praise truth, but invite lying to be their guest. *Lettish*

18162. The poorest truth is better than the richest lie. *American*

18163. Though a lie be swift, the truth overtakes it. *Italian*

18164. Truth ever gets above falsehood as oil above water. *Spanish (Cervantes)*

18165. Truth gives a short answer; lies go round about. *German*

18166. Truth is violated by a lie or by silence. *Latin*

18167. Truth tramples on a lie as oil on water. *Spanish*

18168. Truth will conquer; falsehood will kill. *Hindi*

Two Masters *see* Divided Loyalty

Tyranny

18169. A tyrant never knows true friendship, nor perfect liberty. *American*

18170. A tyrant's breath is another's death. *American*

18171. Better the tyranny of the cat than the justice of the mouse. *Lebanese*

18172. Dictators ride to and fro upon tigers from which they dare not dismount. *Hindi*

18173. Happy the tyrant who dies in bed. *Greek*

18174. Kings will be tyrants from policy, when subjects are rebels from principle. *American*

18175. One tyrant helps another tyrant. *Greek*

18176. Tyranny is a lovely eminence, but there is no way down from it. *Greek (Solon)*

18177. Tyrants are a money-loving race. *Greek (Sophocles)*

18178. Tyrants imitate God and dwindle into the brute. *American*

18179. What is more cruel than a tyrant's ear? *Latin (Juvenal)*

Ugliness

18180. An ugly woman dreads the mirror. *Japanese*

18181. Don't dare kiss an ugly girl—she'll tell the world about it. *American*

18182. If all the world were ugly deformity would be no monster. *American*

18183. No one blames a man for being ugly. *Greek*

18184. The uglier the face, the more it chides the looking-glass. *German*

18185. There is an ugly person in every family. *Russian*

18186. They took away the mirror from me because I was ugly, and gave it to the blind woman. *Spanish*

Unanimity

18187. If we all pulled on one side, the world would be overturned. *American*

18188. Unanimity is the best fortress. *Danish*

Uncertainty

18189. All between the cradle and the coffin is uncertain. *American*

18190. Between the hand and the mouth the soup is often spilt. *French*

18191. Catch not at the shadow, and lose the substance. *English*

18192. In grasping at uncertainties we lose that which is certain. *Latin (Plautus)*

18193. May-be's are no aye [always] honey-bees. *Scottish*

18194. May-be's fleena [fly not] at this time o' the year. *Scottish*

18195. The book o' may-be's is very braid [broad]. *Scottish*

18196. There's a sliddery stane [stone] before the ha' [hall] door. *Scottish*

18197. There's nae [no] sun sae [so] bright but clouds will owercast it. *Scottish*

18198. Ye watna [know not] what wife's ladle may cog your kail [stir your dish of broth]. *Scottish*

Unchangeableness

18199. A leopard does not change his spots. *Latin*

18200. Can the Ethiopian change his skin, or the leopard his spots? *English*

18201. Crows are never the whiter for washing themselves. *English*

18202. Once a beggar, always a beggar. *American*

18203. The leopard can't change his spots. *American*

18204. Wash a dog, comb a dog, still a dog remains a dog. *English*

Understanding *see also* Heart

18205. A nod for a wise man, and a rod for a fool. *Hebrew (Ben Syra)*

18206. As good is he that heareth and understandeth not, as he that hunteth and taketh not. *French*

18207. Each one brings his understanding to market. *German*

18208. God grant me to contend with those that understand me. *English*

18209. He that best understands the world, least likes it. *American (Franklin)*

18210. If you understand the world, you don't like it; if you like it, you don't understand it. *American*

18211. If you wish to know the character of the prince, look at his ministers; if you wish to understand the man, look at his friends; if you wish to know the father, observe his son. *Chinese*

18212. It goes without saying. *American*

18213. Let every man talk of what he understands. *Spanish*

18214. Nothing human is foreign to a man who is at home with the plain folks on Main Street. *American*

18215. One may be acquainted with everybody in the empire, but know the hearts of only a few. *Chinese*

18216. Only the nightingale can understand the rose. *American*

18217. Other folks' burdens kill the ass. *Spanish (Cervantes)*

18218. Pinch yourself and know how others feel. *Japanese*

18219. Ten lands are sooner known than one man. *Yiddish*

18220. The deep sea can be fathomed, but who knows the hearts of men? *Malay*

18221. The fat sow knows not what the hungry sow suffers. *Danish*

18222. The finest wealth is that of the understanding. *American*

18223. The heart has ears. *Russian*

18224. The superior man needs but one word; the swift horse needs but one lash. *Chinese*

18225. The understanding is ever the dupe of the heart. *French*

18226. The wise man understands with half a word. *French*

18227. To a good listener a few words. *Spanish*

18228. To a quick ear half a word. *English*

18229. To understand a stammerer, you ought to stammer yourself. *Latin*

18230. Travelers on horseback know nothing of the toil of those who travel on foot. *Japanese*

18231. Tribulation brings understanding. *Latin*

18232. Understanding is the wealth of wealth. *Arabic*

18233. We may talk this and talk that, but it is because we do not understand one another. *Yoruba*

18234. We never know what a man is till we have money dealings with him. *English*

18235. What is not understood is always marvelous. *Latin*

18236. What we do not understand we do not possess. *German (Goethe)*

18237. Who has not understanding, let him have legs. *Italian*

18238. With all thy getting, get understanding. *Bible*

Undertaking

18239. Who undertakes too much seldom succeeds. *Dutch*

Undoing

18240. One hour's cold will suck out seven years' heat. *American*

Unexpected

18241. Expect the unexpected. *Latin (Heraclitus)*

18242. It [beer] gets spilled when it is ready. *Zulu*

18243. Look out for the unexpected. *American*

18244. Nothing so certain as the unexpected. *English*

18245. Unlooked-for comes oft. *German*

Unhappiness *see also* Misery; Misfortune

18246. Is there anything men take more pains about than to make themselves unhappy? *American (Franklin)*

18247. The wounds of the unhappy endure through the night. *Latin*

18248. These six — the peevish, the niggard, the dissatisfied, the passionate, the suspicious, and those who live upon others' means — are forever unhappy. *Sanskrit*

18249. When we sing everybody hears us; when we sigh, nobody hears us. *Russian*

Unimportance *see* Cause and Effect; Ends and Means; Insignificance; Trifles

Uninvited Guests *see also* Guests

18250. He that comes unbidden goes unthanked. *Dutch*

18251. He that comes unca'd [uncalled] sits unsair'd [unserved]. *Scottish*

Unity *see also* Cooperation; Collaboration

18252. A common danger unites even the bitterest enemies. *Greek (Aristotle)*

18253. A sheaf without a sheaf-band is straw. *Russian*

18254. A single arrow is easily broken, but not ten in a bundle. *Greek (Homer)*

18255. A single bamboo pole does not make a raft. *Chinese*

18256. A threefold cord is not quickly broken. *Bible*

18257. A triple rope is not easily broken. *Latin*

18258. Behold, how good and how pleasant it is for brethren to dwell together in unity. *Bible*

18259. By uniting we stand, by dividing we fall. *English (Dickinson)*

18260. Fighting without concert, they suffer universal defeat. *Latin (Tacitus)*

18261. Helping each other, even boys can hold back a lion. *Ethiopian*

18262. In union there is strength. *American*

18263. Many straws may bind an elephant. *Hindi*

18264. Mony [many] hounds may soon worry ae [one] hare. *Scottish*

18265. One bell does not make a concert. *Italian*

18266. One for all, all for one. *American*

18267. Rich together, poor if separated. *Laotian*

18268. Shouther to shouther stands steel and pouther. *Scottish*

18269. Strength united is greater. *Latin*

18270. String [added to] string will bind even a leopard. *Oji*

18271. The shoe will hold with the sole. *Italian*

18272. The sole holdeth with the upper leather. *English*

18273. The work of many is strong. *Greek (Homer)*

18274. They put four heads in one hood. [They unite the intelligence of four persons.] *French*

18275. Things which of themselves avail nothing, when united become powerful. *Latin (Ovid)*

18276. Three, helping one another, bear the burden of six. *English*

18277. Three, if they unite against a town, will ruin it. *Arabic*

18278. To row together. *Latin*

18279. Twa [two] wits is better nor ane [than one]. *Scottish*

18280. Two small antelopes beat a big one. *Oji*

18281. Union gives strength to the humble. *Latin*

18282. Union is strength. *English*

18283. Union makes power. *French*

18284. Union makes strength. *German*

18285. United, even the weak are strong. *German*

18286. United we stand, divided we fall. *American*

18287. Unity among the small makes the lion lie down hungry. *Swahili*

18288. Valor acquires strength by union. *Latin*

18289. We must all hang together, or assuredly we shall all hang separately. *American (Franklin)*

18290. When spider webs unite, they can tie up a lion. *Ethiopian*

18291. Willows are weak, yet they bind other wood. *Italian*

Universality

18292. Crows are black all the world over. *American*

18293. When it's a question of money, everybody is of the same religion. *American*

Unknown

18294. Everything unknown is taken for magnificent. *Latin*

18295. It's not safe to wade in unknown water. *American*

Unpredictability *see also* Unexpected

18296. Devils live in a quiet pond. *Russian*

18297. God comes to see without a bell. *Spanish*

18298. The devil's boots don't creak. *Scottish*

18299. The feet of the avenging deities are clad in wool. *Latin*

Untimeliness *see also* Appropriateness; Prematureness; Punctuality; Timeliness

18300. To indulge in a joke when surrounded by mourners. *Latin*

Unwelcome *see also* Uninvited Guests

18301. He is as welcome as the first day in Lent. *Dutch*

18302. He is as welcome as the snow in harvest. *Scottish*

18303. He is as welcome as water in a riven ship. *Scottish*

18304. He threw my coat out the door, and I happened to be in it. *Yiddish*

Unwillingness *see also* **Willingness**

18305. It is sheer folly to take unwilling hounds to the chase. *Latin (Plautus)*

18306. Nothing is easy to the unwilling. *English*

18307. Nothing is so easy but it becomes difficult when done reluctantly. *Latin*

Upbringing

18308. Give a child his will and a whelp his fill, / Both will surely turn out ill. *English (Spurgeon)*

18309. No man is born wise and good; it's his upbringing that really counts. *American*

18310. Train up a child in the way he should go; and when he is old he will not depart from it. *Bible*

Urgency

18311. The iron is in the fire. *Latin*

18312. When a man's house burns, it's not good playing at chess. *English*

Use *see also* **Cost; Saving and Spending; Usefulness; Value; Worth; Worthlessness**

18313. A man that keeps riches and enjoys them not, is like an ass that carries gold and eats thistles. *English*

18314. A piece of incense may be as large as the knee but, unless burned, emits no fragrance. *Malay*

18315. A used plow shines; standing water stinks. *German*

18316. A well which is drawn from is improved. *Latin*

18317. Drawn wells are seldom dry. *English*

18318. Drawn wells have sweetest water. *English*

18319. Even a ring of iron is worn away by constant use. *Latin (Ovid)*

18320. In vain does a man possess property if he makes no use of it. *Latin*

18321. Not possession, but use, is the only riches. *English*

18322. The gown is hers that wears it; and the world is his who enjoys it. *English*

18323. Wealth is not his who gets it, but his who enjoys it. *English*

18324. What's in use wants no excuse. *Spanish*

18325. Wine in the bottle does not quench thirst. *English*

Usefulness *see also* **Buying and Selling; Purpose; Use; Value; Worth**

18326. A cloak is not made for a single shower of rain. *Italian*

18327. A layin' hen is better than a standin' mill. *Scottish*

18328. A stone that is fit for the wall, is not left in the way. *English*

18329. A useful burden becomes light. *American*

18330. Better than beauty is a camel. *Arabic*

18331. Everything is good for something. *American*

18332. He that is worst may still hold the candle. *English*

18333. If an ass is invited to a wedding it's merely to carry wood. *American*

18334. If you can't push, pull; if you can't pull, please get out of the way. *American*

18335. Keep a thing seven years and ye'll find a use for it. *Scottish*

18336. Lay a thing by and it'll come o' use. *Scottish*

18337. Nothing is more useful than the sun and salt. *Latin*

18338. That which is despised is often most useful. *Latin*

18339. To everything its use. *Latin*

18340. Unless what we do is useful, glory is vain. *Latin*

18341. We often despise what is most useful to us. *Greek (Aesop)*

18342. What is useful cannot be base. *Latin*

Vacillation *see also* **Hesitation; Indecision**

18343. His opinions are like water in the bottom of a canoe, going from side to side. *Efik*

Vagrancy

18344. A vagrant is everywhere at home. *American*

18345. An honest man is seldom a vagrant. *American*

18346. The true vagrant is the only king above all comparison. *American*

Vagueness

18347. Almost and very nigh saves many a lie. *English*

Valor *see also* **Bravery; Courage; Heart; Heroes and Heroism**

18348. Hidden valor is as bad as cowardice. *Latin*

18349. Valor delights in the test. *Latin*

18350. Valor even in an enemy is worthy of praise. *Latin*

Value *see also* **Cheapness; Cost; Use; Usefulness; Worth**

18351. A dear ship stands long in haven. *Scottish*

18352. A man is valued according to his own estimate of himself. *American*

18353. Dear weeps but once, cheap is always weeping. *Hindi*

18354. Every man is valued in this world as he shows by his conduct that he wishes to be valued. *French (La Bruyere)*

18355. He counts his ha'penny gude siller [good silver]. *Scottish*

18356. Men understand the worth of blessings only when they have lost them. *Latin (Plautus)*

18357. One leg of a lark's worth the whole body of a kite. *English*

18358. One who makes light of himself is slighted by others. *American*

18359. Pebbles lie undisturbed, but jewels do not. *American*

18360. The cat that catches no mice does not earn his keep. *American*

18361. The worth o' a thing is what it will bring. *Scottish*

18362. There is nothing but is good for something. *American*

18363. Things are worth what they will fetch at a sale. *Latin*

18364. What is dust to some is gunpowder to others. *Afghani*

Vanity *see also* **Women and Vanity**

18365. A peacock has too little in its head and too much in its tail. *Swedish*

18366. Admiring himself like a peacock. *Latin*

18367. An ounce of vanity spoils a hundredweight of merit. *French*

18368. Each bird loves to hear himself sing. *English*

18369. Every ass loves to hear himself bray. *English*

18370. Every man thinks his copper gold. *German*

18371. Every vixen praises her own tail. *Polish*

18372. God made us, and we admire ourselves. *Spanish*

18373. I see the vanity through the holes of thy coat. [Referring to cynics.] *Greek*

18374. I would not live alway: for my days are vanity. *Bible*

18375. Make not thy tail broader than thy wings. *French*

18376. Pride that dined with vanity supped with poverty. *English*

18377. Such pains they take to look pretty. *Latin (Juvenal)*

18378. The cow rails at the pig for being black. *Chinese*

18379. The kettle calls the sauce-pan smutty. *Turkish*

18380. The more women look in their glass the less they look in their house. *American*

18381. The nakedness of the indigent world could be easily clothed with the trimmings of the vain. *Irish*

18382. The one-eyed man mocks the man who squints. *American*

18383. They come to see and be seen. *Latin (Ovid)*

18384. Those who scratch their hair with one finger. [To avoid mussing it.] *Latin (Juvenal)*

18385. Vainglory bears no grain. *French*

18386. Vanity has no greater foe than vanity. *French*

18387. Vanity is not all confined to one sex. *English*

18388. Vanity is the sixth sense. *American*

18389. Vanity of vanities; all is vanity. *Bible*

18390. Verily every man at his best state is altogether vanity. *Bible*

18391. Virtue would not go far, if a little vanity walked not with it. *English*

18392. Woe unto them that draw iniquity with cords of vanity. *Bible*

18393. Ye hae [have] little need o' the Campsie wife's prayer, "That she might aye [always] be able to think enough o' hersel'." *Scottish*

18394. "Your feet are crooked, your hair is good for nothing," said the pig to the horse. *Russian*

Variety *see also* **Change; Diversity; Newness; Novelty**

18395. Nothing pleases which is not freshened by variety. *Latin (Publilius Syrus)*

18396. Variety is charming / And not at all alarming. *English*

18397. Variety is pleasing. *Greek*

18398. Variety is sweet in all things. *Greek*

18399. Variety is the soul of pleasure. *Hebrew*

18400. Variety's the very spice of life, / That gives it all its flavor. *English (Cowper)*

18401. Want of variety leads to satiety. *English*

Vengeance *see* **Retaliation; Retribution; Revenge; Women and Revenge**

Venture and Investment *see also* **Boldness; Gambling; Risk**

18402. A nimble sixpence is better than a slow shilling. *English*

18403. Don't throw good money after bad. *American*

18404. He that dares not venture must not complain of ill luck. *English*

18405. He that ventures not fails not. *French*

18406. He that would catch a fish must venture his bait. *American*

18407. He who does not bait his hook catches nothing. *English*

18408. If a little does not go, much cash will not come. *Chinese*

18409. If you've nothing to lose, you can try everything. *Yiddish*

18410. Lay on more wood; ashes give money. *English*

18411. Money begets money. *Italian*

18412. Money draws money. *Yiddish*

18413. Money gains money, and not man's bones. *Spanish*

18414. Naething [nothing] venture, naething win. *Scottish*

18415. Ne'er misca' a Gordon in the raws [rows or lines] o' Stra'bogie. *Scottish*

18416. Nothing stake, nothing draw. *English*

18417. Nothing venture, nothing have. *English*

18418. Nothing ventured, nothing gained. *American*

18419. One must lose a minnow to catch a salmon. *French*

18420. Some seeds will grow, others will die. *Zulu*

18421. Tak your venture, as mony a gude ship has done. *Scottish*

18422. Throw a brick to attract a gem. *Chinese*

18423. 'Tis money that begets money. *English*

18424. To make any gain some outlay is necessary. *Latin (Plautus)*

18425. Unless you enter the tiger's den you cannot take the cubs. *Japanese*

18426. Venture a small fish to catch a great one. *English*

18427. Who does not venture gets neither horse nor mule. *French*

18428. Who ventures nothing has no luck. *Spanish*

18429. Who ventures wins. *German*

18430. With empty hand men may none haukes lure. *English (Chaucer)*

18431. You must risk a small fish to catch a big one. *French*

Vexation

18432. We can more easily endure that which shames than that which vexes us. *Latin (Plautus)*

Vice *see also* Good and Evil; Vice and Virtue

18433. All vices are less serious when they are open. *Latin*

18434. Every vice is downward in tendency. *Latin*

18435. He who plunges into vice is like one who rolls from the top of a precipice. *Chinese*

18436. If vice were profitable, the virtuous man would be the sinner. *Latin*

18437. No vice remains within bounds. *Latin*

18438. One hates not the person but the vice. *Italian*

18439. The vice which offends no one is not really a vice. *French (Montaigne)*

18440. Vice is nourished by concealment. *Latin*

18441. Vice knows she's ugly, so puts on her mask. *American (Franklin)*

18442. Vice ruleth where Gold reigneth. *English*

18443. Vice would be frightful if it did not wear a mask. *English*

18444. Vices are learned without a master. *English*

18445. Vices are their own punishment. *Greek (Aesop)*

18446. Vices creep into our hearts under the name of virtues. *Latin*

18447. We bear with accustomed vices; we reprove those that are new. *Latin*

18448. What maintains one vice would bring up two children. *English*

18449. What were vices have become the fashion of the day. *Latin (Seneca)*

Vice and Virtue *see also* Good and Evil; Vice

18450. As virtue is its own reward, so vice is its own punishment. *English*

18451. Fools, in avoiding vice, run to the opposite extreme. *Latin*

18452. Great abilities produce great vices as well as virtues. *Greek*

18453. Learning virtue means unlearning vice. *Latin*

18454. Our virtues are most frequently but vices in disguise. *French (La Rochefoucauld)*

18455. The first step to virtue is to abstain from vice. *American*

18456. The good hate vice because they love virtue. *Latin*

18457. Vice has more martyrs than virtue. *English (Colton)*

18458. Vice is summary, virtue is slow. *Latin*

18459. Vice makes virtue shine. *American*

18460. Vice often rides triumphant in virtue's chariot. *English*

18461. Vices often become virtues; hatred is respectable in wartime. *American*

18462. Virtue and vice cannot dwell under the same roof. *German*

18463. Virtue may not always make a face handsome, but vice will certainly make it ugly. *American (Franklin)*

18464. We please more often by our vices than by our virtues. *French (La Rochefoucauld)*

Vicissitudes

18465. Cares and joys abound, as seasons fleet. *American*

18466. Happy the man who can endure with calm the highest and the lowest fortune. *American*

18467. No rest can be found on fortune's restless wheel. *American*

18468. Sing before breakfast, cry before night. *English*

18469. The highest spoke in fortune's wheel may soon turn lowest. *Latin*

18470. Yesterday's abyss may turn into today's shoal. *Japanese*

Victory

18471. He who has conquered his own coward spirit has conquered the world. *American*

18472. He who has victory, has right. *German*

18473. He who returns good for evil obtains the victory. *American*

18474. In victory, the hero seeks the glory, not the prey. *American*

18475. It is more difficult to look upon victory than upon battle. *American*

18476. Love victory, but despise the pride of triumph. *American*

18477. Often the victor triumphs but to fall. *Greek*

18478. One trouble with the world is that there are always more victors than spoils. *American*

18479. Pursue not a victory too far: you may provoke the foe to desperate resistance. *American*

18480. Victory does not like rivalry. *Latin*

Vigilance *see* Watchfulness

Violence

18481. Gunpowder is hasty eldin [fuel]. *Scottish*

18482. Nothing good comes of violence. *American*

18483. Violence does even justice unjustly. *American*

Virility

18484. A red-headed man will make a good stallion. *American*

Virtue *see also* Morality; Talent and Virtue; Women and Virtue

18485. All the virtues are in peril when filial piety is attacked. *Chinese*

18486. Assume a virtue, if you have it not. *English (Shakespeare)*

18487. Birth is nothing where virtue is not. *French*

18488. Blood is inherited but virtue is achieved. *American*

18489. Conquer by means of virtue. *Latin*

18490. He hath no mean portion of virtue that loveth it in another. *English*

18491. He is ill clothed that is bare of virtue. *American (Franklin)*

18492. He who dies for virtue does not perish. *Latin*

18493. He who has nothing but virtues is not much better than he who has nothing but faults. *Swedish*

18494. Hear no evil, see no evil, speak no evil. *American*

18495. Heaven wills that virtue be proved by trials. *Arabic*

18496. Honor is the reward of virtue. *Latin*

18497. I wrap myself in my virtue. *Latin*

18498. In virtue are riches. *Latin*

18499. It is a small thing to starve; it is a serious matter to lose one's virtue. *Chinese*

18500. It is impossible for fortune to conquer virtue. *Latin*

18501. It is virtue to flee vice. *Latin*

18502. No one can be happy without virtue. *Latin*

18503. No way is barred to virtue. *Latin*

18504. Our virtues would be proud if our vices whipped them not. *English*

18505. Poverty does not destroy virtue, nor wealth bestow it. *Spanish*

18506. Purchase the next world with this; you will win both. *Arabic*

18507. Seek virtue, and of that possest, to providence resign the rest. *American (Franklin)*

18508. Silver is less valuable than gold, and gold than virtue. *Latin (Horace)*

18509. Successful villainy is called virtue. *Latin (Seneca)*

18510. The excellency of hogs is — fatness; of men — virtue. *American (Franklin)*

18511. The first step to virtue is to love virtue in another. *American*

18512. The memory of the just is blessed. *Bible*

18513. The path of the just is as the shining light. *Bible*

18514. The perfect good is the exercise of virtue. *Greek*

18515. Through virtue lies the road to peace. *Latin*

18516. Virtue alone has majesty in death. *English (Young)*

18517. Virtue alone is the sign of a noble soul. *French*

18518. Virtue and happiness are mother and daughter. *American (Franklin)*

18519. Virtue and honesty are cheap at any price. *American*

18520. Virtue brings honor, and honor vanity. *English*

18521. Virtue conquers envy. *Latin*

18522. Virtue crowns her worshippers. *Latin*

18523. Virtue even in rags will keep warm. *Latin*

18524. Virtue flourishes in misfortune. *German*

18525. Virtue has no greater enemy than wealth. *Italian*

18526. Virtue is a shield. *Latin*

18527. Virtue is abune [above] value. *Scottish*

18528. Virtue is an anchor. *Latin*

18529. Virtue is despised if it be seen in a threadbare cloak. *English*

18530. Virtue is harmony. *Greek*

18531. Virtue is its own reward. *English*

18532. Virtue is not hereditary. *Chinese*

18533. Virtue is not left to stand alone. *Chinese*

18534. Virtue is nothing if not difficult. *Latin*

18535. Virtue is praised, and starves. *Latin*

18536. Virtue is stronger than a battering ram. *Latin*

18537. Virtue is the base for the prosperity of an empire. *Chinese*

18538. Virtue is the health of the soul. *French (Joubert)*

18539. Virtue is the only true nobility. *Latin*

18540. Virtue is the path of praise. *Greek*

18541. Virtue joins man to God. *Latin (Cicero)*

18542. Virtue lies halfway between two opposite vices. *Latin (Horace)*

18543. Virtue lives beyond the grave. *Latin*

18544. Virtue may be gay, yet with dignity. *Latin*

18545. Virtue must be followed for its own sake. *French*

18546. Virtue ne'er grows auld [old]. *Scottish*

18547. Virtue of itself is sufficient for happiness. *Greek*

18548. Virtue often trips and falls on the sharp-edged rock of poverty. *French*

18549. Virtue only is necessary. *Latin*

18550. Virtue our leader, fortune our companion. *Latin*

18551. Virtue overcomes envy. *Latin*

18552. Virtue passes current all over the world. *Greek*

18553. Virtue proceeds through toil. *Greek*

18554. Virtue survives the grave. *Irish*

18555. Virtue, when concealed, has no value. *Latin*

18556. Virtue which parlays is near a surrender. *Latin*

18557. Virtue will triumph. *American*

18558. Virtue withers without opposition. *Latin*

18559. Virtues all agree, but vices fight one another. *American*

18560. We love justice greatly, and just men but little. *French*

18561. Where there is not virtue, there can be no liberty. *Arabic*

18562. Whether I am praised or blamed, I can advance in virtue. *Chinese*

18563. With virtue one may conquer the world. *Chinese*

18564. You make a virtue of necessity. *Latin*

Vision

18565. When there is no vision, the people perish. *Bible*

Visiting *see also* Guests; Hospitality; Uninvited Guests

18566. A long stay changes friendship. *French*

18567. Friends are lost by calling often and calling seldom. *Gaelic*

18568. Friendship increases by visiting friends, but by visiting seldom. *American (Franklin)*

18569. Kenned [known] folks are nae [not] company. *Scottish*

18570. Leave welcome aye behint [behind] you. [Do not overstay your welcome.] *Scottish*

18571. The man who does not visit me in time of war will not be welcome in time of peace. *Arabic*

18572. Visitors, if they did not visit, would do nothing. *American*

18573. Visits always give pleasure; if not in arriving, then in departing. *Portuguese*

18574. Visits should be short, like a winter's day. *American*

Vituperation

18575. We can bear evil deeds better than evil tongues. *American*

Vivacity

18576. The vivacity that increases with years is not far from folly. *American*

18577. Vivacity in youth is often mistaken for genius, and solidity for dullness. *American*

18578. Vivacity is the gift of woman. *American*

18579. Vivacity is the health of the spirit. *American*

Voice

18580. A sweet voice is often a devil's arrow that reaches the heart. *American*

18581. All voice, and beyond that, nothing. *Latin*

18582. He who has no voice in the valley will have none in the council. *Spanish*

18583. The living voice moves. *Latin*

18584. The voice is the guardian of the mind. *American*

18585. The voice is the music of the heart. *American*

18586. The voice of him that crieth in the wilderness. *Bible*

18587. The voice of the pigeon in the spit is not like the voice of the pigeon in the tree. *American*

Voluptuousness

18588. Voluptuousness, like justice, is blind, but that is the only resemblance between them. *American*

Vows *see* Promises

Vulgarity

18589. Never descend to vulgarity even in joking. *Latin*

18590. No medicine can cure a vulgar man. *Chinese*

18591. Success will popularize the grossest vulgarity. *American*

18592. To endeavor to work upon the vulgar with fine sense is like attempting to hew blocks with a razor. *American*

18593. Vulgar minds growl beneath their load; the brave bear theirs without repining. *American*

18594. Vulgarity defiles fine garments more than mud. *Latin*

Vulnerability *see also* Common Sense; Weakness; Weak Links

18595. A man may worship fire for a hundred years, but still he will burn. *Persian*

18596. A thunderbolt strikes a tall house most often. *American*

18597. Even the lion must defend himself against the flies. *English*

18598. Girls and glass are always in danger. *Italian*

18599. Glasses and lasses are bruckle [brittle] wares. *Scottish*

18600. Let him that has a glass skull not take to stone-throwing. *Italian*

18601. Let him that has glass tiles [panes] not throw stones at his neighbor's house. *Italian*

18602. Man is the only animal that can be skinned more than once. *American*

18603. Nothing is so secure as not to be in danger of the attack, even by the weak. *Latin (Quintus Curtius)*

18604. The bigger the man, the better the mark. *American*

18605. The cockroach is always wrong where the fowl is concerned. *Trinidad Creole*

18606. The cockroach never wins its cause when the chicken is judge. *Haitian Creole*

18607. The village is in a bad way whose doctor has gout. *Welsh*

18608. To have the knife by the blade. *Belizean Creole*

18609. When cockroach make dance, him no ax fowl. *Haitian Creole*

18610. Who carries butter on his head should not walk in the sun. *Yiddish*

18611. Who has a head of wax must not come near the fire. *French*

18612. Who hath skirts of straw needs fear the fire. *Spanish*

18613. Who mixes himself with the draff will be eaten by the swine. *Danish*

18614. Your life is like a tobacco-pipe [or the shank of a tobacco-pipe]. *Efik*

Waiting *see also* Patience

18615. Everything comes to those who wait. *French*

18616. He who can wait obtains what he wishes. *Italian*

18617. He who waits for another man's platter has a cold meal. *Spanish*

18618. If you wait upon fortune, you'll never be sure of your dinner. *American*

18619. Learn to labor and to wait. *American (Longfellow)*

18620. Seven never waited for one. *Russian*

18621. The future belongs to him who knows how to wait. *Russian*

18622. They also serve who only stand and wait. *English (Milton)*

18623. To know how to wait is the great secret of success. *French*

18624. "Wait" is a hard word to the hungry. *German*

Walls

18625. A wall between preserves love. *American*

18626. It is bad to lean against a falling wall. *Danish*

18627. When a wall is cracked and lofty, its fall will be speedy. *Chinese*

Want *see* Necessity; Need

Wantonness

18628. As wanton as a wet hen. *Scottish*

War *see also* Peace; War and Peace

18629. A wise man should try everything before resorting to war. *Latin*

18630. A's [all's] fair in war. *Scottish*

18631. After the war many heroes present themselves. *Romanian*

18632. Distant drum, sweet music. *Turkish*

18633. Even the winner of a war suffers from lack of bread. *Czech*

18634. God is on the side of the big battalions. *French*
18635. Gold and riches — the causes of war. *Latin*
18636. He that makes a good war makes a good peace. *Italian*
18637. He that preacheth up war, when it may be avoided, is the devil's chaplain. *English*
18638. He who has land has war. *Italian*
18639. He who likes war, let him have it in his own house. *Serbian*
18640. In war it is best to tie your horse to a strange manger. *Danish*
18641. In war it is not permitted to make a mistake twice. *Greek*
18642. In war, you become ashes if you lose — and charcoal if you win. *Malaysian*
18643. It is a bad war from which no one returns. *German*
18644. Let him who does not know what war is go to war. *Spanish*
18645. Little reason is there in arms. *Latin*
18646. Mind avails most in war. *Latin*
18647. Talk of the war, but do not go to it. *Spanish*
18648. That war is only just which is necessary. *American*
18649. The right of war: let him take who can take. *French*
18650. The war god hates those who hesitate. *Greek*
18651. They make a desert and call it peace. *Latin (Tacitus)*
18652. To die or conquer are the terms of war. *Greek*
18653. War begun, hell let loose. *Italian*
18654. War brings scars. *English*
18655. War does not spare the brave, but the coward. *Greek*
18656. War gives no opportunity for repeating a mistake. *Latin*
18657. War, hunting, and love have a thousand pains for one pleasure. *Spanish*
18658. War is death's feast. *American*
18659. War is deceit. *Lebanese*
18660. War is hell. *American (Sherman)*
18661. War is sweet to those who have not experienced it. *Latin*
18662. War is the trade of kings. *English (Dryden)*
18663. War loves to seek its victims in the young. *Greek*
18664. War should neither be feared nor provoked. *Latin (Pliny)*
18665. War's sweet to them that never tried it. *Scottish*
18666. Weapons bode peace. *Scottish*
18667. When drums beat laws are dumb. *Scottish*
18668. When war comes, the devil makes hell bigger. *German*
18669. When war is raging, the laws are dumb. *Latin*

War and Peace *see also* Peace; War

18670. Better to have bread in peace than a fat calf in war. *Hungarian*
18671. Even if you have the strength of an elephant and the courage of a lion, peace is better than war. *Iranian*
18672. Fame will be won in peace as well as in war. *Latin*
18673. If you desire peace be ever prepared for war. *American*
18674. Of mortal war you can make peace well. *French*
18675. Peace feeds, war wastes; peace breeds, war consumes. *Danish*
18676. Peace hath her victories no less renown'd than war. *English (Milton)*
18677. Peace is more powerful than war. *Latin*
18678. Peace with a cudgel in hand is war. *Portuguese*
18679. War makes thieves, and peace hangs them. *Italian*

Wariness *see* Carefulness; Caution; Vigilance; Watchfulness

Warning

18680. A dog will bark ere he bites. *English*
18681. A wreck on shore is a beacon at sea. *Dutch*
18682. Dogs ought to bark before they bite. *English*
18683. He was slain that had warning, not he that took it. *English*
18684. The dog that bites does not bark in vain. *Italian*
18685. The tempest threatens before it comes; houses creak before they fall. *Latin*

Waste

18686. Cast not pearls to swine. *English*
18687. He's nae gude [not a good] weaver that leaves lang thrums [waste threads]. *Scottish*
18688. Much water flows in the dam, whilst the miller sleeps. *Danish*
18689. Quey caufs are dear veal. [Young cows are too valuable to be sold as veal.] *Scottish*
18690. The sow has been greeted with music. *Latin*
18691. To sing to an ass. *Latin*
18692. Waste makes want. *English*
18693. Waste not, want not. *English*
18694. Wilfu' waste maks woefu' want. *Scottish*

Waste of Time *see also* Delay; Deliberation; Opportunity; Timeliness

18695. As good have no time as make no good use of it. *English*
18696. Dost thou love life? Then do not squander time; for that's the stuff life is made of. *American (Franklin)*
18697. However the fool delays, the day does not delay. *French*
18698. Lost time is never found again, and what we call time enough always proves little enough. *English*
18699. What an amount of good time you lose over a bad matter. *Latin (Seneca)*
18700. Prodigality of time produces poverty of mind as well as of estate. *American (Franklin)*
18701. The greatest sacrifice is the sacrifice of time. *Greek*
18702. The shortest day is too long to waste. *American*
18703. The time best employed is that which one wastes. *French*

18704. They who sing through the summer must dance in the winter. *English*

18705. Those who make the worst use of time, most complain of its shortness. *French (La Bruyere)*

18706. Time lost cannot be recalled. *English*

18707. Time tint [lost] is ne'er found. *Scottish*

18708. Time wasted is existence; used, is life. *English (Young)*

18709. What greater crime than loss of time? *English*

Watchfulness *see also* Carefulness; Caution; Circumspection

18710. A girl, a vineyard, an orchard, and a beanfield are hard to watch. *American*

18711. A mariner must have his eye upon rocks and sands, as well as upon the North Star. *English*

18712. A watchman is the guarantee of peace. *Tunisian*

18713. Be ever vigilant, but never suspicious. *American*

18714. Beware of storms by day and thieves by night. *Chinese*

18715. Beware of the forepart of a woman, the hind part of a mule, and every side of a priest. *Scottish*

18716. Beware of the man who kisses your child; he'll be kissing your wife in due time. *American*

18717. Don't set a fox [or a wolf] to watch the geese. *American*

18718. He has eyes in the back of his head. *Latin*

18719. He is most free from danger, who, even when safe, is on guard. *American*

18720. If the pilot slumber at the helm, the very wind that wafts us toward the port, may dash us on the shoals. *American*

18721. It is good to get out of the net, but better not to get into it. *American*

18722. It is the enemy who keeps the sentinel watchful. *American*

18723. Open eyes are the best signpost. *American*

18724. Sleep not in time of peril. *Latin*

18725. The master's eye makes the horse fat. *Greek*

18726. The master's eye will do more work than both his hands. *English*

18727. The sleeping saint is no match for the vigilant villain. *American*

18728. To him that watches, everything is revealed. *Italian*

18729. Watch your step. *American*

18730. Who busy hath need of a hundred eyes; who sells hath enough of one. *English*

Water

18731. Water washes everything. *Portuguese*

Weak Links

18732. The hedge is trodden down where it seems to lean [i.e., at its weakest point]. *Latin*

18733. The thread breaks where it is thinnest. *Spanish*

18734. Where it is weakest there the thread breaketh. *English*

18735. Where something is thin, that is where it tears. *Russian*

Weakness *see also* Vulnerability; Weak Links

18736. Be not like the dumb cattle, driven. *American*

18737. Best dealing with an enemy when you take him at his weakest. *American*

18738. Every man has his weak side. *Greek*

18739. In a just cause the weak overcome the strong. *Greek*

18740. The weakest goes to the wall. *English (Shakespeare)*

18741. The weakest must hold the candle. *French*

18742. Weak food is best for weak stomachs. *American*

18743. Where it is weakest there the thread breaketh. *English*

Wealth *see also* Money; Poverty; Rich and Poor

18744. A fu' purse maks a man speak. *Scottish*

18745. A fu' purse never lacks friends. *Scottish*

18746. A golden bit does not make a better horse. *Latin*

18747. A great estate is not gotten in a few hours. *French*

18748. A great fortune in the hands of a fool is a great misfortune. *English*

18749. A great fortune is a great slavery. *Latin (Publilius Syrus)*

18750. A gude year winna [will not] mak him, nor an ill year mar him. *Scottish*

18751. A man of wealth is a slave to his possessions. *American*

18752. A man that keeps riches and enjoys them not, is like an ass that carries gold and eats thistles. *English*

18753. A man's wealth may be superior to him. *African*

18754. A rich man has mair [more] cousins than his faither had kin. *Scottish*

18755. A rich man is either a rogue or the heir of a rogue. *Latin*

18756. A rich man is never ugly in the eye of a girl. *American*

18757. A rich man knows not his friends. *American*

18758. A rich man's foolish sayings pass for wise ones. *American*

18759. A shroud has no pockets. *Scottish*

18760. All ask if a man be rich, none if he be good. *American*

18761. Among us most sacred of all is the majesty of wealth. *Latin*

18762. An ass is but an ass though laden with gold. *American*

18763. An excess of hoarded wealth is the death of many. *Latin (Juvenal)*

18764. As money grows, greed for greater riches follows after. *Latin*

18765. At the door of the rich are many friends. *Hebrew*

18766. Command your wealth, else that will command you. *English*

18767. Common sense among men of fortune is rare. *Latin*

18768. Elbow grease makes wealth increase. *American*

18769. Everyone is kin to the rich man. *Italian*

18770. Get what you can, and keep what you hae [have], that's the way to get rich. *Scottish*

18771. God regards pure hands, not full. *Latin*

18772. Gold goes in at any gate, except Heaven's. *English*

18773. Gold goes to the Moor [i.e., to the man without a conscience]. *Portuguese*

18774. Gold hath been the ruin of many. *Bible*

18775. Gold is not grown from seed, but only springs up in diligent and economical families. *Chinese*

18776. Gold is tested by fire; man by gold. *Chinese*

18777. Gold is the greatest enemy in the world. *Japanese*

18778. Gold will not buy everything. *Italian*

18779. Great wealth implies great loss. *Chinese (Laotse)*

18780. Great wealth troubles its owner, as too much food causes discomfort to the eater. *Chinese*

18781. He alone is rich who makes proper use of his riches. *American*

18782. He does not possess wealth, it possesses him. *American (Franklin)*

18783. He enjoys riches most who needs them least. *Latin*

18784. He has wealth who knows how to use it. *Latin*

18785. He heapeth up riches and knoweth not who shall gather them. *Bible*

18786. He is not fit for riches who is afraid to use them. *English*

18787. He is not rich who is not satisfied. *American*

18788. He is rich, that is satisfied. *English*

18789. He is richest that has fewest wants. *Latin (Cicero)*

18790. He that has siller [silver] in his purse may want a head on his shoulders. *Scottish*

18791. He that is drunk with wine gets sober; he that is drunk with wealth does not. *Zanzibar*

18792. He that maketh haste to be rich shall not be innocent. *Bible*

18793. He that never fails never grows rich. *Italian*

18794. He who hastens to be rich incurs peril. *Chinese*

18795. He who multiplies riches multiplies cares. *American (Franklin)*

18796. He who wants riches, wants them at once. *Latin*

18797. How you come by it no one asks; but wealth you must have. *Latin*

18798. I never knew a silent rich man. *French*

18799. If the superior man desires wealth, he gets it in a proper fashion. *Chinese*

18800. If you have money you are able to speak; if you have clothing you can be polite. *Chinese*

18801. If your riches are yours, why don't you take them with you to t'other world? *American (Franklin)*

18802. Is it not sheer madness to live poor to die rich? *Latin (Juvenal)*

18803. It is easier for a camel to go through the eye of a needle, than for a rich man to enter into the Kingdom of God. *Bible*

18804. It's we who earn money; we are not earned by it. *Lettish*

18805. Lay not up for yourselves treasures upon earth where moth and rust doth corrupt. *Bible*

18806. Little wealth, little care. *English*

18807. Many a man would have been worse if his estate had been better. *American*

18808. Many an Irish property was increased by the lace of a daughter's petticoat. *Irish*

18809. Men make wealth and women preserve it. *Italian*

18810. Money, as it increases, becomes either the master or the slave of its owner. *Latin (Horace)*

18811. Money comes to money. *American*

18812. Money is a good passe-partout. [It gains admittance anywhere.] *French*

18813. Money rules the world. *Dutch*

18814. Morals are corrupted by the worship of riches. *Latin*

18815. Much coin, much care. *Latin*

18816. Much industry and little conscience make a man rich. *German*

18817. No just man ever became rich all at once. *Greek*

18818. Nothing prevails against wealth. *Latin*

18819. Of lawful wealth the devil takes the half; of unlawful, the whole and the owner, too. *Turkish*

18820. Our last garment is made without pockets. *Italian*

18821. Pawn your last shirt — only to be rich. *Yiddish*

18822. Pearls around the neck — stones upon the heart. *Yiddish*

18823. Real wealth consists not in having, but in not wanting. *Latin*

18824. Rich for yourself, poor for your friends. *Latin*

18825. Rich fowk [folk] hae routh [plenty] o' freends. *Scottish*

18826. Rich men are everywhere at home. *German*

18827. Riches abuse them who know not how to use them. *English*

18828. Riches and cares are inseparable. *American*

18829. Riches and virtue do not often keep each other company. *American*

18830. Riches are first to be sought for; after wealth, virtue. *Latin (Horace)*

18831. Riches are like muck, which is useless in a heap, but spread abroad makes the earth fruitful. *English*

18832. Riches are often abused, but never refused. *Danish*

18833. Riches are the pillar of the world. *African*

18834. Riches bring oft harm, and ever fear. *English*

18835. Riches can solder up an abundance of flaws. *Spanish*

18836. Riches cover a multitude of woes. *Greek*

18837. Riches either serve or govern the possessor. *Latin*

18838. Riches fly away as an eagle toward heaven. *Bible*

18839. Riches have wings. *English*

18840. Riches rather enlarge than satisfy appetites. *English*

18841. Riches serve a wise man, but command a fool. *French*

18842. Riches, the incentives to evil, are dug out of the earth. *Latin*

18843. So he be rich, even a barbarian pleases. *Latin*

18844. Some people are masters of money, and some its slaves. *Russian*

18845. The abuse of riches is worse than the want of them. *American*

18846. The acquisition of wealth is a great toil, its possession a great terror, its loss a great tribulation. *Latin*

18847. The ass loaded with gold still eats thistles. *German*

18848. The best choice is wealth. *Welsh*

18849. The foolish sayings of the rich pass for wise saws. *Spanish*

18850. The house laughs with silver. *Latin*

18851. The larger a man's roof, the more snow it collects. *Persian*

18852. The lust for wealth can never bear delay. *Latin*

18853. The man of means is by no means honored: it's his money that receives our respect. *American*

18854. The rich and ignorant are sheep with golden wool. *American*

18855. The rich can eat with only one mouth. *German*

18856. The rich man has more relations than he knows. *French*

18857. The rich never lack relatives. *American*

18858. The richest man carries nothing away with him but his shroud. *French*

18859. The river does not become swollen with clear water. *Italian*

18860. The shortest way to riches is by contempt of riches. *Latin*

18861. There is no better friend in misfortune than gold. *German*

18862. There is no revenge upon the rich. *Spanish*

18863. There is pain in acquiring wealth, pain in keeping it, pain in losing it, and pain in spending it—why have so much sorrow? *Sanskrit*

18864. To be rich, one must have a relation at home with the devil. *Italian*

18865. To become rich one has only to turn one's back on God. *French*

18866. To gain wealth is easy; to keep it, hard. *Chinese*

18867. To have acquired wealth is with many not to end their troubles but to change the nature of their troubles. *Latin (Seneca)*

18868. Virtue and riches seldom settle on one man. *Italian*

18869. We must spurn riches, the diploma of slavery. *Latin*

18870. Wealth breeds satiety; satiety, outrage. *Greek*

18871. Wealth conquered Rome after Rome had conquered the world. *Italian*

18872. Wealth excuses folly. *Latin*

18873. Wealth gotten by vanity is diminished. *Bible*

18874. Wealth has made mair [more] men covetous than covetousness has made men wealthy. *Scottish*

18875. Wealth in the widow's house, kail but [without] salt. *Scottish*

18876. Wealth is best known by want. *English*

18877. Wealth is like rheumatism; it falls on the weakest parts. *English*

18878. Wealth is not acquired by our own labors, but inherited. *Latin*

18879. Wealth is not his that has it, but his that enjoys it. *Italian*

18880. Wealth lightens not the heart and care of man. *Latin*

18881. Wealth, like an index, reveals the character of men. *Latin*

18882. Wealth, like want, ruins mony [many]. *Scottish*

18883. Wealth makes wit waver. *Scottish (Scott)*

18884. Wealth makes worship. *English*

18885. Wealth maketh many friends. *Bible*

18886. Wealth serves for heroism; wine for bravery. *Chinese*

18887. Wealth unused might as well not exist. *Greek (Aesop)*

18888. What ye want up and doun ye hae [have] hither and yont. *Scottish*

18889. When riches increase, the body decreaseth. *English*

18890. Where gold speaks every tongue is silenced. *Italian*

18891. Who would be rich in a year gets hanged in half a year. *Spanish*

18892. Without a rich heart, wealth is an ugly beggar. *American (Emerson)*

18893. Would you become rich? Be a pig for seven years. *Yiddish*

18894. You may speak with your gold, and make other tongues dumb. *Italian*

Weapons

18895. A man of courage never wants weapons. *American*

18896. A weapon is an enemy even to its owner. *Turkish*

18897. The robber and the cautious traveler both carry swords; the one uses it as a means of attack, the other as a means of defense. *Latin (Ovid)*

18898. They who fight with golden weapons are sure to prove their right. *Dutch*

Wear

18899. Everything is the worse for wearing. *American*

18900. It is better to wear out than to rust out. *American*

Weariness *see also* Rest

18901. The ox when weariest is most surefooted [or treads surest]. *Latin*

Weather

18902. A poor man's rain. [Rain at night that does not interfere with the labor of outdoor workers.] *English*

18903. After clouds a clear sun. *Latin*

18904. Change of weather is the discourse of fools. *English*

18905. Everybody talks about the weather, but nobody does anything about it. *American (Twain)*
18906. Fair weather cometh out of the north. *Bible*
18907. On a hot day mu!e yourself the more. *Spanish*

Weddings *see also* Brides

18908. A man may weep upon his wedding day. *English (Shakespeare)*
18909. A shotgun marriage won't last longer than the honeymoon. *American*
18910. Happy is the bride that the sun shines on; happy is the corpse that the rain rains on. *Scottish*
18911. Marriage in May is unlucky. *Russian*
18912. Marry in Lent, live to repent. *English*
18913. Marry in May, repent alway. *Latin (Ovid)*

Weeping

18914. A small tear relieves a great sorrow. *English*
18915. Better the child cry than the old man. *Danish*
18916. Better the cottage where one is merry than the palace where one weeps. *Chinese*
18917. He who weeps from the heart can provoke even the blind to tears. *Russian*
18918. It is as much intemperance to weep too much, as to laugh too much. *Latin (Tacitus)*
18919. Love is loveliest when embalmed in tears. *American*
18920. Man is the weeping animal born to govern all the rest. *American*
18921. Men given to tears are good. *Greek*
18922. More tears are shed in playhouses than in churches. *American*
18923. Scorn the proud man that is ashamed to weep. *American*
18924. Shed tears boldly: weeping is nature's mark to know an honest heart by. *American*
18925. Tears are no proof of cowardice. *American*
18926. Tears are the natural penalties of pleasure. *American*
18927. Tears hinder sorrow from becoming despair. *American*
18928. Tears of joy are the dew in which the sun of righteousness is mirrored. *American*
18929. There is a certain kind of pleasure in weeping. *Latin (Ovid)*
18930. There's no seeing one's way through tears. *English*
18931. They who are sad find somehow sweetness in tears. *Greek (Euripides)*
18932. Weeping makes the heart grow lighter. *Yiddish*
18933. When the vulture dies, the hen does not weep. *German*
18934. Who would recognize the unhappy if grief had no language? *Latin (Publilius Syrus)*

Welcome

18935. Harsh is the voice which would dismiss us, but sweet is the sound of welcome. *Latin*
18936. He who brings is welcome. *German*
18937. He's as welcome as snaw [snow] in hairst [harvest]. *Scottish*
18938. He's as welcome as water in a riven ship. *Scottish*
18939. His room 's better than his company. *Scottish*
18940. His worth is warrant for his welcome. *American*
18941. Small cheer and great welcome make a merry feast. *American*
18942. Stay nae langer [no longer] in a friend's house than ye're welcome. *Scottish*
18943. Welcome is the best cheer. *Greek*
18944. Welcome's the best dish in the kitchen. *Scottish*
18945. Who comes seldom is welcome. *Italian*

Wholesomeness

18946. All sweets are not wholesome. *American*

Wickedness *see also* Badness; Evil

18947. A wicked companion invites us all to hell. *American*
18948. A wicked man is afraid of his own memory. *American*
18949. A wicked man is his own hell. *English*
18950. A wicked man's gift hath a touch of his master. *English*
18951. Even the wicked hate vice in others. *English*
18952. God bears with the wicked, but not forever. *Spanish*
18953. He that lives wickedly can hardly die honestly. *English*
18954. He who brings aid to the wicked, grieves for it later. *Latin*
18955. Most men are wicked. *Greek*
18956. Never was the wicked wise. *Greek*
18957. No man ever became wicked all at once. *Latin*
18958. No man is so wicked as to wish to appear wicked. *Latin*
18959. The sun shines even on the wicked. *Latin*
18960. The sure way to wickedness is through wickedness. *Latin (Seneca)*
18961. The triumphing of the wicked is short. *Bible*
18962. The way of the wicked is as darkness. *Bible*
18963. The wicked shun the light as the devil shuns the cross. *Dutch*
18964. The wickedness of a few is the calamity of all. *Latin*
18965. There is no peace, saith the Lord, unto the wicked. *Bible*
18966. Wicked ears are deaf to wisdom's voice. *Greek*
18967. Wicked men cannot be friends. *Greek*
18968. Wickedness proceedeth from the wicked. *Bible*
18969. Ye have ploughed wickedness, ye have reaped iniquity. *Bible*

Widows

18970. A buxom widow must be either married, buried or shut up in a convent. *Spanish*
18971. A girl receives — a widow takes, her husband. *American*
18972. A rich widow weeps with one eye and laughs with the other. *Portuguese*
18973. A widow is a rudderless boat. *Chinese*

18974. Better a young widow than an old maid. *Yiddish*

18975. He that marries a widow and three children marries four thieves. *English*

18976. He that marries a widow will often have a dead man's head thrown into his dish. *Spanish*

18977. In the widow's house there's no fat mouse. *Turkish*

18978. Ne'er marry a widow unless her first man was hanged. *Scottish*

18979. One can with dignity be wife and widow but once. *French*

18980. Slanders cluster thick around a widow's door. *Chinese*

18981. The rich widow's tears soon dry. *Danish*

18982. Widows are always rich. *English*

Wife *see* Husbands and Wives; Marriage; Wives: Choosing a Wife

Will

18983. A fat kitchen, a lean will. *German*

18984. A man's will is his heaven. *Danish*

18985. He that winna [will not] when he may, shanna [shall not] when he wad [would]. *Scottish*

18986. He who is firm in will molds the world to himself. *German (Goethe)*

18987. He who wills is the man who can. *French*

18988. He who wills the end wills the means. *English*

18989. If we cannot do what we will, we must will what we can. *Yiddish*

18990. No one can rob us of our free will. *Greek (Epictetus)*

18991. Nothing is impossible to the man that can will. *American*

18992. Tak your ain [own] will and ye'll no dee o' the pet. *Scottish*

18993. Tak your ain [own] will o't, as the cat did o' the haggis—first ate it, and then creepit [crept] into the bag. *Scottish*

18994. The good or ill of man lies within his own will. *Greek (Epictetus)*

18995. The man who has the will to undergo all labor may aspire to any goal. *Greek*

18996. The means were wanting, not the will. *Latin*

18997. The will cannot be compelled. *Latin*

18998. The will does it. *German*

18999. The will is the soul of the work. *German*

19000. The will of even a common man cannot be taken away from him. *Chinese (Confucius)*

19001. There is nothing good or evil save in the will. *Greek*

19002. Though the power be wanting, the will deserves praise. *Latin (Ovid)*

19003. To him that wills, ways are seldom wanting. *Scottish*

19004. Where the will is ready, the feet are light. *English*

19005. Where there's a will there's a way. *Spanish*

19006. Will is character in action. *American*

19007. Will is the cause of woe. *English*

19008. Will will have wilt though will woe win. *English*

Willfulness

19009. A wilfu' man maun hae [must have] his way. *Scottish*

19010. A wilfu' man never wanted wae [lacked woe]. *Scottish*

19011. A wilfu' man should be unco [uncommonly] wise. *Scottish*

19012. A wilful fault has no excuse, and deserves no pardon. *English*

19013. He hears na [not] at that ear. *Scottish*

19014. He wa'd na gie ae [would not give an] inch o' his will for a span o' his thrift. *Scottish*

19015. Wilful will do it. *English*

19016. Wilfulness is more terrible than slavery. *Russian*

19017. Ye breed o' oor laird, ye'll no do right and ye'll tak nae wrang. *Scottish*

19018. Ye'll neither dance nor haud the candle. *Scottish*

19019. Ye're like a sow, ye'll neither lead nor drive. *Scottish*

Willingness

19020. A man may lead a horse to the water, but four-and-twenty cannot gar [make] him drink. *Scottish*

19021. A voluntary burden is not a burden. *Italian*

19022. A willing helper does not wait to be called. *Danish*

19023. A willing mind makes a light foot. *English*

19024. All lay load on the willing horse. *English*

19025. Better a friendly refusal than an unwilling promise. *German*

19026. He that cannot is always willing. *Italian*

19027. He that hath love in his breast hath spurs in his sides. *English*

19028. He that will does more than he can. *Portuguese*

19029. He who is willing is able. *German*

19030. Help him who is willing to work, not him who shrinks from it. *Latin*

19031. I am willing but unable. *Latin*

19032. It is bad coursing with unwilling hounds. *Dutch*

19033. It is no good leading the ox to the water if he is not thirsty. *French*

19034. Nothing is difficult to a willing mind. *English*

19035. Nothing is troublesome that we do willingly. *American (Jefferson)*

19036. The willing dancer is easily played to. *Serbian*

19037. To be willing is to be able. *French*

19038. When a man's / Willing and eager, God joins in. *Greek (Aeschylus)*

19039. Where the will is prompt the legs are nimble. *Italian*

19040. Where the will is ready the feet are light. *German*

19041. You cannot make an ass drink when he does not wish to. *French*

Wine *see also* Drinking and Drunkenness

19042. Bronze is the mirror of the form; wine, of the heart. *Greek*

19043. Corn shall make the young men cheerful, and new wine the maids. *Bible*

19044. Give, in return for old wine, a new song. *Latin*

19045. I like best the wine another pays for. *Greek*

19046. If sack and sugar be a fault, God help the wicked! *English (Shakespeare)*

19047. Inflaming wine dulls the noble heart. *Greek*

19048. Its sinfulness is greater than its use. *Koran*

19049. Neither do men put old wine into new bottles. *Bible*

19050. No one so wise but wine makes a fool of him. *German*

19051. Of what use is the cup of gold if the wine be sour? *German*

19052. Since the wine is drawn it must be drunk. *French*

19053. The best wine has its lees. *French*

19054. The master's wine is in the butler's gift. *Latin*

19055. Thick wine is better than clear water. *Italian*

19056. Truth and folly dwell in the wine cask. *Danish*

19057. When the wine is in, the wit is out. *Italian*

19058. Where there is no wine there is no love. *Greek*

19059. Wine carries no rudder. *Latin*

19060. Wine enters the stomach, and business grows ripe in the brain. *Chinese*

19061. Wine gives courage and makes men apt for passion. *Latin*

19062. Wine in excess keeps neither secrets nor promises. *Spanish*

19063. Wine is a cunning wrestler: it catches you by the feet. *Latin*

19064. Wine is a mocker; strong drink is raging. *Bible*

19065. Wine is one thing; drunkenness another. *Latin*

19066. Wine is the milk of old men. *French*

19067. Wine kindles wrath. *Latin (Seneca)*

19068. Wine reveals one's inner mind. *Japanese*

19069. Wine to the poet is a winged steed. *Greek*

19070. Wine will not keep in a foul vessel. *French*

Winning and Losing *see also* Gambling; Profit and Loss; Risk; Venture

19071. At the end of the game you'll see who's the winner. *English*

19072. Give losers leave to talk. *English*

19073. He that blows best bears away the horn. *Scottish*

19074. It is a silly game where nobody wins. *Italian*

19075. Let him laugh, who is on the right side of the hedge. *English*

19076. Let him laugh who wins. *English*

19077. Losers are always in the wrong. *Spanish*

19078. The conqueror weeps, the conquered is ruined. *Latin*

19079. The victor is always justified. *Bosnian*

19080. The world is on the side of the man left standing. *Arabic*

19081. There are games in which it is better to lose than win. *Latin (Plautus)*

19082. They laugh that win. *English (Shakespeare)*

19083. When ane winna [one will not], twa canna [two cannot] cast out. *Scottish*

19084. When two play, one must lose. *American*

19085. Who wins, plays best. *German*

19086. Win't and wear't. *Scottish*

Winter

19087. As the days lengthen, so the storms strengthen. *English*

19088. Every mile is two in winter. *English (Herbert)*

19089. If Winter comes, can Spring be far behind? *English (Shelley)*

19090. The daytime grows, the cold grows, says the fisherman. *Italian*

Wisdom *see also* Fools and Folly; Wisdom and Folly

19091. A man may be born to a heritage, but wisdom comes only with length of days. *Yoruba*

19092. A mind enlightened is like heaven; a mind in darkness is like hell. *Chinese*

19093. A wise head maks [makes] a close mouth. *Scottish*

19094. A wise lawyer never gangs [goes] to law himsel. *Scottish*

19095. A wise man gets learning frae [from] them that hae nane o' their ain [have none of their own]. *Scottish*

19096. A wise man hears one word and understands two. *Yiddish*

19097. A wise man is not wise in everything. *French*

19098. A wise man is out of the reach of fortune. *English*

19099. A wise man needs three assistants. *Chinese*

19100. A wise man sees as much as he ought, not as much as he can. *French*

19101. A wise man who knows proverbs reconciles difficulties. *Yoruba*

19102. A wise man will overrule the stars. *Latin*

19103. A wise man — a strong man. *German*

19104. A word to the wise is sufficient. *American*

19105. Be ye therefore wise as serpents, and harmless as doves. *Bible*

19106. Better be mad with all the world than wise alone. *French*

19107. Better be wise than rich. *Spanish*

19108. Dare to be wise. *Latin*

19109. Dust never stains a polished mirror; nor does vice generate in an enlightened mind. *Chinese*

19110. Enlightened men pronounce sentence on themselves. *Chinese*

19111. He is not called wise who knows good and ill, but he who can recognize of two evils the lesser. *Hebrew*

19112. He is not wise that is not wise for himself. *Greek*

19113. He is very wise who is not foolish for long. *Latin*

19114. He is wise enough that can keep himself warm. *English*

19115. He is wise that is 'ware in time. *Scottish*

19116. He is wise to no purpose, who is not wise for himself. *Latin*

19117. He knows much who knows how to hold his tongue. *English*

19118. He that has grown to wisdom does not hurry. *Italian*

19119. He that's wise by day is no fool by night. *English*

19120. He who is wise before his time will die before he is old. *Latin*

19121. He's wise that kens [knows] when he's weel enough. *Scottish*

19122. He's wise that's timely wary. *Scottish*

19123. How cautious are the wise! *Greek (Homer)*

19124. In much wisdom is much grief. *Bible*

19125. In youth and beauty wisdom is but rare. *Greek (Homer)*

19126. It becomes all wise men to confer and converse. *Latin*

19127. It is easier to be wise for others than for yourself. *French*

19128. It is not good to be always wise. *German*

19129. It is not wise to be wiser than is necessary. *French*

19130. It takes a wise man to recognize a wise man. *Greek*

19131. Loss, misfortune, the way to wisdom. *Polish*

19132. Nae [no] man is wise at a' times nor on a' things. *Scottish*

19133. No man is the only wise man. *Latin*

19134. No man is wise at all times. *Latin (Pliny)*

19135. No man is wise enough by himself. *Latin*

19136. No man was ever wise by chance. *Latin*

19137. Not by age but by capacity is wisdom attained. *Latin*

19138. Observation, not old age, brings wisdom. *Latin*

19139. Send a wise man on an errand and say nothing to him. *English*

19140. That is good which is wisdom in the end. *Dutch*

19141. That man is wise who speaks little. *Latin*

19142. That man is wisest who realizes that his wisdom is worthless. *Greek (Socrates)*

19143. The doors of wisdom are never shut. *American*

19144. The first step to wisdom is to recognize things which are false. *Latin*

19145. The gods laugh at the wisdom of men. *French*

19146. The heart of the wise man is like still water. *Cameroonian*

19147. The heart of the wise should reflect all objects, without being sullied by any. *Chinese (Confucius)*

19148. The man who knows most knows most his own ignorance. *American*

19149. The mark of wisdom is to read the present aright. *Greek*

19150. The Pole is wise after the damage is done. *Polish*

19151. The price of wisdom is above rubies. *Bible*

19152. The tongue of a wise man lieth behind his heart. *Arabic (Ali Ibn-abi-talib)*

19153. The wise are always at peace. *Arabic*

19154. The wise find pleasure in water; the virtuous find pleasure in hills. *Chinese*

19155. The wise learn many things from their foes. *Greek*

19156. The wise man alone is free, and every fool is a slave. *Greek*

19157. The wise man carries wealth within himself. *Greek (Menander)*

19158. The wise man does not hang his knowledge on a hook. *English*

19159. The wise man does not lay up treasure. *Chinese (Laotse)*

19160. The wise man has learned from the dunce more than once. *American*

19161. The wise man has long ears and a short tongue. *German*

19162. The wise man knows he knows nothing; the dunce thinks he knows it all. *American*

19163. The wise man knows that he does not know; the ignorant man imagines that he knows. *Spanish*

19164. The wise man strikes twice against the same stone. *Russian*

19165. The wisest man is he who does not think he is so. *French*

19166. Three things produce wisdom — truth, consideration and suffering. *Welsh*

19167. We are wiser than we know. *American (Emerson)*

19168. When wisdom fails, luck helps. *Danish*

19169. Wisdom adorns riches and shadows poverty. *Greek*

19170. Wisdom at proper times will forget. *Latin*

19171. Wisdom comes alone through suffering. *Greek (Aeschylus)*

19172. Wisdom doesn't always speak in Greek and Latin. *American*

19173. Wisdom first teaches what is right. *Latin*

19174. Wisdom giveth life to them that have it. *Bible*

19175. Wisdom in a poor man is a diamond set in lead. *American*

19176. Wisdom is a good purchase, though we pay dear for it. *English*

19177. Wisdom is always an overmatch for strength. *Latin*

19178. Wisdom is in the head and not in the beard. *Swedish*

19179. Wisdom is not only to be acquired, but enjoyed. *Latin (Cicero)*

19180. Wisdom is oftentimes nearer when we stoop / Than when we soar. *English (Wordsworth)*

19181. Wisdom is only found in truth. *German (Goethe)*

19182. Wisdom is the conquerer of fortune. *Latin*

19183. Wisdom is the mother of all arts. *German*

19184. Wisdom is the only liberty. *Latin*

19185. Wisdom is the principal thing; therefore get wisdom; and with all thy getting get understanding. *Bible*

19186. Wisdom is to the soul what health is to the body. *French*

19187. Wisdom may come out of the mouths of babes. *American*

19188. Wisdom never lies. *Greek*

19189. Wisdom often exists under a shabby coat. *Latin (Cicero)*

19190. Wisdom triumphs over chance. *Latin (Juvenal)*

19191. Woe unto them that are wise in their own eyes, and prudent in their own sight. *Bible*

19192. You may be a wise man though you can't make a watch. *English*

Wisdom and Folly *see also* Fools and Folly; Wisdom

19193. A fool is a fine counselor for a wise man. *French*

19194. A fool is happier thinking weel o' himsel than a wise man is in ithers thinking weel o' him. *Scottish*

19195. A fool is wise if he holds his tongue. *French*

19196. A fool knows more in his own house than a wise man in another's. *Scottish*

19197. A fool may earn money, but it takes a wise man to keep it. *Scottish*

19198. A fool may eke [also] a wise man often guide. *English (Chaucer)*

19199. A fool may gie [give] a wise man counsel. *Scottish*

19200. A fool may speir [ask] mair questions than a wise man can answer. *Scottish*

19201. A fool says what he knows, and a wise man knows what he says. *Yiddish*

19202. A fool sees not the same tree that a wise man sees. *English (Blake)*

19203. A fool who can keep silent is counted among the wise. *Yiddish*

19204. A rich man's foolish sayings pass for wise ones. *English*

19205. A thousand of the blind, a thousand of the sighted. [Meaning that there are as many fools as wise men, or as many ignorant persons as there are knowledgeable.] *Japanese*

19206. A wise man can nourish a thousand people; a fool can only keep himself. *Chinese*

19207. A wise man's guess is truer than a fool's certainty. *Arabic*

19208. Better a slap from a wise man than a kiss from a fool. *Yiddish*

19209. Better be a fool at a feast than a wise man at a fray. *Scottish*

19210. Better be foolish with all than wise by yourself. *French*

19211. Better to lose with a wise man than win with a fool. *Yiddish*

19212. Even a fool, when he holdeth his peace, is counted wise. *Bible*

19213. Every fool has his wisdom. *Polish*

19214. Every owl is stupid in the daytime. *Polish*

19215. Fools are aye [always] fond o' flittin', and wise men o' sittin'. *Scottish*

19216. Fools big [build] houses and wise men buy them. *Scottish*

19217. Fools make feasts and wise men eat them. *Scottish*

19218. Fools prepare the banquets and wise men enjoy them. *Italian*

19219. Fools ravel [confute] and wise men redd [counsel]. *Scottish*

19220. Fools tie knots and wise men loose them. *English*

19221. Fruitful trees bend down; the wise stoop; a dry stick and a fool can be broken, not bent. *Sanskrit*

19222. He is no wise man that cannot play the fool upon occasion. *English*

19223. He who lives without folly is not so wise as he thinks. *French (La Rochefoucauld)*

19224. He who thinks himself wise has an ass near at hand. *Spanish*

19225. It is a profitable thing, if one is wise, to seem foolish. *Greek (Aeschylus)*

19226. It needs great wisdom to play the fool. *American*

19227. It needs greater wisdom not to play the fool. *American*

19228. Learn wisdom by the follies of others. *Italian*

19229. Man's chief wisdom consists in knowing his follies. *French (La Rochefoucauld)*

19230. Nae [no] man can play the fule sae [so] weel as the wise man. *Scottish*

19231. No man is so wise but that he has a little folly remaining. *German*

19232. None is so wise but the fool overtakes him. *English*

19233. None so wise but he is sometimes foolish. *French*

19234. One wise man's verdict outweighs all the fools. *American*

19235. Play the fule weel an [if] ye be wise. *Scottish*

19236. Rather in hell with a wise man than in paradise with a fool. *Yiddish*

19237. Some men are wise, and some are otherwise. *English*

19238. The dunce wonders, the wise man asks. *American*

19239. The folly of one man is the fortune of another. *English*

19240. The greatest fool may ask more than the wisest man can answer. *English (Colton)*

19241. The heart of a fool is in his mouth, but the mouth of a wise man is in his heart. *Hebrew*

19242. The wisdom of the world is foolishness with God. *Bible*

19243. The wise make jests and fools repeat them. *American*

19244. The wise man alone is free, and every fool is a slave. *Greek*

19245. The wise man conceals his wisdom; the fool displays his foolishness. *Yiddish*

19246. The wise man has learned from the dunce more than once. *American*

19247. The wise man yields to the fool, and the fool rejoices. *Polish*

19248. The wise man's eyes are in his head; but the fool walketh in darkness. *Bible*

19249. The wise seek wisdom, the fool has found it. *German*

19250. 'Tis wisdom sometimes to seem a fool. *English*

19251. To flee from folly is the beginning of wisdom. *Latin*

19252. To succeed in this world, one must have the appearance of a fool and be wise. *French* (Montesquieu)

19253. Too much wisdom is folly. *German*

19254. What good is wisdom to a fool? *Polish*

19255. What's the good of being wise when foolishness serves? *Yiddish*

19256. When wise men play the fool, they do it with a vengeance. *Italian*

19257. Who are a little wise, the best fools be. *English (Donne)*

19258. Who lives without folly is not so wise as he thinks. *French (La Rochefoucauld)*

19259. Wisdom rises upon the ruins of folly. *English*

19260. Wise men learn by other men's mistakes, fools by their own. *English*

19261. Wise men make proverbs and fools repeat them. *American*

19262. Wise men propose, and fools determine. *American*

Wisdom and Virtue *see also* Wisdom; Virtue

19263. Wisdom and virtue are like the two wheels of a cart. *Japanese*

Wishes and Wishing *see also* Wishful Thinking

19264. After the doing, wishing is in vain. *French*

19265. Bode [wish for] a robe and wear it, bode a pock [a sack] and bear it. *Scottish*

19266. Bode [wish for] gear [money, property] and get it. *Scottish*

19267. Bode [wish] for a silk gown and ye'll get a sleeve o't. *Scottish*

19268. Boden [wished for] gear [money, property] stinks. *Scottish*

19269. Dinna [do not] sigh for him, but send for him; if he be unhanged he'll come. *Scottish*

19270. "If" an' "an" spoil mony [many] a gude charter. *Scottish*

19271. If "ifs" an' "ans" were kettles an' pans, there would be no use for tinklers [tinkers]. *Scottish*

19272. If man could have half his wishes, he would double his troubles. *American (Franklin)*

19273. If things are not as you wish, wish them as they are. *Yiddish*

19274. If wishes were butter-cakes, beggars might bite. *English*

19275. If wishes were horses, beggars would ride. *English*

19276. If wishes were thrushes, beggars would eat birds. *English*

19277. If wishes were true, peasants would be kings. *French*

19278. If wishes would bide, beggars would ride. *English*

19279. Men easily believe what they wish to believe. *Latin*

19280. The evil wish is most evil to the wisher. Greek

19281. Thy wish was father, Harry, to that thought. *English (Shakespeare)*

19282. We cannot wish for what we don't know. *French*

19283. What one has wished for in youth, in old age one has in abundance. *German (Goethe)*

19284. Who has no money must have no wishes. *Italian*

19285. Wish not for soft things, lest thou earn the hard. *Greek*

19286. Wishers and woulders are never good householders. *English*

19287. Wishes were ever fools. *English (Shakespeare)*

19288. Wishes won't wash dishes. *American*

19289. Wishing of all employments is the worst. *English (Young)*

19290. With wishing comes grieving. *Italian*

19291. Ye'll get as muckle [much] for ae [one] with this year as for twa [two] fernyear [the preceding year]. *Scottish*

19292. You can't get rich by wishing. *Yiddish*

19293. You cannot have all you wish for. *Latin*

Wishful Thinking *see also* Hope; Wishes and Wishing

19294. Believe that you have it, and it is yours. *Latin*

Wit *see also* Common Sense; Humor; Jests and Jesting; Laughter

19295. A man of wit would often be at a loss, were it not for the company of fools. *French (La Rochefoucauld)*

19296. A' the wit o' the warld's no in ae pow [one head]. *Scottish*

19297. Better a witty fool than a foolish wit. *English (Shakespeare)*

19298. Even wit is a burden when it talks too long. *Latin*

19299. Every ditch is full of after-wits. *Italian*

19300. Gude wit jumps. *Scottish*

19301. He has mair [more] wit in his wee finger than ye hae in your hale bouk [whole bulk, compass]. *Scottish*

19302. He has some sma' wit, but a fool has the guiding o't. *Scottish*

19303. It is a sort of wit to know how to use the wit of others. *Latin*

19304. Little wit in the head makes much work for the feet. *American*

19305. Muckle [much] head, little wit. *Scottish*

19306. Tak wit i' your anger. *Scottish*

19307. The wit one wants [i.e., lacks] spoils what one has. *French*

19308. Use your wit as a shield, not as a dagger. *American*

19309. Want o' wit is waur nor [worse than] want o' gear [money, goods, property]. *Scottish*

19310. Weak men had best be witty. *English*

19311. Wit bought is better than Wit taught. *English*

19312. Wit is folly unless a wise man hath the keeping of it. *English*

19313. Wit is never good till it be bought. *English*

19314. Your wit will ne'er worry you. *Scottish*

Wives: Choosing a Wife *see also* Courtship

19315. A bustling mother makes a slothful daughter. *Latin*

19316. A diamond daughter turns to glass as a wife. *Dutch*

19317. A dink [neat, trim] maiden aft maks a dirty wife. *Scottish*

19318. A fair wife without a fortune is a fine house without furniture. *English*

19319. A light-heeled mother makes a heavy-heeled daughter. *English*

19320. A pitiful mother makes a scabby daughter. *Dutch*

19321. A poor man who marries a wealthy woman gets a ruler and not a wife. *Greek*

19322. A tenderhearted mother rears a scabby daughter. *Italian*

19323. A woman and a melon are hard to choose. *French*

19324. All are good maids, but whence come the bad wives? *English*

19325. An indulgent mother makes a frowsy daughter. *French*

19326. As you would have a daughter, so choose a wife. *Italian*

19327. Be careful to marry a woman who lives near to you. *Greek*

19328. Better wed over the mixen [dung heap] than over the moor. [Better marry someone from close to home.] *Scottish*

19329. Choose a wife with her nightcap on. *Scottish*

19330. Choose neither a wife nor linen by candlelight. *Spanish*

19331. Choose a good woman's daughter though her father were the devil. *Gaelic*

19332. For a wife and a horse go to your neighbor. *Italian*

19333. Go down the ladder when you marry a wife; go up when you choose a friend. *Hebrew*

19334. If you want a neat wife, go chuse her on a Saturday. *American (Franklin)*

19335. In choosing a wife and buying a sword we ought not trust another. *English*

19336. Judge of the daughter by the mother. *Latin*

19337. One should buy a house ready made and a wife to make. *French*

19338. Refuse the wife who has but one fault but seek after one with two. *Welsh*

19339. She hath broken her elbow at the church door. [She has grown idle after marriage.] *English*

19340. Take no woman for a wife in whom you cannot find a flaw. *Gaelic*

19341. The best and worst thing to man for his life, is good or ill choosing his good or ill wife. *English*

19342. The gude or ill hap o' a gude or ill life is the gude or ill choice o' a gude or ill wife. *Scottish*

19343. To choose a wife, two heads are not enough. *German*

Woes

19344. By telling our woes we often assuage them. *French*

19345. Their causes are hidden, but our woes are clear. *Latin (Ovid)*

19346. Waes [woes] unite faes [foes]. *Scottish*

Womanizing *see also* Men and Women

19347. He that loves Glass without G, / Take away L, and that is he. *English*

Women *see also* Discipline and Women; Husbands and Wives; Marriage; Men and Women; Women and Age; Women and Clothes; Women and Education; Women and Intelligence; Women and Jealousy; Women and Money; Women and Revenge; Women and Secrets; Women and Talking; Women and Tears; Women and Their Bodies; Women and Trustworthiness; Women and Vanity; Women and Variability; Women and Virtue; Women Saying No; Women's Advice; Women's Work; Women in Authority

19348. A foolish woman is clamorous. *Bible*

19349. A good-looking woman in a house is the foe of all the plain ones. *Chinese*

19350. A handsome woman is always right. *German*

19351. A lazy woman tries to carry everything at once. *Chinese*

19352. A maid that giveth yieldeth. *Italian*

19353. A mule and a woman do what is expected of them. *Spanish*

19354. A ship and a woman are ever repairing. *Scottish*

19355. A truth-telling woman has few friends. *Danish*

19356. A woman and a cherry paint themselves for their own hurt. *Spanish*

19357. A woman and a hen are well nigh lost by gadding. *Spanish*

19358. A woman at a window, as grapes on the highway. *Italian*

19359. A woman can love a poor boy better than a rich dotard. *Hebrew*

19360. A woman dares all things when she loves or hates. *Latin*

19361. A woman is known by her walking and drinking. *Spanish*

19362. A woman is most merciless when shame goads on her hate. *Latin (Juvenal)*

19363. A woman is the weaker vessel. *Bible*

19364. A woman of charm is as rare as a man of genius. *Spanish (de Madariaga)*

19365. A woman should be good for everything at home, for nothing abroad. *Greek*

19366. A woman should stand by a woman. *Greek*

19367. A woman smells sweet when she smells of nothing. *Latin*

19368. A woman sometimes scorns what best contents her. *English (Shakespeare)*

19369. A woman who meditates alone meditates evil. *Latin*

19370. A woman's gude either for something or naething. *Scottish*

19371. A woman's heart sees more than ten men's eyes. *Swedish*

19372. A woman's in pain, a woman's in woe, a woman is ill when she likes to be so. *Italian*

19373. A woman's mind is moved by the meanest gifts. *Latin*

19374. All women are good — for something or nothing. *English*

19375. An ill-tempered woman is the devil's doornail. *Danish*

19376. As fierce as hell, or fiercer still, / A woman piqued who has her will. *English (Byron)*

19377. As is the body, so is the soul of tender women frail. *Latin*

19378. As the good man saith, so say we; / As the good woman saith, so must it be. *English*

19379. Being but a woman, raise not the sword. [Don't offer to help when you can be of no service.] *Latin*

19380. Clergy and women are all one. *French*

19381. Deceit, weeping, spinning, God hath give to women kindly, while they may live. *English*

19382. Empty rooms make ladies foolish. *French*

19383. Every woman thinks herself lovable. *Latin*

19384. Fair maidens are mostly unlucky, clever young men are seldom good-looking. *Chinese*

19385. Find the woman. [Cherchez la femme.] *French*

19386. Fire, the sea, and woman; these are three ills. *Latin*

19387. Frailty, thy name is woman! *English (Shakespeare)*

19388. Heaven has no rage like love to hatred turn'd, / Nor hell a fury like a woman scorn'd. *English (Congreve)*

19389. In men every mortal sin is venial; in women every venial sin is mortal. *Italian*

19390. It is because of men that women dislike each other. *French*

19391. It is not the most beautiful women whom men love most. *French*

19392. Keep a mistress seven years and you'll find her as useful as a wife. *American*

19393. Mills and women ever want something. *Italian*

19394. Modesty is the beauty of women. *Gaelic*

19395. Most women don't need rouge to make them pretty. *Chinese*

19396. Nature meant woman to be her masterpiece. *American*

19397. No argument can convince a woman or a stubborn ass. *American*

19398. No fish without bones; no woman without a temper. *American*

19399. Nothing is worse than a woman — even a good one. *Greek*

19400. Of women, Miris, the parrot, and the crow, the minds of these four you cannot know. *Assamese*

19401. Once a woman has given you her heart you can never get rid of the rest of her. *American*

19402. Plain women are as safe as churches. *American*

19403. Priests and women never forget. *German*

19404. Put the light out and all women are alike. *German*

19405. She had rather kiss than spin. *English*

19406. She hath broken her leg above the knee. [Her baby is illegitimate.] *English*

19407. She wad na hae the walkers, and the riders gaed by. [She is unmarried because she set her sights too high.] *Scottish*

19408. Sometimes a hen crows as if she were a cock. *Russian*

19409. The great ambition of women is to inspire love. *French*

19410. The hearts of women sicken for love more than do the hearts of men. *Greek (Euripides)*

19411. The laughter, the tears, and the song of a woman are equally deceptive. *Latin*

19412. The preparations of a woman are as long as the legs of a goose. *Russian*

19413. The sea, and fire, and woman, are three evils. *Greek*

19414. The three most pleasant things: A cat's kittens, a goat's kid, and a young woman. *Irish*

19415. The woman in finery, the house in filth, but the doorway swept. *Spanish*

19416. The woman that deliberates is lost. *American*

19417. The woman who likes washing can always find water. *American*

19418. The woman who spares her lover spares herself too little. *Latin*

19419. The woman you keep keeps you. *American*

19420. There are three without rule: A mule, a pig, and a woman. *Irish*

19421. There is never a lawsuit but a woman is at the bottom of it. *Latin*

19422. There is no accounting for the actions of a woman. *French*

19423. There is no mischief but a woman is at the heart of it. *American*

19424. There is no mischief done, but a woman is one. *English*

19425. There is no such poison in the green snake's mouth or the hornet's sting, as in a woman's heart. *Chinese*

19426. There is someone to pick up every fallen woman. *Lebanese*

19427. There's hardly a strife in which a woman has not been a prime mover. *American*

19428. To a foolish woman a violin is more pleasing than a distaff. *Italian*

19429. To defame the servant is to defame the mistress. *Chinese*

19430. Two women are worse than one. *Latin*

19431. Ugliness is the guardian of women. *Hebrew*

19432. We ask four things for a woman — that virtue dwell in her heart, modesty in her forehead, sweetness in her mouth, and labor in her hands. *Chinese*

19433. What a woman wills, God wills. *French*

19434. Whatever a woman will she can. *Italian*

19435. When a candle is taken away, every woman is alike. *Greek*

19436. When a woman reigns, the devil governs. *Italian*

19437. When an ass climbs a ladder, we may find wisdom in women. *Hebrew*

19438. Where the devil can't manage, he'll send a woman. *Polish*

19439. While there's a world it's woman that will govern it. *American*

19440. Who would keep his house clean, let him not admit woman, priest or pigeon. *French*

19441. With one smile she overthrows a city; with another, a kingdom. *Chinese*

19442. With women one should never venture to joke. *German*

19443. Woman complains, woman mourns, woman is ill, when she chooses. *French*

19444. Woman is a mystery to men but women are wise to each other. *American*

19445. Woman is by nature generally extravagant. *Greek*

19446. Woman is made of glass. *Spanish (Cervantes)*

19447. Woman is the handsomest in animal creation. *Hebrew*

19448. Woman, like good wine, is a sweet poison. *Turkish*

19449. Woman must have her way. *American*

19450. Women and bairns [children] lein [conceal] what they kenna [know not]. *Scottish*

19451. Women and calendars are good only for a year. *Spanish*

19452. Women and elephants never forget. *American*

19453. Women and glass are always in danger. *Portuguese*

19454. Women and hens through too much gadding are lost. *Italian*

19455. Women and their wills are dangerous ills. *American*

19456. Women and wine, dice and deceit, mak wealth sma' [make wealth small] and want great. *Scottish*

19457. Women and workmen are difficult to handle. *Japanese*

19458. Women are always in extremes. *American*

19459. Women are necessary evils. *American*

19460. Women are one and all a set of vultures. *Latin*

19461. Women are silver dishes into which we put golden apples. *German*

19462. Women are strong when they arm themselves with their weaknesses. *French*

19463. Women are very short-sighted. [Women appreciate only what is before their eyes.] *Chinese*

19464. Women are watches that keep bad time. *German*

19465. Women are worthless wares. *Latin*

19466. Women, being the weaker vessel, are ever thrust to the wall. *English (Shakespeare)*

19467. Women, dying maids, lead apes in hell. *English*

19468. Women have always some mental reservation. *French*

19469. Women have no rank. *French (Napoleon I)*

19470. Women know a point more than the devil. *Italian*

19471. Women pardon great infidelities more easily than little ones. *French*

19472. Women rouge that they may not blush. *Italian*

19473. Women when injured are generally not easily appeased. *Latin*

19474. Women's jars breed men's wars. *English*

19475. Women's thoughts are afterthoughts. *Japanese*

19476. Wrinkles disfigure a woman less than ill nature. *French*

Women and Age

19477. A woman is as old as she admits. *American*

19478. A woman is no older than she looks. *French*

19479. A woman of sixty, the same as a girl of six, runs to the sound of the timbrel. *Hebrew*

19480. Death laughs when old women frolic. *Latin (Publilius Syrus)*

19481. It is safer to irritate a dog than an old woman. *Latin*

19482. Old maids lead apes in hell. *English*

19483. Old wives were aye [always] gude maidens. *Scottish*

19484. The hell of women is old age. *French (La Rochefoucauld)*

19485. The old gray mare, she ain't what she used to be. *American*

19486. The only secret a woman can keep is that of her age. *American*

19487. The rouged beauty cannot regain the bloom of youth. *Chinese*

19488. The rouged beauty repudiates age, the jolly profligate never speaks of poverty. *Chinese*

19489. What though she be toothless and bald as a coote? *English*

19490. Women and music should never be dated. *English (Goldsmith)*

19491. Young, she's a Kuanin [goddess of mercy]; old, she's a monkey. *Chinese*

Women and Clothes

19492. A foolish woman is known by her petticoats. [The number she wears correlates with her wealth.] *Dutch*

19493. A lady is always known by her boots and her gloves. *French*

19494. A maid aft seen and a gown aft worn are disesteemed and held in scorn. *Scottish*

19495. Choose your wife on Saturday, not on Sunday. *Scottish*

19496. He who teaches a woman letters feeds more poison to a terrible asp. *Greek (Menander)*

19497. No woman is ugly if she is well dressed. *Portuguese*

19498. Silk was invented so that woman could go naked in clothes. *Arabic*

19499. The swarthy dame, dressed fine, decries the fair one. *Spanish*

19500. The woman who dresses well draws her husband from another woman's door. *Spanish*

19501. Three tenths of her good looks are due to nature, seven tenths to dress. *Chinese*

19502. Ugly women finely dressed are the uglier for it. *English*

Women and Intelligence

19503. A wise woman is twice a fool. *Latin*

19504. Intelligence is the ornament of every serious woman. *Lebanese*

19505. Long are a woman's locks, but short a woman's wits. *Russian*

19506. Stupidity in a woman is unfeminine. *American*

19507. The hair of the woman is long, but her wit is short. *Cheremis*

19508. Women are wise on a sudden, but fools upon premeditation. *Italian*

19509. Women have long hair and short wits. *Yiddish*

Women and Jealousy *see also* Jealousy

19510. A jealous woman has no flesh upon her breast, for however much she may feed upon jealousy, she will never have enough. *Yoruba*

19511. A jealous woman is worse than a witch. *American*

19512. A jealous woman sets the whole house afire. *Latin*

19513. It is impossible to be more jealous than a woman. *Chinese*

19514. Jealousy is inborn in women's hearts. *Greek*

19515. Nine women in ten are jealous. *Chinese*

Women and Money *see also* Dowries

19516. A beautiful woman smiling, bespeaks a purse weeping. *Italian*

19517. A woman prefers a man without money to money without a man. *Greek*

19518. A woman without dower has no liberty to speak. *Greek*

19519. Nothing agreeth worse / Than a lady's heart and a beggar's purse. *English*

19520. Nothing more unbearable than a wealthy woman. *Latin*

19521. When a handsome woman laughs, you may be sure her purse weeps. *English*

19522. Women are able to share adversity, but not prosperity. *Chinese*

Women and Revenge

19523. A woman's vengeance has no bounds. *American*

19524. No one rejoices more in revenge than woman. *Latin (Juvenal)*

19525. Vengeance should be left to women. *Italian*

Women and Secrets

19526. A woman always thinks it takes two to keep a secret. *American*

19527. How hard it is for women to keep counsel! *English (Shakespeare)*

19528. To a woman and a magpie tell what you would speak in the marketplace. *Spanish*

Women and Talking

19529. A man's words are like an arrow; a woman's, like a broken fan. *Chinese*

19530. A noble man is led far by woman's gentle words. *German (Goethe)*

19531. A smooth tongue is better than smooth locks. *Danish*

19532. A squaw's tongue runs faster than the wind's legs. *American*

19533. A woman has never spoiled anything through silence. *German*

19534. A woman who talks like a man, and a hen which crows like a cock, are no good to anyone. *French*

19535. A woman's hair is long; her tongue is longer. *Russian*

19536. A woman's strength is in her tongue. *Welsh*

19537. A woman's tongue is her sword, and she does not let it rust. *Chinese*

19538. A woman's tongue is only three inches long, but it can kill a man six feet tall. *Japanese*

19539. All women are good Lutherans; they would rather preach than hear mass. *Danish*

19540. Arthur could not tame a woman's tongue. *Welsh*

19541. Foxes are all tail, and women are all tongue. *French*

19542. I am woman, needs must I speak. *English (Chaucer)*

19543. Kind words and few are a woman's ornament. *Danish*

19544. Maidens must be seen and not heard. *English*

19545. Many women, many words. *English*

19546. One tongue is enough for a woman. *English*

19547. She is as quiet as a wasp in one's nose. *English*

19548. Silence gives grace to a woman. *Greek (Sophocles)*

19549. Silence is a fine jewel for a woman, but it is little worn. *English*

19550. Silence is the best ornament of women. *Latin*

19551. Ten measures of speech descended on the world; women took nine and men one. *Hebrew*

19552. The nightingale will run out of songs before a woman runs out of conversation. *Spanish*

19553. The only silent women are those who have no tongues. *Russian*

19554. Three women and one goose make a market. *Danish*

19555. Three women, three geese, and three frogs make a fair. *German*

19556. Three women will make as much noise as a market. *Latin*

19557. Two women and a goose make a market. *Italian*

19558. Women will have the last word. *American*

Women and Tears *see also* Crying

19559. A woman's tears and a dog's limping are not real. *Spanish*

19560. A woman's tears are a fountain of craft. *Italian*

19561. As great pity to see a woman weep, as a goose go barefoot. *English*

19562. It's as hard to see a woman crying as it is to see a barefooted duck. *Irish*

19563. It's nae mair ferlie [no more a wonder] to see a woman greet [weep] than to see a goose gang barefit [barefoot]. *Scottish*

19564. Take a lass with the tear in her eye. *English*

19565. Those women who grieve least make the most lamentation. *Latin*

19566. Woman complains, woman mourns, woman is ill, when she chooses. *French*

19567. Women laugh when they can and weep when they will. *French*

Women and Their Bodies

19568. A fat wife is like a blanket in winter. *Pakistani*

19569. A goose, a woman, and a goat are bad things, lean. *Portuguese*

19570. A woman and a greyhound must be small in the waist. *Spanish*

19571. Show me rotundity and I will show you beauty. *Arabic*

Women and Trustworthiness *see also* Women and Infidelity; Women and Secrets

19572. A bag of fleas is easier to keep guard over than a woman. *German*

19573. A dog is faithful, women never. *Turkish*

19574. A woman's word is a bundle of water. *Hindi*

19575. Believe one word in forty that a woman speaks. *Turkish*

19576. For half so boldly can there no man / Swear and lyen as a woman can. *English (Chaucer)*

19577. I write a woman's oaths in water. *Greek*

19578. In infancy, the father should guard her; in youth, her husband should guard her; and in old age her children should guard her; for at no time is a woman properly to be trusted with liberty. *Sanskrit*

19579. The man who trusts a woman may as well trust the weather. *Russian*

19580. Trust not a woman, even when dead. [Because she may be feigning death.] *Latin*

19581. Trust not a woman: she will tell thee what she has just told her companion. *Wolof*

19582. Trust not in kings, horses or women. *Persian*

19583. Trust your dog to the end, and a woman to the first opportunity. *American*

Women and Vanity

19584. A woman who looks much in the glass spins but little. *French*

19585. An ugly woman dreads the mirror. *Japanese*

19586. Every woman loves the woman in the looking-glass. *German*

19587. Tell a woman she's a beauty and the devil will tell her ten times. *Spanish*

19588. The fox loves cunning, the wolf covets the lamb, and a woman longs for praise. *Latin*

19589. The more a woman admires her face, the more she ruins her house. *Spanish*

19590. There never was a mirror that told a woman she was ugly. *French*

19591. Women and girls must be praised, whether it be true or false. *German*

Women and Variability

19592. A woman's mind is like the wind in a winter's night. *Scottish*

19593. Because is a woman's reason. *Scottish*

19594. Every woman has the divine privilege of changing her mind. *American*

19595. Ladies have leave to change their minds. *American*

19596. She can change her mind like the wind. *English (Byron)*

19597. Winter weather and women's thoughts change often. *American*

19598. Woman is as variable as a feather in the wind. *Italian*

19599. Woman is ever varying and changeable. *Latin (Virgil)*

19600. Woman's heart is as changeable as a cat's eyes. *Japanese*

19601. Women are as fickle as April weather. *American*

Women and Virtue *see also* Chastity; Virtue

19602. A bad woman is worse than a bad man. *English*

19603. A fair woman without virtue is like stale wine. *American*

19604. A maid's virtue is unlimited; a wife's resentment without end. *Chinese*

19605. A storehouse of evil is a woman if she is depraved. *Latin*

19606. A virtuous woman commands her husband by obeying him. *Latin*

19607. A virtuous woman is a crown to her husband. *Bible*

19608. A wicked woman is a magazine of evils. *Latin*

19609. A woman finds it easier to do ill than well. *Latin*

19610. A woman without virtue is one of three things—selfish, jealous or malicious. *Chinese*

19611. A woman's virtues need not be of the famous or uncommon kind; her face need not be beautiful, her conversation need not be eloquent; and her work need not be surpassingly exquisite. *Chinese*

19612. All wickedness is but little to the wickedness of a woman. *Bible*

19613. Avoid three things: A snake, a smooth-tongued man, and a wanton woman. *Japanese*

19614. Better a de'il than a daw [a drab, a slattern]. *Scottish*

19615. Every woman would rather be beautiful than good. *German*

19616. How unhappy the woman who is loved and virtuous at the same time. *French (La Rochefoucauld)*

19617. If women were little as they are good, / A pease-cod would make them a gown and a hood. *Italian*

19618. The three virtues of a woman: obey the father, obey the husband, obey the son. *Chinese*

19619. There are only two good women in the world: the one is dead, the other not found. *German*

19620. Virtue is doubly pleasing in one whose form is beautiful. *Latin (Virgil)*

19621. Women are saints in church, angels in the street, devils in the kitchen, and apes in bed. *American*

19622. Women are the devil's nets. *American*

Women in Authority

19623. A petticoat government. *Japanese*

19624. A woman for a general, and the soldiers will be women. *Latin*

19625. A woman's general: what should we fear? *English (Shakespeare)*

Women Saying No *see also* Denial; Refusal; Resistance

19626. A woman's nay is no denial. *English*

19627. And whispering, "I will ne'er consent," consented. *English (Byron)*

19628. Between a woman's "yes" and "no" / There is not room for a pin to go. *Spanish (Cervantes)*

19629. Coyly resisting. [Dulce resistens.] *Latin*

19630. Do as the maids do, say no and take it. *English*

19631. Have you not heard it said full oft, / A woman's nay doth stand for nought? *English (Shakespeare)*

19632. Maids' nays are nothing; they are shy / But do desire what they deny. *English (Herrick)*

19633. Nineteen nay-says o' a maiden are ha'f a grant. *Scottish*

19634. Saying "No," a woman shakes her head lengthwise. *Japanese*

19635. Yielded with coy submission, modest pride, / And sweet reluctant amorous delay. *English (Milton)*

Women's Advice

19636. A woman's advice helps at last. *English*

19637. A woman's advice is of little value, but he who won't take it is a fool. *Spanish (Cervantes)*

19638. It is said of old that woman's counsel is fatal counsel. *English*

19639. Take the first advice of a woman and not the second. *Latin*

19640. Take your wife's first advice, not her second. *Spanish*

19641. Woman's counsel is either too dear or too cheap. *Latin*

19642. Women beat men in evil counsel. *Latin*

19643. Women's advice is often fatal. Icelandic

19644. Wommenes counseil been ful ofte colde [is too often fatal]. *English (Chaucer)*

19645. Yit a woman's avyse [advice] helpys at the last. *English*

Women's Work

19646. A woman's work and washing of dishes is never at an end. *English*

19647. Women's wark [work] is never dune. *Scottish*

Wonders

19648. A wonder lasts but nine days. *English*

19649. No wonder is greater than any other wonder, and if once explained, ceases to be a wonder. *American*

19650. Stones have been known to move and trees to speak. *American*

19651. Wonder lasts but nine nights in a town. *Scottish*

Wooing *see* Courtship

Words *see also* Fair Words; Good Words; Plain Talk; Promises; Smooth Words; Soft Words; Speaking; Thought and Language; Words and Deeds

19652. A word does not make a hole in the head. *Yiddish*

19653. A word isn't a bird; if it flies out you'll never catch it again. *Russian*

19654. A word spoken in due season, how good it is! *Bible*

19655. Better one living word than a hundred dead ones. *Dutch*

19656. Better one word before than two after. *Yiddish*

19657. By thy words thou shalt be condemned. *Bible*

19658. Do not go forth on the gale with every sail set into an ocean of words. *Greek*

19659. Empty words—sound without thought. *Latin (Virgil)*

19660. Enough words, little wisdom. *American*

19661. Every word in its proper place. *Yiddish*

19662. Evil words corrupt good manners. *Dutch*

19663. He that speaks lavishly shall hear as knavishly. *English*

19664. In a multitude of words there will surely be error. *Chinese*

19665. It befits the brave to combat ill with words. *Greek (Homer)*

19666. It is bitter fare to eat one's own words. *Danish*

19667. Let thy words be few. *Bible*

19668. Loyal words have the secret of healing grief. *Greek (Menander)*

19669. Many words: an unsound heart. *Turkish*

19670. Our words have wings, but fly not where we would. *American*

19671. Syllables govern the world. *American*

19672. The spoken word cannot be swallowed. *Russian*

19673. The words of the wise are as goads. *Bible*

19674. Thorns and thistles sting very sure; but old maids' tongues sting more. *American*

19675. Tongue breaketh bone, and herself hath none. *English*

19676. Why should I spare words? They cost nothing. *Latin*

19677. Without knowing the force of words, it is impossible to know men. *Chinese (Confucius)*

19678. Word by word the book is made. *Chinese*

19679. Words and feathers the wind carries away. *Spanish*

19680. Words are fools' pence. *English*

19681. Words are like bees: they have honey and a sting. *American*

19682. Words are the only things that last forever. *American*

19683. Words are the voice of the heart. *Chinese*

19684. Words are the wings of actions. *American*

19685. Words become seeds. Korean

19686. Words don't chink. *Latin*

19687. Words, like glass, darken whatever they do not help to see. *American*

19688. Words may either conceal character or reveal it. *Latin*

19689. Words provoke to senseless wrath. *Greek*
19690. Words repeated have, as another sound, another sense. *French*
19691. Words should be weighed and not counted. *Yiddish*
19692. Words spoken in an evening, the wind carrieth away. *Italian*
19693. Words, words, words. *English (Shakespeare)*
19694. Wounds heal, but not ill words. *Spanish*

Words and Deeds *see also* Action; Boasting; Good Deeds; Good Words; Oaths; Promises; Swearing; Threat(s)

19695. A dog which barks much is never good at hunting. *Portuguese*
19696. A great ruser [braggart] was ne'er a gude rider. *Scottish*
19697. A long tongue is a sign of a short hand. *Spanish*
19698. A man of words and not of deeds is like a garden full of weeds. *English*
19699. A mere voice, and nothing more. *Latin*
19700. A scholar's ink lasts longer than a martyr's blood. *Irish*
19701. A tree is known by its fruit, and not by its leaves. *American*
19702. A' his buz [talk, noise] shakes nae corn. *Scottish*
19703. Actions speak louder than words. *American*
19704. All talk is no cider. *American*
19705. Bachelors' wives and maids' children are always well taught. *English*
19706. Better one "take it" than two "you will have it." *French*
19707. Between promising and performing a man may marry his daughter. *Portuguese*
19708. Between saying and doing many a pair of shoes is worn out. *Italian*
19709. Big words seldom go with good [or great] deeds. *Danish*
19710. Bold in design, but timid in execution. *Latin*
19711. Brag's a good dog, but Holdfast's a better. *English*
19712. "Can do" is easily carried about wi' ane [one]. *Scottish (Scott)*
19713. Deeds not words are required. *Latin*
19714. Don't put it in my ear, but in my hand. *Russian*
19715. Easier said than done. *French*
19716. Every word is vain that is not completed by deed. *Greek*
19717. Expect nothing from him who promises a great deal. *American*
19718. Fair [or fine] words butter no parsnips. *English*
19719. Fine words do not grease the cabbage. *German*
19720. For mad words, deaf ears. *French*
19721. From saying to doing is a long step [or a long stretch]. *French*
19722. Good actions speak for themselves; they need no tin horn. *American*
19723. Good words fill not a sack. *English*
19724. Good words make us laugh; good deeds make us silent. *French*
19725. Good words without deeds / Are rushes and reeds. *English*
19726. Great barkers are nae [no(t)] biters. *Scottish*
19727. Great talkers, little doers. *English*
19728. He loses his thanks who promises and delays. *Latin*
19729. He makes a great row but does nothing. *Latin (Seneca)*
19730. He who gives fair words feeds you with an empty spoon. *English*
19731. He who speaks evil only differs from him who does evil in that he lacks opportunity. *Latin (Quintilian)*
19732. Help by actions, not by words. *Latin*
19733. His deeds do not agree with his words. *Latin (Cicero)*
19734. His wind shakes no corn. *Scottish*
19735. Ill workers are aye gude [always good] onlookers. *Scottish*
19736. It is as easy to draw back a stone thrown with force from the hand, as to call back a word once spoken. *American*
19737. It is better to light a candle than to curse the darkness. *Chinese*
19738. It is easier to know how to do something than it is to do it. *Chinese*
19739. It is not the hen which cackles most that lays most eggs. *Dutch*
19740. It is one thing to boast, another to fight. *Latin*
19741. It is one thing to cackle and another to lay an egg. *Ecuadorian*
19742. It is one thing to promise and another to perform. *American*
19743. It is weel said, but who will bell the cat? *Scottish*
19744. It's a long step from saying to doing. *Spanish*
19745. Leaves enough, but few grapes. *English*
19746. Less counsel and more hands. *German*
19747. Let a man be bad if [i.e., if only] his tongue be good. *Wolof*
19748. Many words will not fill the bushel. *English*
19749. Maybe was never a guid [good] honey bee. *Scottish*
19750. Meikle crack [much chatting] fills nae [no] sack. *Scottish*
19751. Men who ape the saint and play the sinner. *Latin (Juvenal)*
19752. Men's words are ever bolder than their deeds. *German*
19753. Mony words fills not the furlot. *Scottish*
19754. More noise than wool. *English*
19755. Much bruit, little fruit. *French*
19756. Not words but knocks. *Latin*
19757. One "take this" is better than two of "will give." *Spanish*
19758. One here-it-is [or take-this] is better than two you-shall-have-it's. *French*
19759. One take-this is better than two thou-shalt-haves. *English*
19760. Praise without profit puts little in the pocket. *English*
19761. Promise little and do much. *Talmud*

19762. Promises may make friends, but 'tis performances that keep them. *English*

19763. Prove your words by your deeds. *Latin*

19764. "Say well" and "Do well" end with one letter; / "Say well" is good, but "Do well" is better. *English*

19765. Saying and doing are two different things. *Italian*

19766. Saying gangs [goes] cheap. *Scottish*

19767. Saying is one thing, and doing, another. *French*

19768. She loves the poor well, but cannot abide beggars. *English*

19769. Slow in words, swift in deeds. *Chinese*

19770. Smooth words in place of gifts. *Latin*

19771. Some things are easier said than done. *Latin (Plautus)*

19772. Speaking much is a sign of vanity, for he that is lavish in words is a niggard in deed. *American*

19773. Speech is the mirror of action. *Greek*

19774. Suit the action to the word, the word to the action. *English (Shakespeare)*

19775. Talk does not cook rice. *Chinese*

19776. Talkers are no doers. *English (Shakespeare)*

19777. Talking is easier than doing, and promising than performing. *German*

19778. The cow that moos much gives little milk. *Polish*

19779. The planting of one tree is worth the prayers of a whole year. *Turkish*

19780. The superior man is modest in speech, but surpassing in his actions. *Chinese (Confucius)*

19781. The tongue is more to be feared than the sword. *Japanese*

19782. The word once spoken flies beyond recall. *Latin*

19783. There is a great distance between doing and saying. *Hindi*

19784. There's muckle [much] between the word and the deed. *Scottish*

19785. They can do least who boast loudest. *Latin*

19786. They talk like angels but they live like men. *English (Johnson)*

19787. Think of many things, do one. *Portuguese*

19788. Thunder without rain is like words without deeds. *American*

19789. Thy actions to thy words accord. *English (Milton)*

19790. Trust on the deed and not in gay speeches. *English (Lyly)*

19791. We have not to talk, but to steer the vessel. *Latin (Seneca)*

19792. We promise according to our hopes, and perform according to our fears. *French (La Rochefoucauld)*

19793. Well done is better than well said. *American (Franklin)*

19794. Who has not a wife clothes her well; who has not children feeds them well. *Italian*

19795. Who promises much and does little dines a fool on hope. *German*

19796. Words are but sands; 'tis money buys lands. *English*

19797. Words are female, deeds are male. *Italian*

19798. Words are good, but fowls lay eggs. *English*

19799. Words are the daughters of the earth, and deeds are the sons of heaven. *Hindi*

19800. Words butter no parsnips. *English*

19801. Words gang [go] wi' the wind but dunts hard [blows] are out of season. *Scottish*

19802. Words make a woman, deeds make a man. *Russian*

19803. Words may pass, but blows fall heavy. *English*

19804. Words may shew a man's wit, but actions his meaning. *American (Franklin)*

19805. Words pay no debts. *Latin* (Terence)

19806. Words show the wit of a man, but actions his meaning. *English*

19807. Words will build no walls. *Greek*

19808. Words will not do for my aunt, for she does not trust even deeds. *Spanish*

19809. Work and vote as you talk and pray. *American*

19810. Work as if you were to live 100 years, pray as if you were to die to-morrow. *American (Franklin)*

19811. Works have a stronger voice than words. *Latin*

Work and Workers

19812. A burthen cheerfully borne becomes light. *Latin (Ovid)*

19813. A good laborer is better than a bad priest. *German*

19814. A ploughman on his feet is higher than a gentleman on his knees. *American*

19815. A thin meadow is soon mowed. *American*

19816. A woman's work is never done. *American*

19817. A work well begun is half done. *Greek*

19818. All things are easy that are done willingly. *English*

19819. As is the workman, so is the work. *American*

19820. At the working man's house hunger looks in, but dares not enter. *American (Franklin)*

19821. Be the first in the field and the last to the couch. *Chinese*

19822. Come unto me, all ye that labor and are heavy laden. *Bible*

19823. Each one to his own trade. *French*

19824. Finish the work you have set for yourself. *Latin*

19825. Girn [grin] when ye bind, and laugh when ye loose. *Scottish*

19826. God walks among the pots and pipkins. *Latin*

19827. Good material is half the work. *German*

19828. Great is work which lends dignity to man. *Hebrew*

19829. He never did a good day's work who went grumblingly about it. *English*

19830. He that hath a trade hath an estate. *American (Franklin)*

19831. He who does not kill hogs will not get black puddings. *Spanish*

19832. He who would rest must work. *Italian*

19833. I hae muckle [have much] to do and few to do for me. *Scottish*

19834. I have bestowed upon you labor in vain. *Bible*

19835. If any would not work, neither should he eat. *Bible*

19836. If you want work well done, select a busy man. *American*

19837. If your plough be jogging you may have food for your horses. *American*

19838. In all labor there is profit. *Bible*

19839. In the sweat of thy brow shalt thou eat bread. *Bible*

19840. It is a poor art that maintains not the artisan. *Italian*

19841. It is not the long day but the heart that does the work. *Italian*

19842. It is not the part of a man to fear sweat. *Latin*

19843. It is not with saying, "Honey," "Honey," that sweetness will come into the mouth. *English*

19844. It may be hard to work, but it must be harder to want. *American*

19845. Labor conquers all things. *Latin*

19846. Labor has a bitter root but a sweet taste. *Danish*

19847. Labor helps, but you get more by luck. *American*

19848. Labor is in no way disgraceful. *Greek (Hesiod)*

19849. Labor is often the father of pleasure. *French*

19850. Labor warms, sloth harms. *Dutch*

19851. Life grants no boon to man without much toil. *Latin*

19852. Life is in labor. *Russian*

19853. Light is the task when many share the toil. *Greek (Homer)*

19854. Long talk makes short work. *American*

19855. Man is born unto labor. *Bible*

19856. Many hands make light work. *Latin*

19857. Never was good work done without much trouble. *Chinese*

19858. No mill, no meal. *English*

19859. No profit grows where is no pleasure ta'en. *English (Shakespeare)*

19860. Not a long day, but a good heart, rids work. *English*

19861. Nothing is achieved without toil. *Latin (Horace)*

19862. Nothing to be got without pains but poverty. *English*

19863. O sweet solace of labor! *Latin*

19864. Only horses work, and they turn their back on it. *American*

19865. People labor all their lives to be rich that they might live without labor. *American*

19866. Plough deep whilst sluggards sleep, / And you shall have corn to sell and to keep. *English*

19867. Pray and work and you shall be saved. *Polish*

19868. Pray and work. *Latin*

19869. Sour work — sweet sleep. *German*

19870. Suffer that you may be wise; labor that you may have. *Spanish*

19871. Sweet is the memory of past labor. *Greek*

19872. The day is short, the work is much. *Hebrew*

19873. The labor is in itself a pleasure. *Latin*

19874. The labor we delight in physics pain. *English (Shakespeare)*

19875. The laborer is worthy of his hire. *Bible*

19876. The man who does not teach his child a trade brings him up to steal. *Persian*

19877. The man who enjoys the fruits of his labor is greater than the man who fears heaven. *Palestinian Talmud*

19878. The needle conquers the weaver. *Lebanese*

19879. The workman is known by his work. *American*

19880. There are mair [more] wark-days than life-days. *Scottish*

19881. There belangs mair [belongs more] to a ploughman than whistling. *Scottish*

19882. There is no labor in the labor of love, and there is love in honest labor. *American*

19883. They were never first at the wark [work] that bade God speed the wark. *Scottish*

19884. Think of ease, and work on. *American*

19885. To him that toils God owes glory. *Greek*

19886. To labor [or to work] is to pray. *Latin*

19887. To work for naething maks folk dead sweer [unwilling, indolent]. *Scottish*

19888. Toil is the sire of fame. *Greek*

19889. Wark bears witness wha [who] does weel. *Scottish*

19890. What profit hath a man of all the labor which he taketh under the sun. *Bible*

19891. What you get by your own labor is sweet to the taste. *American*

19892. Where there are too many there is little work. *German*

19893. White siller [silver] is wrought in black pitch. *Scottish*

19894. Whither shall the ox go, where he will not have to plough? *English*

19895. Why seekest thou rest, since thou art born to labor? *Latin*

19896. Without work there is no bread. *Polish*

19897. Work done expects money. *Portuguese*

19898. Work has a bitter root but sweet fruit. *German*

19899. Work is a fine fire for frozen fingers. *American*

19900. Work is the sustenance of noble minds. *Latin*

19901. Work is worship. *Arabic*

19902. Work legs and hae [have] legs, hain [spare] legs and tine [lose] legs. *Scottish*

19903. Workmen are easier found than masters. *American*

19904. Ye hae [have] wrought a yoken [the time that a horse should be in a cart] and loosed in time. *Scottish*

World

19905. All the world's a stage, / And all the men and women merely players. *English (Shakespeare).*

19906. Do well and right, and let the world sink. *English (Herbert)*

19907. How weary, stale, flat and unprofitable, / Seem to me all the uses of this world. *English (Shakespeare)*

19908. Huge though the world is, I always miss when I hit at it. *Malay*

19909. In the world there must be of all sorts. *Spanish*

19910. Of this world each man has as much as he takes. *Italian*

19911. So goeth the world: now woe, now weal. *English (Chaucer)*

19912. The world is a ladder for some to go up and some down. *Italian*

19913. The world is a mother. *Lebanese*

19914. The world is governed with little wisdom. *Italian*

19915. The world is wiser than it was. *French*

19916. The world likes to be cheated. *Dutch*

19917. This world is a round gulf, and he who cannot swim must go to the bottom. *Spanish*

19918. You must either imitate or loathe the world. *Latin*

Worldliness

19919. Be wisely worldly, be not worldly wise. *English (Quarles)*

19920. A troubled heart is a worm to the bones. *Latin*

Worry

19921. All his troubles are carried under one hat. *American*

19922. Carefulness bringeth age before the time. *Bible*

19923. Do not anticipate trouble, or worry about what may never happen. Keep in the sunlight. *American (Franklin)*

19924. Don't invent imaginary evils when we have plenty of real ones. *Irish*

19925. Early risers are robust; anxious people have poor health. *Chinese*

19926. How much pain have cost us the evils which have never happened. *American (Jefferson)*

19927. If you have anxieties, go to sleep. *Moorish.*

19928. In this world only three things dispel anxiety: women, horses and books. *Arabic*

19929. It's a poor man that always counts his sheep. *Latin (Ovid)*

19930. Jealousy and anger shorten life, and anxiety brings on old age too soon. *Bible*

19931. Let every fox worry about its own tail. *American*

19932. Let tomorrow take care of tomorrow. *English*

19933. Living in worry invites death in a hurry. *American*

19934. Man does not live a hundred years, yet he worries himself enough for a thousand. *Chinese*

19935. One who fears the falling dust [or leaves] will break his skull. *Chinese*

19936. One who is afraid that his bones [or eyes] will decay before he is dead. *Chinese*

19937. Stupidity is without anxiety. *German (Goethe)*

19938. Taking things philosophically is easy if they don't concern you. *American*

19939. The mind that is anxious about the future is wretched. *Latin (Seneca)*

19940. To carry care to bed is to sleep with a pack on your back. *American*

19941. What I don't know doesn't worry me. *Yiddish*

19942. Worries go down better with soup than without. *Yiddish*

19943. Ye're feared for the day ye never saw. *Scottish*

19944. Ye're like a hen on a het girdle [i.e., griddle]. *Scottish*

Worth *see also* Use; Usefulness; Value

19945. According to a man's worth is the worth of his land. *French*

19946. According to what you have, such is your worth. *Latin*

19947. An inch of a nag is worth a span of an aver [colt]. *English*

19948. Everyone is worth as much as he has. *German*

19949. Great things cannot be bought for small sums. *Latin*

19950. Humble worth and honest pride gar [make] presumption stand aside. *Scottish*

19951. She'll wear like a horse-shoe, aye the langer the clearer. *Scottish*

19952. So much is a man worth as he esteems himself. *French*

19953. The ass does not know what his tail is worth until is has gone. *Italian*

19954. The game is not worth the candle. *French*

19955. The mair [more] cost the mair honour. *Scottish*

19956. The play won't pay for the candles. *English*

19957. The rat's head is worth more than the lion's tail. *Spanish*

19958. The sun is nae waur [no worse] for shining on the midden [dung hill]. *Scottish*

19959. The worth o' a thing is best ken'd [known, understood] by the want o't. *Scottish*

19960. Things are only worth what one makes them worth. *French*

19961. We know a good thing when we have lost it. *French*

19962. What is not needed is dear at an obol [a coin of small denomination]. *Latin*

19963. Whoso would know what he is worth let him never be surety. *Italian*

19964. Worth makes the man. *English (Pope)*

19965. Worth may be blamed but ne'er be shamed. *Scottish*

19966. Worthy things happen to the worthy. *Latin*

19967. You are worth as much as you possess. *Spanish (Cervantes)*

Worthlessness *see also* Buying and Selling; Cost; Purpose; Usefulness; Value; Worth

19968. A good edge is good for nothing, if it has nothing to cut. *English*

19969. A useless life is early death. *German (Goethe)*

19970. He who is of no use to himself is of no use to anyone else. *Yiddish*

19971. He's a fifth wheel to the wagon. *American*

19972. I would not purchase it at the price of a rotten nut. *Latin*

19973. It is a great misfortune to be of use to nobody; scarcely less to be of use to everybody. *Spanish (Gracián)*

19974. It is not worth a button. *English*

19975. Nothing is useless to a person of sense. *French*

19976. The most worthless things on earth are these four: rain on a barren soil, a lamp in sunshine, a beautiful woman given in marriage to a blind man, and a good deed to one who is ungrateful. *Arabic*

19977. There is nothing so vile as not to be good for something. *German*

19978. Though living, dead for all useful purposes. *Latin*

19979. To be employed in useless things is half to be idle. *English*

19980. What should a cow do with a nutmeg? *English*

19981. You can't put beauty into the pot, nor loveliness into the kettle. *American*

Wrath *see* Anger

Wretchedness *see also* Misery; Suffering

19982. Let him be wretched who thinks himself so. *Spanish*

19983. The wretched are in haste to hear their wretchedness. *Latin*

Wrinkles *see also* Aging

19984. A good life keeps off wrinkles. *American*

Writing

19985. By writing you learn to write. *Latin*

19986. Either write things worth reading, or do things worth writing. *American (Franklin)*

19987. He is not a good scribe who writes well, but he who erases well. *Russian*

19988. He who can't write says the pen is bad. *Yiddish*

19989. He who writes, rests himself. *Wolof*

19990. If you want to be a good writer, write. *Greek*

19991. Paper endures anything. *French*

19992. Paper is patient. *German*

19993. Scribblers are a conceited and self-worshiping race. *Latin (Horace)*

19994. The incurable itch of scribbling. *Latin (Juvenal)*

19995. The pen is mightier than the sword. *American*

19996. The written word remains. *American*

19997. The written word remains, as the empty word perishes. *Latin*

19998. Words fly, writing remains. *Latin*

19999. Writing is the language of the hand. *Hebrew*

Wrong *see also* Good and Evil; Right; Right and Wrong; Sin and Virtue

20000. As a rule men do wrong when they have a chance. *Greek (Aristotle)*

20001. If a thing is done wrong, it is far better that it had not been done at all. *American*

20002. People do wrong, though there is much more to be gained by doing right. *American*

20003. Whoso diggeth a pit shall fall therein. *Bible*

20004. Wrang has nae [no] warrant. *Scottish*

20005. Wrong hears wrong answer given. *Scottish*

Yielding *see also* Surrender; Yielding

20006. Give way to him with whom you contend and you will gain the victory. *Latin*

20007. Giving way stops all war. *German*

20008. The wiser man yields. *German*

20009. Yielding stills [or stops] all war. *German*

Youth *see also* Youth and Old Age

20010. A growing youth has a wolf in his belly. *Italian*

20011. A man whose youth has no follies, will in his maturity have no power. *American*

20012. A raggit cowte [colt] may prove a gude gelding. *Scottish*

20013. A young cowte [colt] will canter, be it uphill or down. *Scottish*

20014. A young trooper should have an old horse. *American*

20015. Being young is a fault which improves daily. *Swedish*

20016. Beware of the young doctor and the old barber. *American*

20017. Enjoy the season of thy prime. *Greek*

20018. Goslings lead the geese to grass. *Italian*

20019. Happy is he who knows his follies in his youth. *English*

20020. He who enters an asylum for the aged at twenty, enjoys happiness too soon. *Chinese*

20021. He who has no hair on his lip can't be trusted to do anything well. *Chinese*

20022. In everything, youths are without experience. *Chinese*

20023. In judging of what a boy will be, notice what is in infancy. *Chinese*

20024. One is young only once. *French*

20025. That ring's to grow on your horn yet. *American*

20026. The devil was handsome when he was young. *American*

20027. The fewer the years, the fewer the treat. *American*

20028. The spirits run riot in youth. *Latin (Ovid)*

20029. The wildest colts make the best horses. *Greek*

20030. The youth of the soul is everlasting, and eternity is youth. *American*

20031. There die as many lambs as wethers. *Spanish*

20032. When we are out of sympathy with the young, our work in the world is over. *American*

20033. Whilst the morning shines, gather the flowers. *Latin*

20034. Ye're but young cocks, your craw's roupy [hoarse]. *Scottish*

20035. Ye're new come ower, your heart's nipping [nip = pinching]. *Scottish*

20036. You may see the man in the boy. *Chinese*

20037. Young heads are giddy, and young hearts are warm. *American*

20038. Youth and white paper take any impression. *English*

20039. Youth flies. *Latin*

20040. Youth has a small head. *Irish*

20041. Youth holds no society with grief. *Greek (Aristotle)*

20042. Youth is the time to make one's mark. *Chinese*

20043. Youth knows no virtue. *German*

20044. Youth, like virgin parchment, is capable of any inscription. *American*

20045. Youth must store up; age must use. *American*

20046. Youth suffers; age knows. *American*

20047. Youth will be served. *American*

20048. Youth will have its fling. *American*

20049. Youth will have its swing. *English*

Youth and Old Age *see also* Youth

20050. A lazy youth, a lousy age. *French*

20051. A man may be old and yet have a youthful heart; a man may be poor and yet his will be undaunted. *Chinese*

20052. A slothful youth produces an old age of beggary. *Latin*

20053. A wild colt may become a sober horse. *Scottish*

20054. A young idler [or gambler], an old beggar. *German*

20055. A young man will be wiser by and by; / An old man's wit may wander ere he die. *English (Tennyson)*

20056. A young saint, an old devil. *English*

20057. A young serving man, an old beggar. *English*

20058. A young twig is easier twisted than an old tree. *American*

20059. A young whore, an old saint. *American*

20060. A young woman married to an old man must behave like an old woman. *American*

20061. Age is more just than youth. *Greek (Aeschylus)*

20062. An angelic boyhood becomes a Satanic old age. *Dutch (Erasmus)*

20063. An old young man will be a young old man. *American (Franklin)*

20064. Become old early if you wish to stay old long. *Latin (Cato)*

20065. Crabbed age and youth cannot live together. *English (Shakespeare)*

20066. Grey and green make the worst medley. *English*

20067. I am what you will be; I was what you now are. *Latin*

20068. If the young man would, and the old man could, there would be nothing undone. *Italian*

20069. If youth but knew; if old age could! *French (Etienne)*

20070. If youth knew, if old age could, there would be nothing which might not be done. *Italian*

20071. If youth knew what age would crave, / It would both get and save. *English*

20072. In the old there is no taste; in the young no insight. *Babylonian Talmud*

20073. In youth we believe many things that are not true; in old age we doubt many truths. *American*

20074. Inferior in youth, quite useless in old age. *Chinese*

20075. Man is like palm-wine: when young, sweet but without strength; in old age, strong but harsh. *Congolese*

20076. Men are like the herbs of the field—while some are sprouting, others are withering. *Babylonian Talmud*

20077. Mother, carry me, and I will carry you. *Bible*

20078. Of a young hermit, an old devil. *French (Rabelais)*

20079. Of young men die many; / Of old men escape not any. *English*

20080. Old age considers; youth ventures. *American*

20081. Old and tough, young and tender. *English*

20082. Old fools are bigger fools than young fools. *French (La Rochefoucauld)*

20083. Old young, young old. *English*

20084. Our youthful sins plague our old age. *Latin*

20085. Rackless youth makes a rueful [or goustie (dreary)] age. *Scottish*

20086. Rashness attends youth, as prudence does old age. *American*

20087. Rashness is the companion of youth, Prudence of old age. *Latin (Cicero)*

20088. Revere your elder, for old excels in wisdom. *Efik*

20089. Royet [wild] lads mak sober men. *Scottish*

20090. Rule youth weill, and eild [old age] will rule the sel [and age will rule itself]. *Scottish*

20091. Slothful youth produces an old age of beggary. *Latin*

20092. The gravity of old age is fairer than the flower of youth. *Arabic*

20093. The old age of an eagle is better than the youth of a sparrow. *Greek*

20094. The old forget, the young don't know. *German*

20095. The old man shows what the young man was. *American*

20096. The young do not know what age is, and the aged forget what youth was. *American*

20097. The young may die, the old must die. *American*

20098. They who would be young when they are old must be old when they are young. *English*

20099. Wanton kitlins may make sober old cats. *Scottish*

20100. What is learned in youth is remembered in old age. *German*

20101. What little Hans didn't learn, big Hans doesn't know. *German*

20102. What little John has not learned, John will not know. *Polish*

20103. What the colt learns in youth he continues in old age. *French*

20104. Where old age is evil, youth can learn no good. *English*

20105. You can't put old heads on young shoulders. *American*

20106. Young angel, old devil. *German*

20107. Young flesh and old fish are best. *English*

20108. Young folk, silly folk, old folk, cold folk. *Dutch*

20109. Young fools fancy that old fools rave, but old fools have forgotten more than young fools know. *Dutch*

20110. Young men soon give, and soon forget, affronts; / Old age is slow in both. *English (Addison)*

20111. Young men think old men fools; old men know young men to be so. *English*

20112. Young men's knocks old men feel. *English*

20113. Young saint, old devil. *American*

20114. Youth and age will never agree. *Scottish*

20115. Youth is a blunder; manhood a struggle; old age a regret. *English (Disraeli)*

20116. Youth is a crown of roses, old age a crown of willows. *Hebrew*

20117. Youth is a garland of roses, age is a crown of thorns. *Hebrew*

20118. Youth, through not knowing, age, through not being able, lose everything. *Spanish*

Zeal *see also* Enthusiasm

20119. Blind zeal only does harm. *German*

20120. If our zeal were true and genuine, we should be more angry with a sinner than with a heretic. *American*

20121. Success is due less to ability than to zeal. *American*

20122. Zeal is a bad servant. *French*

20123. Zeal is blind when it encroaches upon the rights of others. *American*

20124. Zeal is like fire; it needs both feeding and watching. *American*

20125. Zeal is only for wise men, but is found mostly in fools. *American*

20126. Zeal is the fire of love, active for duty — burning as it flies. *American*

20127. Zeal without knowledge is a fire without light. *English*

20128. Zeal without knowledge is the sister of folly. *English*

Bibliography

1530: J. Palsgrave, *L'Éclaircissement de la langue française* (Paris)
1539 (and later): R. Taverner, *Proverbs or Adages with New Additions, Gathered Out of the Chiliades of Erasmus*
1546: J. Heywood, *A Dialogue Containing ... the Proverbs in the English Tongue*
1555: J. Heywood, *Two Hundred Epigrams Upon Two Hundred Proverbs with a Third Hundred Newly Added*
1573: T. Tusser, *Five Hundred Points of Good Husbandry*
1611: R. Cotgrave, *A Dictionary of the French and English Tongues*
1614 (and later): W. Camden, *Remains Concerning Britain*
1616 (and later): T. Draxe, *Bibliotheca Scholastica*
1639: J. Clarke, *Parœmiologia Anglo-Latina*
1640: G. Herbert, *Outlandish Proverbs*
1641: D. Fergusson, *Scottish Proverbs*
1642: G. Torriano, *Select Italian Proverbs*
1651: G. Herbert, *Jacula prudentum* (expanded edition of *Outlandish Proverbs*)
1659: J. Howell, *Parœmiographia*
1659: N.R. Gent, *Proverbs English, French, Dutch, Italian and Spanish*
1660: J. Howell, *Lexicon Tetraglotton. An English-French-Italian-Spanish Dictionary with the Choicest Proverbs*
1662: T. Fuller, *The History of the Worthies of England*
1664: R. Codrington, *A Collection of Many Select and Excellent Proverbs Out of Several Languages*
1666: G. Torriano, *Piazza universale di proverbi italiani*
1670 (and later): J. Ray, *English Proverbs*
1672: W. Walker, *Parœmiologia Anglo-Latina or, English and Latin Proverbs*
1707: J. Mapletoft, *Select Proverbs. Italian, Spanish, French, English, Scottish, British, etc. Chiefly Moral.*
1709: O. Dykes, *Moral Reflexions Upon Select English Proverbs*
1721: J. Kelly, *A Complete Collection of Scottish Proverbs*
1732: T. Fuller, *Gnomologia: Adages and Proverbs; Wise Sentences and Witty Sayings, Ancient and Modern, Foreign and British*
1733-58: B. Franklin, *Poor Richard's Almanack*
1737: A. Ramsay, *A Collection of Scots Proverbs*
1800: J. Ray, A. Ramsay, O. Pescetti and F. Nuñez, *Proverbial Sayings, or a Collection of the Best English Proverbs by John Ray, Scots Proverbs by Allan Ramsay, Italian Proverbs by Orlando Pescetti, Spanish Proverbs by Ferdinand Nuñez. With the Wise Sayings and Maxims of the Ancients*

1814: R. Bland, *Proverbs, Chiefly Taken from the Adagia of Erasmus, with Explanations and Examples from the Spanish, Italian, French and English Languages*
1823: J. Collins, *A Dictionary of Spanish Proverbs*
1824: T.A. Roebuck, *A Collection of Proverbs and Proverbial Phrases in the Persian and Hindustanee Languages*
1824: T. Fielding (J. Wade), *Select Proverbs of All Nations with an Analysis of the Wisdom of the Ancients*
1830: W.M. Logan, *Italian Proverbs*
1832: A. Henderson, *Scottish Proverbs*
1838: W. Bush, *1800 Selected Proverbs of the World, Ancient, Medieval and Modern*
1842: P. Percival, *Tamil Proverbs with Their English Translations*
1842: C. Ward, *National Proverbs in the Principal Languages of Europe*
1851: J. Long, *Bengali Proverbs*
1852: J. Orton, *Proverbs Illustrated by Parallel, or Relative Passages, to Which Are Added Latin, French, Spanish and Italian Proverbs with Translations*
1853: R.C. Trench, *On the Lessons in Proverbs*
1855: H.G. Bohn, *A Hand-Book of Proverbs*
1857: H.G. Bohn, *A Polyglot of Foreign Proverbs, Comprising French, Italian, German, Dutch, Spanish, Portuguese, and Danish*
1862: A. Hislop, *The Proverbs of Scotland*
1865: R.F. Burton, *Wit and Wisdom from West Africa: A Book of Proverbial Philosophy, Idioms, Enigmas, and Laconisms*
1868: M.W. Carr, *A Selection of Telugu Proverbs*
1869: W.C. Hazlitt, *English Proverbs and Proverbial Phrases*
1873: J.A. Mair, *A Handbook of Proverbs: English, Scottish, Irish, American, Shakespearean and Scriptural*
1875: J.L. Burckhardt, *Arabic Proverbs, or the Manners and Customs of the Modern Egyptians, Illustrated from Their Proverbial Sayings Current in Cairo*
1875: W. Scarborough, *A Collection of Chinese Proverbs*
1876: J. Donald, *Scottish Proverbs*
1879: W.K. Kelly, *A Collection of the Proverbs of All Nations*
1881: J. Long, *Eastern Proverbs and Emblems Illustrating Old Truths*
1883: W. Roper, *Weather Sayings*
1885: L. Hearn, *Gombo Zhebes: Little Dictionary of Creole Proverbs*
1885: E.B. Mawr, *Analogous Proverbs in Ten Languages*
1885: J. Knowles, *A Dictionary of Kashmiri Proverbs and Sayings*
1886: S.W. Fallon, *A Dictionary of Hindustani Proverbs*
1886: J. Gray, *Ancient Proverbs and Maxims from Burmese Sources*
1887: R. Christy, *Proverbs, Maxims and Phrases of All Ages*
1888: W.F.H. King, *Classical and Foreign Quotations, Law Terms and Maxims, Proverbs, Mottoes, Phrases, and Expressions in French, German, Greek, Italian, Spanish and Portuguese*
1889: J. Middlemore, *Proverbs, Sayings and Comparisons in Various Languages*
1889: K. Bayyan, *Armenian Proverbs and Sayings*
1890: E.M. Dennys, *Proverbs and Quotations of Many Nations*
1891: J. Christian, *Behar Proverbs*
1895: G. Rochiram, *A Handbook of Sindhi Proverbs with English Renderings and Equivalent Sayings*
1896: A. Cheviot, *Proverbs, Proverbial Expressions, and Popular Rhymes of Scotland*
1896: P.R. Gurdon, *Some Assamese Proverbs*
1897: H. Jensen, *A Classified Collection of Tamil Proverbs*

1897: E.J. Davis, *Osmanli Proverbs and Quaint Sayings*
1898: W.F. Johnson, *Hindi Proverbs with English Translations*
1899: A. Manwaring, *Marathi Proverbs*
1902-04: V.S. Lean, *Collectanea*
1903: N.P. Jamshedgi, *Gujarati Proverbs*
1904: W.J. Shearer, *Wisdom of the World in Proverbs of All Nations*
1904: D. Kidd, *The Essential Kafir*
1905: G. Merrick, *Hausa Proverbs*
1905: A.C. Hollis, *The Masai: Their Language and Folklore*
1906 J.H. Bechtel, *Proverbs: Maxims and Phrases Drawn from All Lands and Times*
1906: G.W. Conklin, *The World's Best Proverbs*
1907: C.F. O'Leary, *The World's Best Proverbs and Short Quotations*
1907: R.J. Wilkinson, *Malay Proverbs on Malay Character*
1909: R.G. Bayan, *Armenian Proverbs*
1910: J. Walker, *Handy Book of Proverbs*
1911: A. Cohen, *Ancient Jewish Proverbs*
1911: M. Goldman, *Proverbs of the Sages: Collection of Proverbs, Ethical Precepts, from the Talmud and Midrashim*
1912: Anon., *National Proverbs: England*
1913: Anon., *National Proverbs: Ireland*
1913: Anon., *National Proverbs: Arabia*
1913: Anon., *National Proverbs: Italy*
1913: Anon., *National Proverbs: Scotland*
1913: Anon., *National Proverbs: China*
1913: Anon., *National Proverbs: Japan*
1914: Anon., *National Proverbs: India*
1914: A.H. Smith, *Proverbs and Common Sayings from the Chinese*
1915: Anon., *National Proverbs: Holland*
1915: K.A. Turner, *National Proverbs: Serbia*
1915 (?): Anon., *National Proverbs: Portugal*
1915 (?): Anon., *National Proverbs: Spain*
1915 (?): Anon., *National Proverbs: Rumania*
1915 (?): Anon., *National Proverbs: Russia*
1920: Anon., *National Proverbs: Wales*
1932: C.H. Plopper, *Chinese Proverbs*
1935 (and later): W.G. Smith, *The Oxford Dictionary of English Proverbs*
1940: O. Huzii, *Japanese Proverbs*
1940: C.E.J. Whitting, *Hausa and Fulani Proverbs*
1948: B. Stevenson, *The Macmillan Home Book of Proverbs, Maxims, and Famous Phrases*
1958: R. Okada, *Japanese Proverbs and Proverbial Phrases*
1977: W. Mieder, *International Bibliography of Explanatory Essays on Individual Proverbs and Proverbial Expressions*
1978: W. Mieder, *Proverbs in Literature: An International Bibliography*
1982: W. Mieder, *International Proverb Scholarship: An Annotated Bibliography*
1984: W. Mieder, *Investigations of Proverbs, Proverbial Expressions, Quotations and Clichés*
1986: W. Mieder, *The Prentice-Hall Encyclopedia of World Proverbs: A Treasury of Wit and Wisdom Through the Ages*
1987: G. Paczolay, *A Comparative Dictionary of Hungarian, Estonian, German, English, Finnish and Latin Proverbs*

1989: W. Mieder, *American Proverbs: A Study of Texts and Contexts*
1990: A.T. Dalfovo, *Lugbara Proverbs*

Keyword Index

References are to entry numbers

Subject Index

References are to entry numbers. References in **bold** *are to proverbs appearing under that head word. Other references are to proverbs that are closely related.*

Source Index

References are to entry numbers